MW01687356

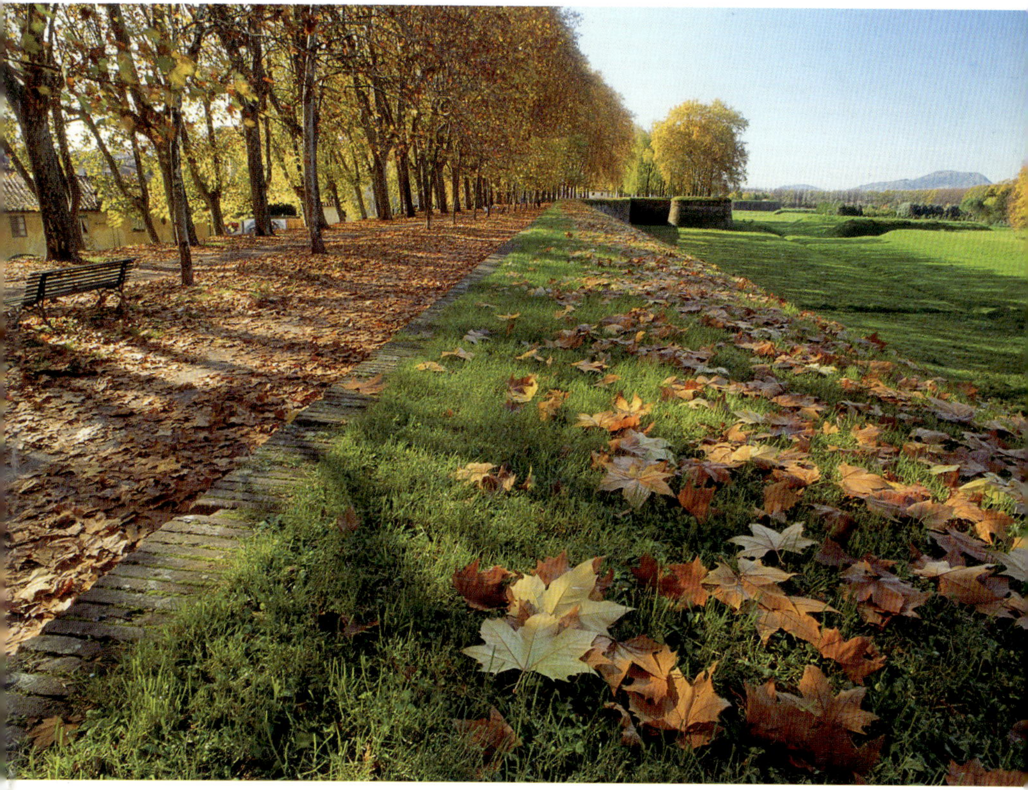

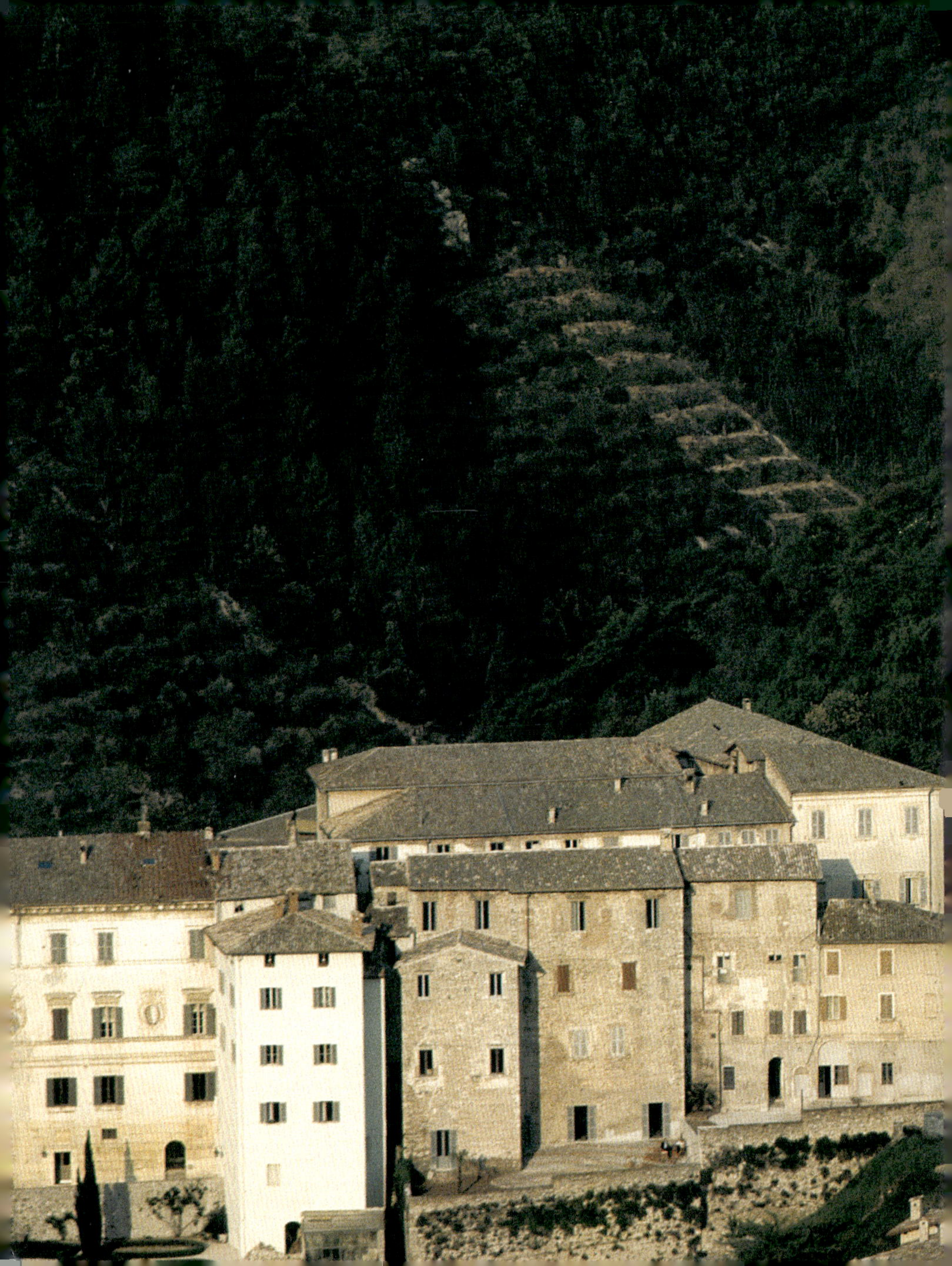

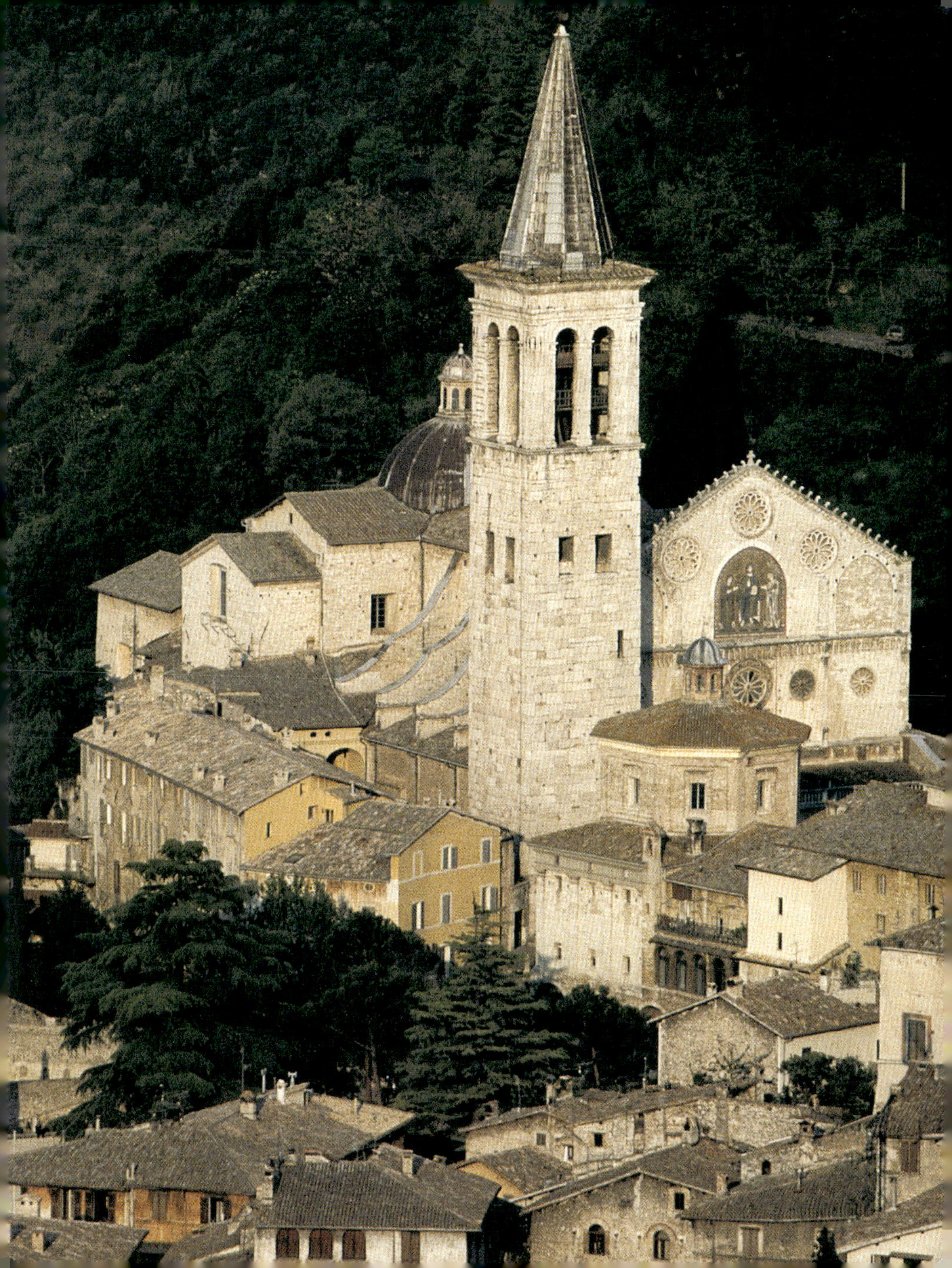

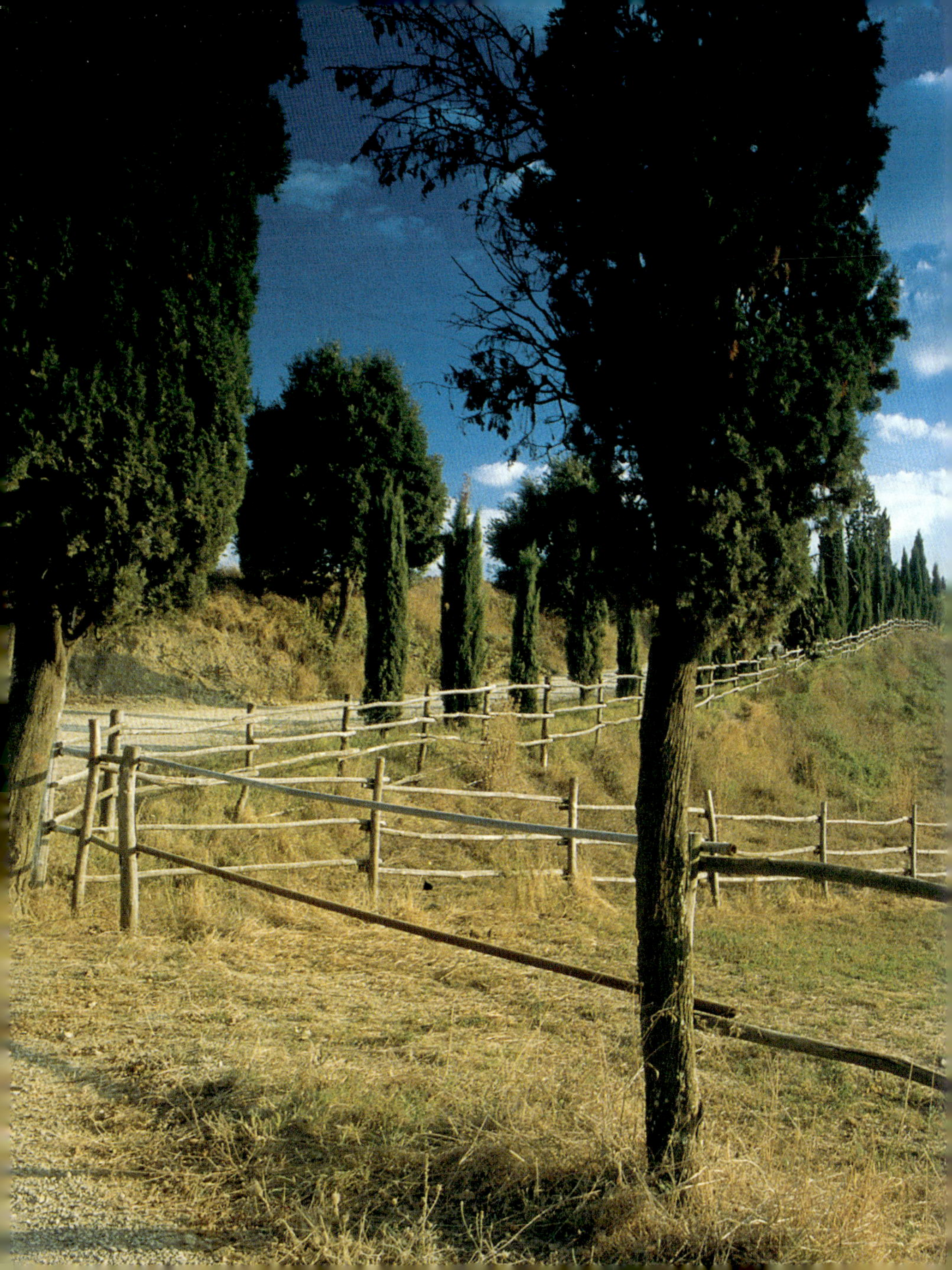

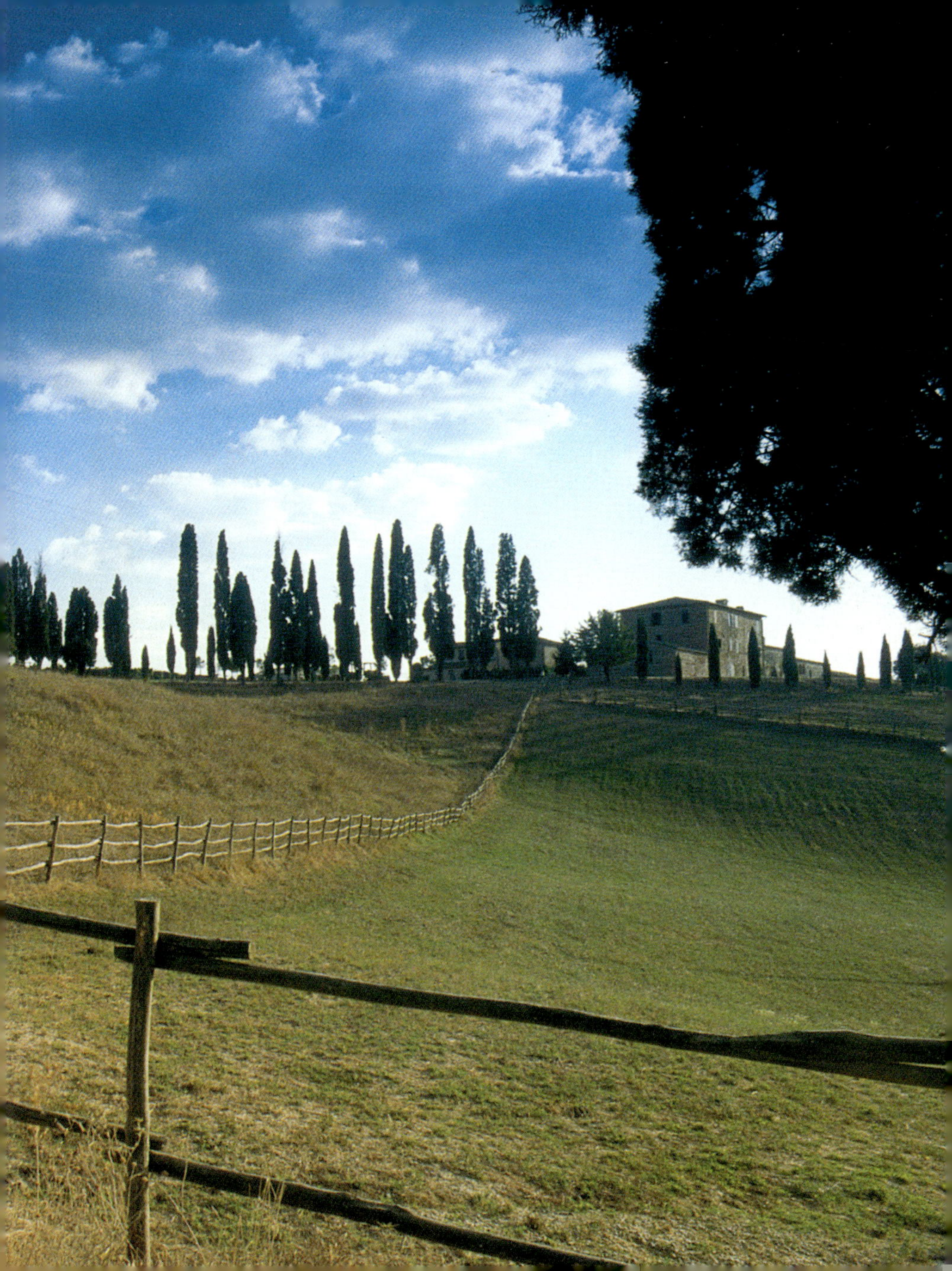

PREVIOUS PAGES:
Baluardo San Frediano, Lucca *(p. 1)*
Spoleto, Terni *(pp. 2-3)*
Cortona, Arezzo *(pp. 4-5)*
Montalcino, Siena *(pp. 6-7)*

FOLLOWING PAGE: Sanremo, Genoa

ITALY

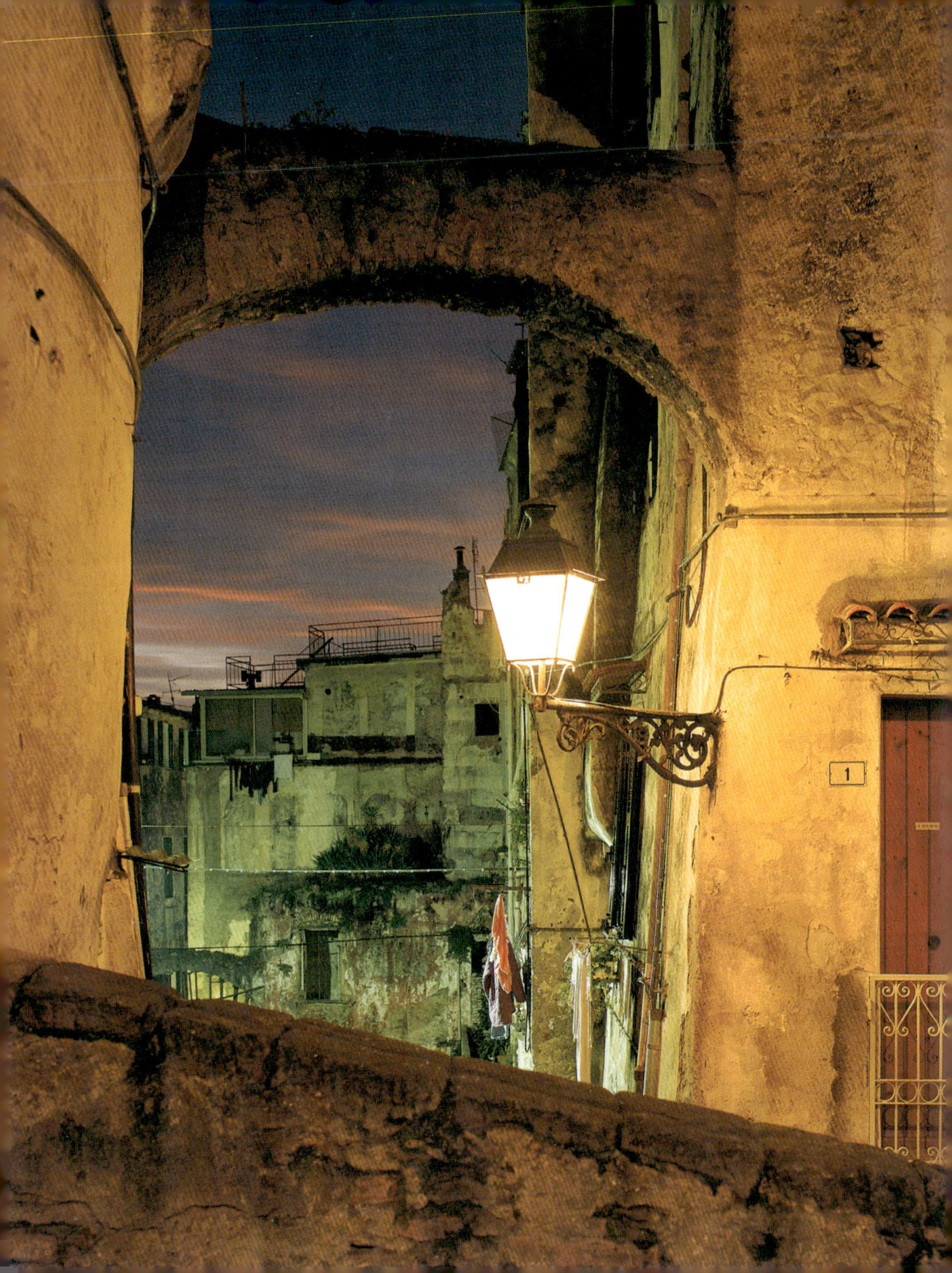
1

ITALY

ANDREA PISTOLESI – GUIDO ALBERTO ROSSI

MONDADORI

Fabio Ratti Editoria S.r.l., Corso Monforte 16, Milano

First edition: October 2002
ISBN 88-370-2013-9

Photographers
Andrea Pistolesi, Guido Alberto Rossi

Texts
Donatella Ceriani

Translations and Editing
Gabriella Cursoli

Design
Oriana Bianchetti

Reproduction
Lineatre service, Milan

Printing
Artes Gráficas, Toledo

INDEX

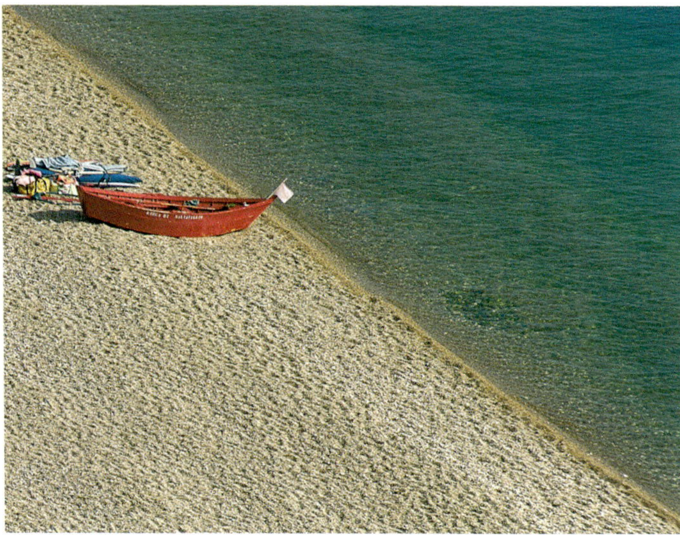

To say that Italy is beautiful, or rather, wonderful is quite a commonplace. Yet which Country can't be defined as such? Are there any lands lacking gorgeous sights and memories of the past? Certainly there aren't. Italy, however, is a special, actually unique place, because not only it is the land where treasures of art and history compete with natural marvels, as charmingly documented in this volume, but also the one in which nature turned into history and history became civilization and art.

I don't think it is easy to find another Country that has been so often a leading character on the worldwide scene over the centuries, yet that is what happened to Italy, the peninsula stretching over the Mediterranean sea and splitting it in two. The Roman civilization – with its arts, laws, roads, town planning, its military power and the adoption of the elections as a means and source of legitimacy – made the Italian peninsula the stimulating hub of a world that has laid the foundations of common Western values and the roots of several Western languages.

Furthermore, Italy kept the role of protagonist during the Middle Ages – in times of destruction and dreadful devastation – thanks to the religious strength of the Roman Church, which found expression in spiritual as well as architectural manifestations such as abbeys, convents and cloisters. Inheriting the Roman Empire legacy, the Church intercepted those people searching for a land to settle in and led them to acknowledge the common beliefs and rules underlying European culture.

Then, once more, Italy was the main character of the Renaissance, generated by a new consideration of the country's memories and identity, both invigorated by refreshed cultural and artistic expressions. That context favoured again a wealth of architectural solutions, classical and innovative experimentation at once, the application of the theory of perspective, the discovery of the central function of man and the importance of music, whose Italian terminology is still used today. Consequently, our country could maintain its remarkably crucial status as far as all the human, scientific and artistic activities were concerned. Unfortunately, however, such a cultural growth failed to promote national unity, which would have allowed Italy to occupy a decisive position amongst the great new European States.

Modern history, from the Enlightenment to the achievement of the national unification, testifies to the capability of Italy and the Italians to constantly conceive original if often troubled ideas. Italy has always been active in forging notions, styles, experiments, creativity, craftsmanship and entrepreneurial abilities which helped to preserve its place amongst the principal countries of the contemporary world.

The photographs by Andrea Pistolesi and Guido Alberto Rossi collected in this book not only display the astonishing beauty of Italy, solely due to the generosity of its Creator who lavished on its coasts, plains and mountains a set of such marvels as few places on earth can boast. They also represent the pages of a narration in which the whole of humanity seeks out and finds its roots, its history, reasons to be moved and to feel grateful for everything that has been devised, implemented and constructed in Italy over the centuries.

It is with this feeling of the universality of Italy – which in many ways and different periods anticipated and fulfilled the most important global achievements in history – that I invite You to enjoy these wonderful pictures.

Silvio Berlusconi

July 2001

HAMLETS AND CASTLES

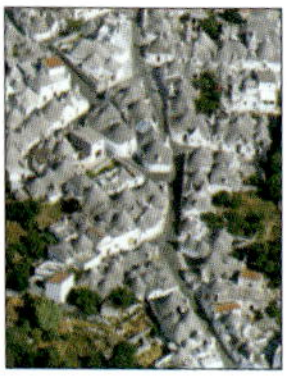

THE TRULLI OF ALBEROBELLO, conic-roofed buildings with dry-stone walls. Born in the Itria valley, Apulia, during the Baroque period, the trulli's complex combinations generated peculiar dwellings *(p. 21)*.

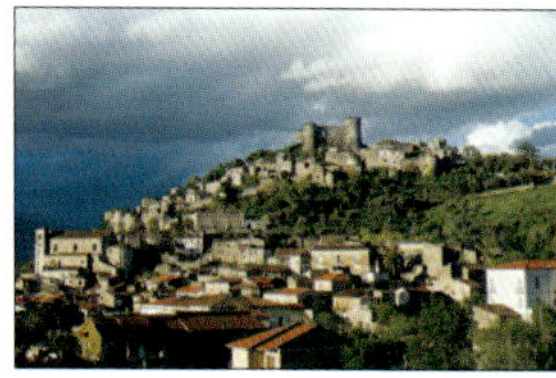

VAIRANO PATENORA, an agricultural centre located on a hill north of Caserta, in the river Volturno Valley. It is overlooked by a 15th-century castle with four battlemented towers *(pp. 22-23)*.

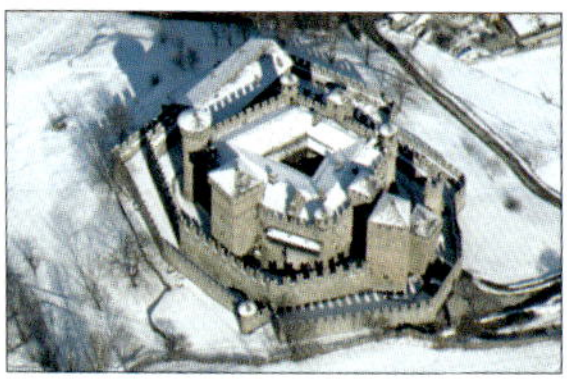

THE FÉNIS CASTLE, enclosed by double battlemented walls, is one of the finest architectural treasures of the Valle d'Aosta. Built in the 16th century, it dominates the valley of the Dora Baltea river *(pp. 24-25)*.

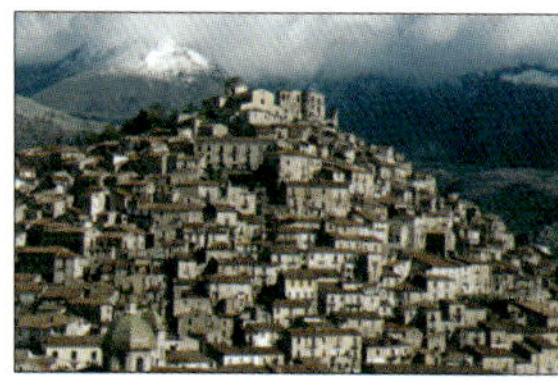

THE VILLAGE OF MORANO CALABRO, characterised by a late medieval structure, is perched on a hill at the foot of Mount Pollino. Its castle's ruins – dating from the Swabian period – overlook it *(pp. 26-27)*.

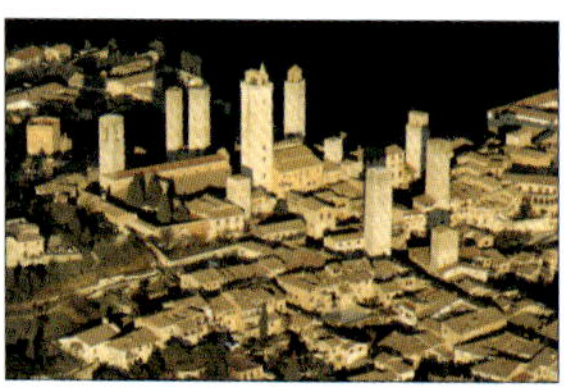

SAN GIMIGNANO, THE TOWERED CITY, with its distinctive medieval look is one of the best-preserved and most fascinating in Tuscany. Today only fourteen towers of the original seventy-six are left *(pp. 28-29)*.

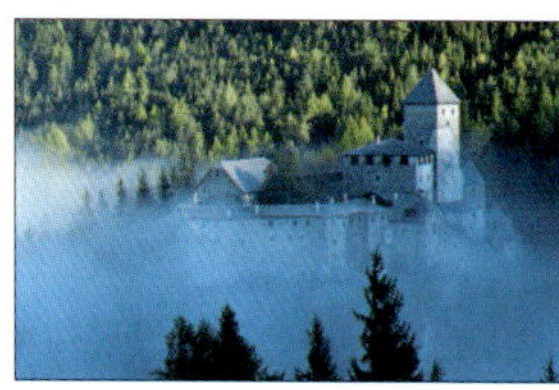

THE TURES CASTLE in Trentino Alto Adige. Built during the 13th–14th century at the entrance of the Aurina Valley, it appears from the fog surrounded by pines, evoking a fairy-like landscape *(pp. 30-31)*.

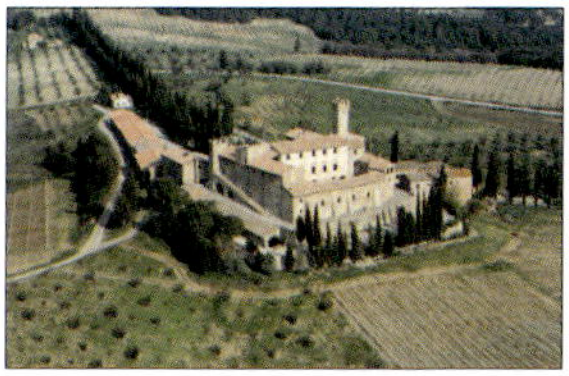

THE HILLS AROUND Montalcino form an agricultural area of outstanding natural beauty, which is also known for producing the Brunello di Montalcino, one of the finest Italian vintage wines *(pp. 32-33)*.

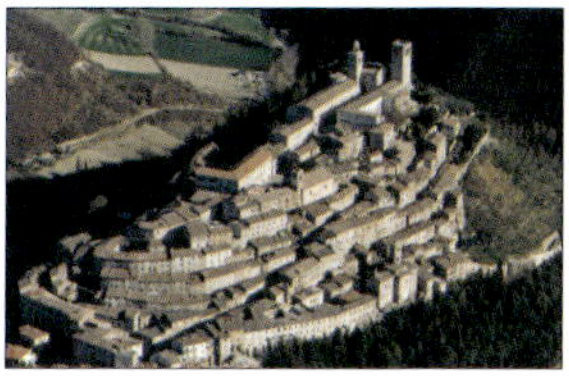

THE ROMANESQUE DUOMO and the crenellated tower, once part of a fortress, overlook Nocera Umbra, built on a hill in the Topino upper valley (*pp. 36-37;* photographed before the earthquake).

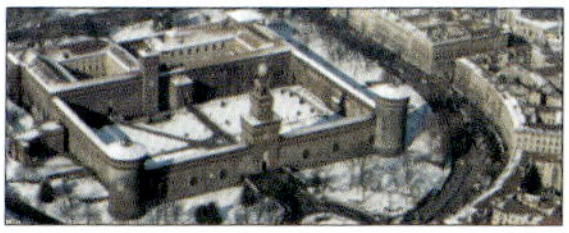

AN UNUSUAL PICTURE of the Sforza Castle, Milan, covered with snow. Built as a fortress in the 14th century, it housed a Renaissance court. Today it contains history and art museums, libraries and archives *(pp. 40-41)*.

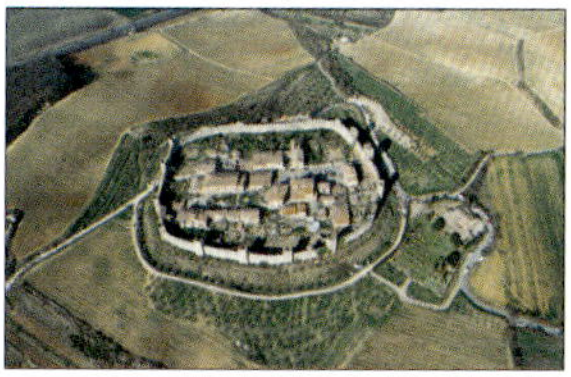

AERIAL VIEW of the fortified village of Monteriggioni, near Siena. Protected by high walls with fourteen towers, it was built at the beginning of the 13th century to supervise Siena's possessions *(pp. 34-35)*.

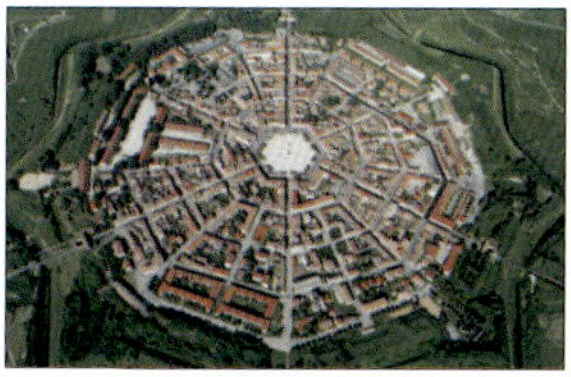

THE TOWN OF PALMANOVA, in Friuli-Venezia Giulia, built at the end of the 16th century as a rampart against the Turkish and Hapsburgian incursions. It expanded into the shape of a nine-point star *(pp. 38-39)*.

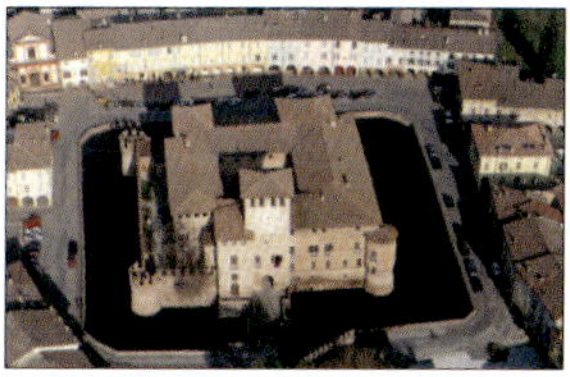

THE 15TH-CENTURY FORTRESS of Fontanellato, surrounded by a moat, was built by the Sanvitale family. A very interesting cycle of frescoes by Parmigianino is kept inside it *(pp. 42-43)*.

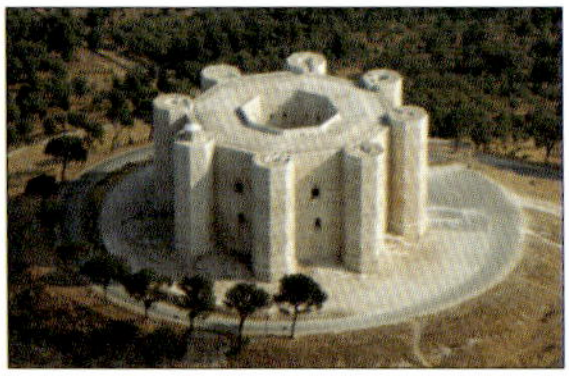

THE ISOLATED CASTEL DEL MONTE, in Apulia. Its distinctive shape, nearly resembling an imperial crown, and its regular and harmonious lines make it one of the most original medieval buildings *(pp. 44-45)*.

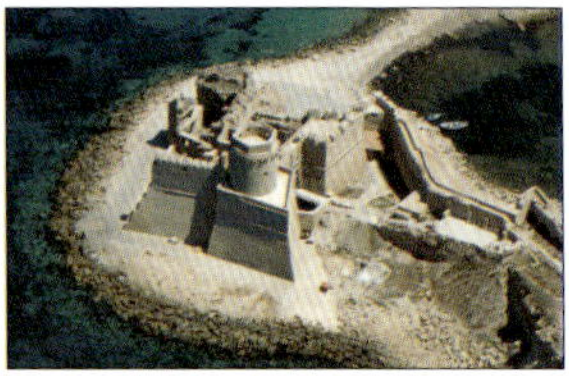

LE CASTELLA, an Aragonian fortress built in the 16th century, is located on a tongue of land not far from Isola di Capo Rizzuto, in the middle of a stunning landscape *(pp. 46-47)*.

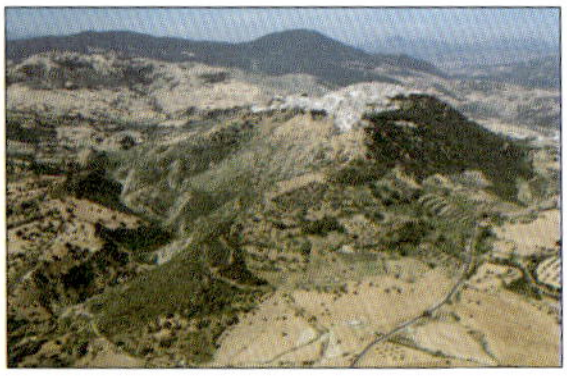

THE TINY VILLAGE OF ROTONDELLA, on the border between Basilicata and Calabria and not very far from the Ionian Sea, rises on the slopes of the Lucania Apennines, in a remote location *(pp. 48-49)*.

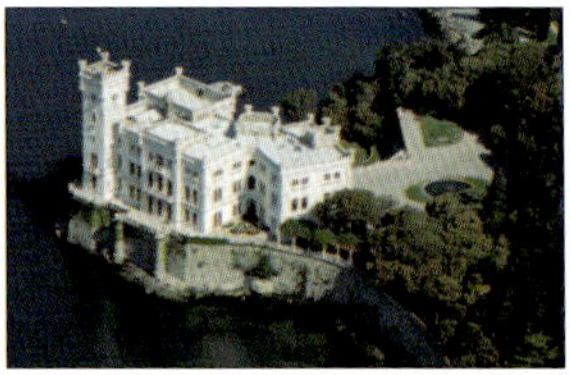

THE MIRAMARE CASTLE, facing the Adriatic Sea, was built in the 1850s on a headland 15 kilometres from Trieste. It is surrounded by a huge park interspersed by little lakes and fountains *(pp. 50-51)*.

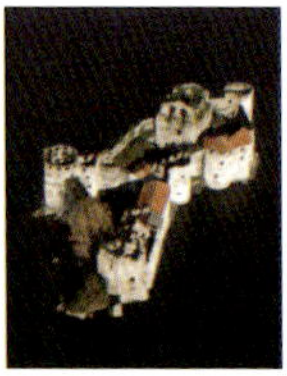

THE RUINS of one of the two castles of Cannero, namely the Vitaliana Castle, built in 1520 by Ludovico Borromeo. The remains are located on a rocky islet of Lake Maggiore, pretty close to the shore *(p. 52)*.

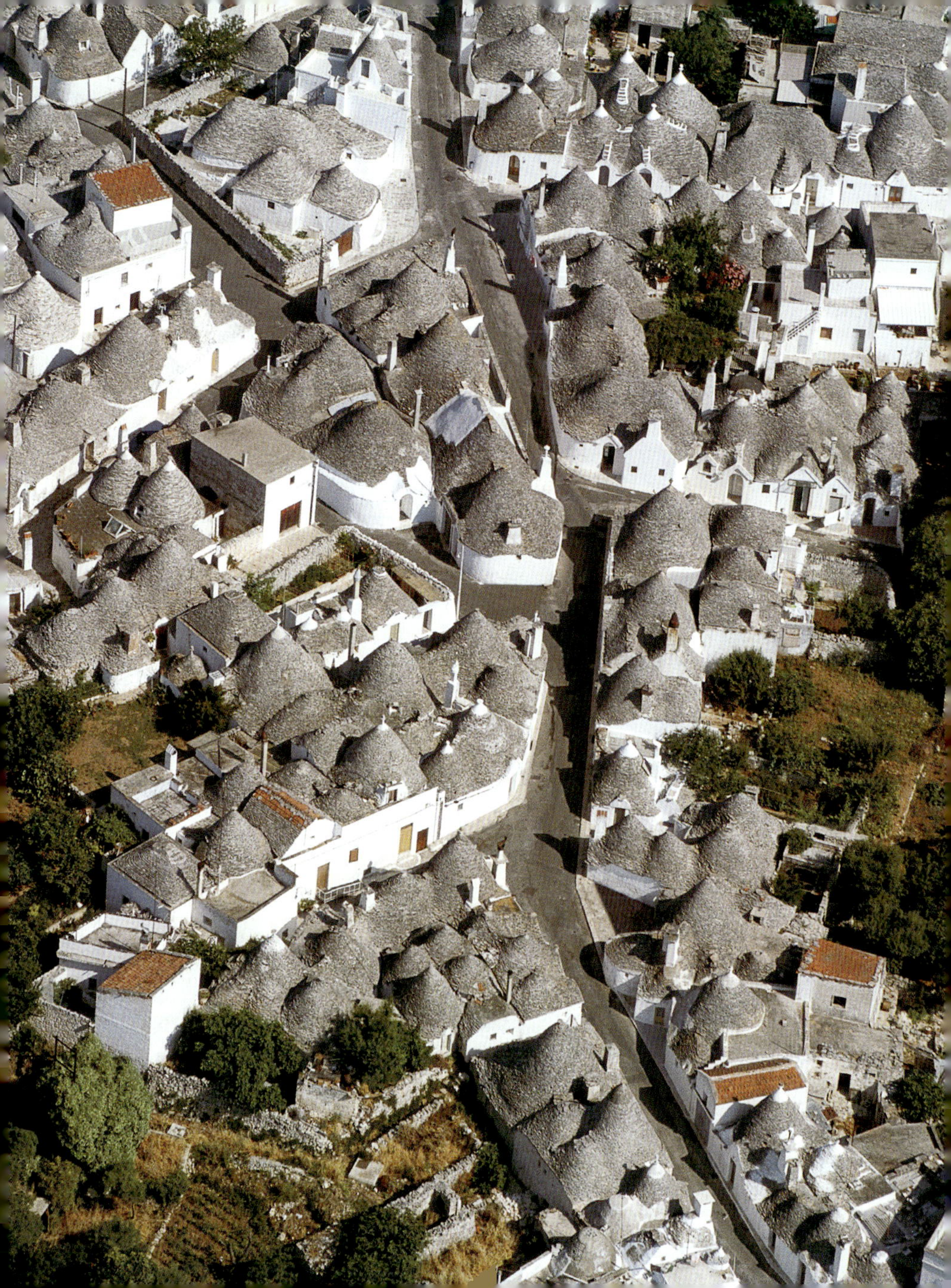

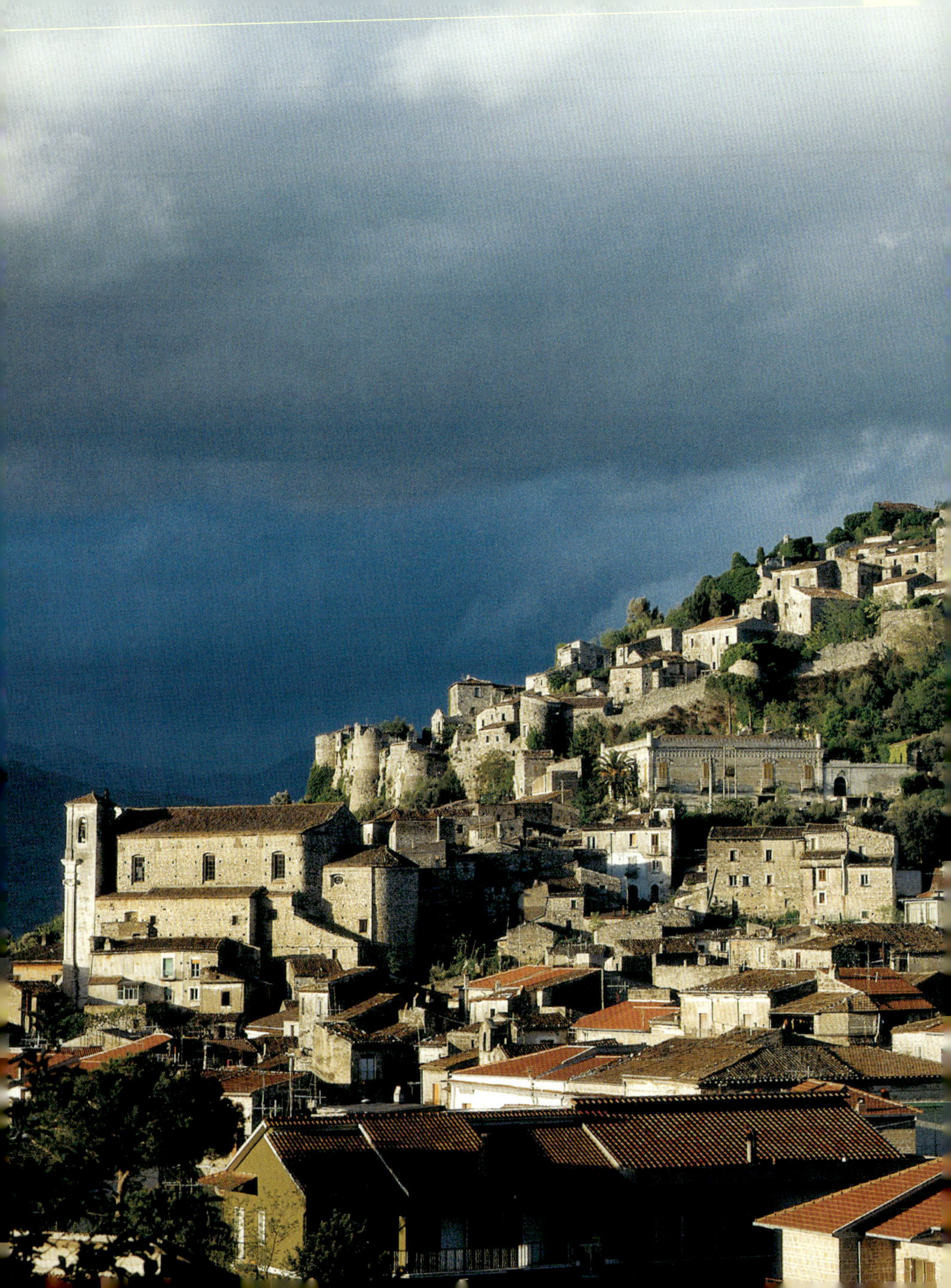

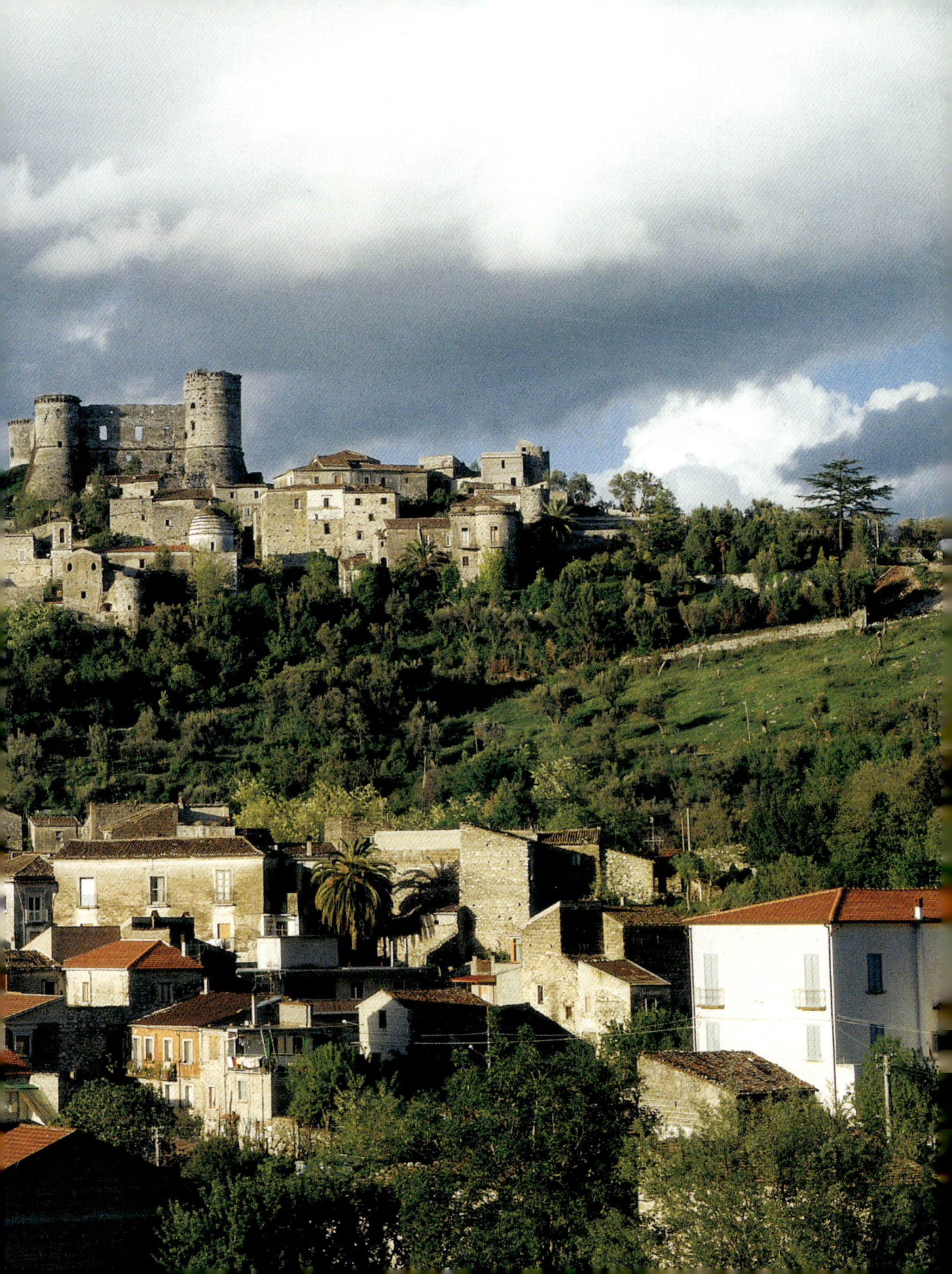

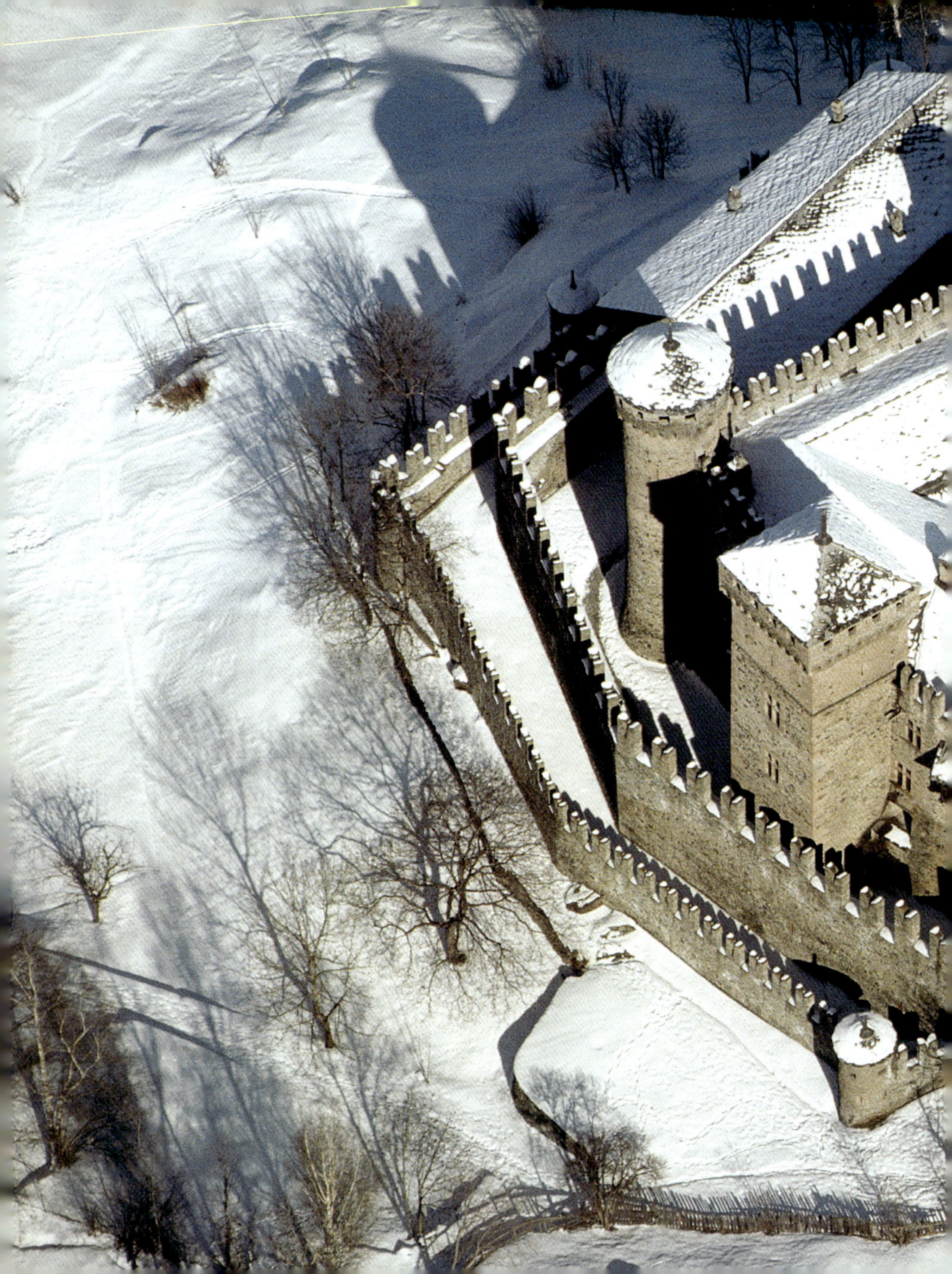

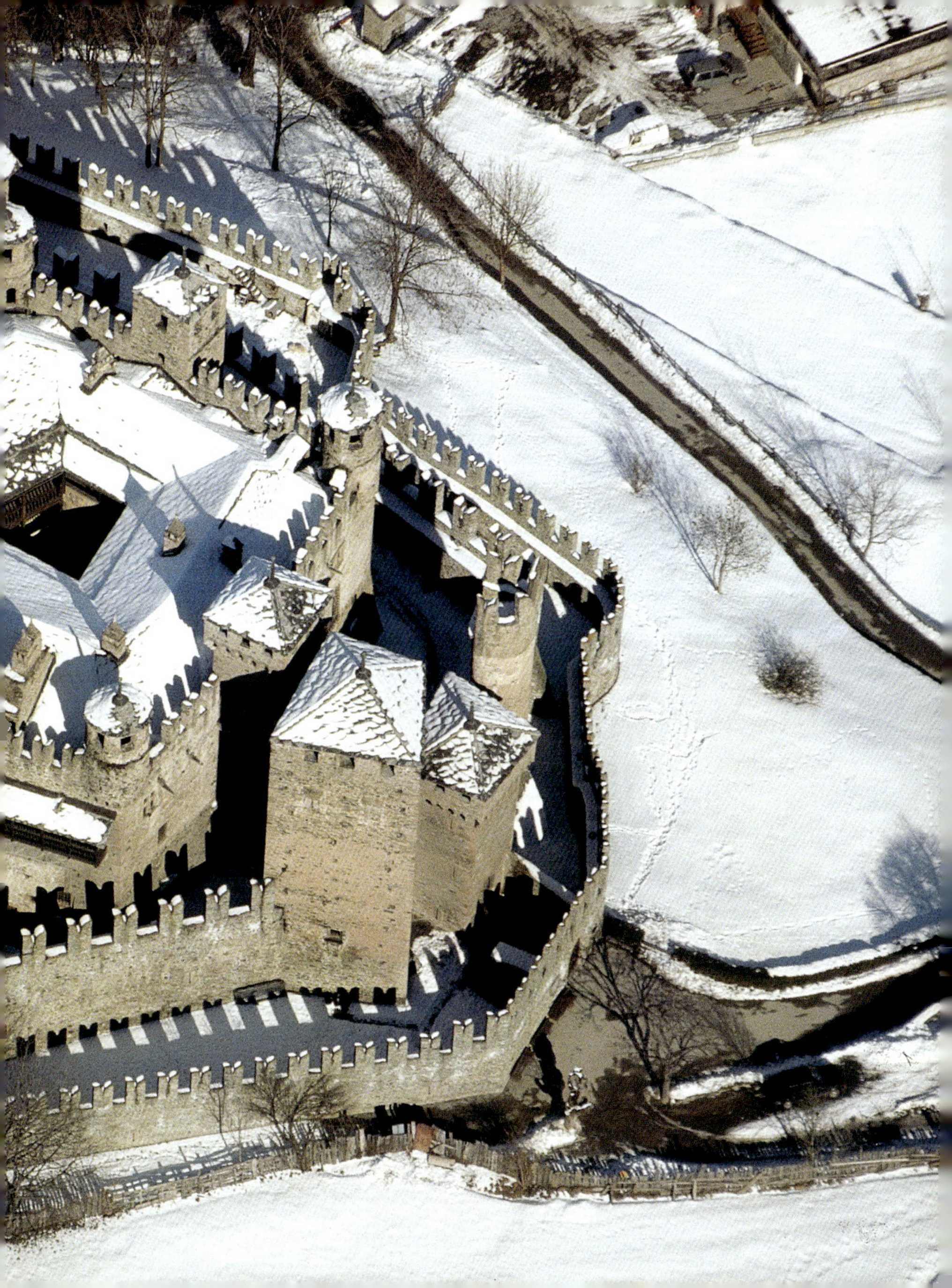

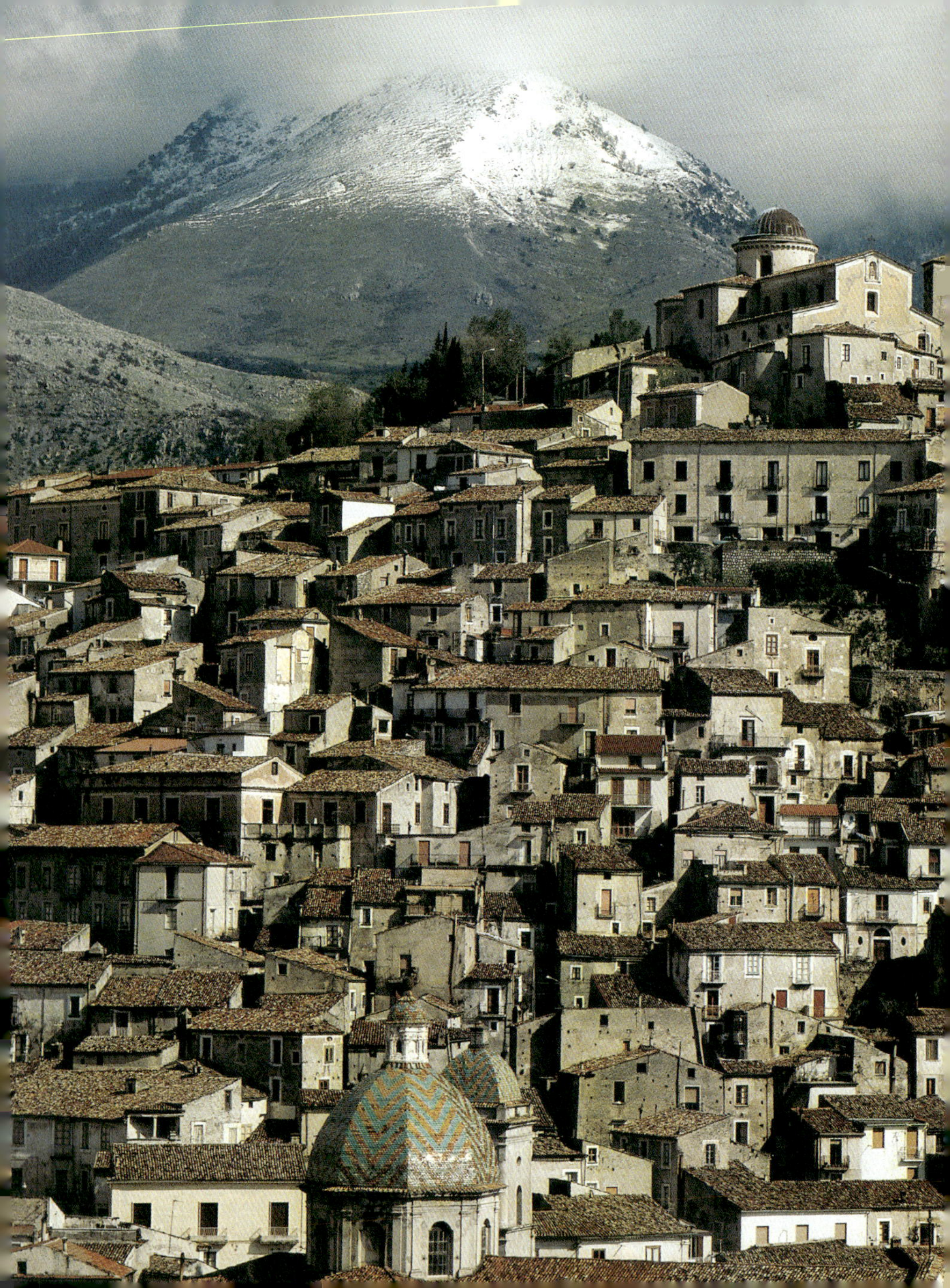

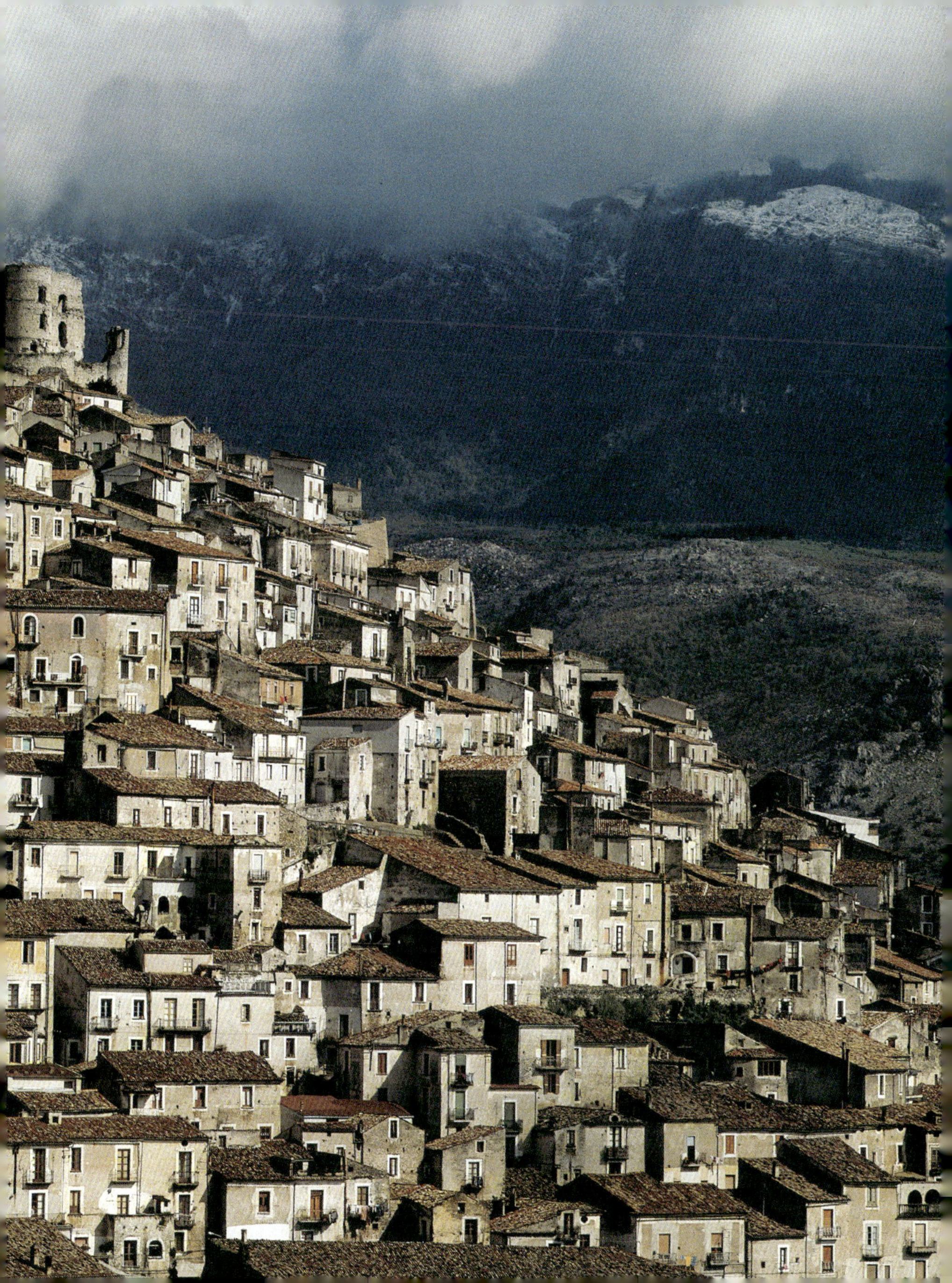

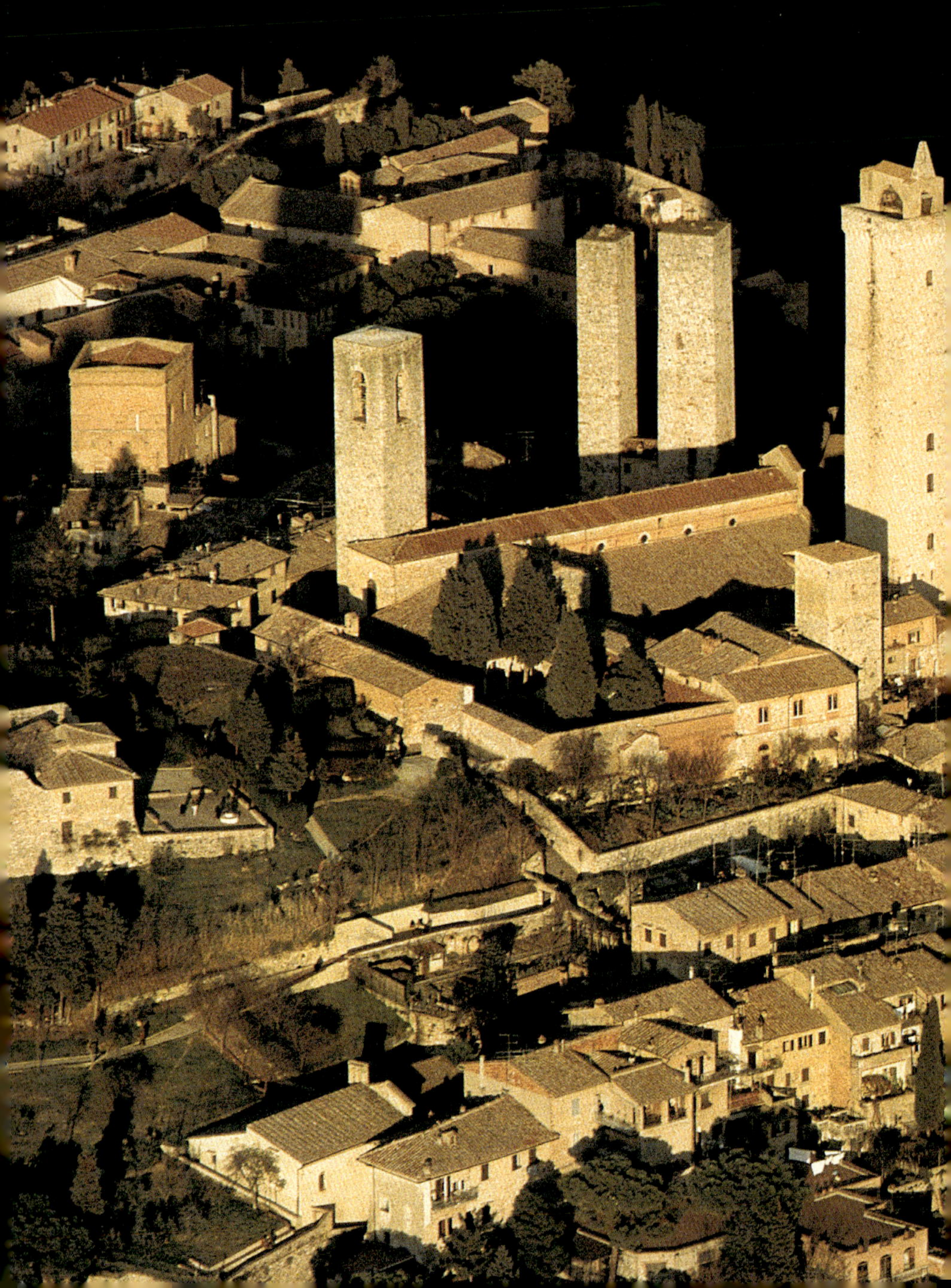

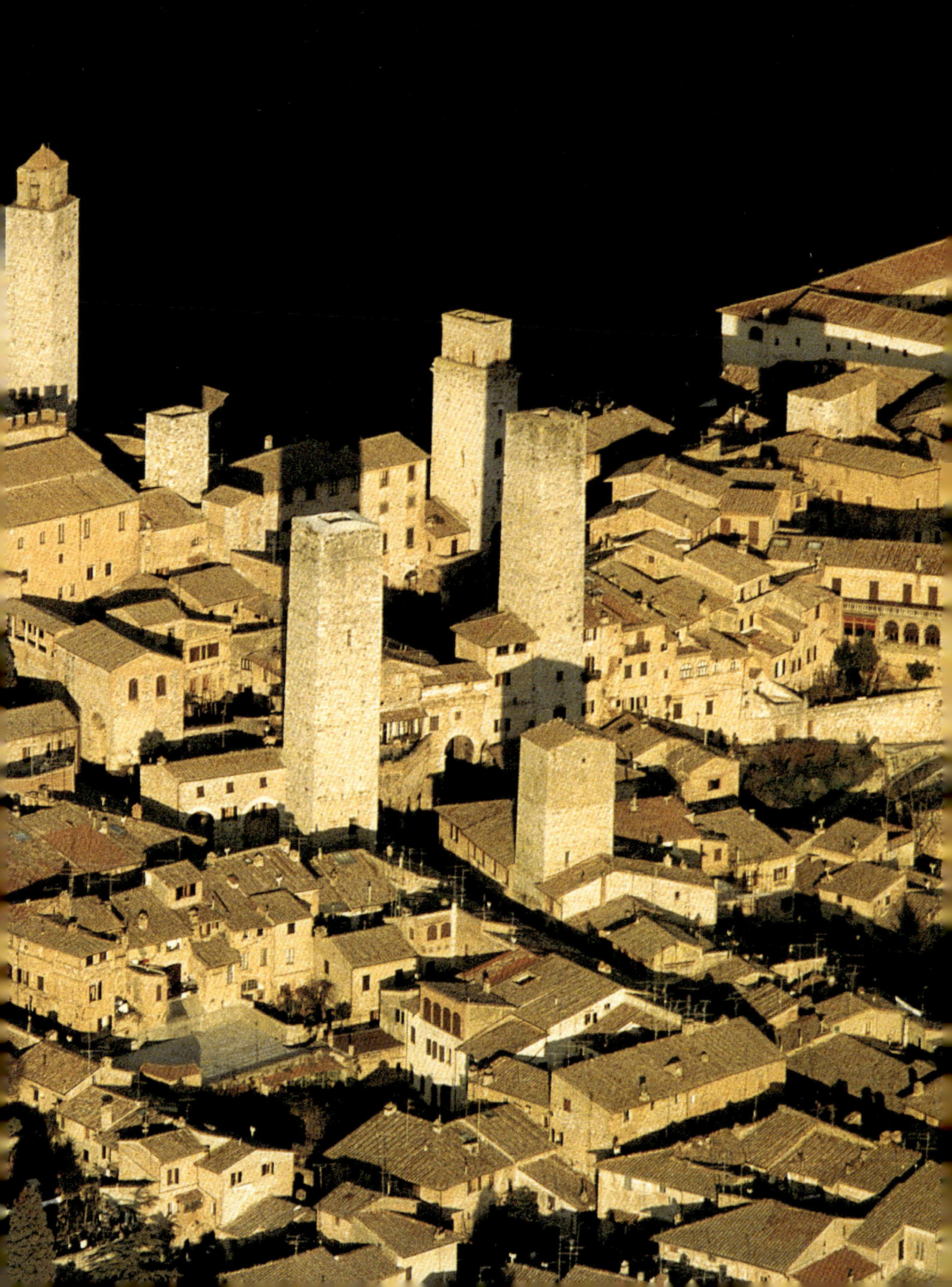

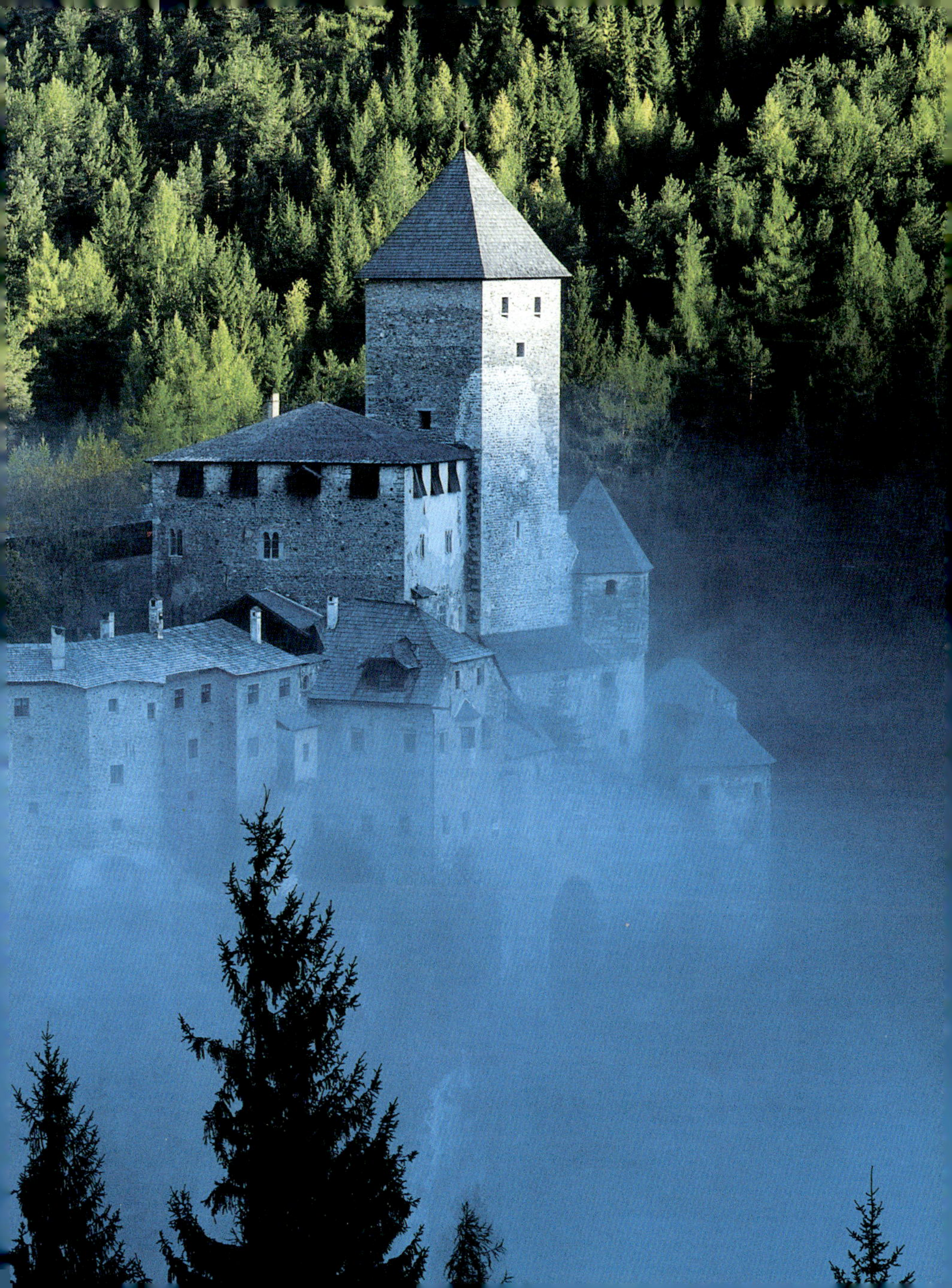

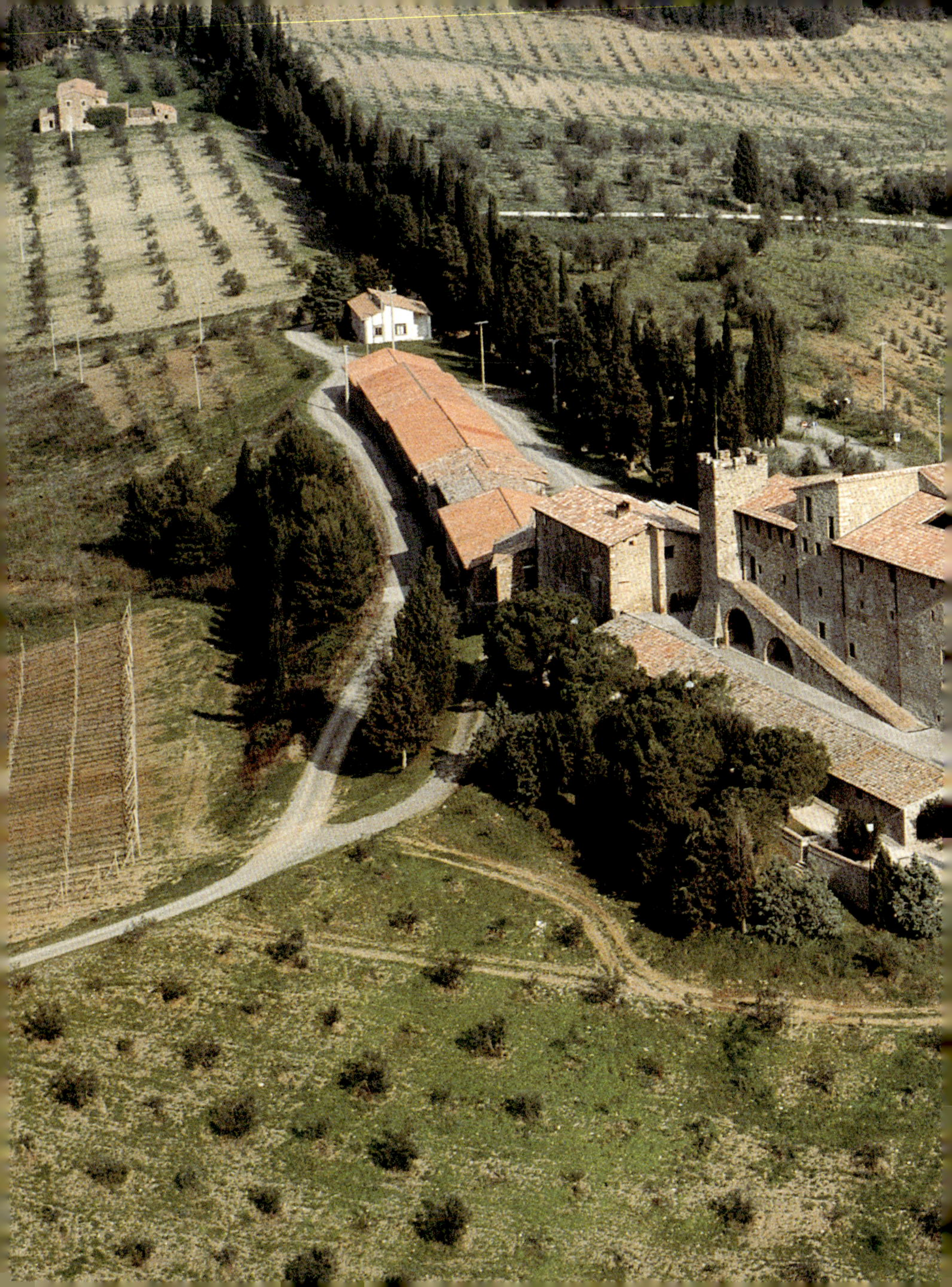

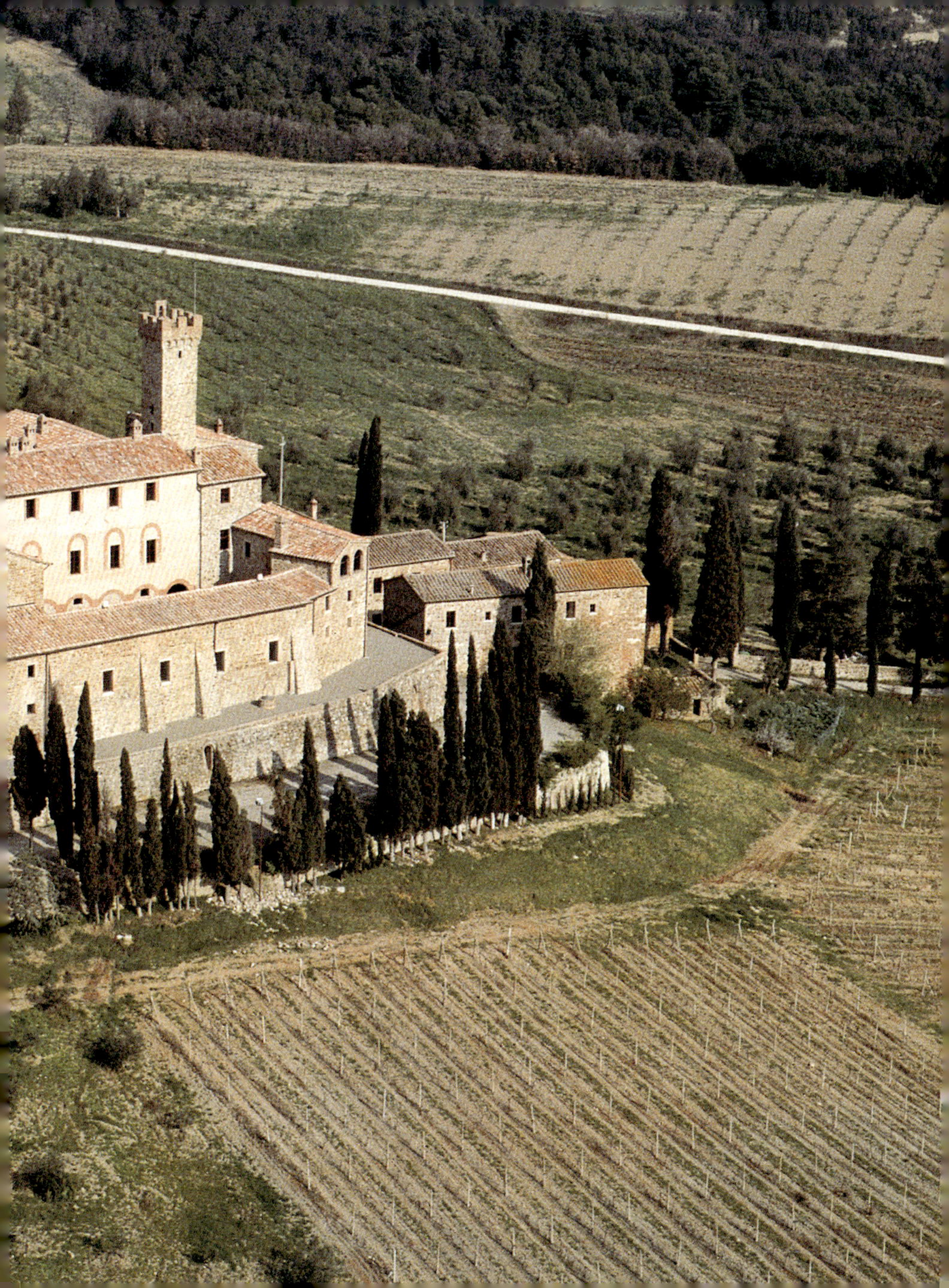

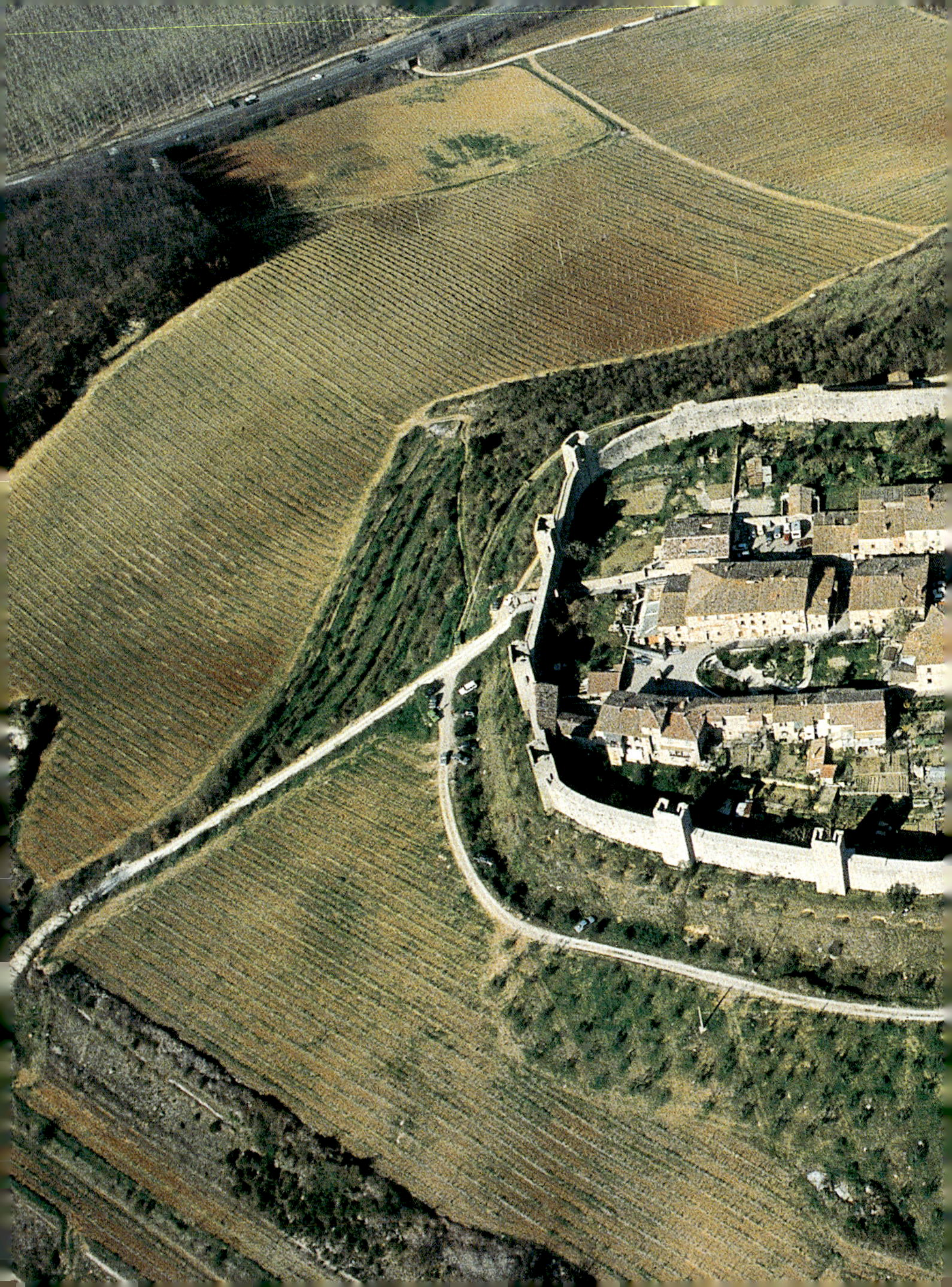

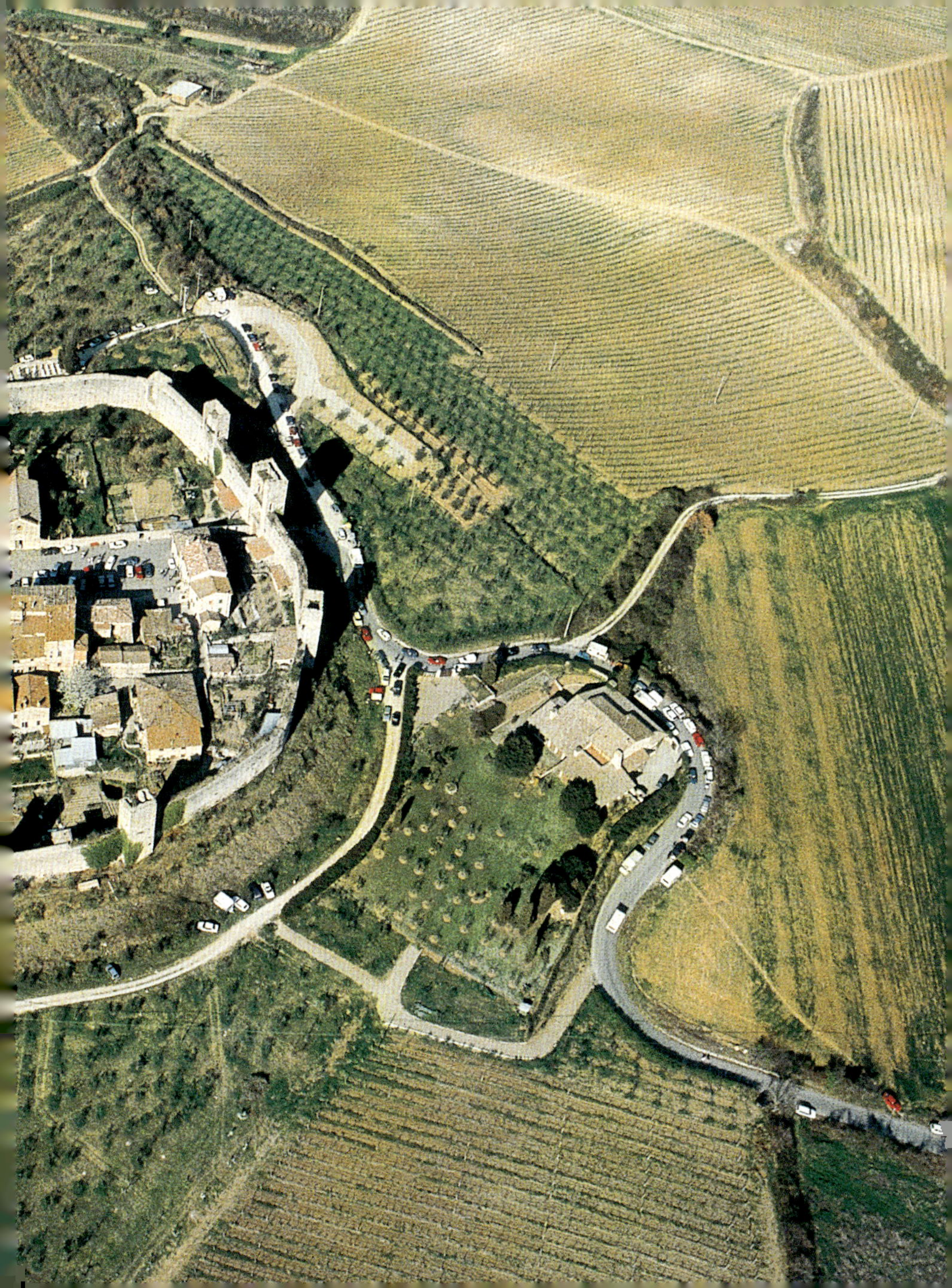

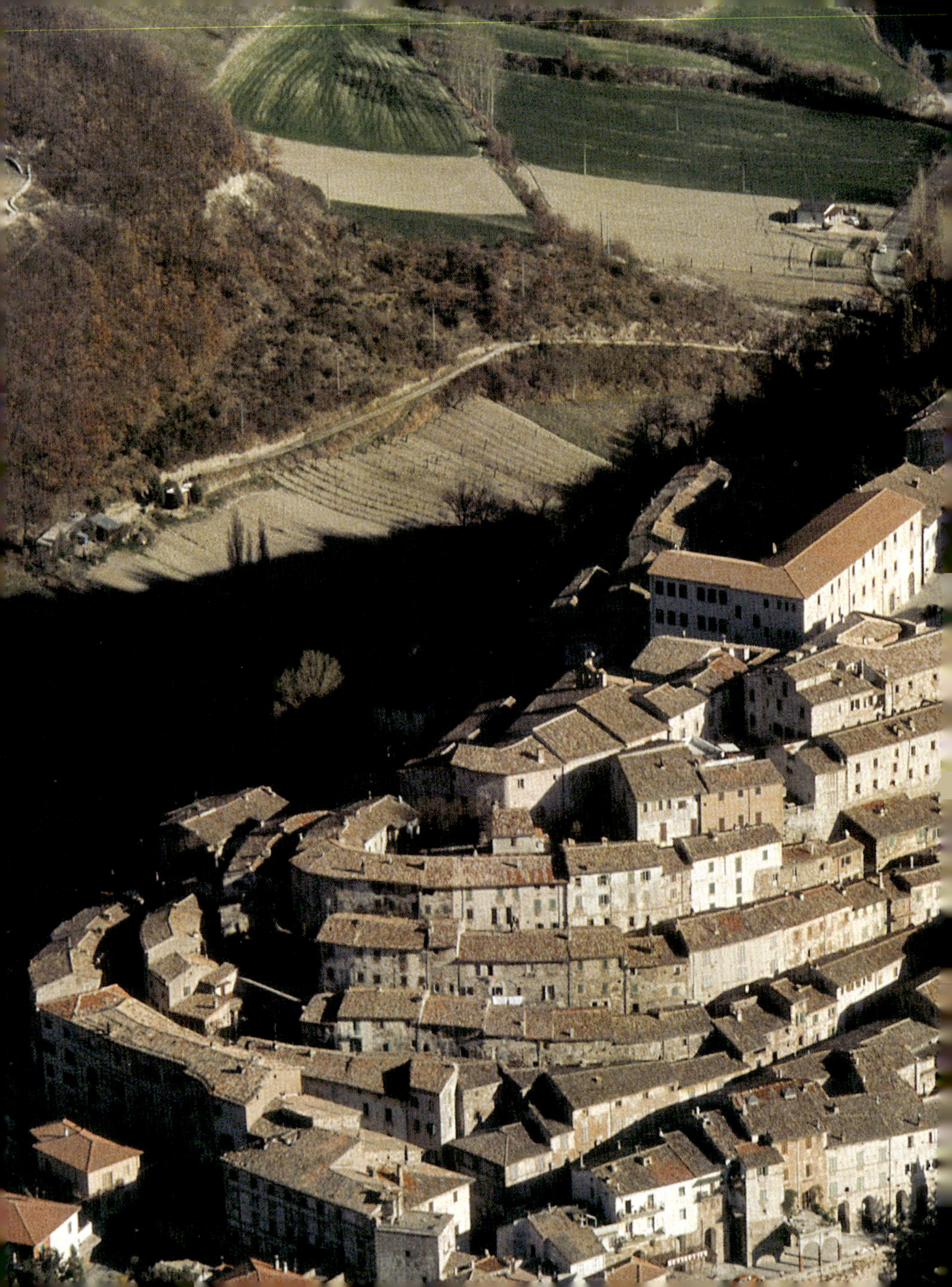

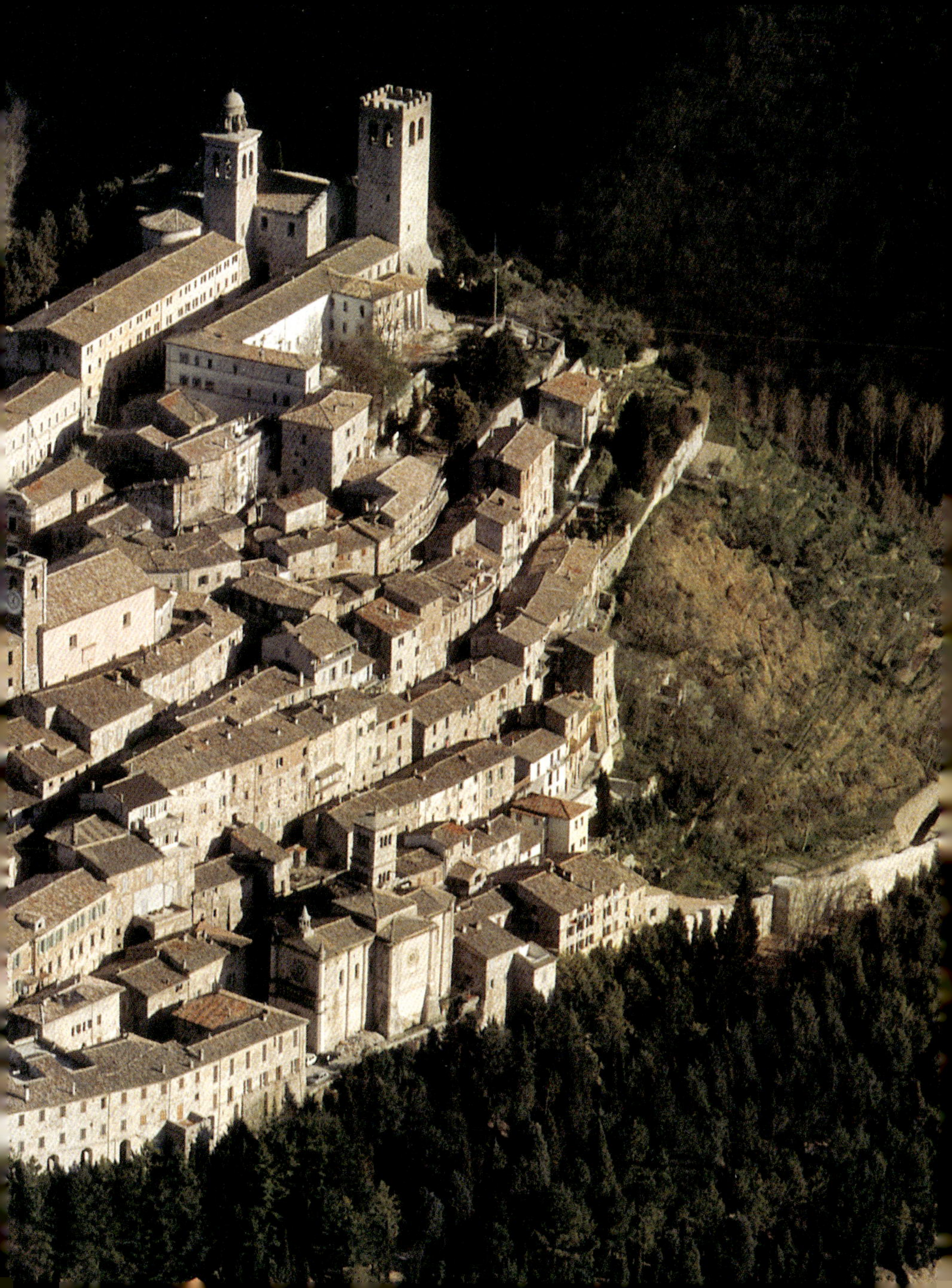

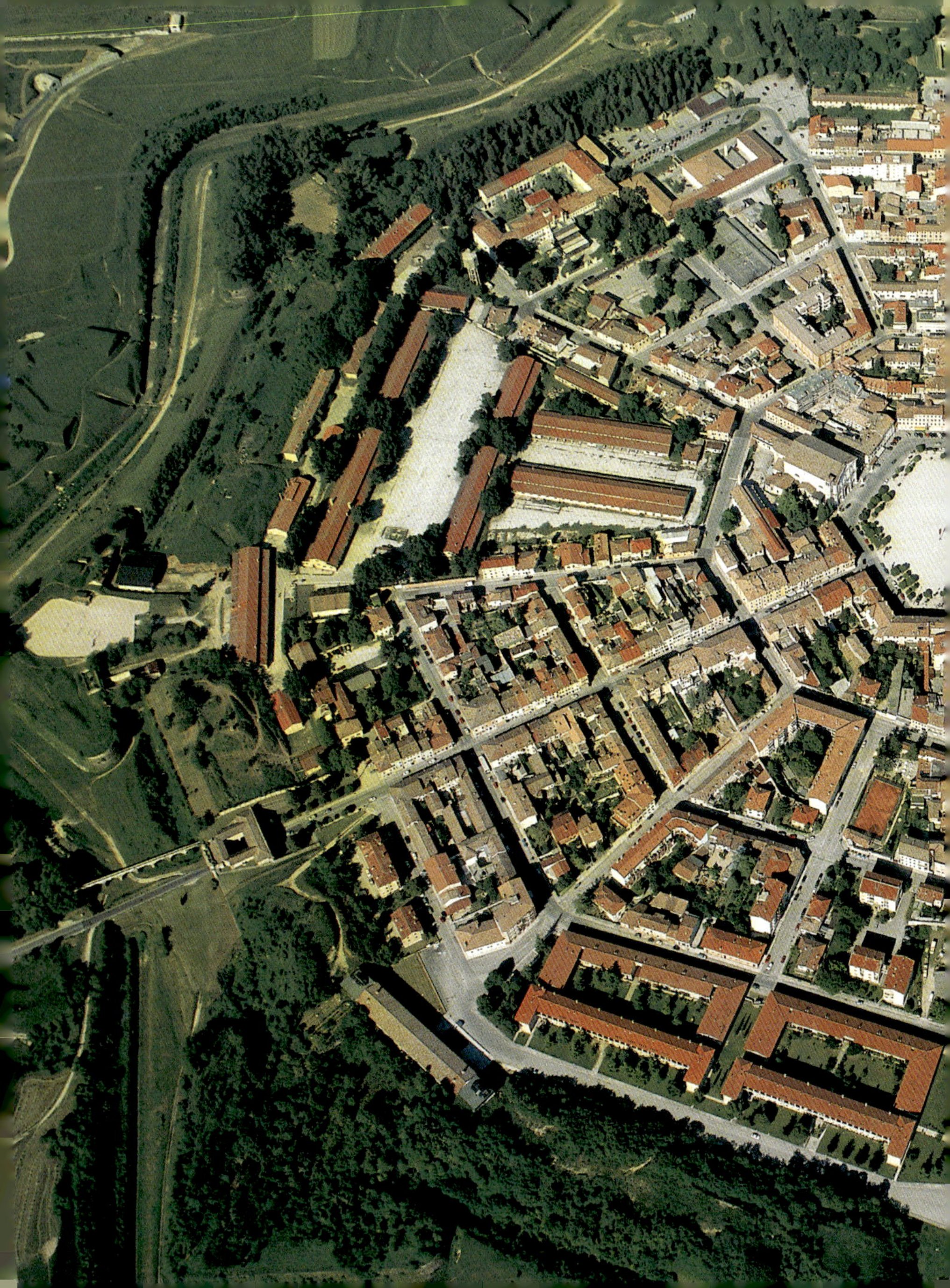

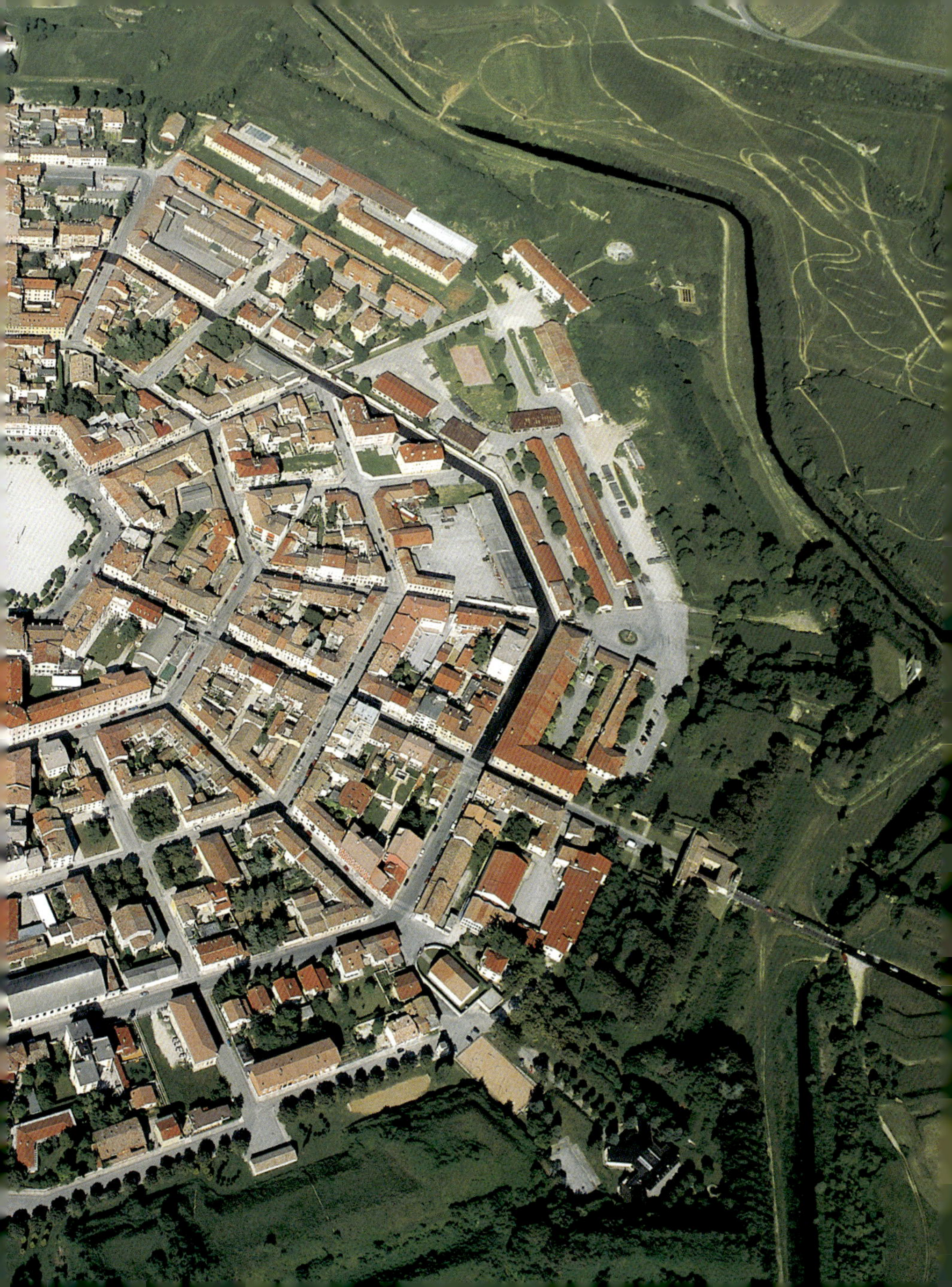

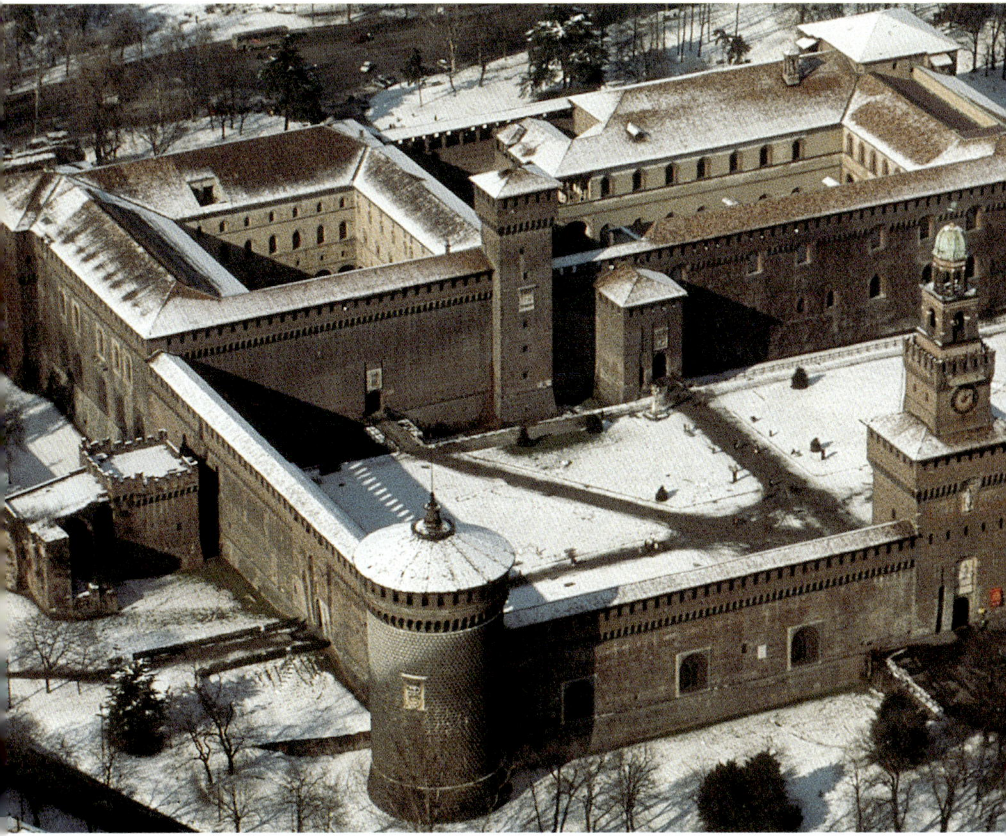

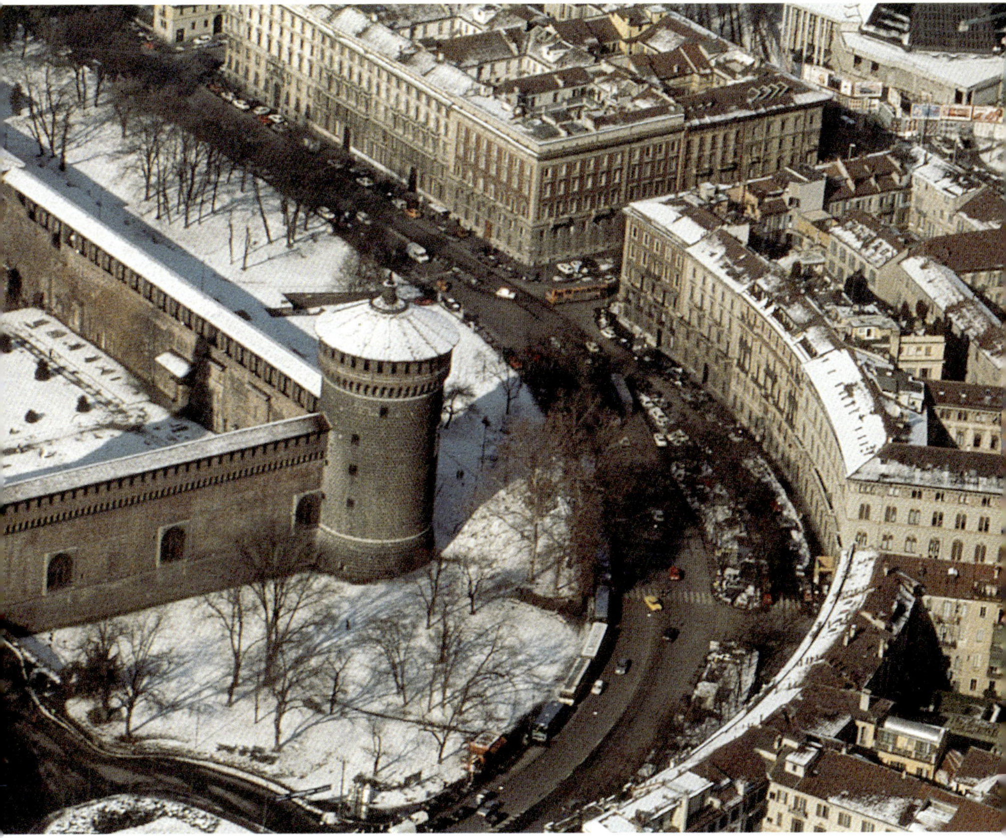

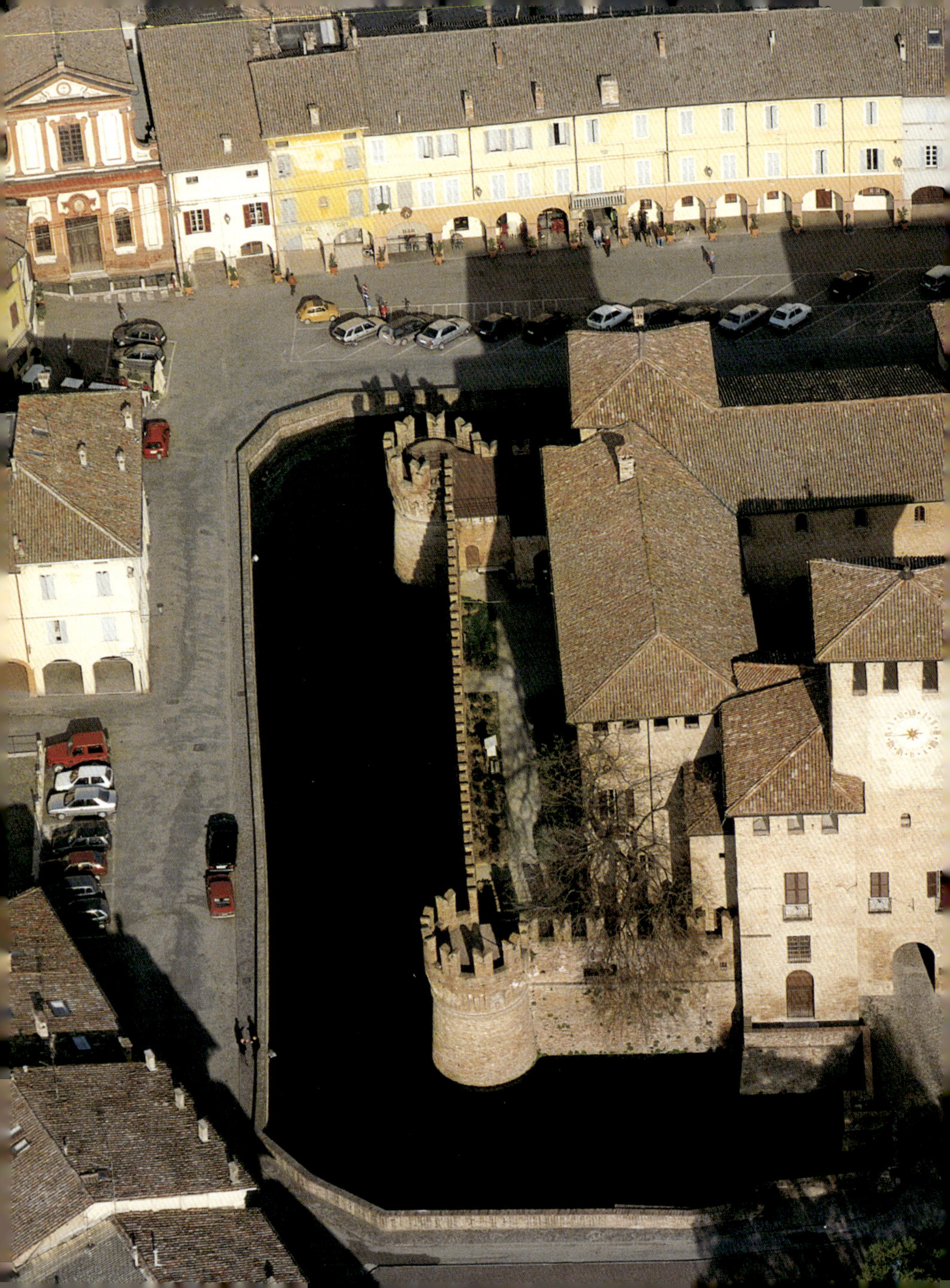

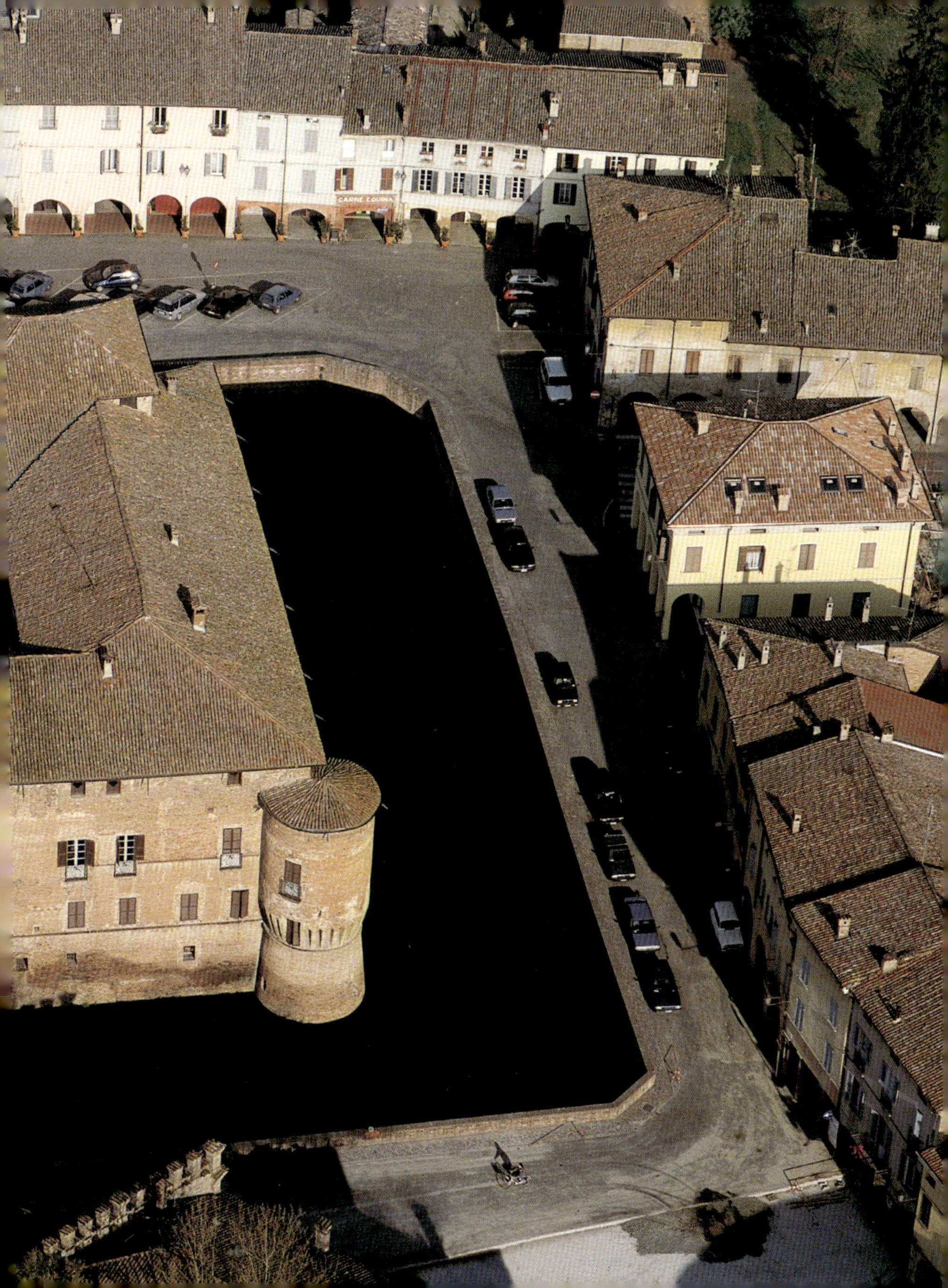
CARNE EQUINA

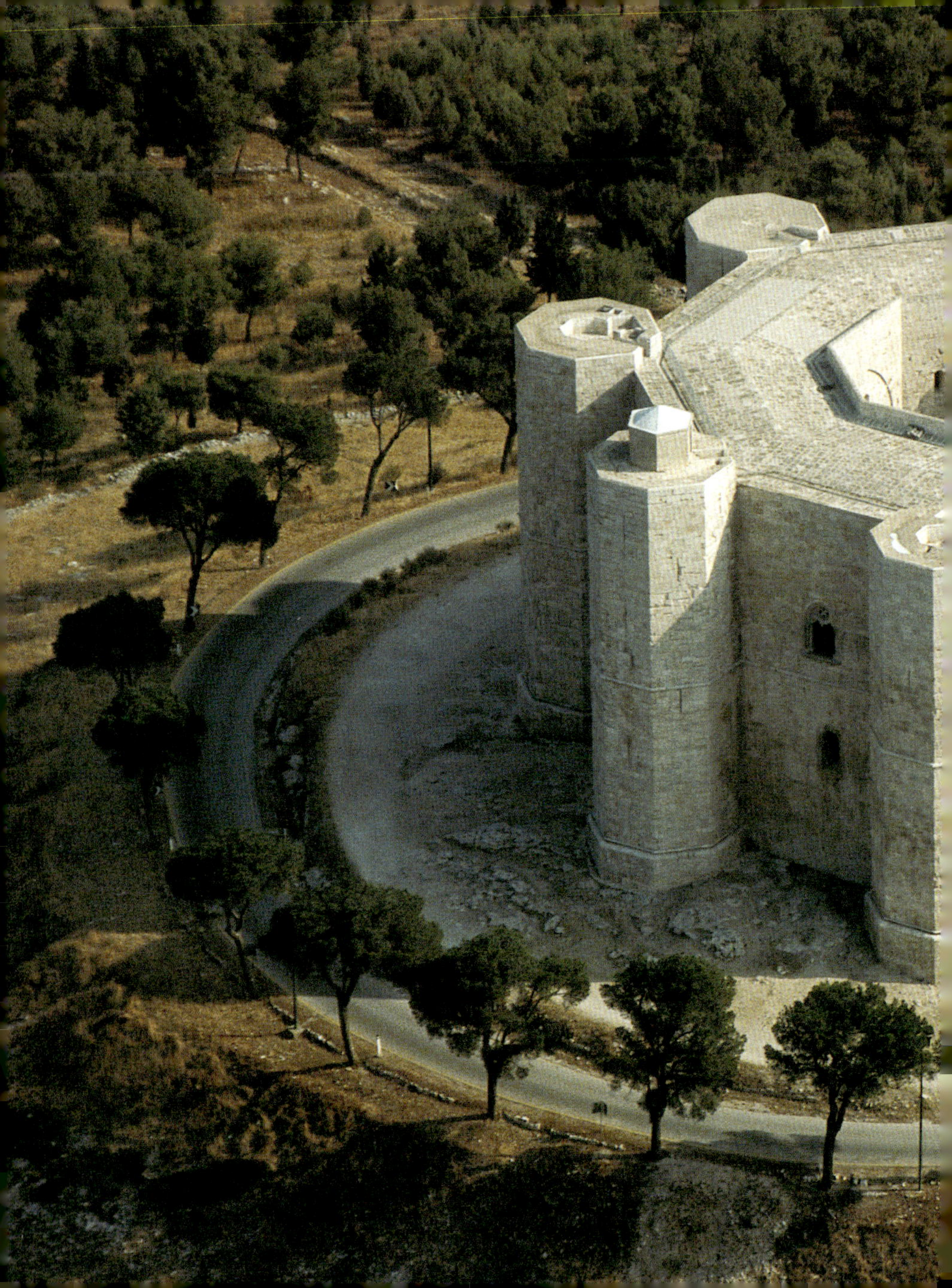

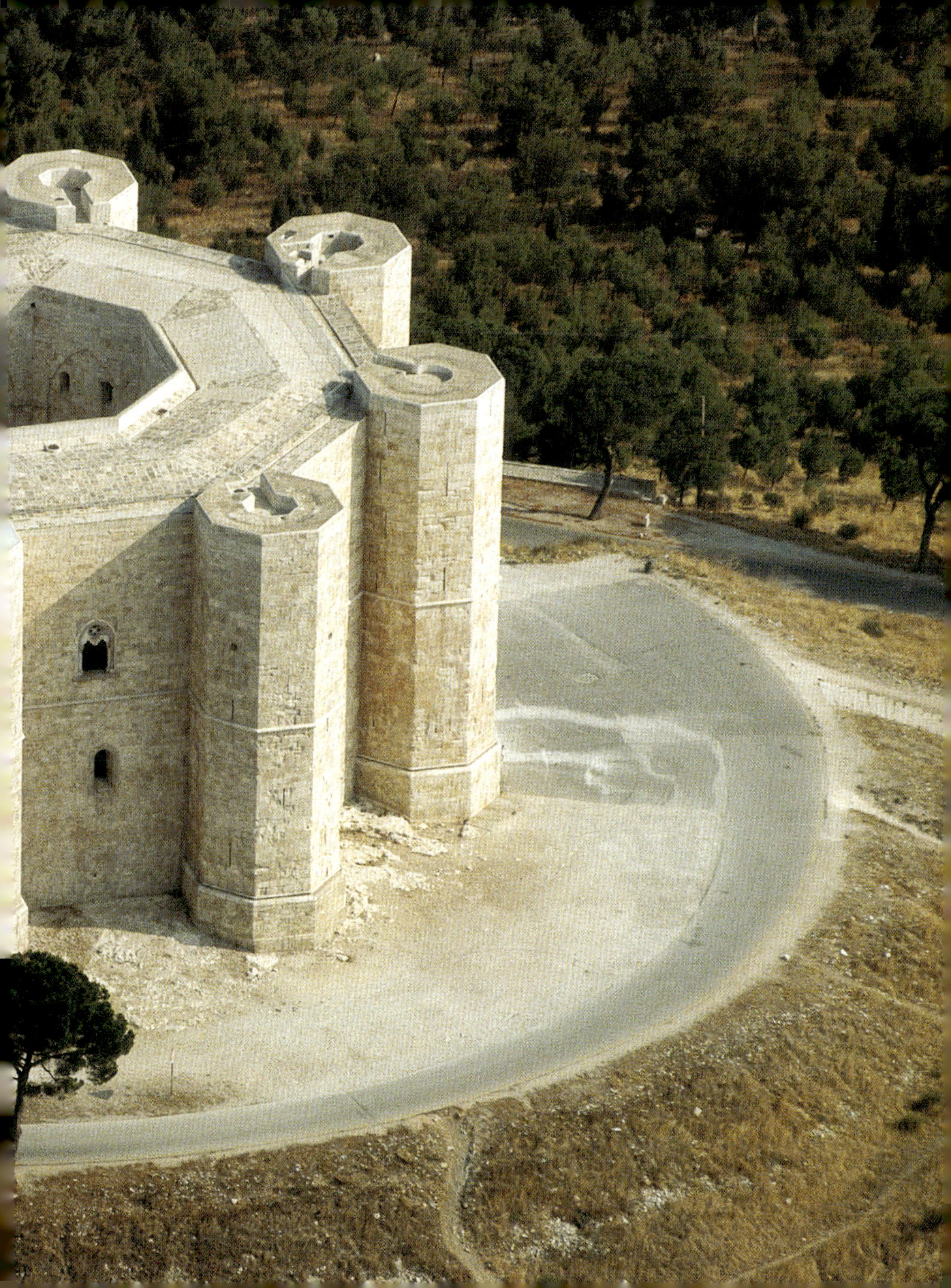

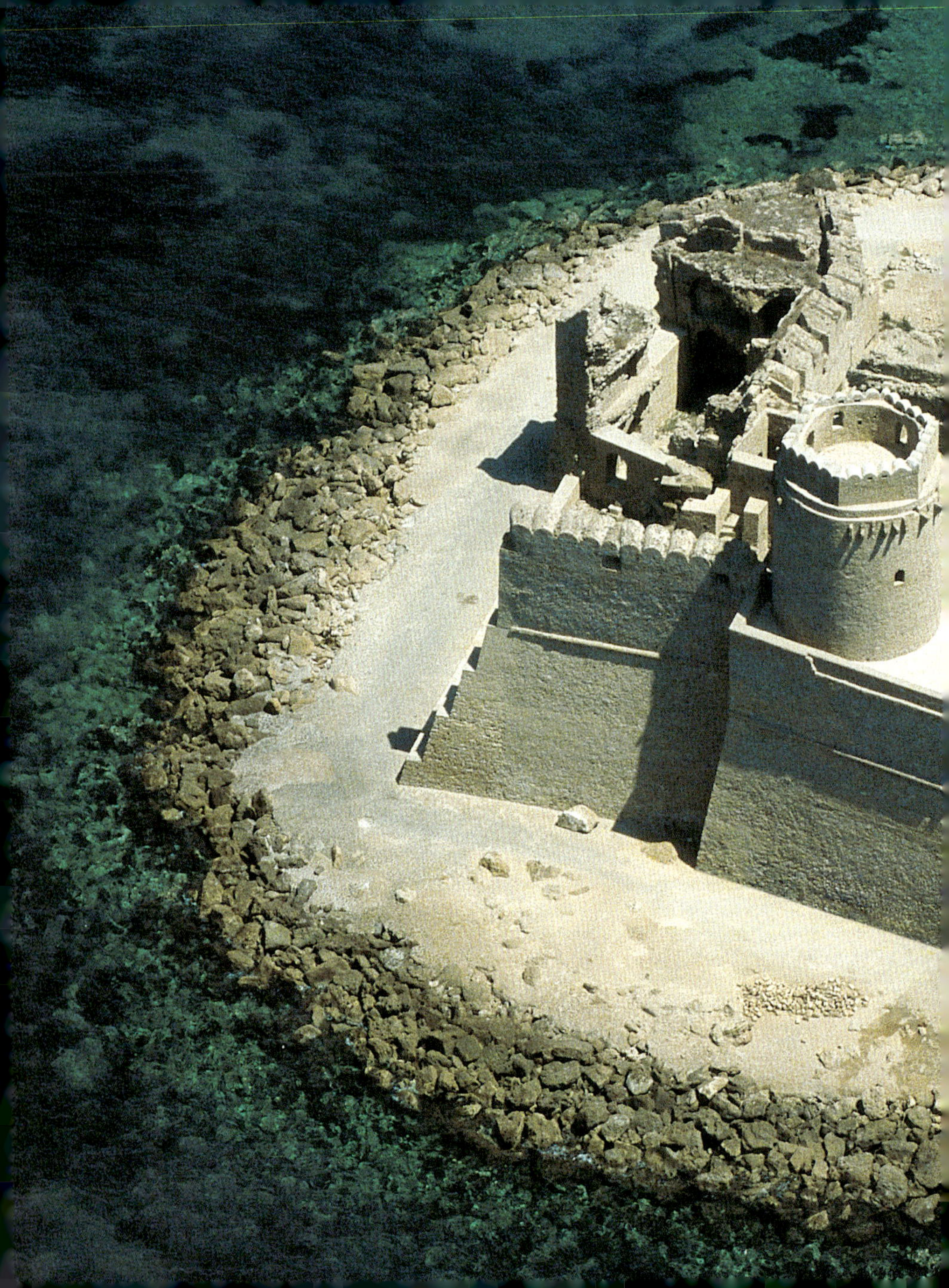

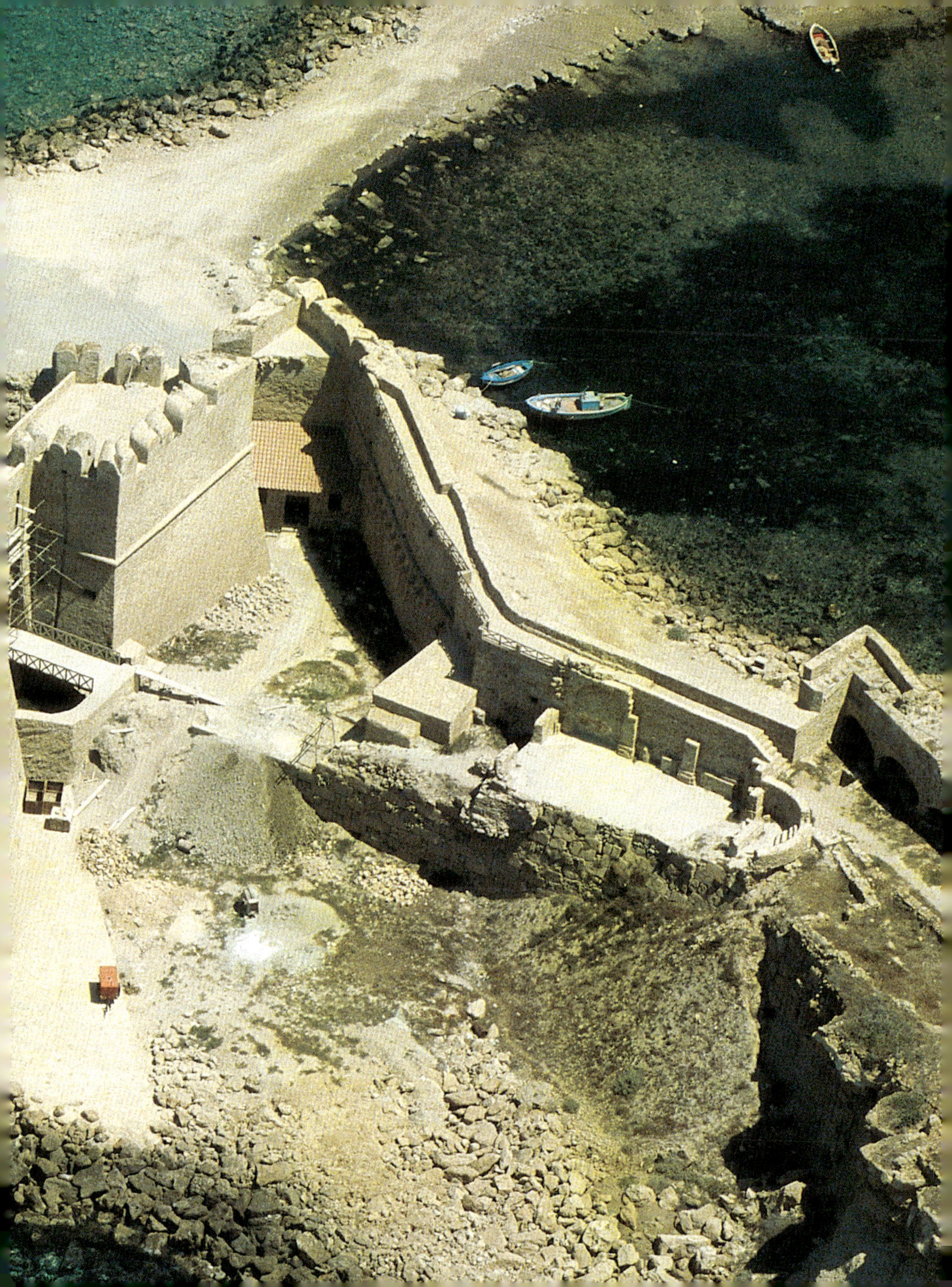

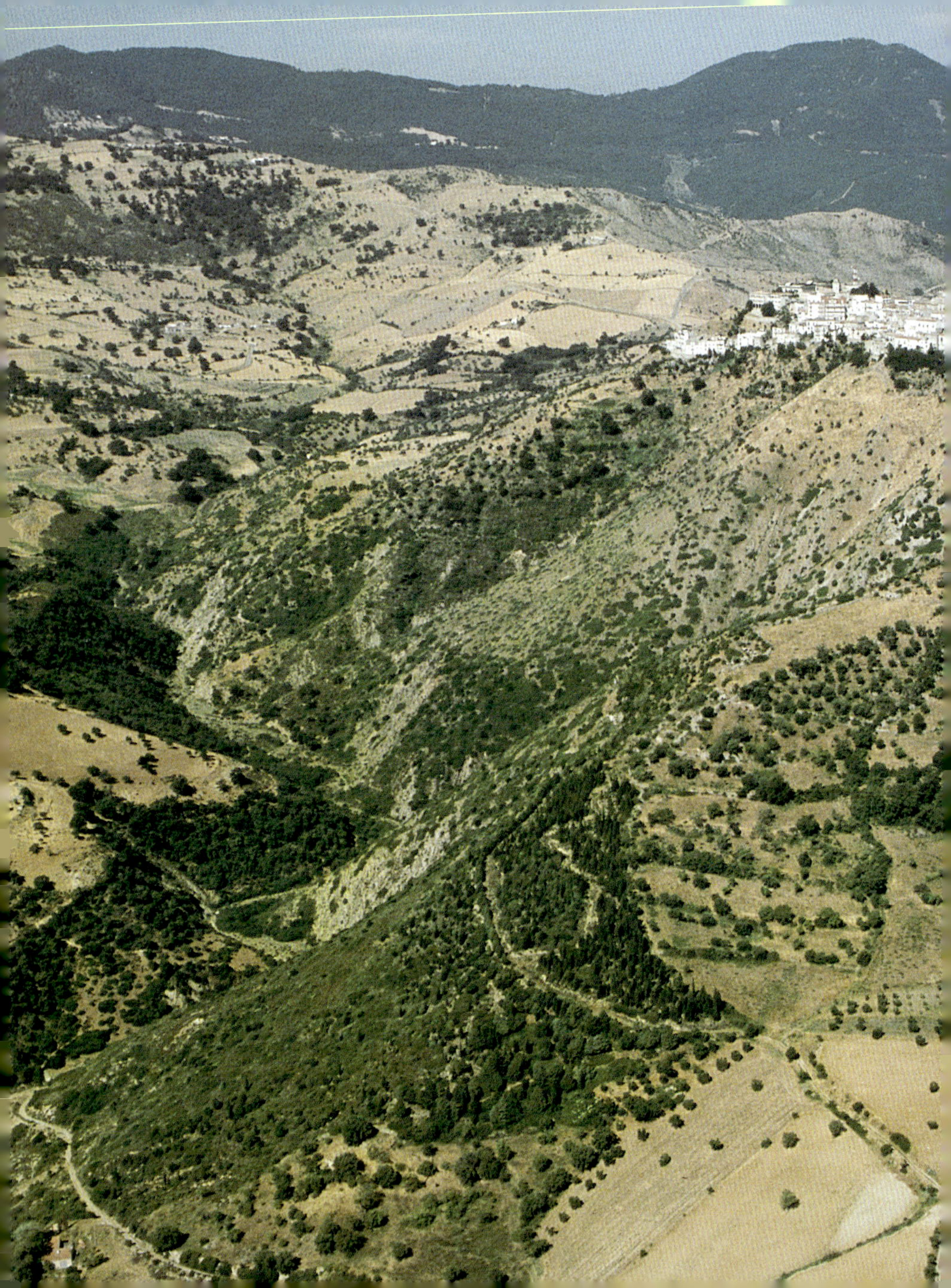

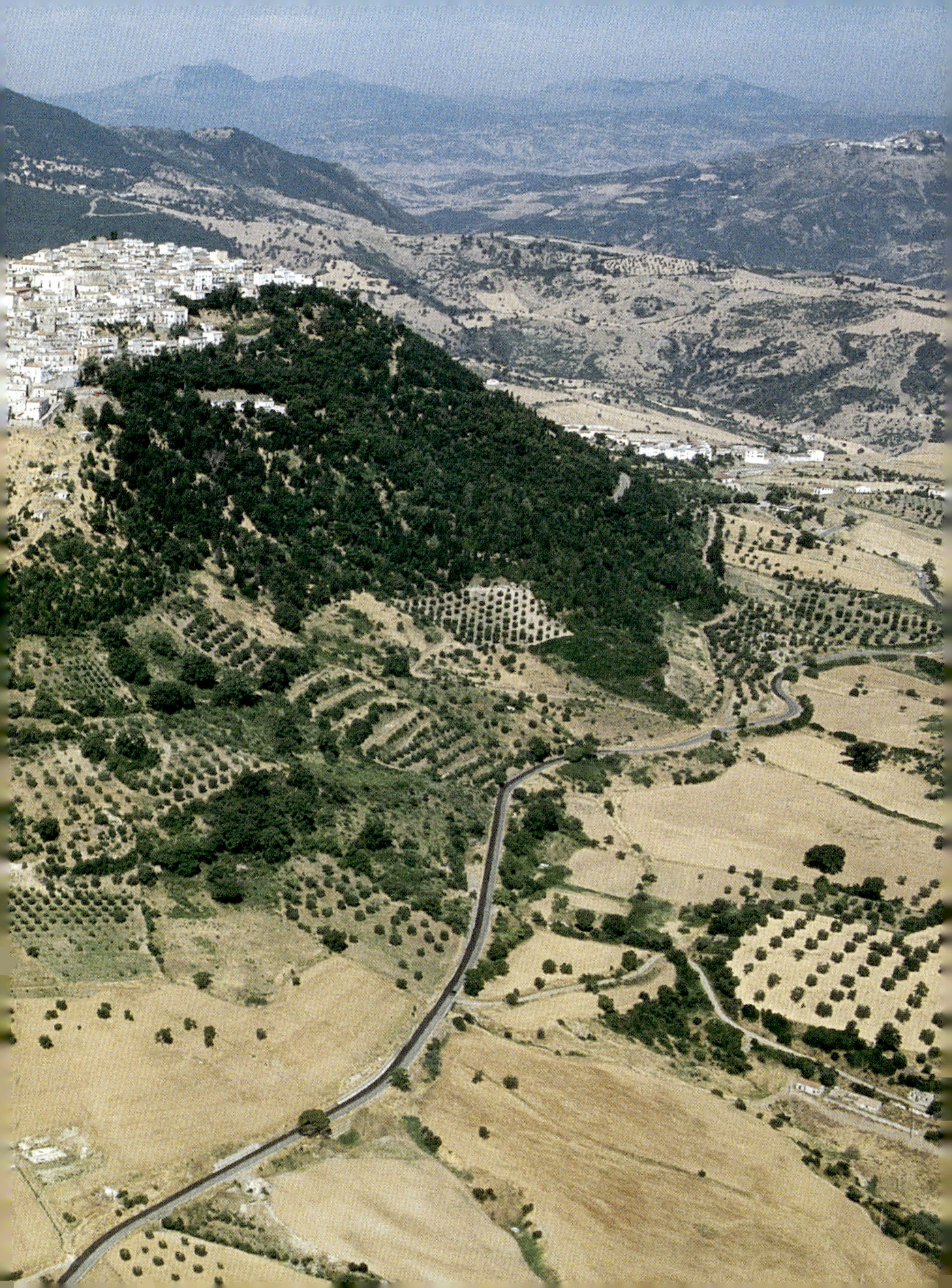

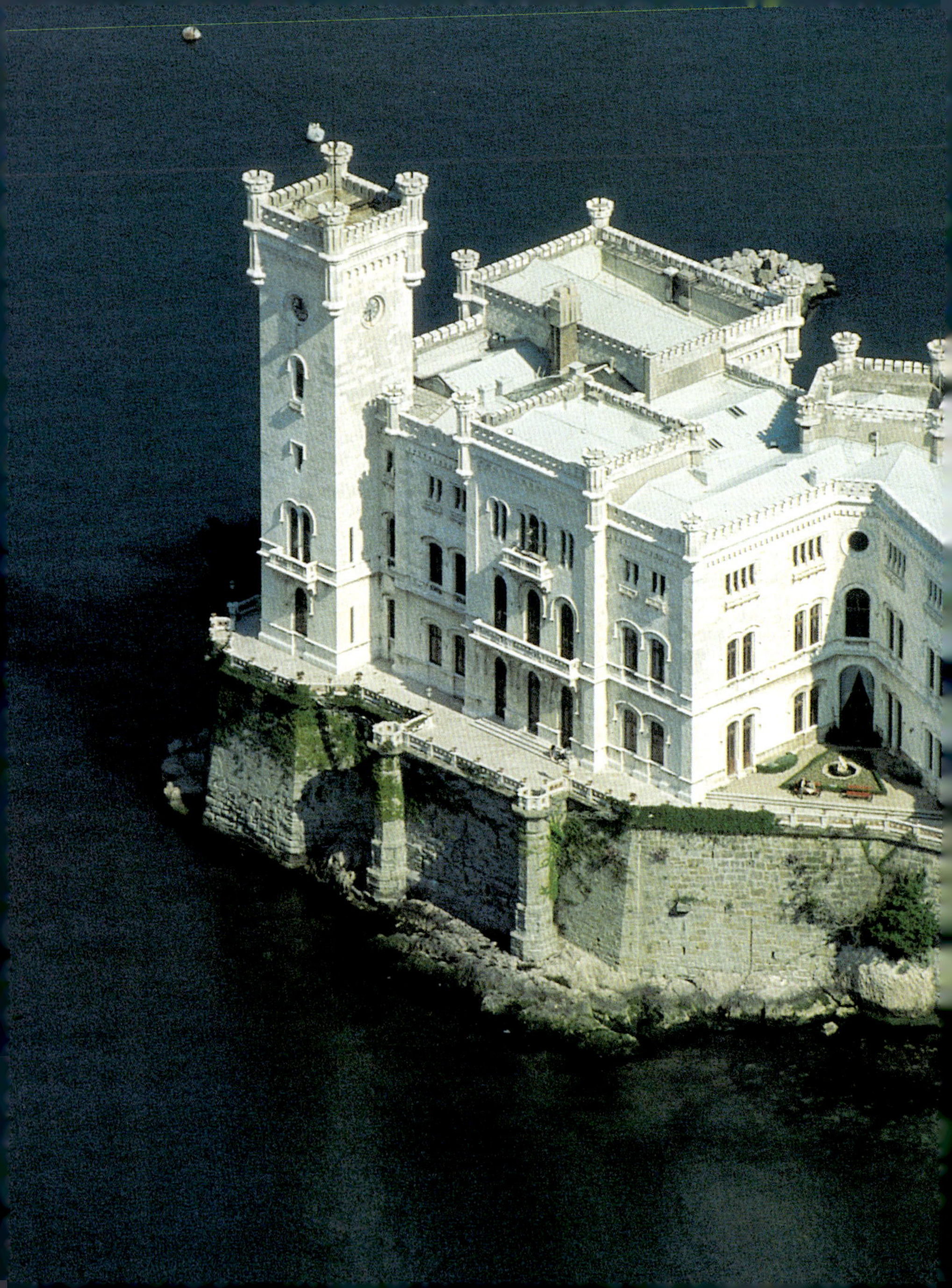

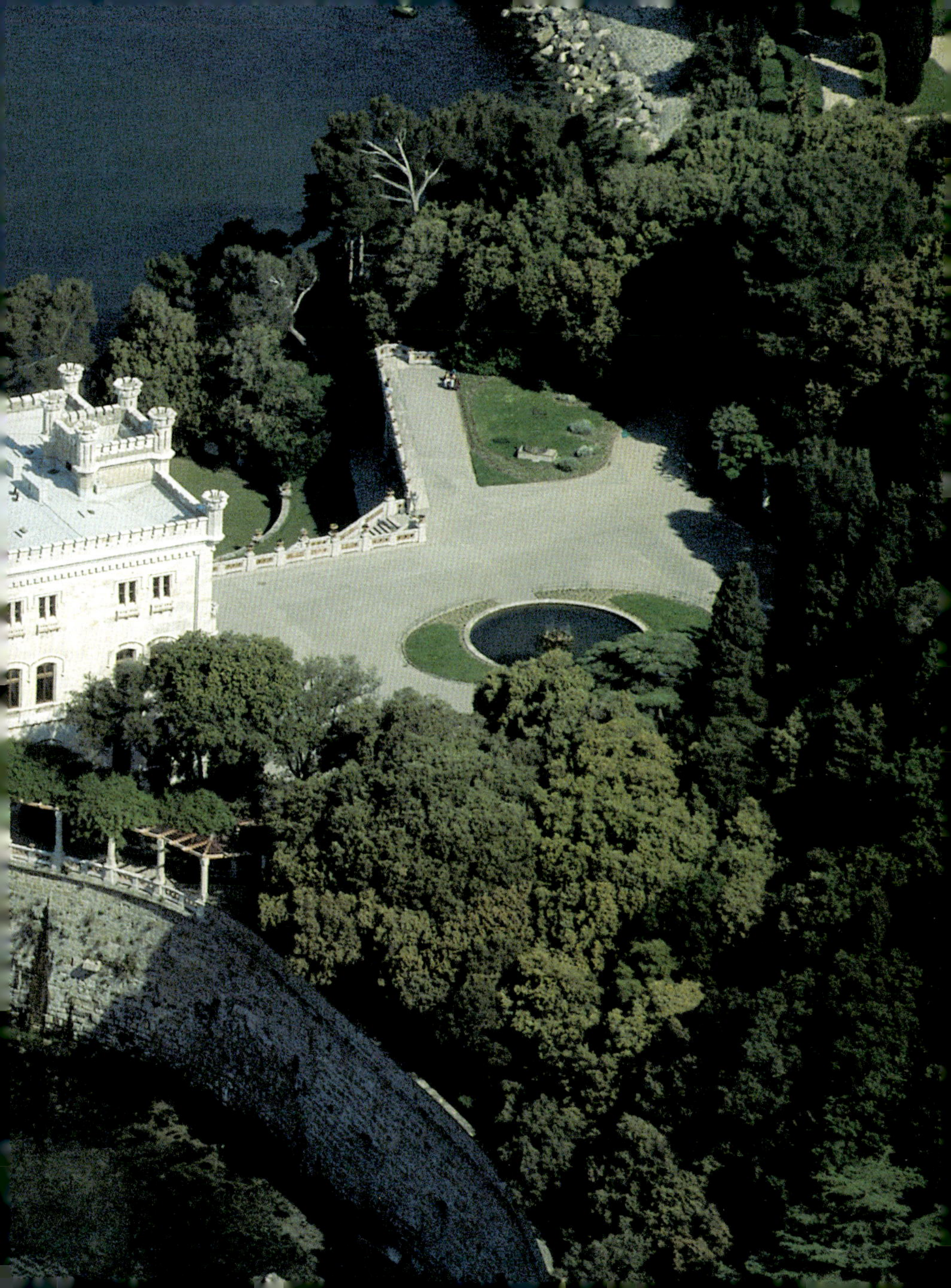

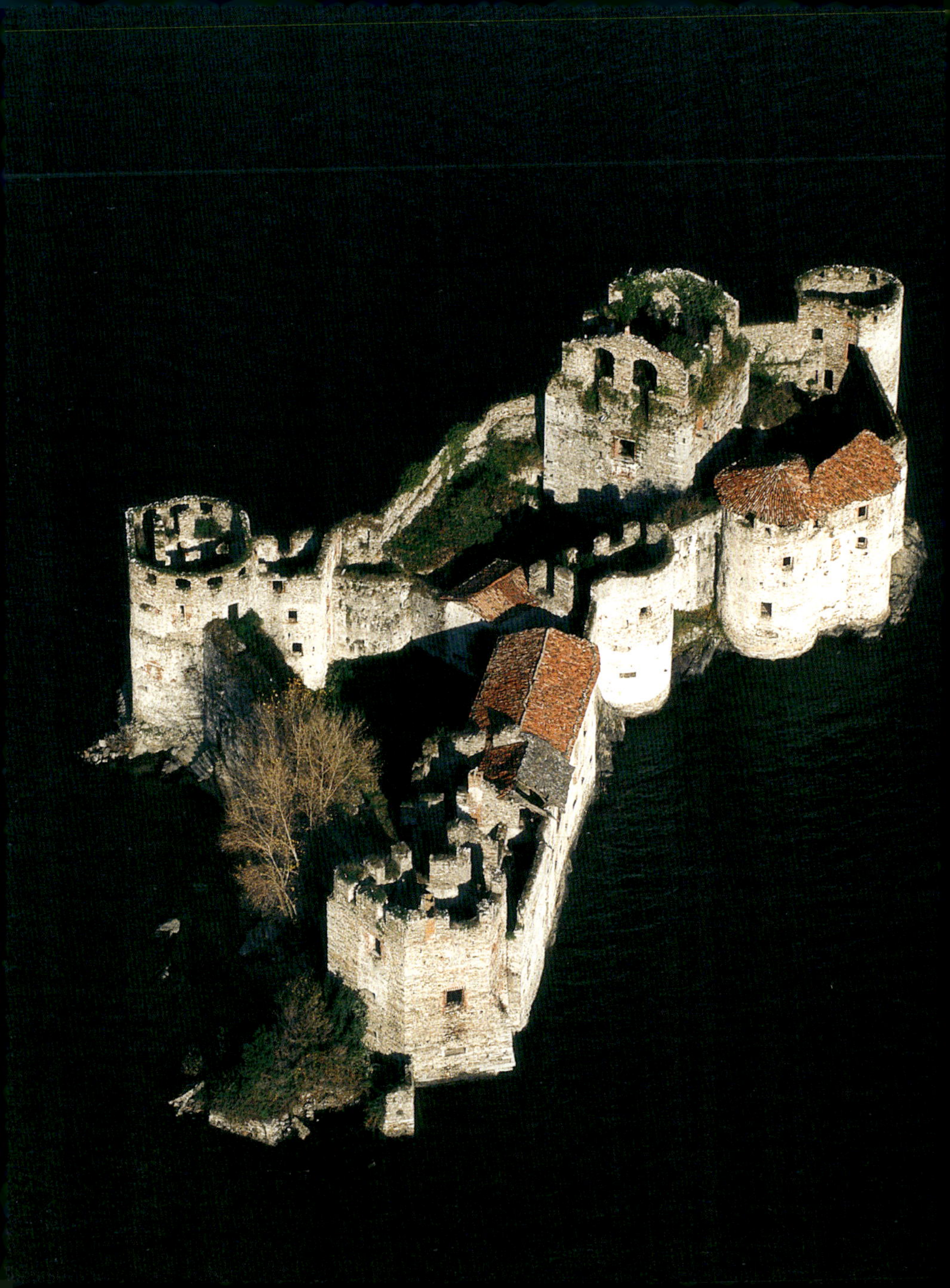

MOUNTAINS AND VOLCANOES

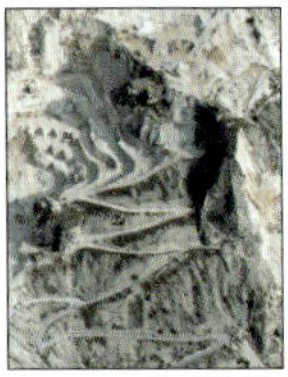

A VIEW OF ONE OF THE GIGANTIC MARBLE caves in the Apuan Alps, Tuscany, renowned for the quality of marble which has been quarried since the Roman age, mainly in the areas of Carrara, Massa and

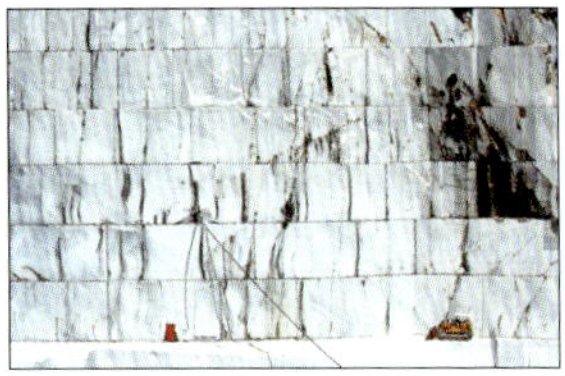

Seravezza. The wild landscape, the blinding brightness of the white caves and the titanic work of the man blend into an outstandingly beautiful scenery *(pp. 57, 58-59)*.

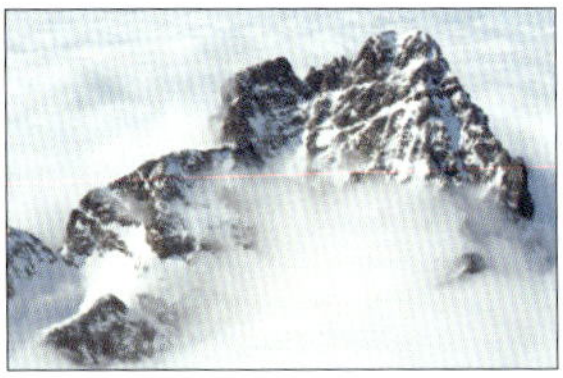

THE MONVISO, an imposing 3,841 metre-high peak of the Cozie Alps, is also called "King of Stone." With its majesty it overlooks the whole Piedmontese plan: at its foot, in the Pian del Re, rises the Po *(pp. 60-61)*.

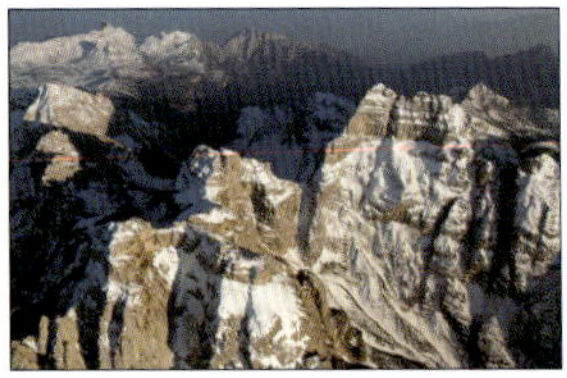

THE IMPOSING DOLOMITES RANGE of the Pale of San Martino presents steep faces and colour-changing spires which play with the light, from dawn's pink shades to sunset's orange hues *(pp. 62-63)*.

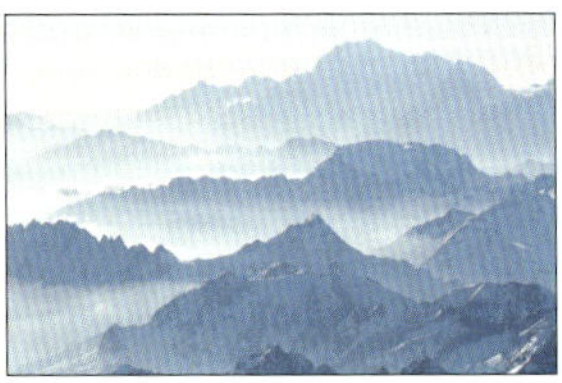

A VIEW OF THE ALPINE RANGE in the Valle d'Aosta reveals a sequence of glaciers and rocky mountains. They include some of the highest European peaks such as Mount Bianco, Mount Cervino and Mount Rosa *(pp. 64-65)*.

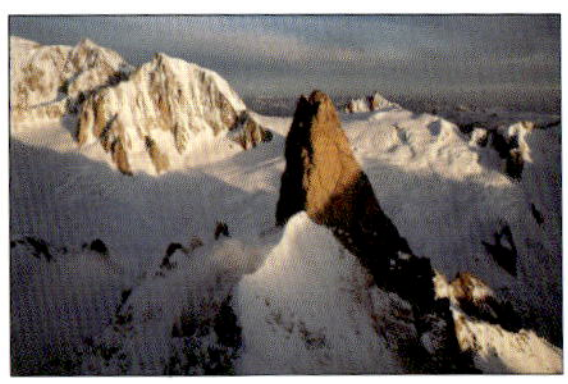

THE DENTE DEL GIGANTE (the Giant's Tooth), a granitic monolith of a distinctive shape, stands out alone amongst the glaciers and canyons of Mount Bianco, the highest peak in Europe *(pp. 66-67)*.

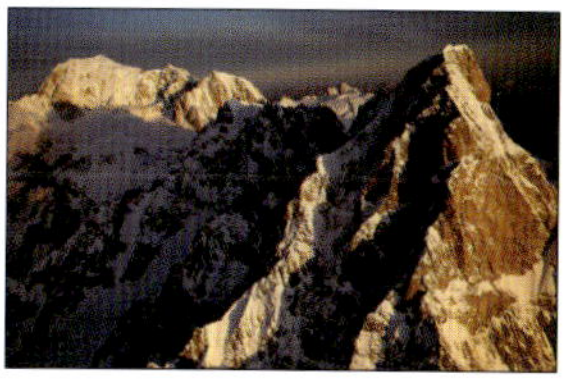

THE GRANDES JORASSES, a range of mountains belonging to the Mount Bianco massif, dominate the Ferret Valley with their astounding beauty. Their highest point is the 4,206 metre-high Walker peak *(pp. 68-69)*.

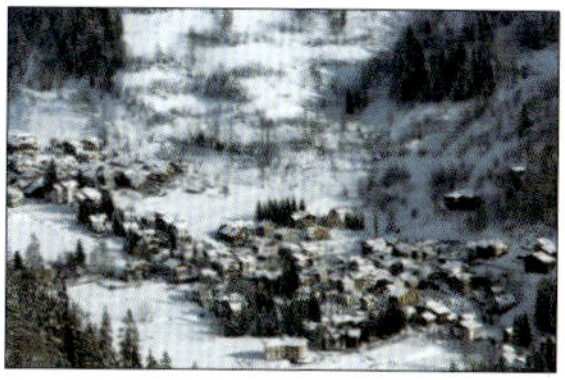

COURMAYEUR covered with snow. The renowned ski resort, surrounded by the untouched natural landscape of the Alps, lies on a valley at the foot of Mount Bianco's rocks and glaciers *(pp. 72-73)*.

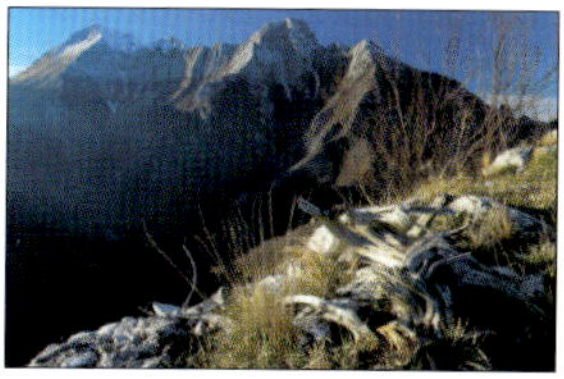

A VIEW OF THE GARFAGNANA ZONE between the Apuan Alps and the Northern Apennines: a huge section of this hilly and mountainous area of Tuscany is a national park *(pp. 76-77)*.

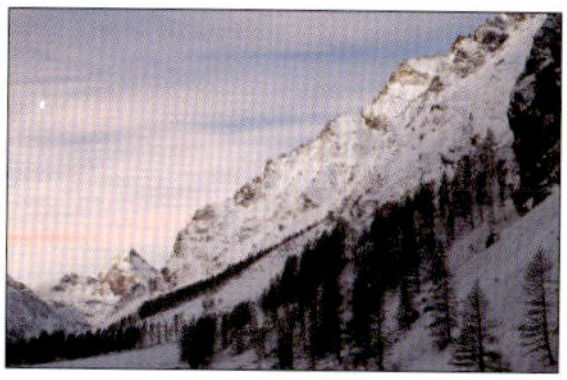

THE RHÊMES VALLEY, where the village of Rhêmes-Notre-Dame is located. A side of the valley, whose natural environment is perfectly preserved, belongs to the Gran Paradiso National Park *(pp. 70-71)*.

SUNSET AT MONTICELLO D'ALBA, in the Langhe. The hamlet is located on the top of a hill where an isolated 13th-century castle rises too. The Monviso peak stands out in the background *(pp. 74-75)*.

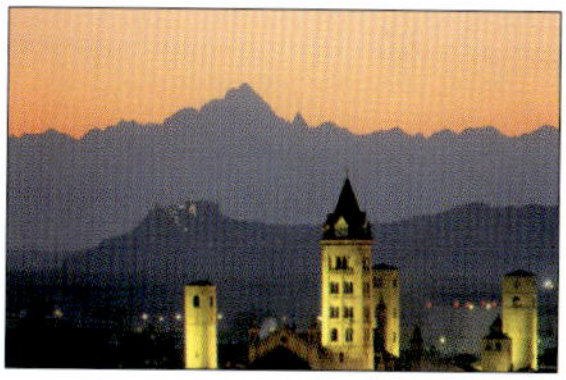

THE OUTLINE OF THE ALPS makes an impressive background to this night view of Alba. Placed in a hilly region rich in vineyards and orchards, the Piedmontese town is mainly known for its fine truffles *(pp. 78-79)*.

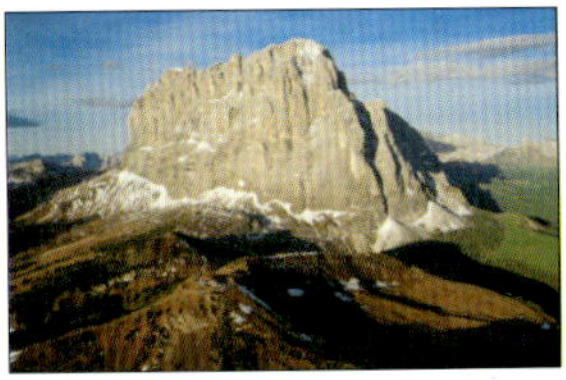

THE SASSOLUNGO, named after its distinctive shape, is actually a set of calcareous rocks of the Dolomites which impressively stands out between the Val di Fassa and the Val Gardena *(pp. 80-81)*.

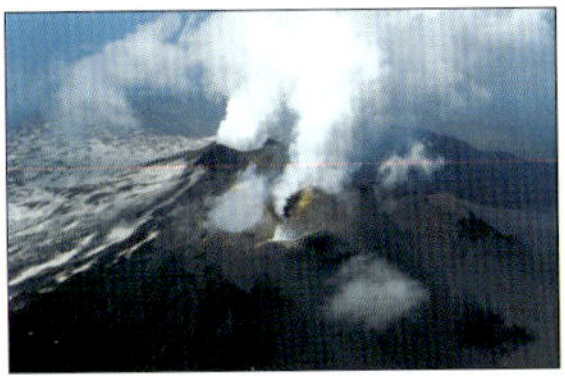

THE ETNA MOUNT, thanks to its ever-steaming craters, is the most important active volcano in Europe. Typical Mediterranean vegetation abounds on its lower levels, where citrus orchards and vineries can be found. Woods grow instead on its upper slopes. Finally, the lava desert prevails at over 3,000 metres, creating a moony landscape that in winter is often covered with snow *(pp. 84-85, 86-87)*.

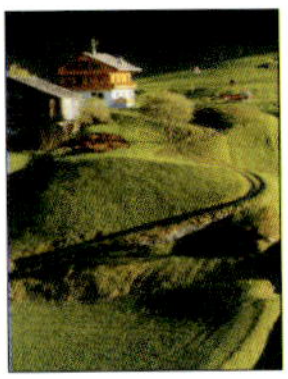

THE BRIGHT GREEN VALLE AURINA near Campo Tures village, in Trentino Alto Adige, is studded with isolated houses surrounded by vast expanses of fields and woods. A 13th-century castle overlooks the valley *(p. 88)*.

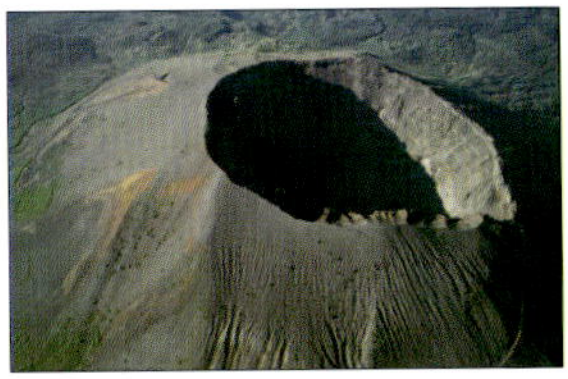

THE ENORMOUS CRATER OF VESUVIUS, whose slopes are covered with vegetation. The volcano overlooking Naples bay is mainly known for the eruption that destroyed Hercolaneum and Pompeii in 79 A.D. *(pp. 82-83)*.

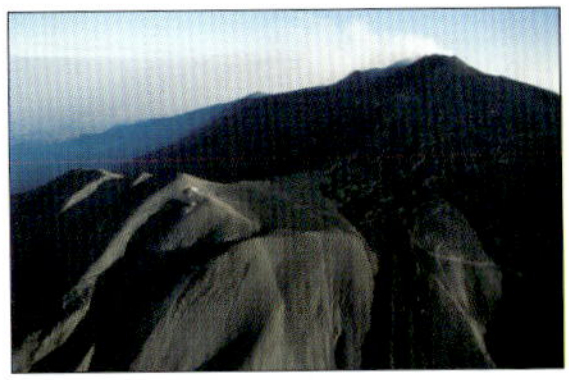

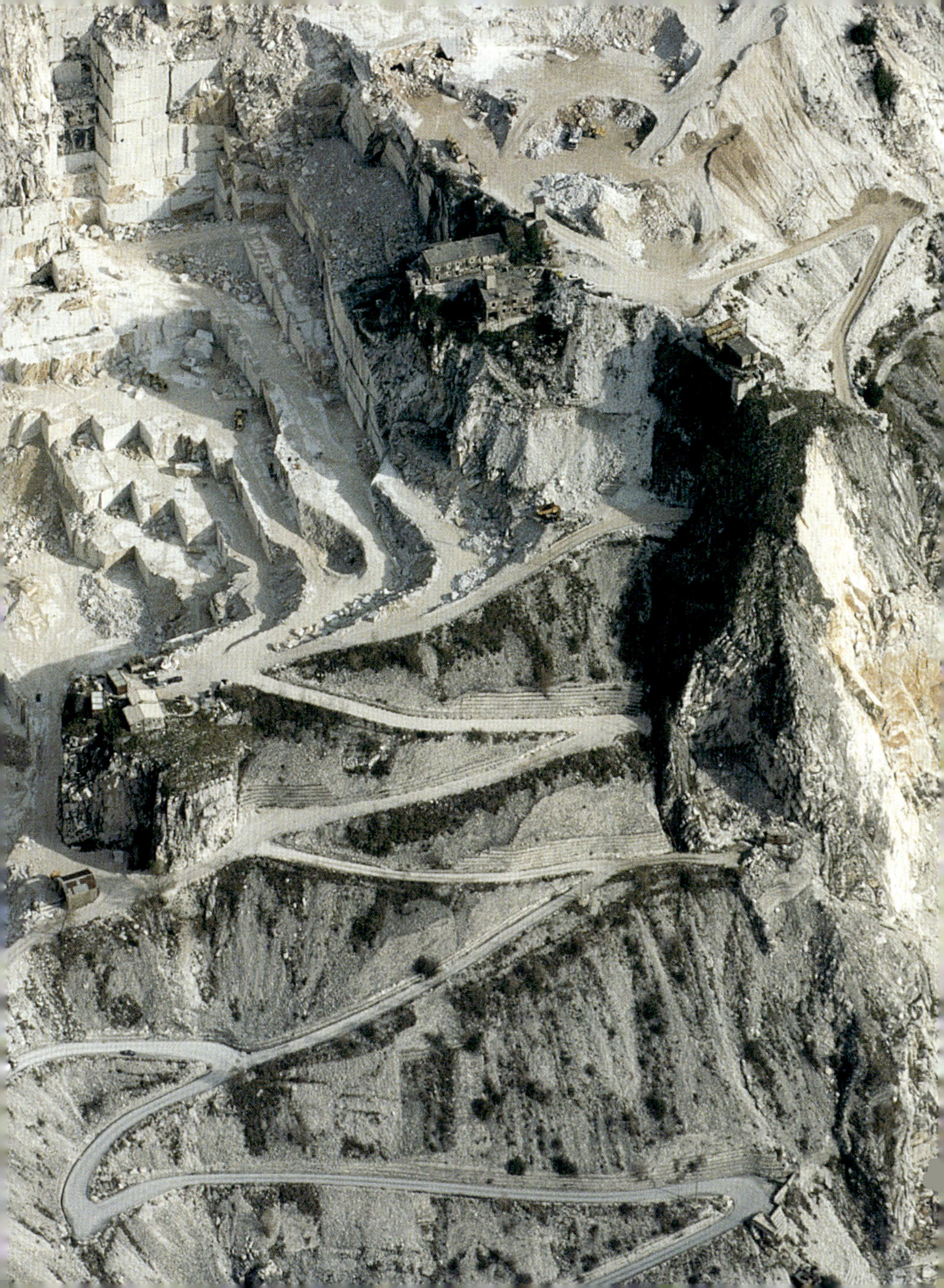

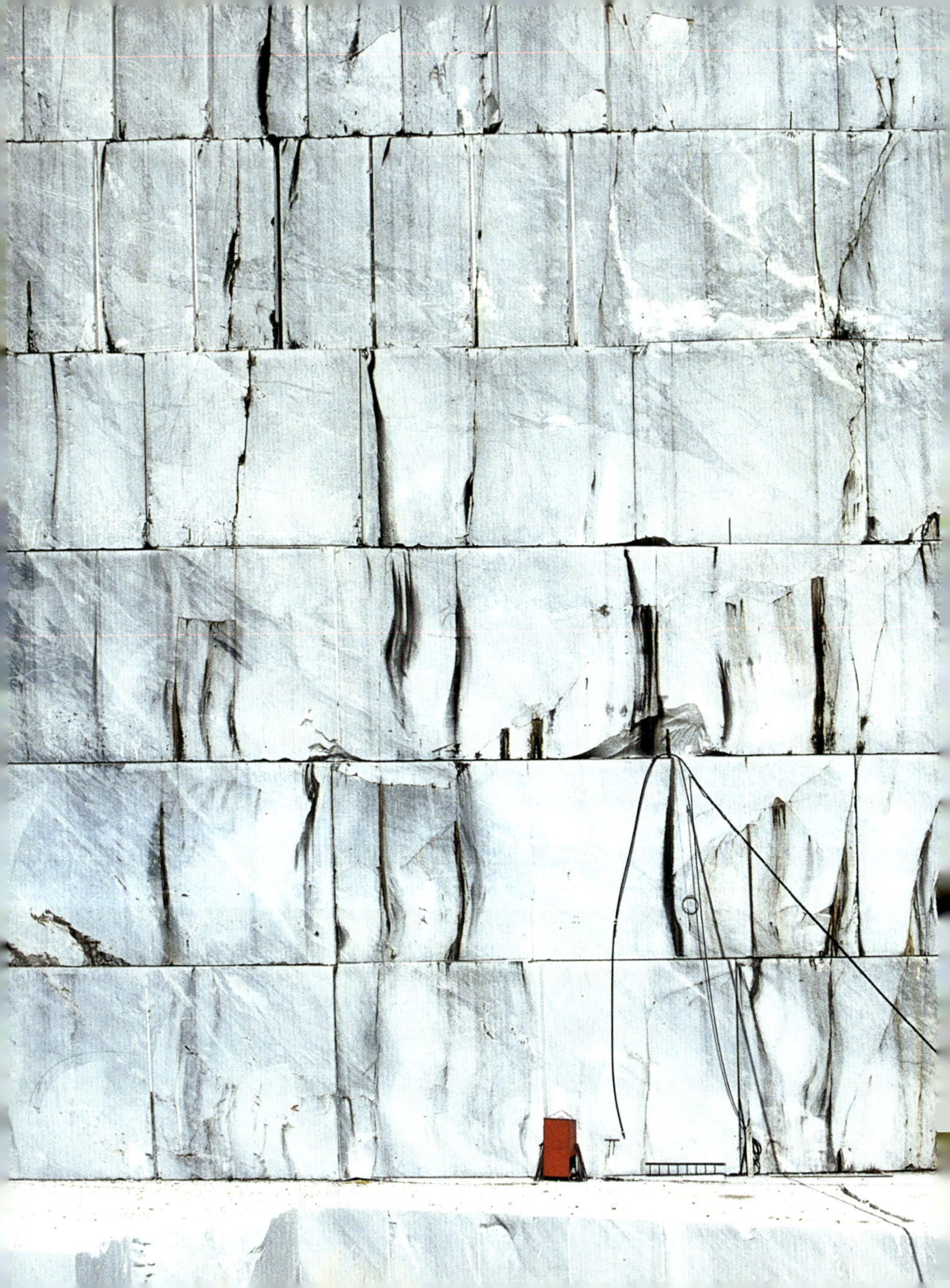

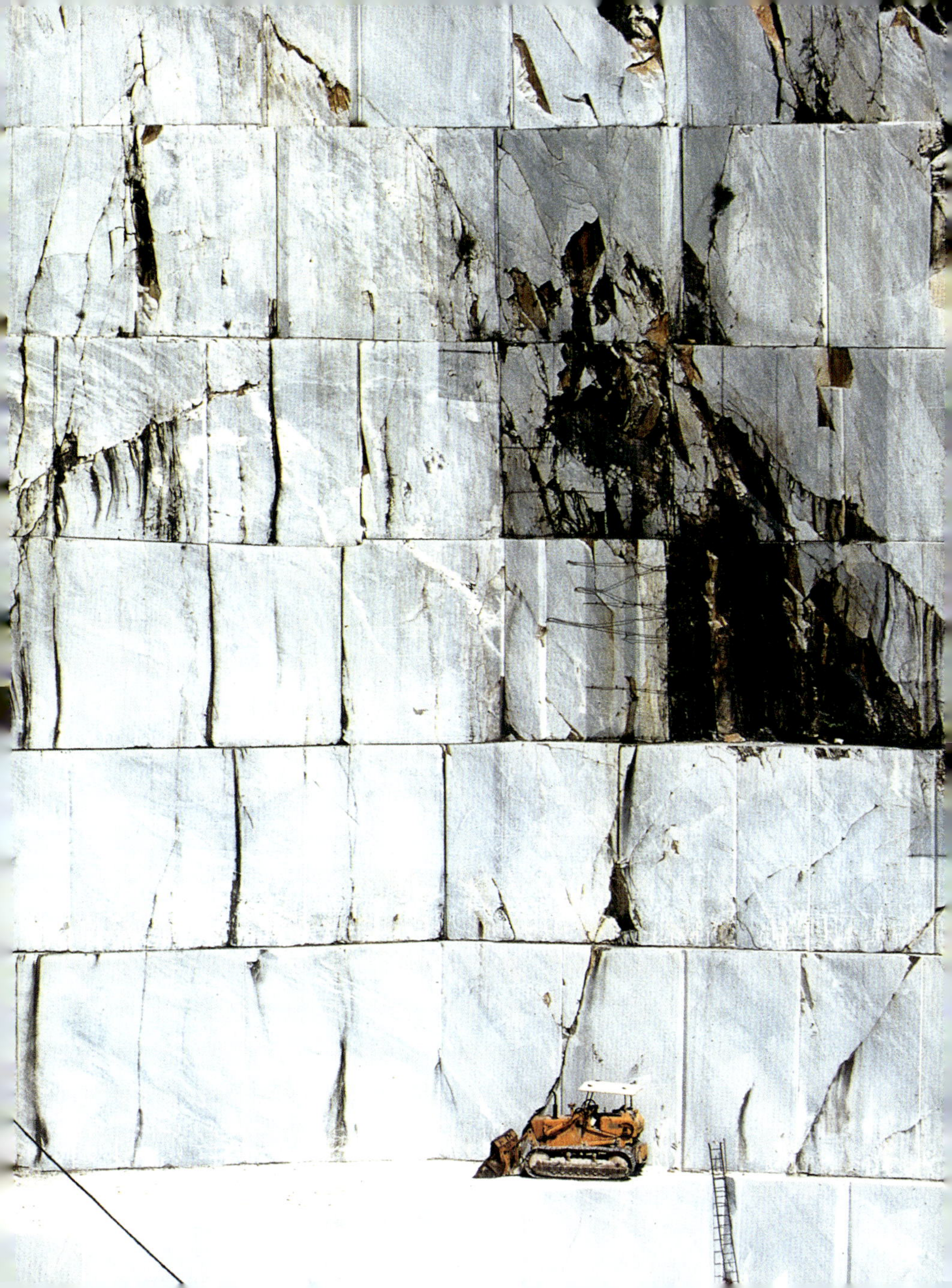

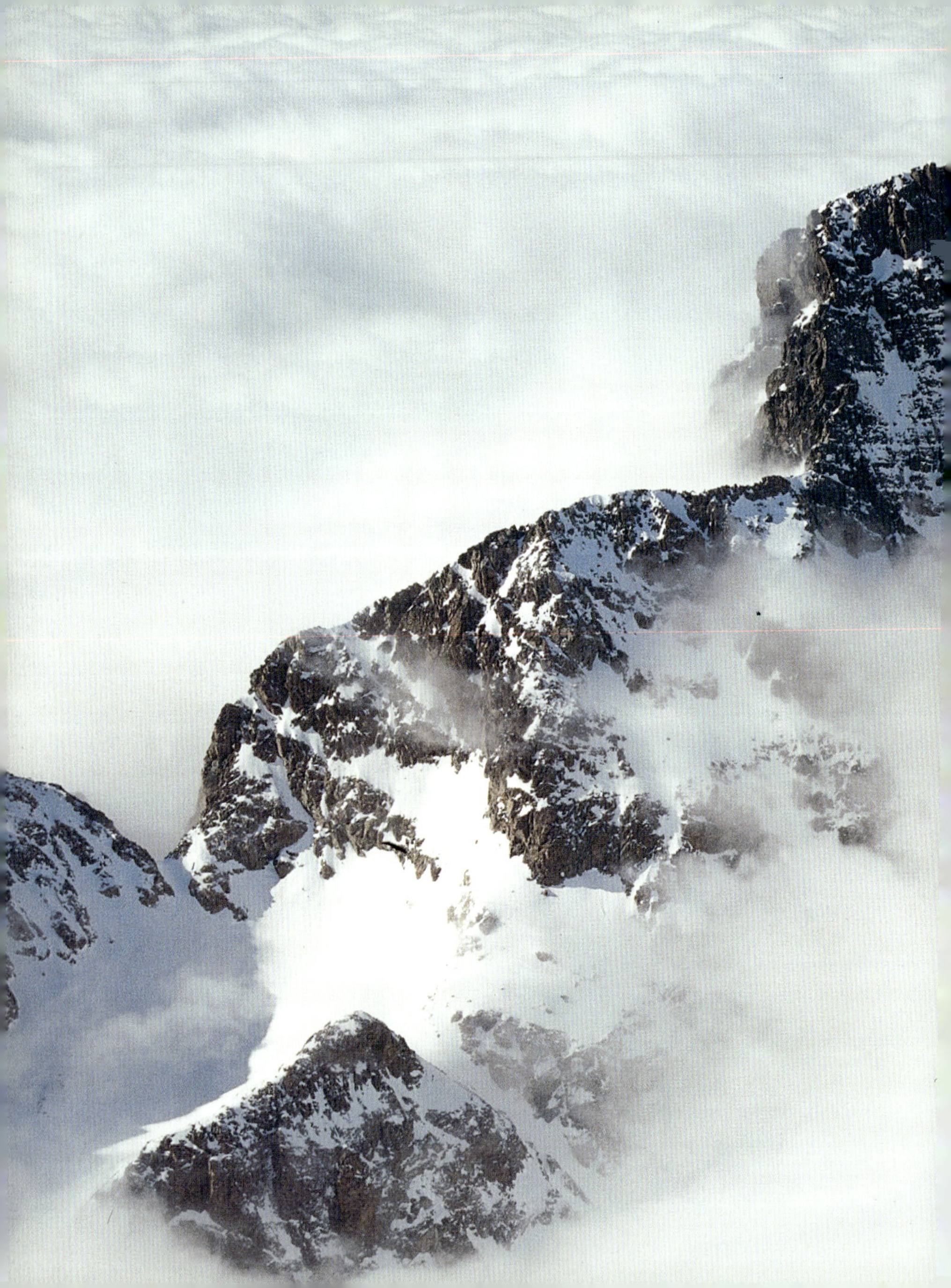

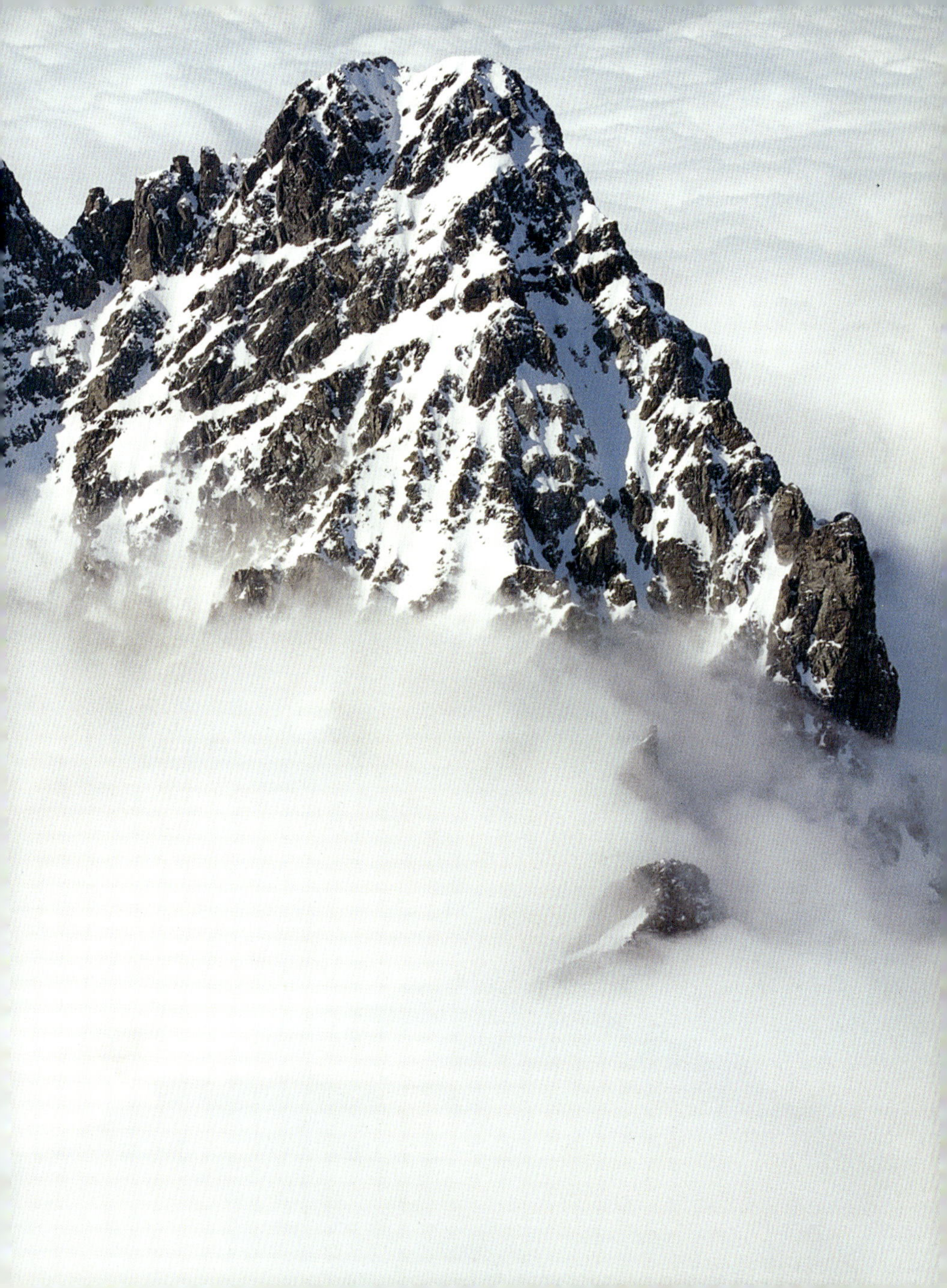

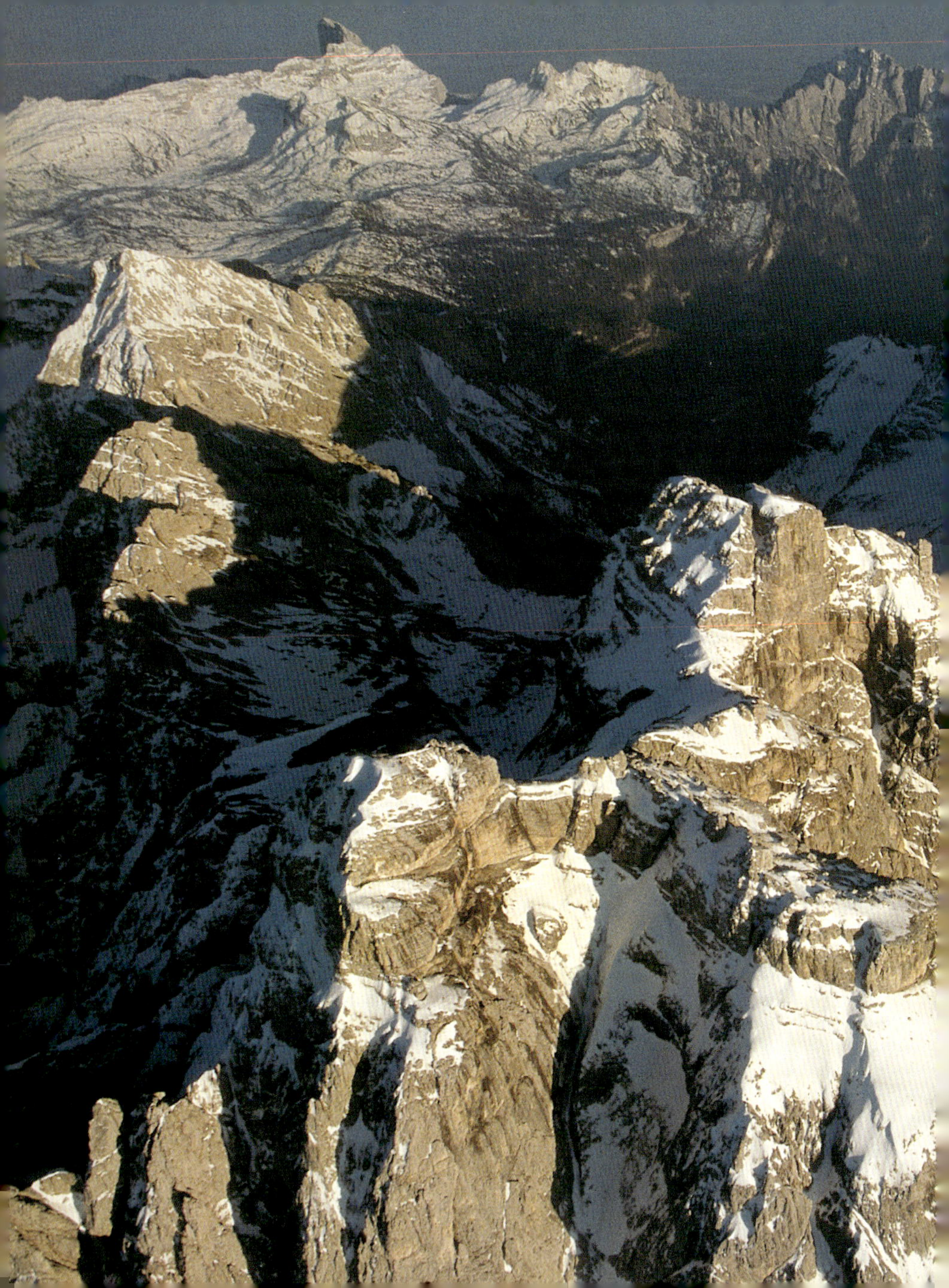

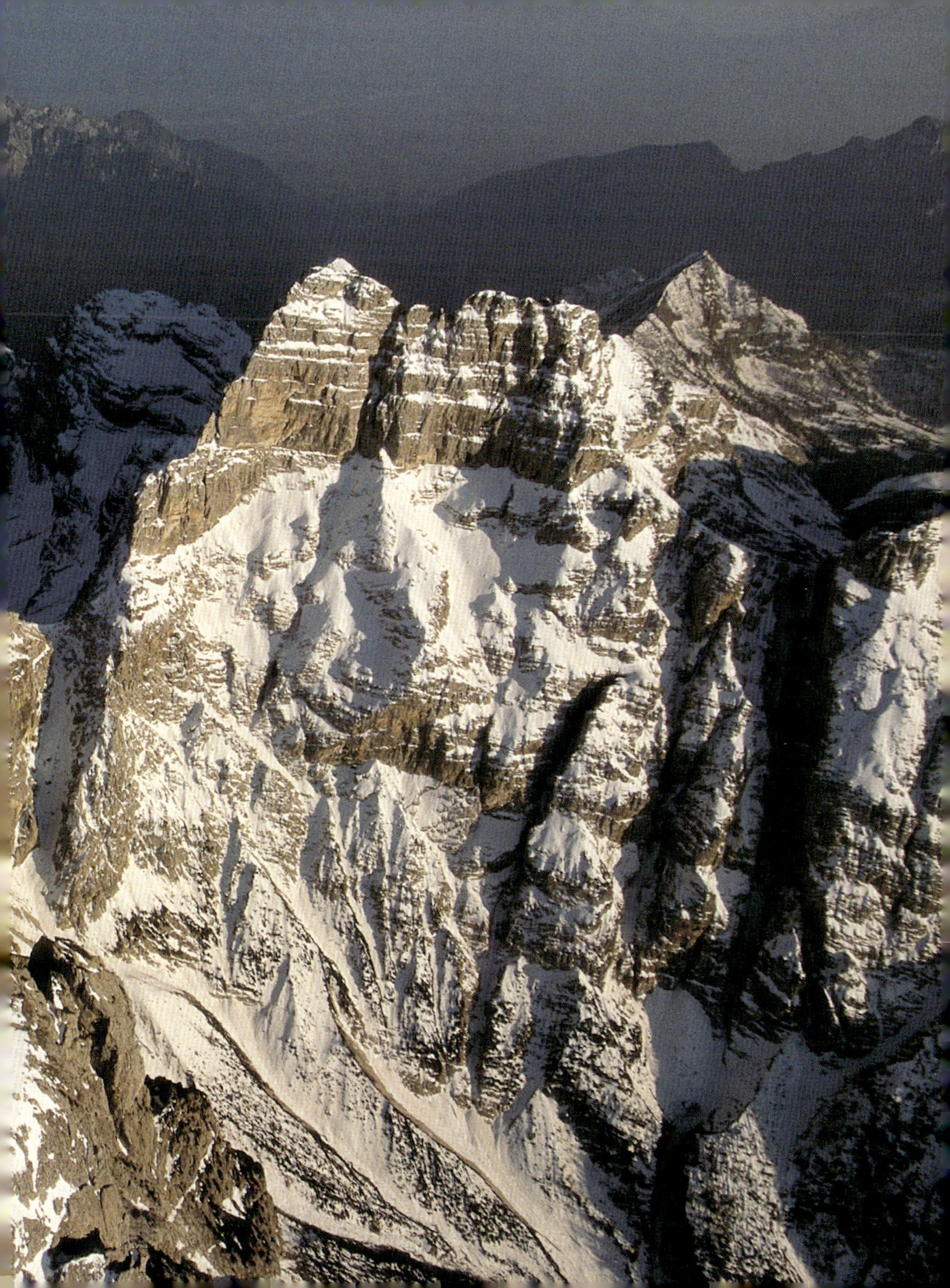

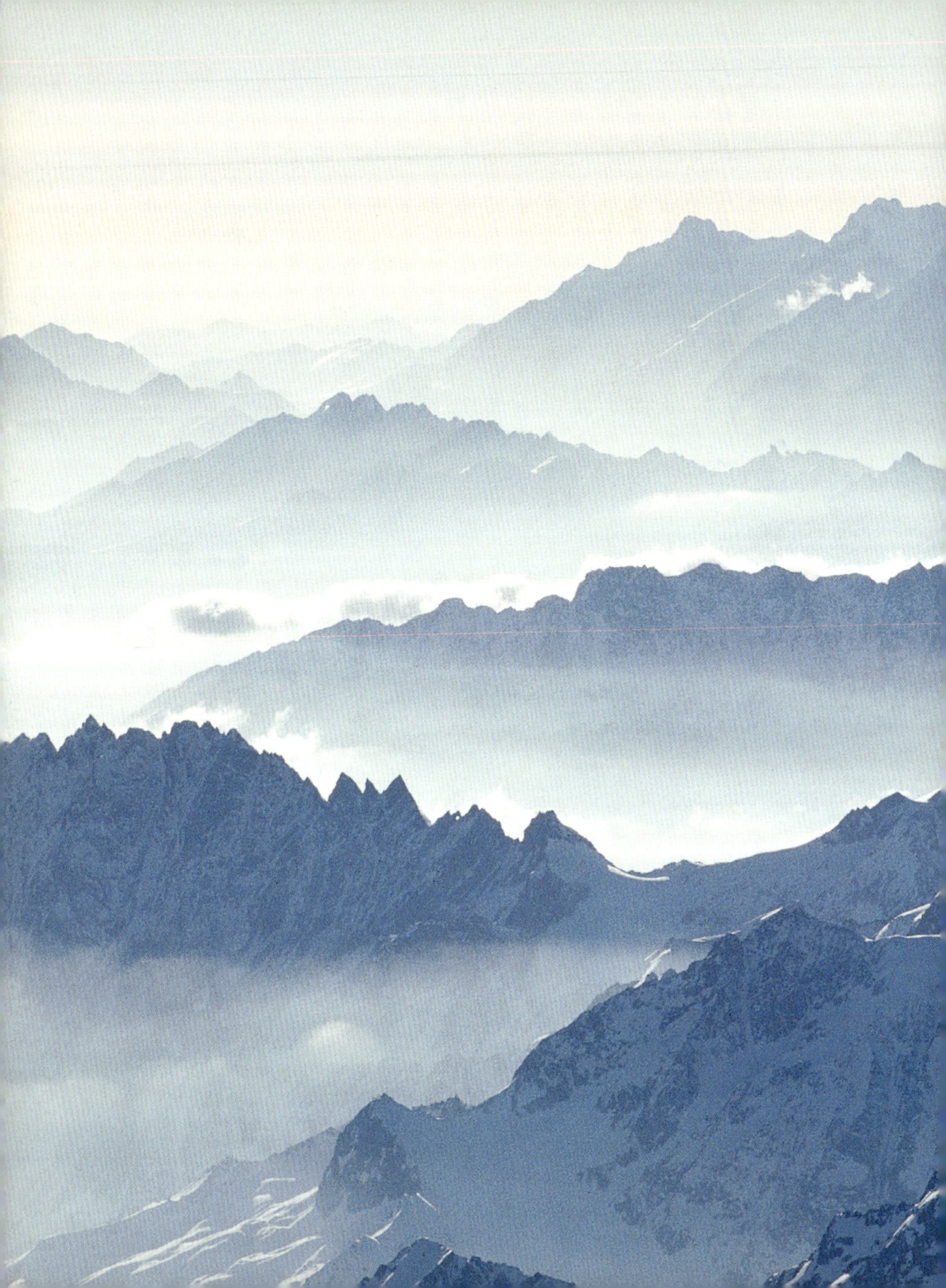

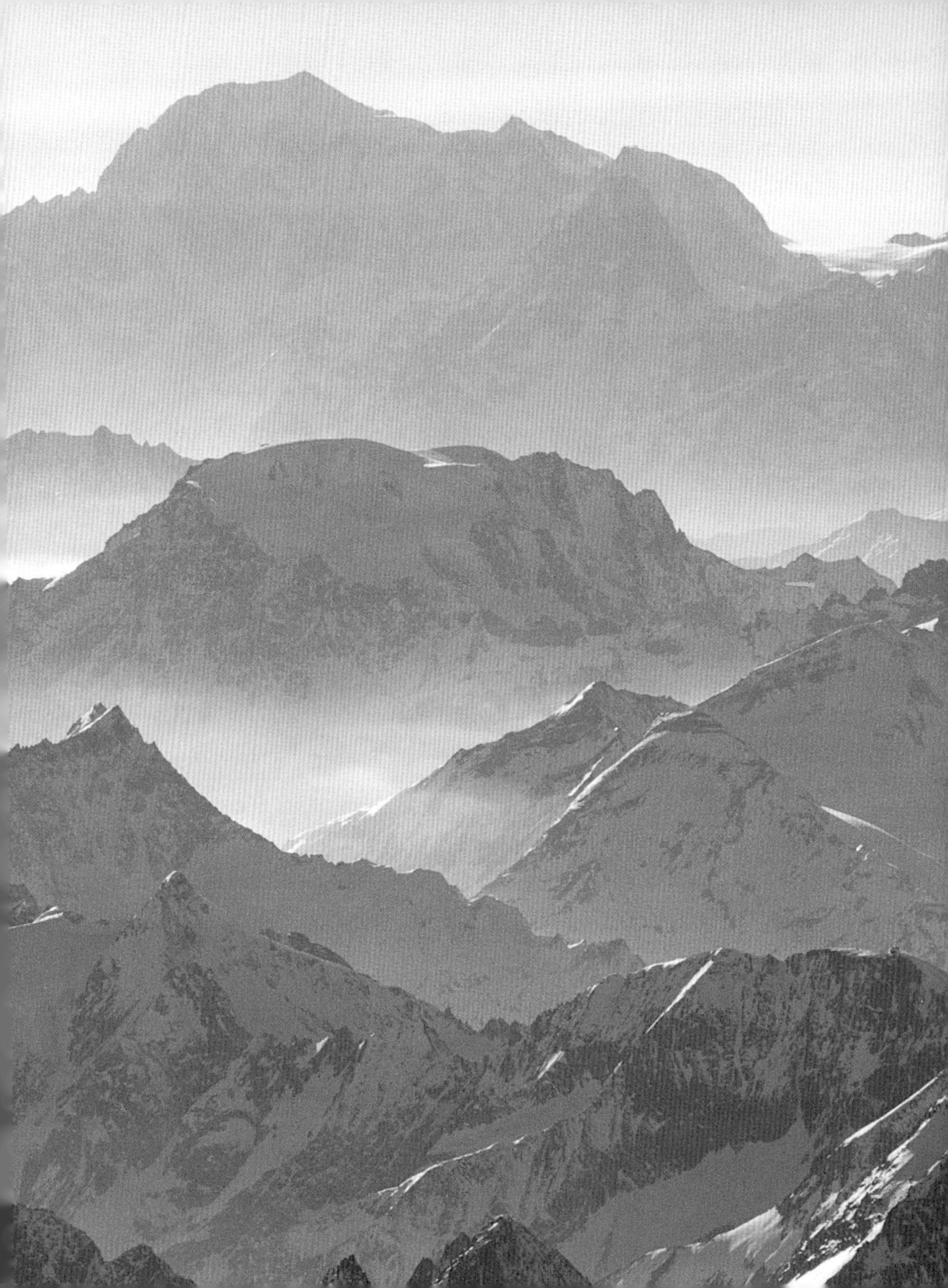

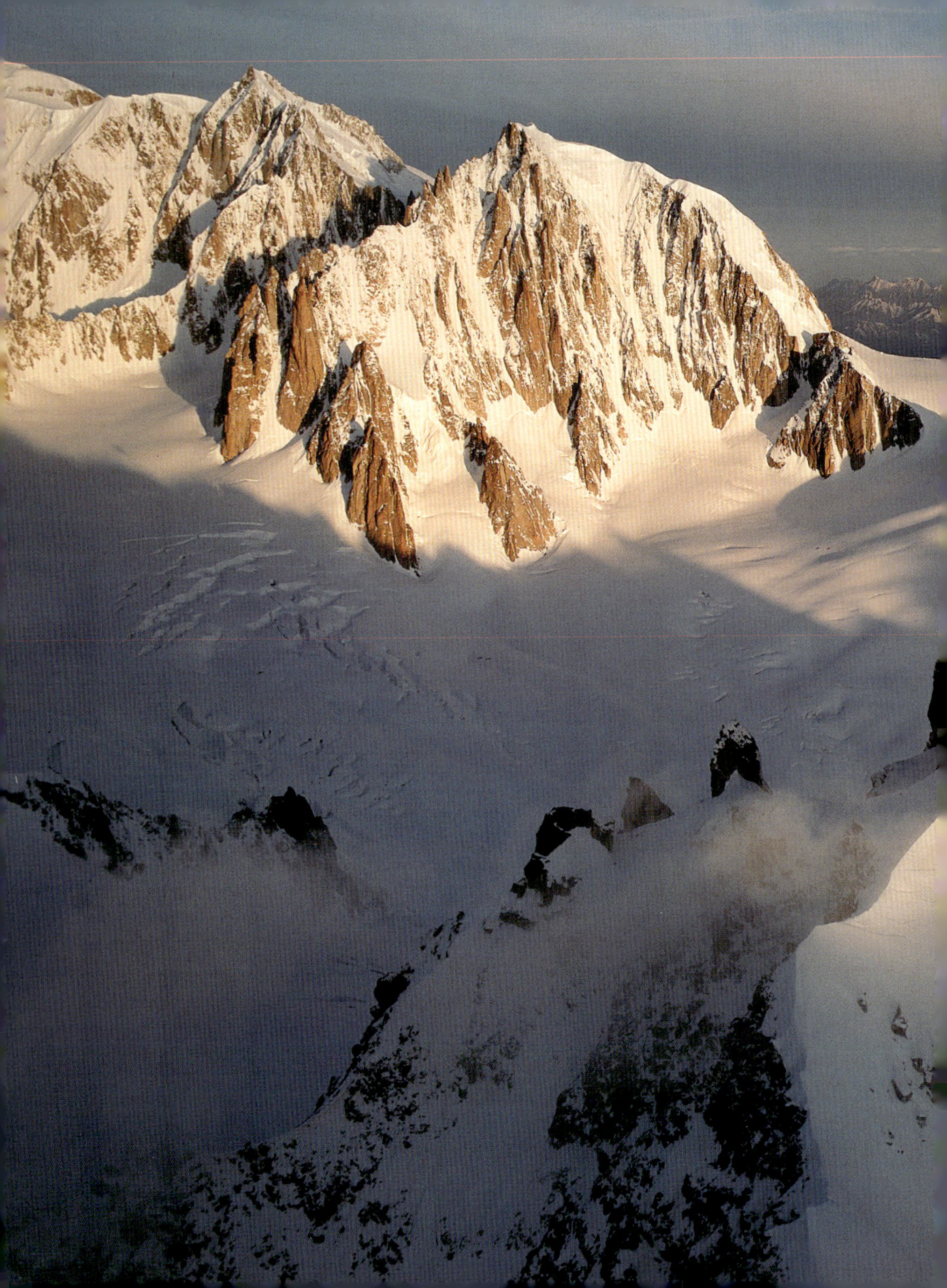

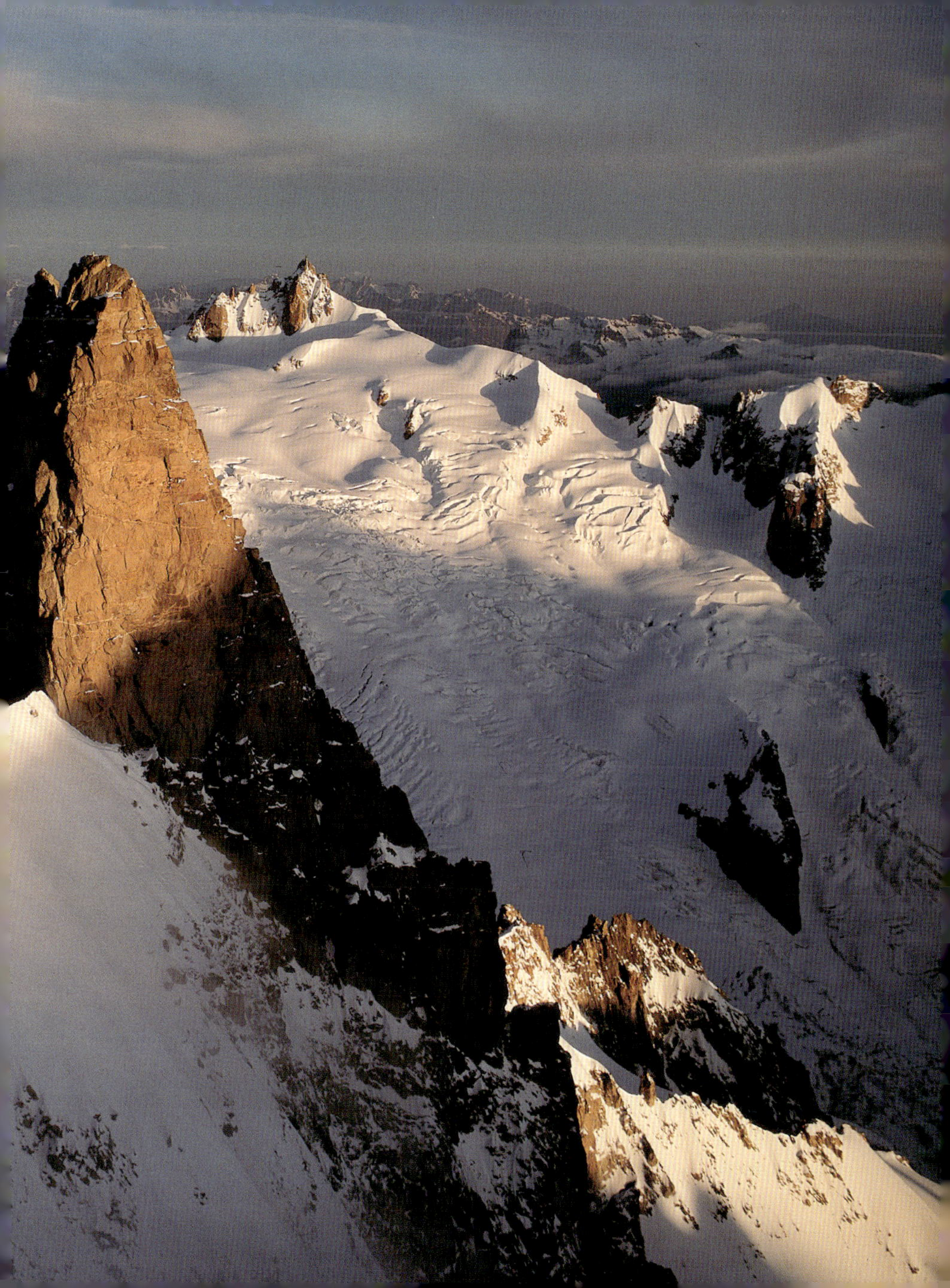

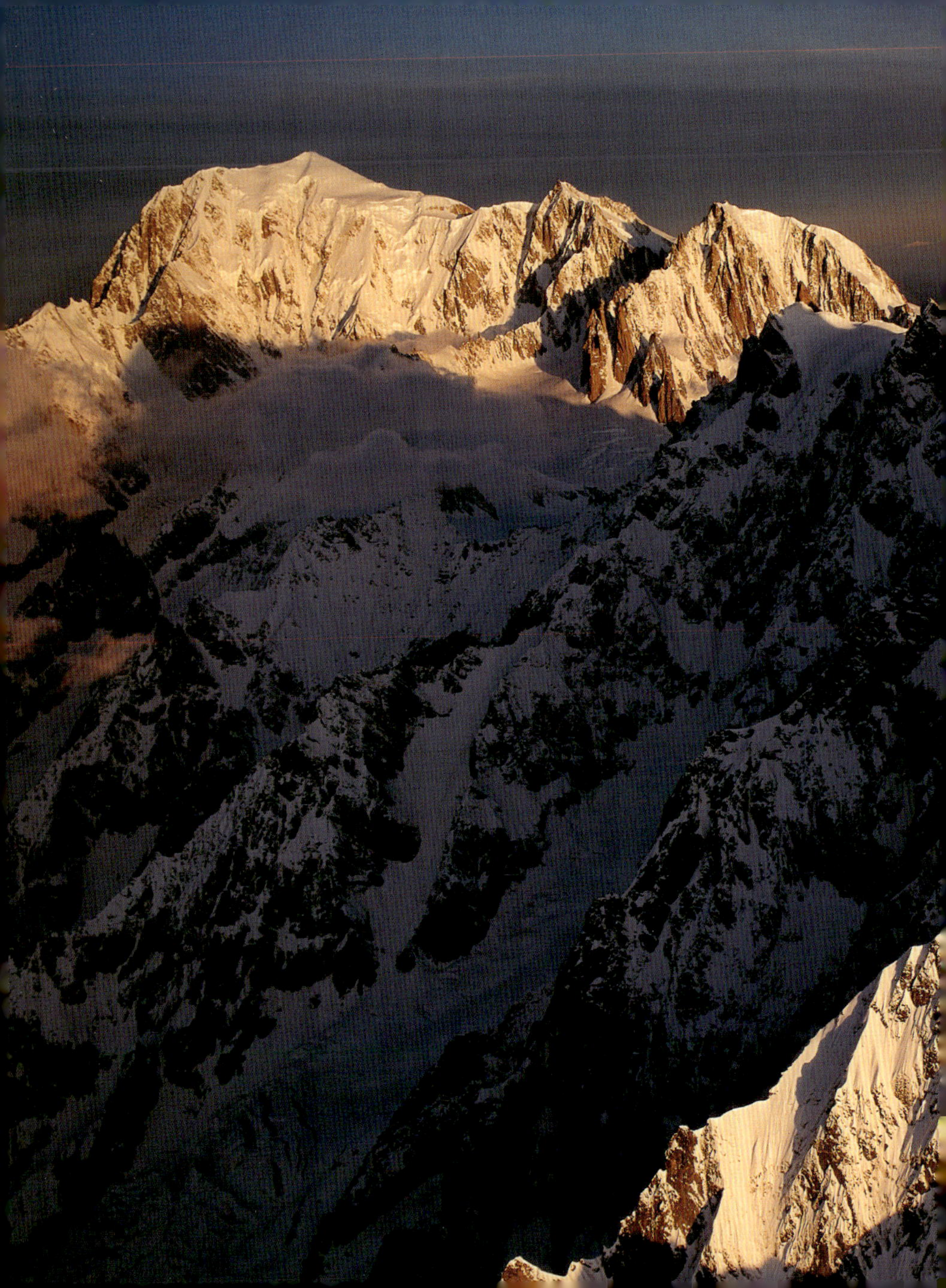

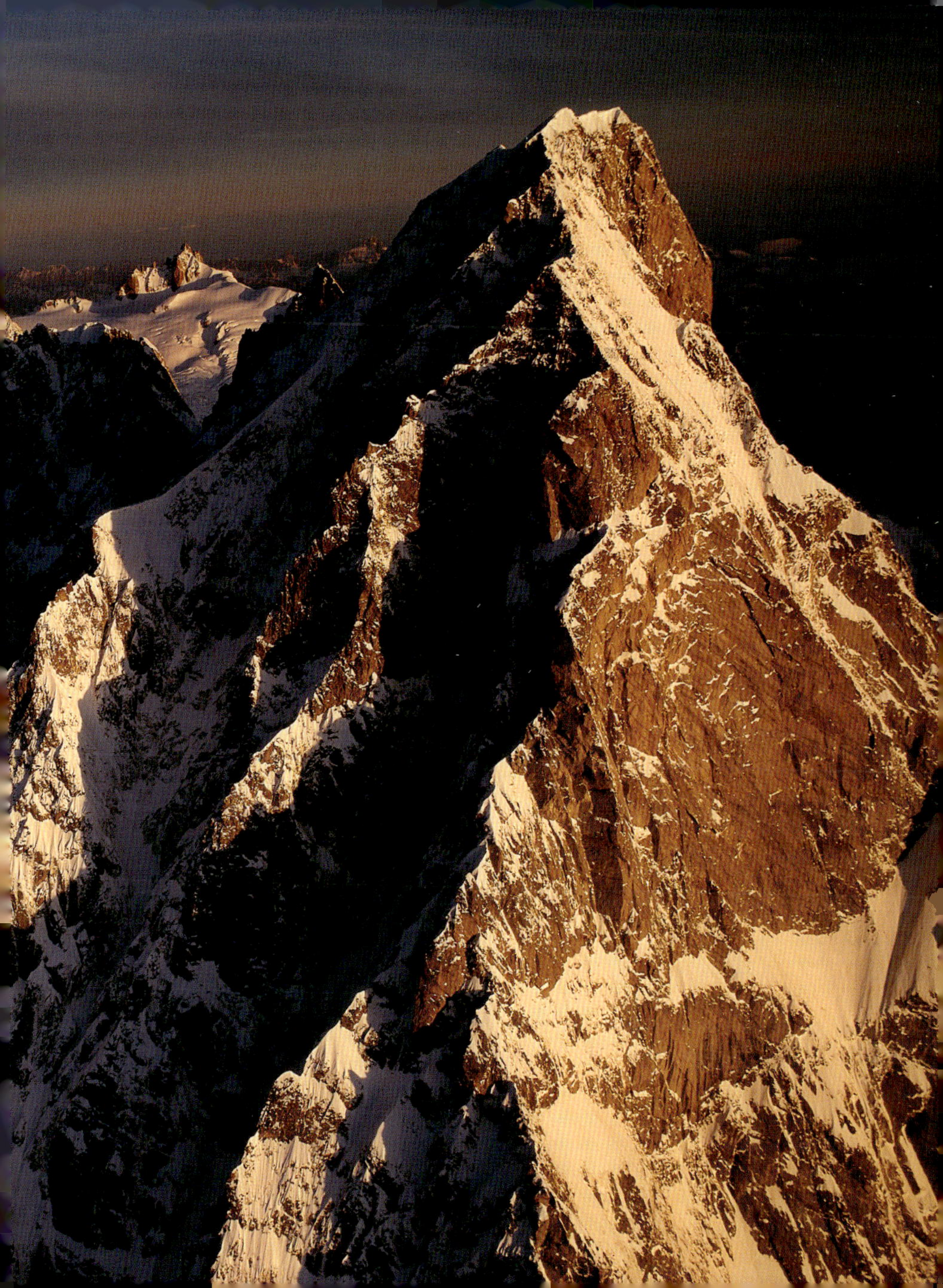

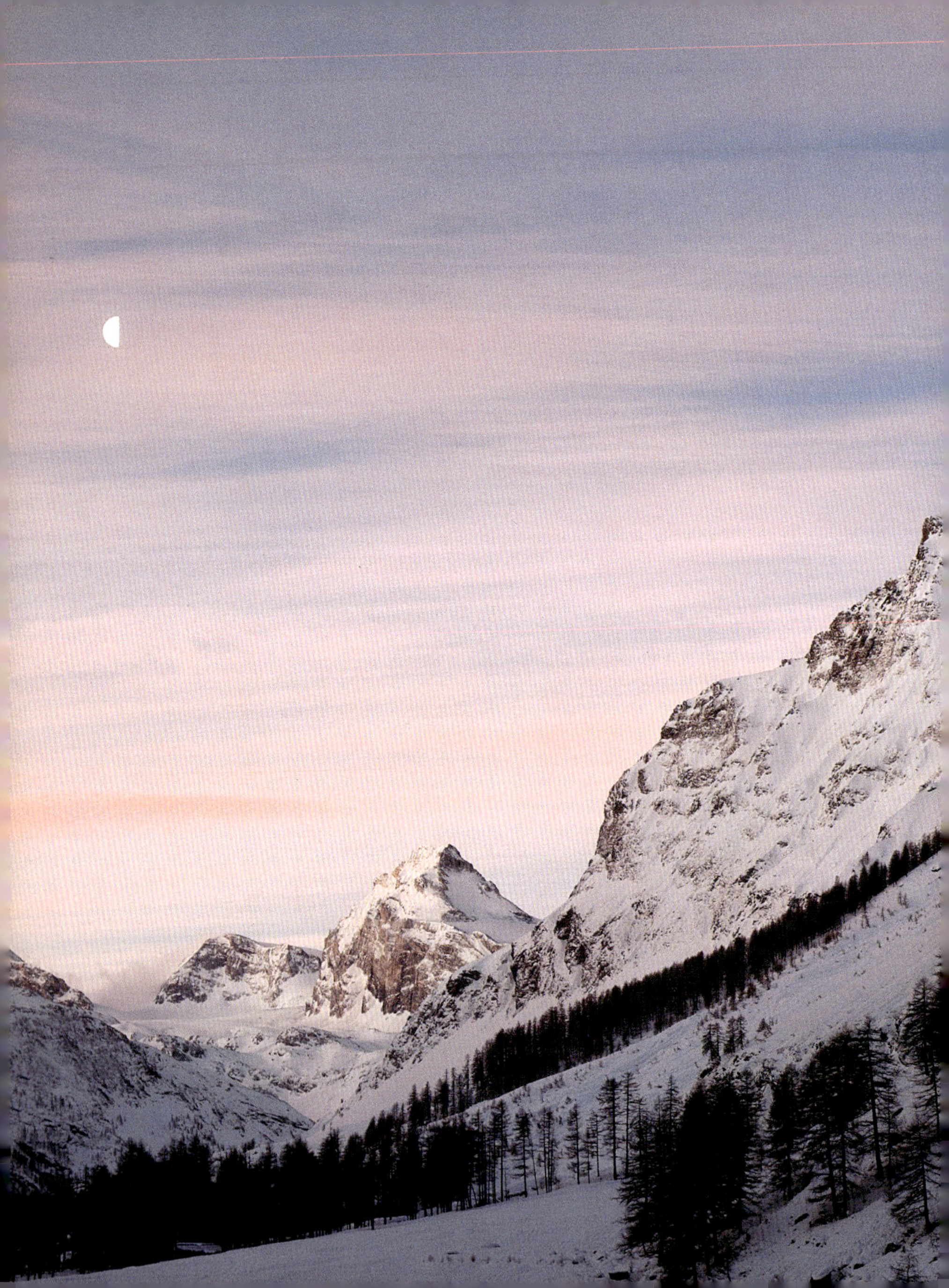

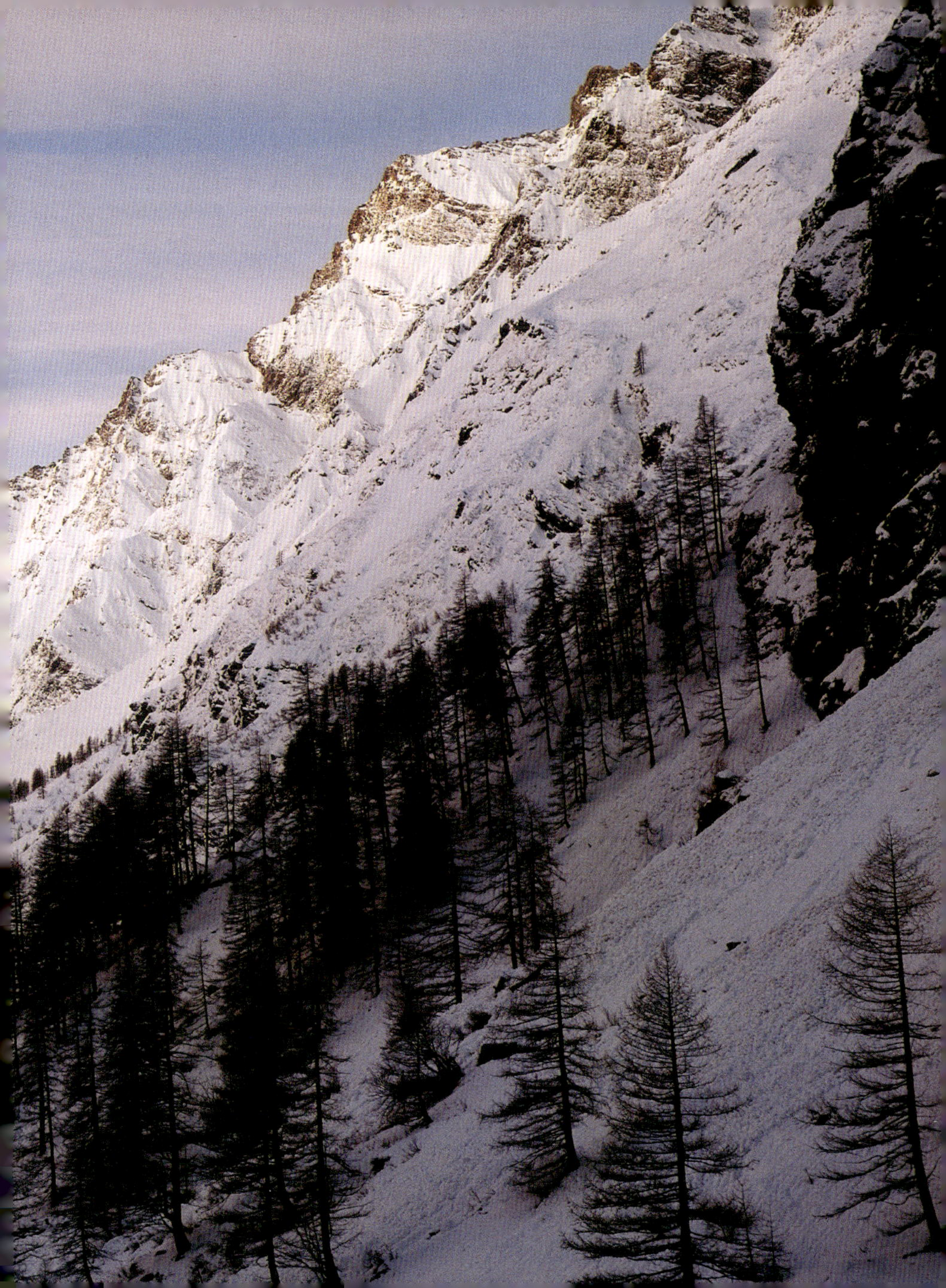

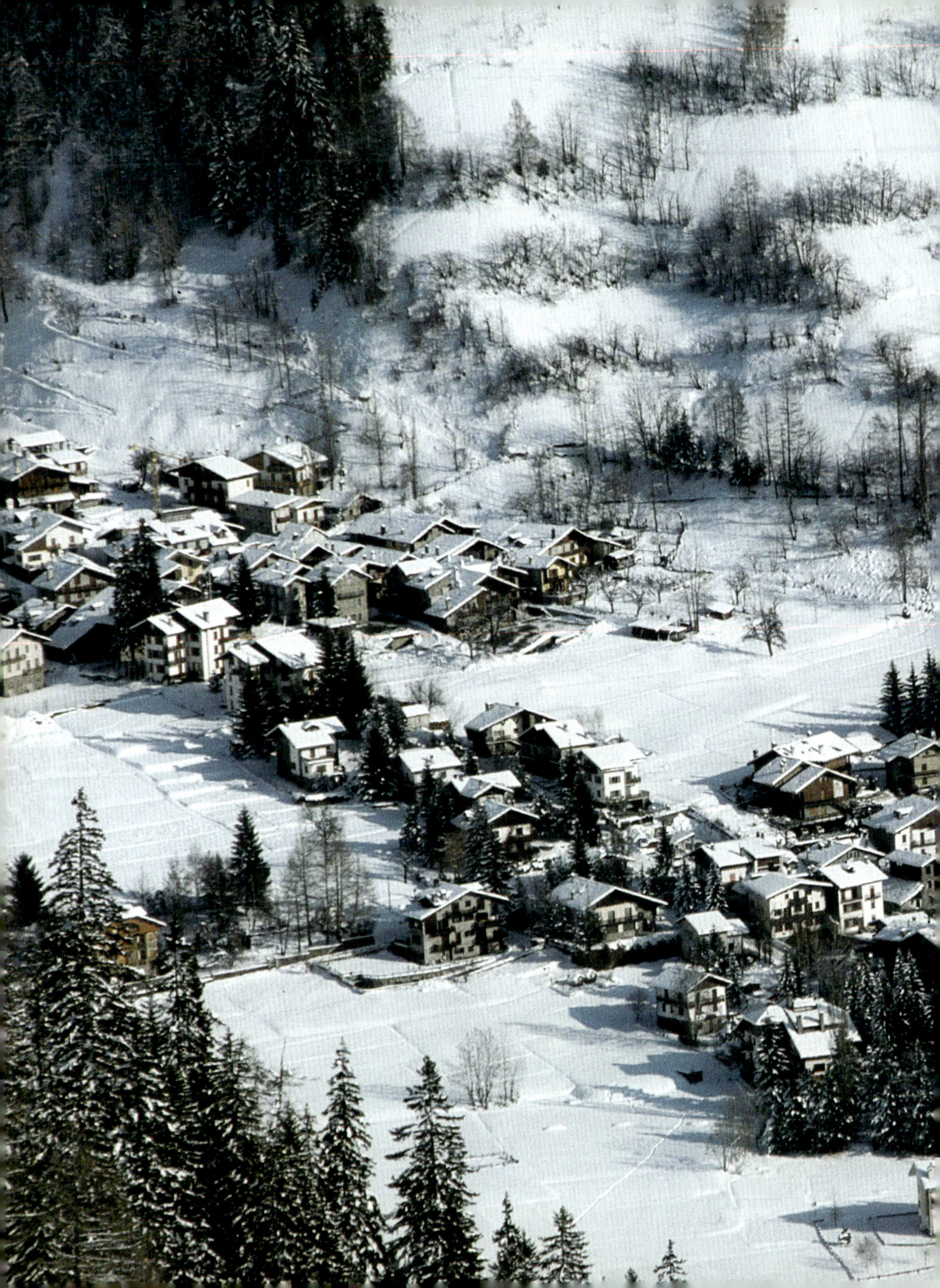

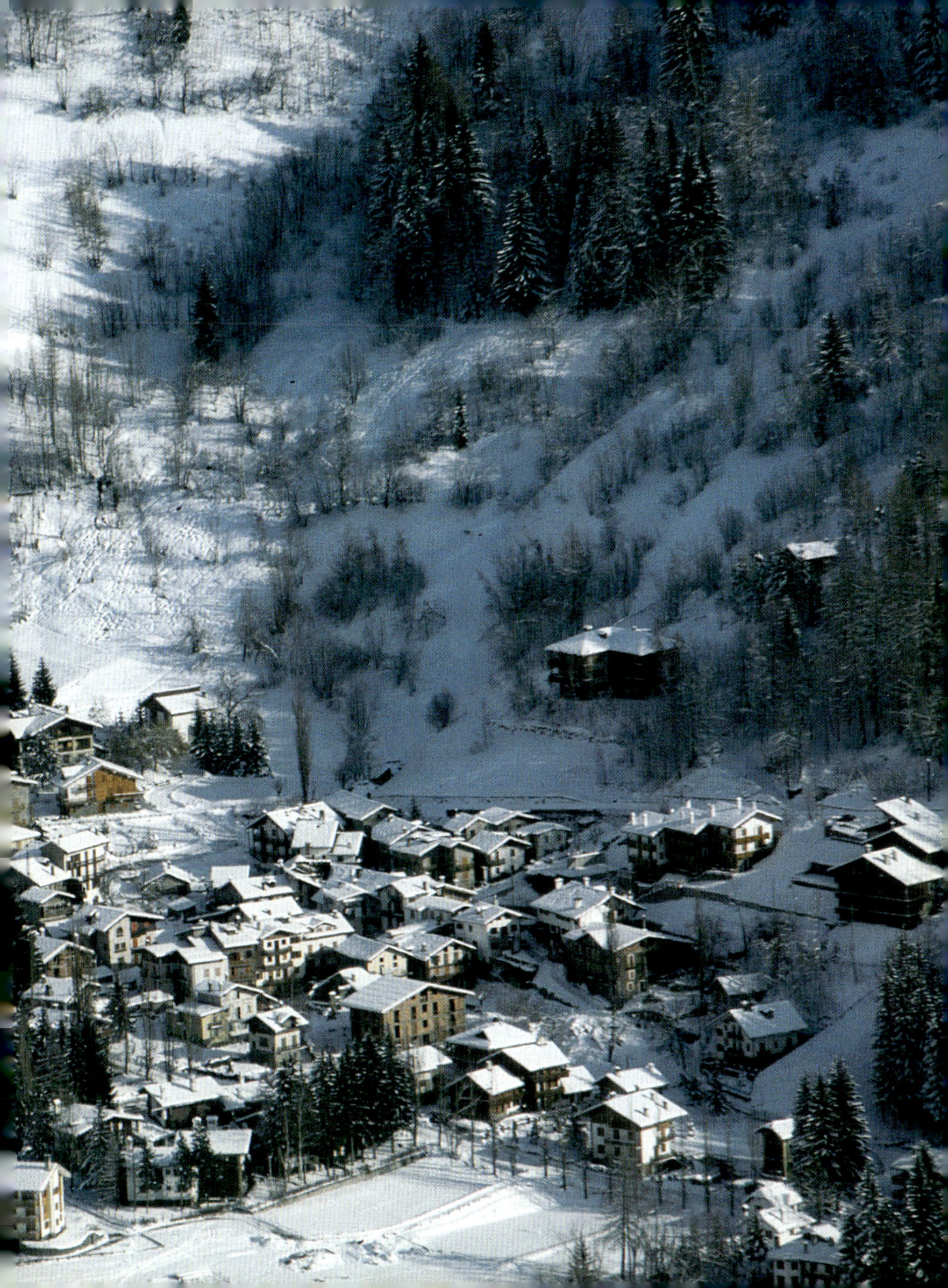

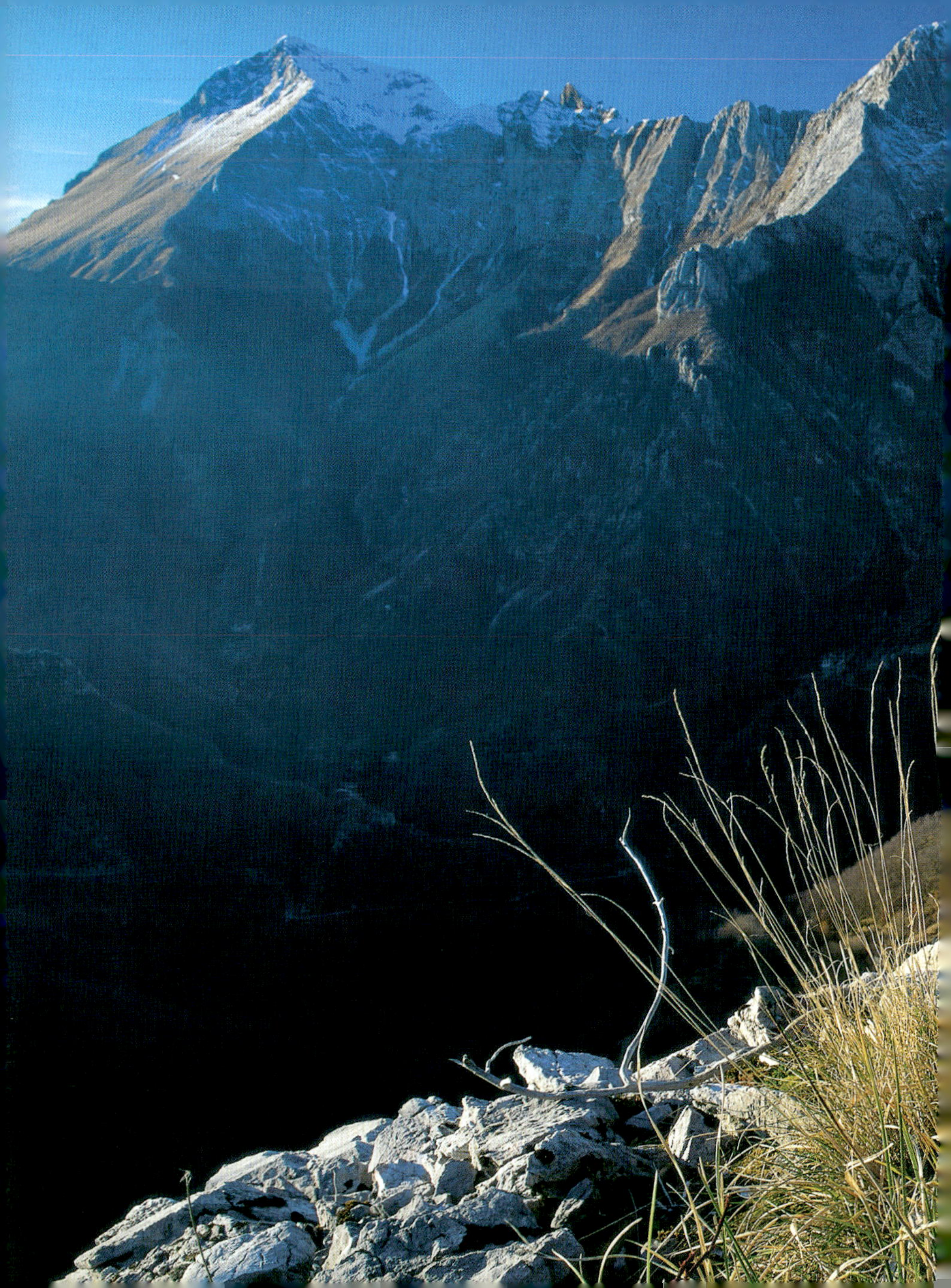

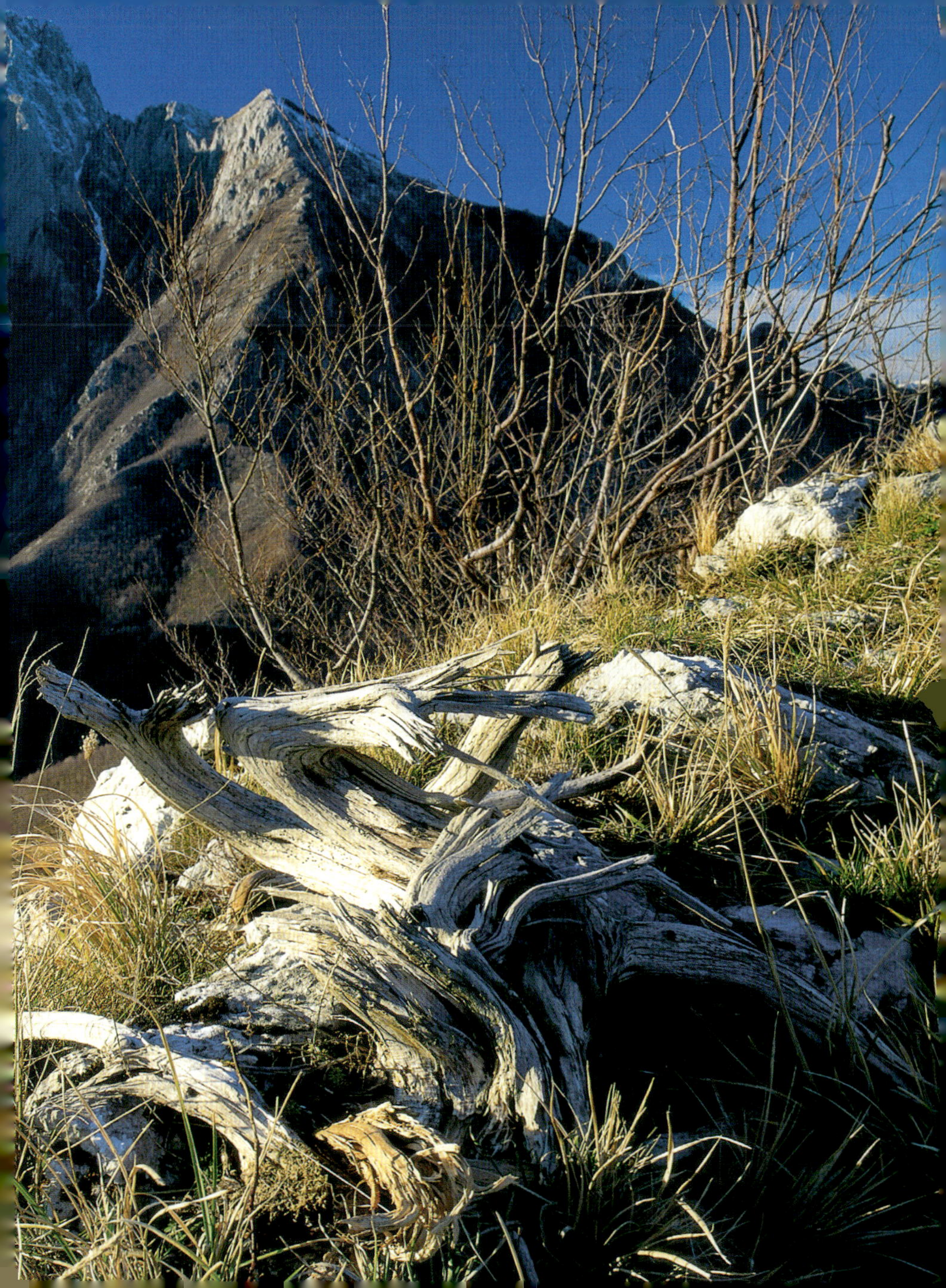

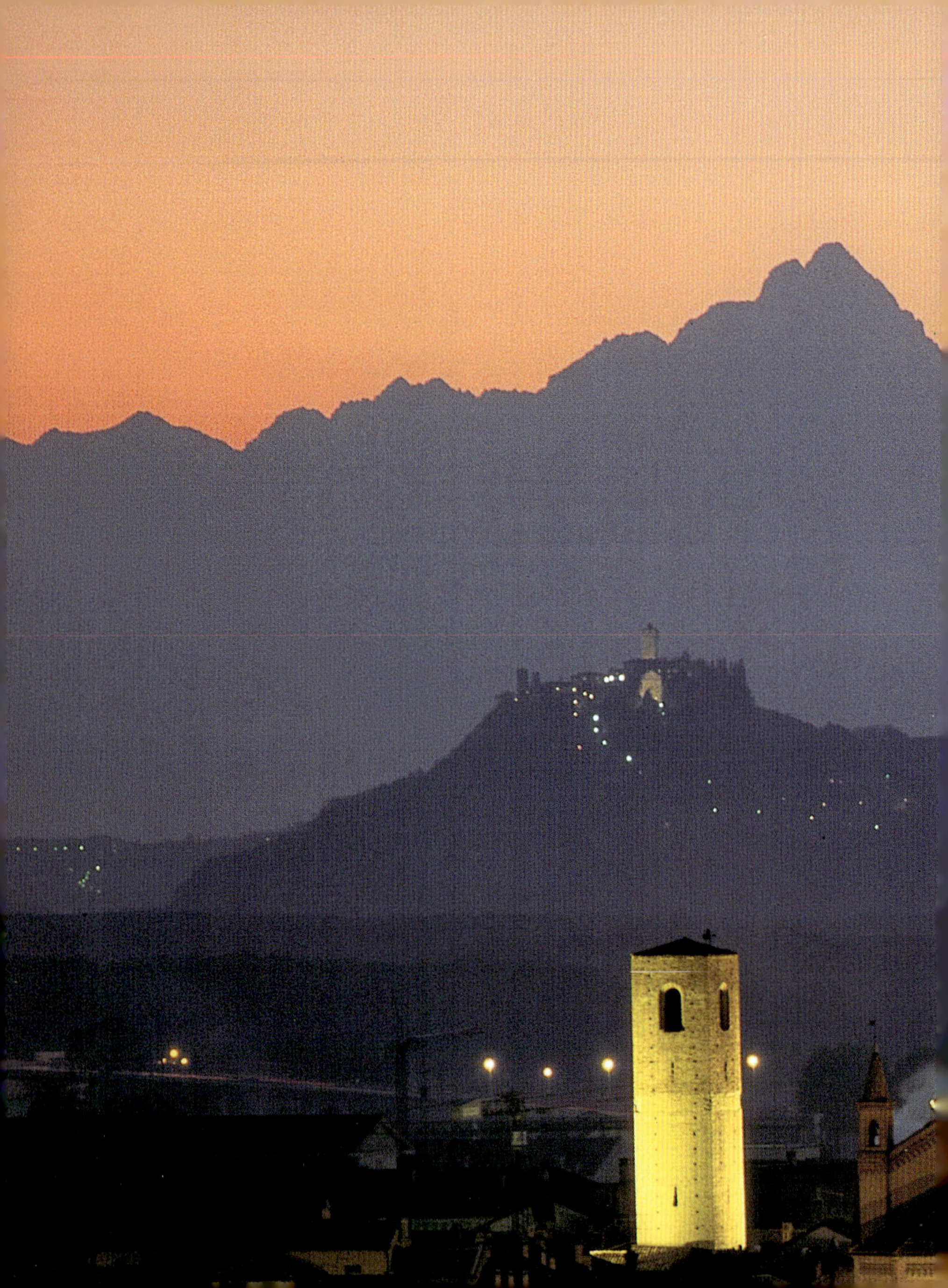

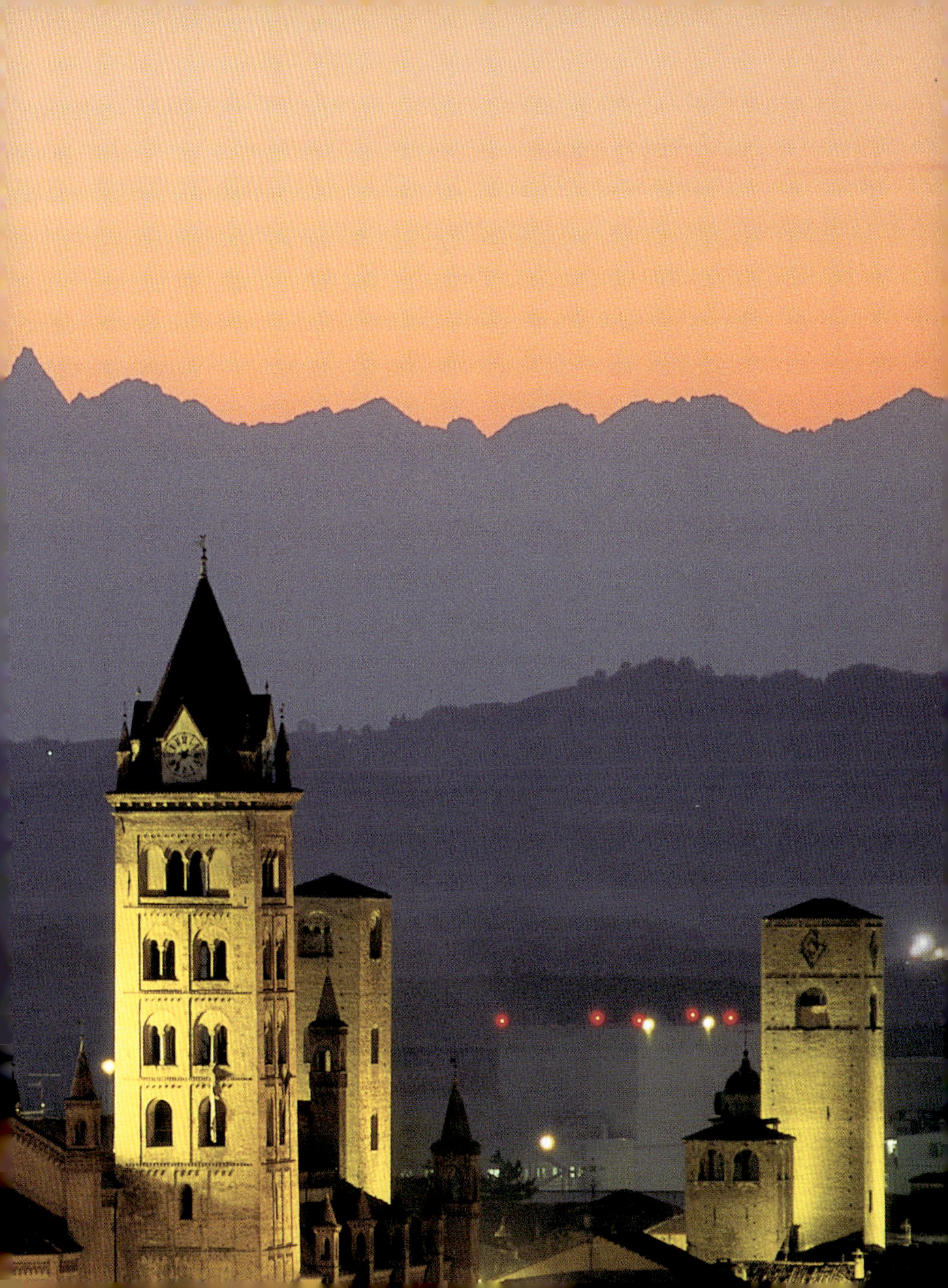

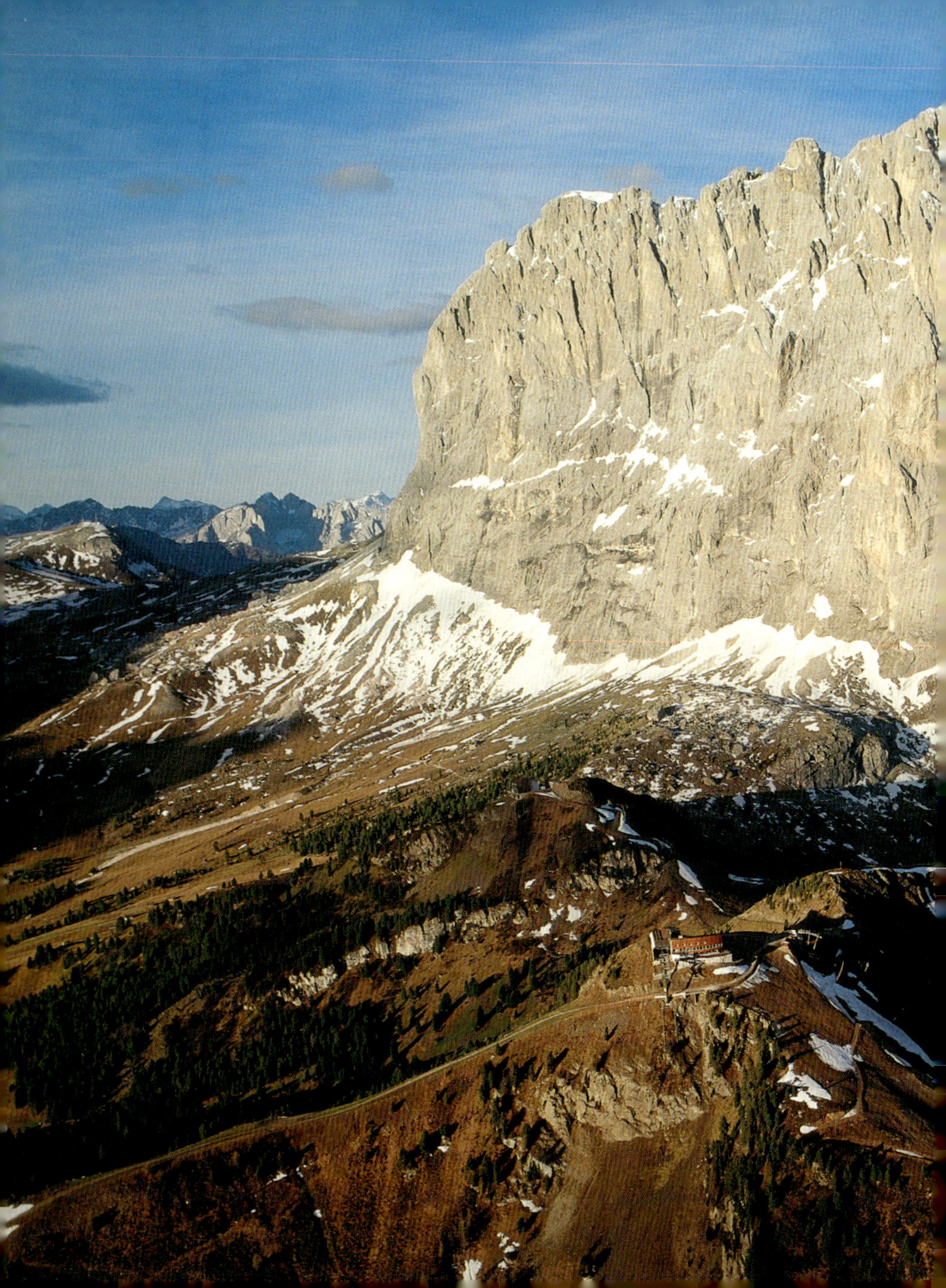

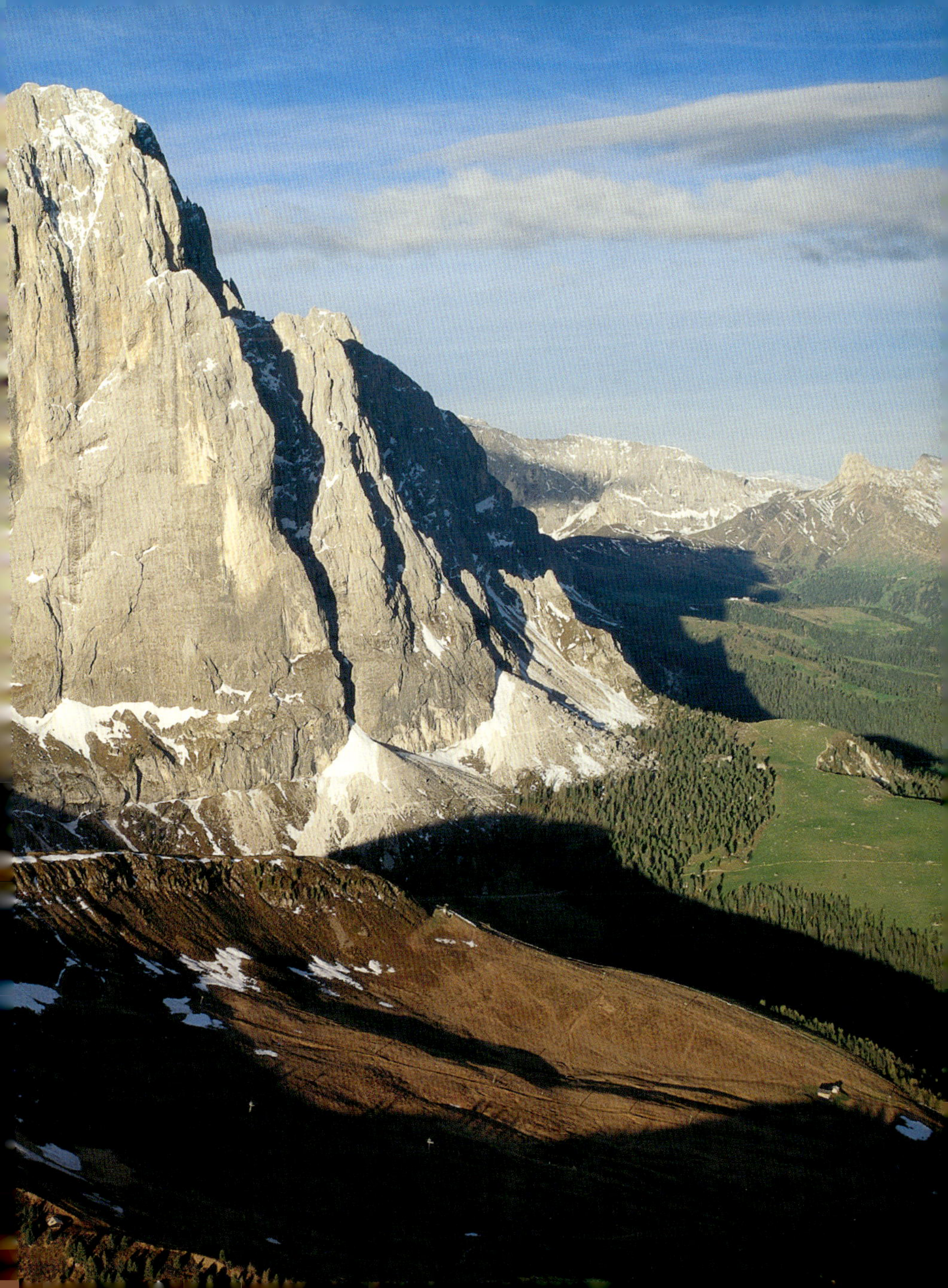

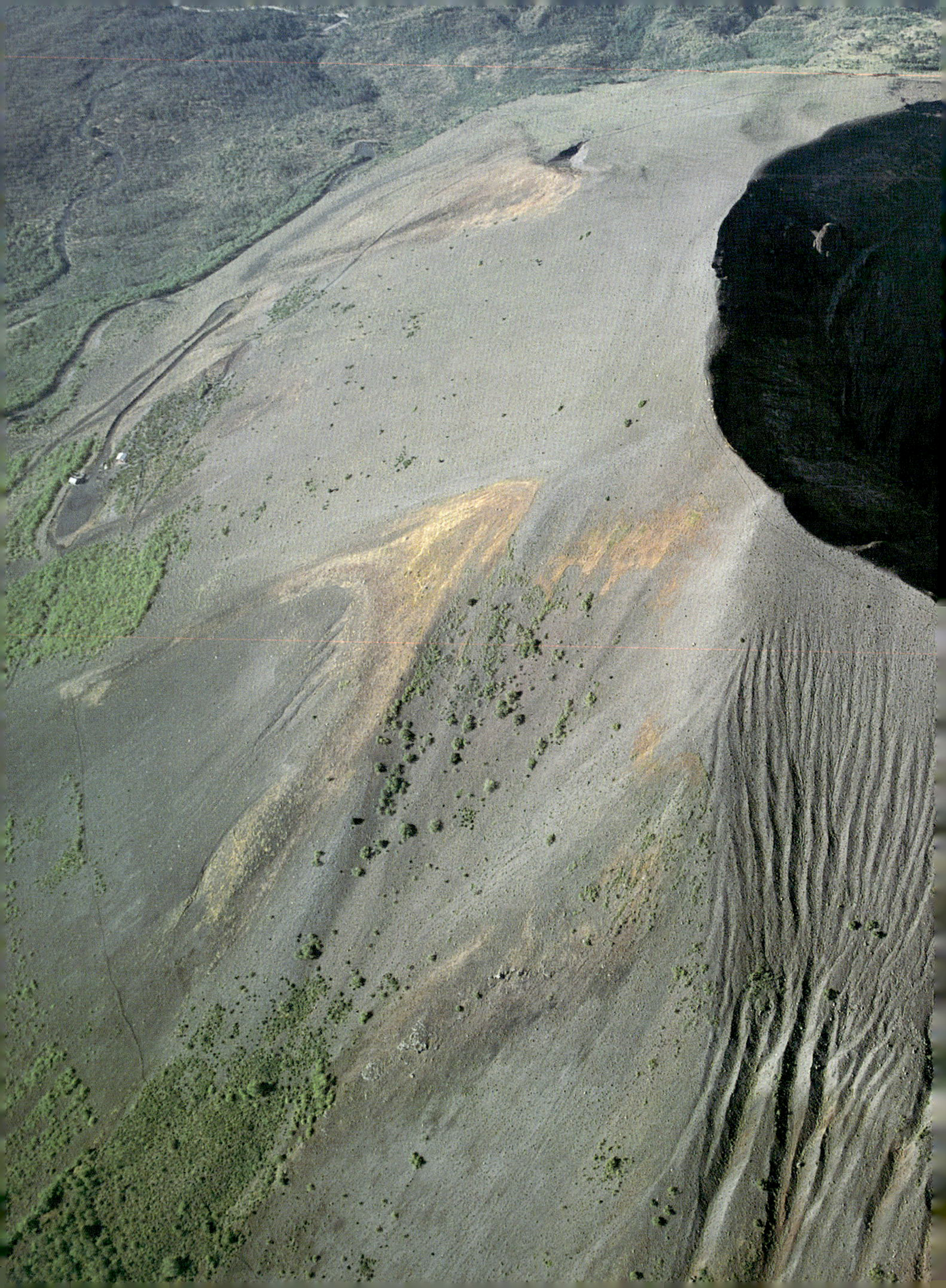

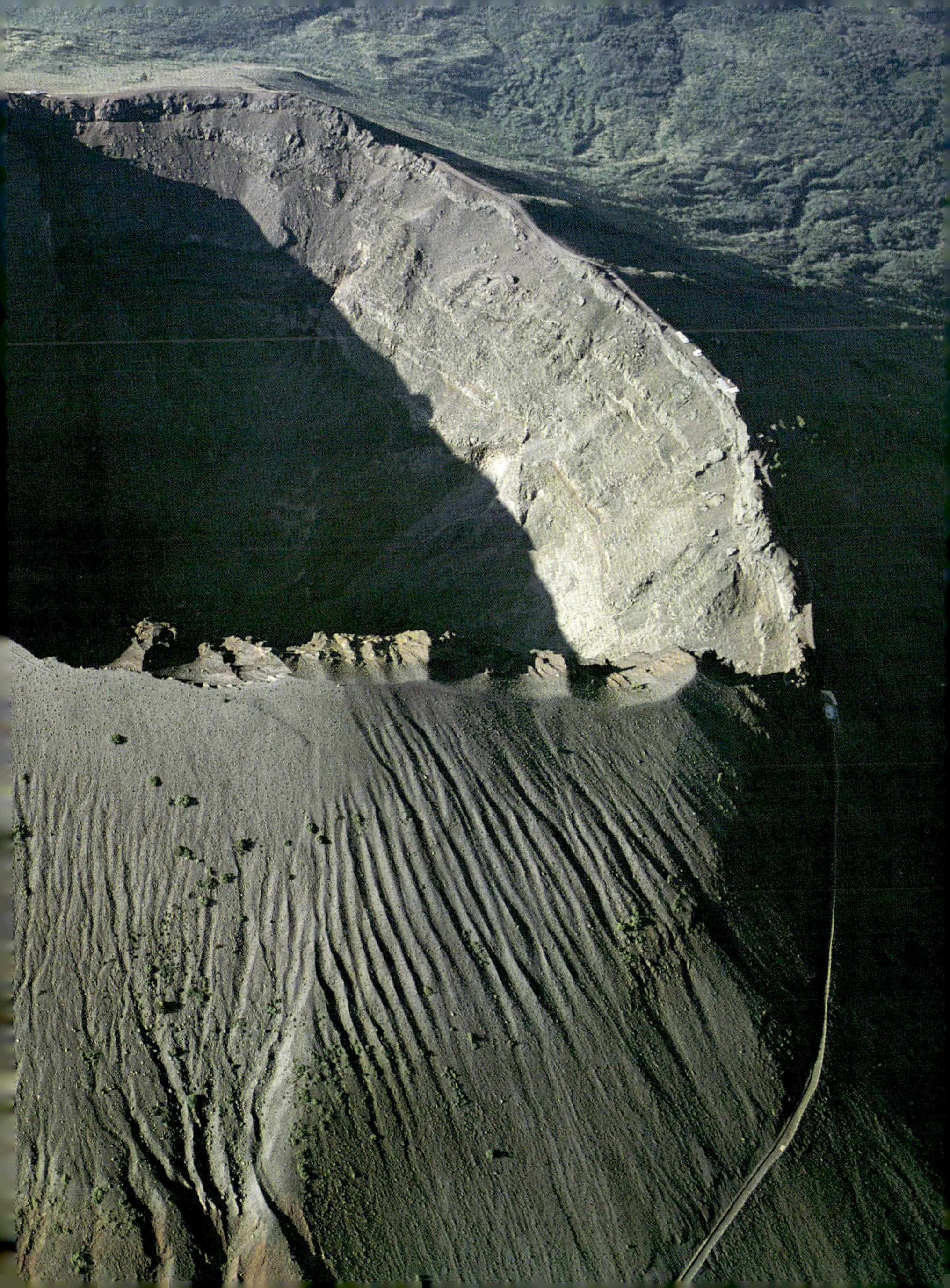

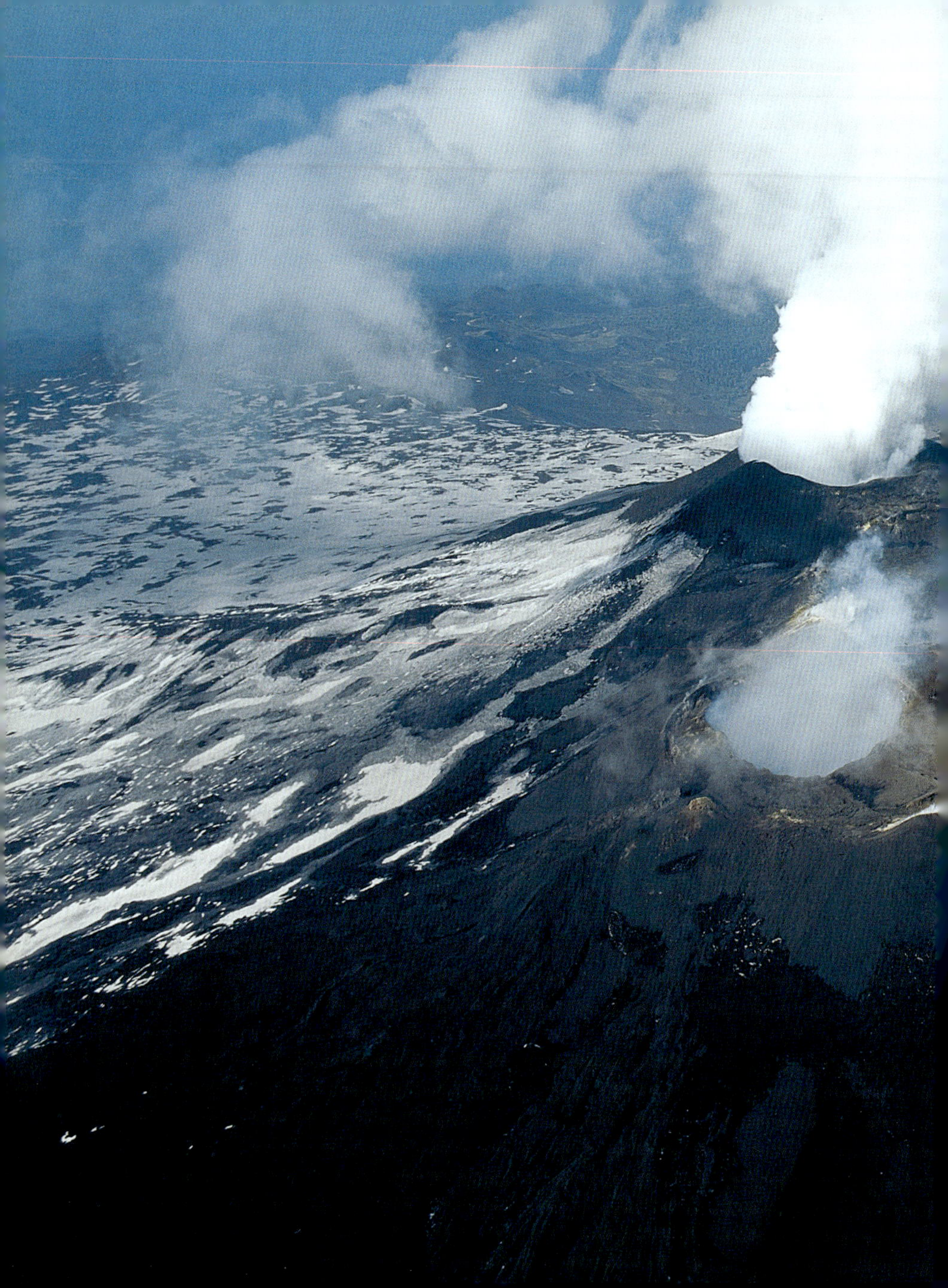

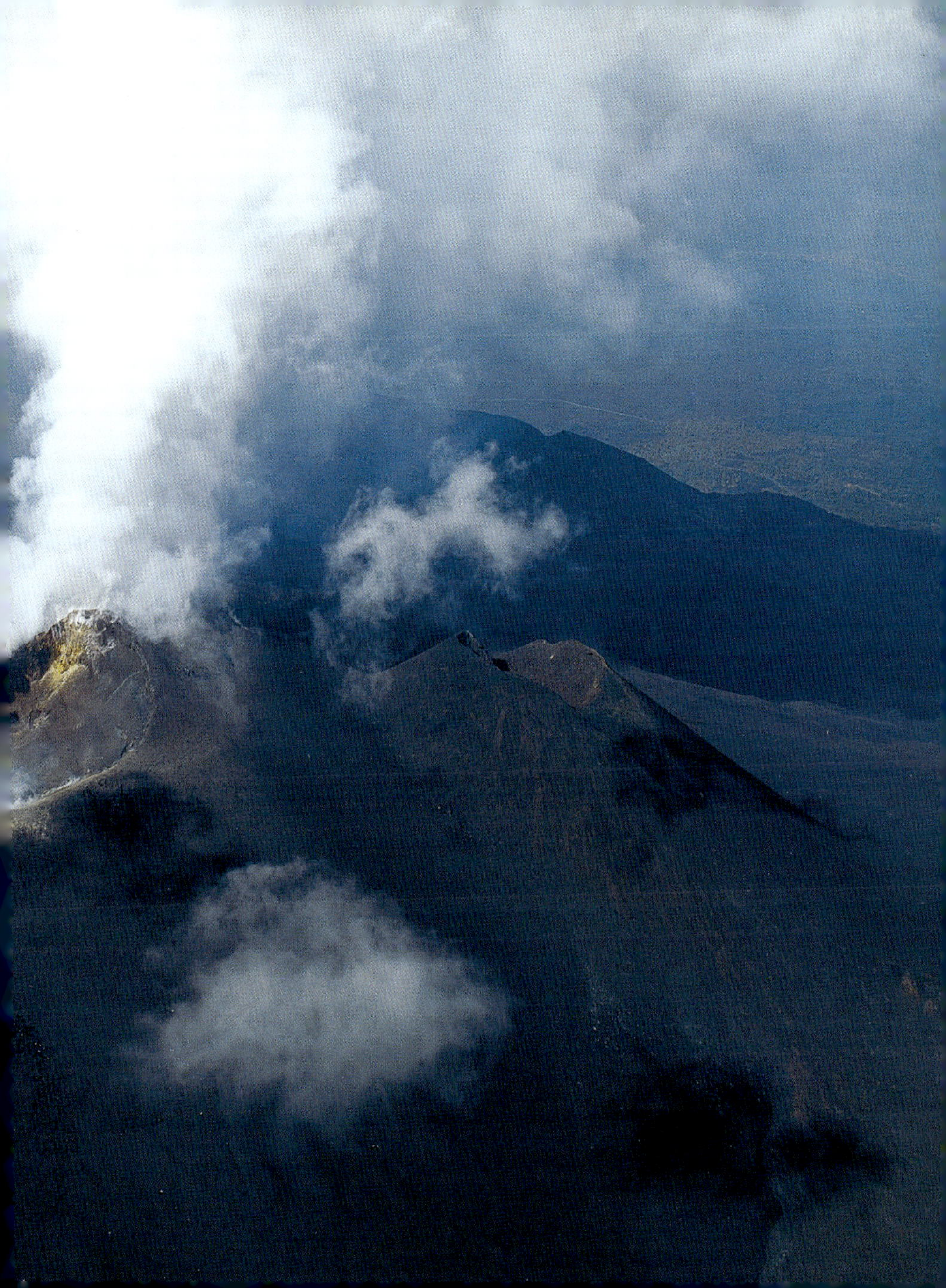

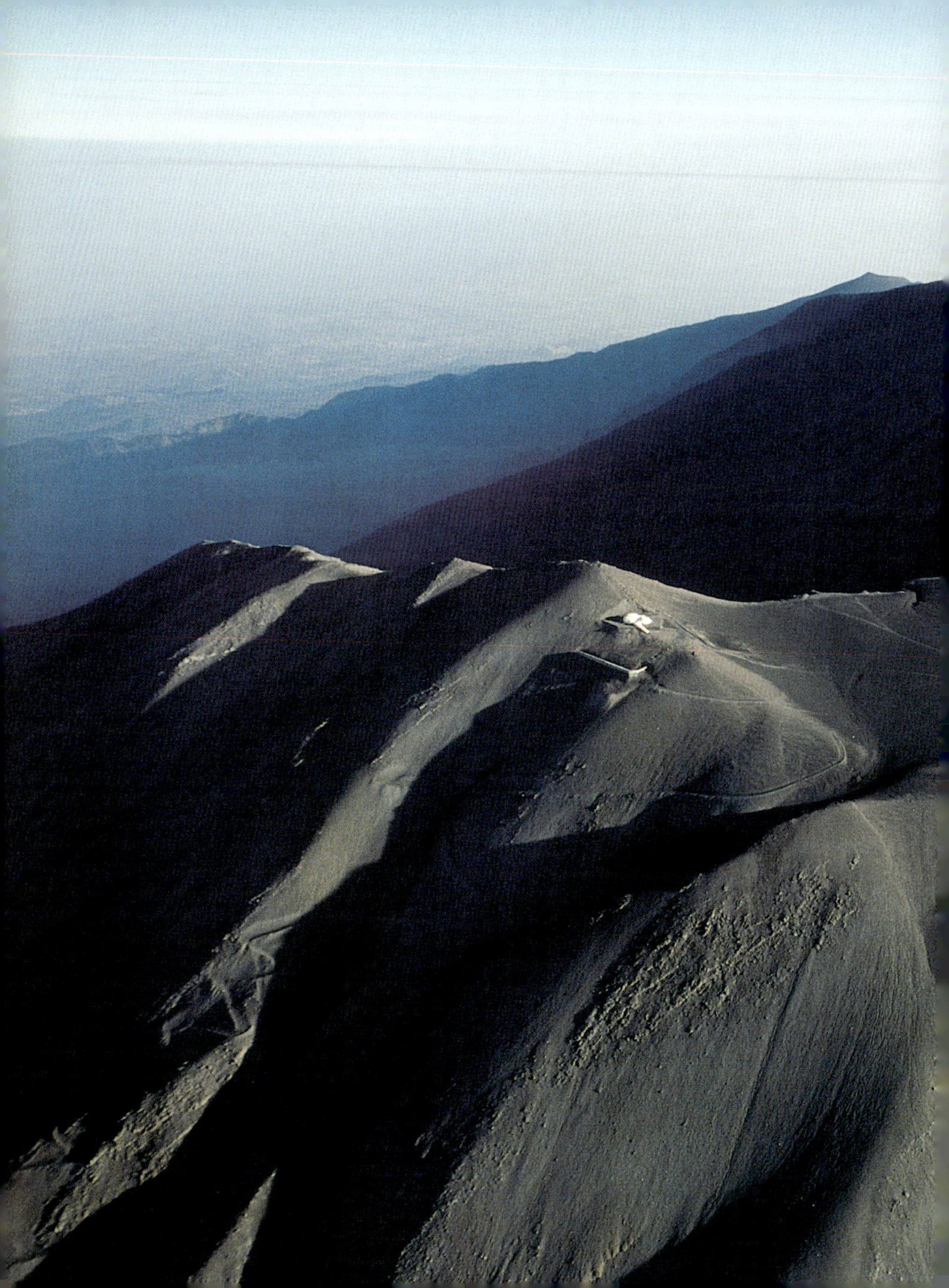

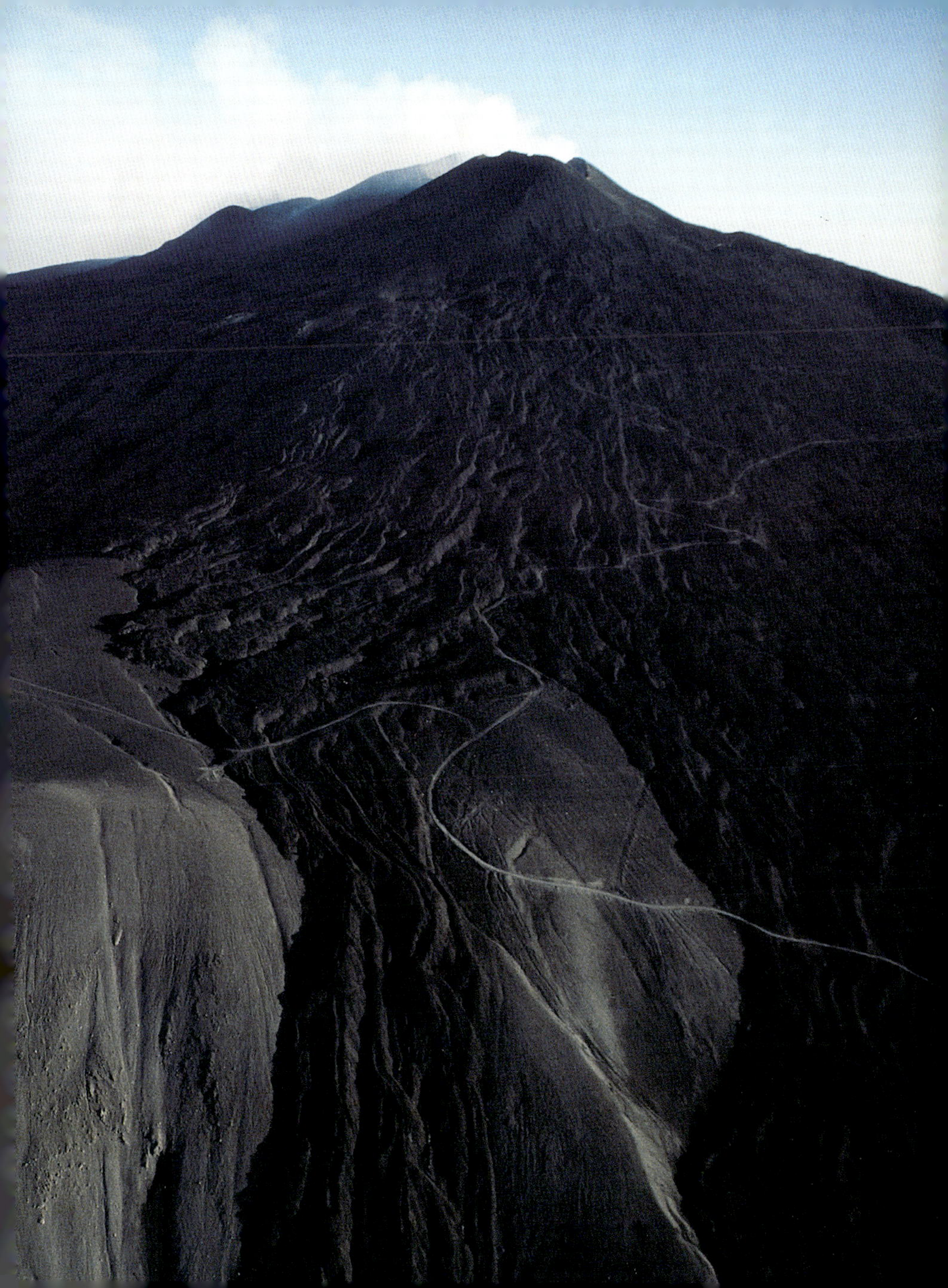

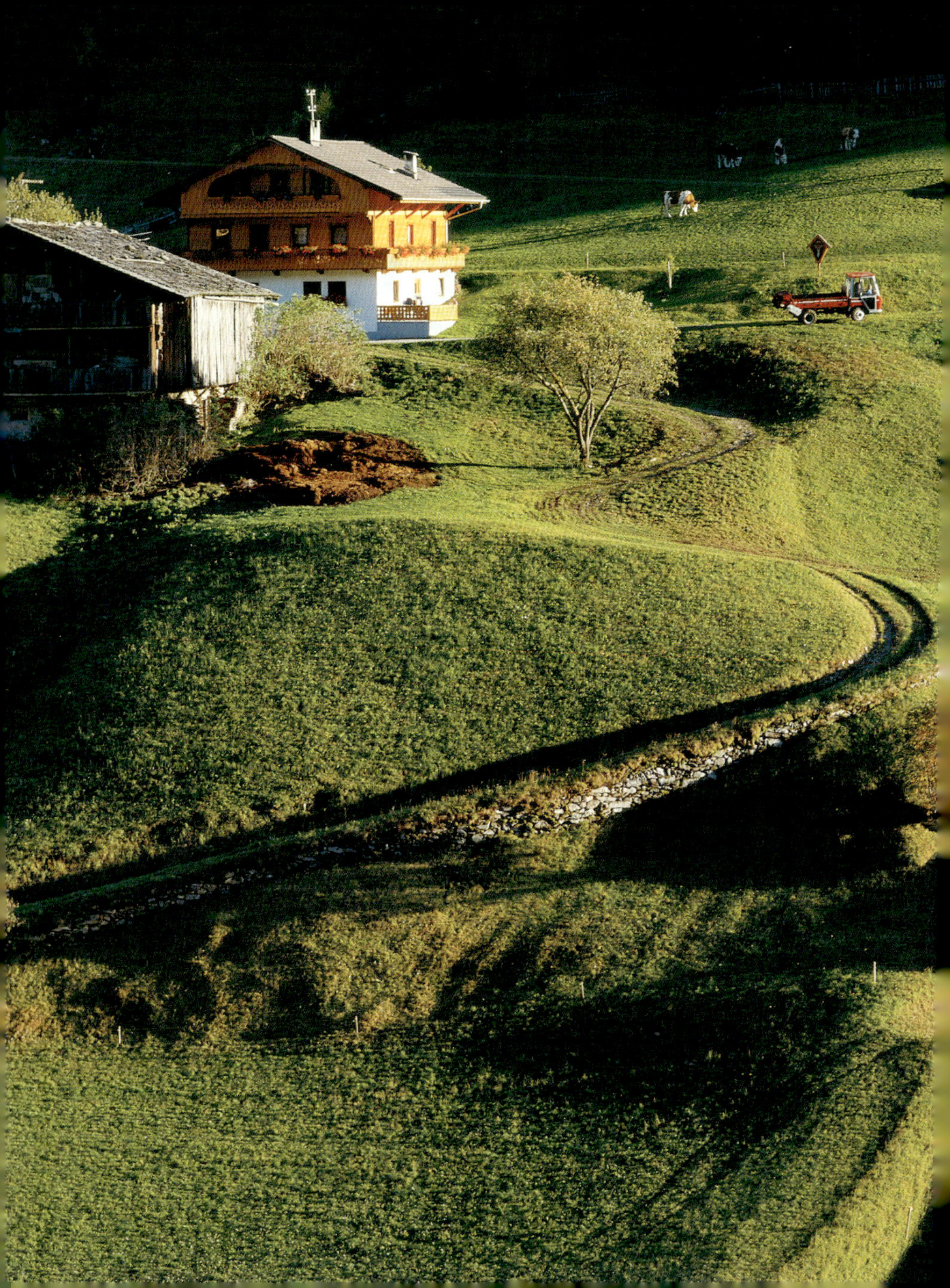

SQUARES
AND CITY VIEWS

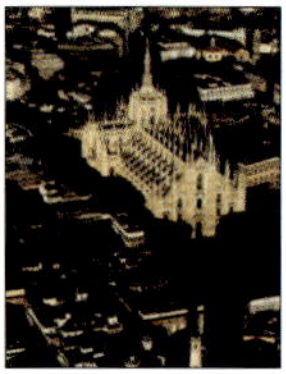

THE DUOMO OF MILAN, the third largest church in the world after Saint Peter's in Rome and Seville Cathedral, rises in central town boasting its mass, many spires and the four metre-high gilt "Madonnina" *(p. 97)*.

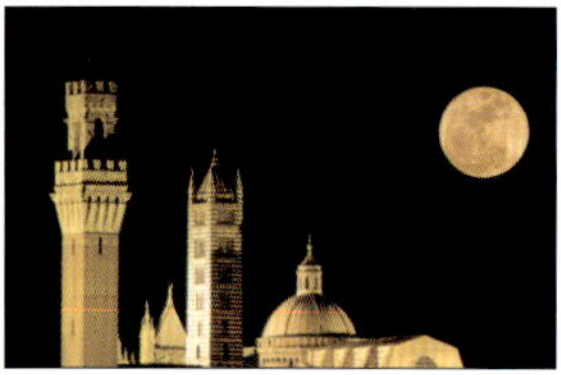

IMPRESSIVE NIGHT VIEW OF SIENA showing the Gothic Duomo, the Romanesque bell tower and the Palazzo Pubblico in the foreground. The latter dominates Piazza del Campo *(pp. 100-101)*.

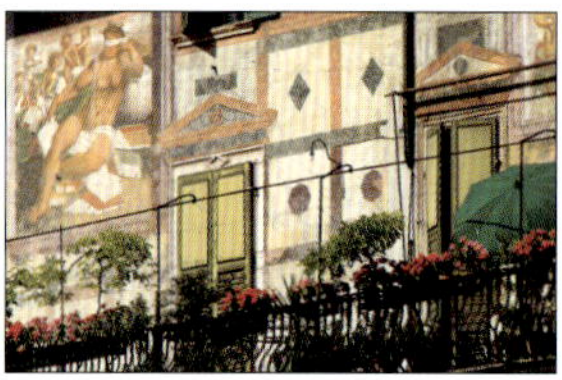

THE FAÇADE OF MAZZANTI HOUSES, decorated with 16th-century frescoes in Piazza delle Erbe, Verona. Built on the site of the Roman forum, the square is surrounded by 14th-century houses and towers *(pp. 104-105)*.

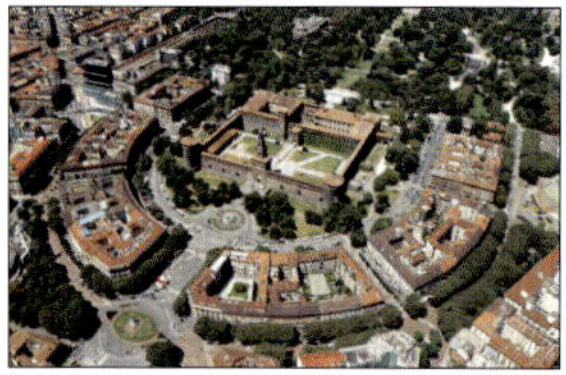

SFORZA CASTLE and Foro Buonaparte, Milan. The castle was built in the 14th century by the Visconti family, and lately owned by the Sforzas, who transformed it in a sumptuous Renaissance court *(pp. 98-99)*.

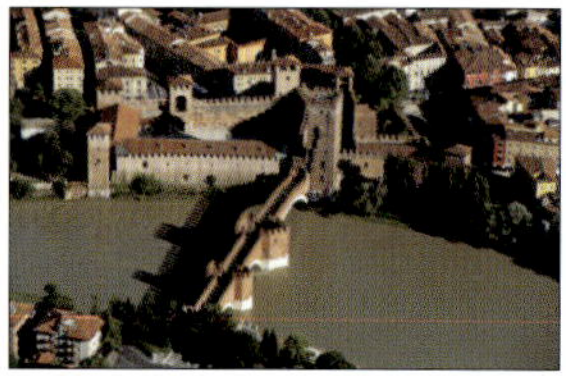

THE PONTE SCALIGERO IN VERONA links the medieval Castelvecchio to the opposite side of river Adige. The three-arcade bridge rests on turreted pillars, and was rebuilt after the 1945 bombings *(pp. 102-103)*.

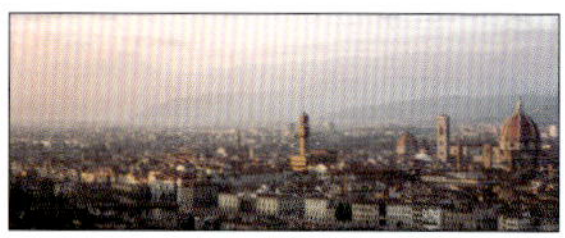

PANORAMA OF FLORENCE, located on the banks of river Arno. The imposing Brunelleschi's Dome, Giotto's Campanile and the 14th-century Palazzo Vecchio stand out proudly *(pp. 106-107)*.

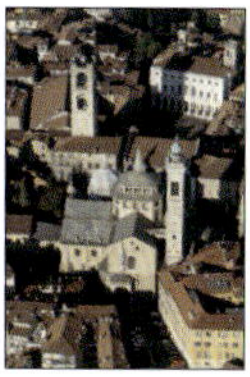

A VIEW OF BERGAMO ALTA, which is the historical part of the town perched on the slopes of a hill. Inside the 16th-century Venetian walls are located ancient streets and medieval and Renaissance buildings *(p. 108)*.

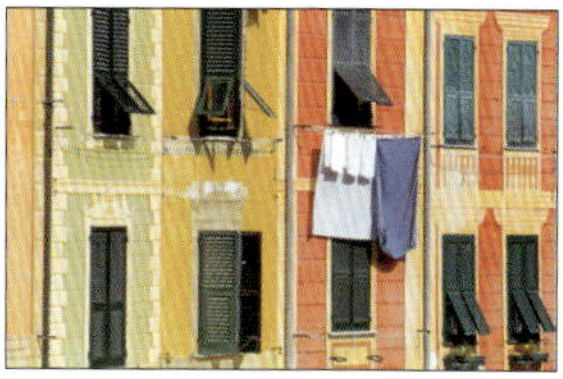

THE OLD STREETS OF PORTOFINO DISPLAY the typical warm Ligurian colours. Once inhabited by sailors, these buildings face the little harbour of Portofino, today a fashionable resort for celebrities *(pp. 110-111)*.

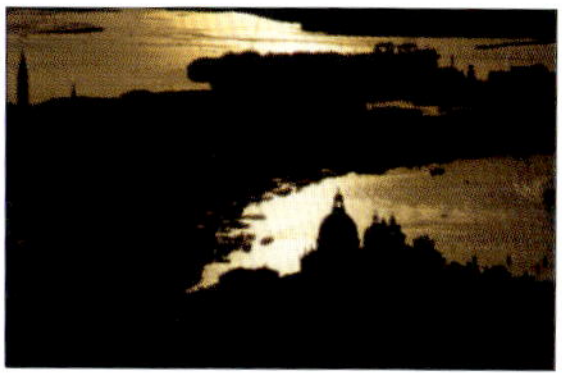

REFLECTIONS OF LIGHT ON THE LAGOON surrounding Venice, one of the most beautiful and celebrated towns in the world for its peculiar geo-morphological features and its gorgeous architecture *(pp. 114-115)*.

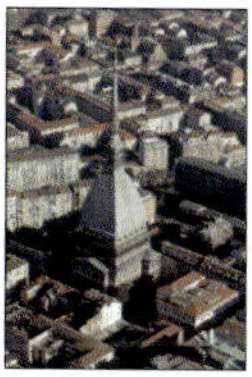

THE MOLE ANTONELLIANA rises in the centre of Turin. Started in 1862 as a Hebraic synagogue, it was eventually completed by the Commune in 1889 and became the symbol of the city *(p. 109)*.

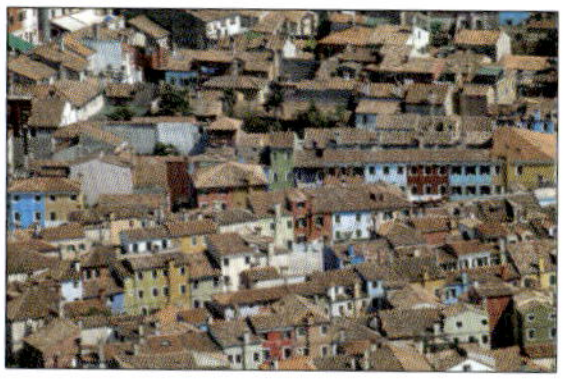

MULTICOLOURED FAÇADES of Burano houses. The most picturesque island of the Venetian Lagoon is also known for lace manufacturing, a craft dating back to the early years of the 16th century *(pp. 112-113)*.

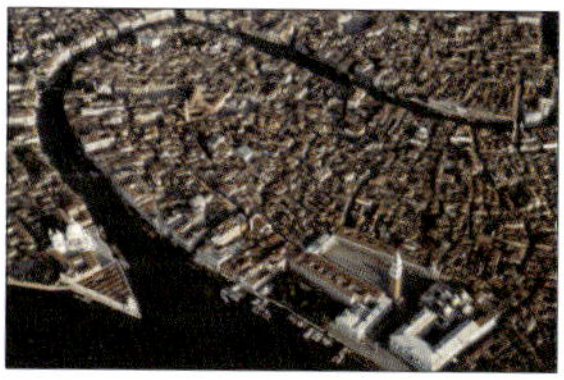

BIRD'S-EYE VIEW OF VENICE and the Grand Canal. The city built on water includes more than 100 islands and canals and more than 400 bridges. It centres round the elegant Piazza San Marco *(pp. 116-117)*.

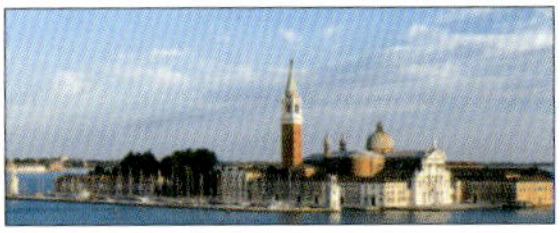

SAN GIORGIO MAGGIORE ISLAND, Venice, faces Saint Mark's quay and houses the church of the same name, designed by Andrea Palladio and finished after his death in 1611 *(pp. 118-119)*.

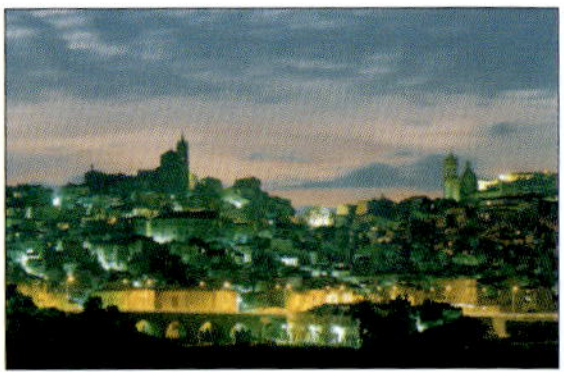

NIGHT VIEW OF CALTAGIRONE, spread on three hills in the heart of Sicily and thus called "Queen of the Mounts." The town had to be rebuilt in 17th-century Baroque style after the 1693 earthquake *(pp. 120-121)*.

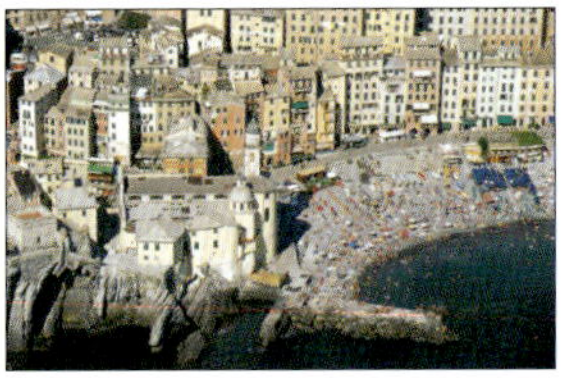

THE HAMLET OF CAMOGLI is distinguished by very colourful period buildings facing the old little harbour, which is overlooked by the church and by Castel Dragone, both built on a rocky headland *(pp. 122-123)*.

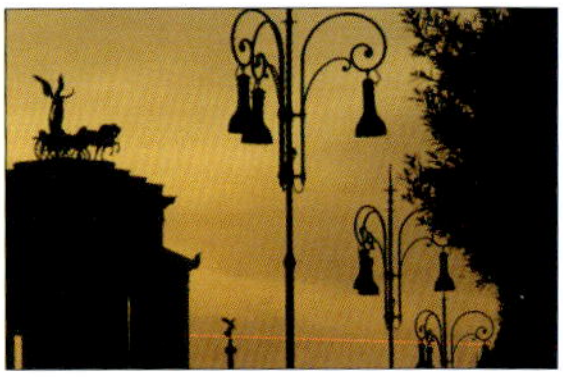

A DETAIL OF THE VITTORIANO, Rome, at sunset. Dedicated to Victor Emmanuel II, the first king of unified Italy, the white limestone *Altare della patria* stands out in its majesty *(pp. 124-125)*.

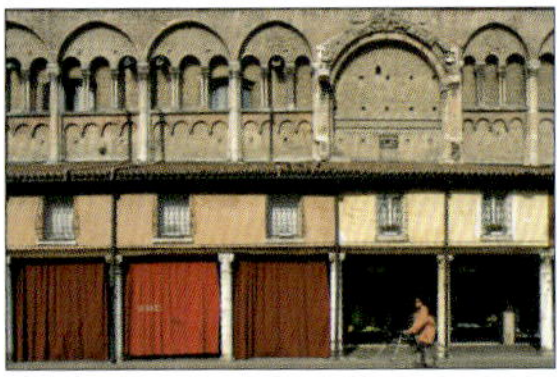

THE LOGGIA DEI MERCANTI in Piazza Trento e Trieste, Ferrara, was built in the 15th century to house the shops still lining the right-hand side of the Cathedral *(pp. 126-127)*.

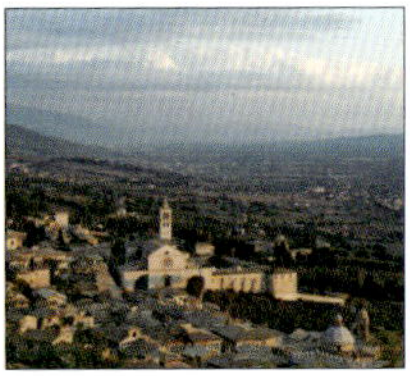

THE 13TH-CENTURY CHURCH OF SANTA CHIARA is one of Assisi's symbols of art and spirituality. The body of the saint, founder of the Clarisse religious order, is kept inside it *(pp. 128-129)*.

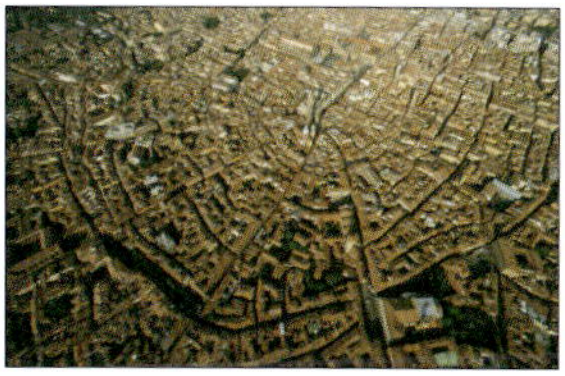

BOLOGNA SEEN FROM ABOVE. Its historical center, based on a medieval plant but marked out by Renaissance and Baroque features, converges on Piazza Maggiore, the ancient seat of the city government *(pp. 130-131)*.

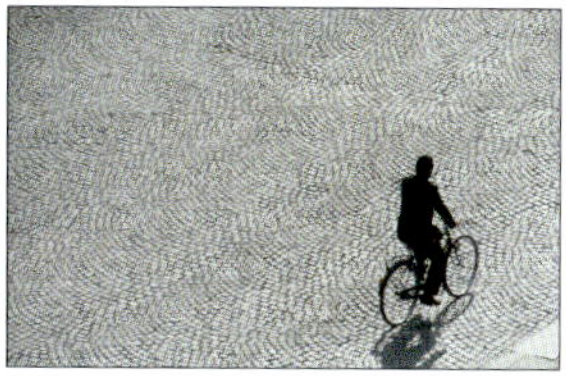

A MAN ON HIS BIKE crosses the cobblestone streets of downtown Ferrara. Scenes like this are frequent in the small town, where short distances favour the two-wheeled means of transport *(pp. 132-133)*.

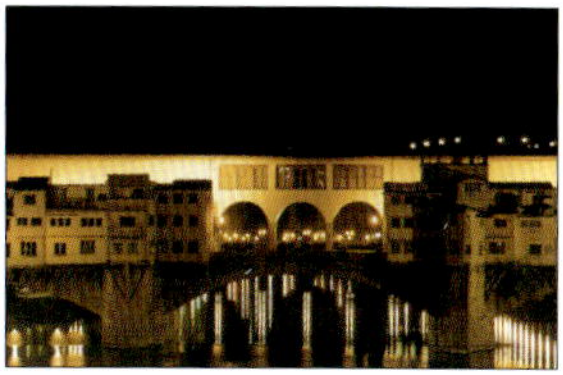

PONTE VECCHIO, Florence's oldest bridge, was built in 1345. Several goldsmith's shops are lined on its sides. They are specialised in making old- and contemporary-style jewellery *(pp. 134-135)*.

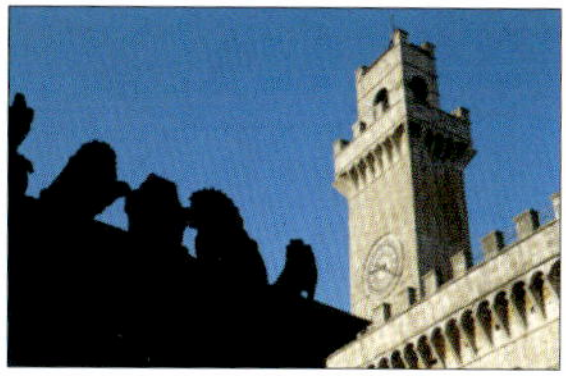

THE 13TH-CENTURY TOWN HALL of Montepulciano, dominated by a two-floor crenellated tower, overlooks Piazza Grande, the huge focal point of the town on the top of a hill *(pp. 136-137)*.

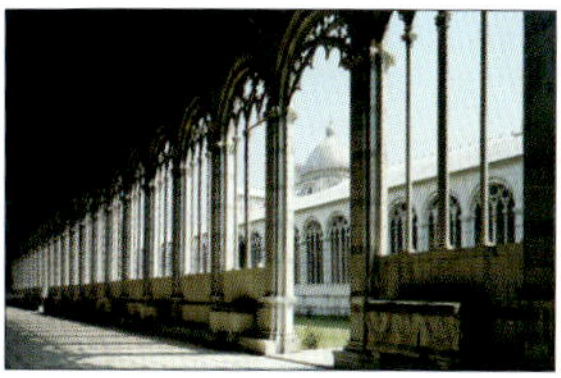

THE CEMETERY IN PIAZZA DEI MIRACOLI, Pisa, built in 1277. The original design foresaw a blind-arched, rectangular marble enclosure around it, one of the most interesting works of Tuscan Gothic style *(pp. 138-139)*.

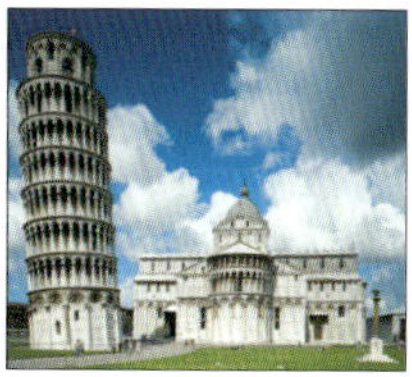

THE LEANING TOWER AND THE DUOMO are the finest examples of Pisan-Romanesque architecture. They are located on the green of Pisa's Piazza del Duomo, called Campo dei Miracoli for its beauty *(pp. 140-141)*.

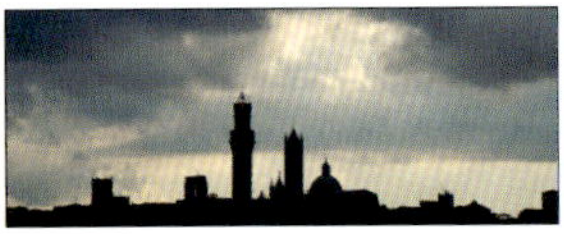

THE DISTINCTIVE OUTLINE OF SIENA. A unique place for its artistic and architectural heritage, the town also boasts an outstanding natural landscape in its neighbourhoods *(pp. 142-143)*.

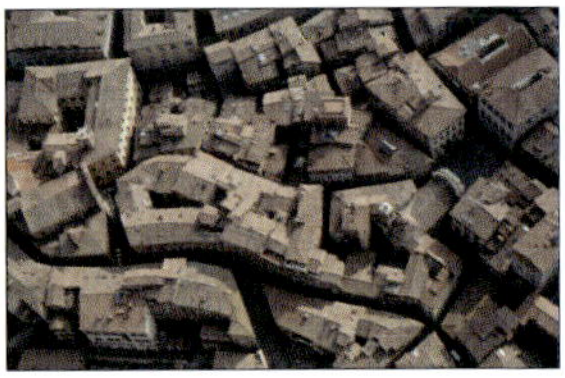

THE ROOFS OF THE HOUSES THAT WIND ALONG the narrow streets of the centre of Siena. The town, built on three clayey hills, has preserved its medieval look and structure *(pp. 144-145)*.

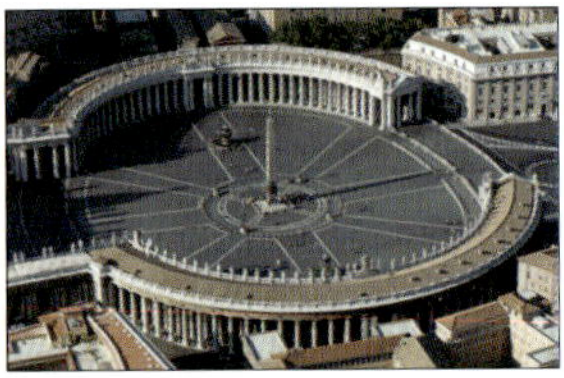

SAINT PETER'S SQUARE, ROME, designed by Bernini in the 17th century. It is bordered by four rows of columns, which look like one to those watching from either focal point of the ellipse *(pp. 146-147)*.

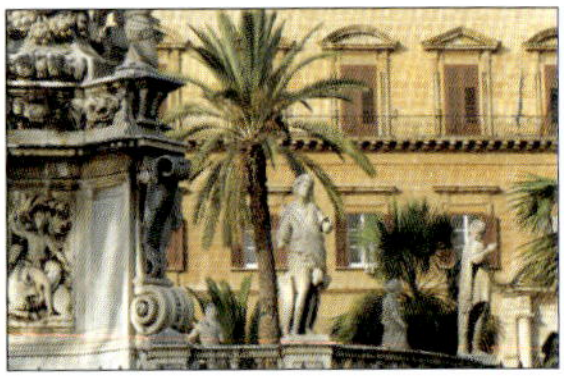

THE MONUMENT TO PHILIP V was raised in 1662 in Palermo's Piazza Vittoria, where is the Palazzo dei Normanni, built by the Arabs in the 11th century and lately transformed into a royal palace *(pp. 148-149)*.

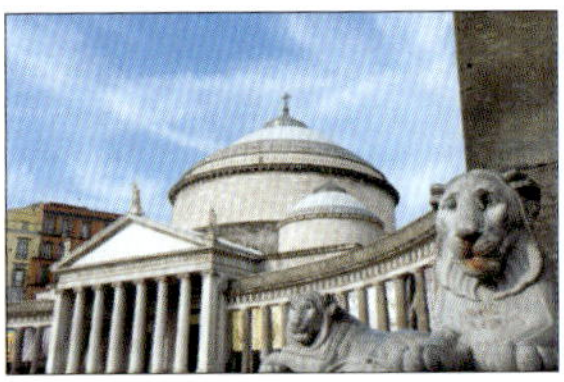

THE MAJESTIC HALF-ELLIPTICAL PIAZZA DEL PLEBISCITO in Naples. In 1810 Joachim Murat wanted it improved by a Doric-style colonnade, which frames the Basilica of Saint Francis of Paola *(pp. 150-151)*.

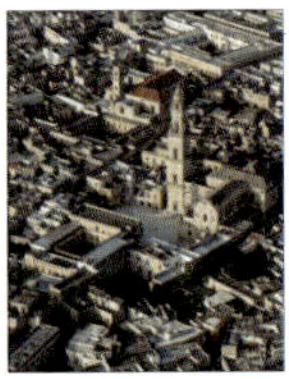

PIAZZA DUOMO is Lecce's main square. It is encircled by Baroque buildings and by the Duomo, built in the 1650s on an earlier 12th-century church and flanked by an imposing five-floor bell tower *(p. 152)*.

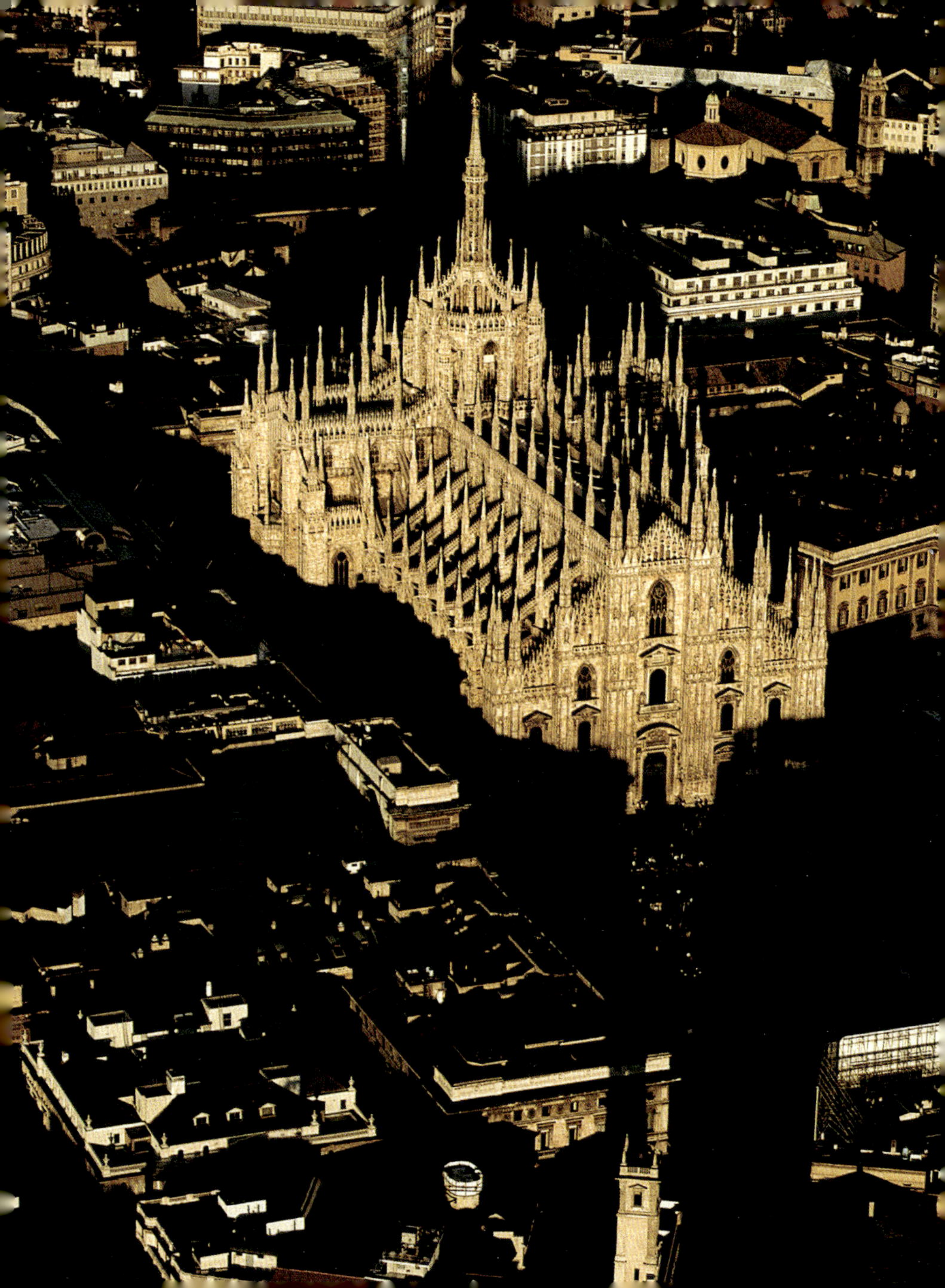

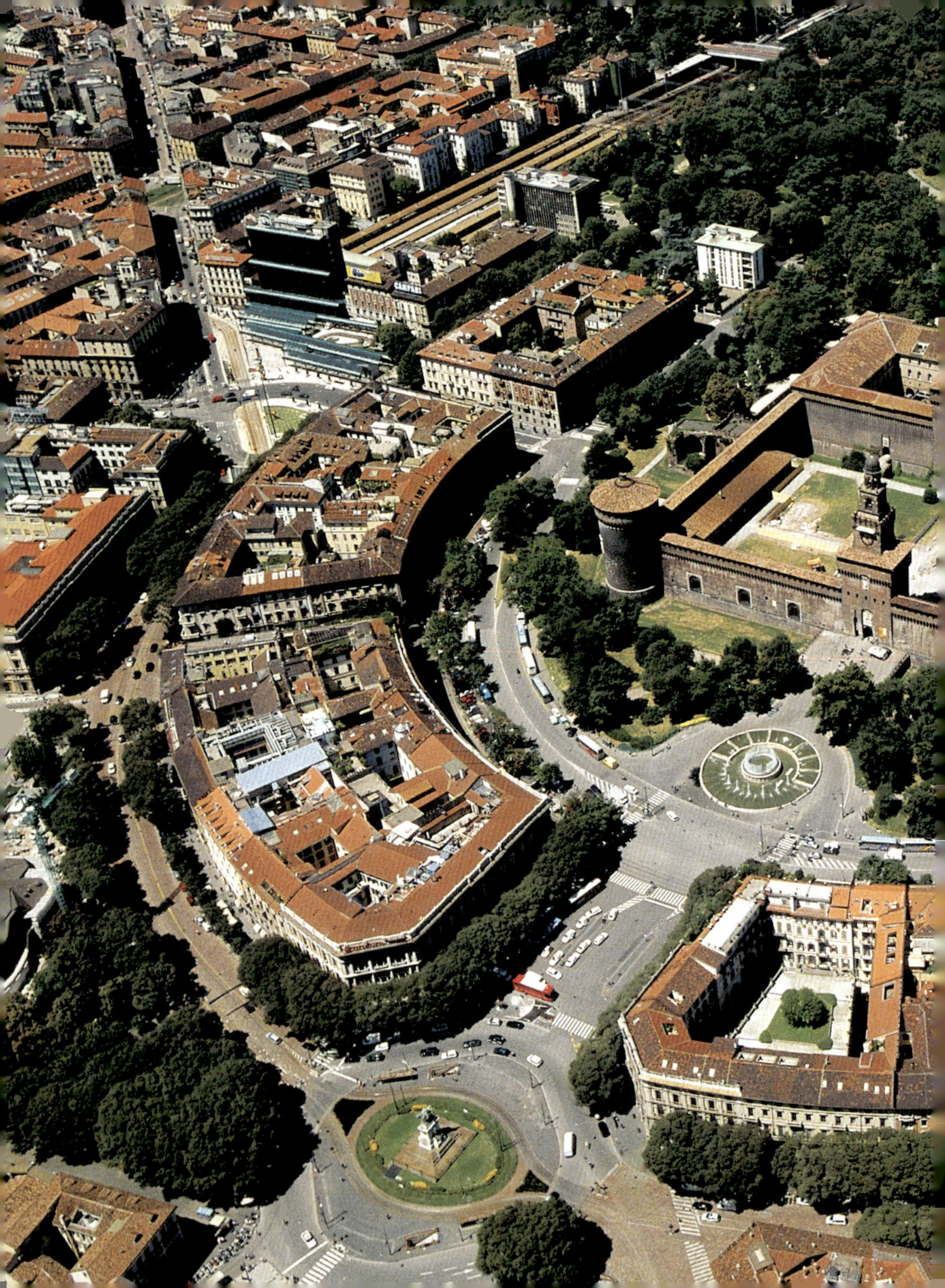

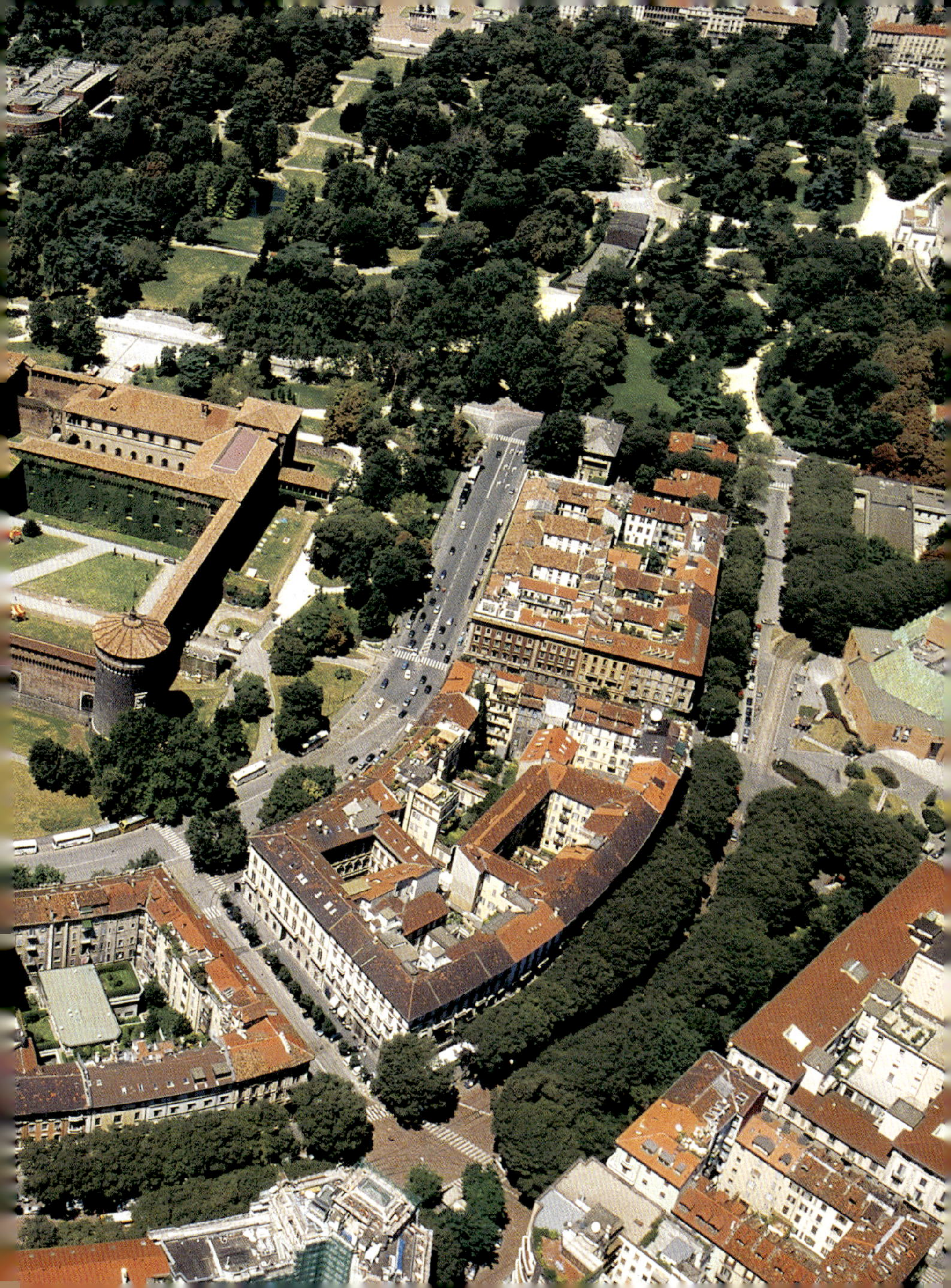

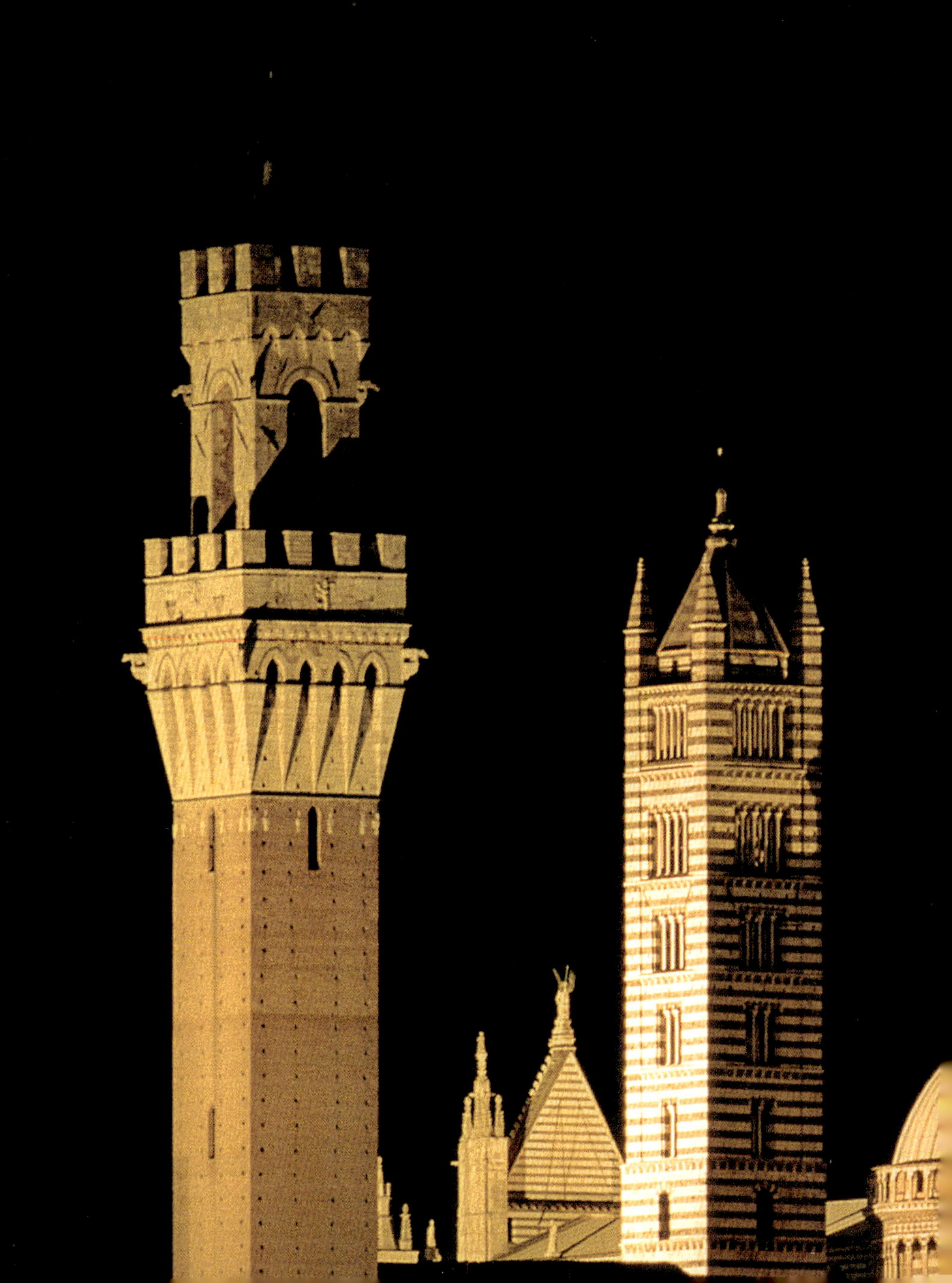

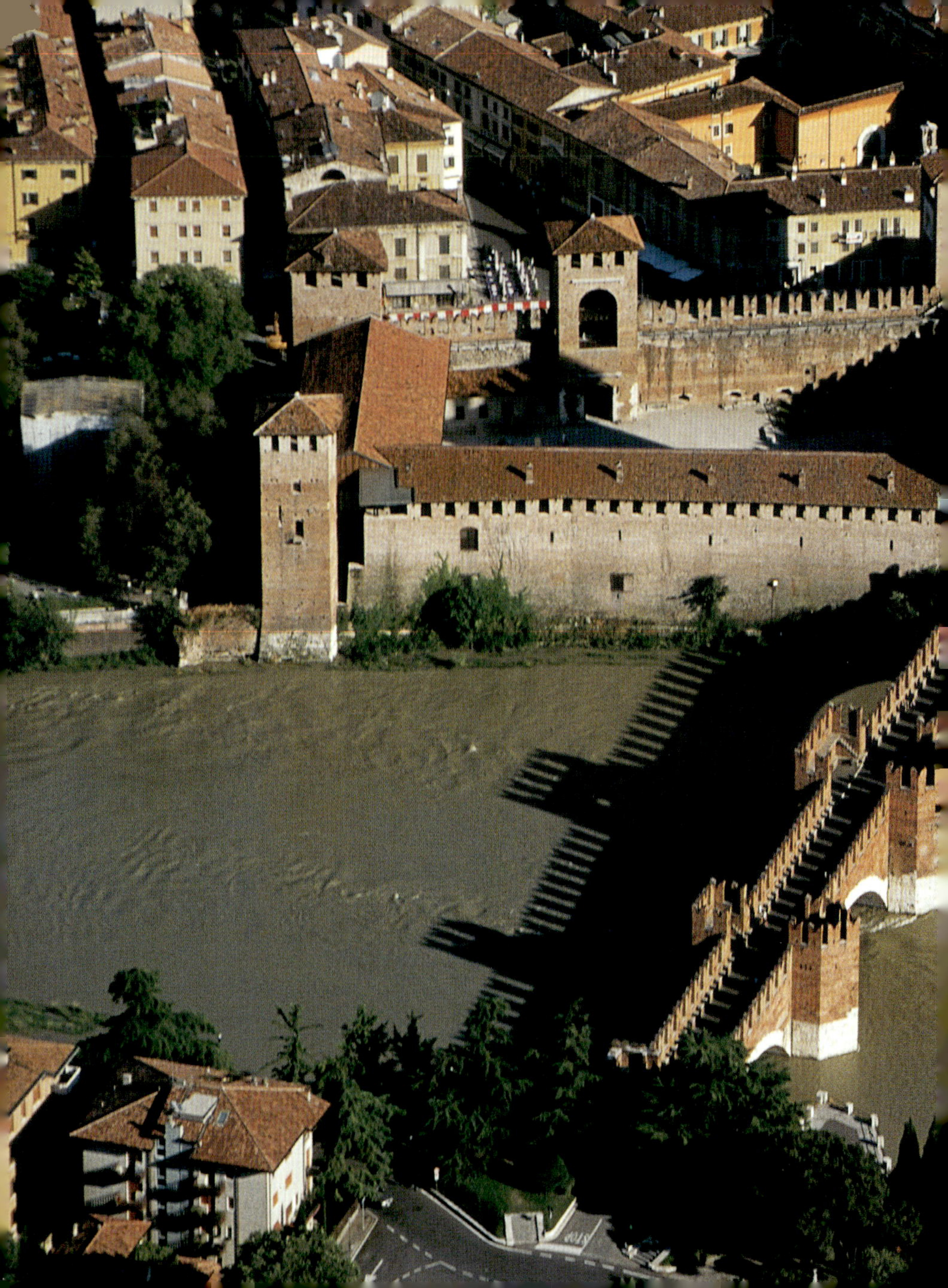

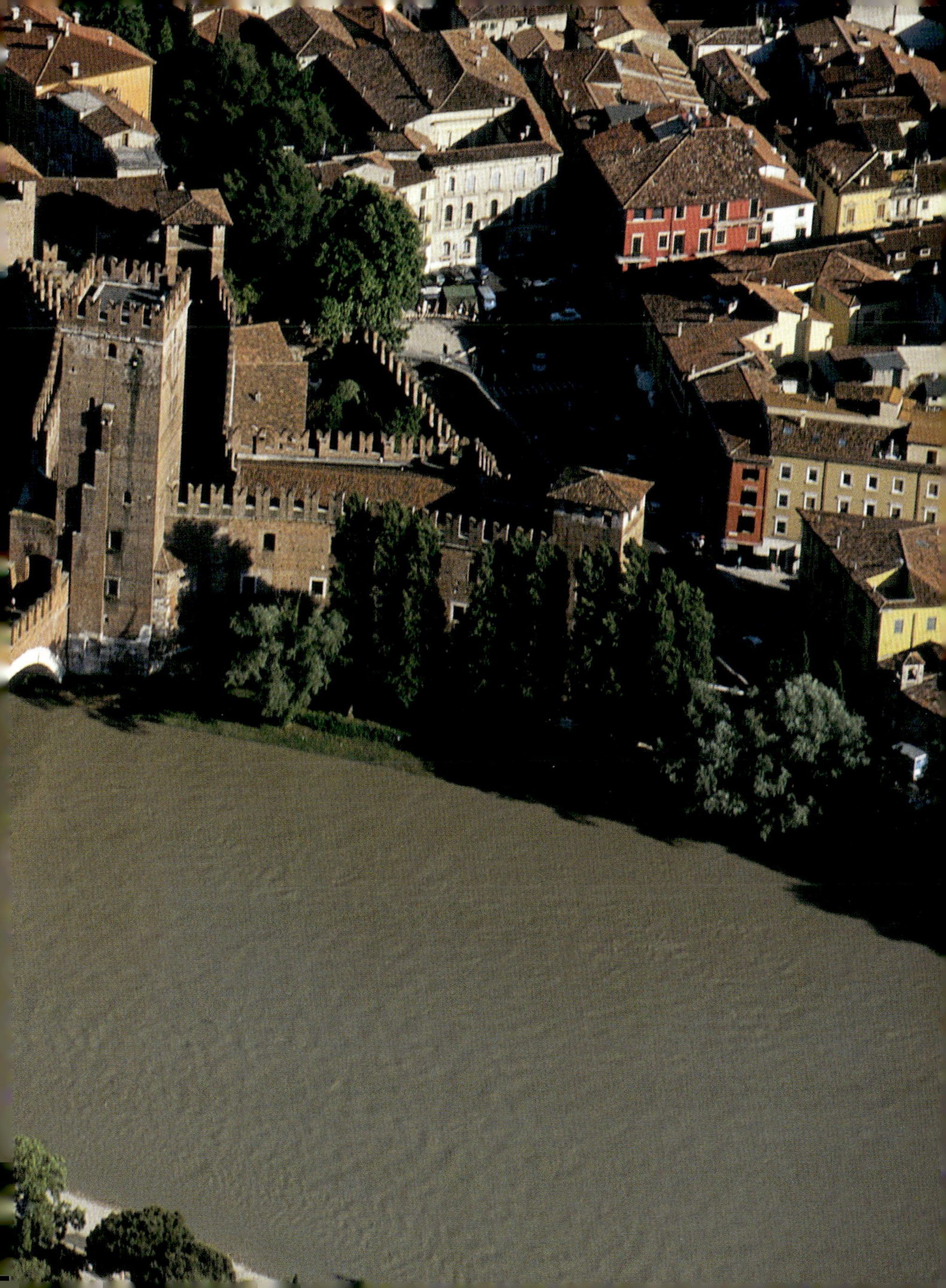

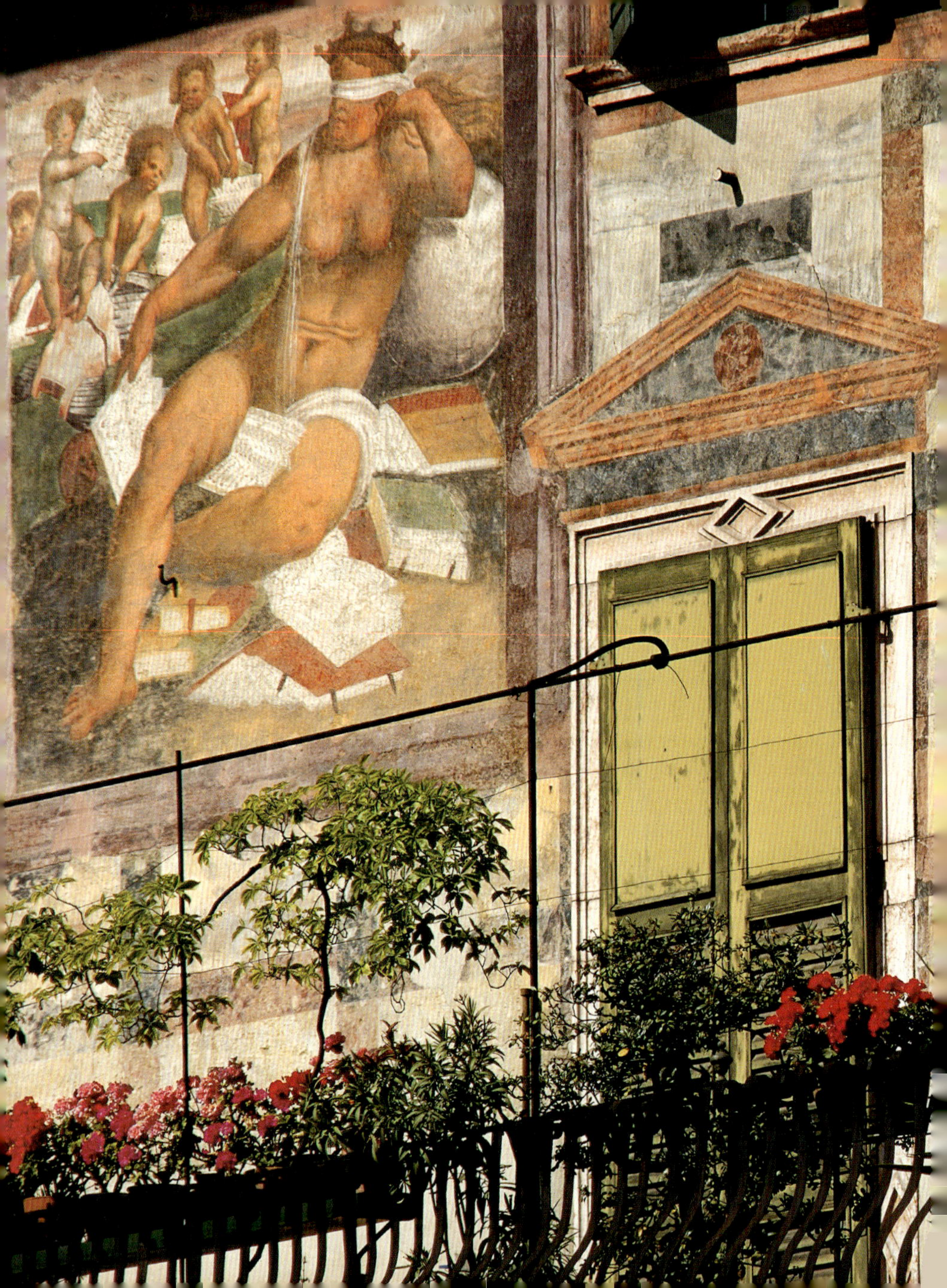

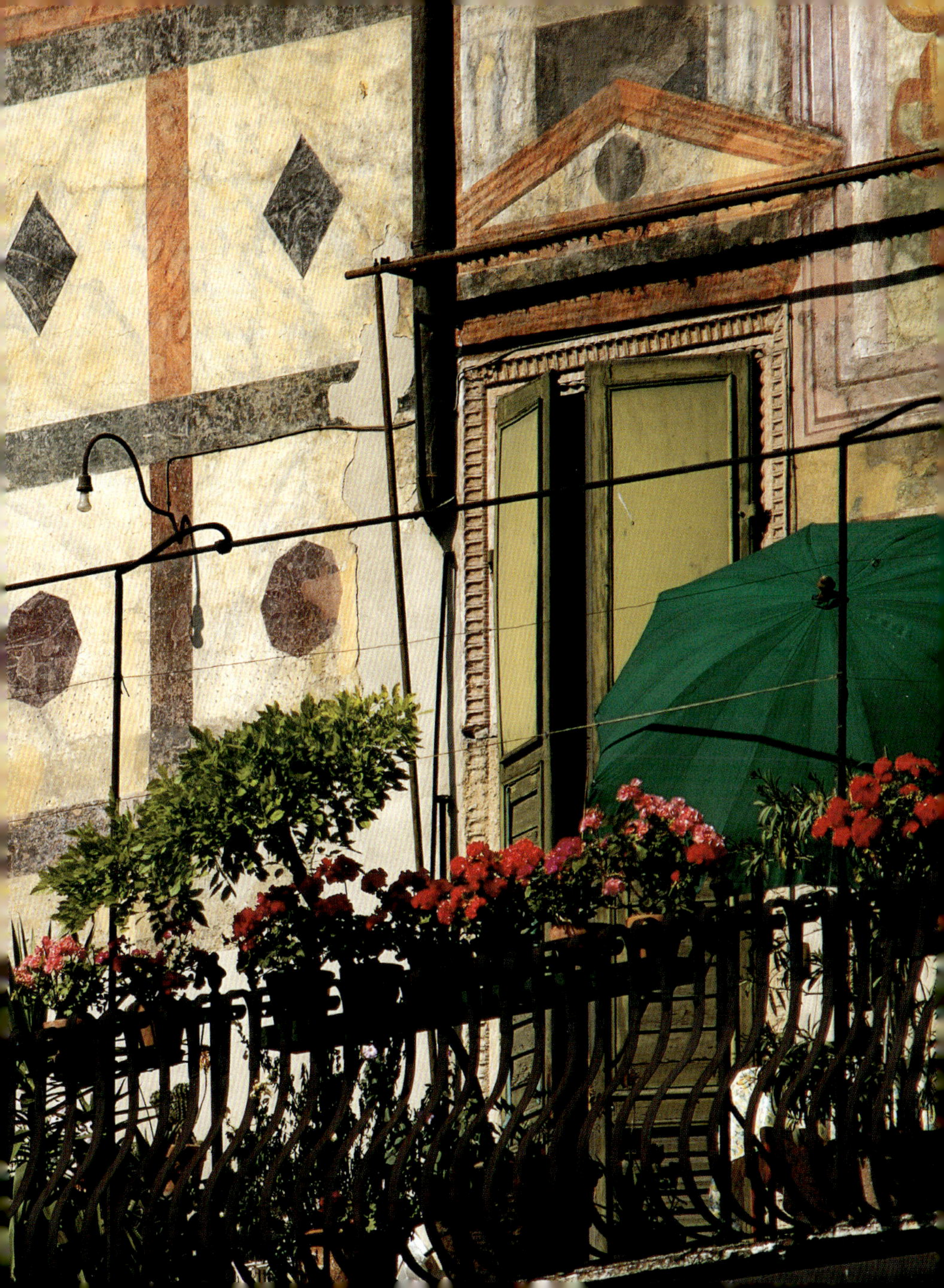

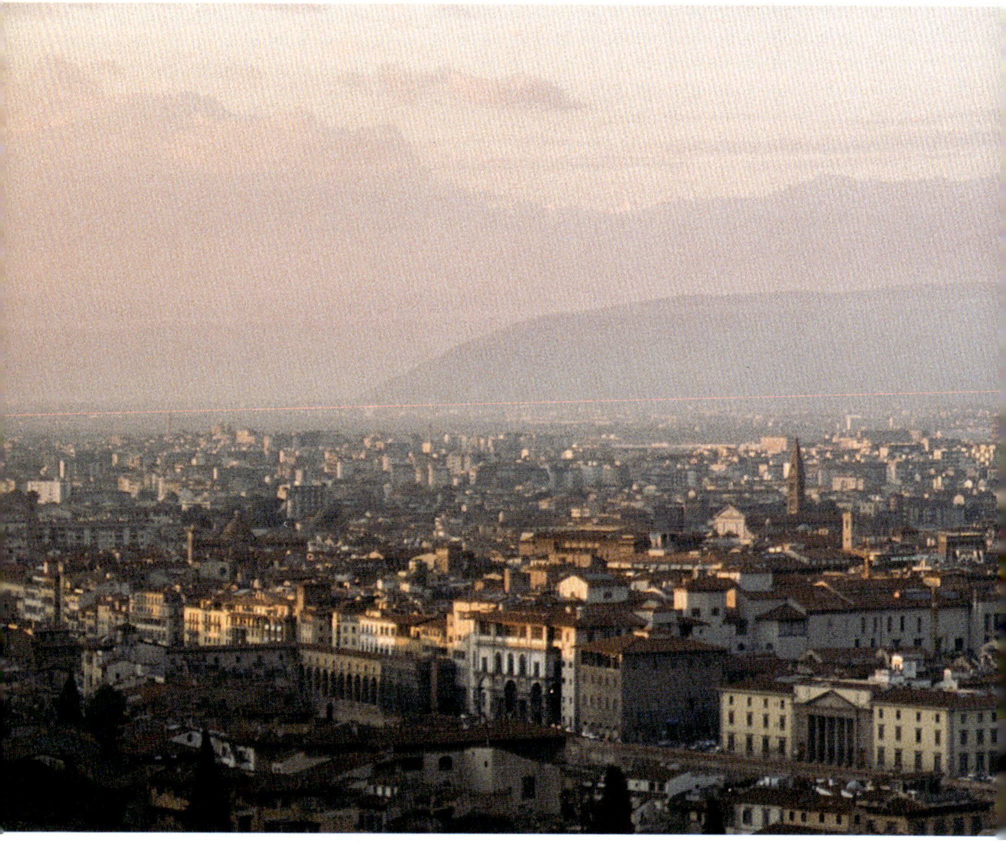

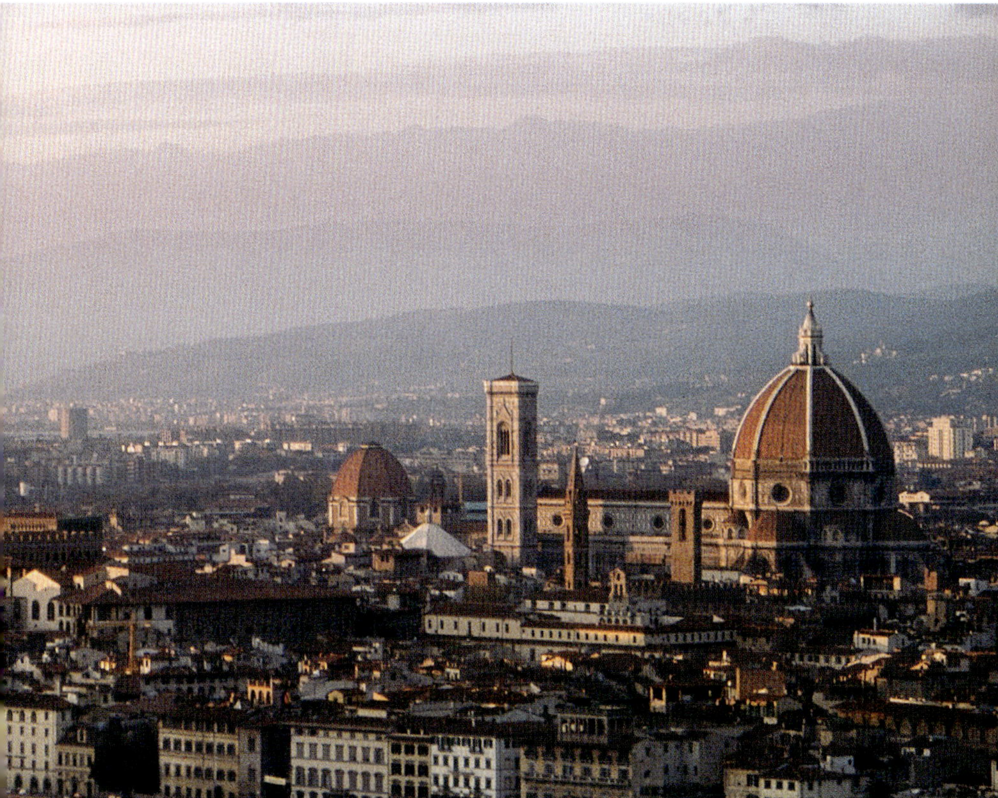

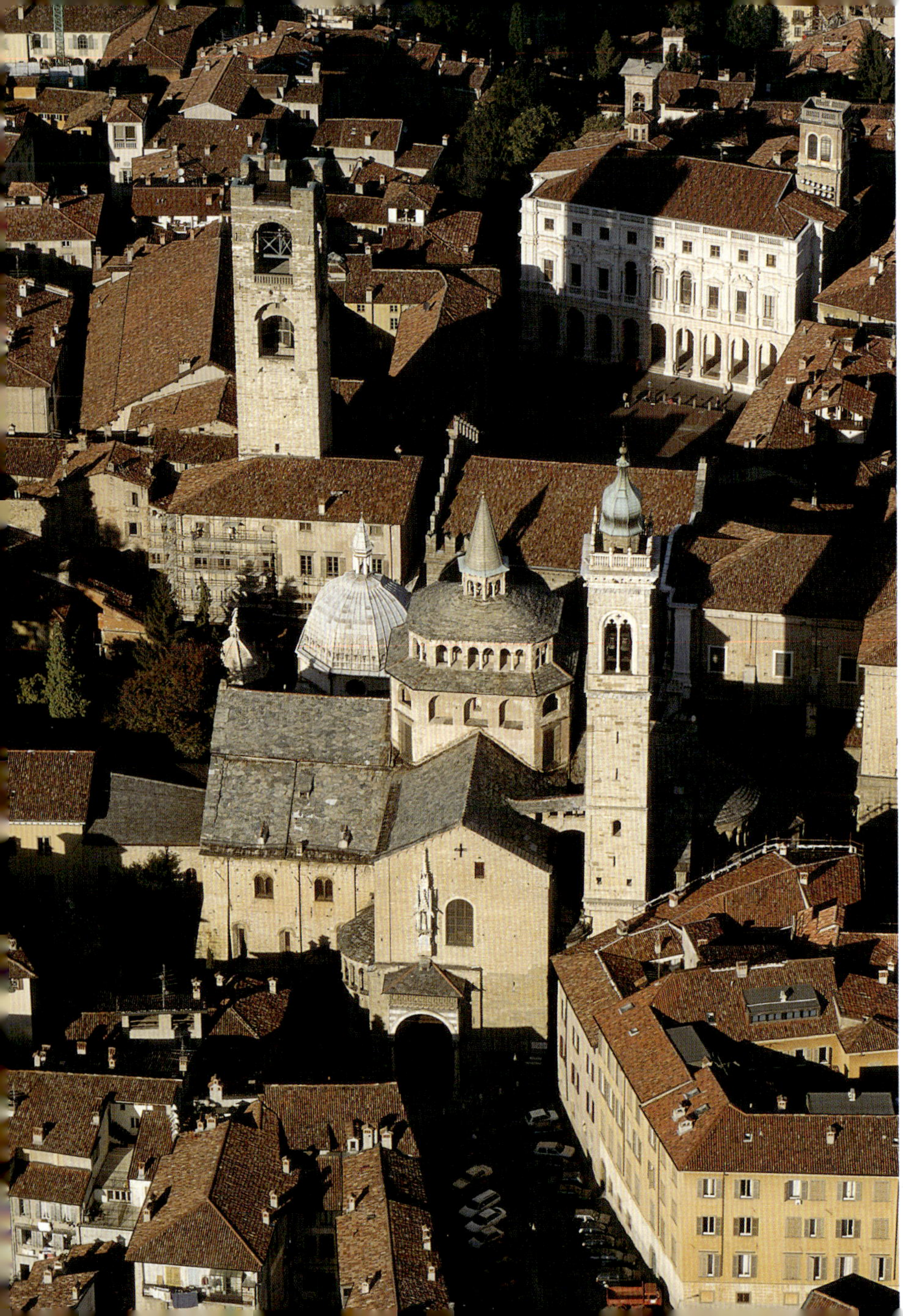

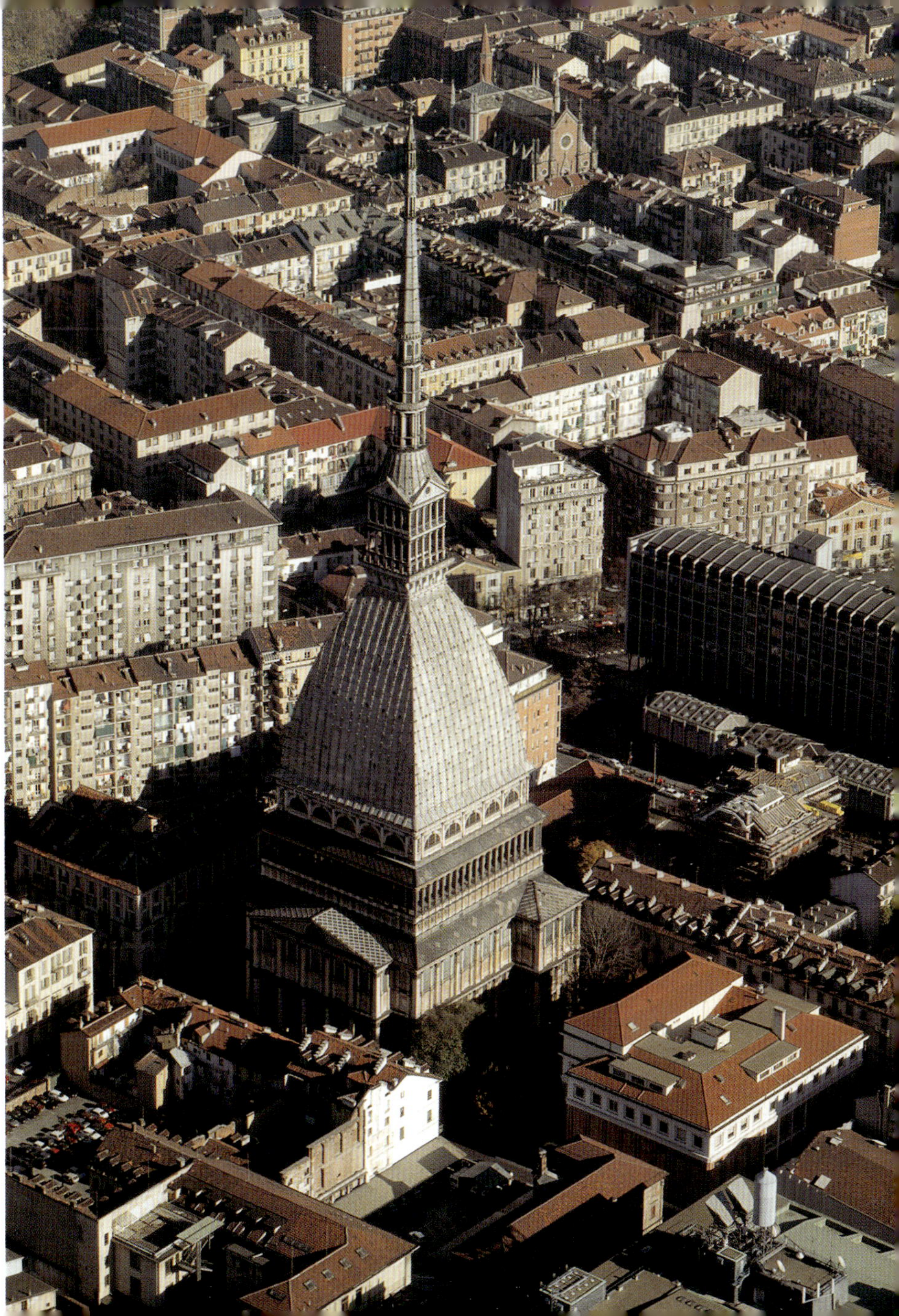

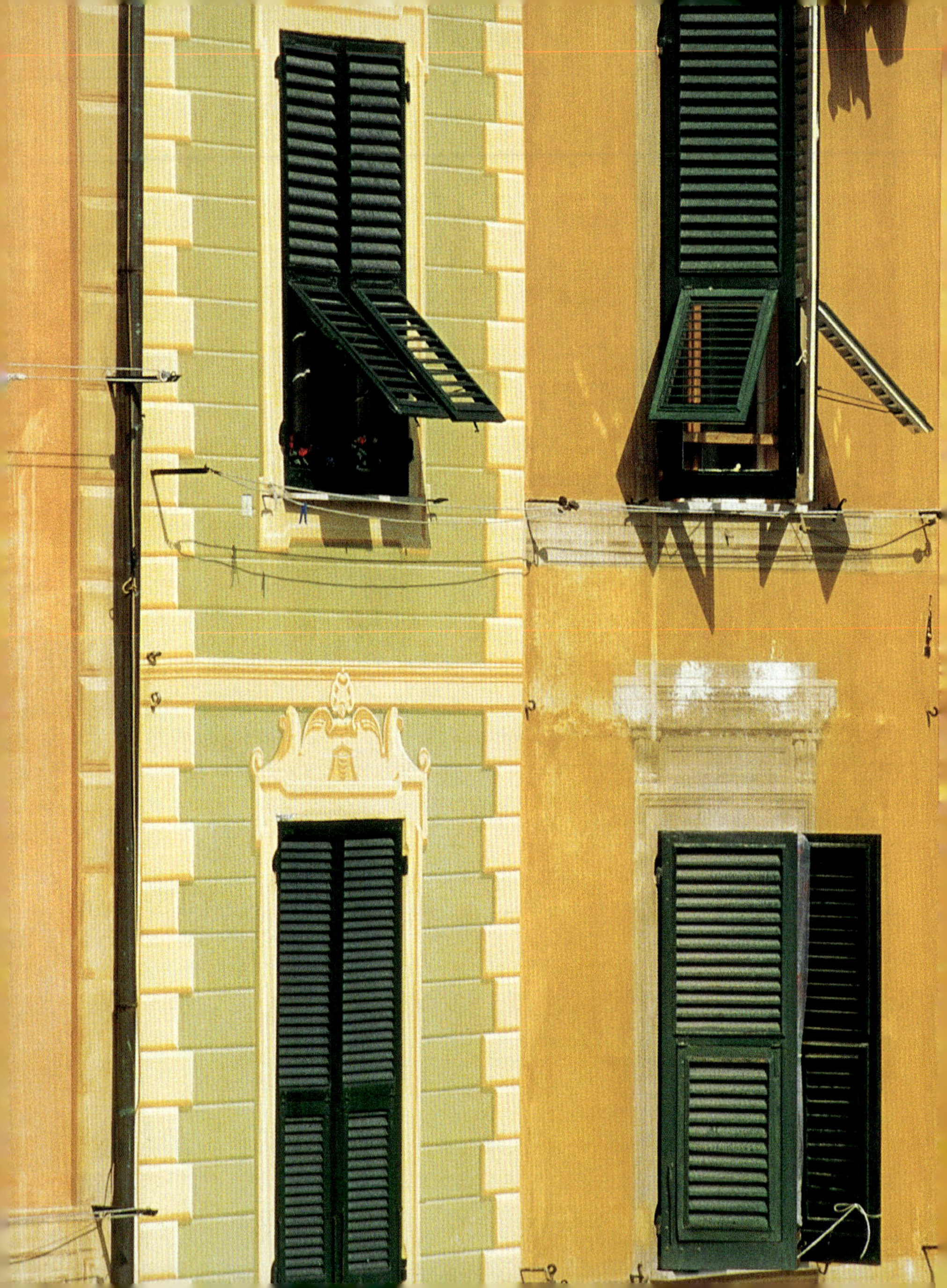

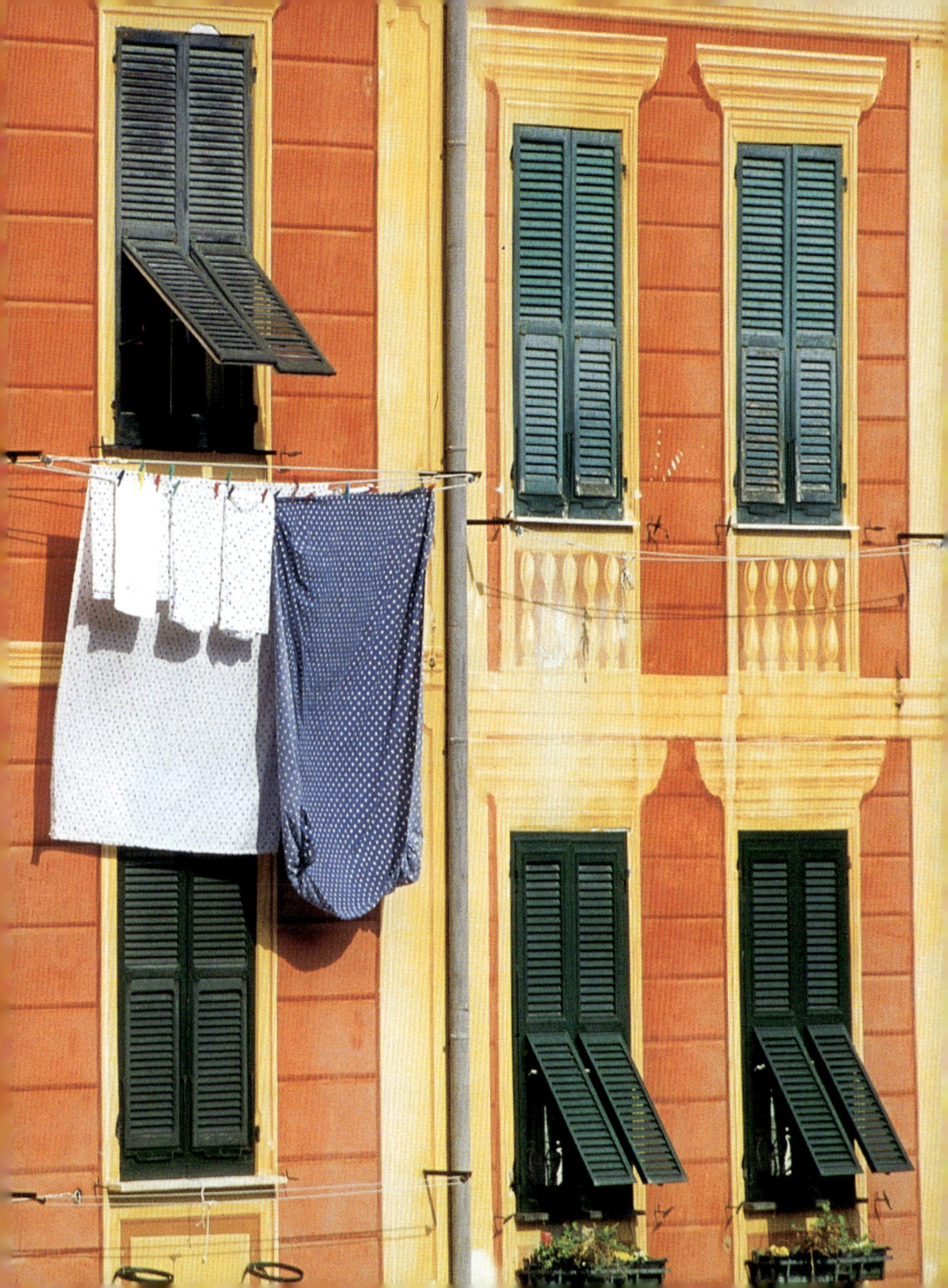

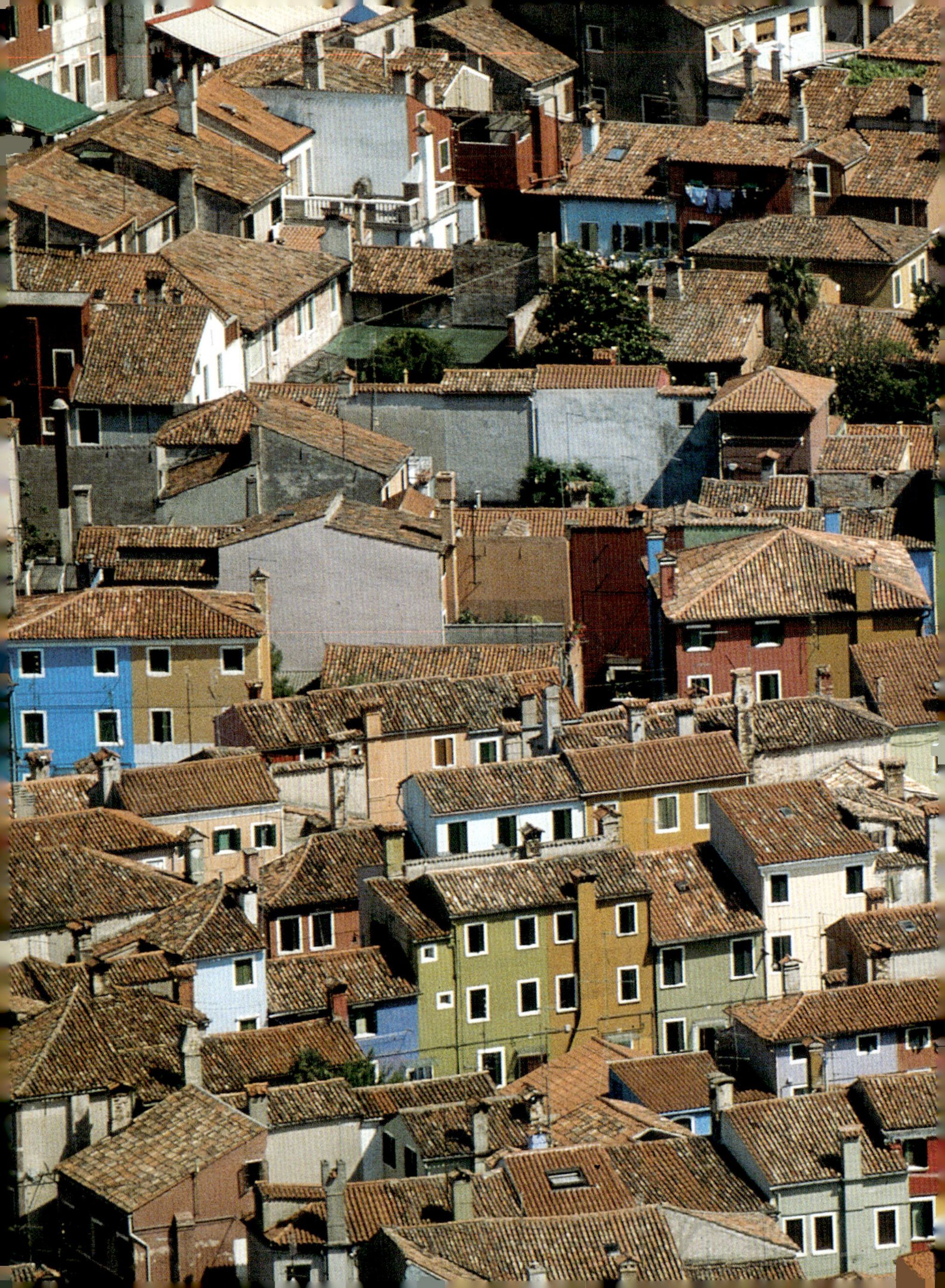

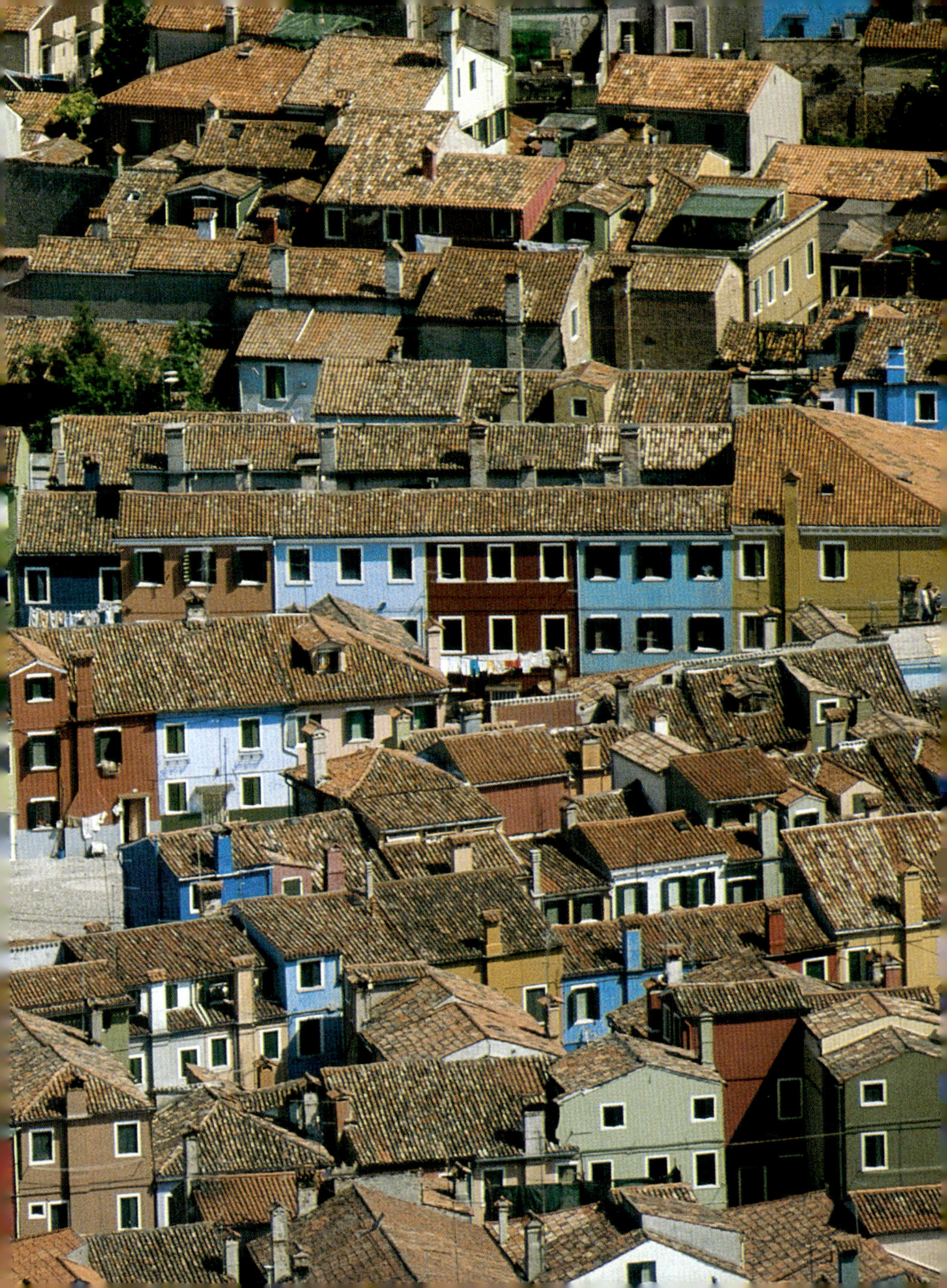

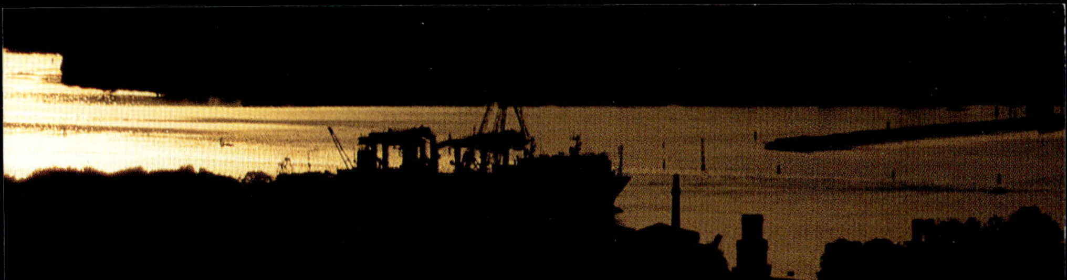

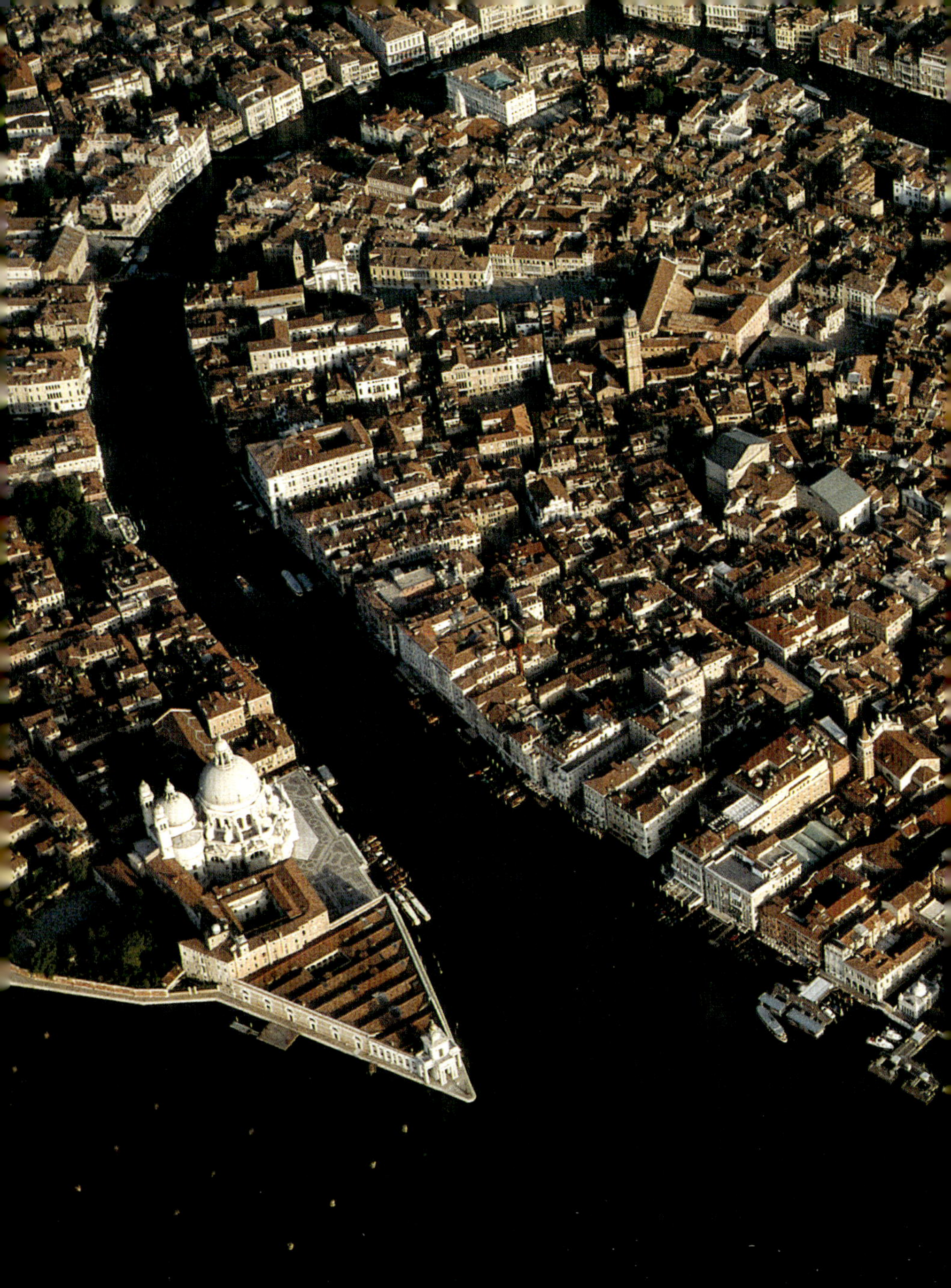

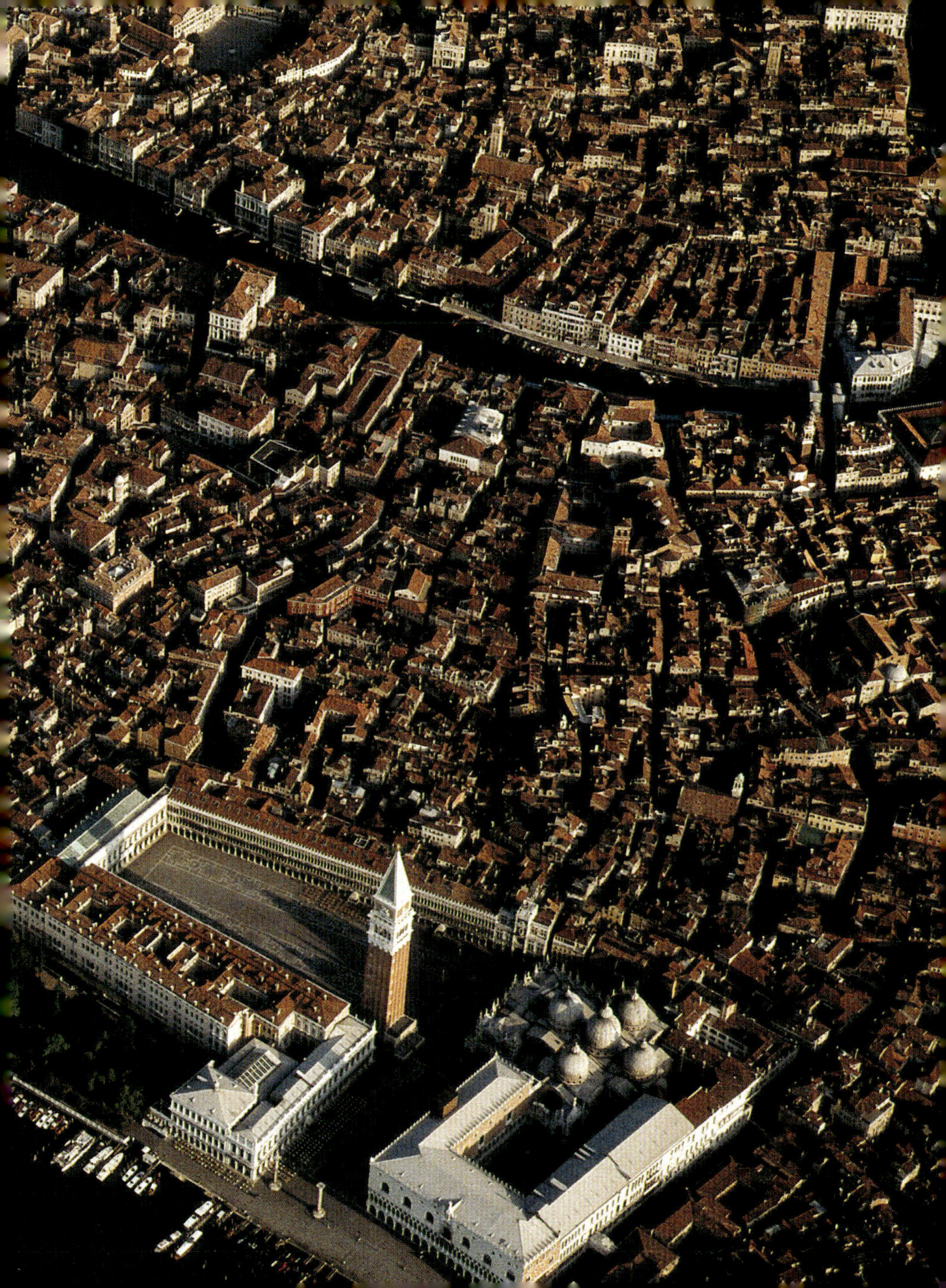

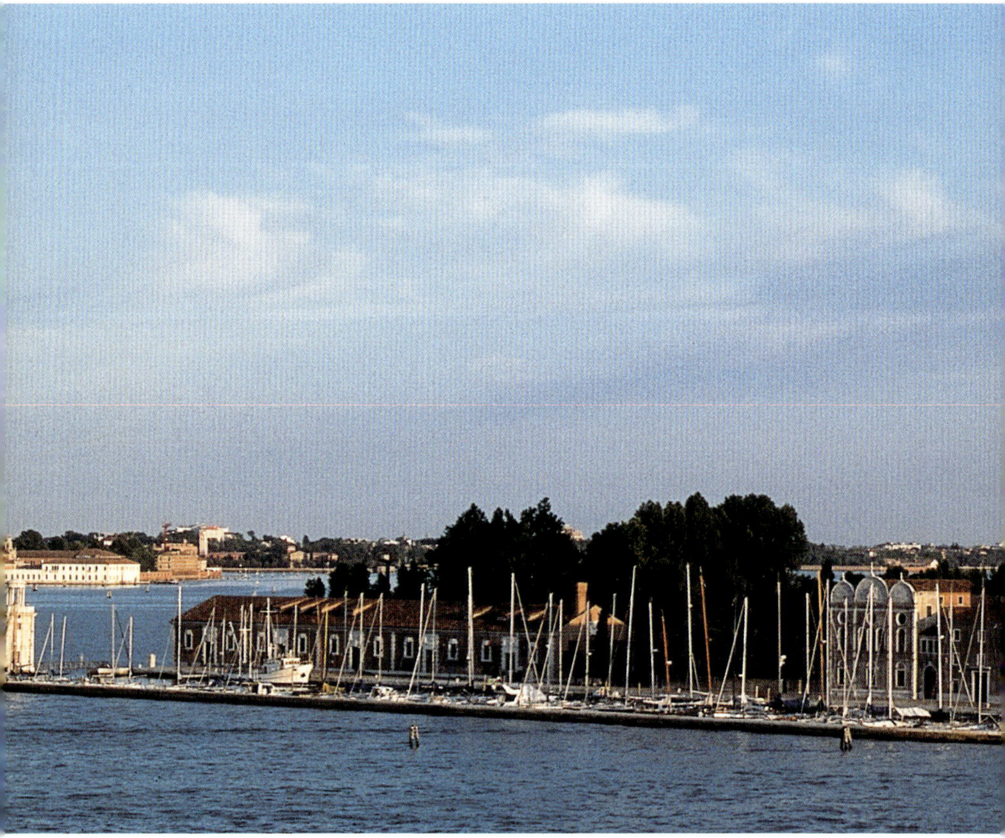

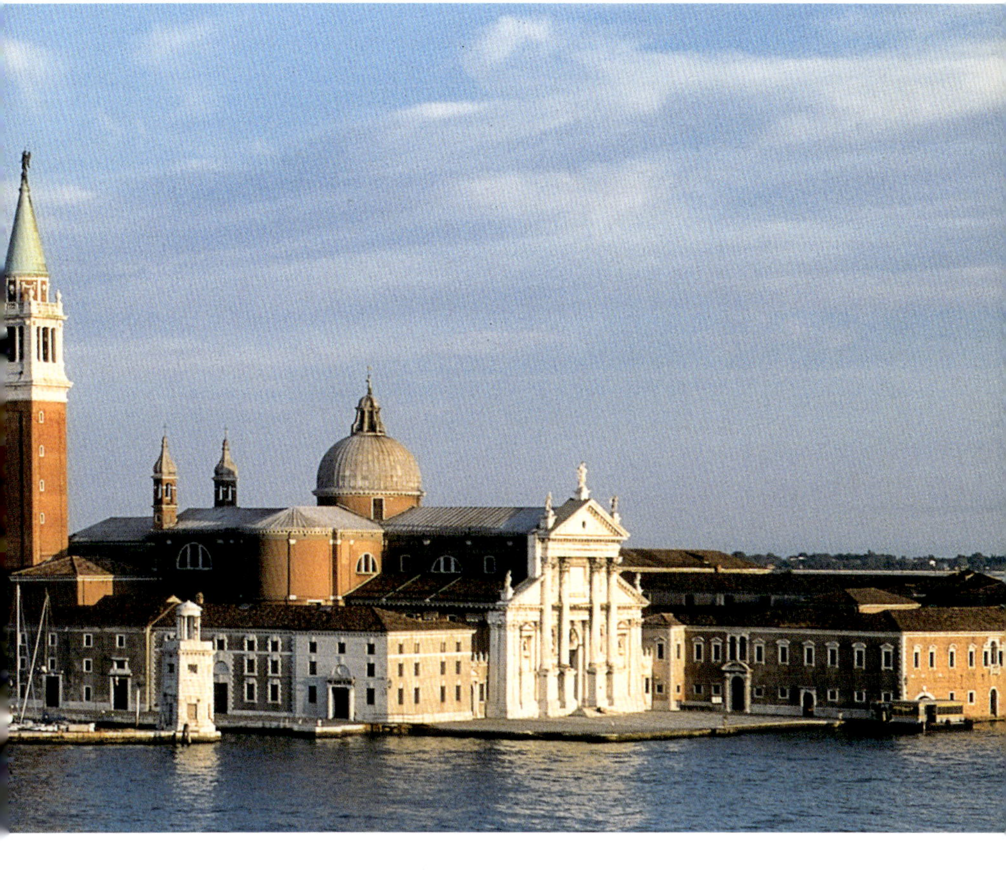

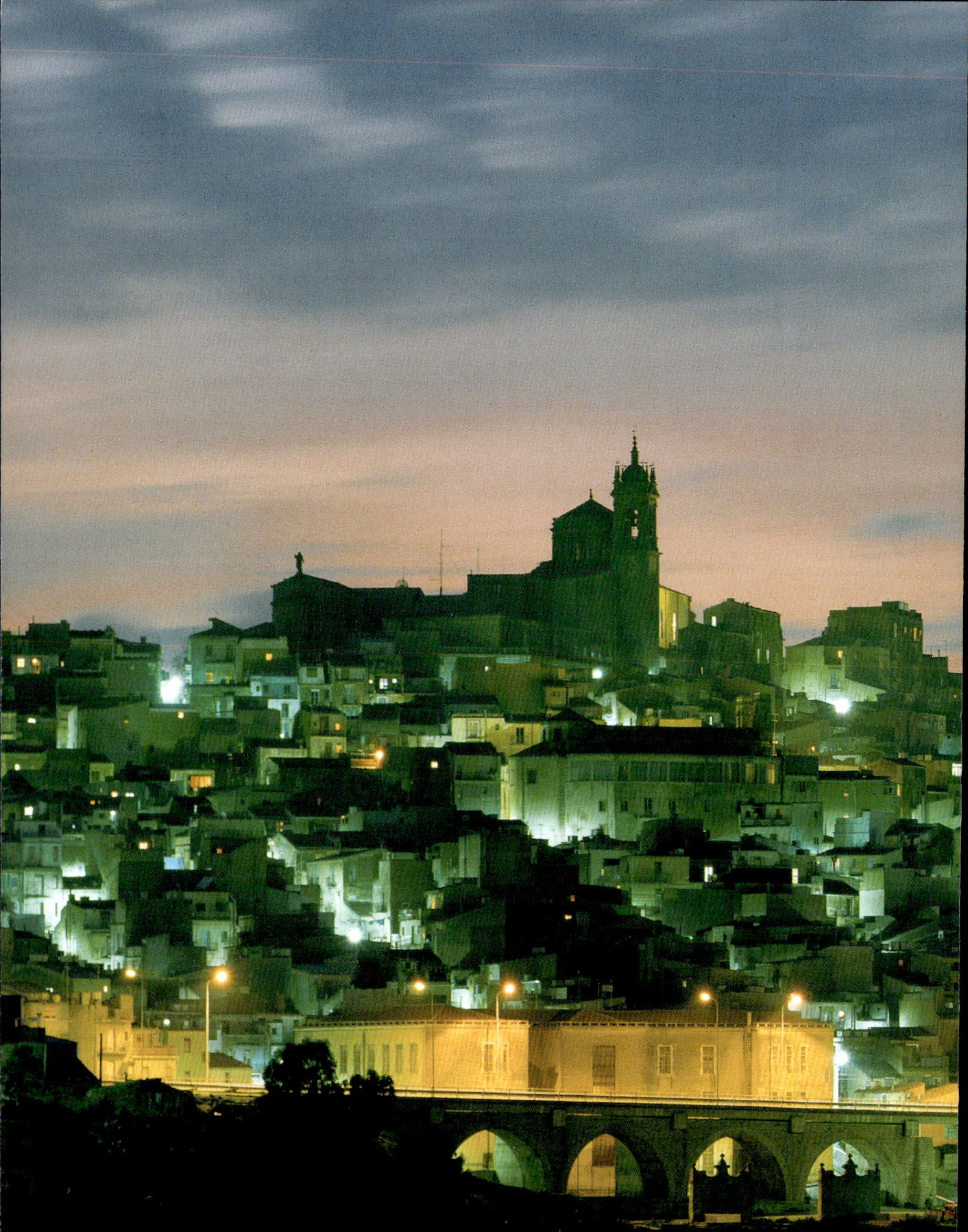

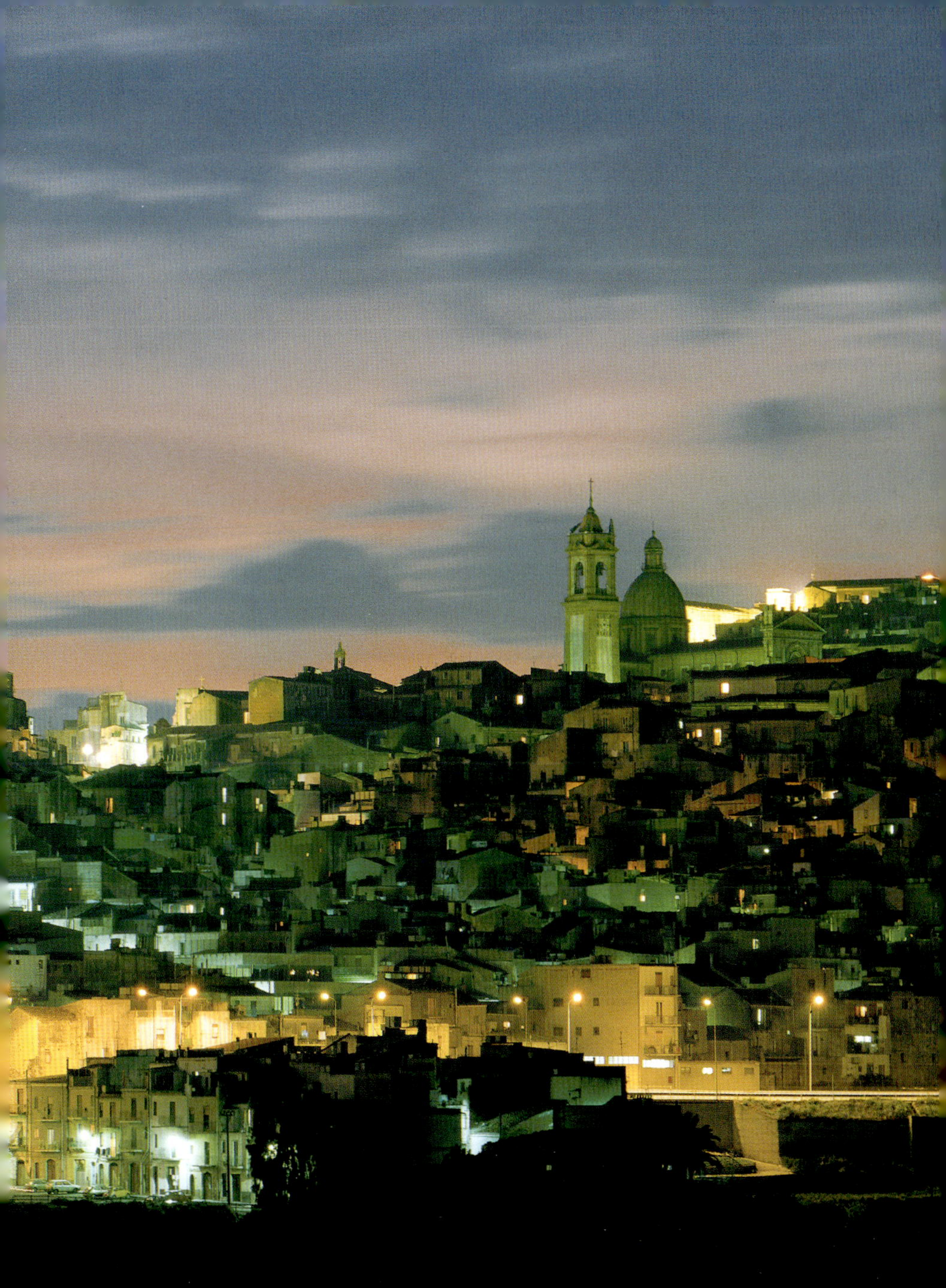

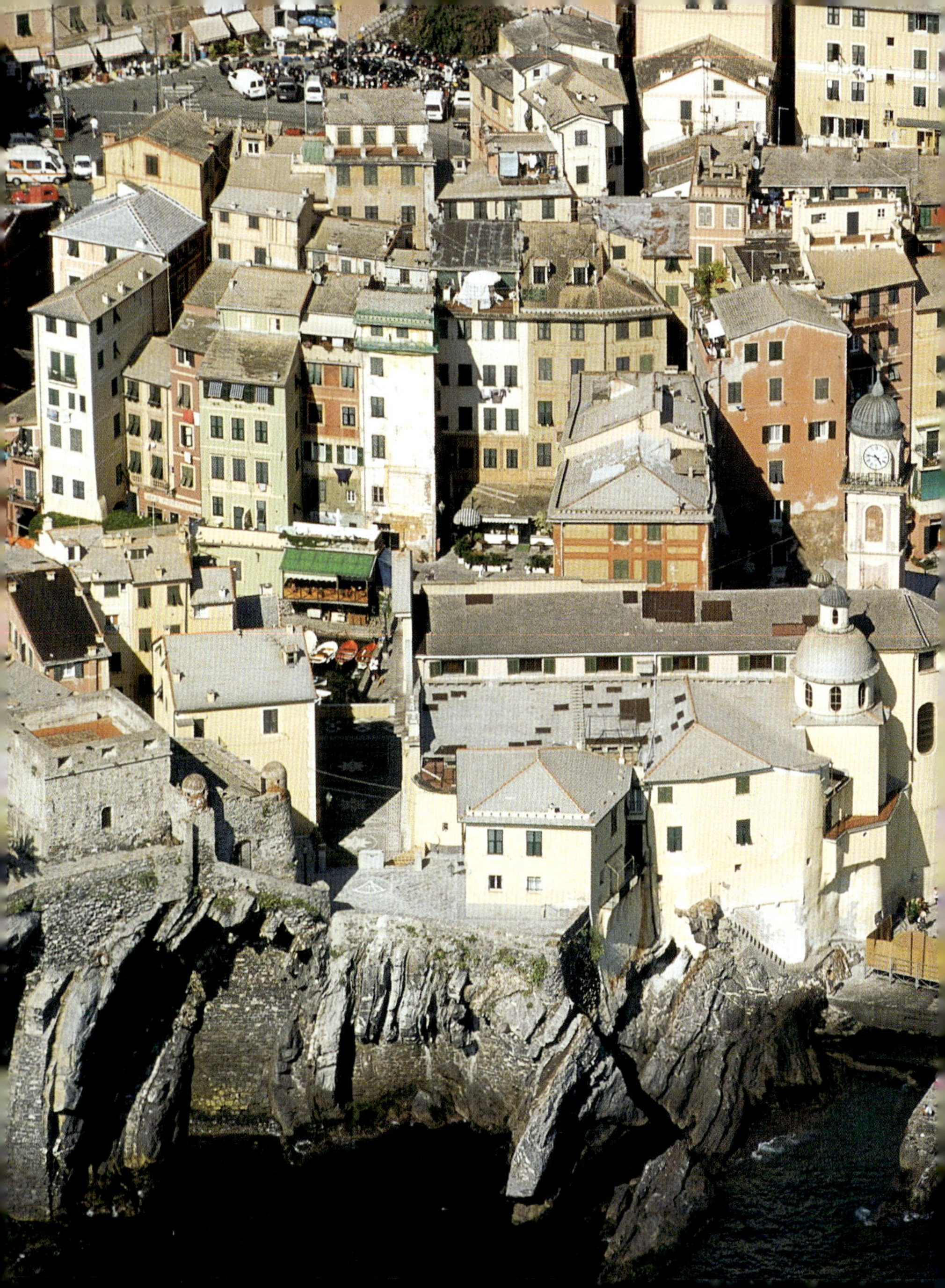

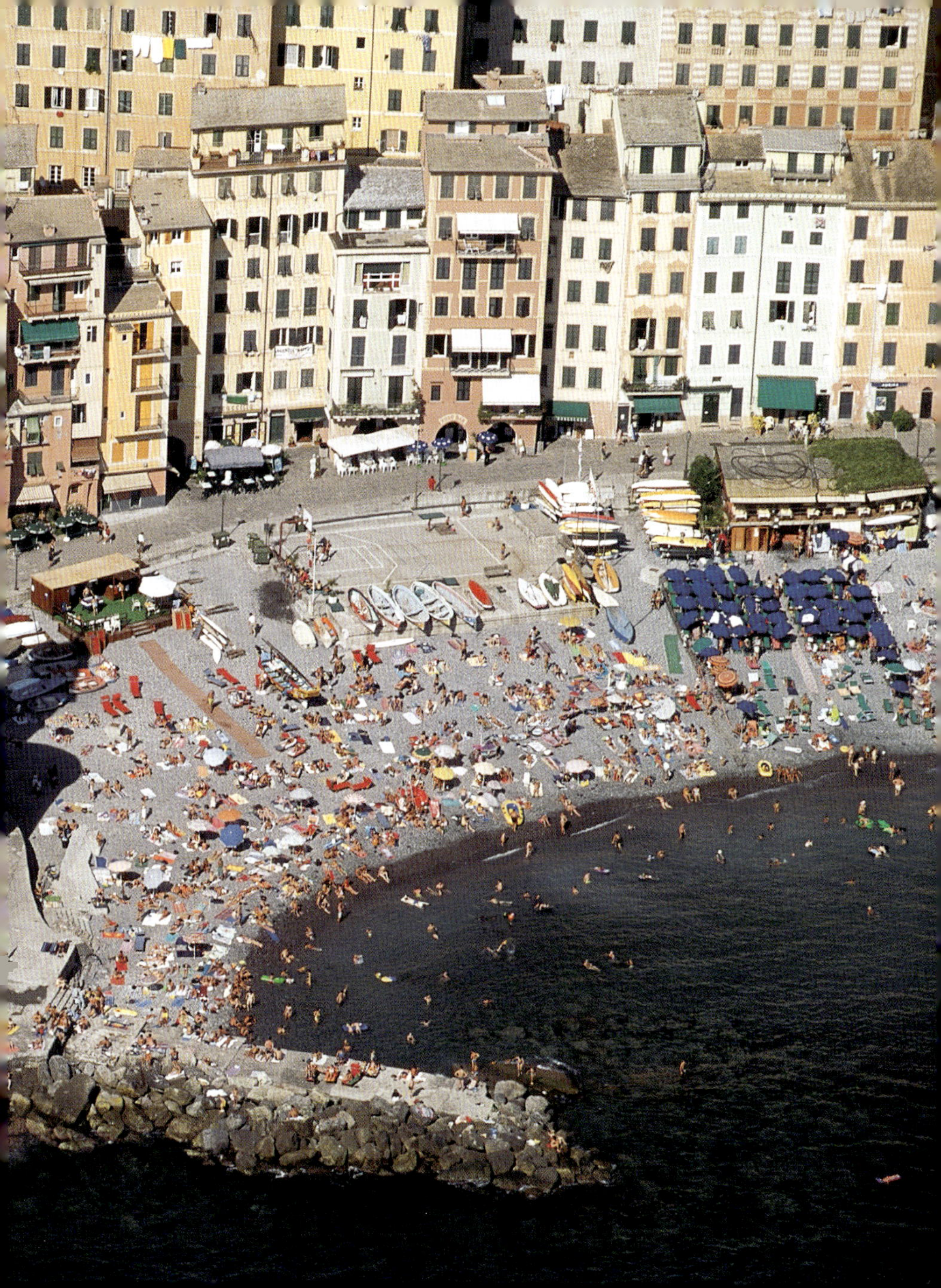

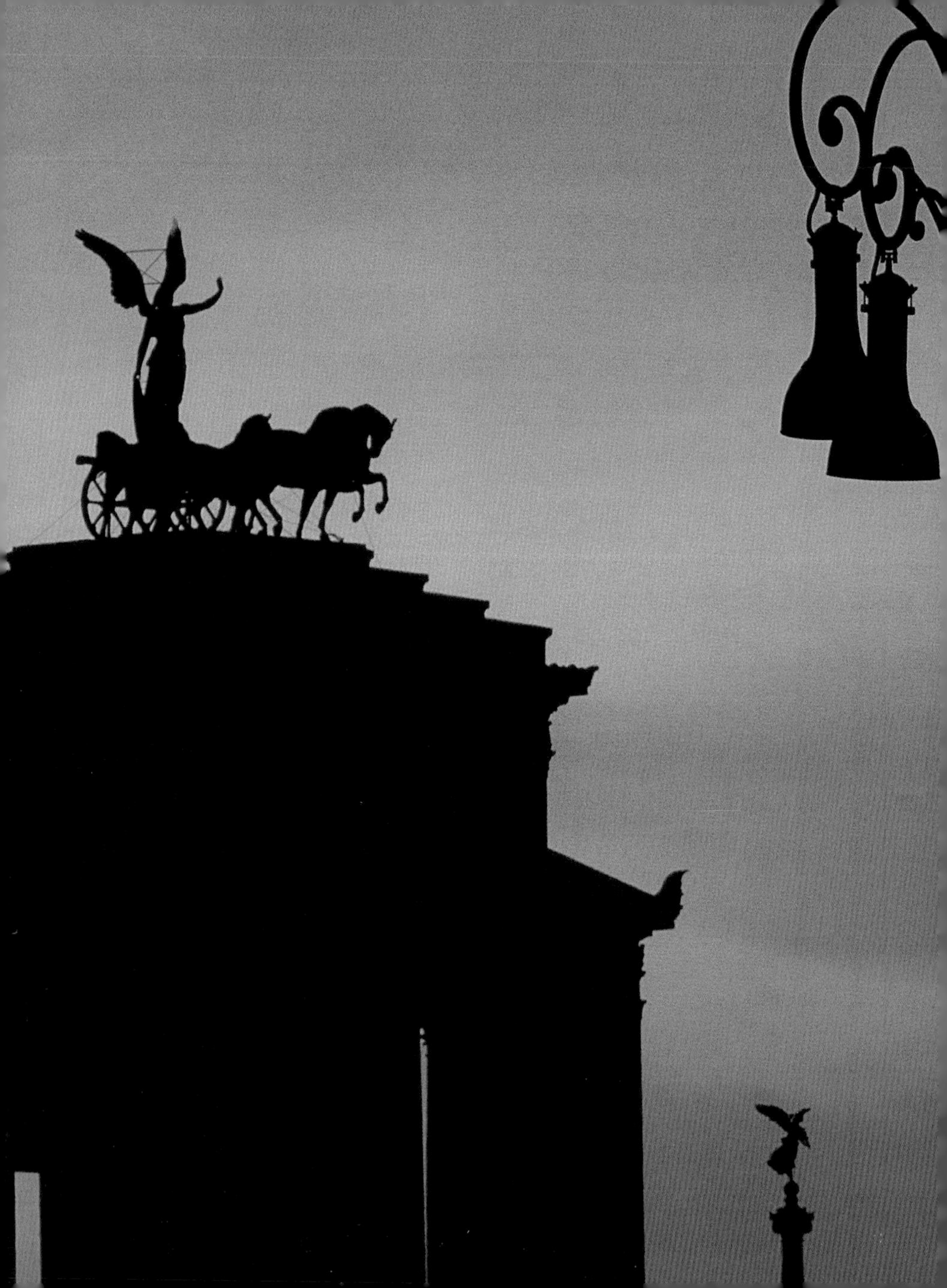

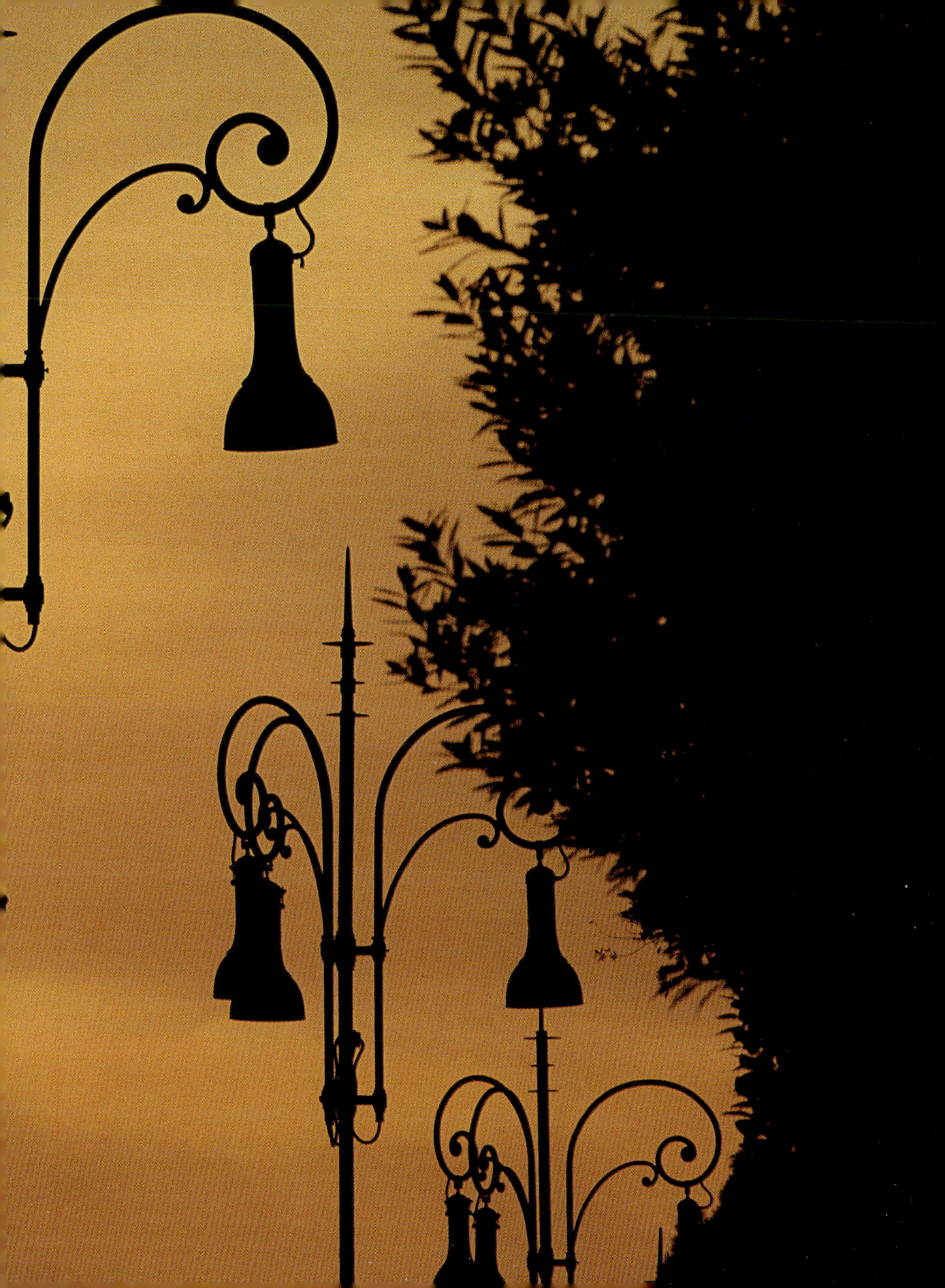

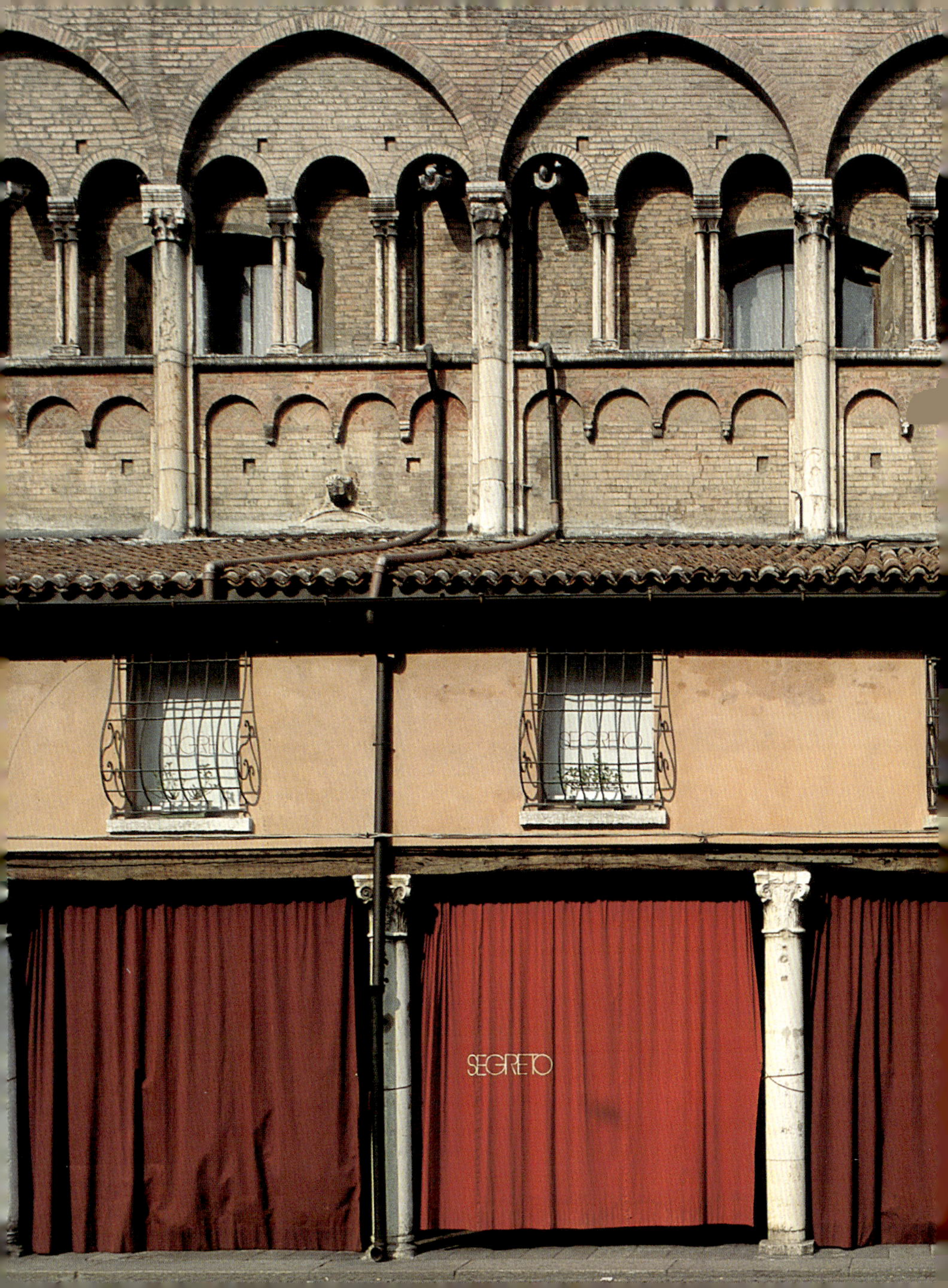
SEGRETO

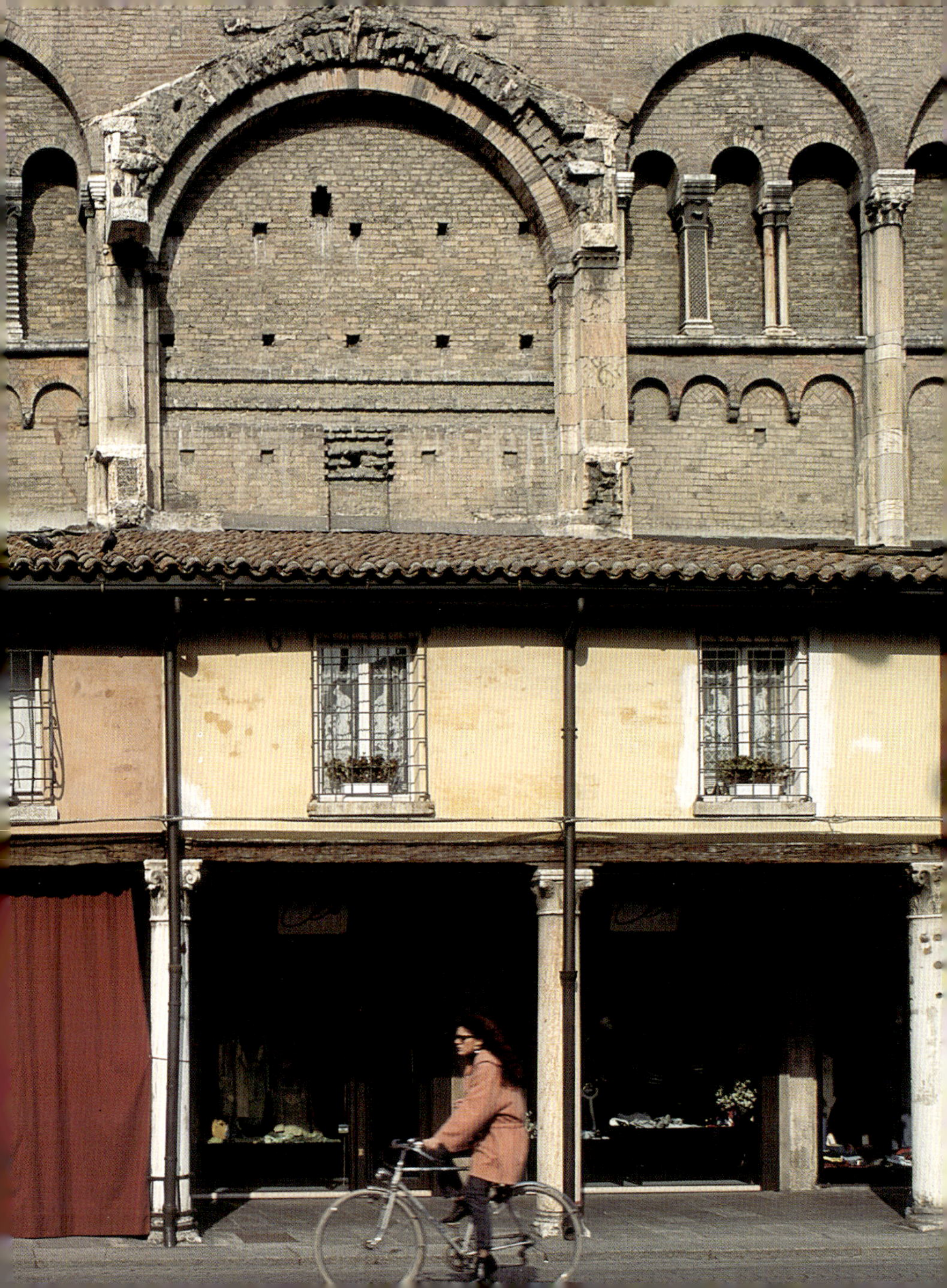

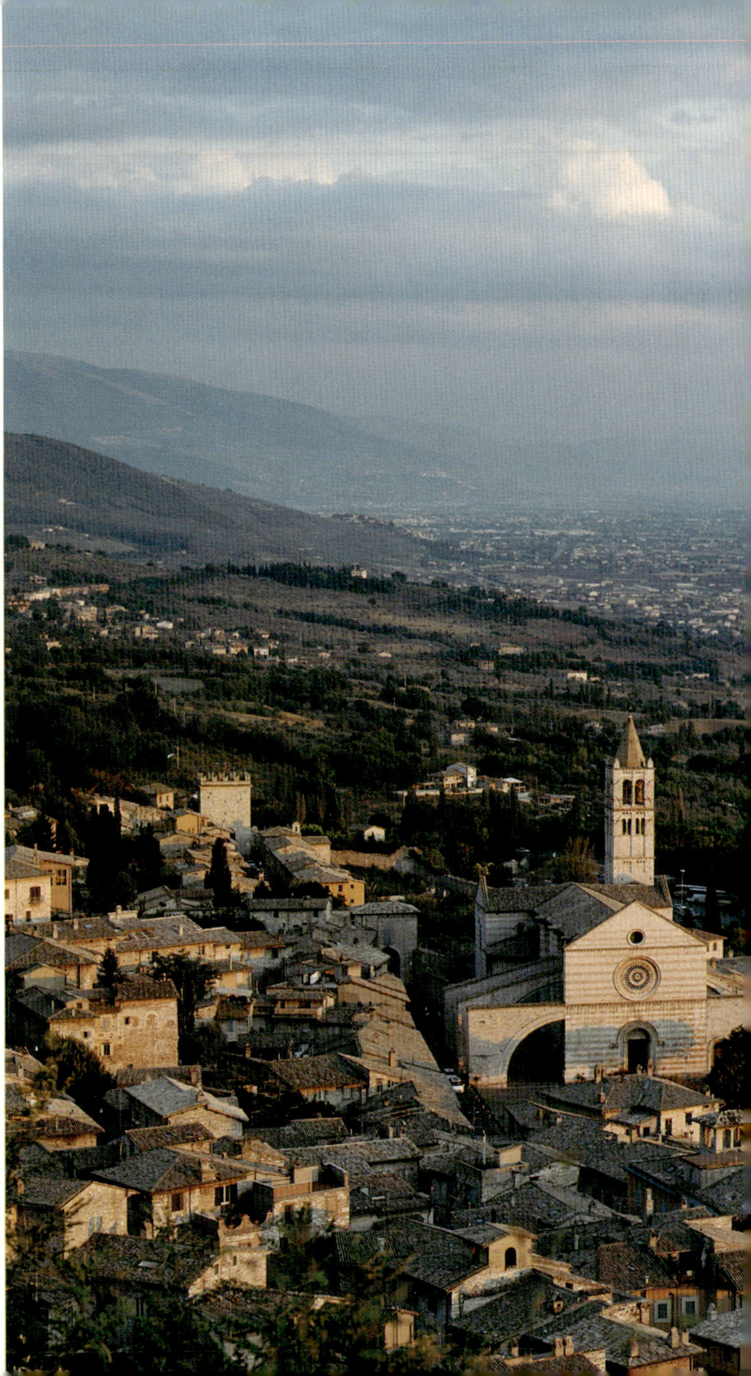

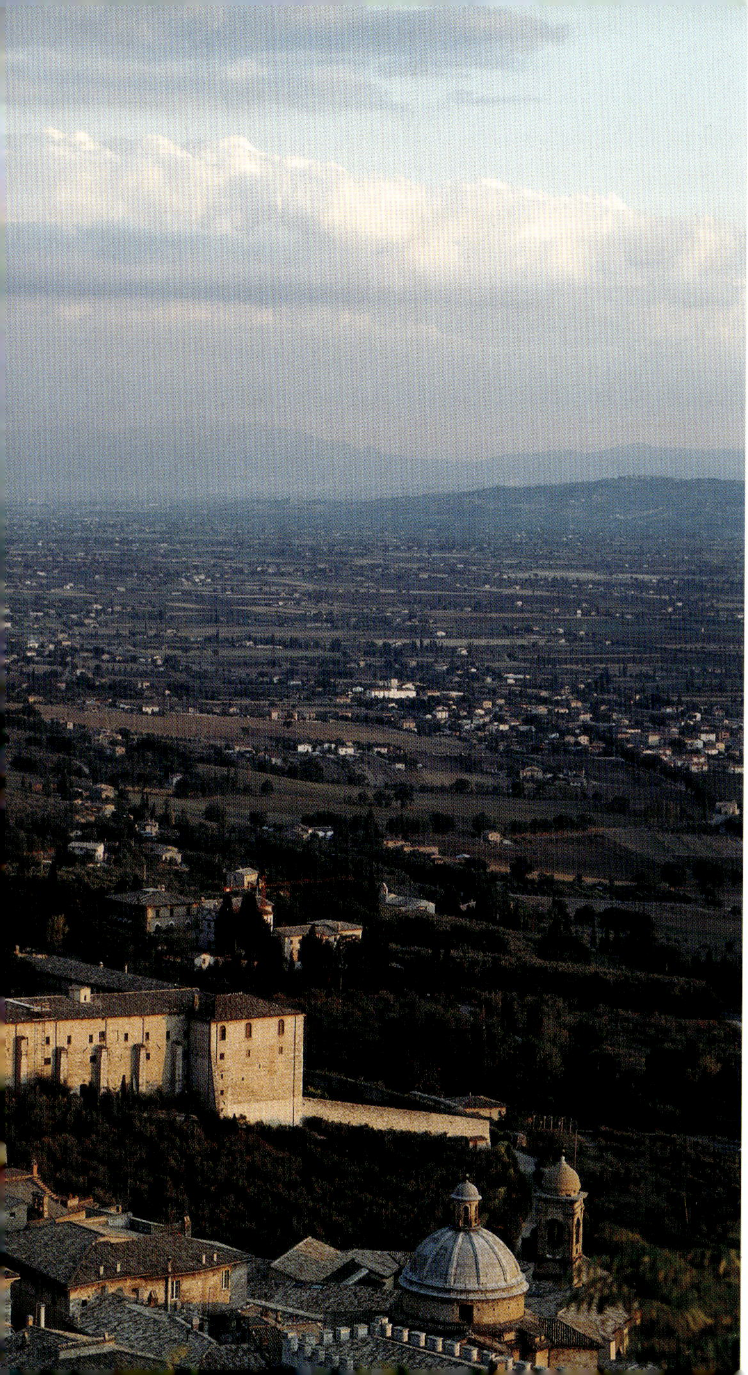

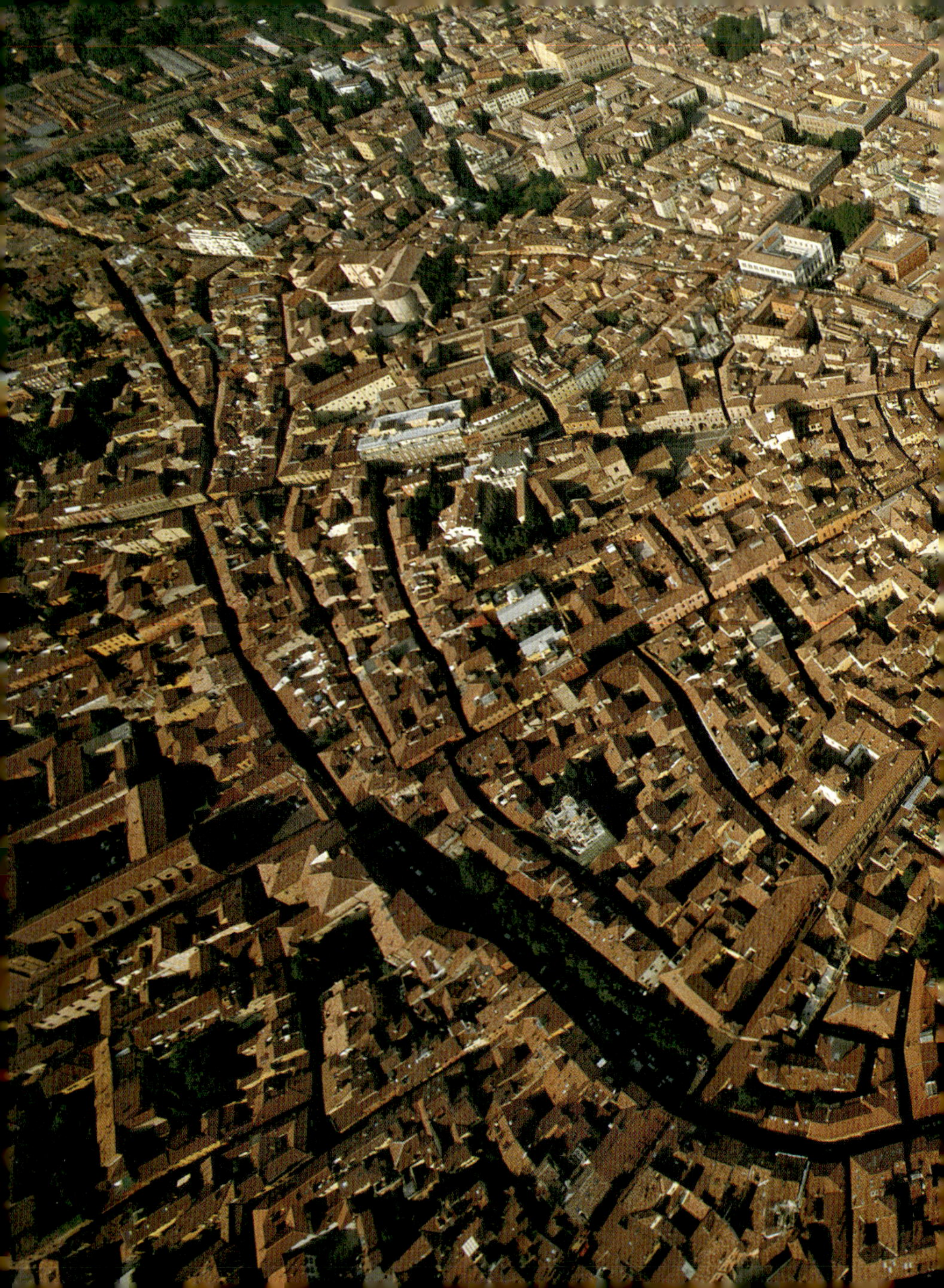

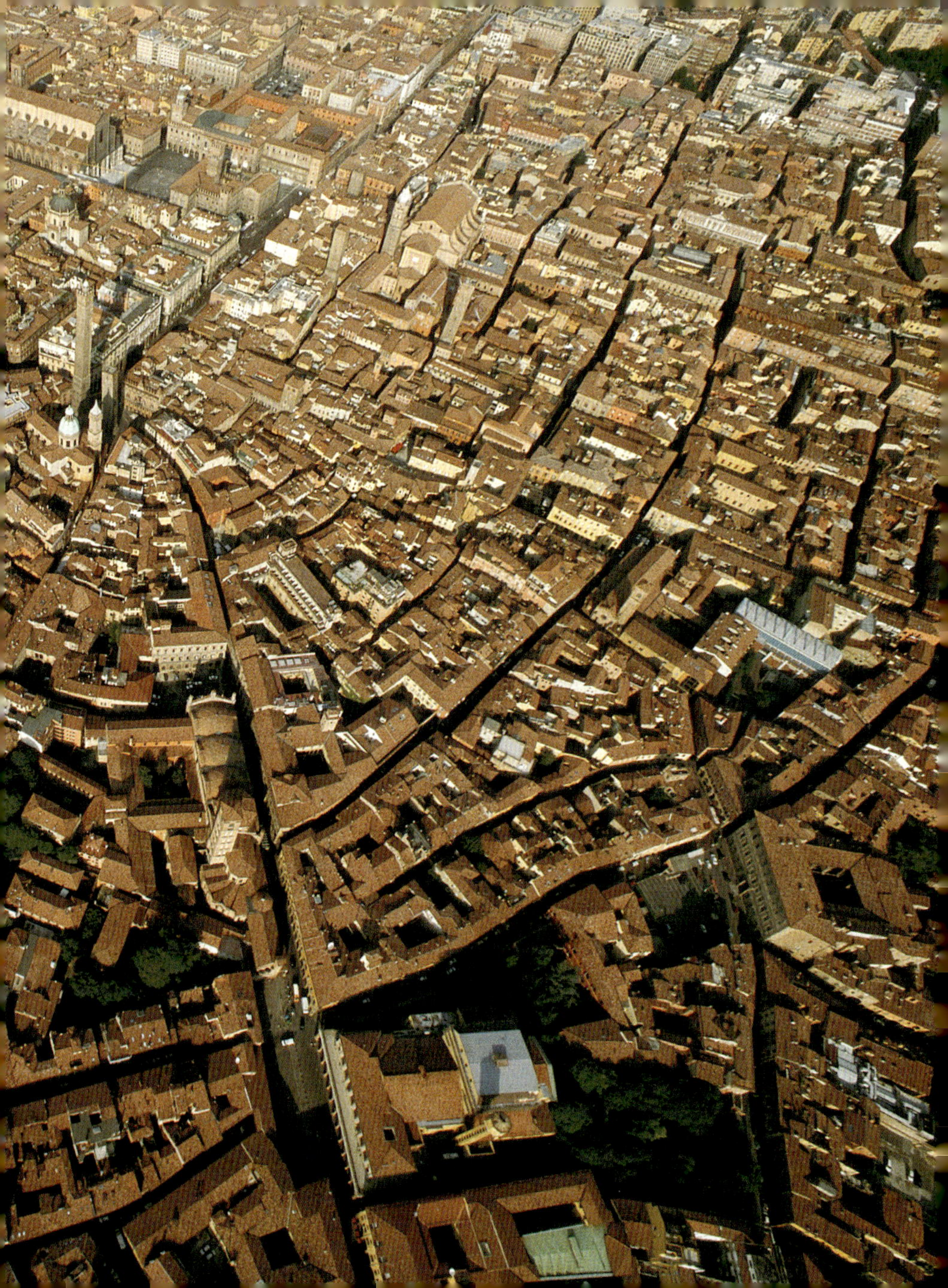

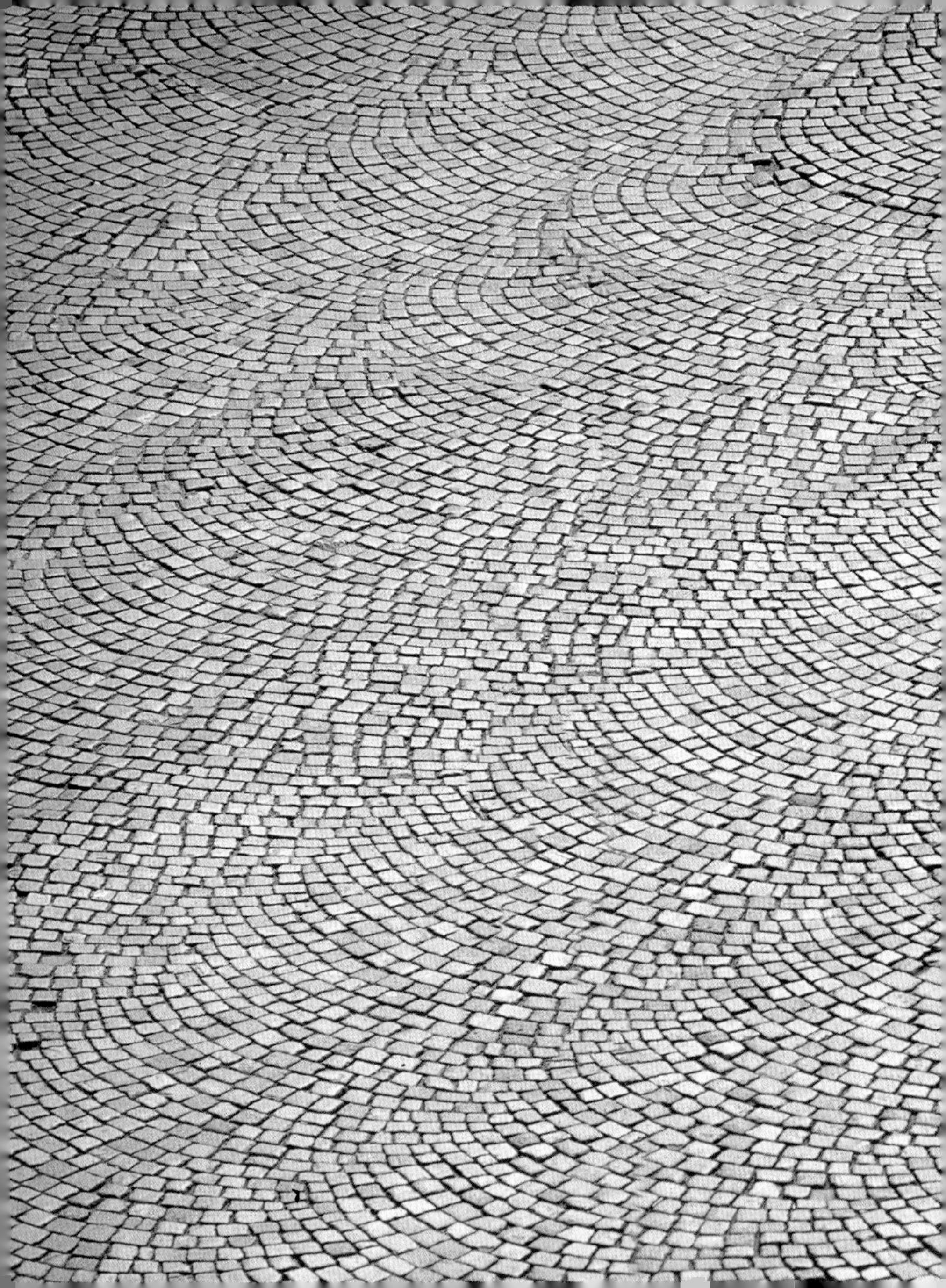

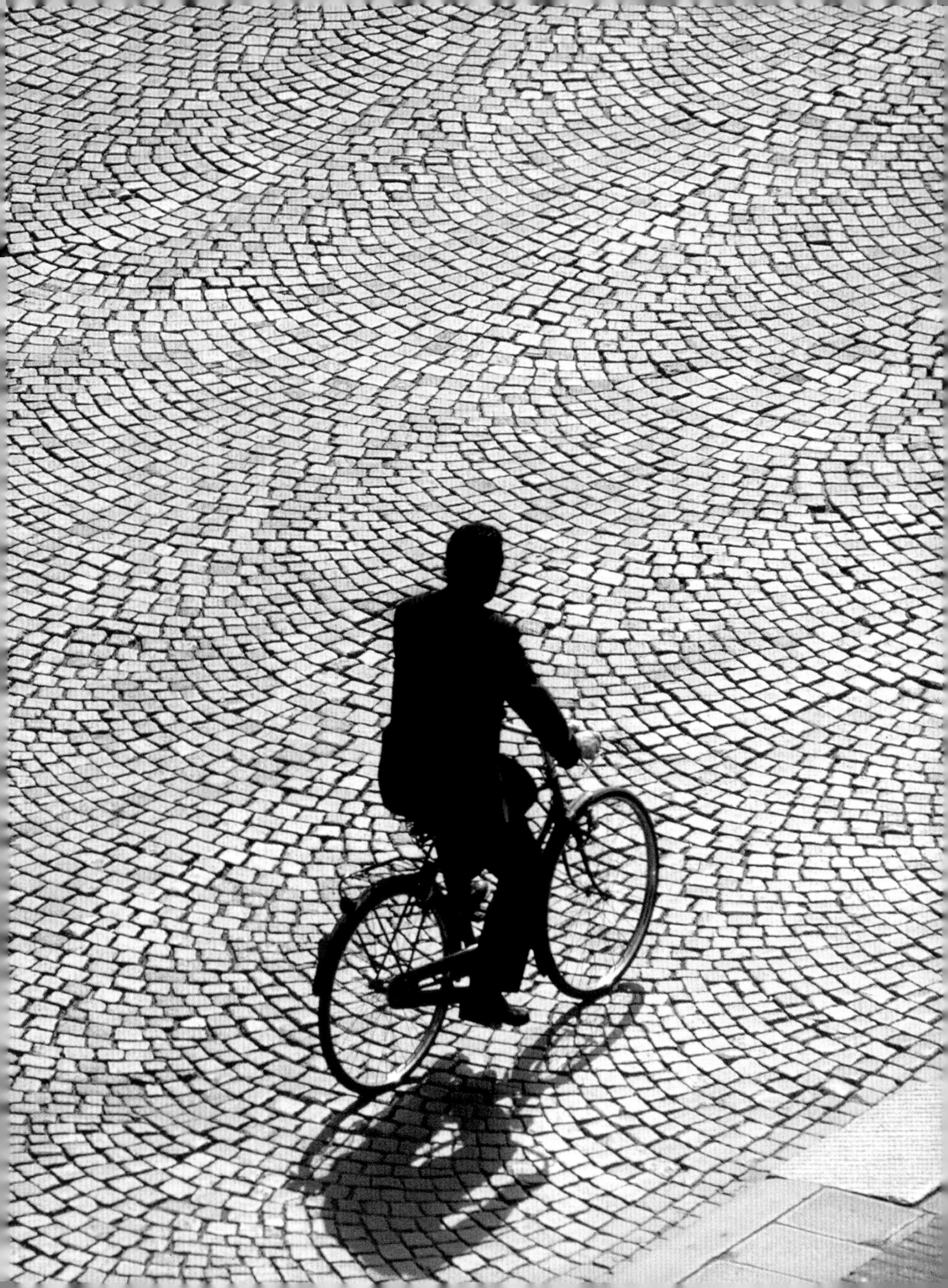

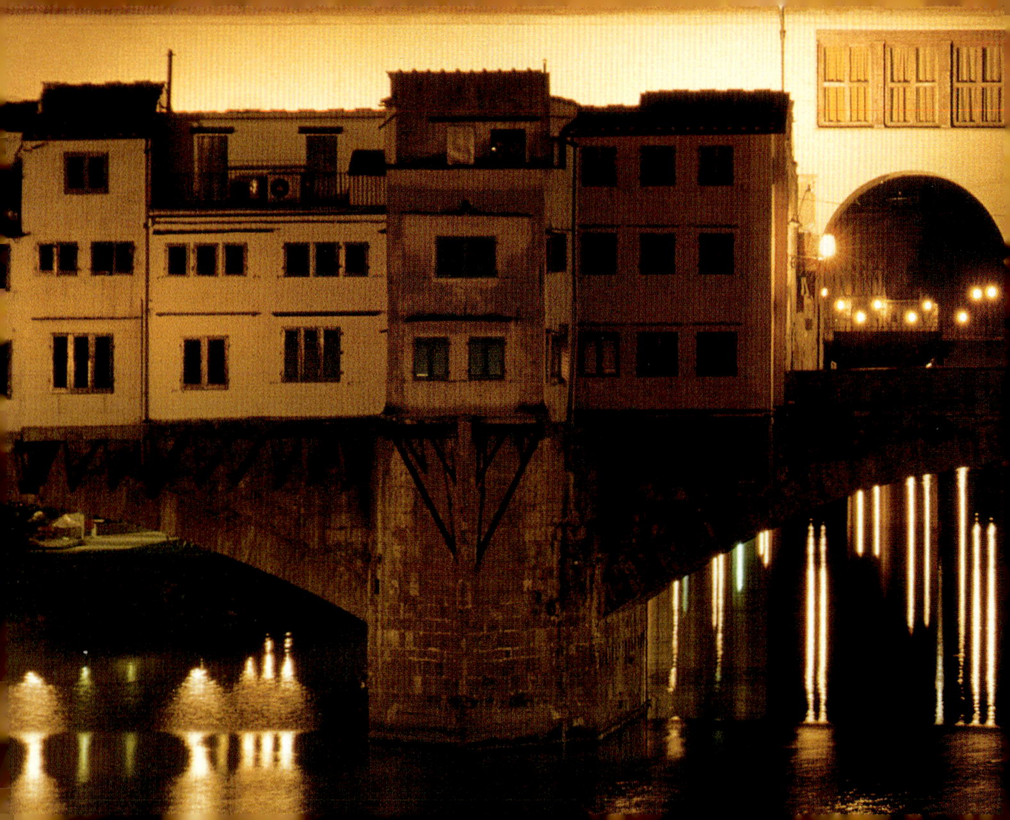

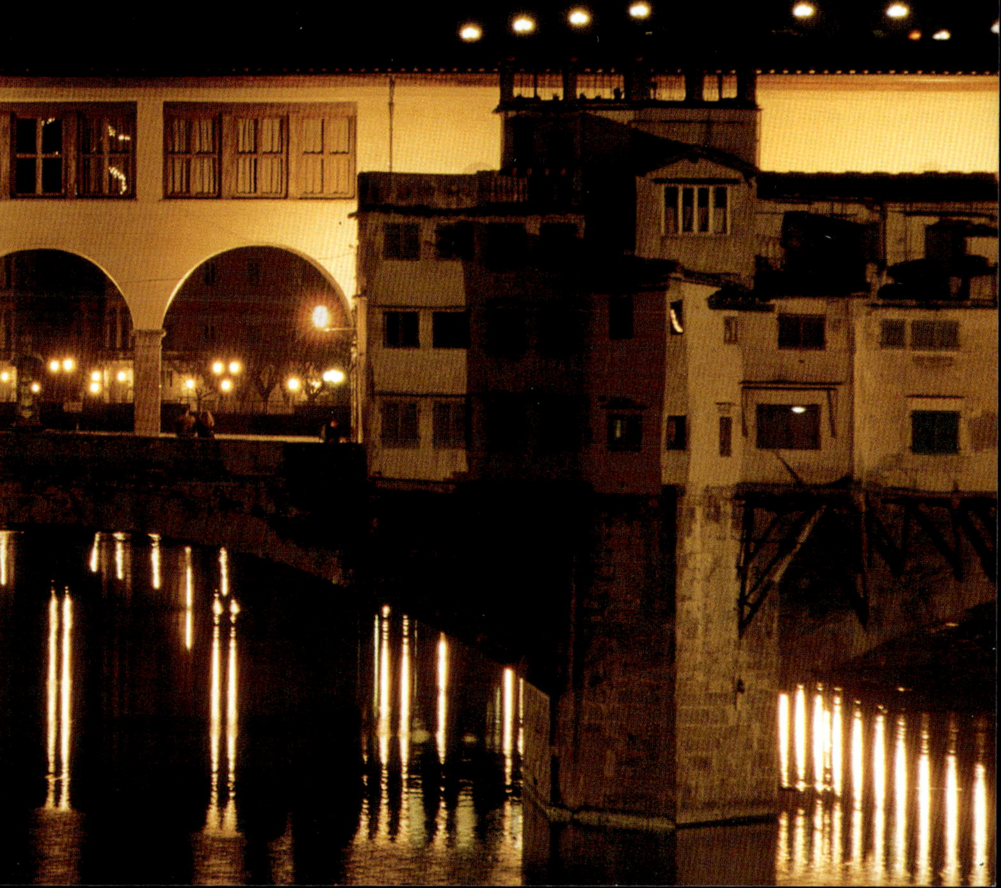

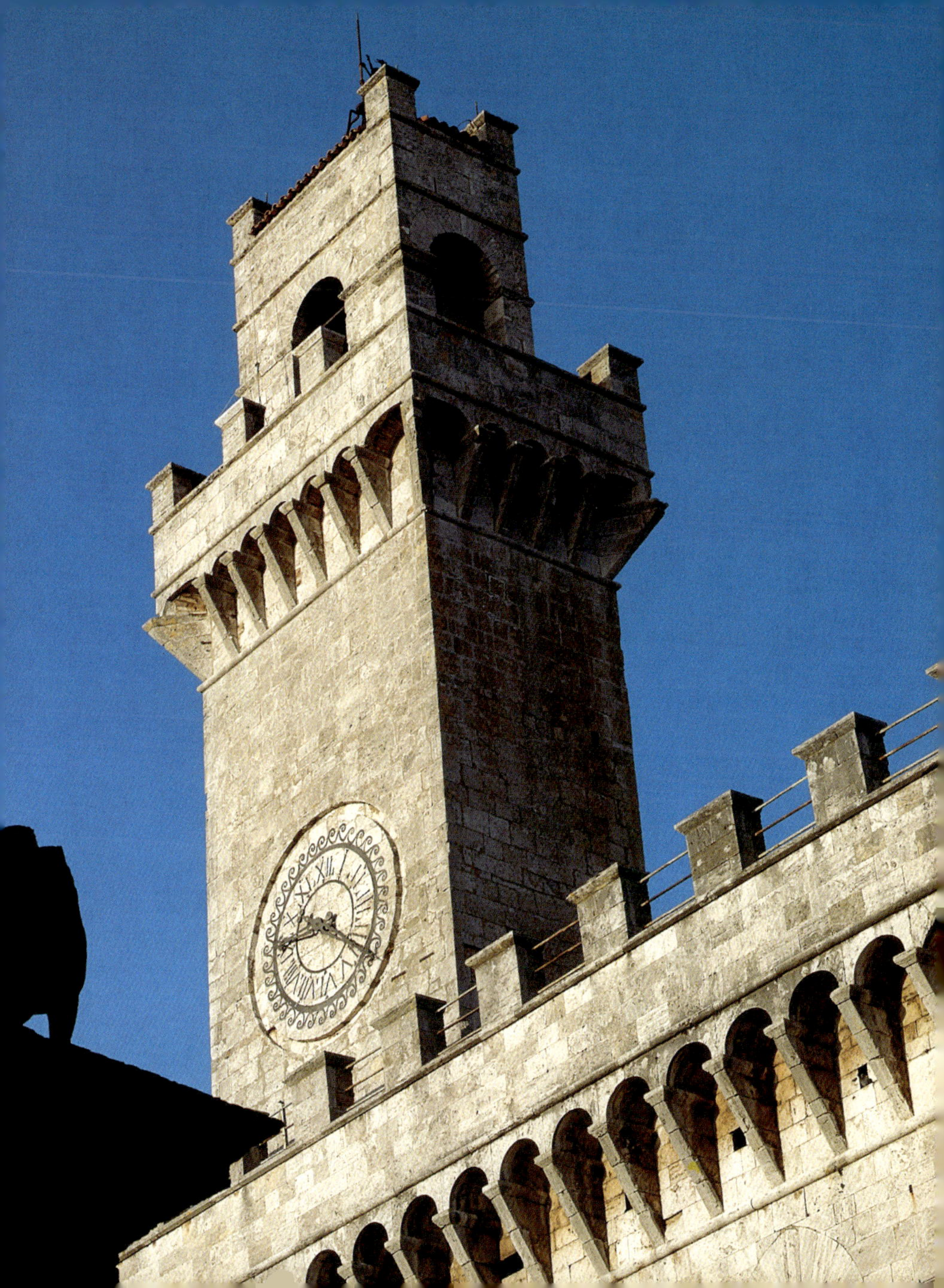

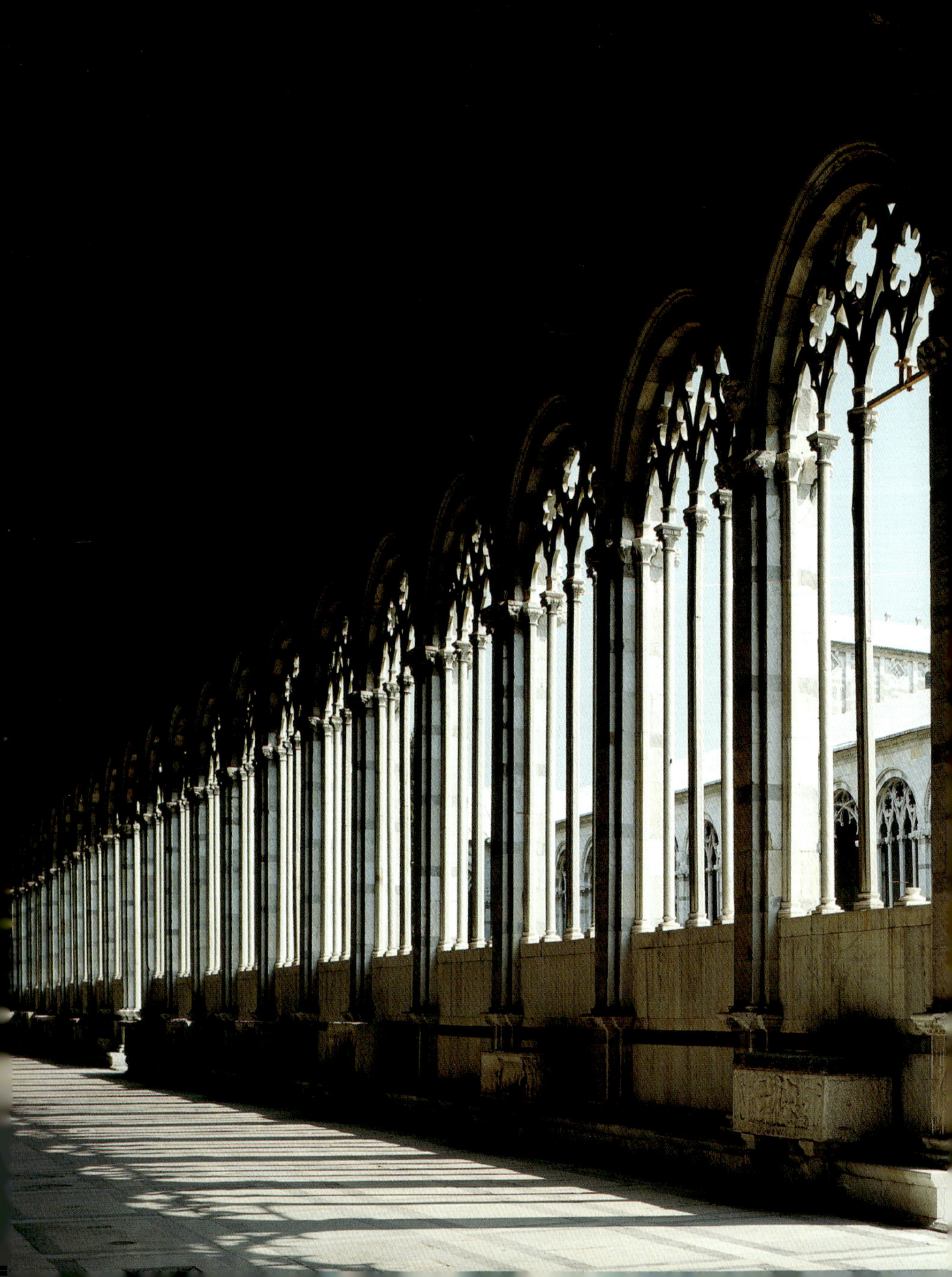

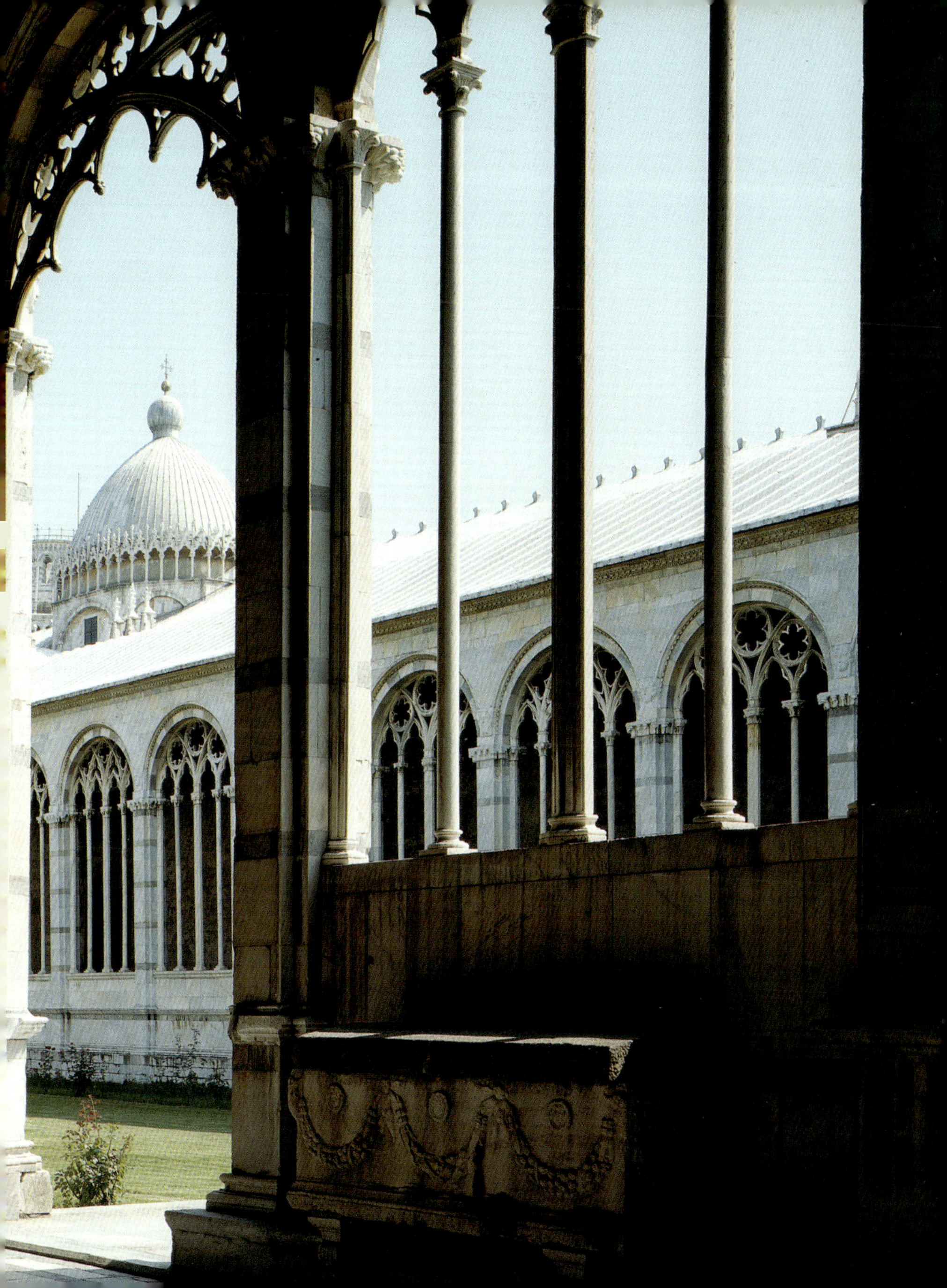

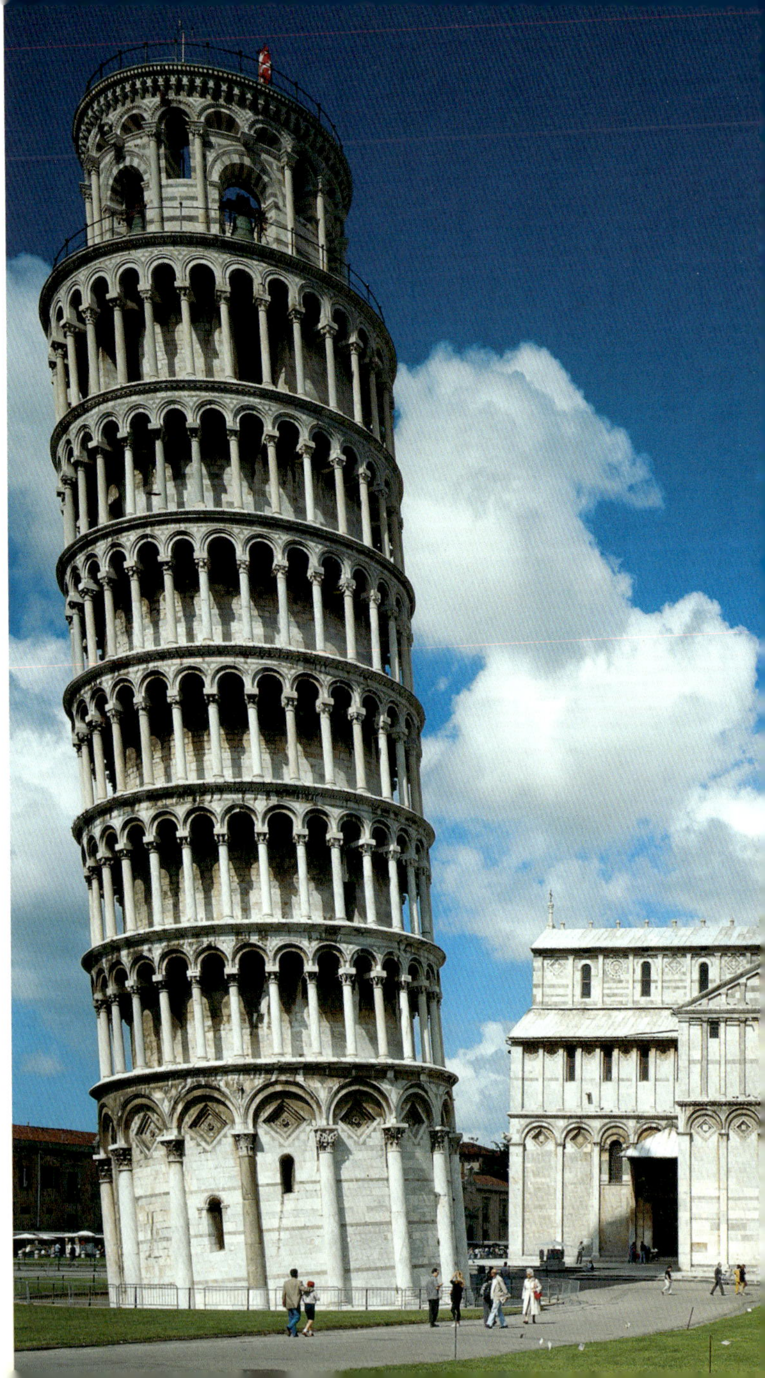

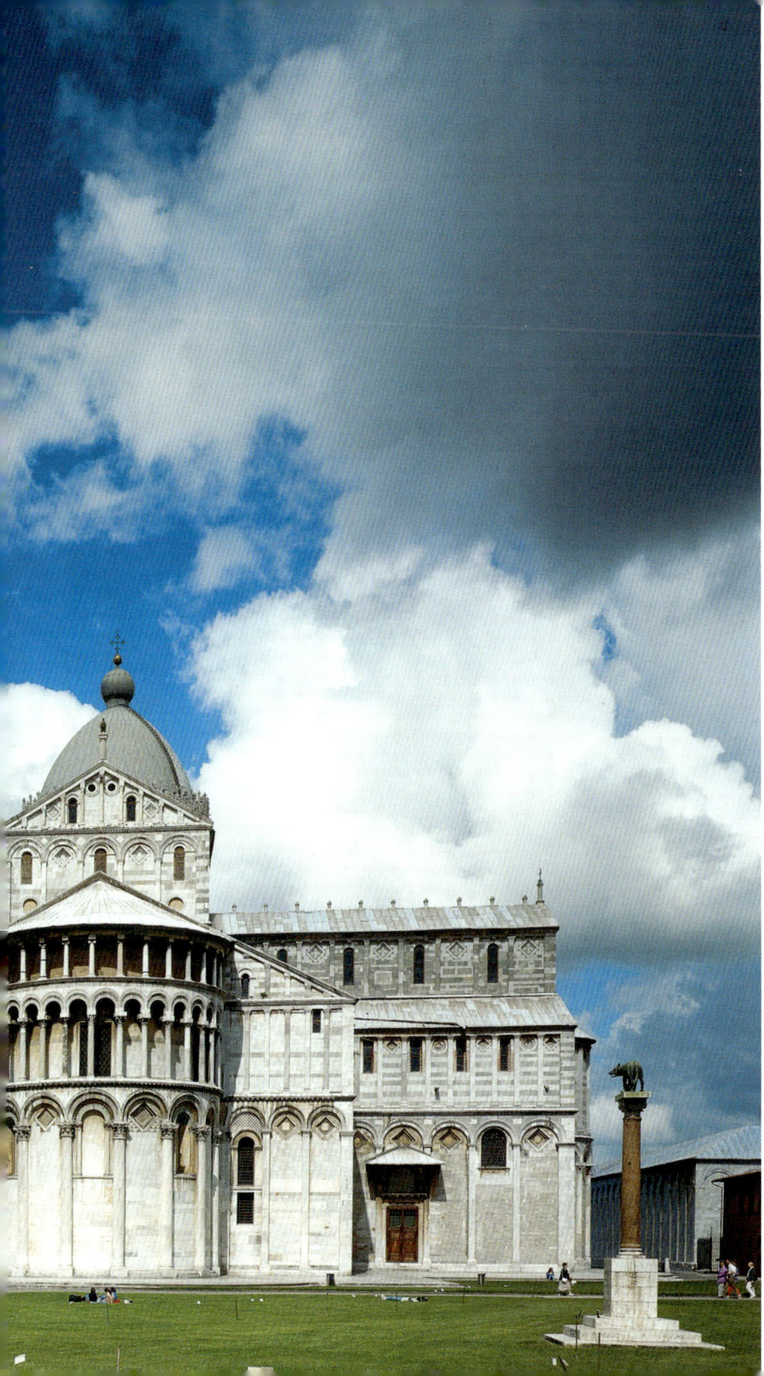

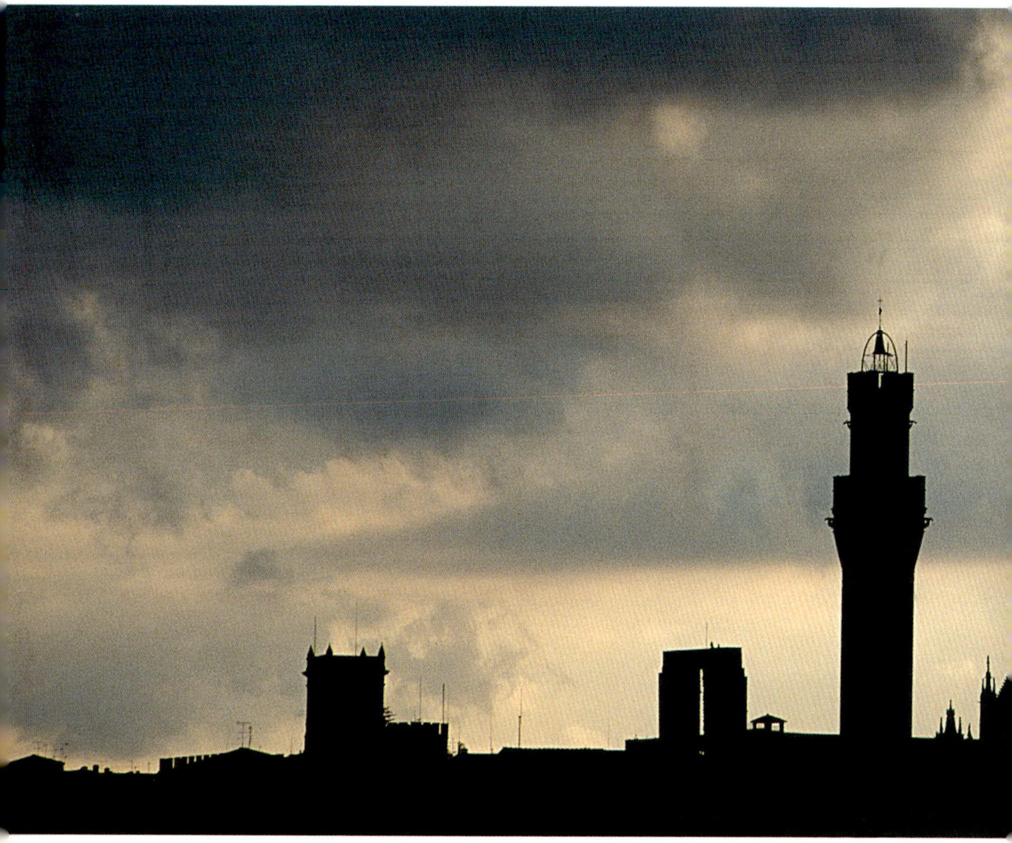

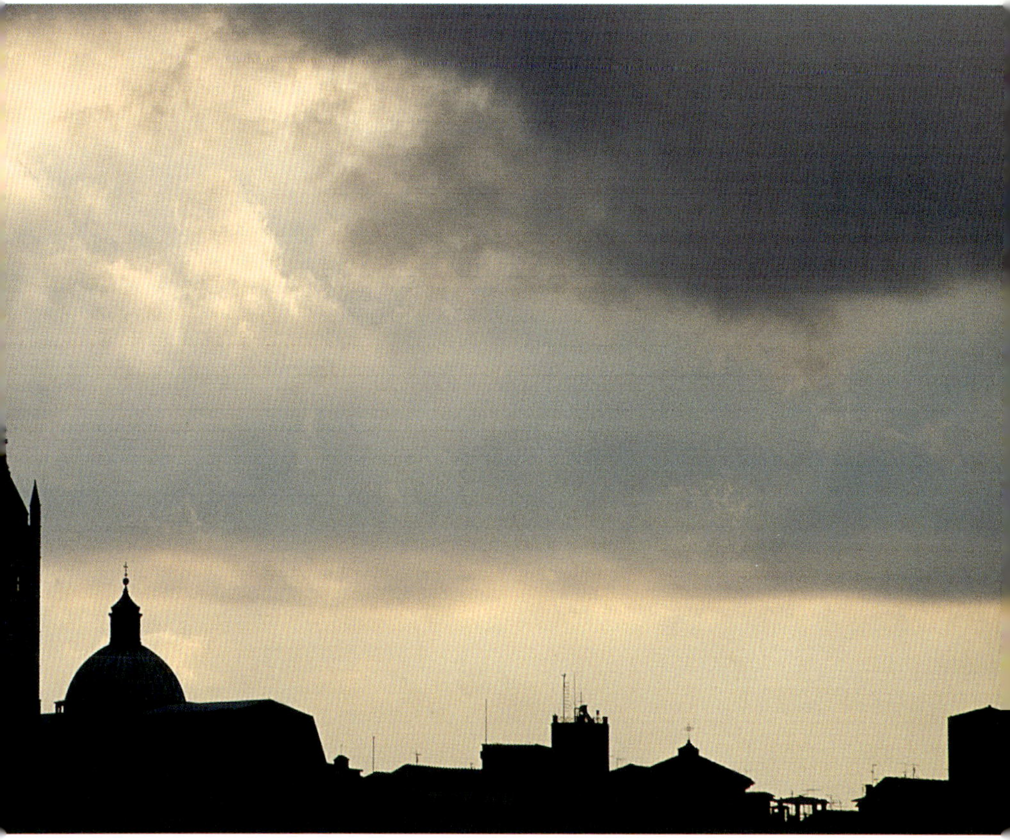

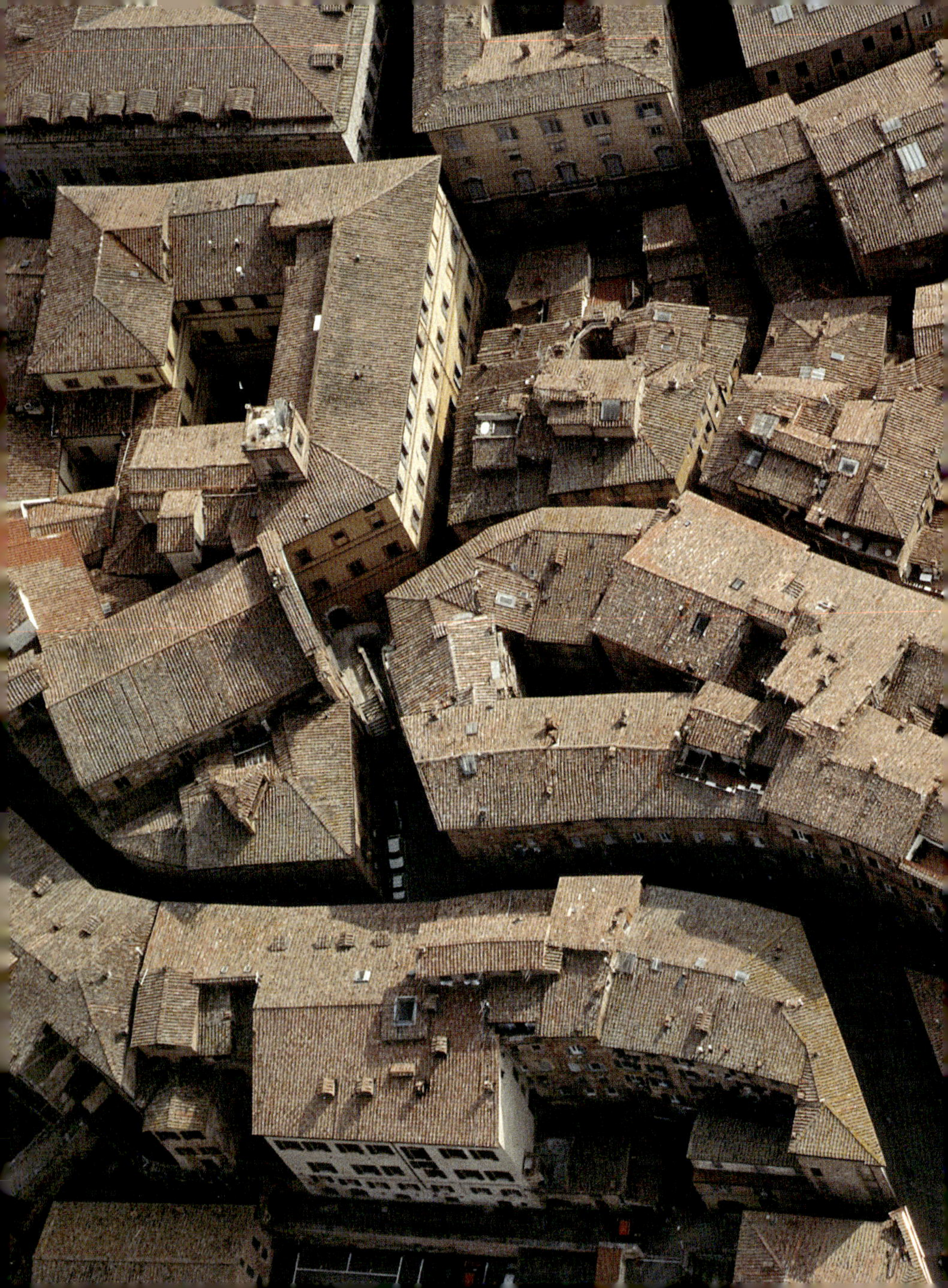

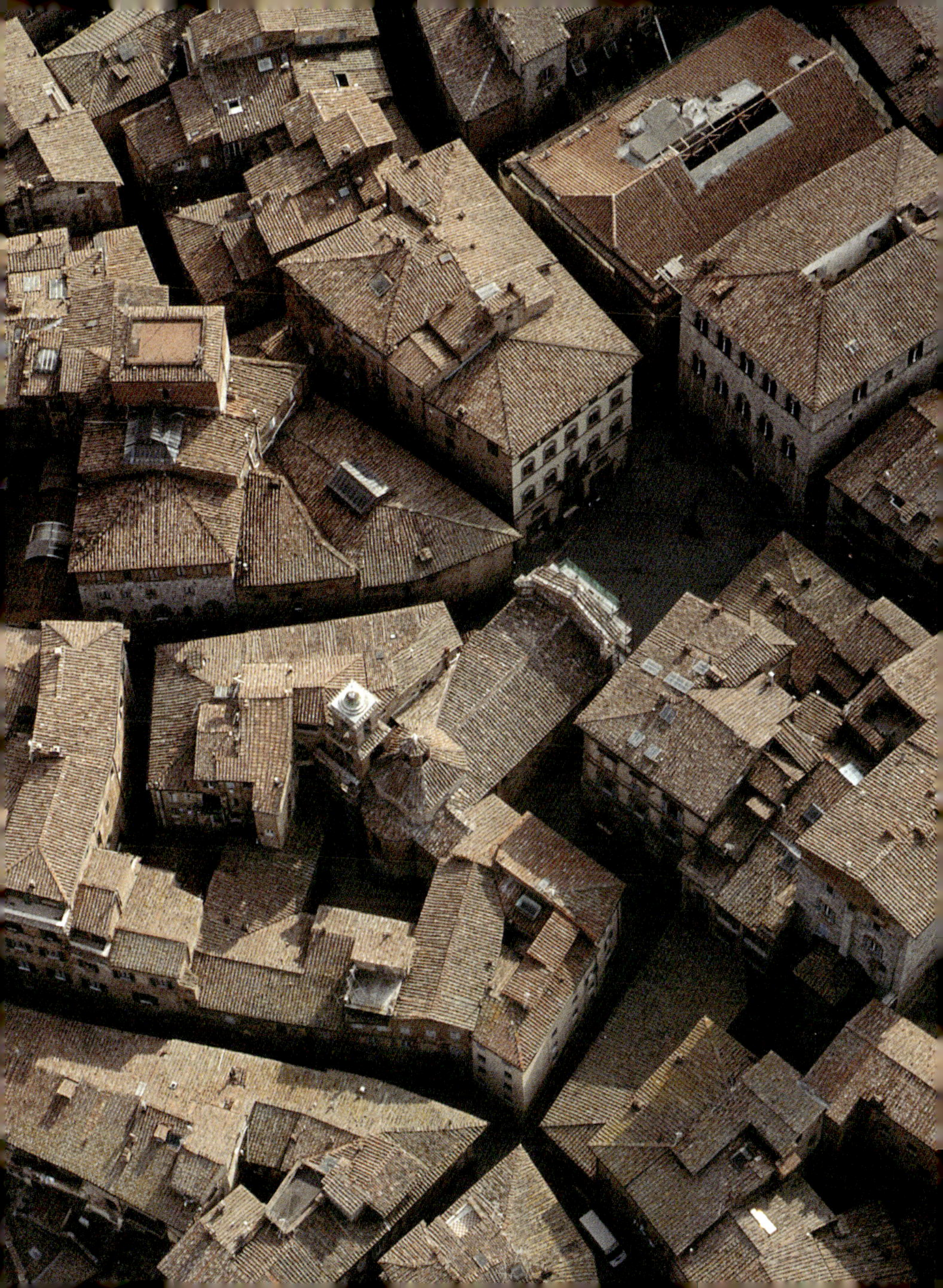

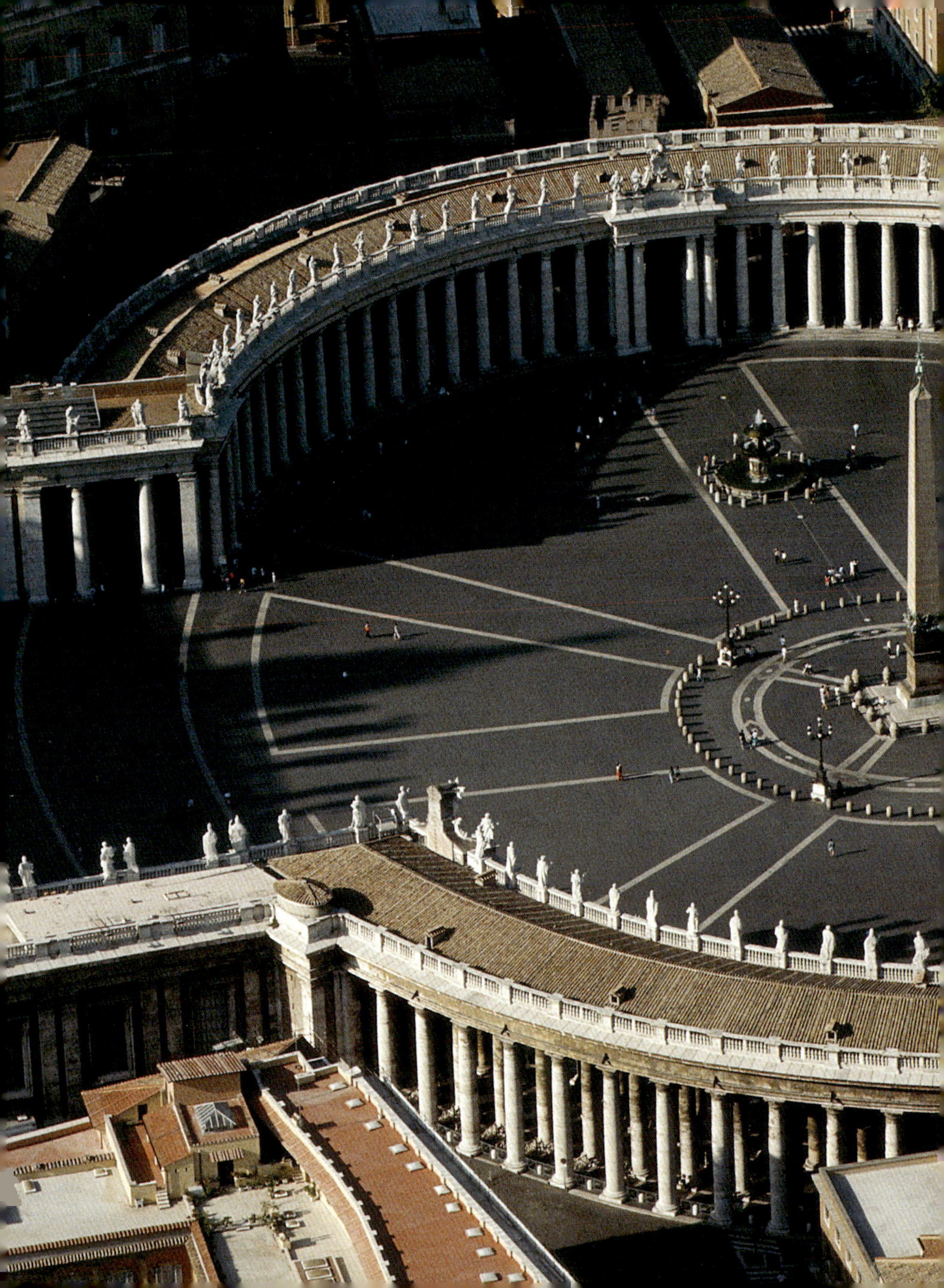

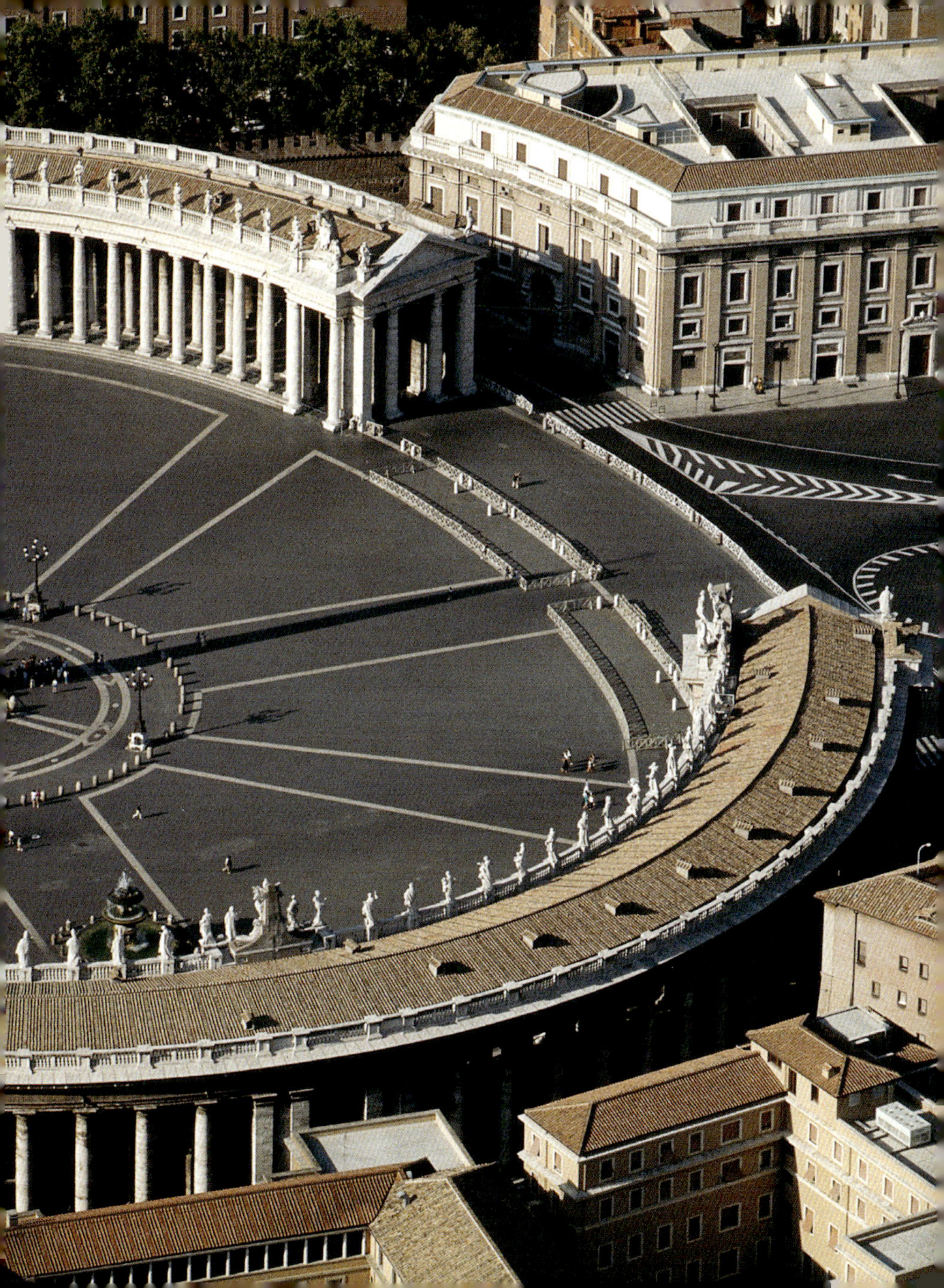

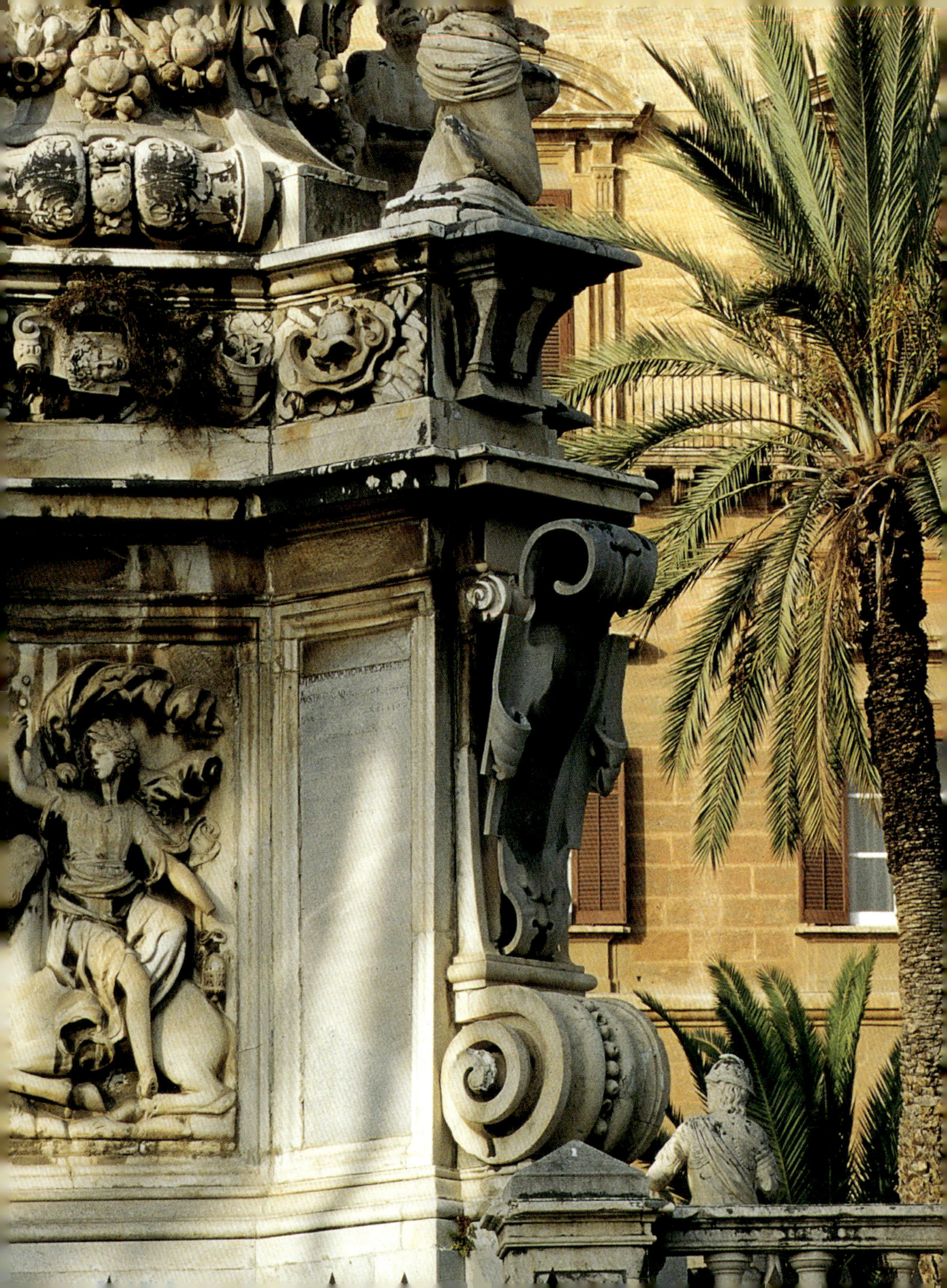

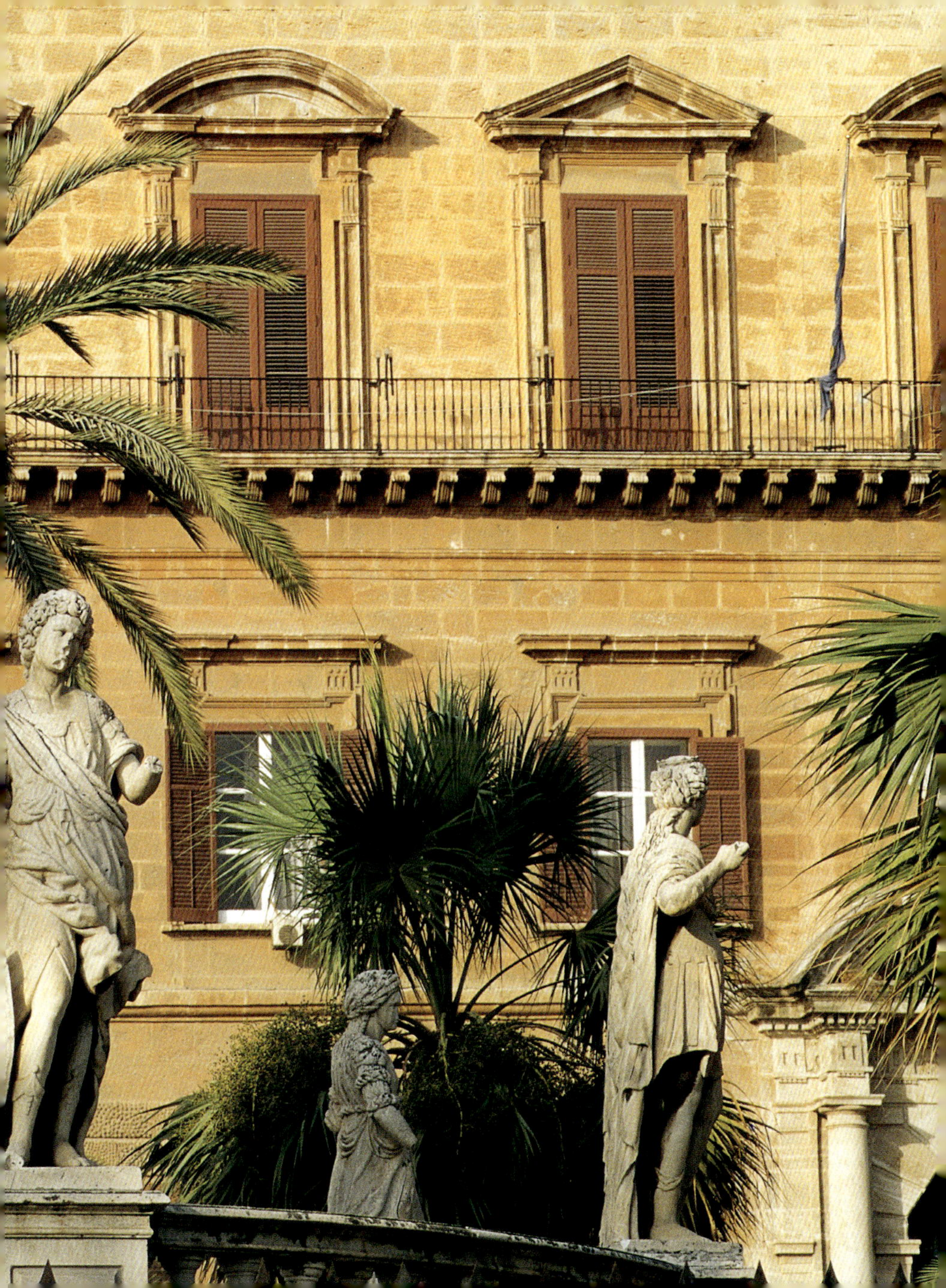

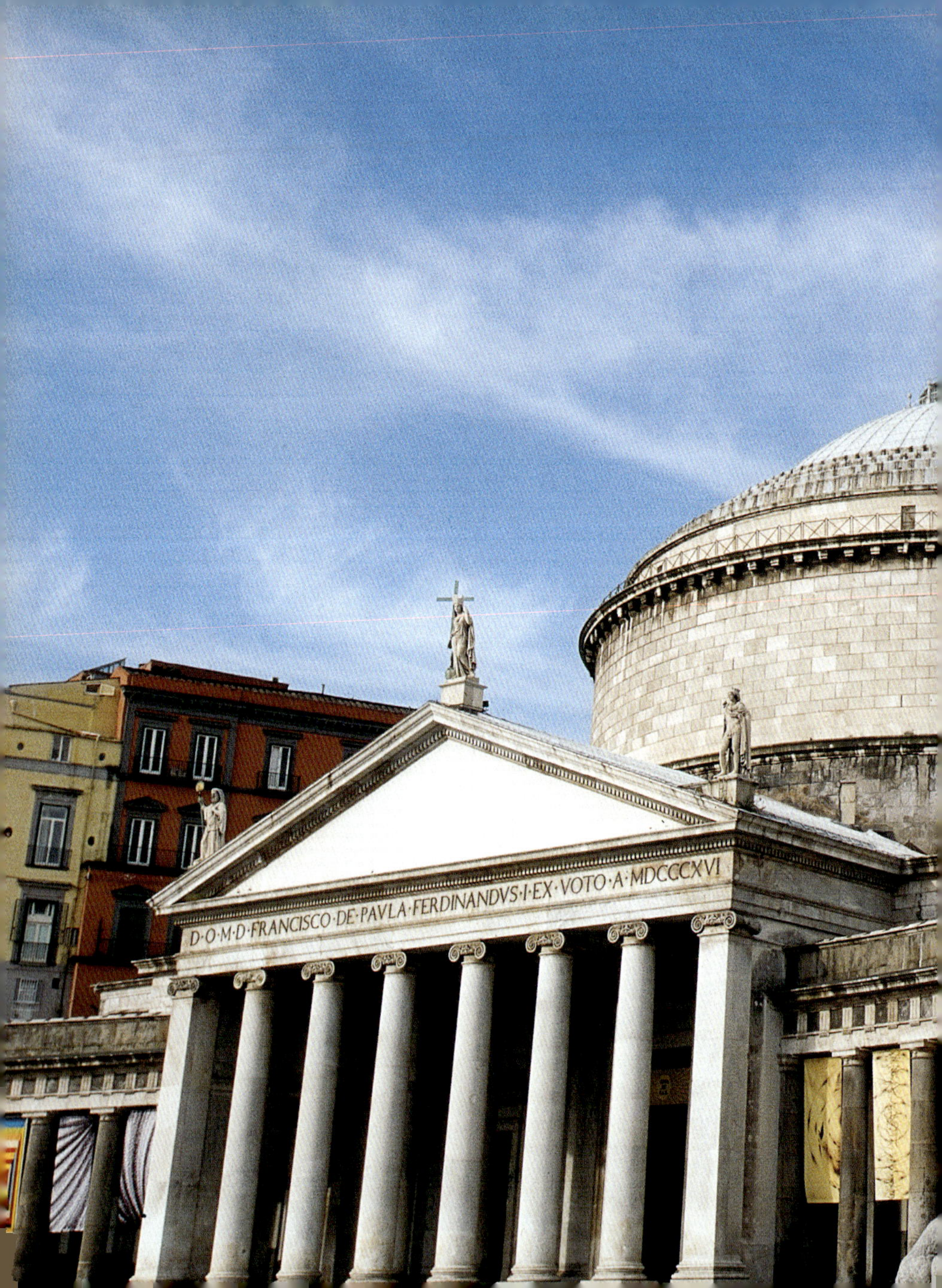
D·O·M·D·FRANCISCO·DE·PAVLA·FERDINANDVS·I·EX·VOTO·A·MDCCCXVI

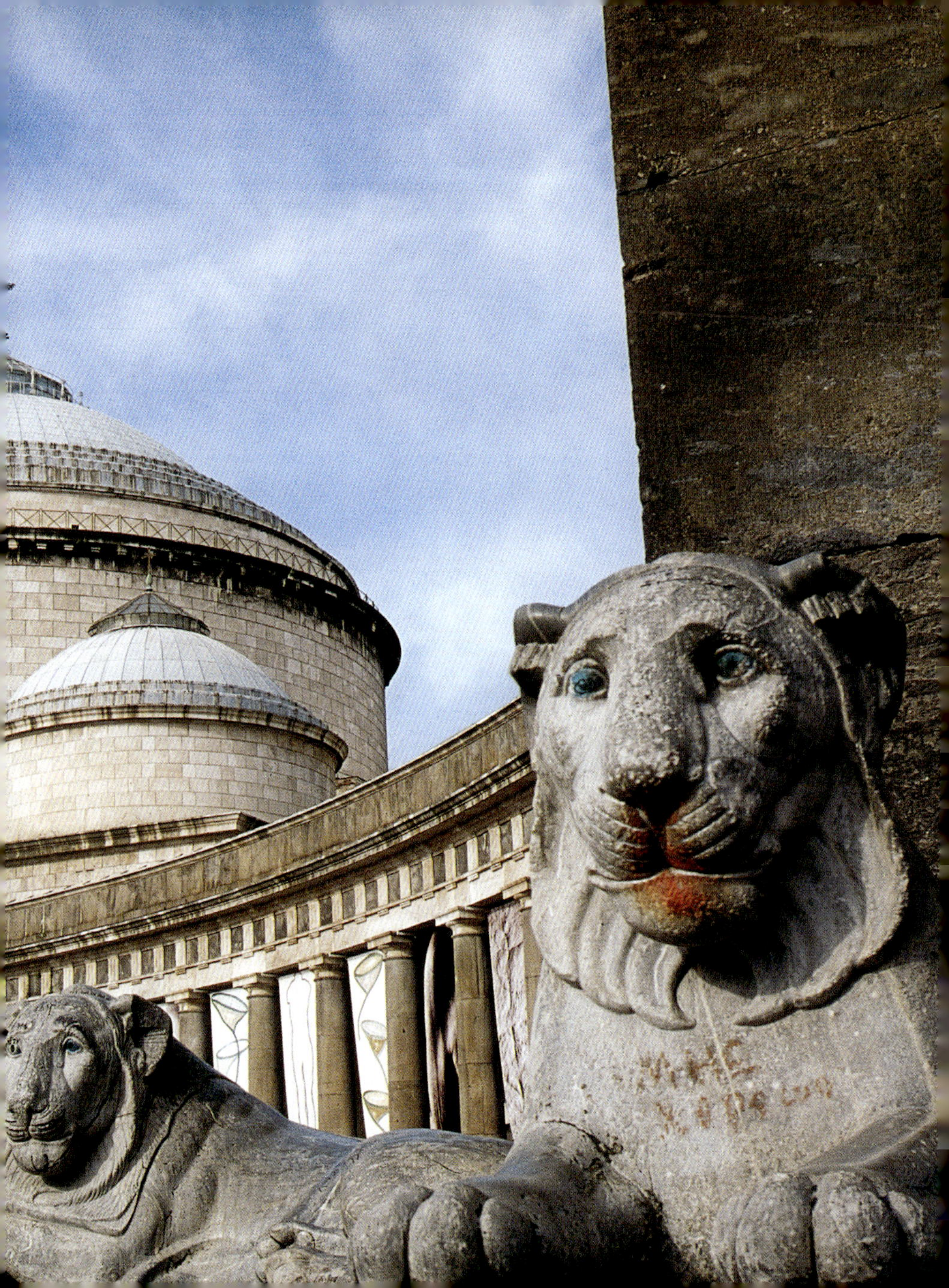

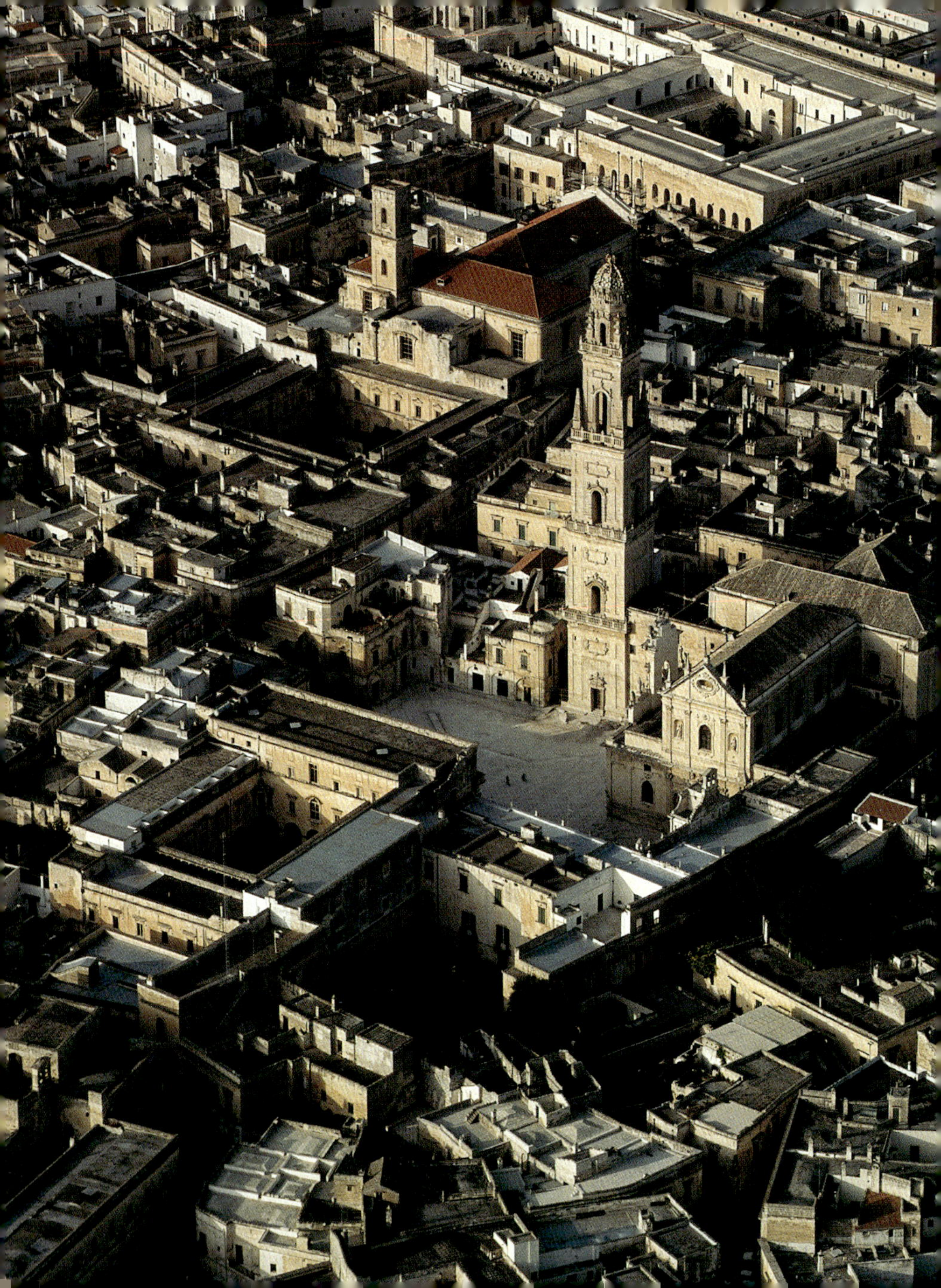

FORMS AND COLOURS OF THE COUNTRY

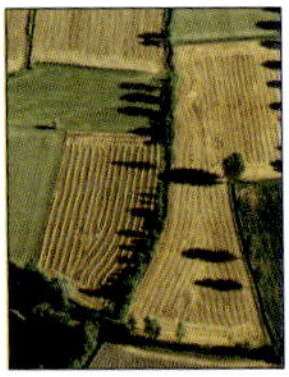

A TYPICAL TUSCAN LANDSCAPE. The tilled land on the hills, edged by boulevards of trees climbing towards farms, villas or castles, creates varying hues of colours ranging from deep green to warm ochre tones *(p. 157)*.

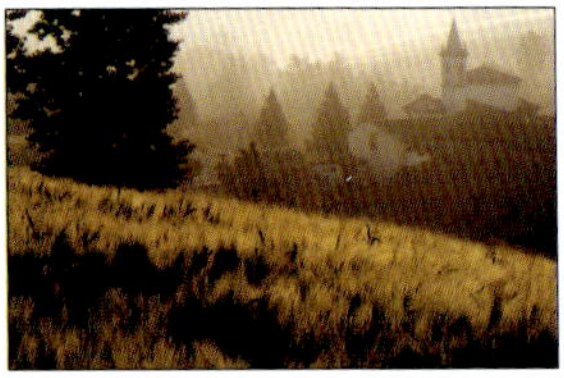

VIEW OF SANTA MARIA DEL SASSO in the Casentino area. This huge region, which expands north of Arezzo, is made of little villages spread amongst hills covered with age-old woods *(pp. 158-159)*.

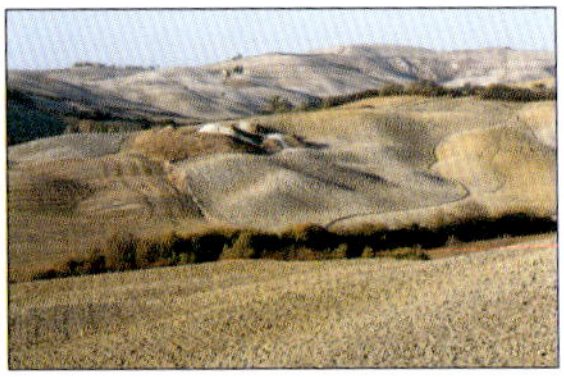

WAVY HILLS around Volterra, the Etruscan town built on a plateau that divides the valleys of the rivers Cecina and Era. They present an unusual and fascinating landscape.

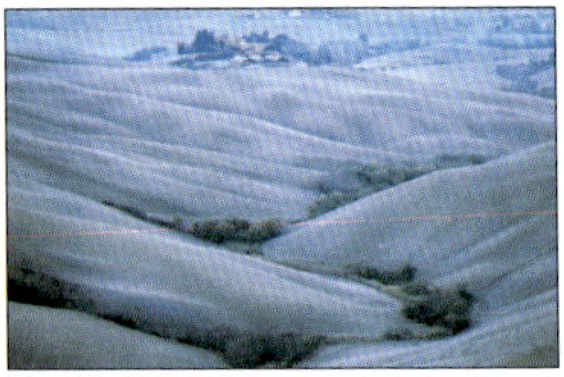

To the west, a clayey sliding ground originated some ledges, called the "balze"; to the north, a sweet fertile countryside expands *(pp. 160-161, 162-163)*.

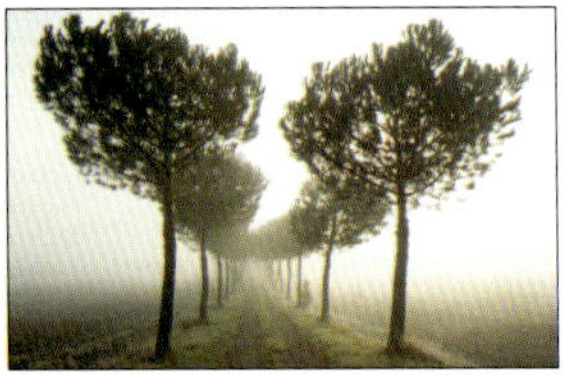

PERSPECTIVE VIEW OF A TREE-LINED AVENUE shrouded in the fog of the countryside around Cortona, the ancient Etruscan town located on the rises north of Lake Trasimeno *(pp. 164-165)*.

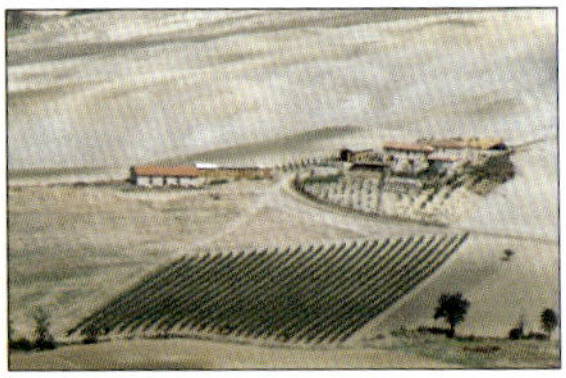

THE HILLY AREA OF MONTALCINO, between the Ombrone and Asso valleys, abounds with vineyards. It is renowned for producing the Brunello di Montalcino, the outstanding local wine *(pp. 166-167)*.

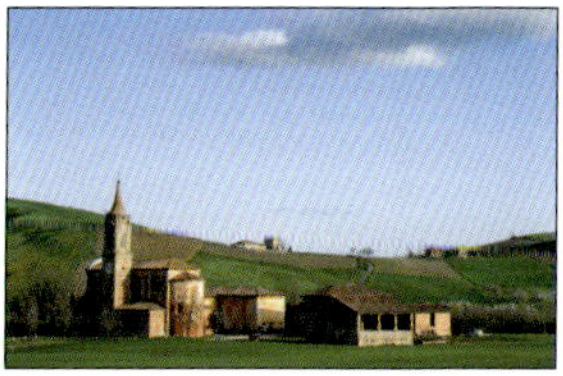

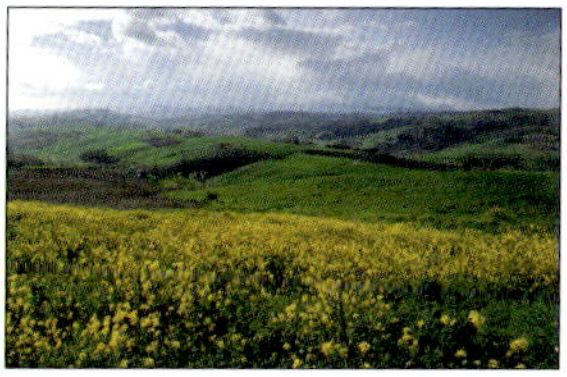

A TINY CHURCH and plain stone-made houses on the Emilia- Romagna hills near the Castle of Serravalle. From this small picturesque medieval hamlet, surrounded by walls and placed on a hummock, it is possible to enjoy fine panoramic views on the neighbouring hills, which are covered with flowers in springtime *(pp. 168-169, 170-171)*.

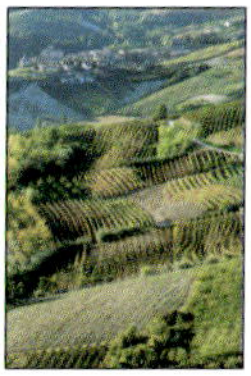

VINE ROWS IN THE LANGHE. The vineries of this area of Southern Piedmont produce first-rate wines known all over the world, such as the Barolo, Barbaresco, Barbera, Dolcetto and Nebbiolo d'Alba *(pp. 172)*.

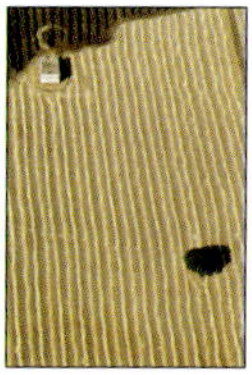

THE TYPICAL YELLOW MUSTARD COLOUR of a recently ploughed field in the Tavoliere delle Puglie. The Tavoliere is the largest plain of Southern Italy, where hard wheat, cotton, tobacco and orchards are raised *(pp. 173)*.

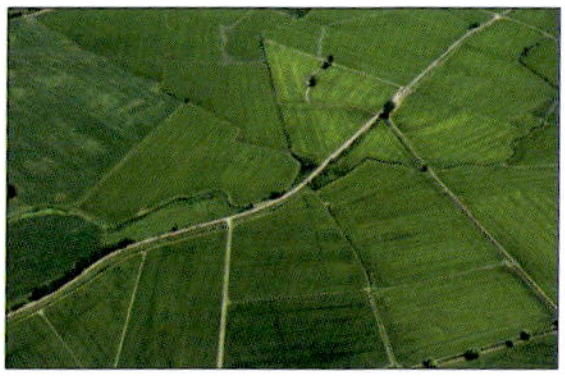

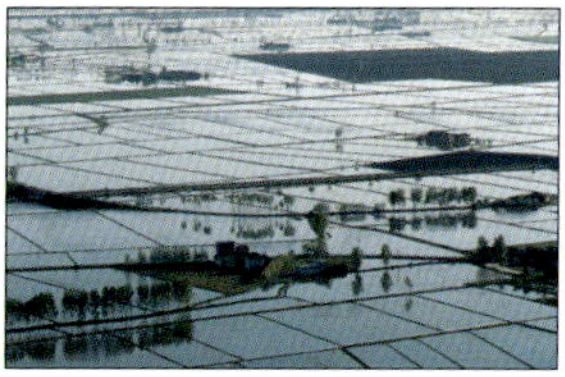

THE IMMENSE GREEN MARSHY EXPANDS of the Piedmontese paddy fields in the Novara and Vercelli countryside constitute one of the most remarkable landscapes of Northern Italy. The sheets of water boast various shades ranging from deep green to pale blue and from blue to silver. They create a very special natural chessboard *(pp. 174-175, 176-177)*.

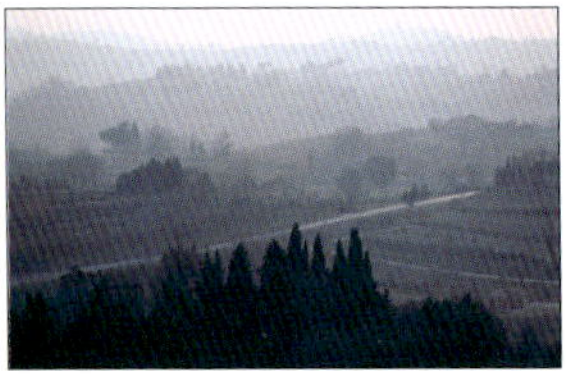

MONTEPULCIANO, erected on a hill ovelooking the Chiana Valley and surrounded by 16th-century fortifications, is immersed in a fairy-like landscape marked by vineries and cypresses *(pp. 178-179)*.

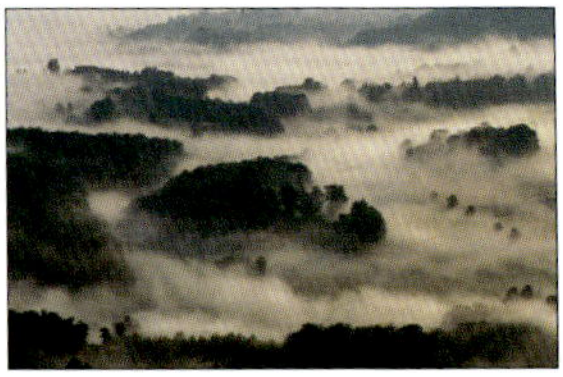

THE LOMBARDY HILLS AROUND VARESE slope down from the Sacro Monte to the lake, wrapped in the fog of the cold, misty winter months. They evoke an atmospheric, almost fairy-like feeling *(pp. 180-181)*.

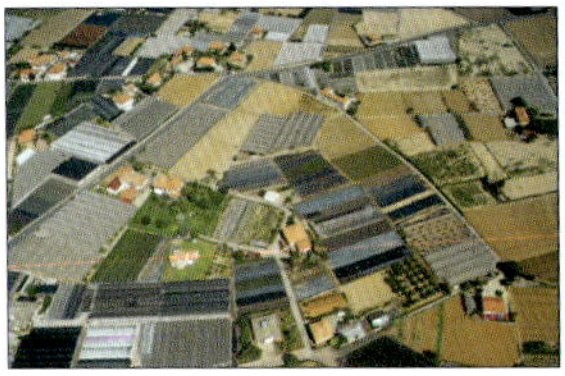

GREENHOUSES AND CULTIVATED LANDS in the plain of Albenga, well-known agricultural and seaside Ligurian resort. The mild climate of the Riviera favours the growth of flowers, fruit and vegetables *(pp. 182-183)*.

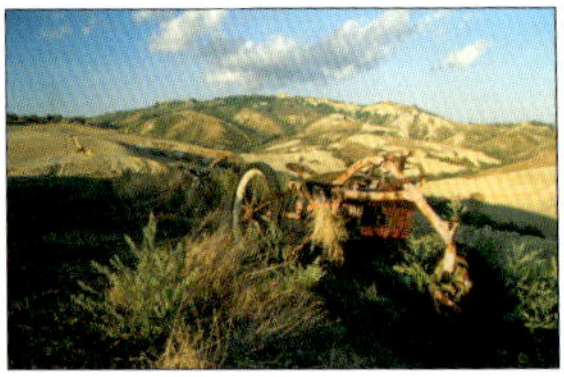

AN ABANDONED PLOUGH on the hills of Volterra. The tilled fields and the uncultivated meadows, interspersed with rows of vines and olive trees, look like the tesserae of a multicoloured mosaic *(pp. 184-185)*.

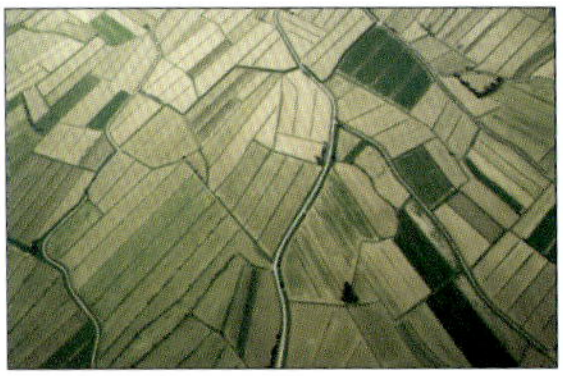

SPECTACULAR BIRD'S-EYE PICTURE of the cultivated fields in Friuli-Venezia Giulia. Moulded by men's work, the land has formed perfectly geometric, almost unreal shapes, based on colour effects *(pp. 186-187)*.

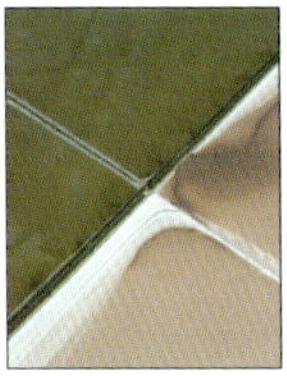

ONE OF THE MANY SALINAS in the countryside near Cagliari. They boast colours ranging from green to white, from pink to brown. Pink flamingoes nest in the neighbouring ponds between August and March *(p. 188)*.

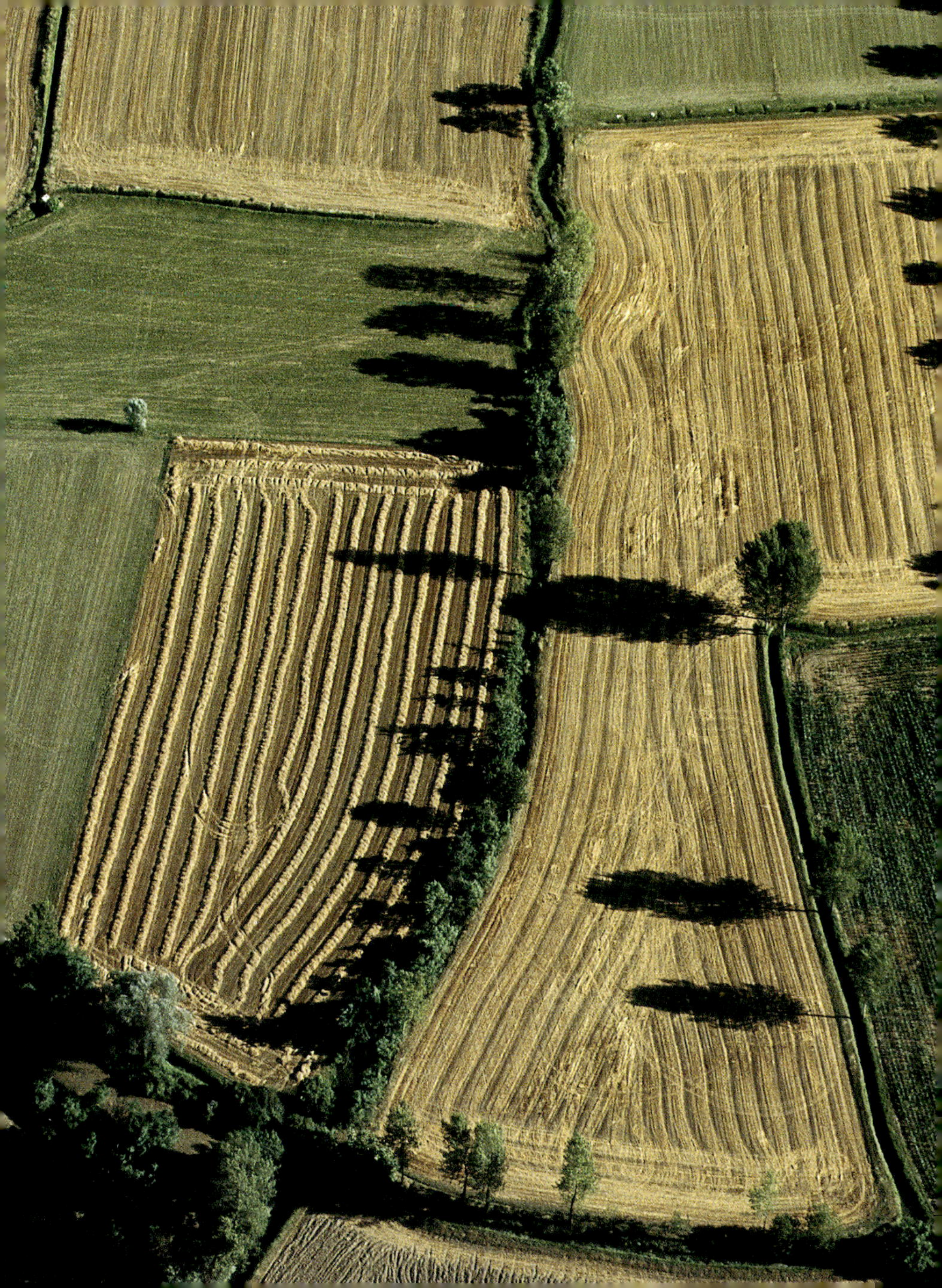

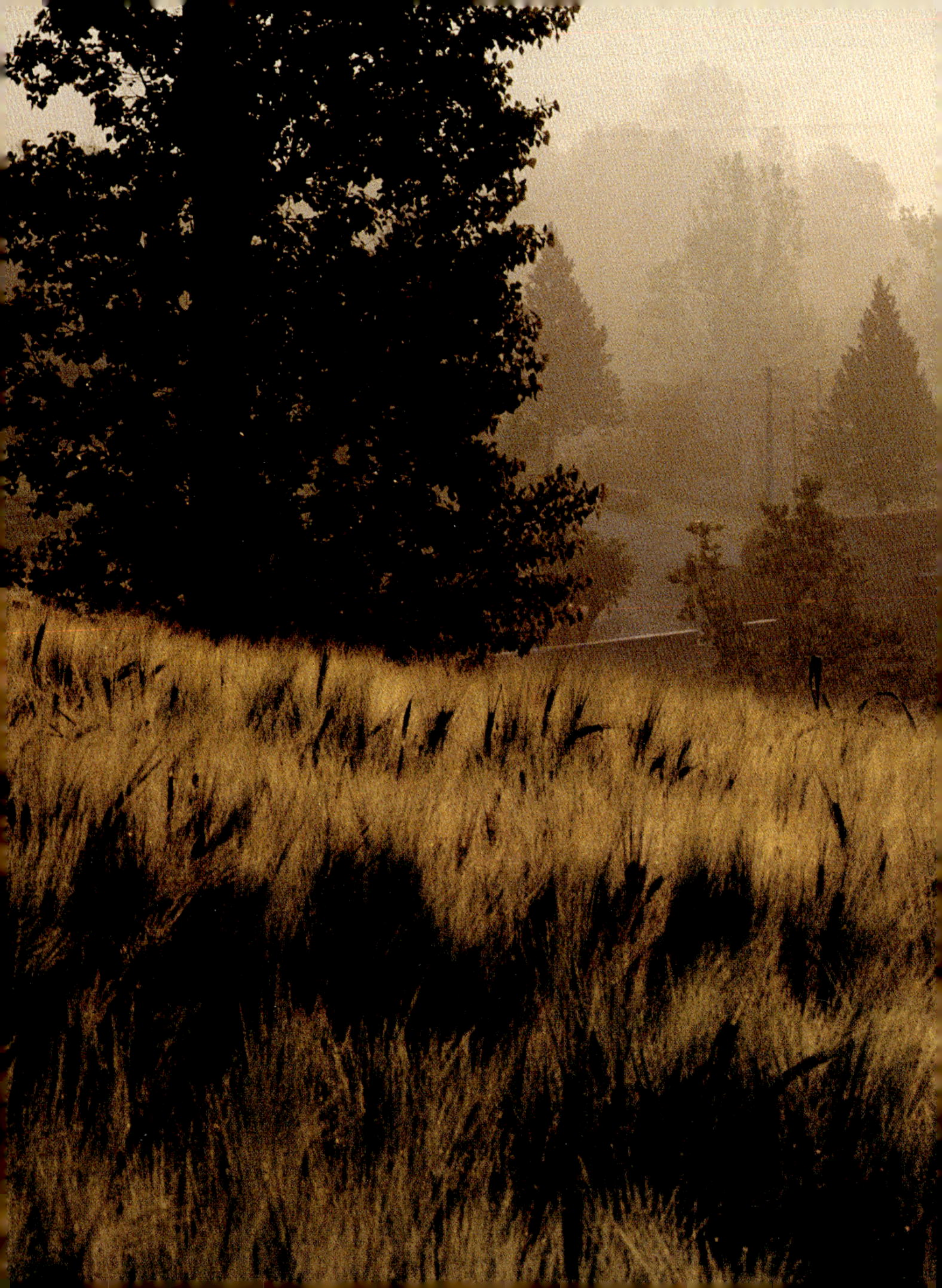

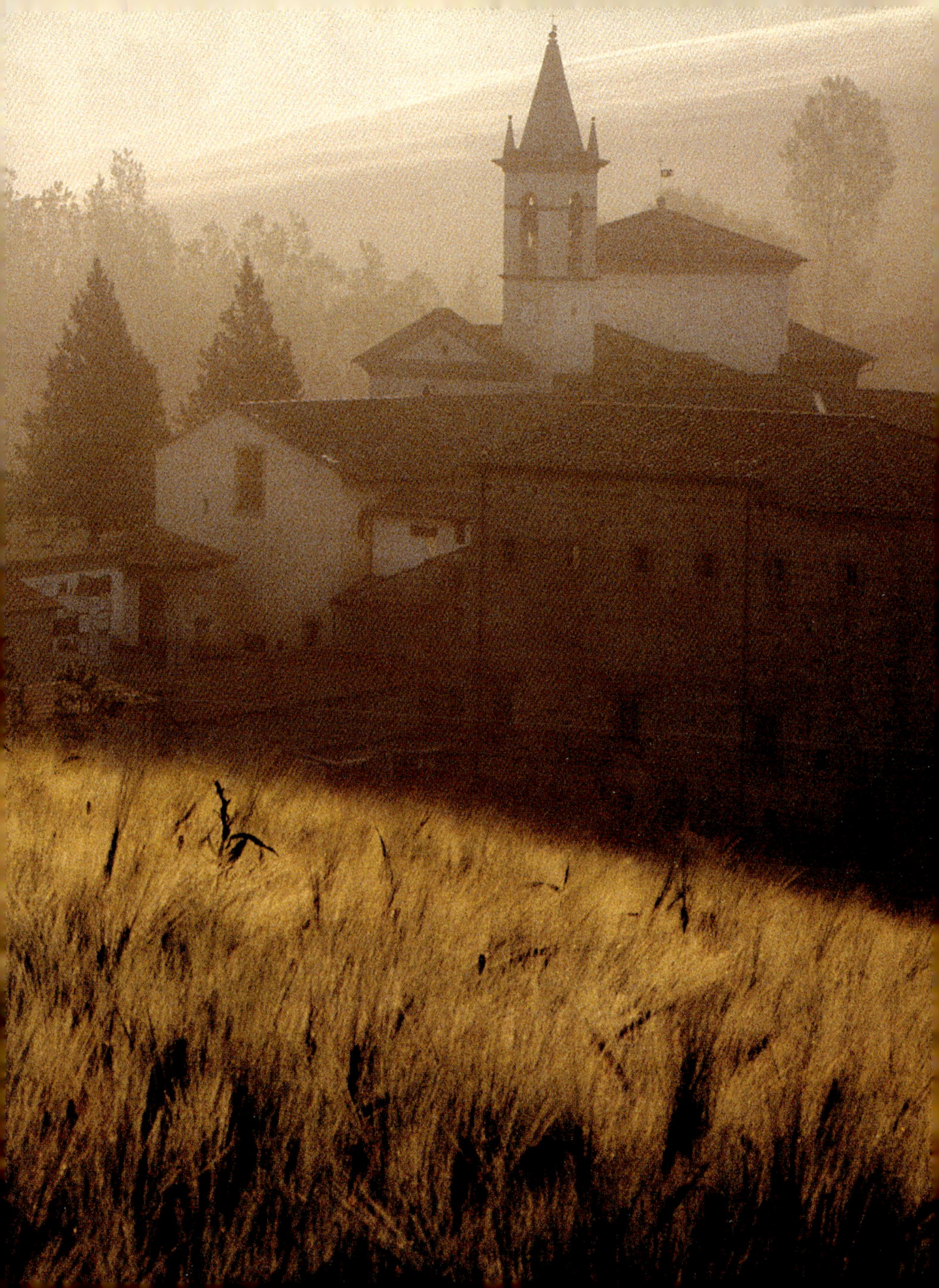

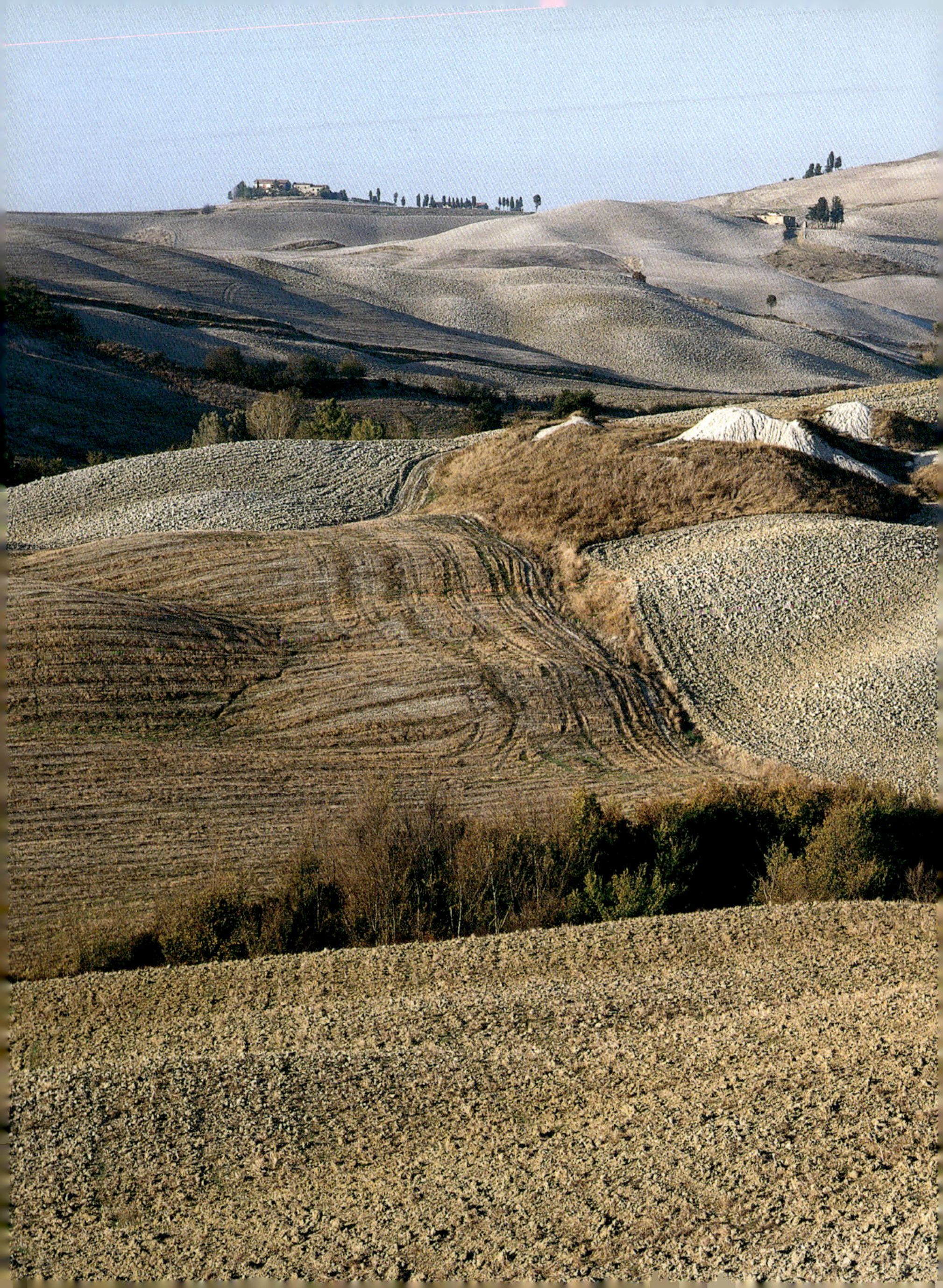

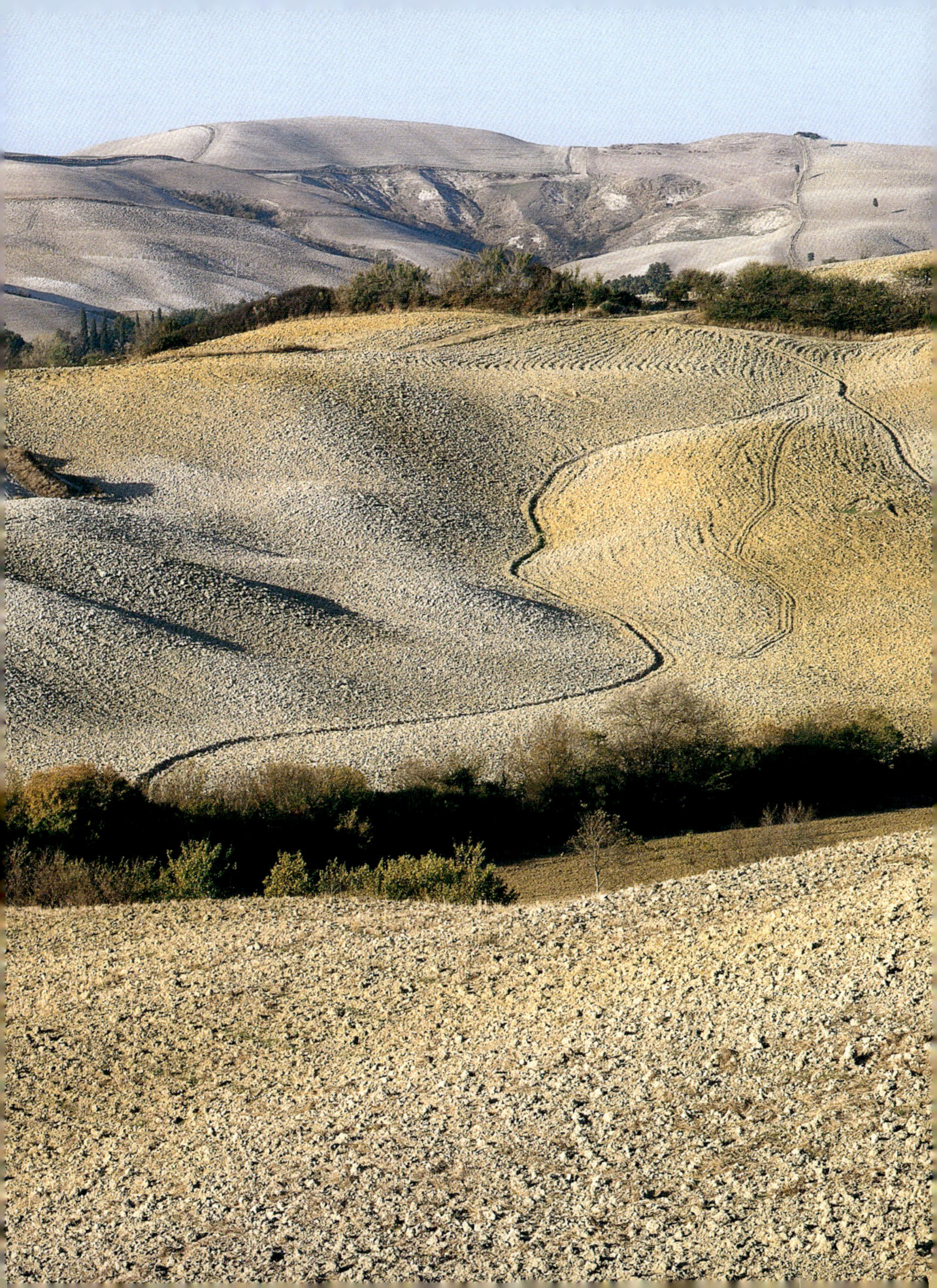

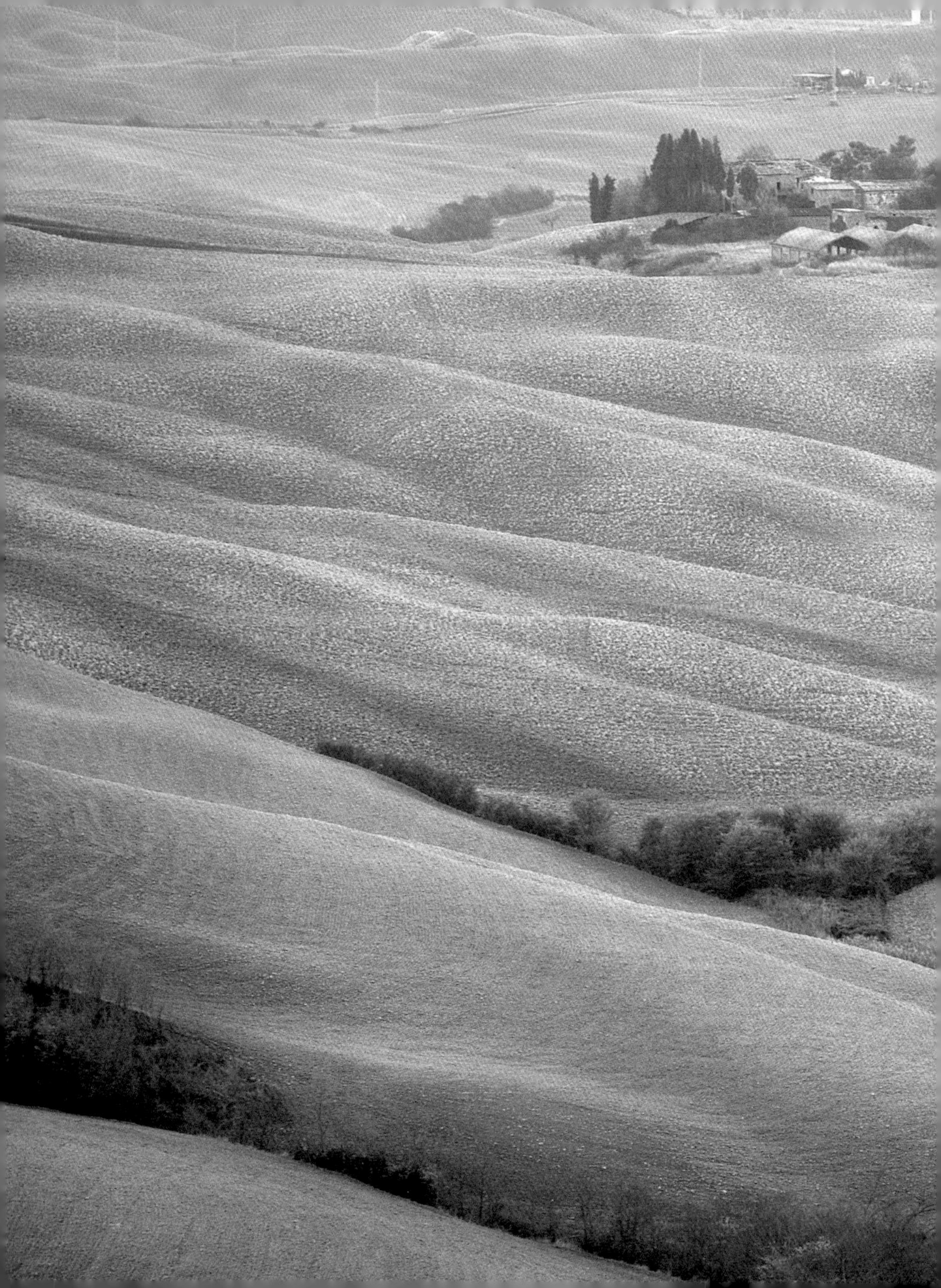

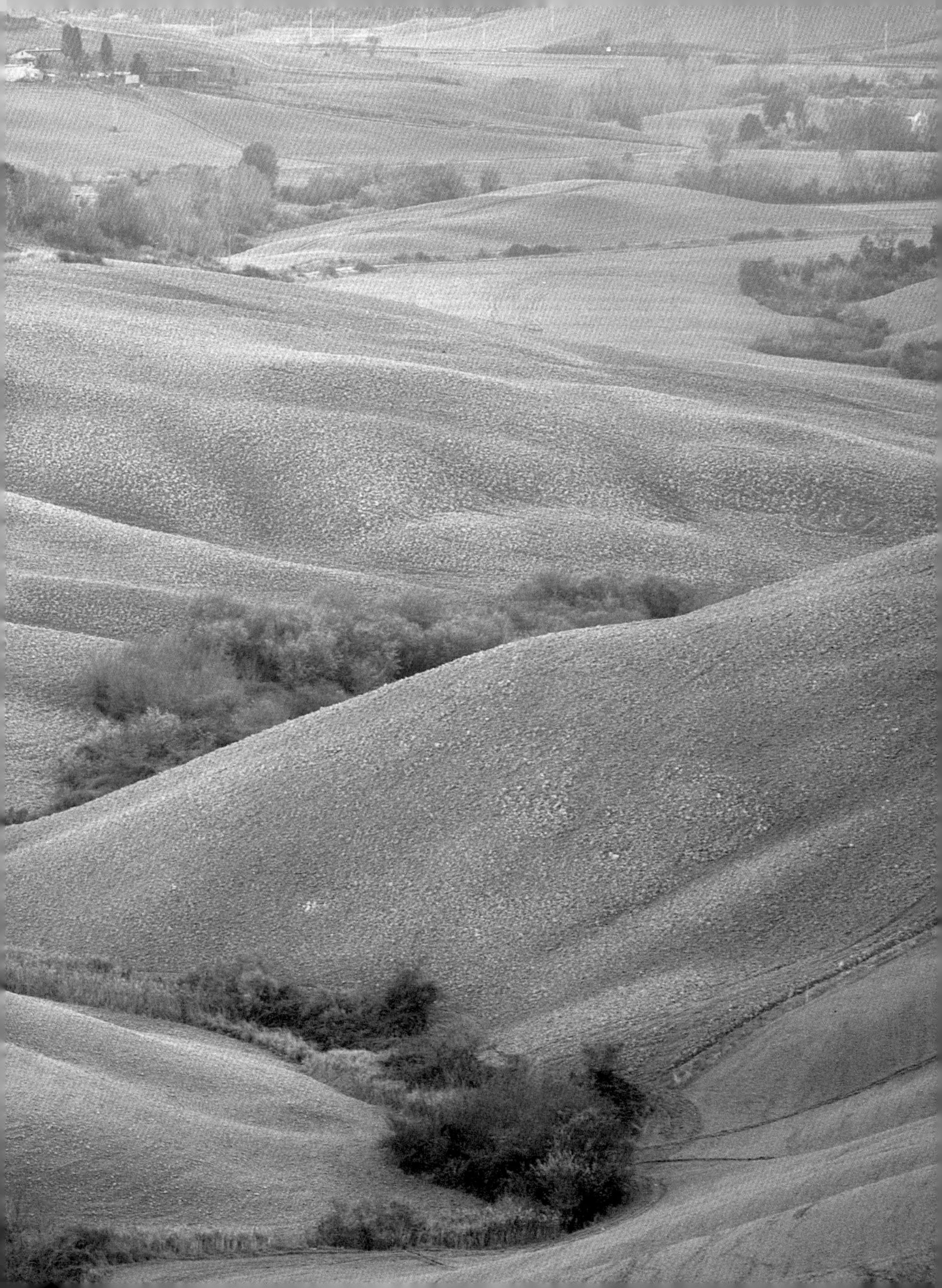

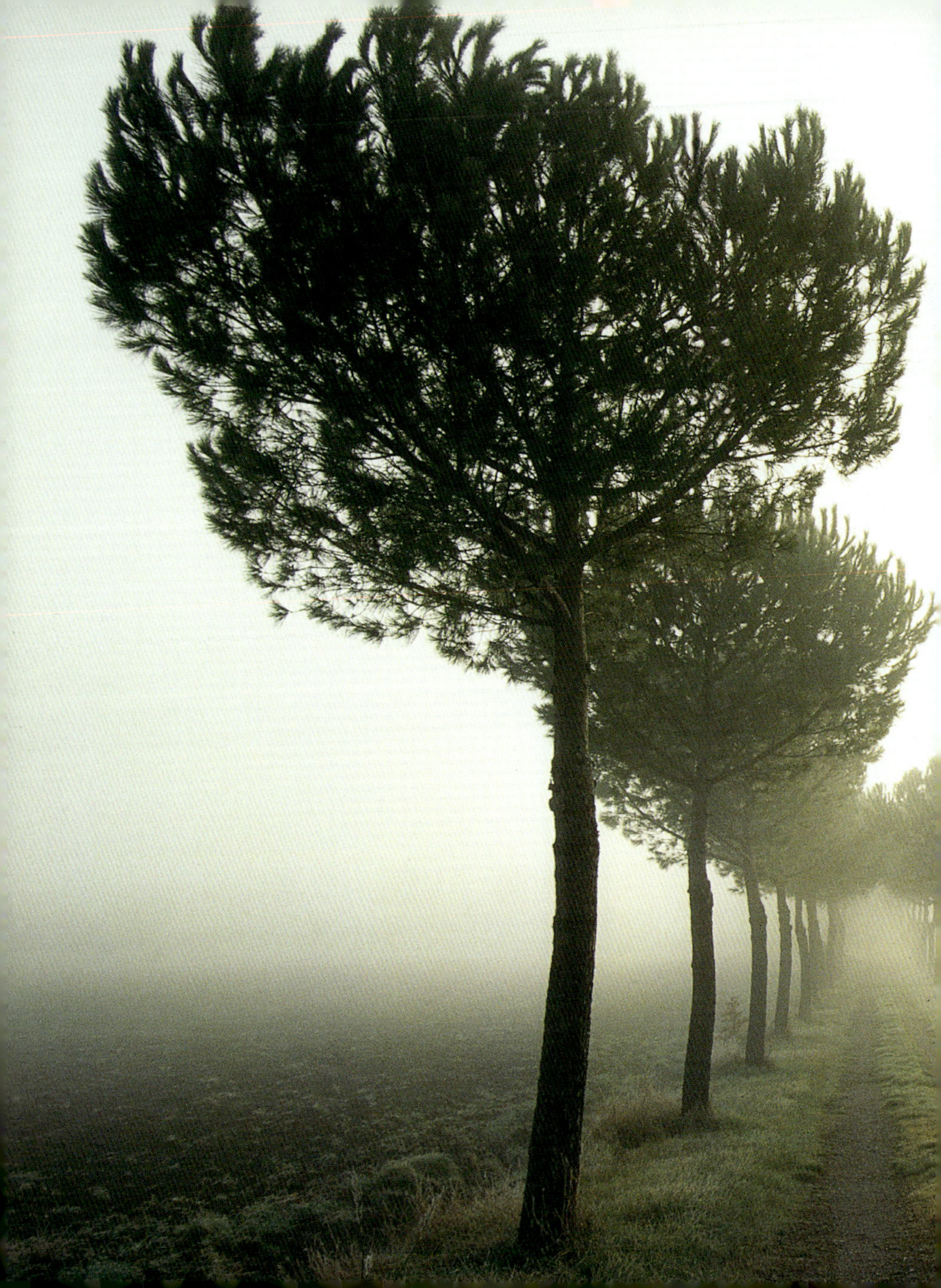

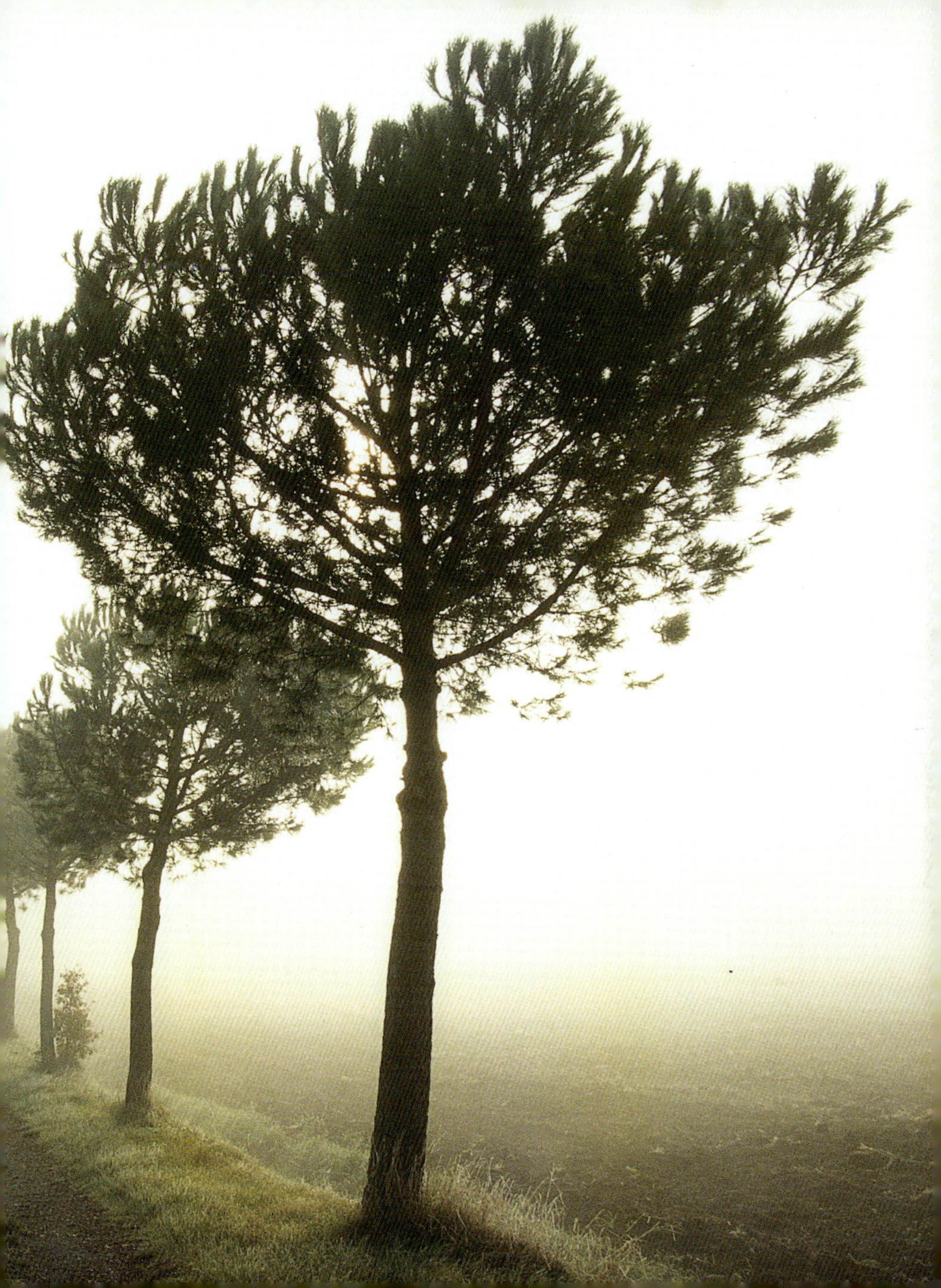

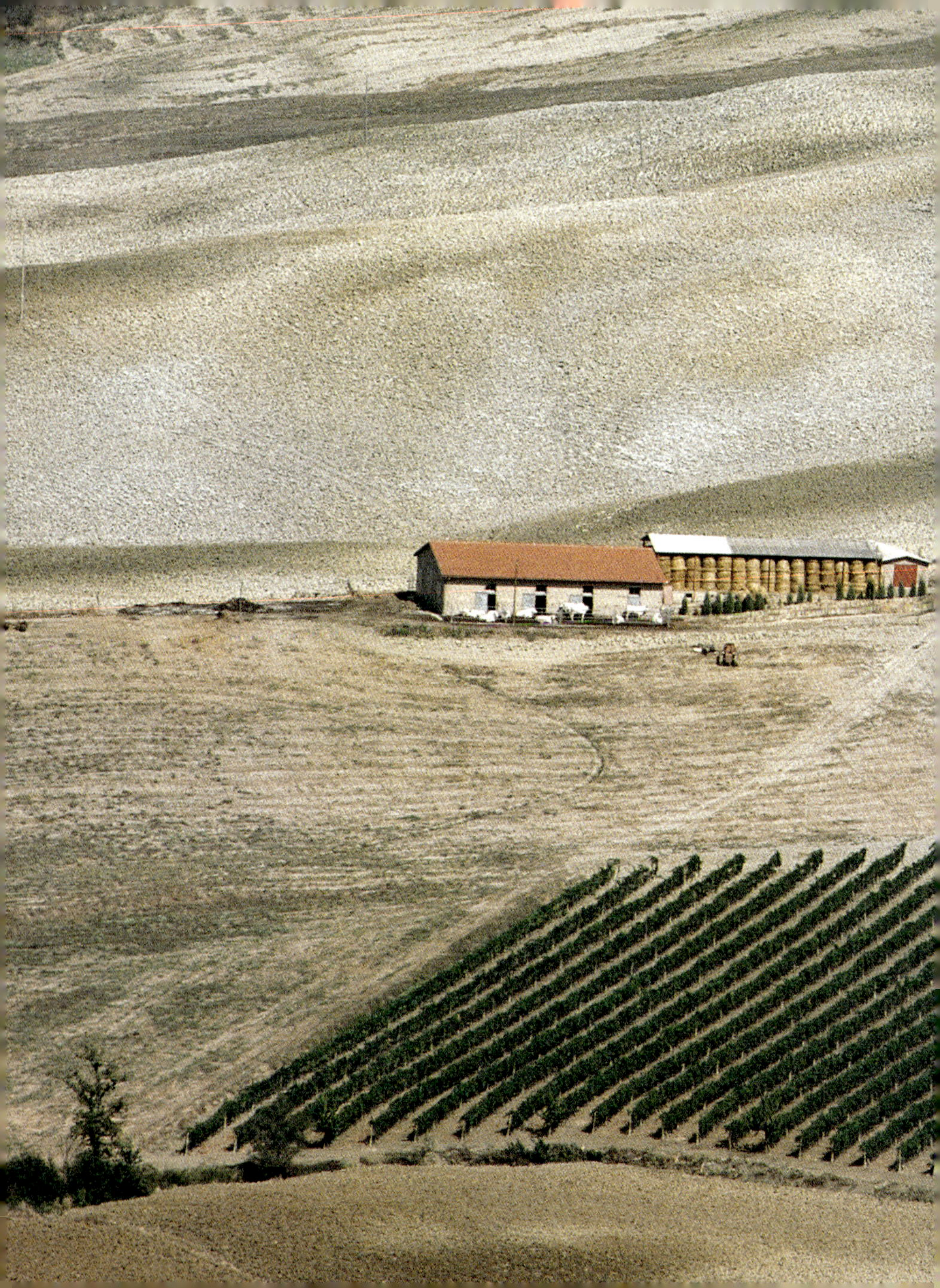

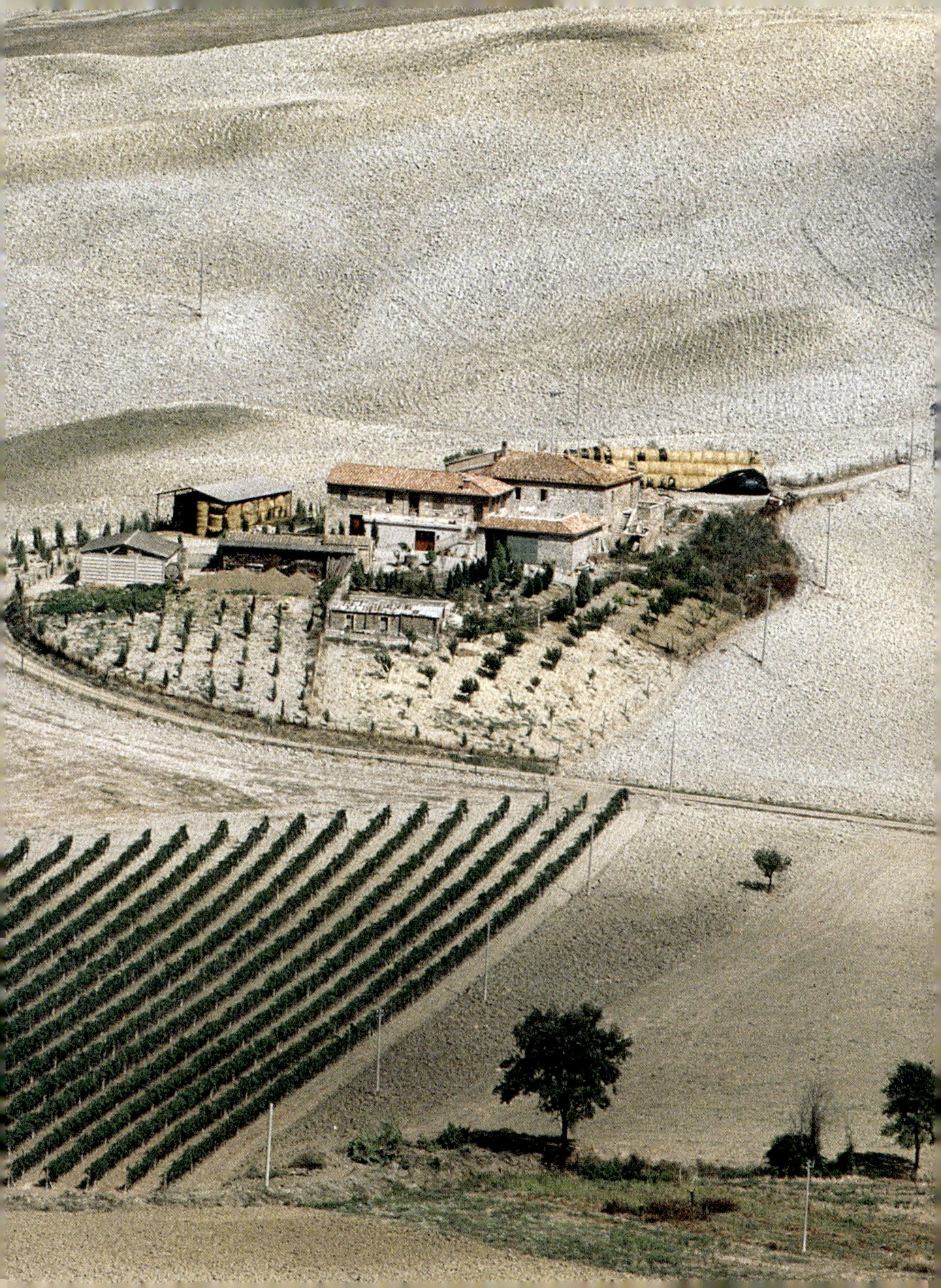

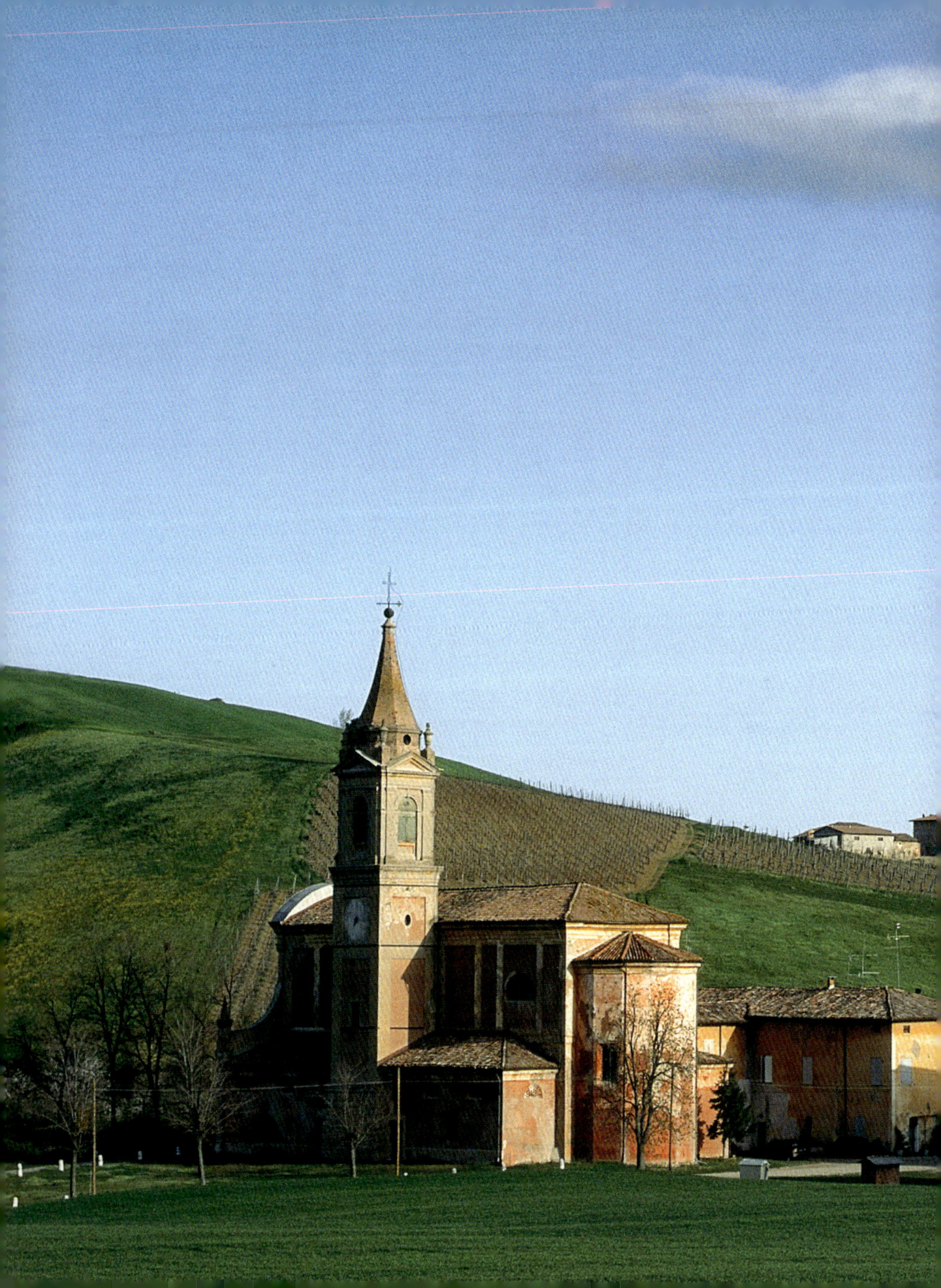

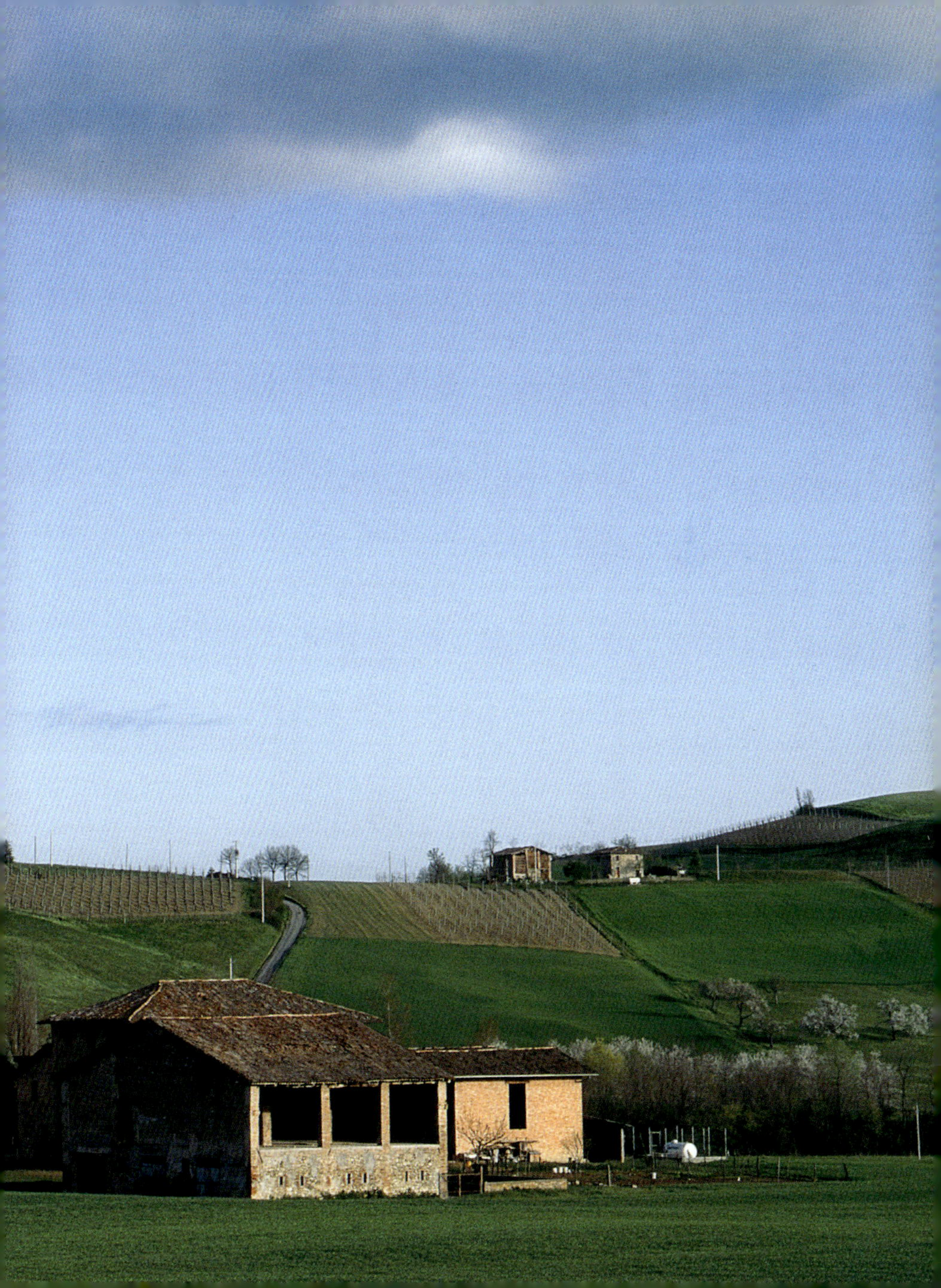

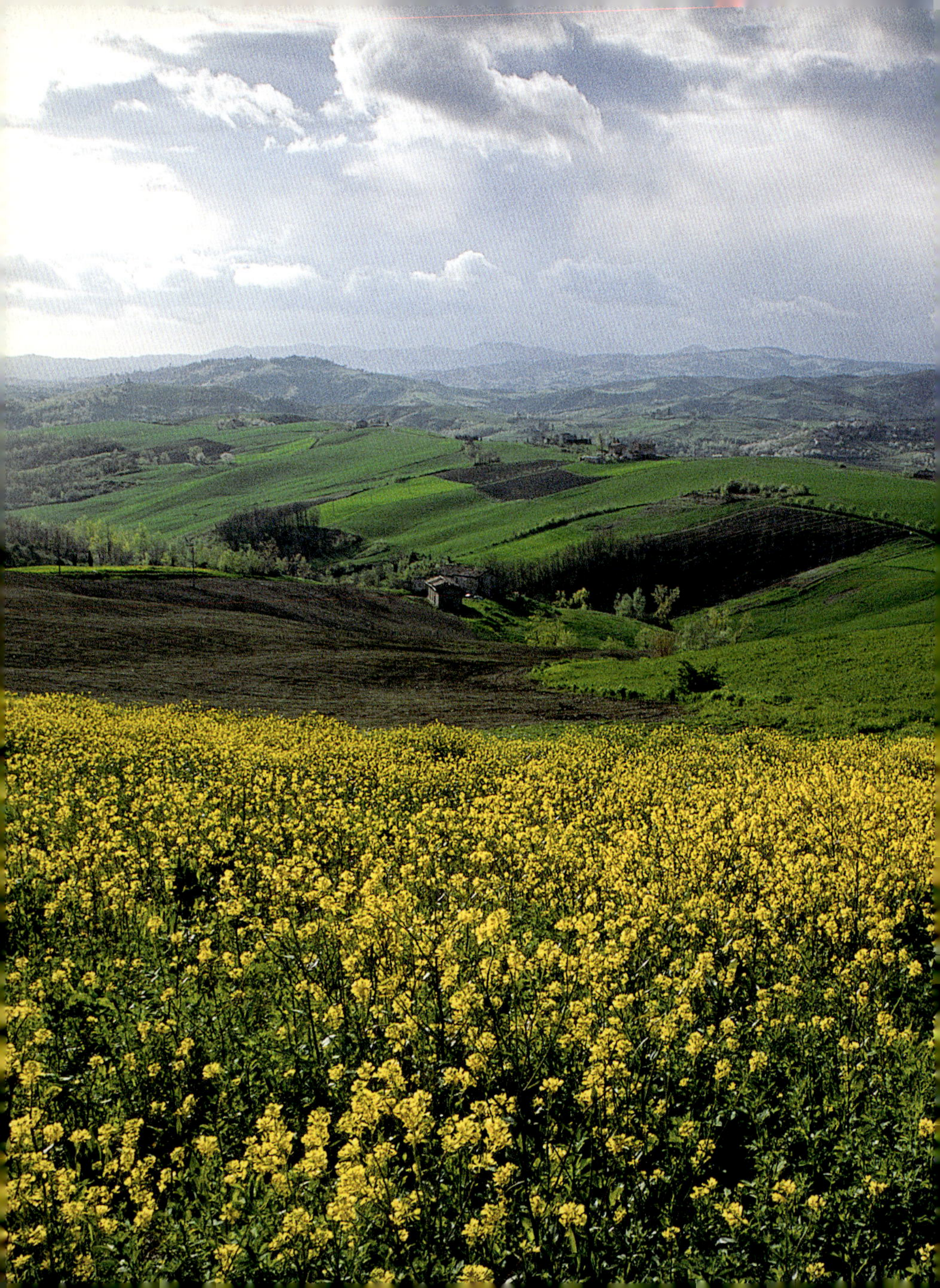

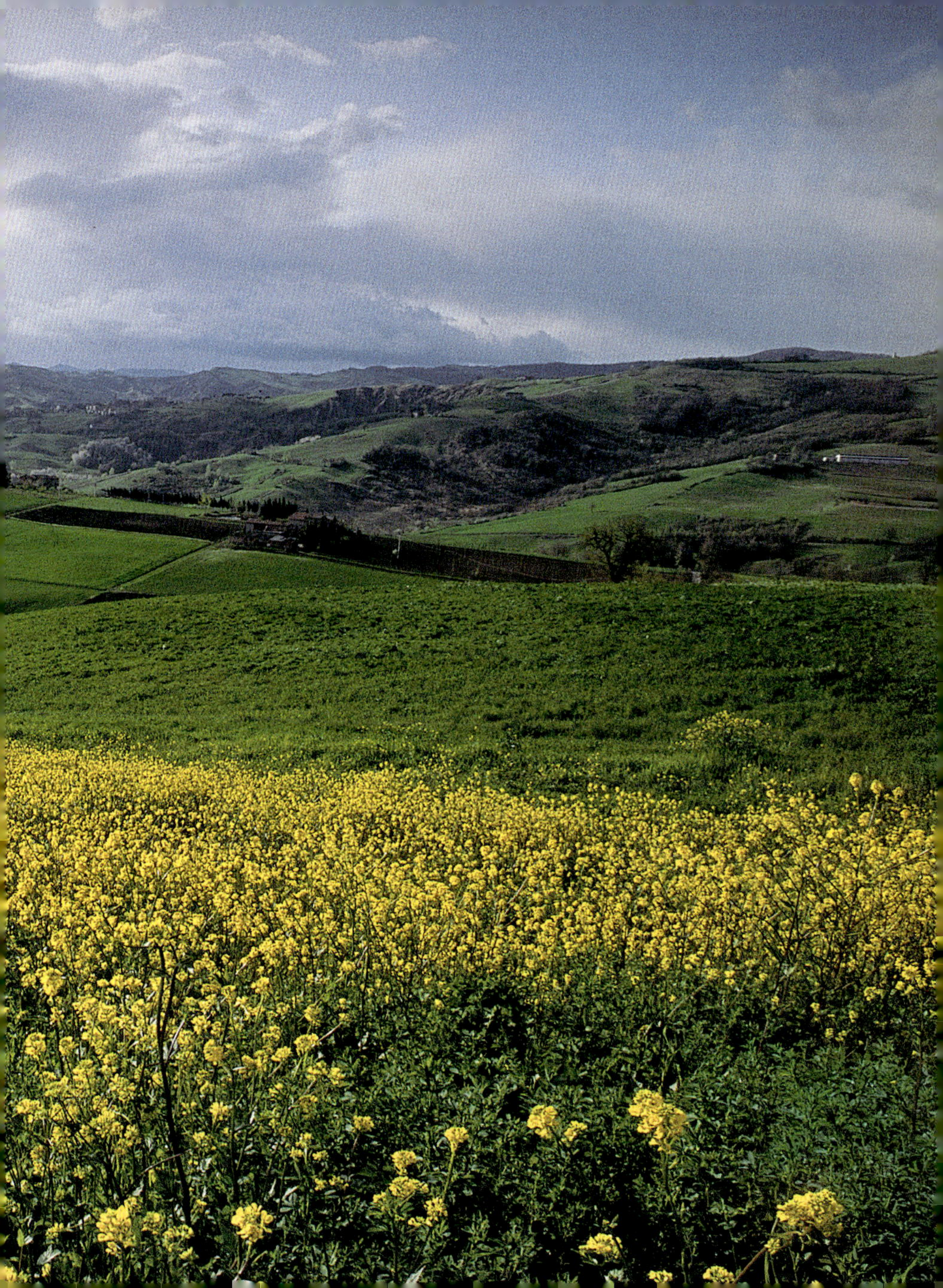

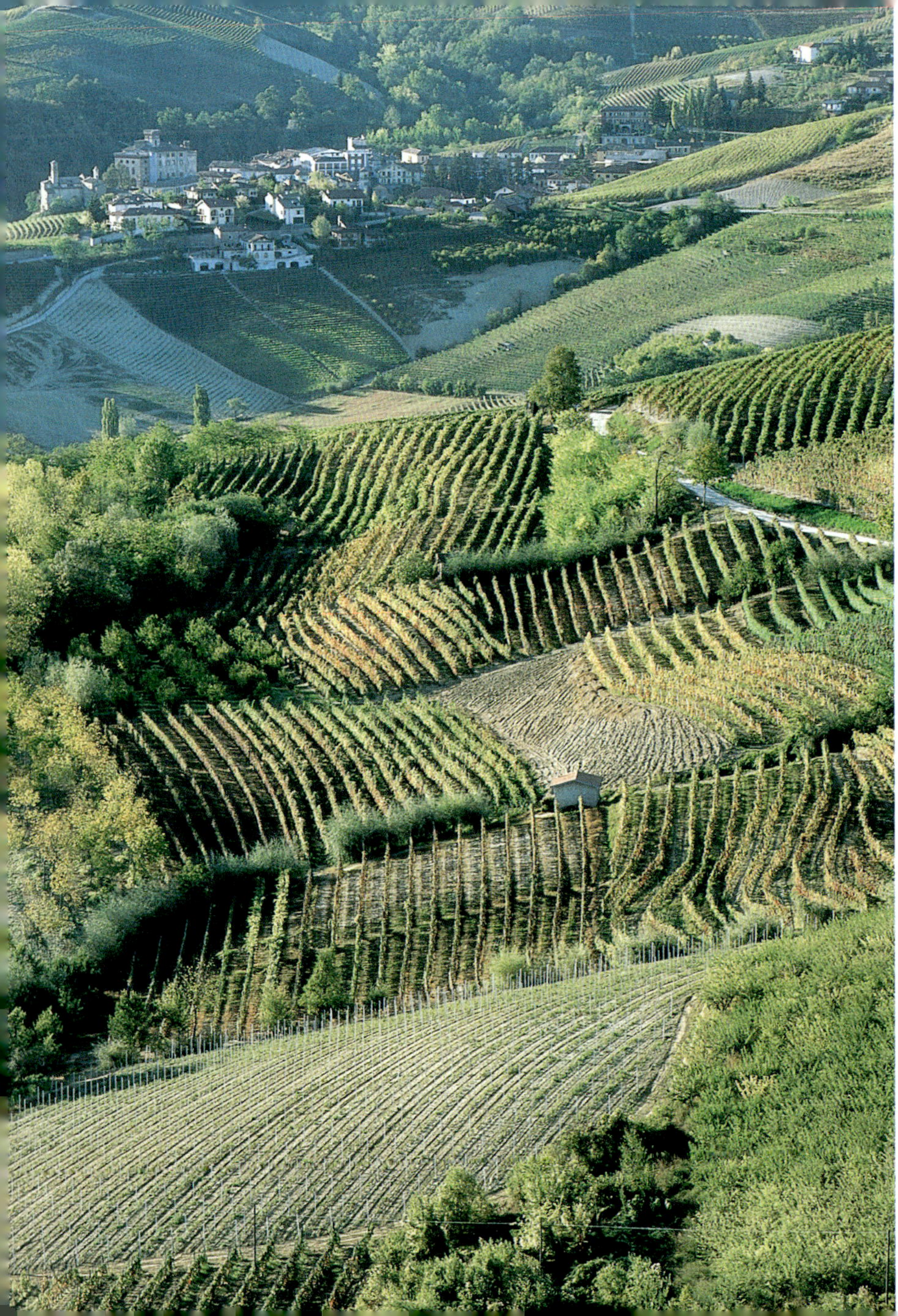

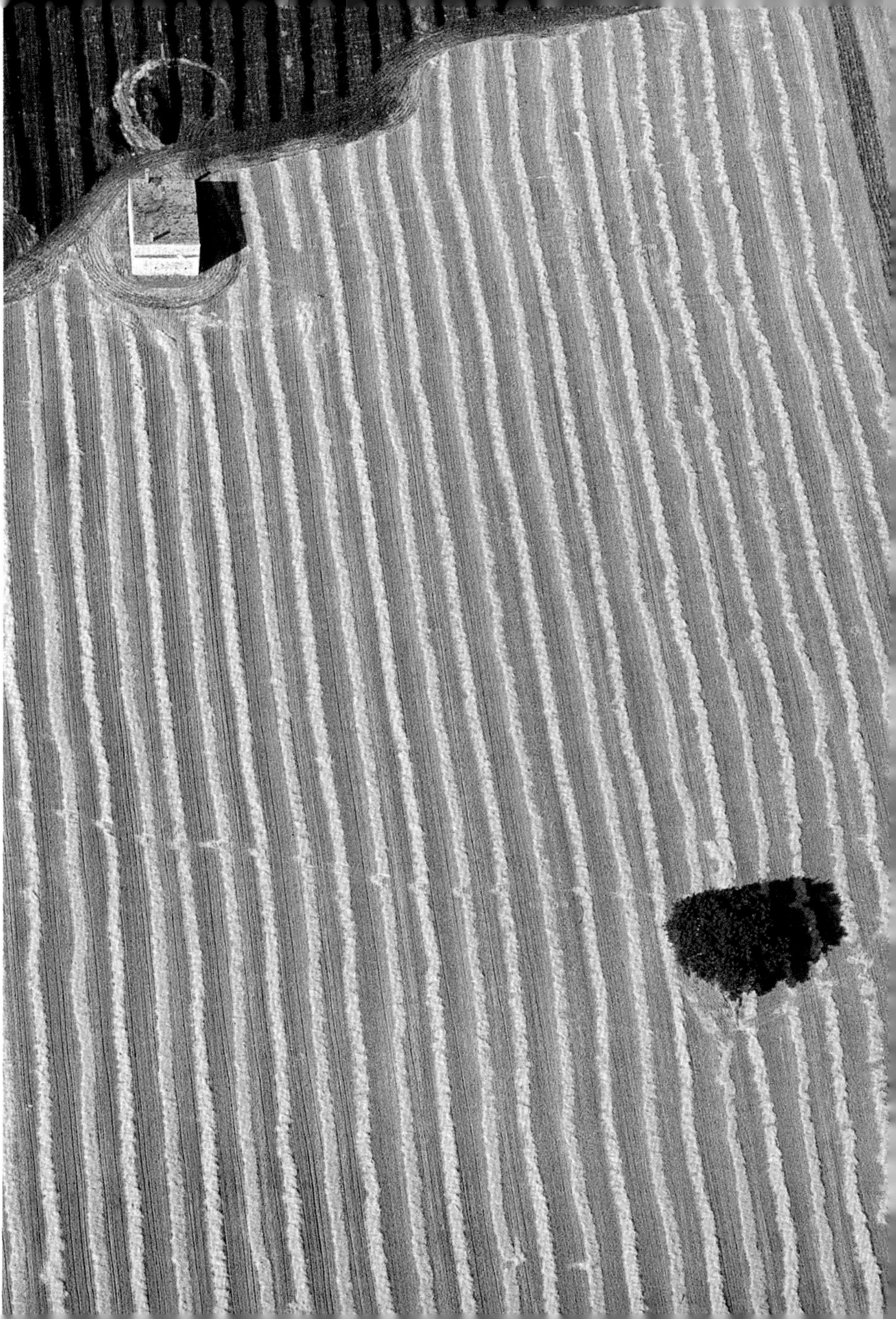

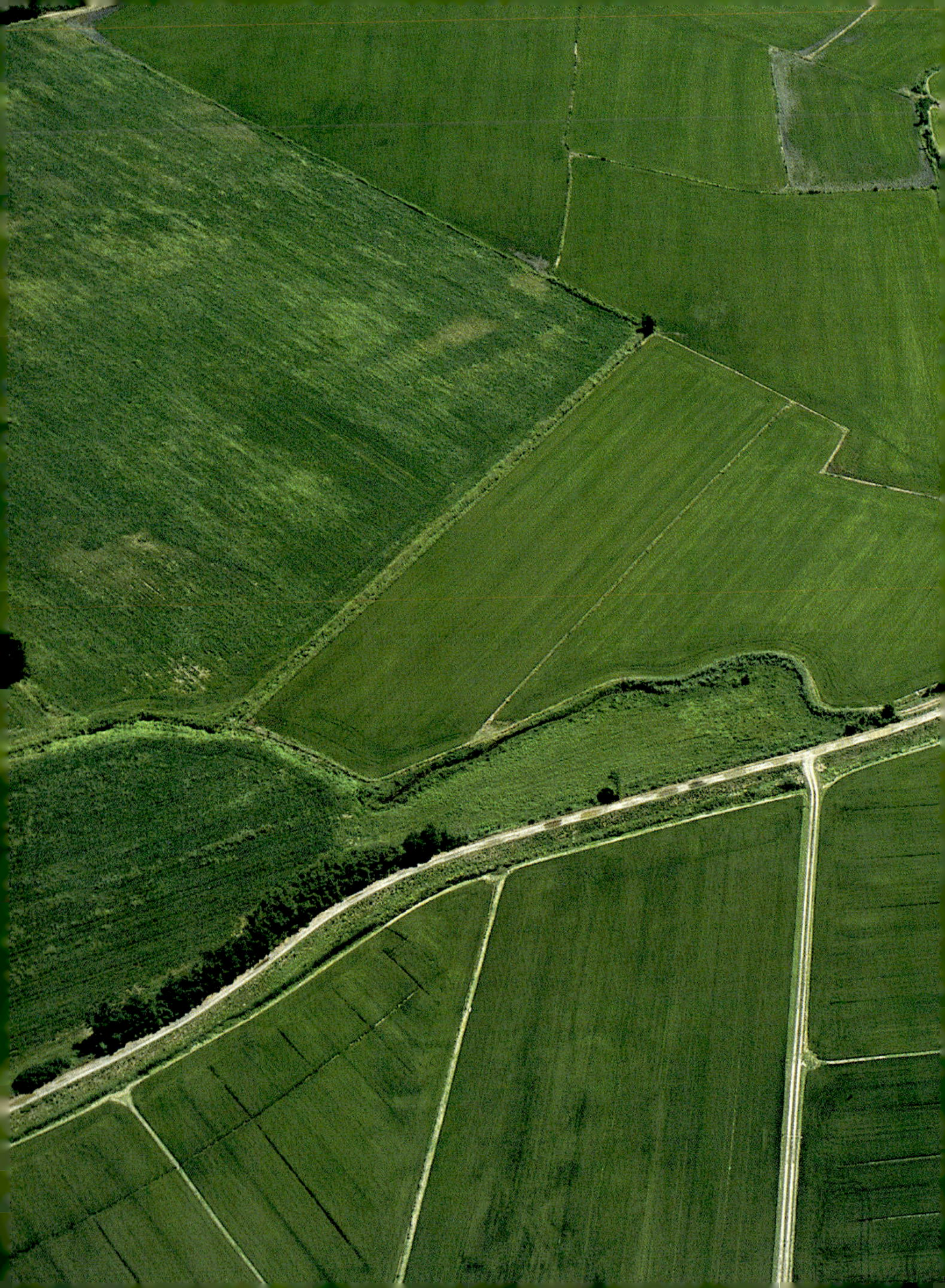

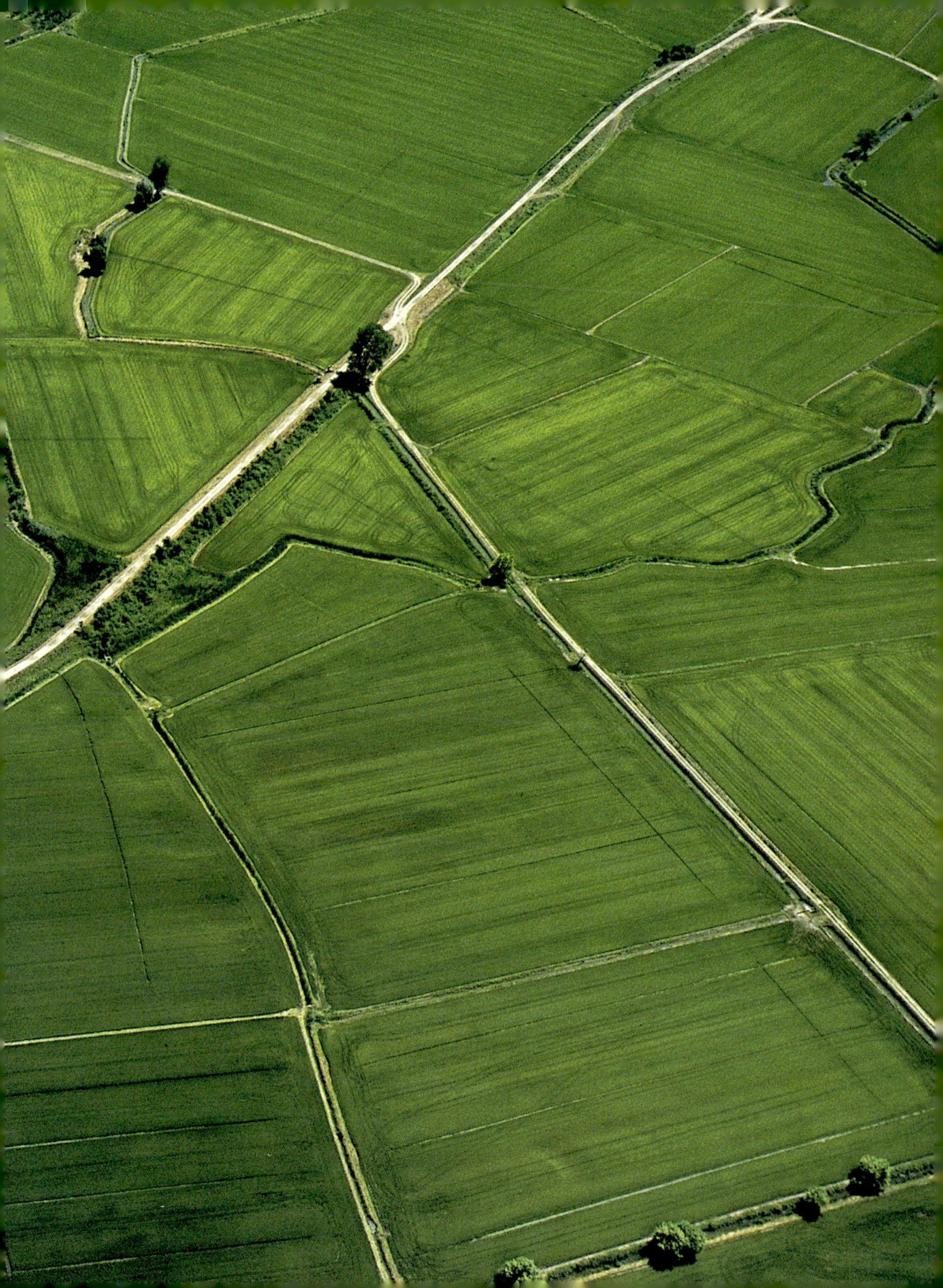

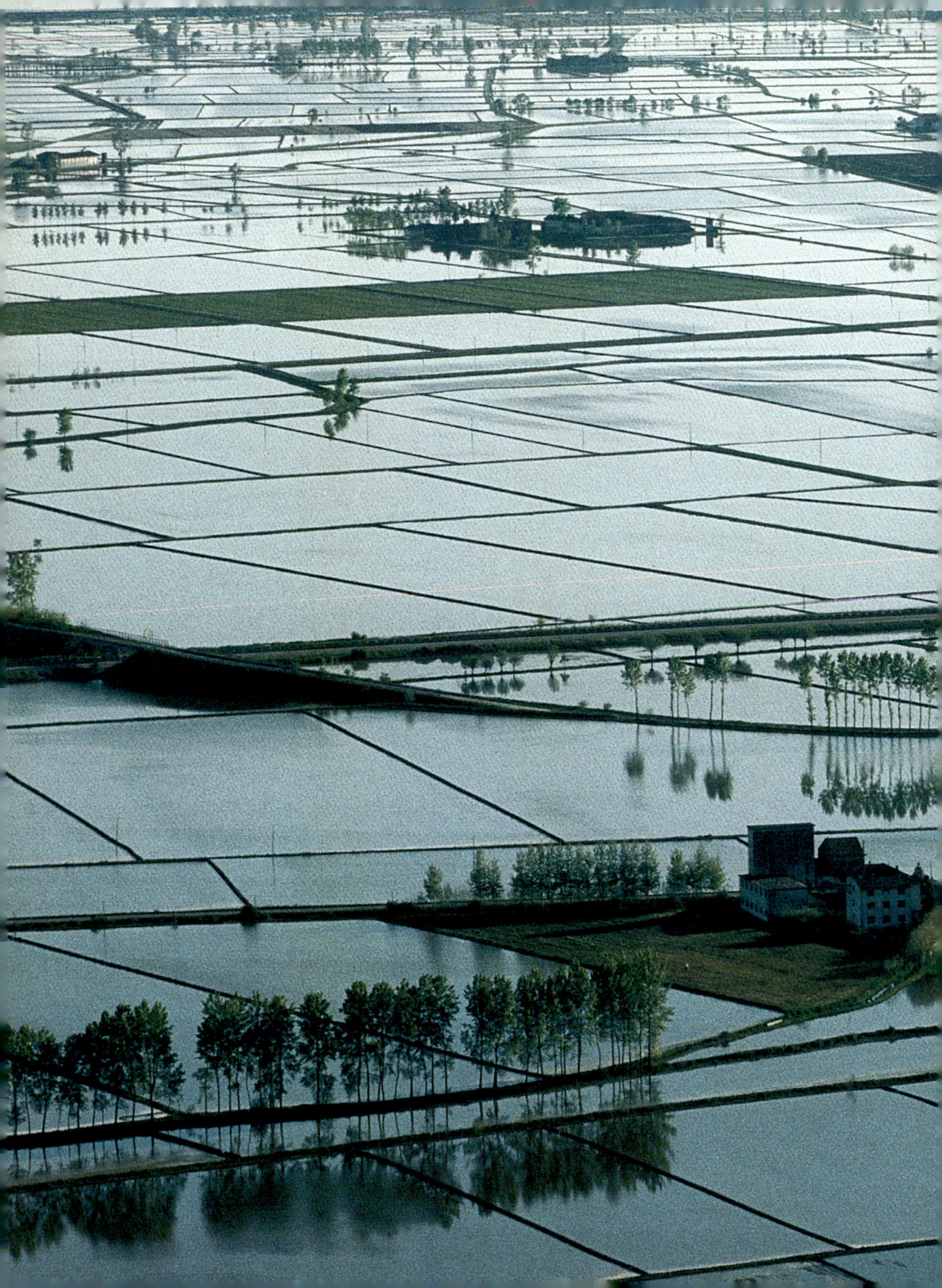

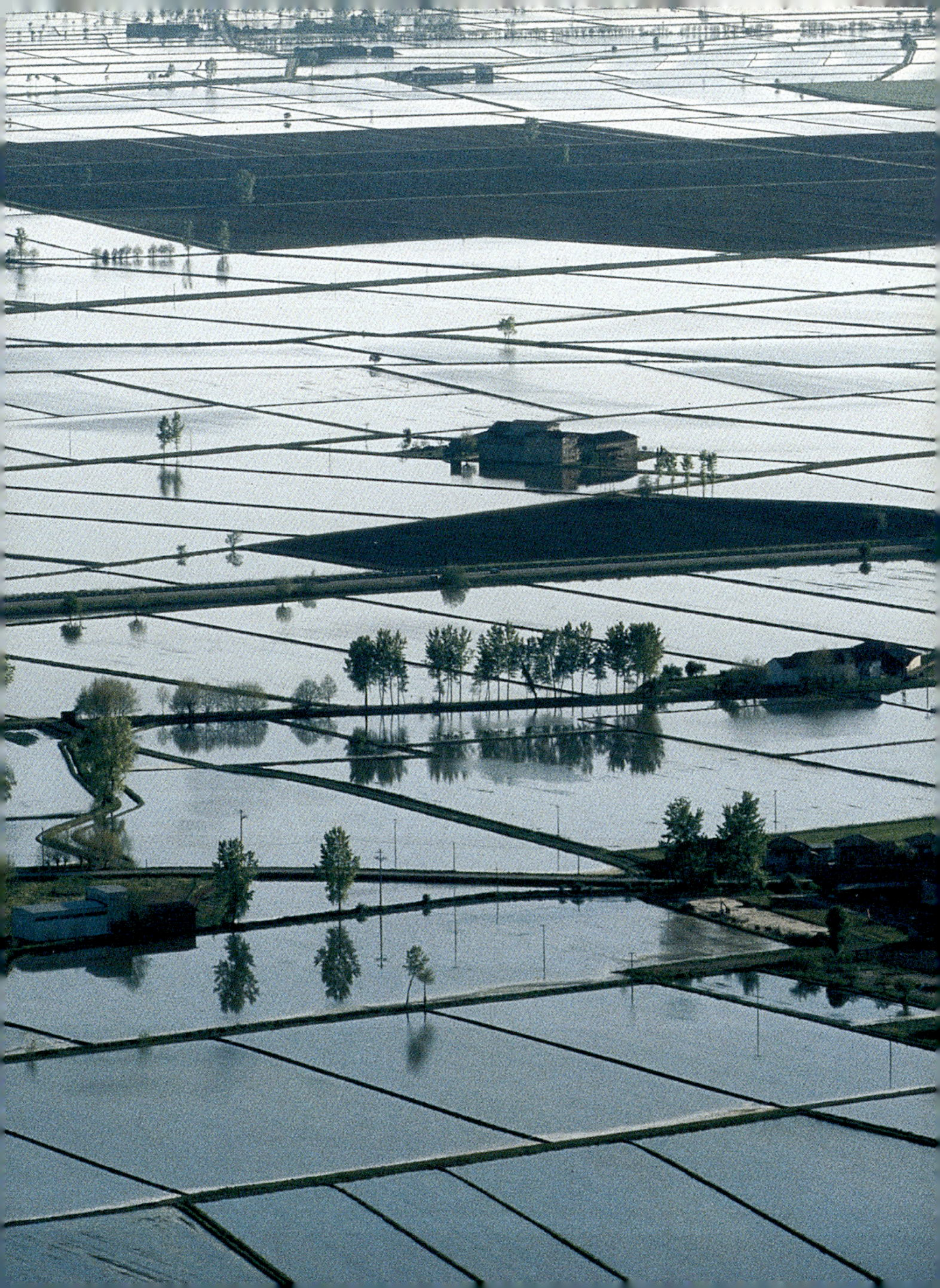

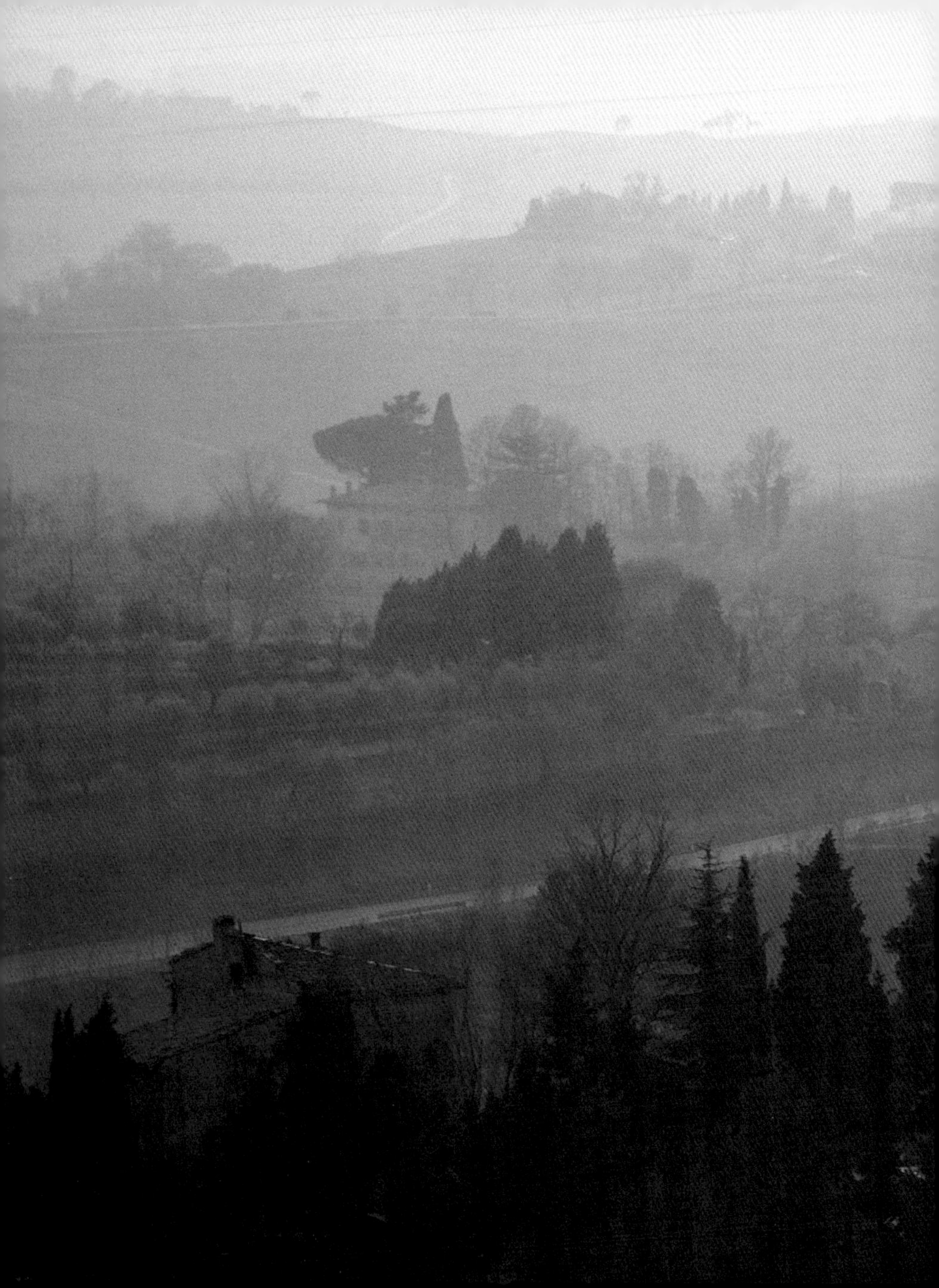

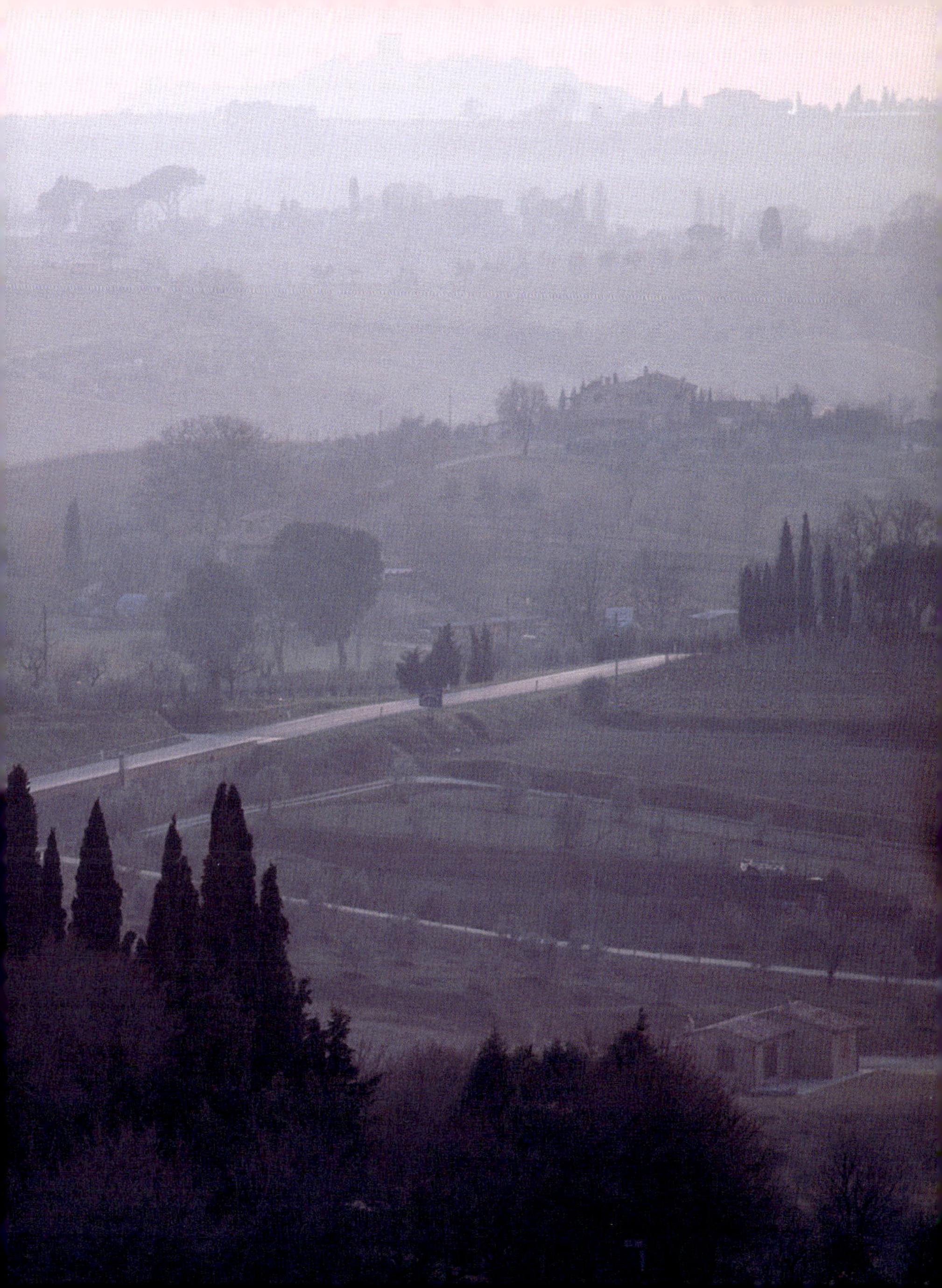

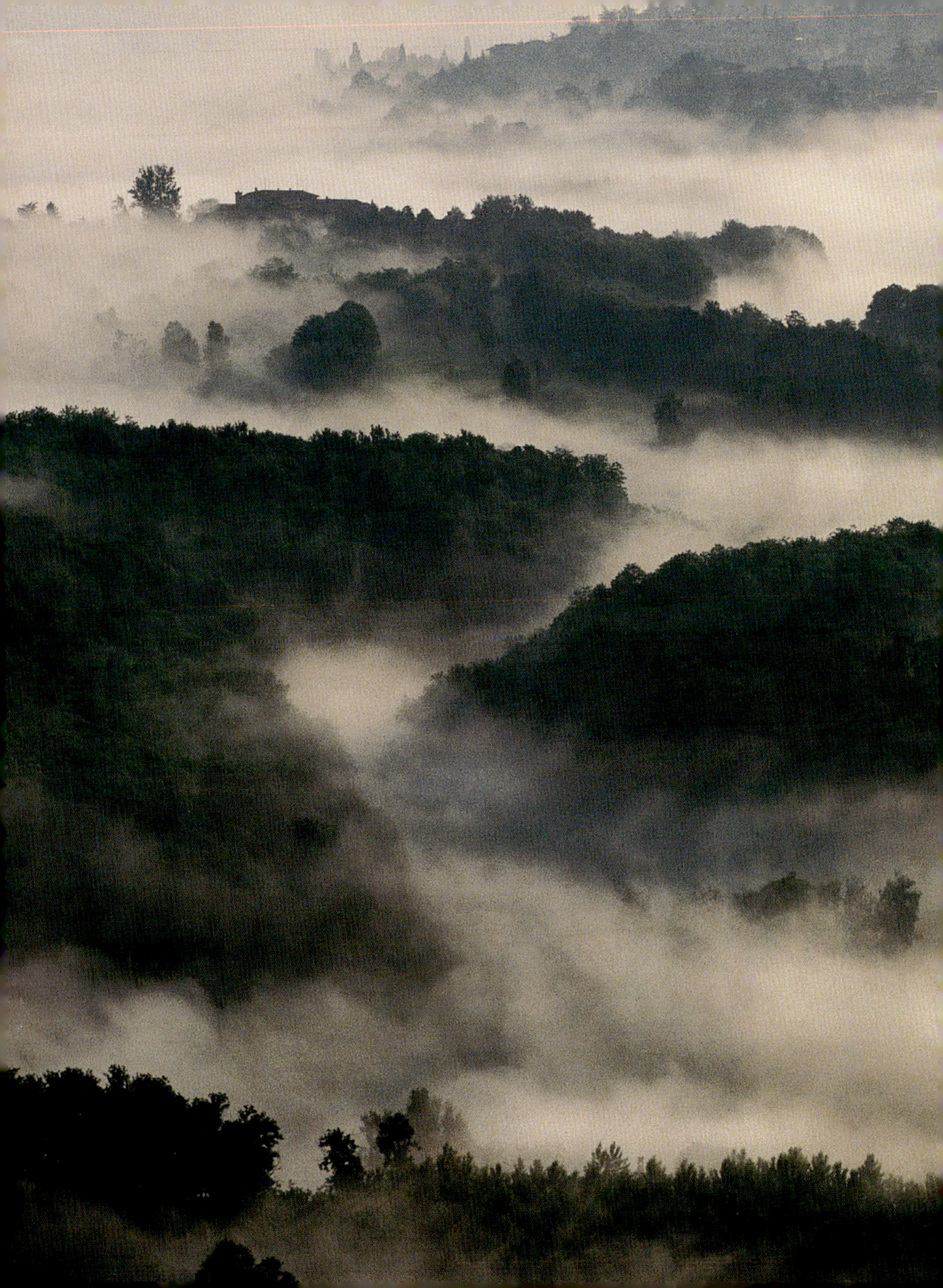

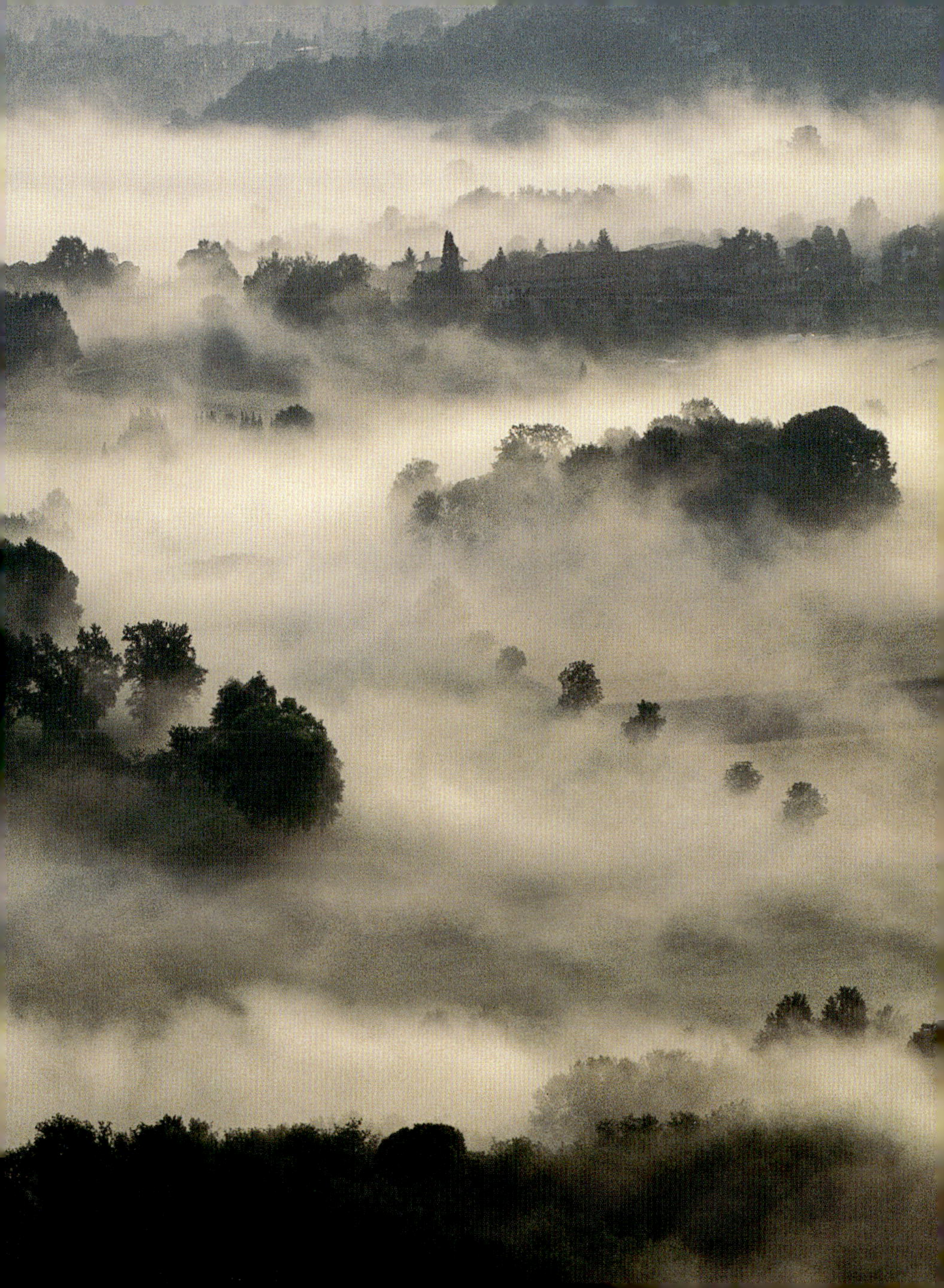

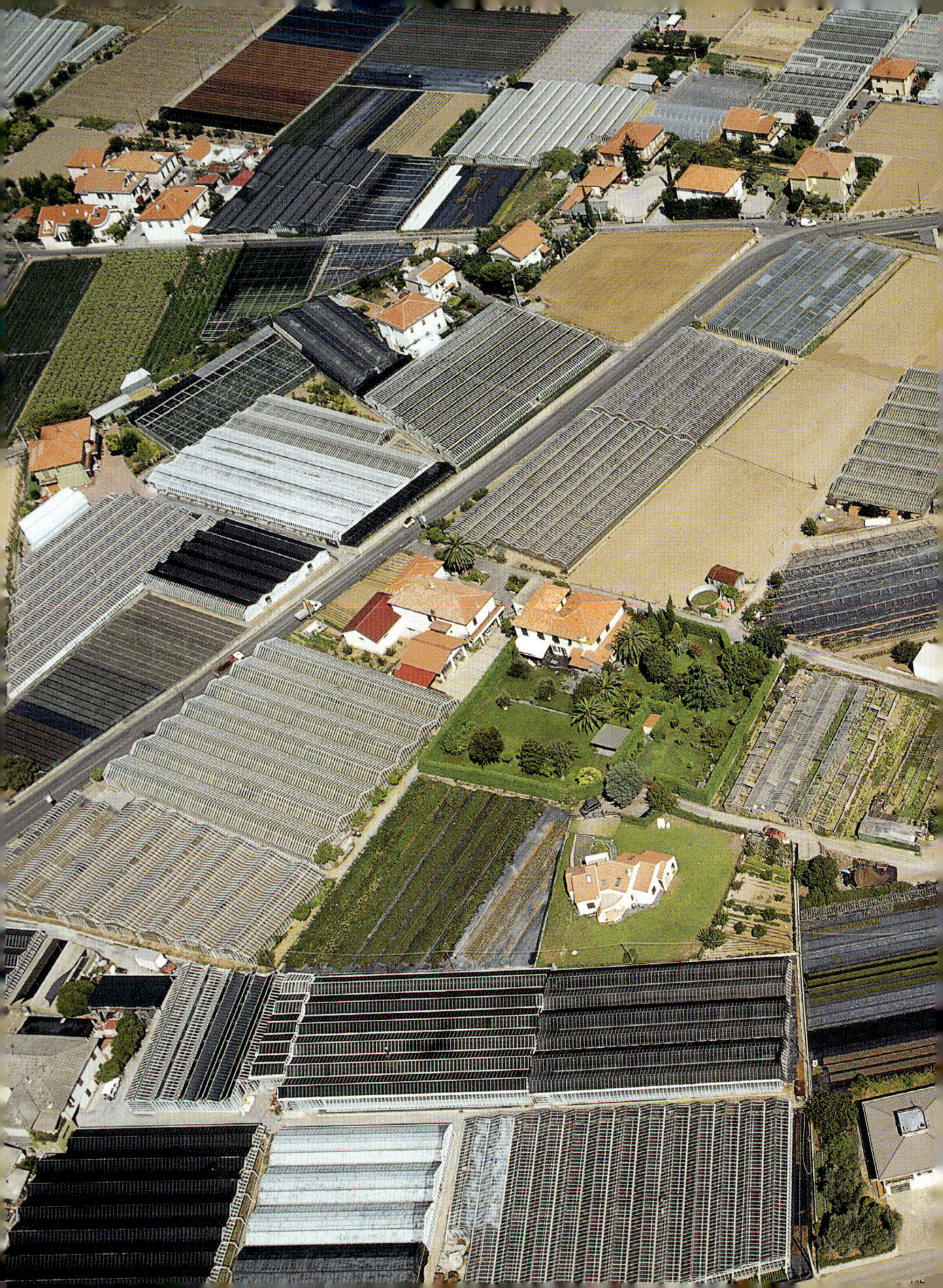

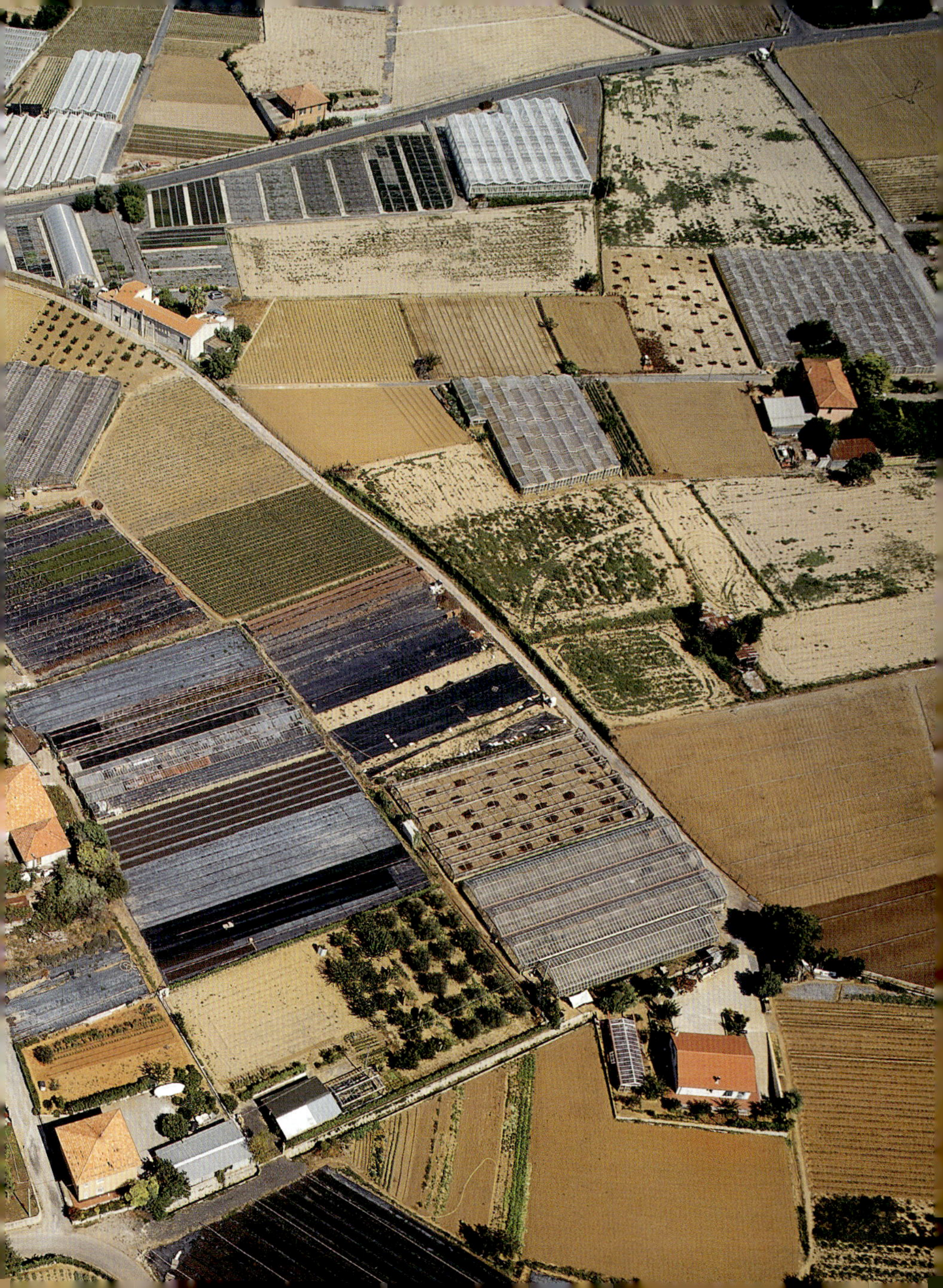

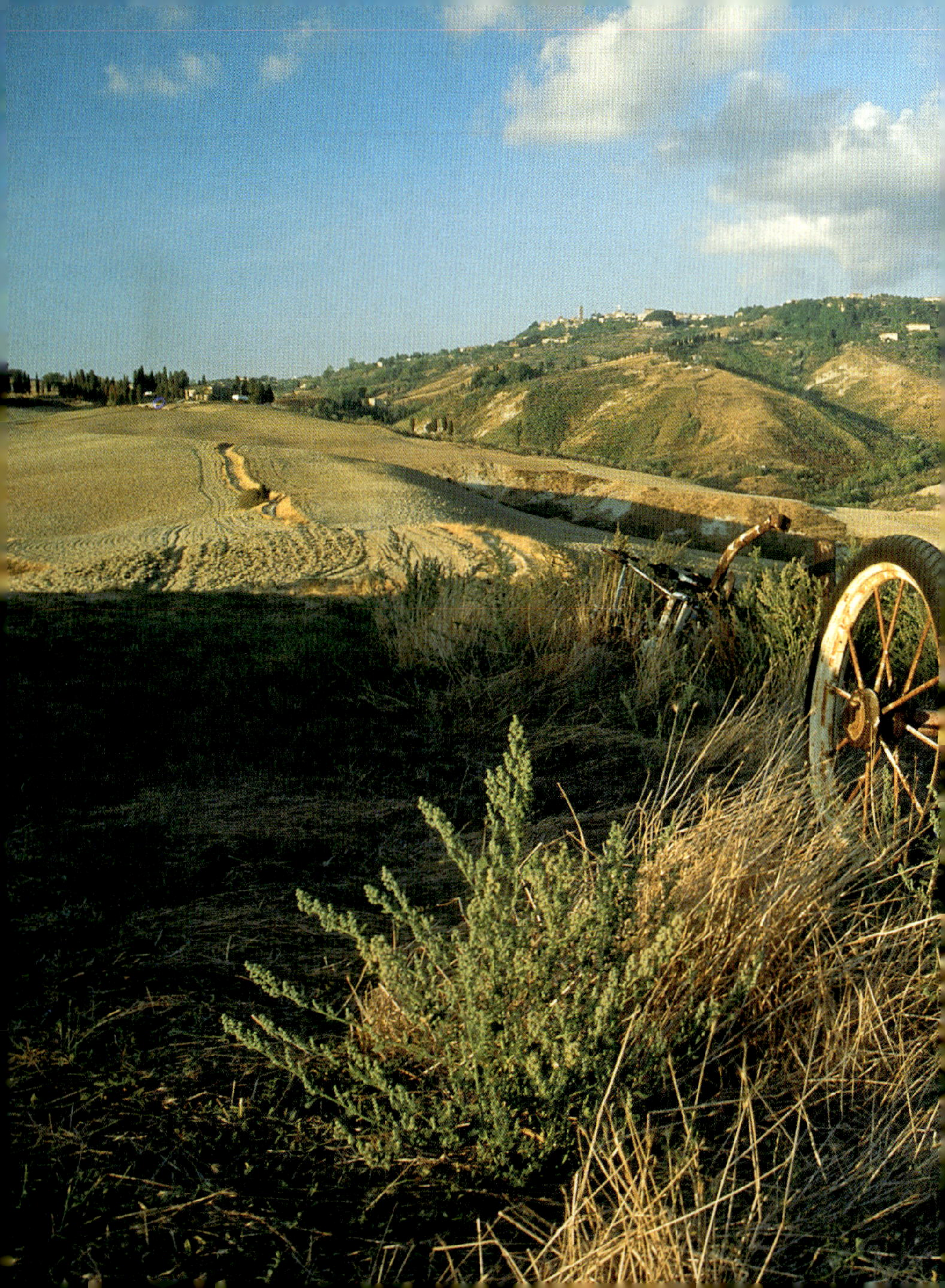

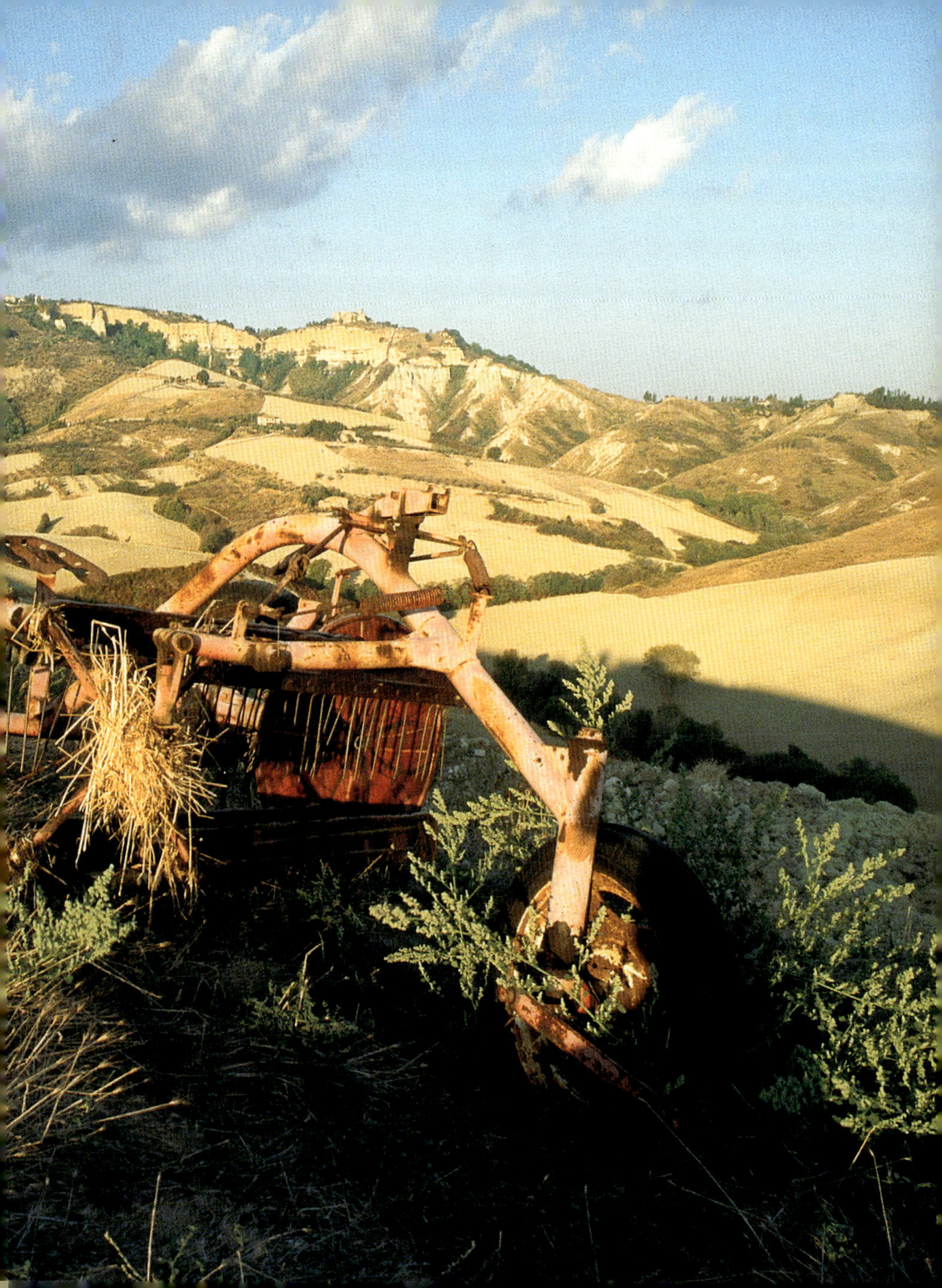

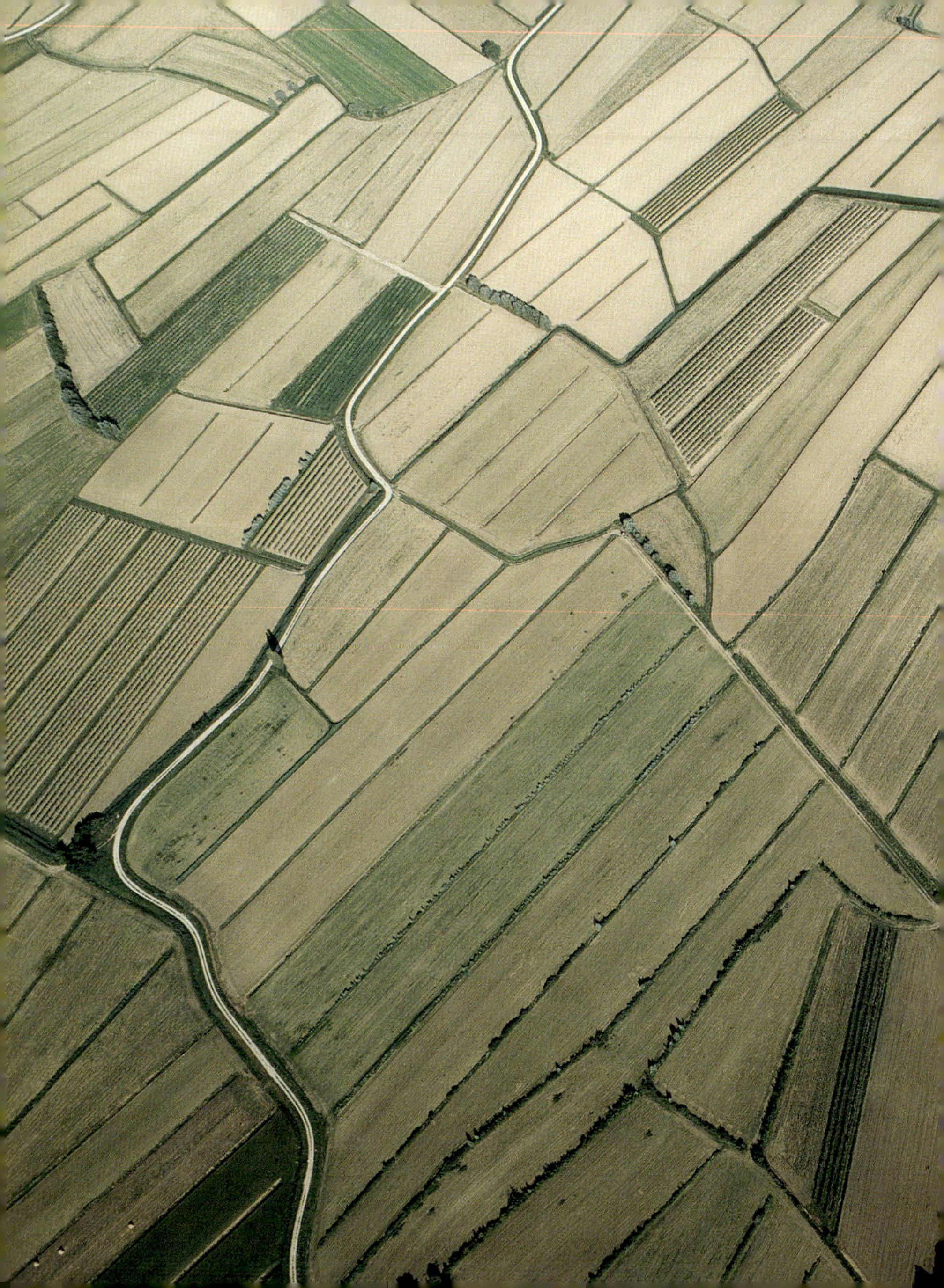

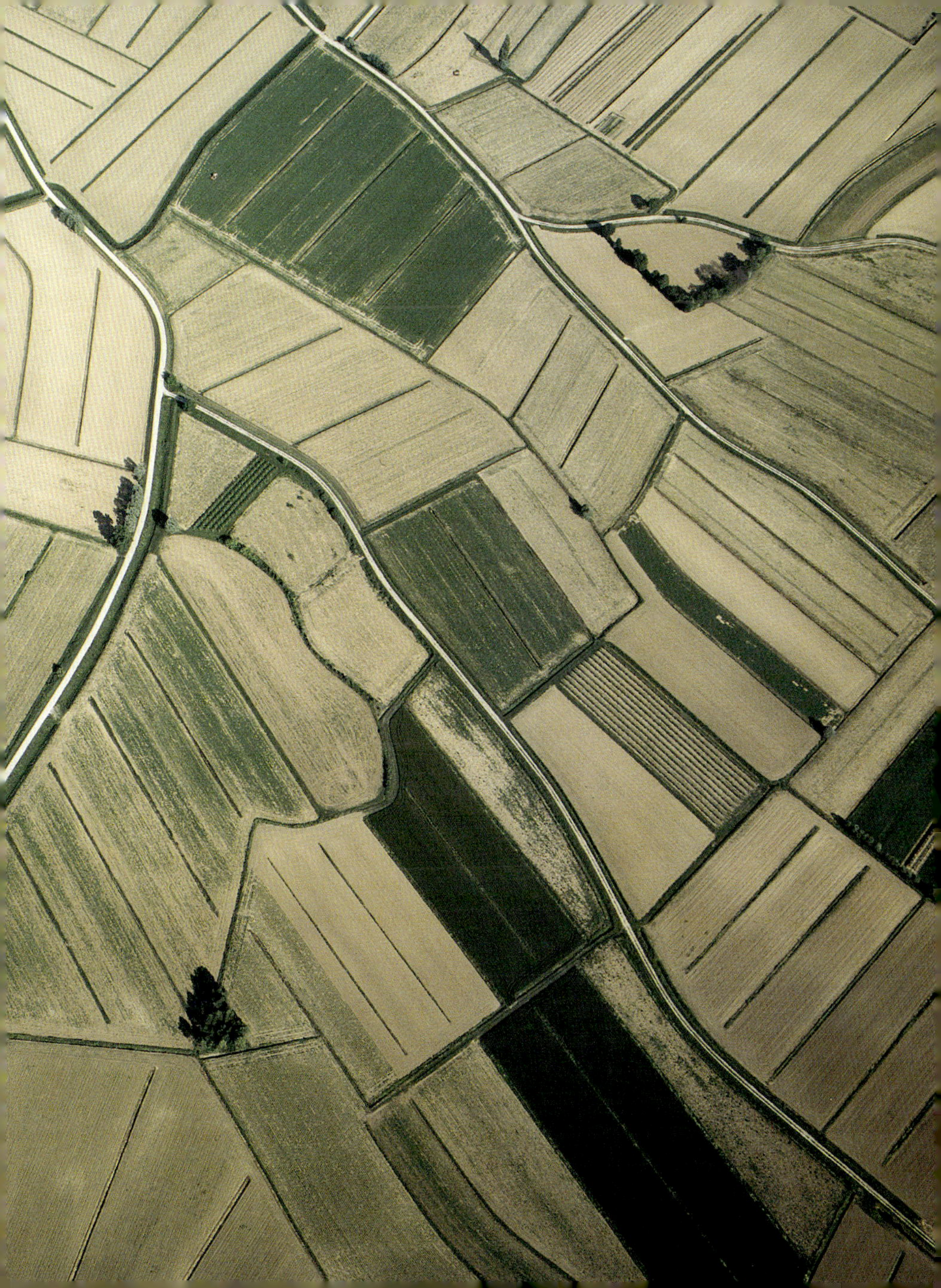

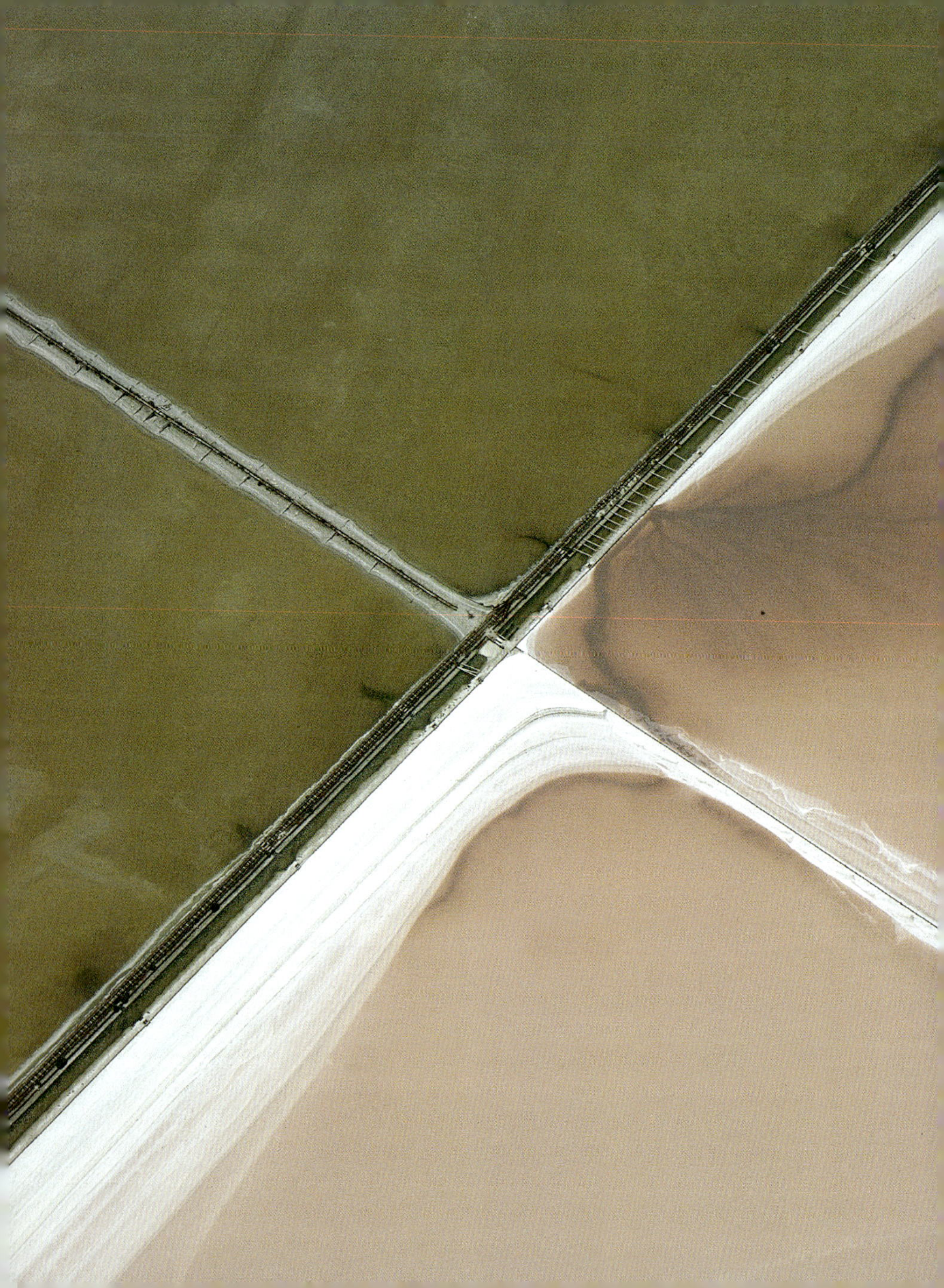

CHURCHES AND MONASTERIES

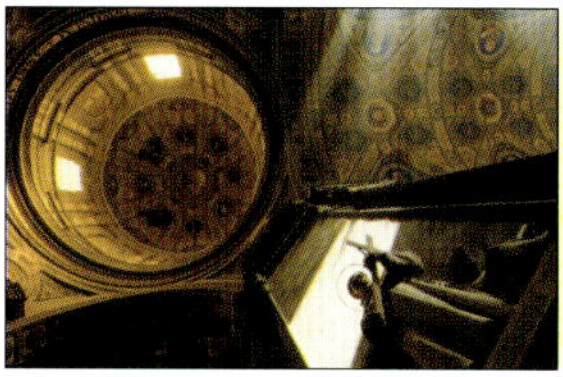

Two striking pictures of the inside of Carpi Cathedral, in Emilia-Romagna. The church was started in 1514 and completed in the 18th century. It presents a Baroque façade and Renaissance interior, including a high dome and altars decorated by stucco frontals and altarpieces. In the apse is kept an interesting 16th-century sculpture of Our Lady of the Assumption, carved in cedarwood *(pp. 193, 194-195)*.

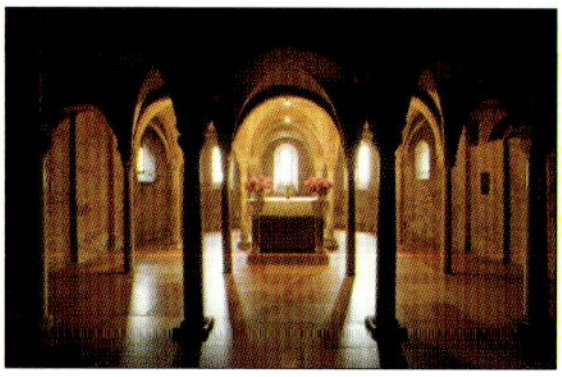

The crypt of Nonantola Abbey is one of the Romanesque architecture's finest. It rests on sixty-four columns with 8th- and 9th- century capitals. King Astolfo founded the Benedictine monastery in 752 *(pp. 196-197)*.

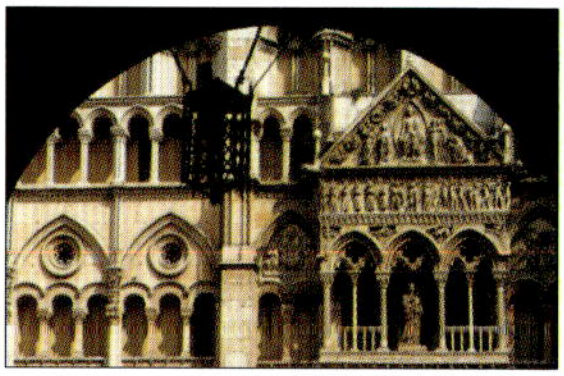

The forecourt and loggia of Ferrara Cathedral's façade, one of the most important medieval monument of the town, in Romanesque style. The bas-reliefs on the tympanum depict the Last Judgement *(pp. 198-199)*.

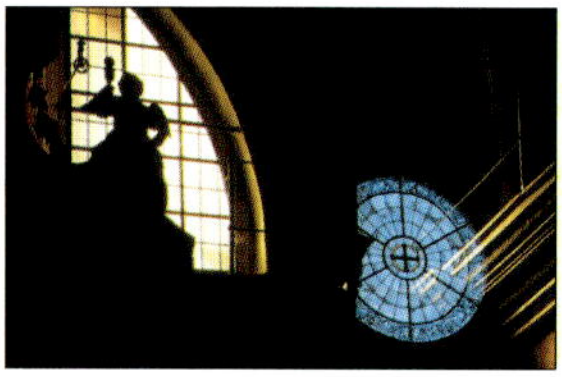

The interior of the Duomo in Alba takes in rays of sun from the outside. Built in Gothic style at the end of the 15th century, restored in the 19th, it still preserves a wood-carved 16th-century choir *(pp. 200-201)*.

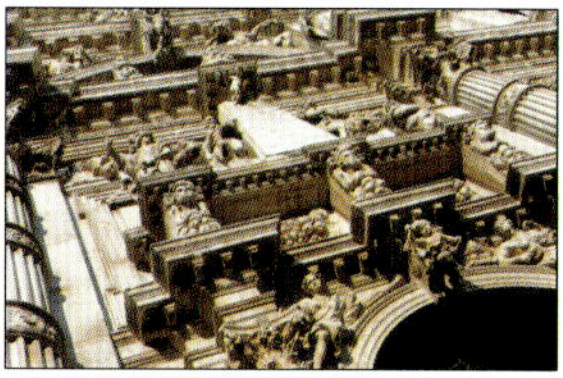

The imposing façade of the 17th-century Church of San Moisè, Venice. Finished in 1688 and lavishly decorated with statues and busts, it is an example of the sumptuous Venetian Baroque art *(pp. 202-203)*.

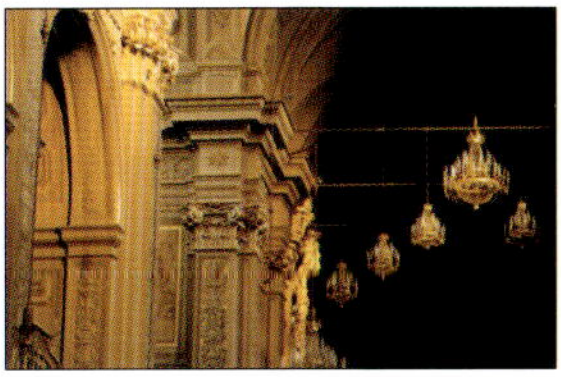

THE MONUMENTAL INTERIOR of the medieval Cathedral of Ferrara. It presents three naves divided by huge pillars; it was renewed during the 18th century and decorated at the end of the 19th century *(pp. 204-205)*.

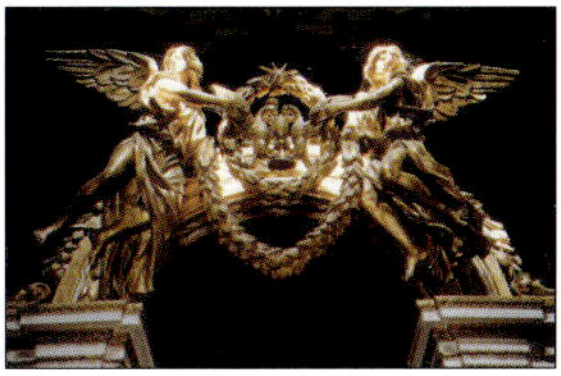

ONE OF THE GILT STUCCOWORKS inside the church of Camaldoli hermitage. Founded in the 11th century, it was refurbished in Baroque style and was the first seat of the Camaldolese order *(pp. 206-207)*.

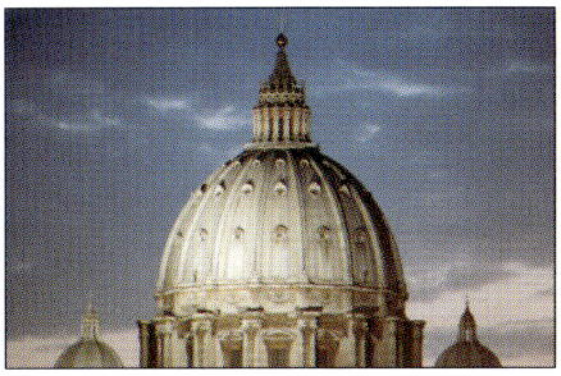

SAN PETER'S IN ROME is the largest cathedral ever built in the world. It was erected on the spot where the first apostle's grave was. The dome – 132.5 metres high – was designed by Michelangelo *(pp. 208-209)*.

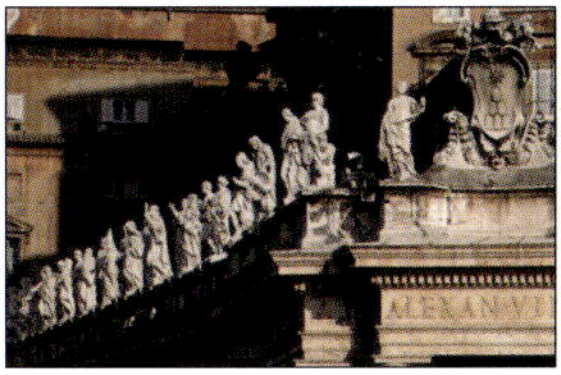

SOME OF THE ONE HUNDRED AND FORTY STATUES of saints crowning Piazza San Pietro's colonnade in Rome. Designed by Gian Lorenzo Bernini, the two hemicycles almost embrace the Vatican basilica *(pp. 210-211)*.

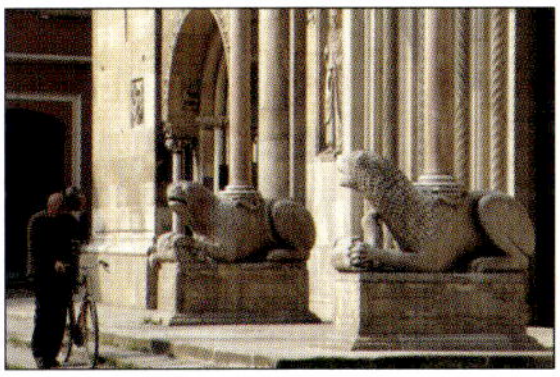

THE DUOMO OF FIDENZA is regarded as one of the finest examples of Romanesque art in the Po Valley. It boasts a façade with three lavishly adorned portals, flanked by two towers *(pp. 212-213)*.

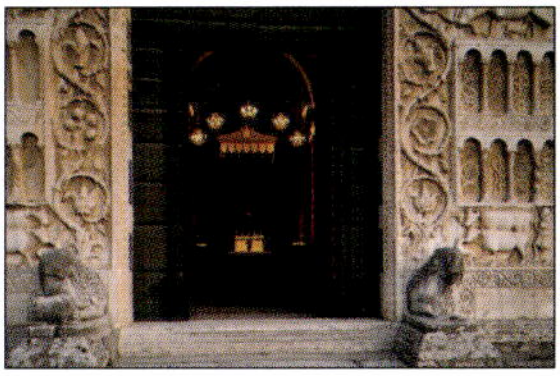

THE PORTAL OF SAINT PETER'S CHURCH, Spoleto, from which the illuminated interior can be seen. The 5th-century church was enlarged in the 12th century; bas-reliefs adorn its façade *(pp. 214-215)*.

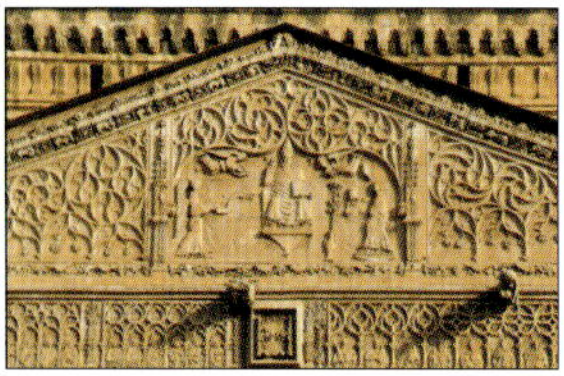

THE CATALAN GOTHIC PORTICO OF PALERMO Cathedral, built in 1430. Its three pointed arches are surmounted by a tympanum on which religious scenes and the town's coat of arms are sculpted *(pp. 216-217)*.

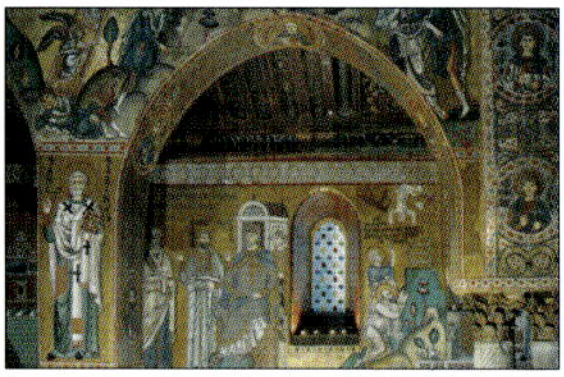

SOME OF THE GILT-BACKGROUND MOSAICS in the Cappella Palatina, Palermo, representing Old and New Testament scenes This masterpiece of Norman art was founded by Ruggero II in 1132 *(pp. 218-219)*.

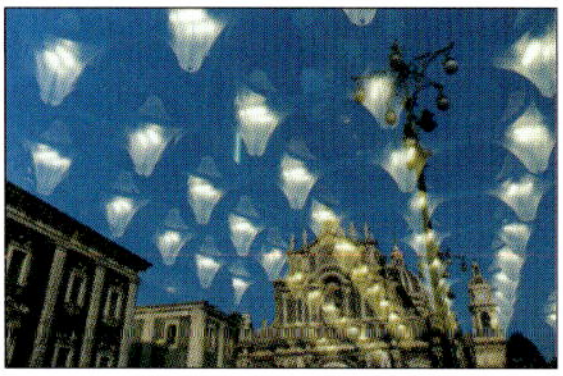

THE CATHEDRAL OF CATANIA seen through the window of a pizzeria in Piazza Duomo. The church retains its original Norman design, although the façade reveals a noticeable Baroque mark *(pp. 220-221)*.

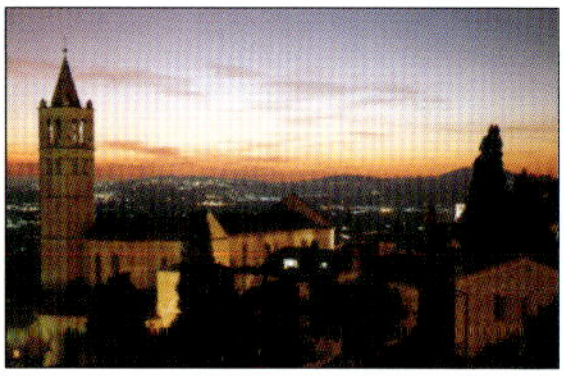

THE EXQUISITELY DESIGNED BASILICA OF SANTA CHIARA in Assisi, placed on a spur of Mount Subasio. Its plain Gothic lines evoke an intense mystical feeling *(pp. 222-223)*.

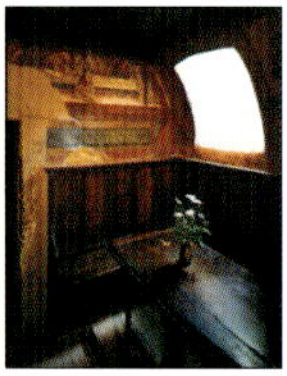

THE EREMO DELLE CARCERI IN ASSISI, immersed in the depth of an oak and ilex wood, was Saint Francis' place of seclusion, prayer and meditation. In 1400 Saint Bernardino da Siena built a small convent there *(p. 224)*.

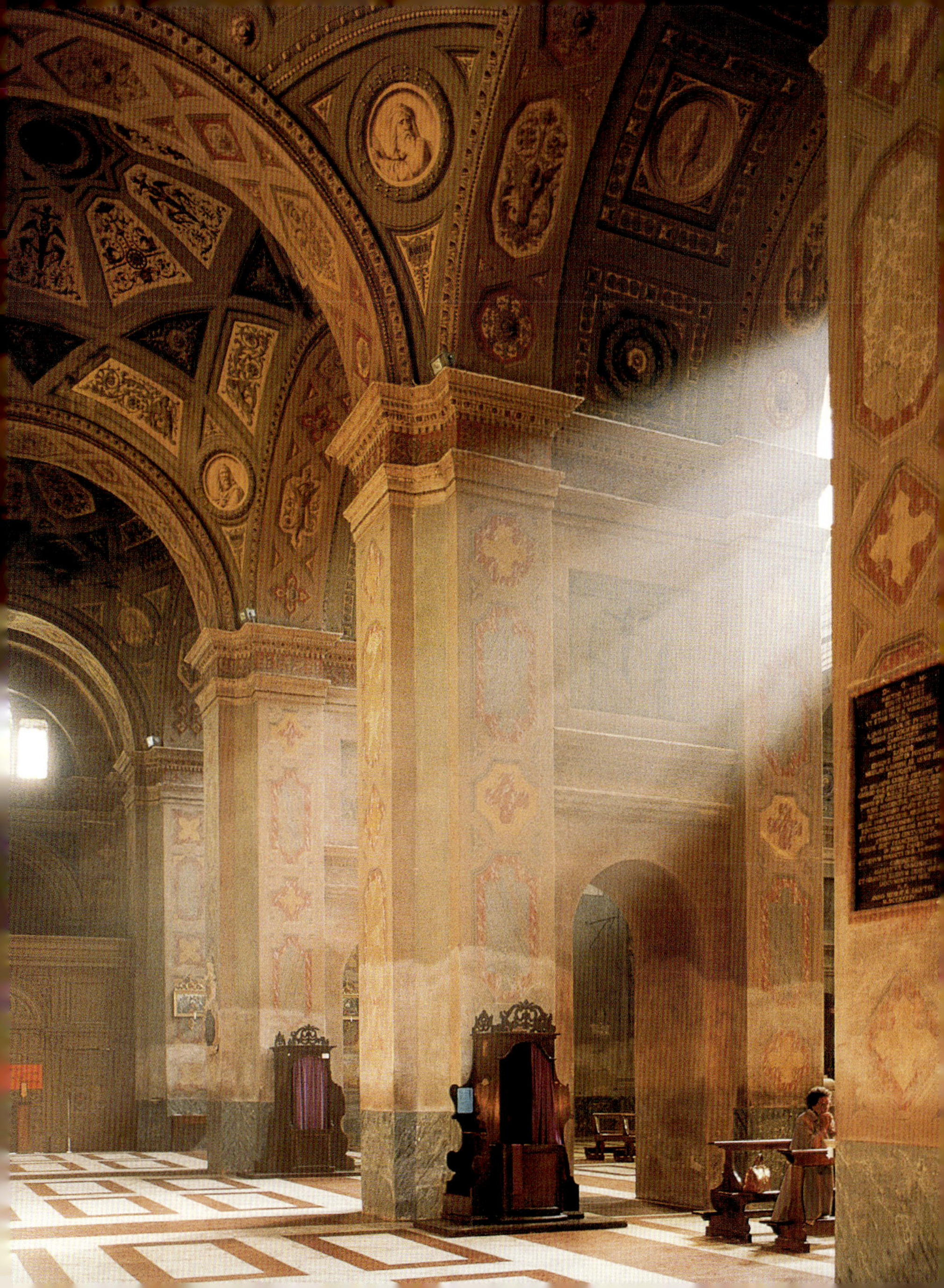

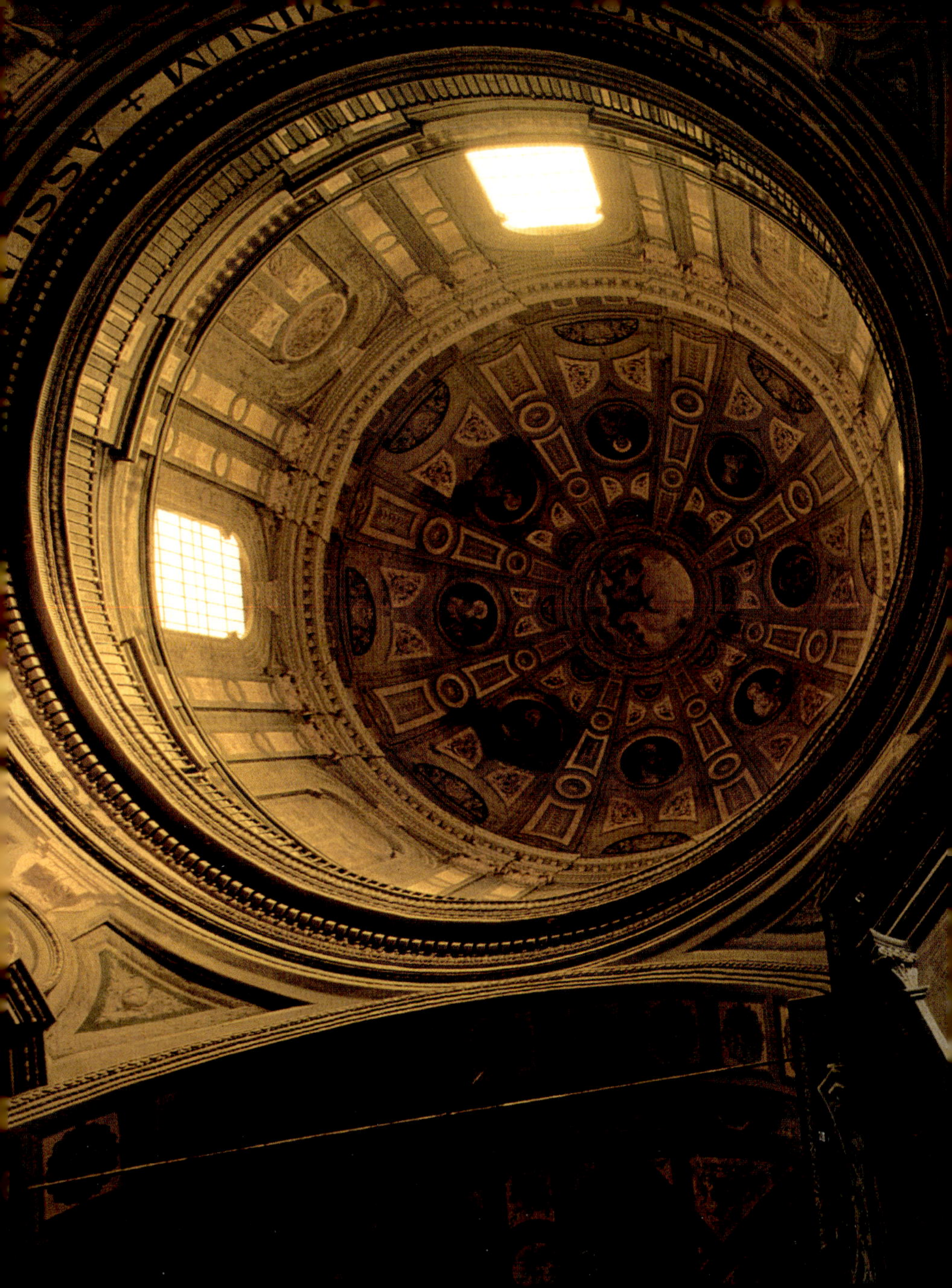

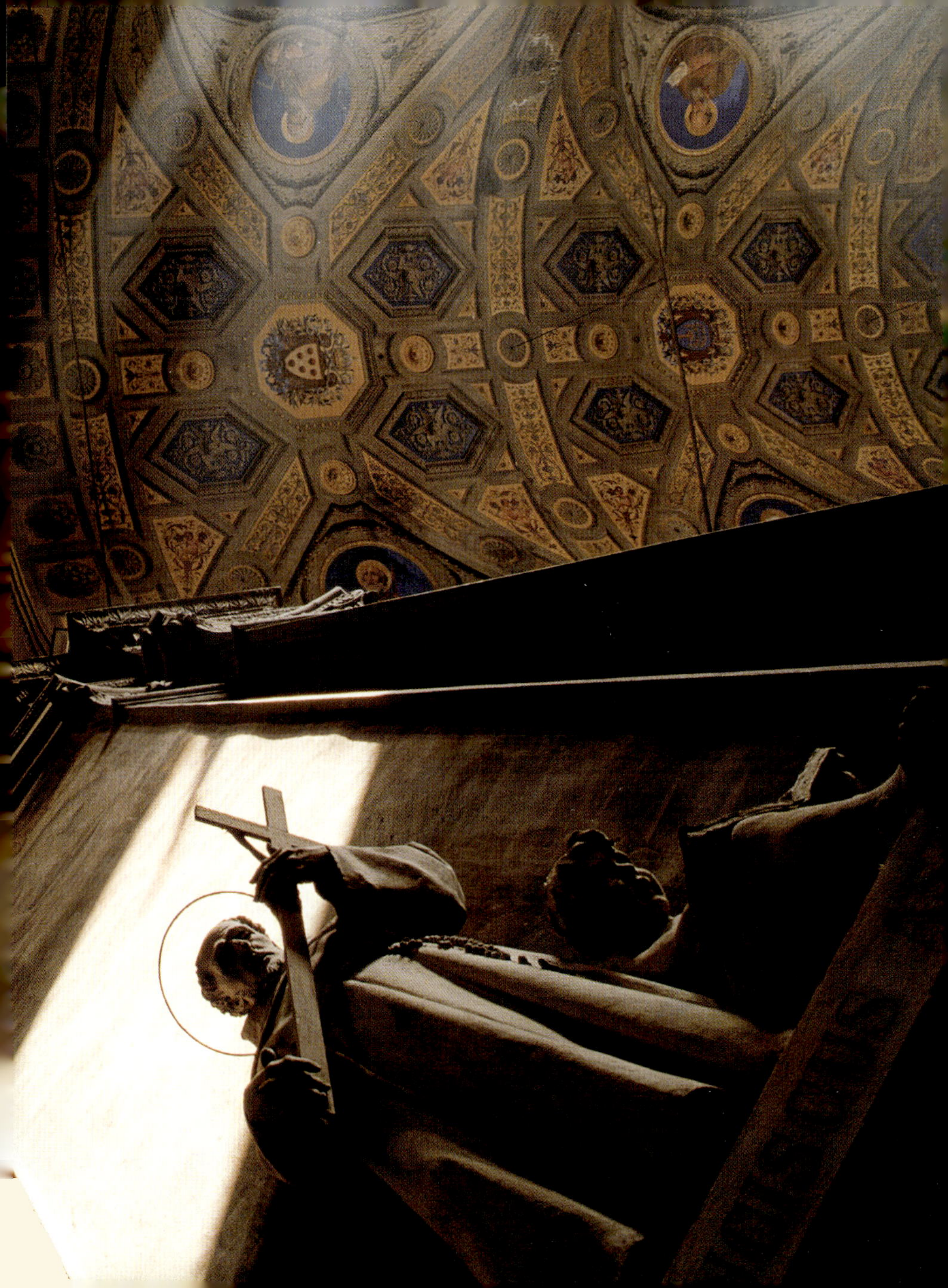

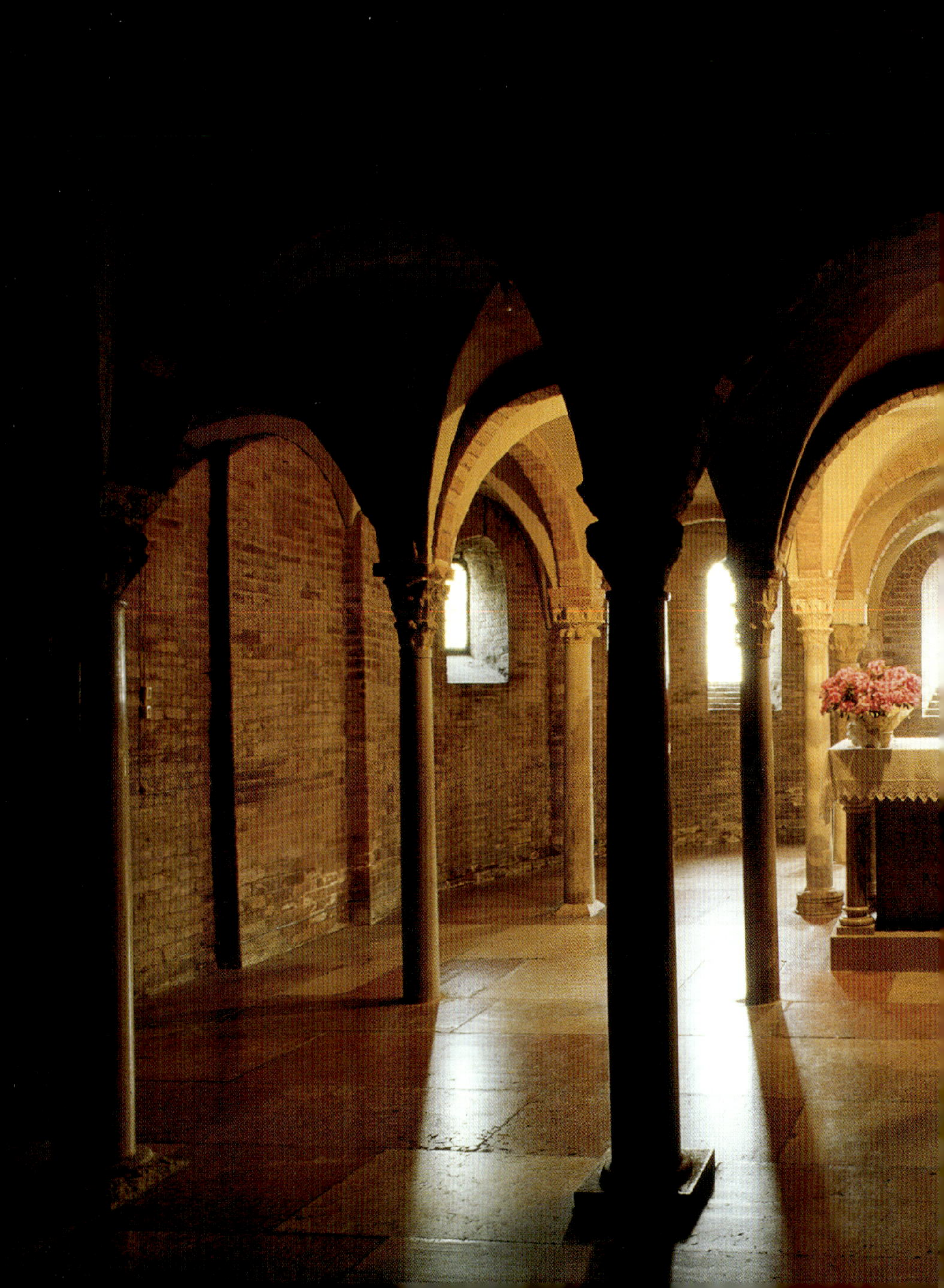

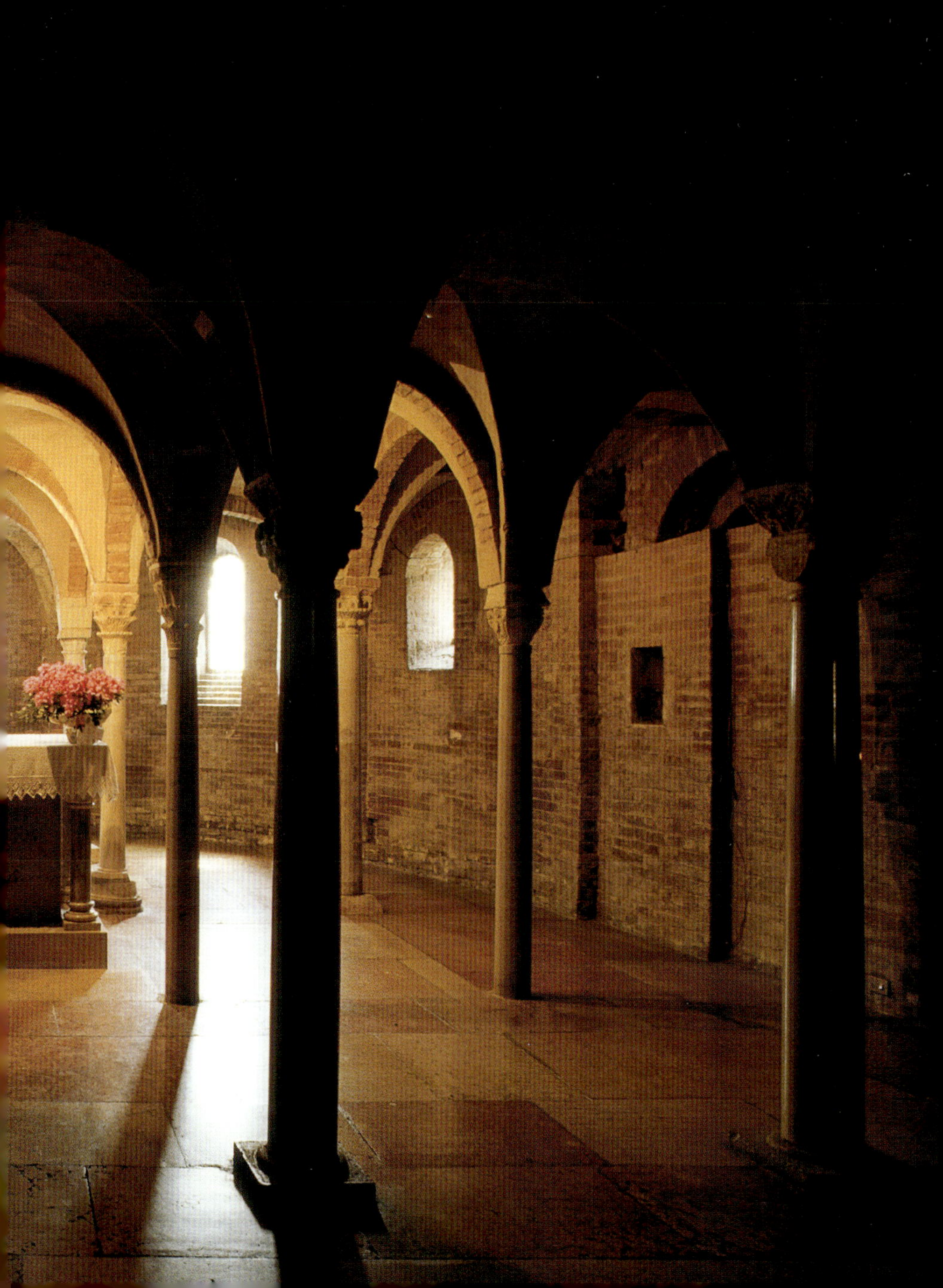

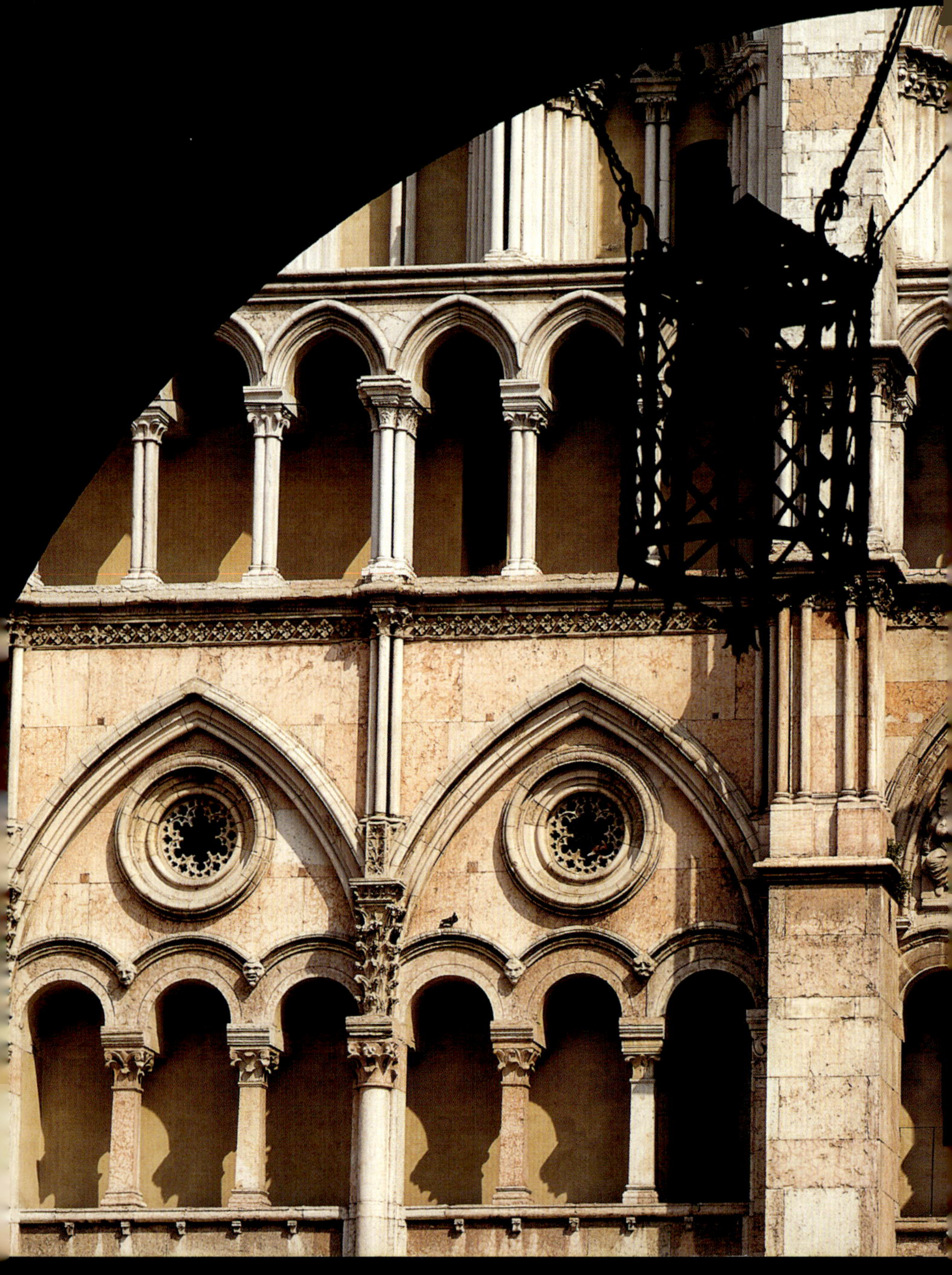

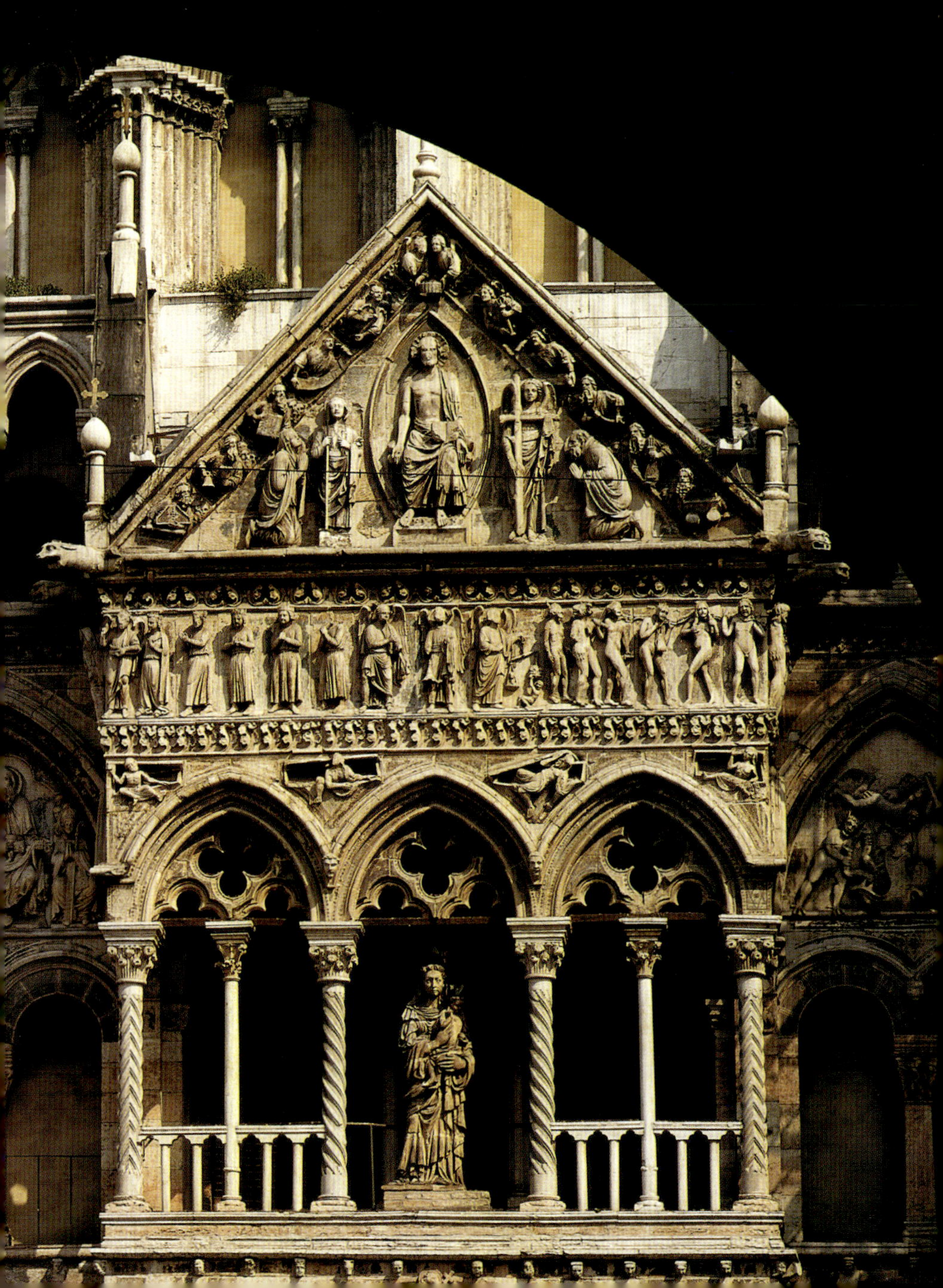

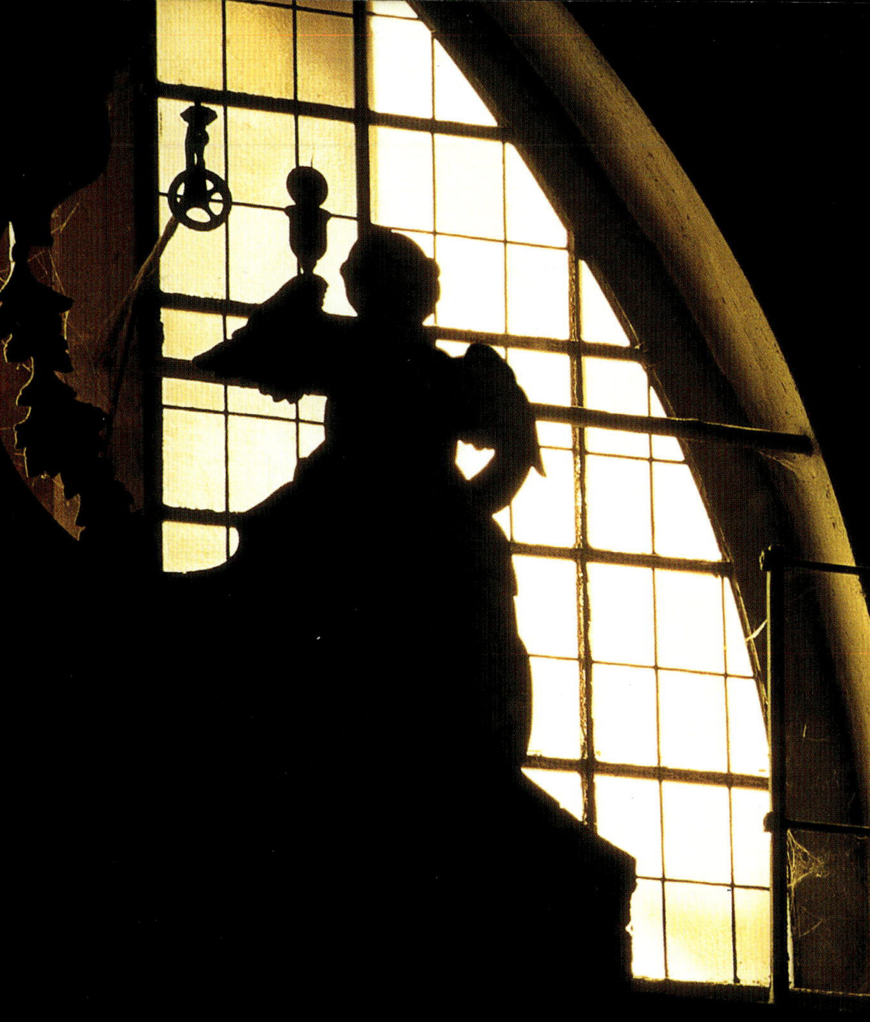

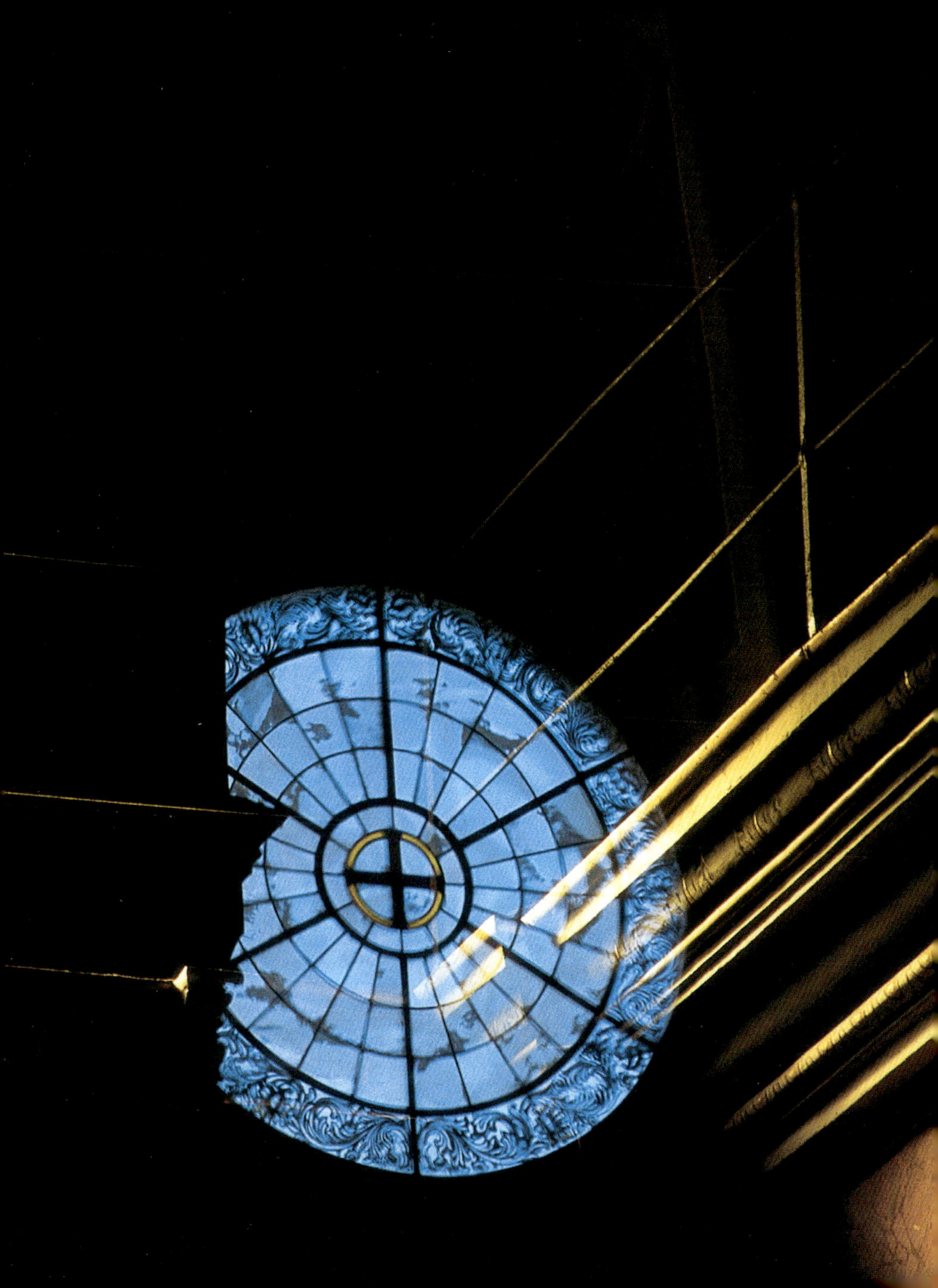

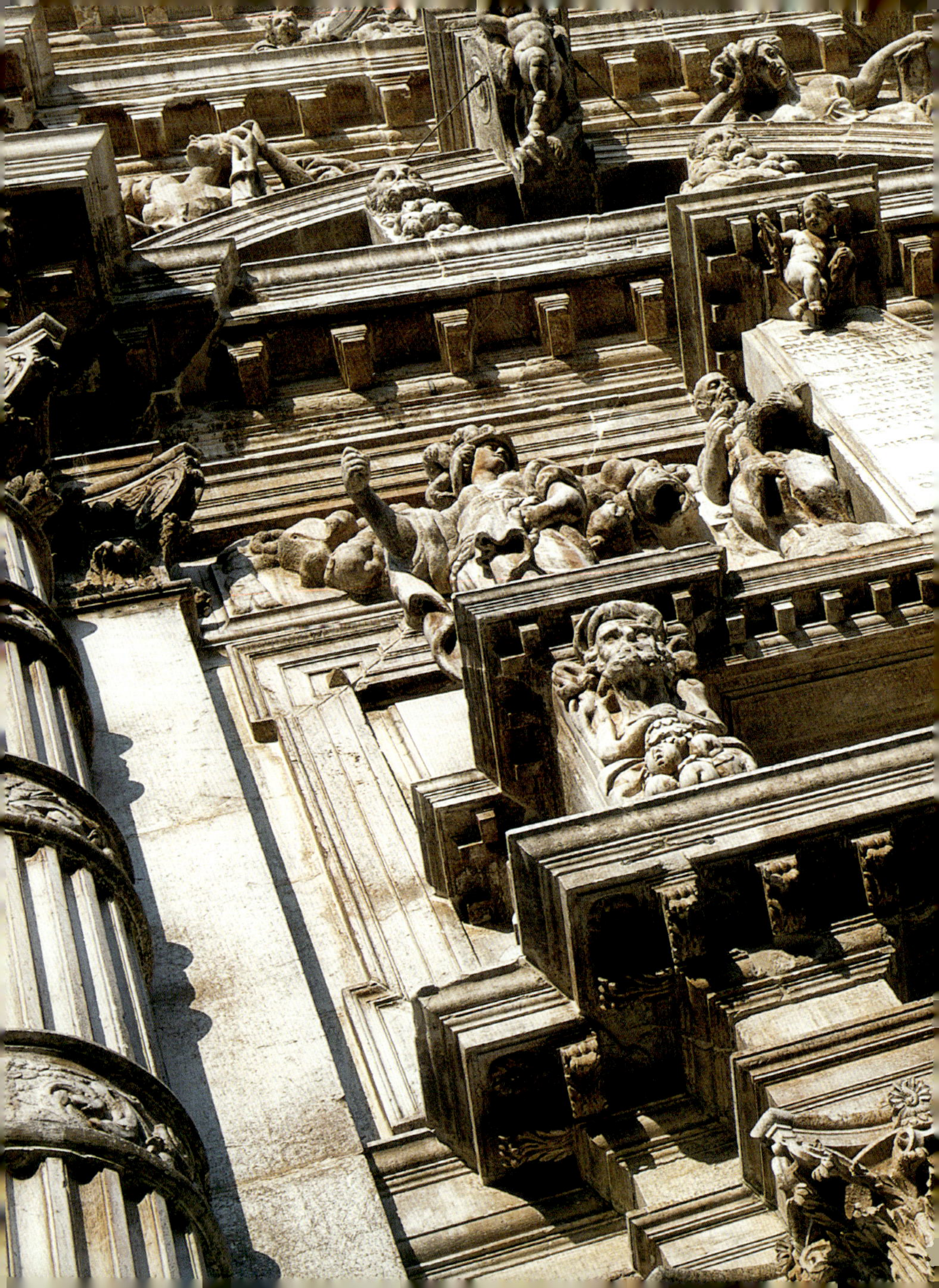

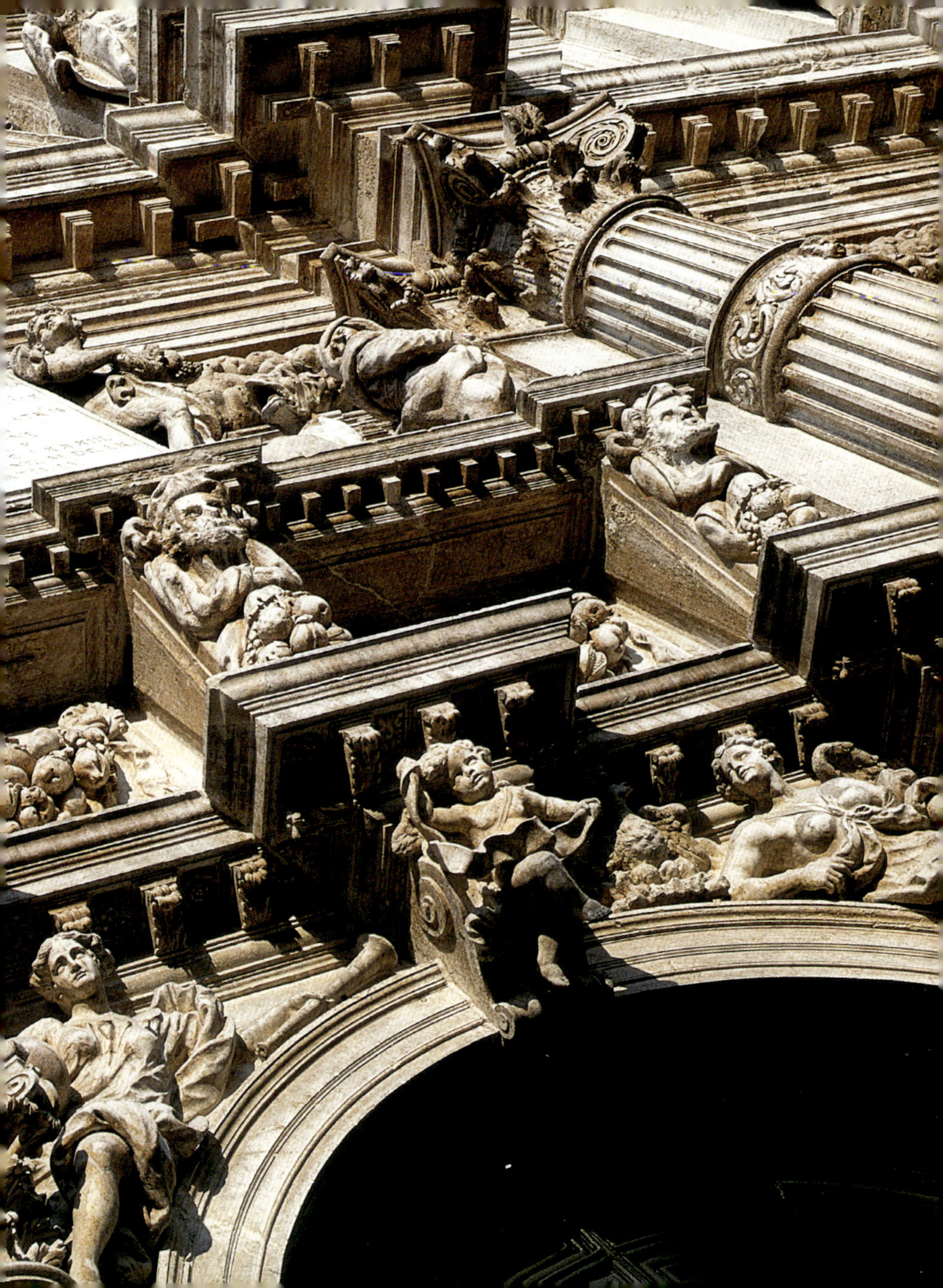

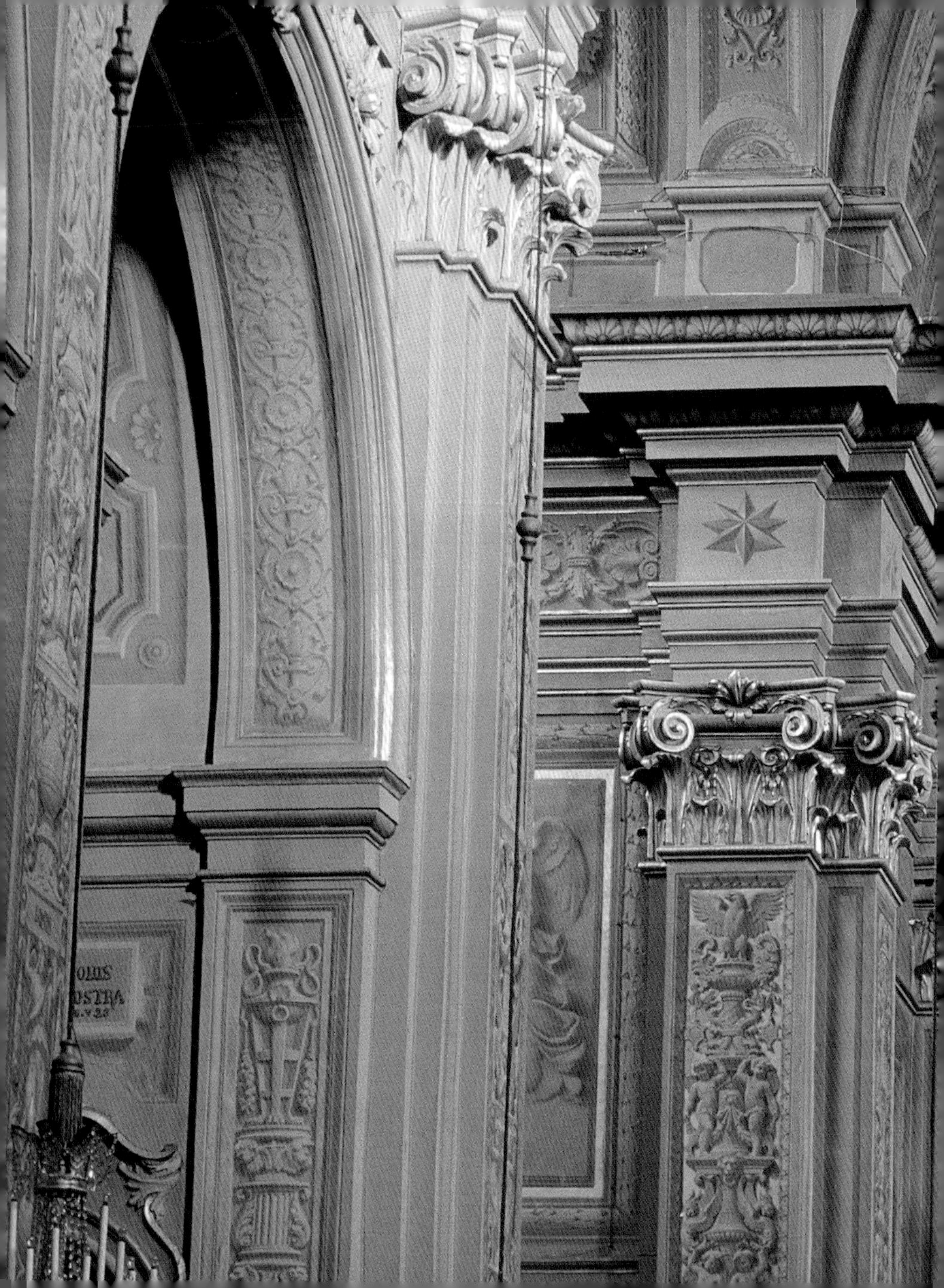

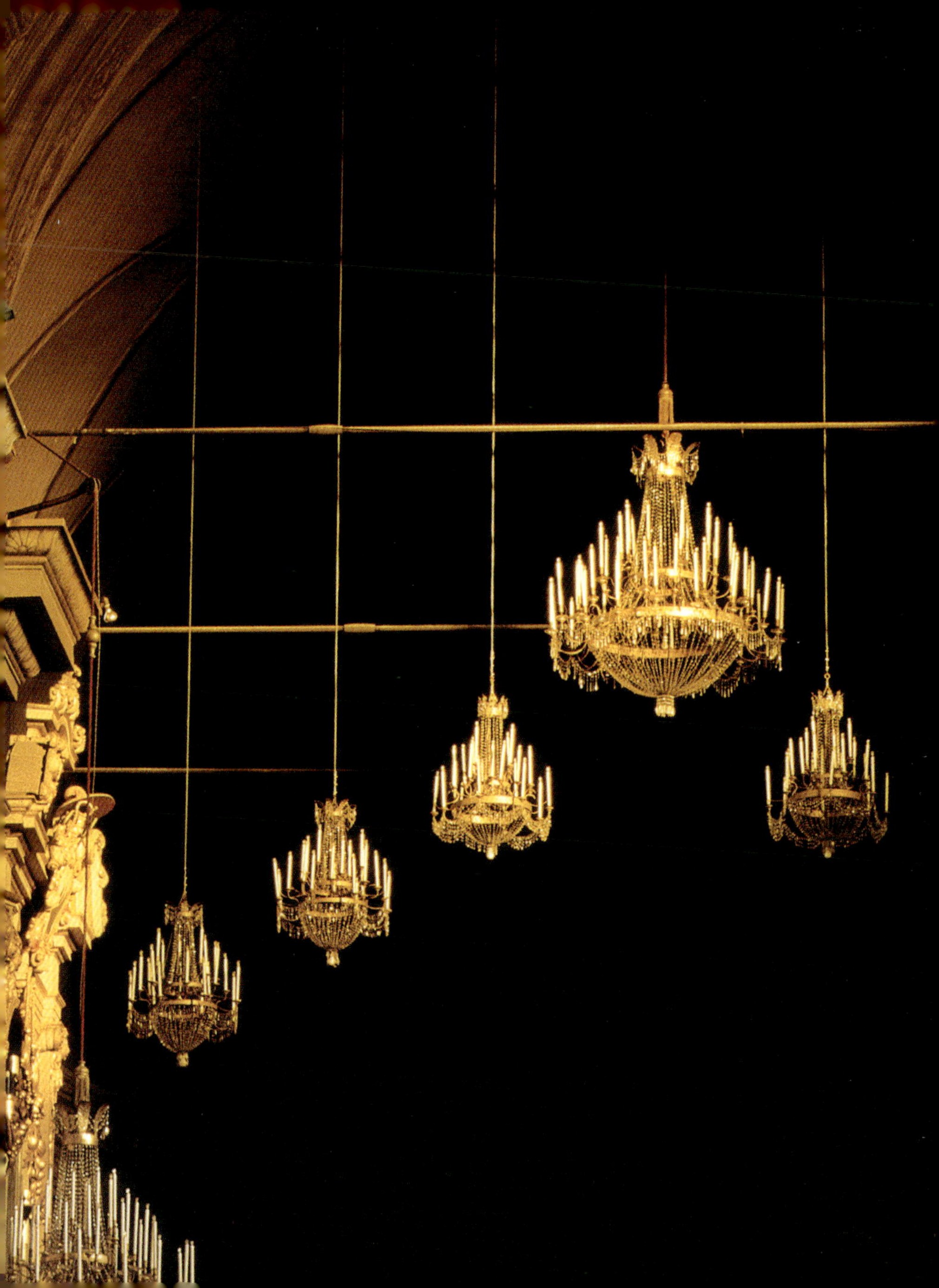

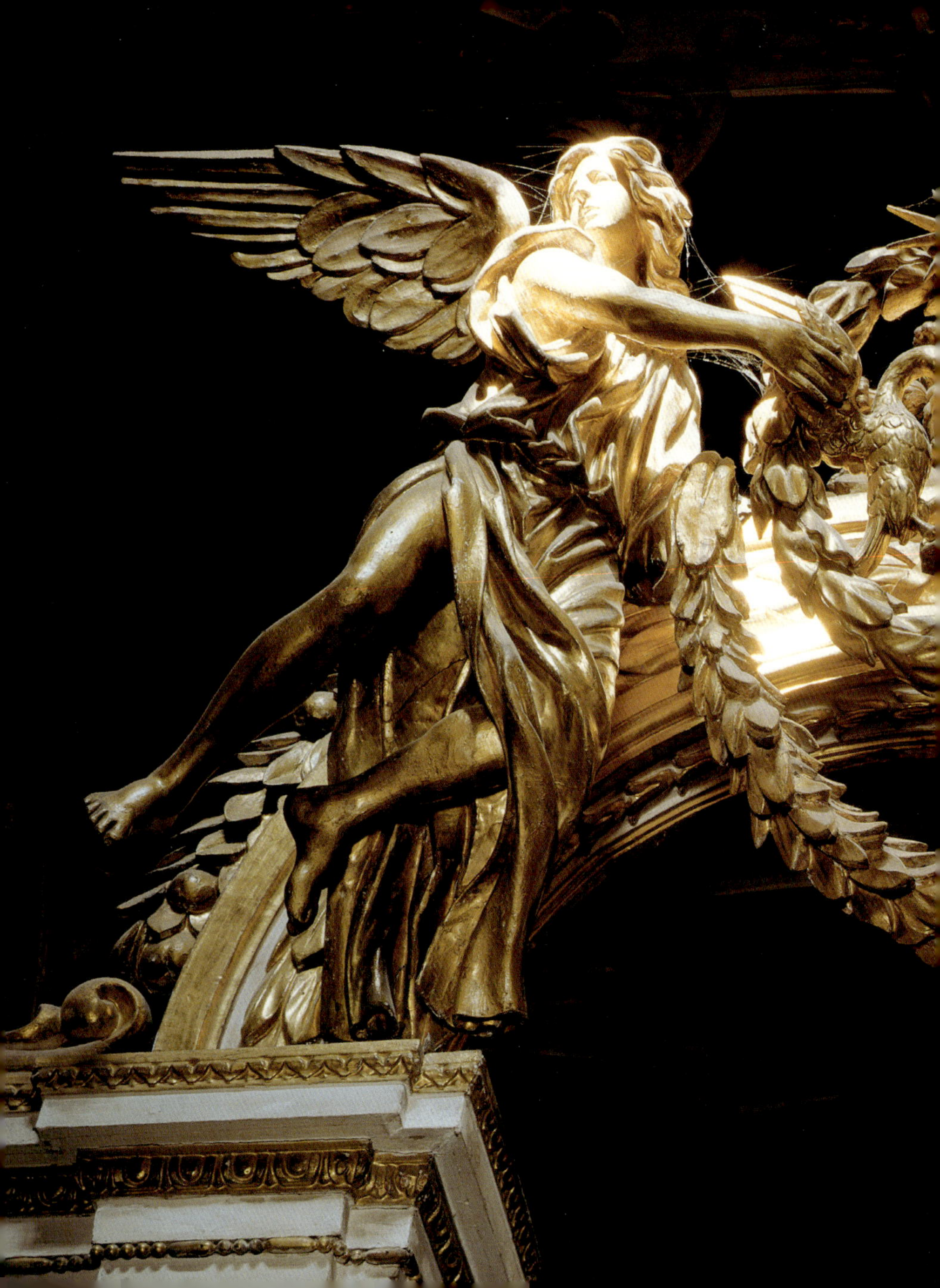

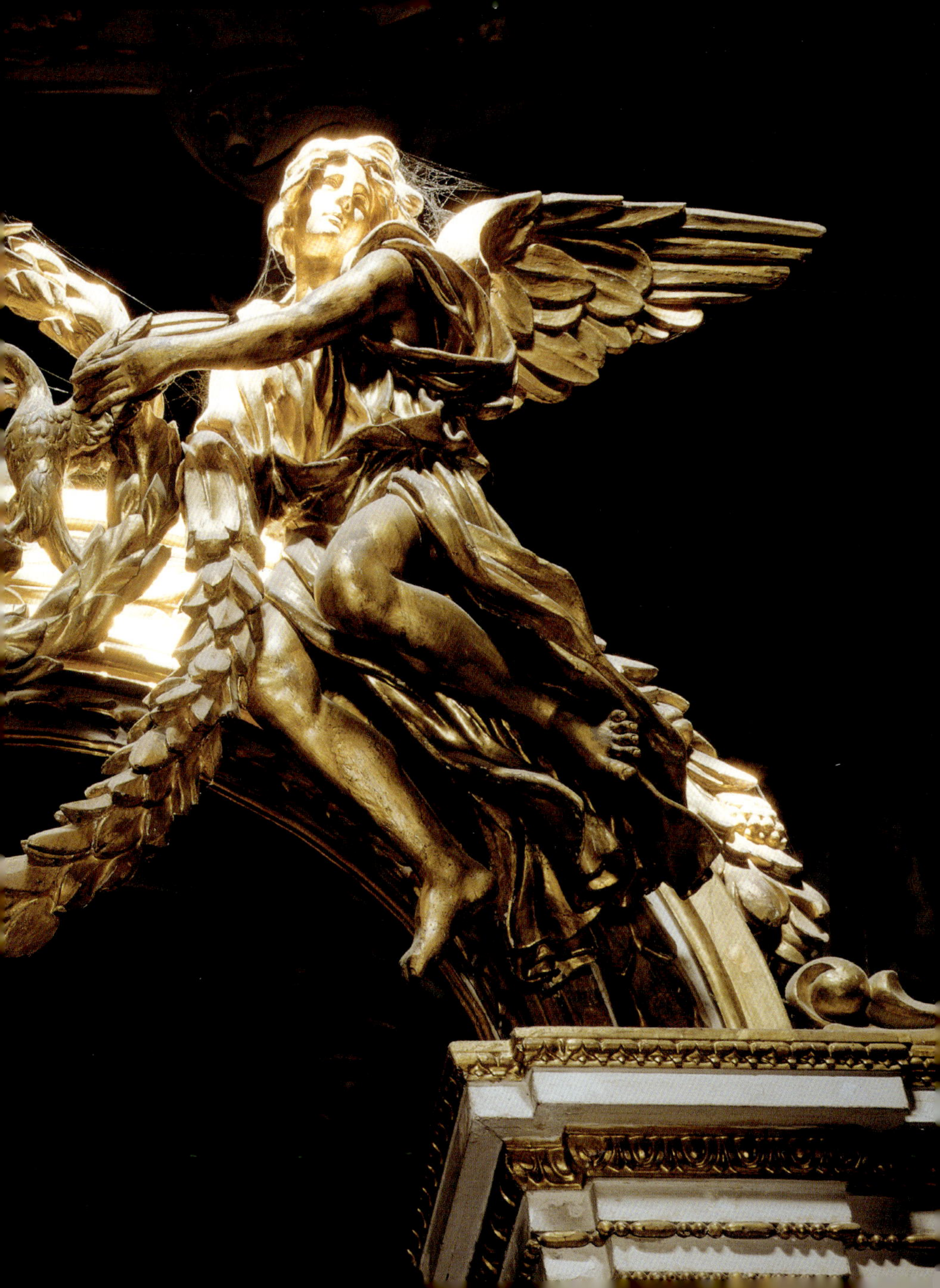

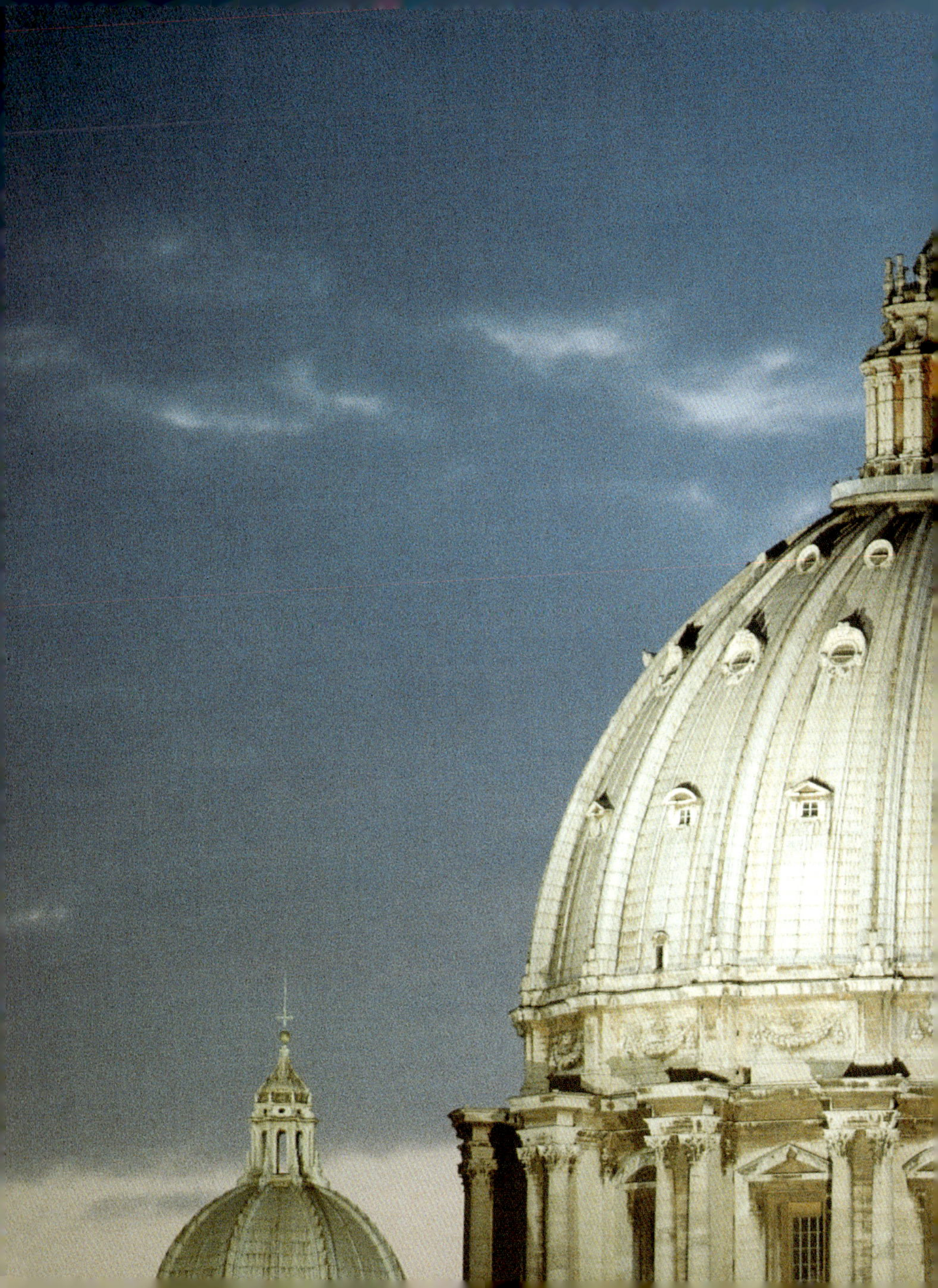

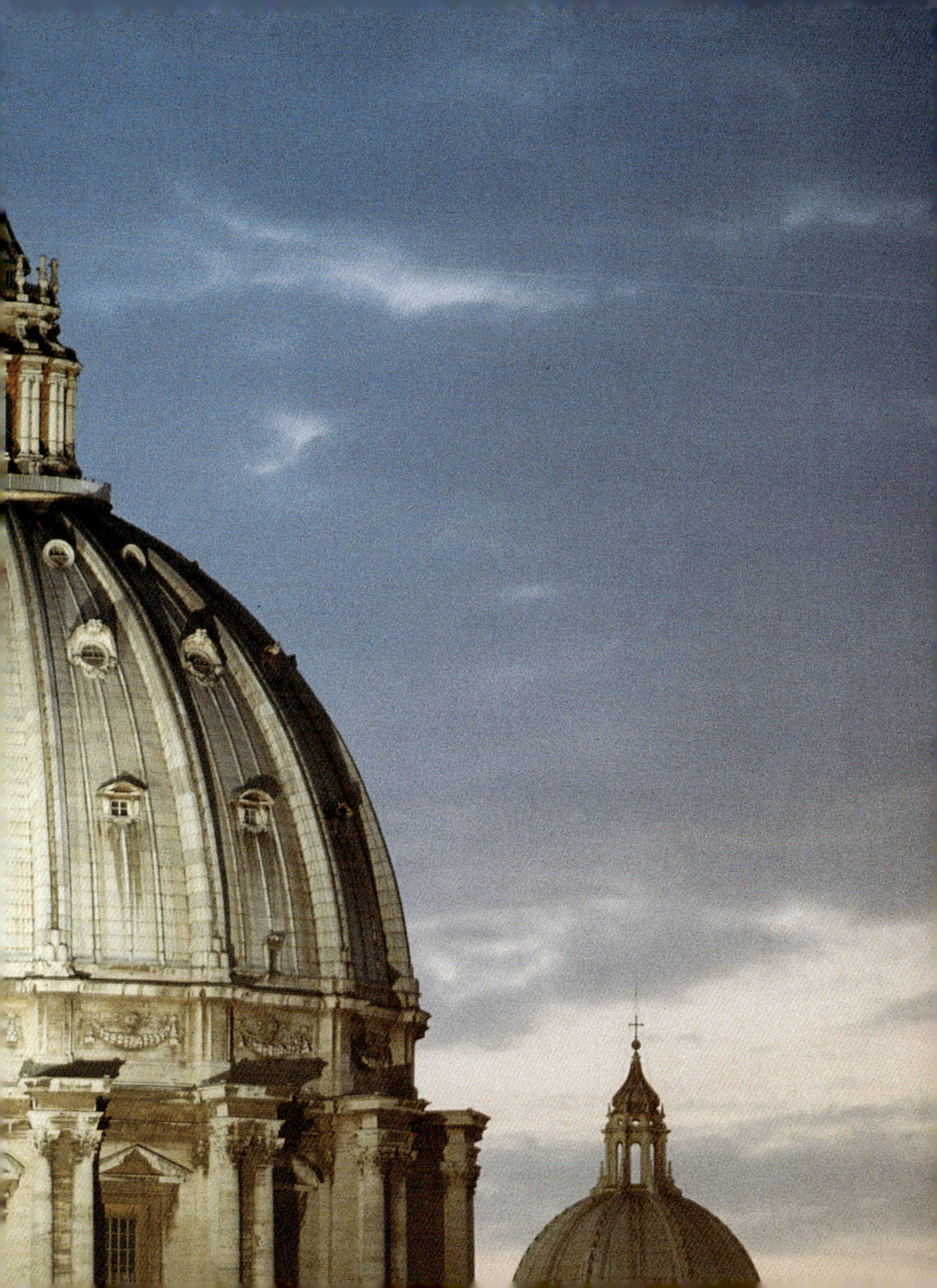

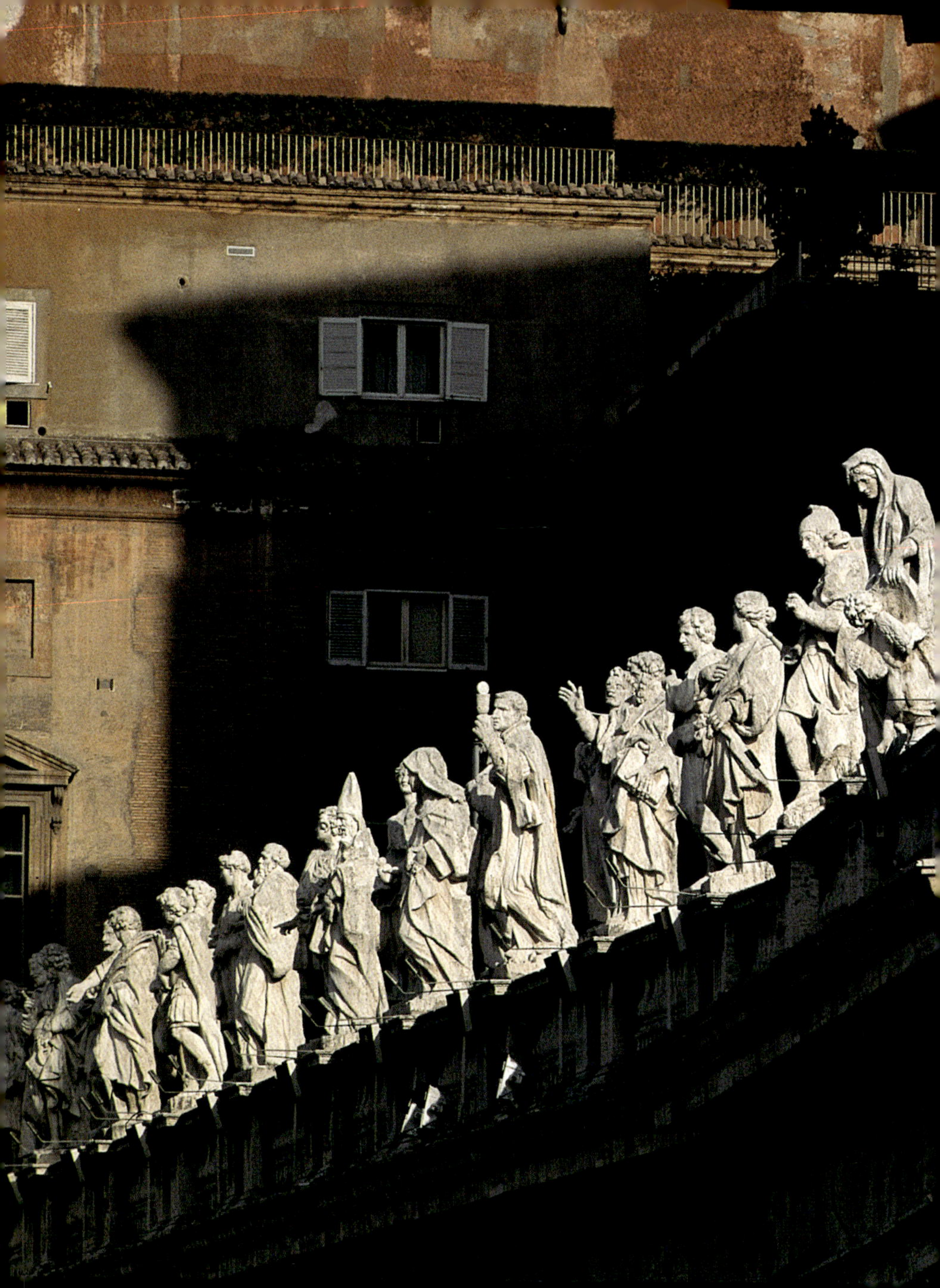

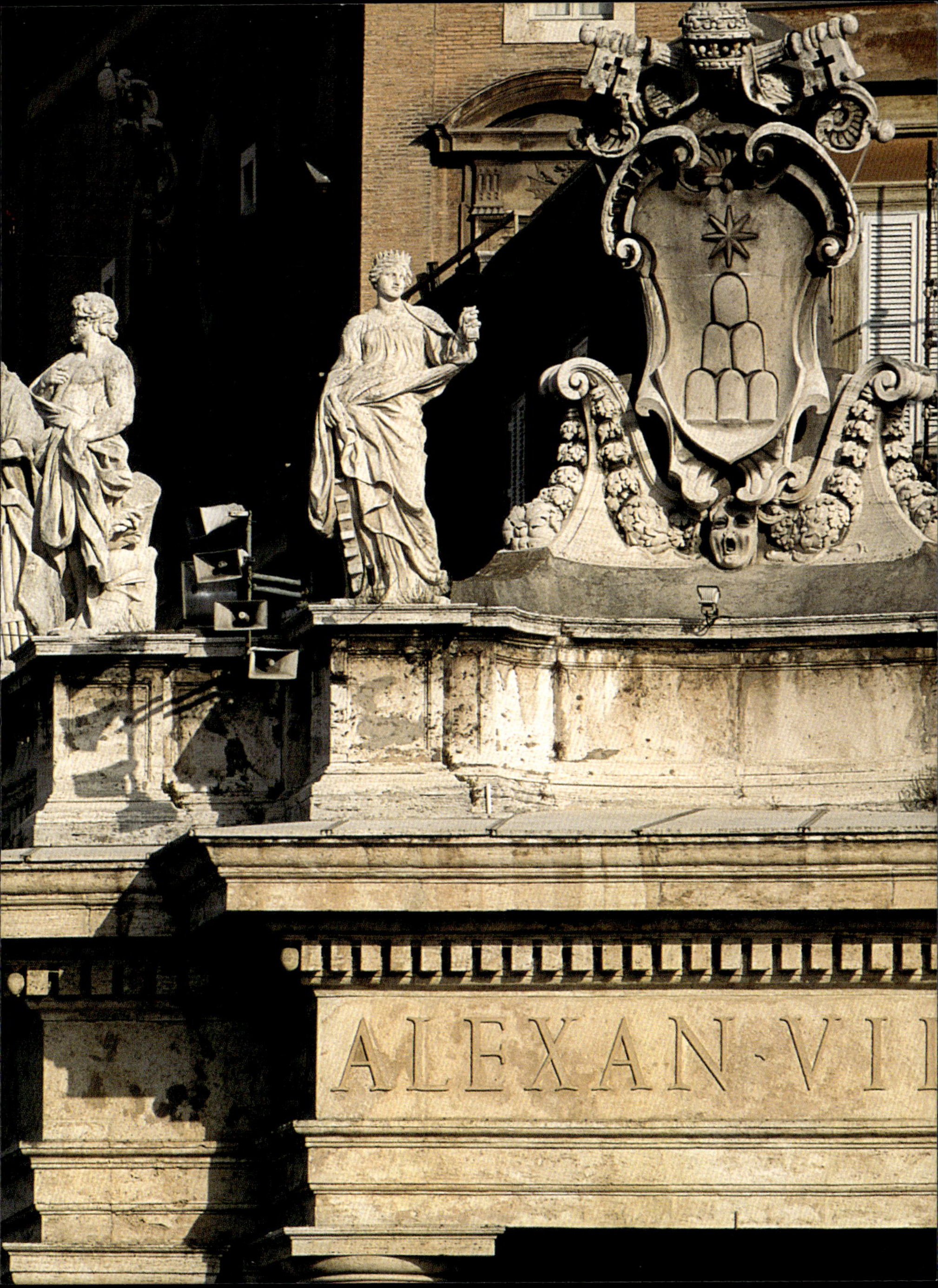
ALEXAN·VI

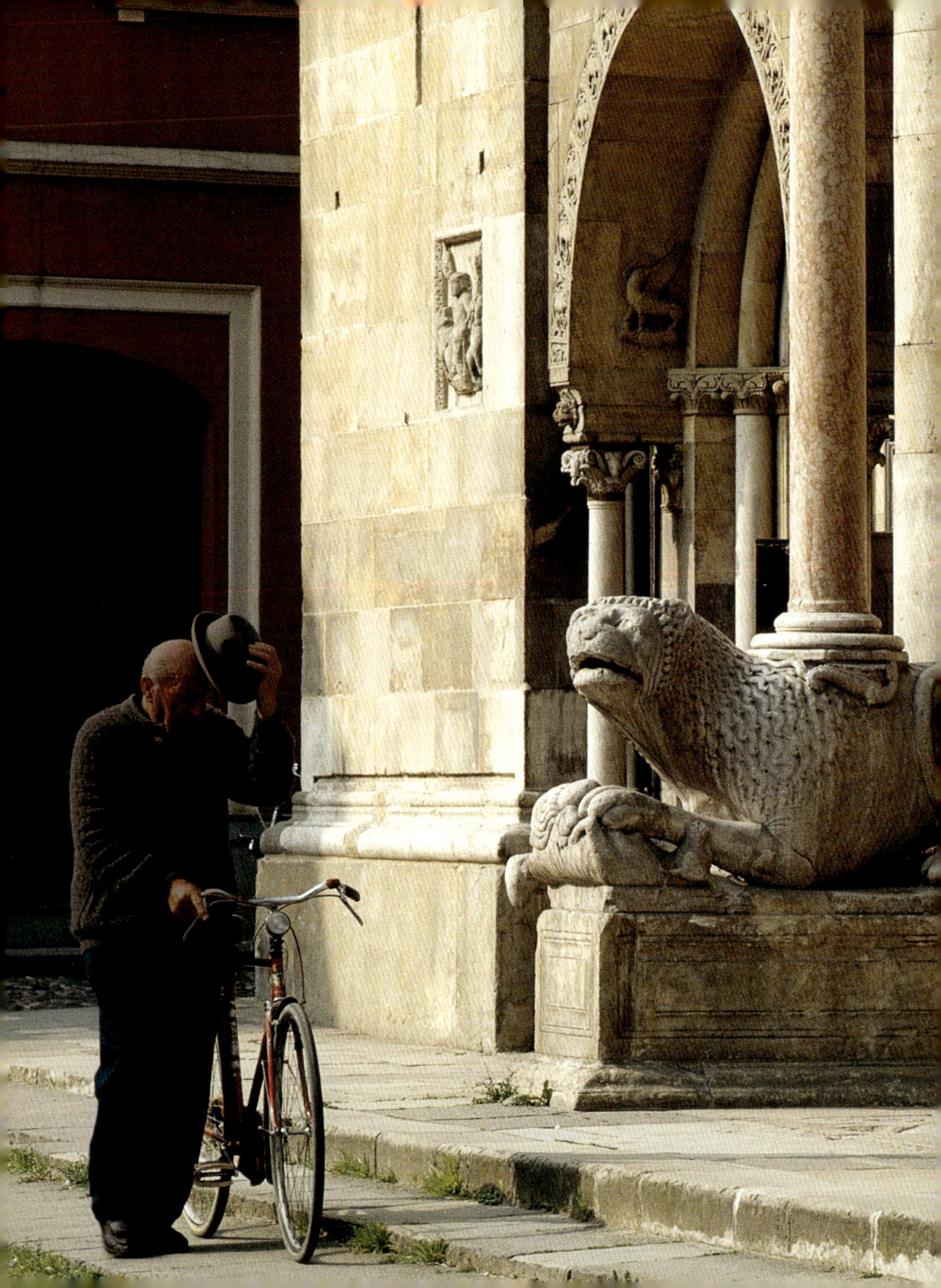

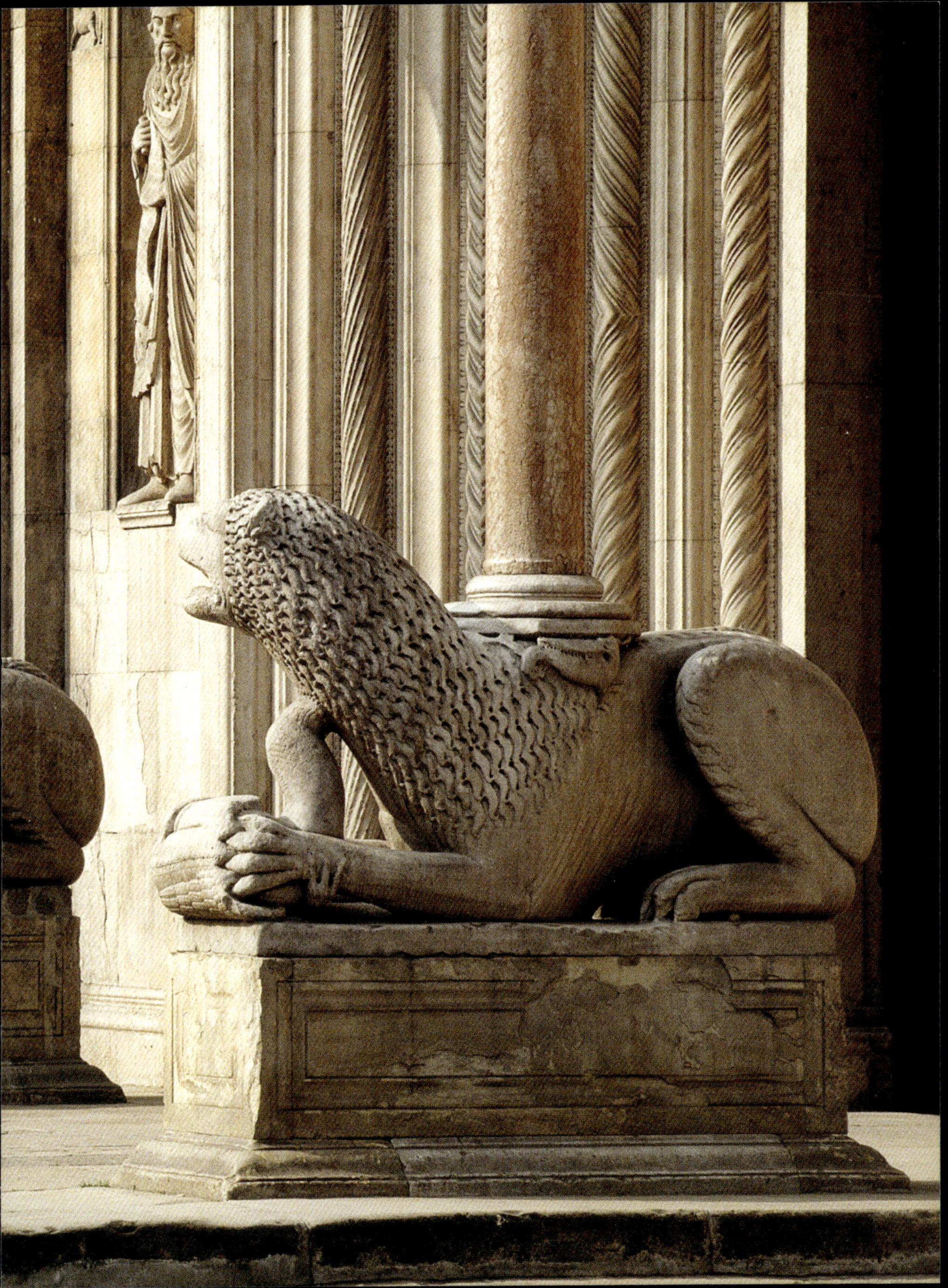

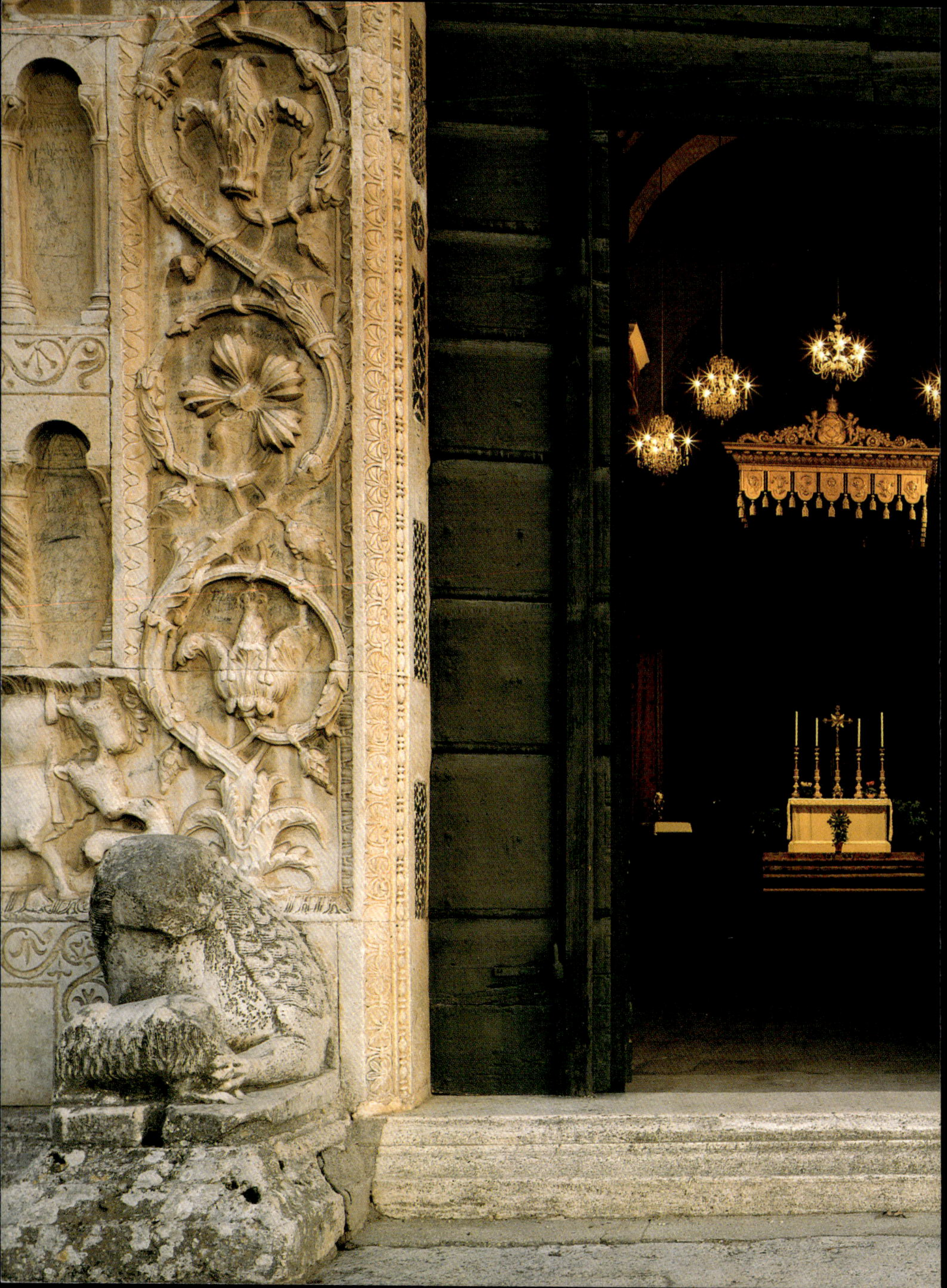

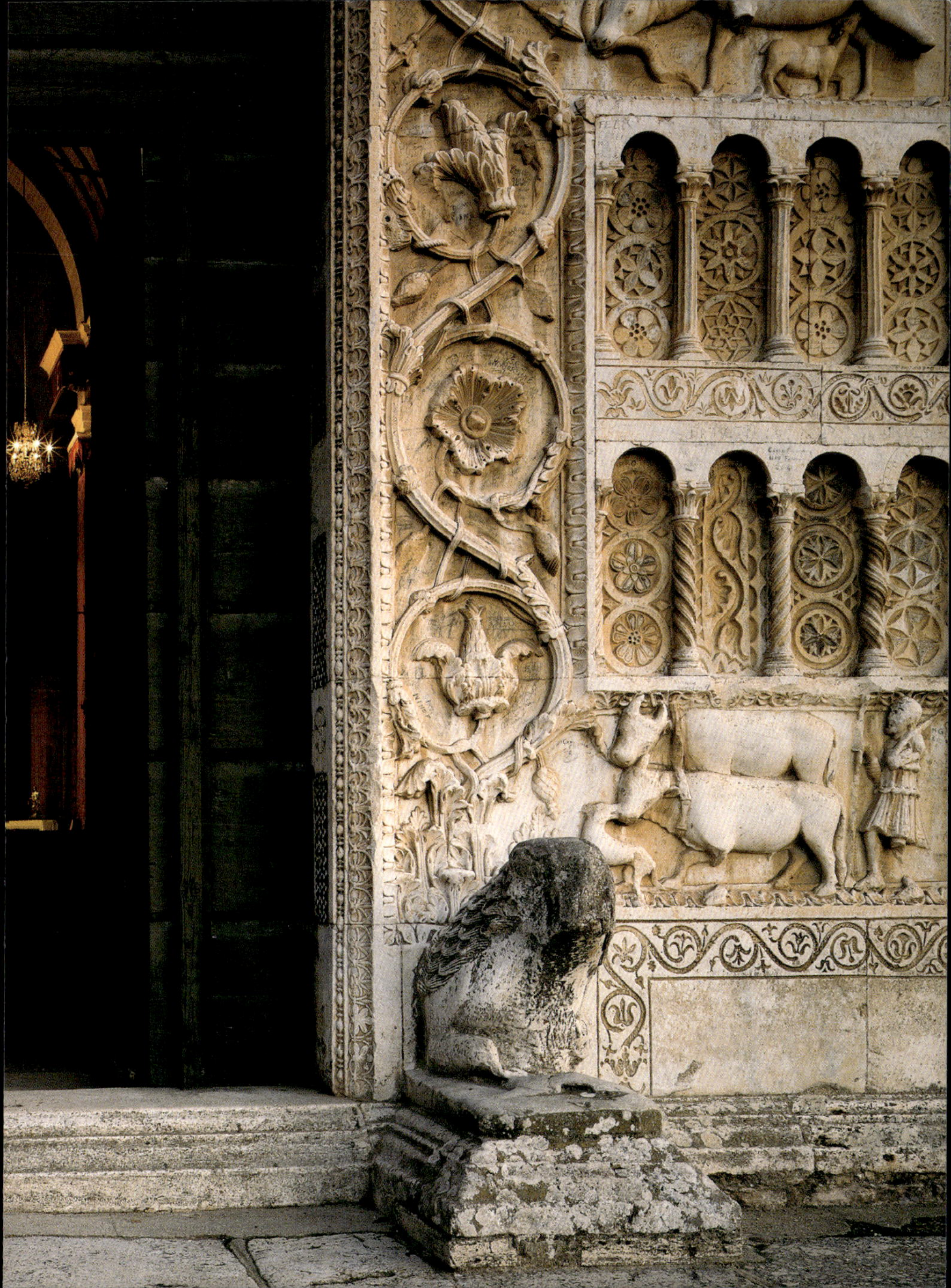

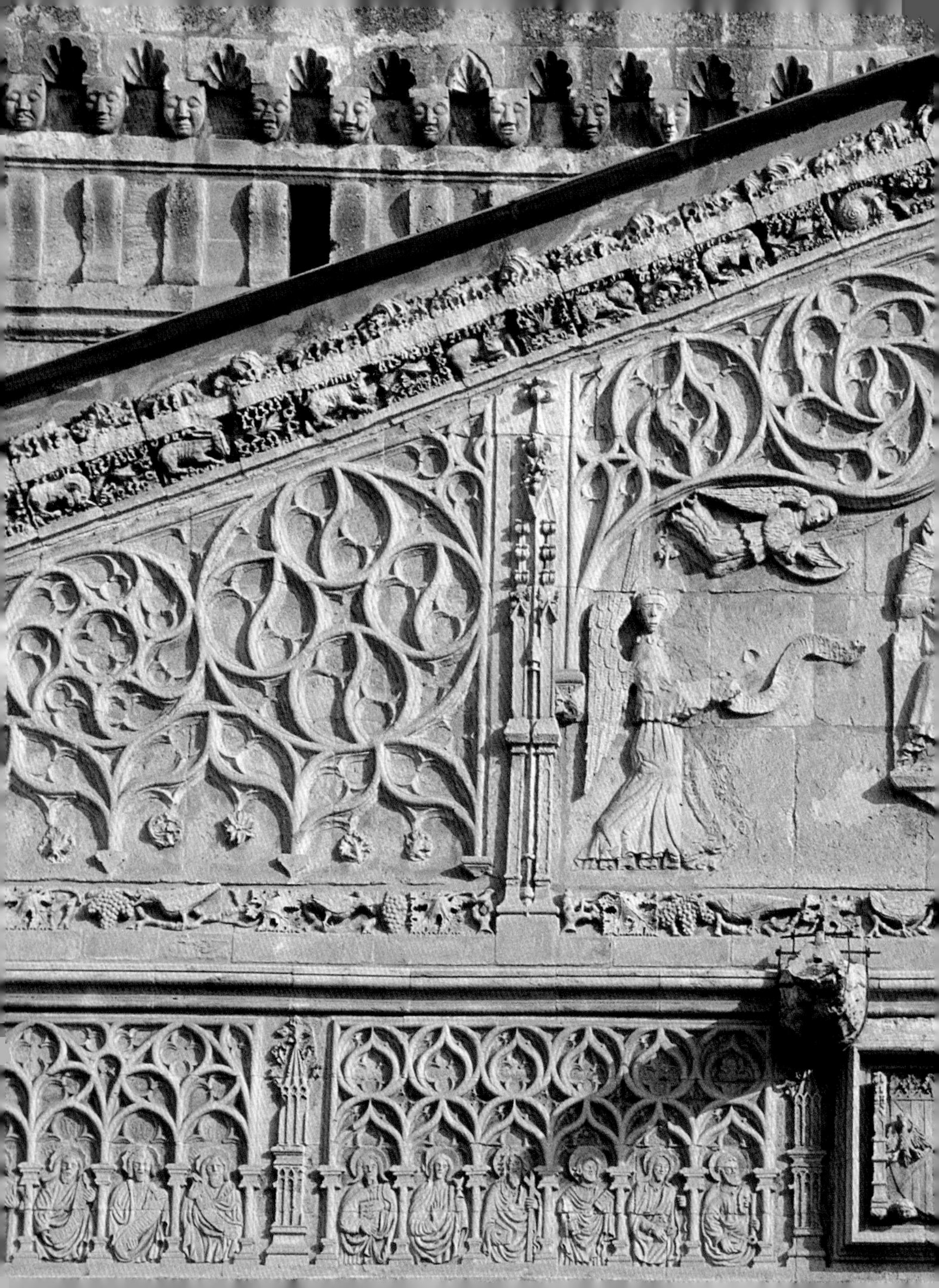

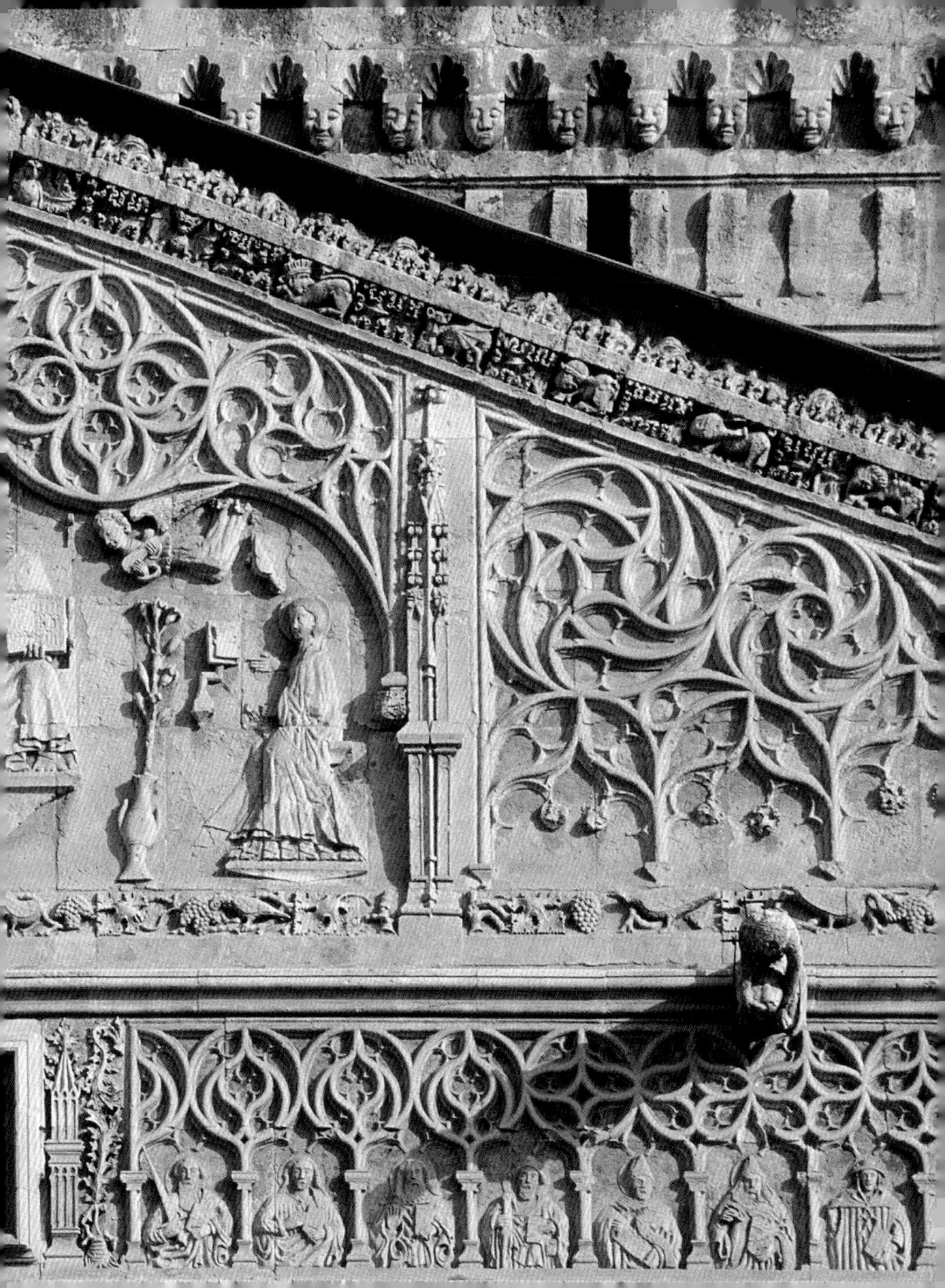

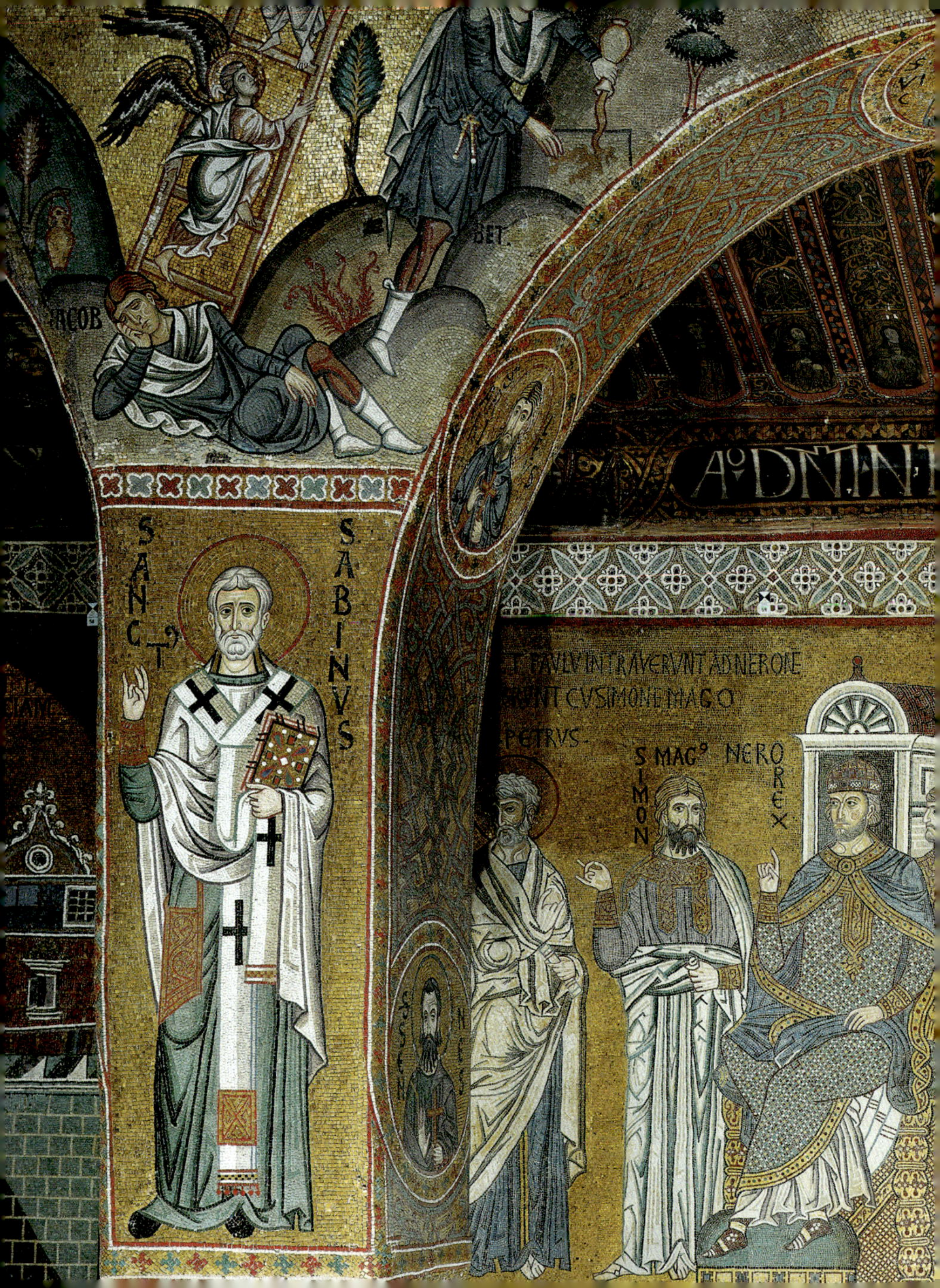

IACOB
BET.
SANCT'
SABINVS
PETRVS
SIMON MAG°
NERO REX

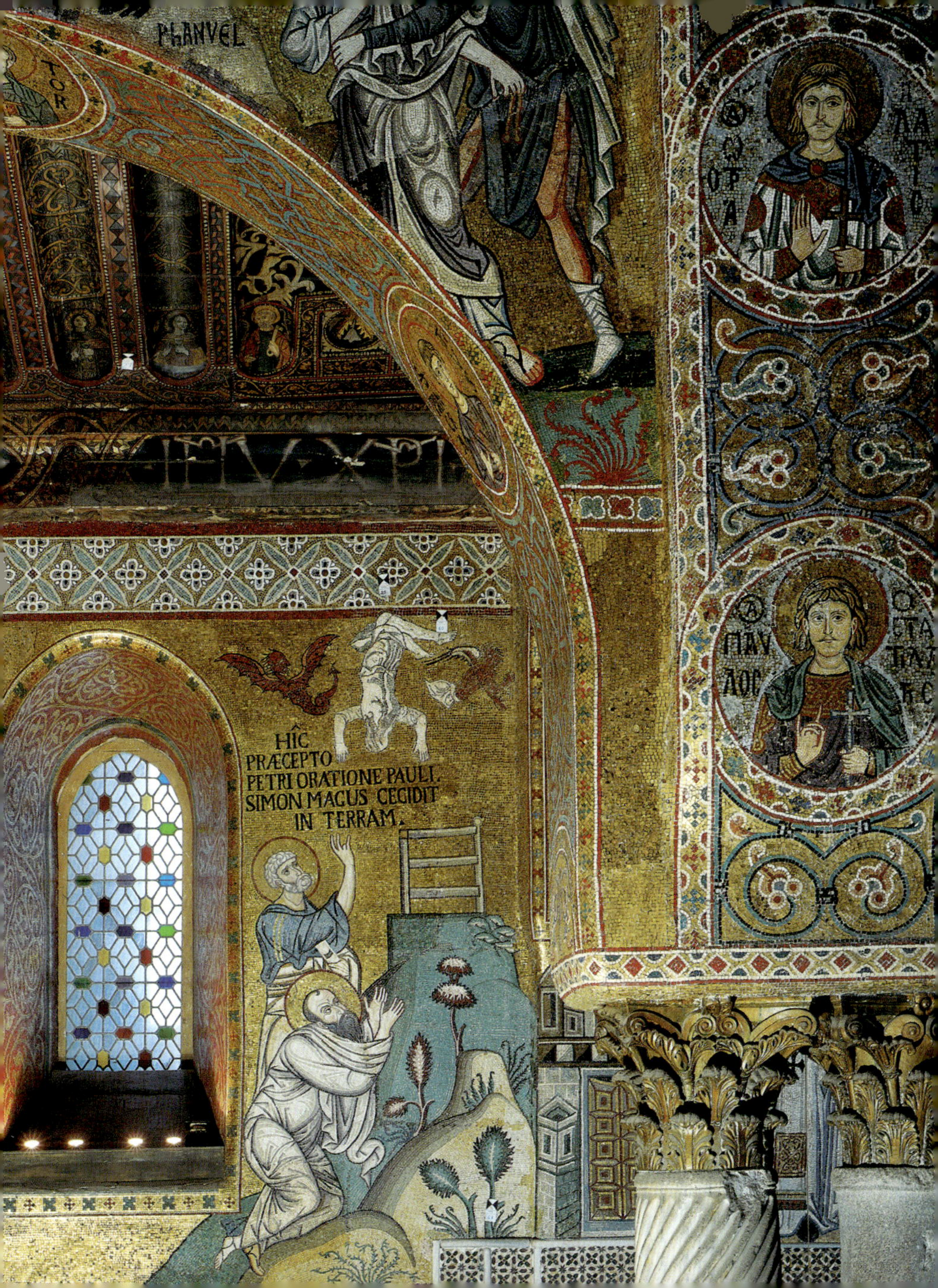
HIC
PRÆCEPTO
PETRI ORATIONE PAULI.
SIMON MAGUS CECIDIT
IN TERRAM.

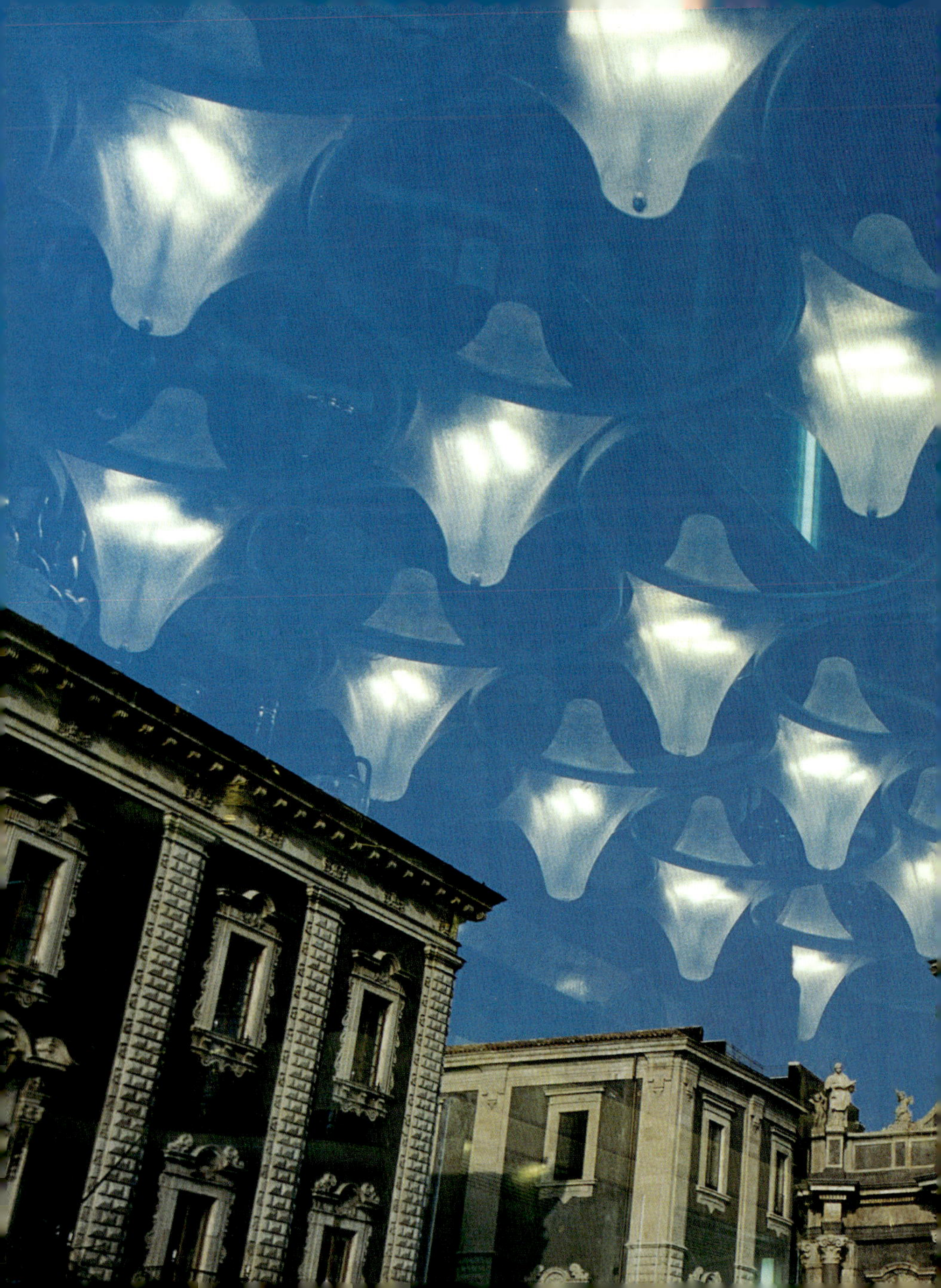

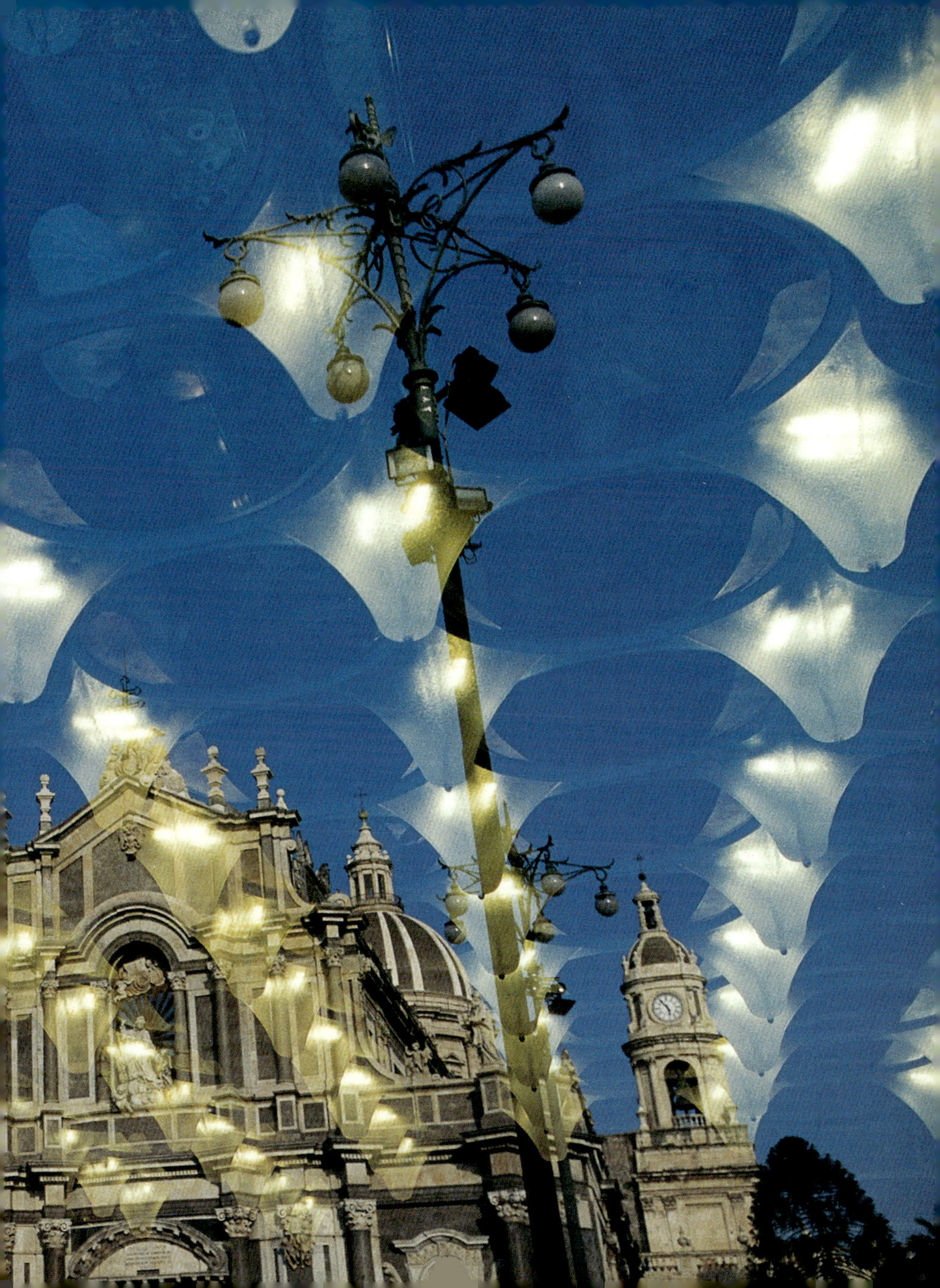

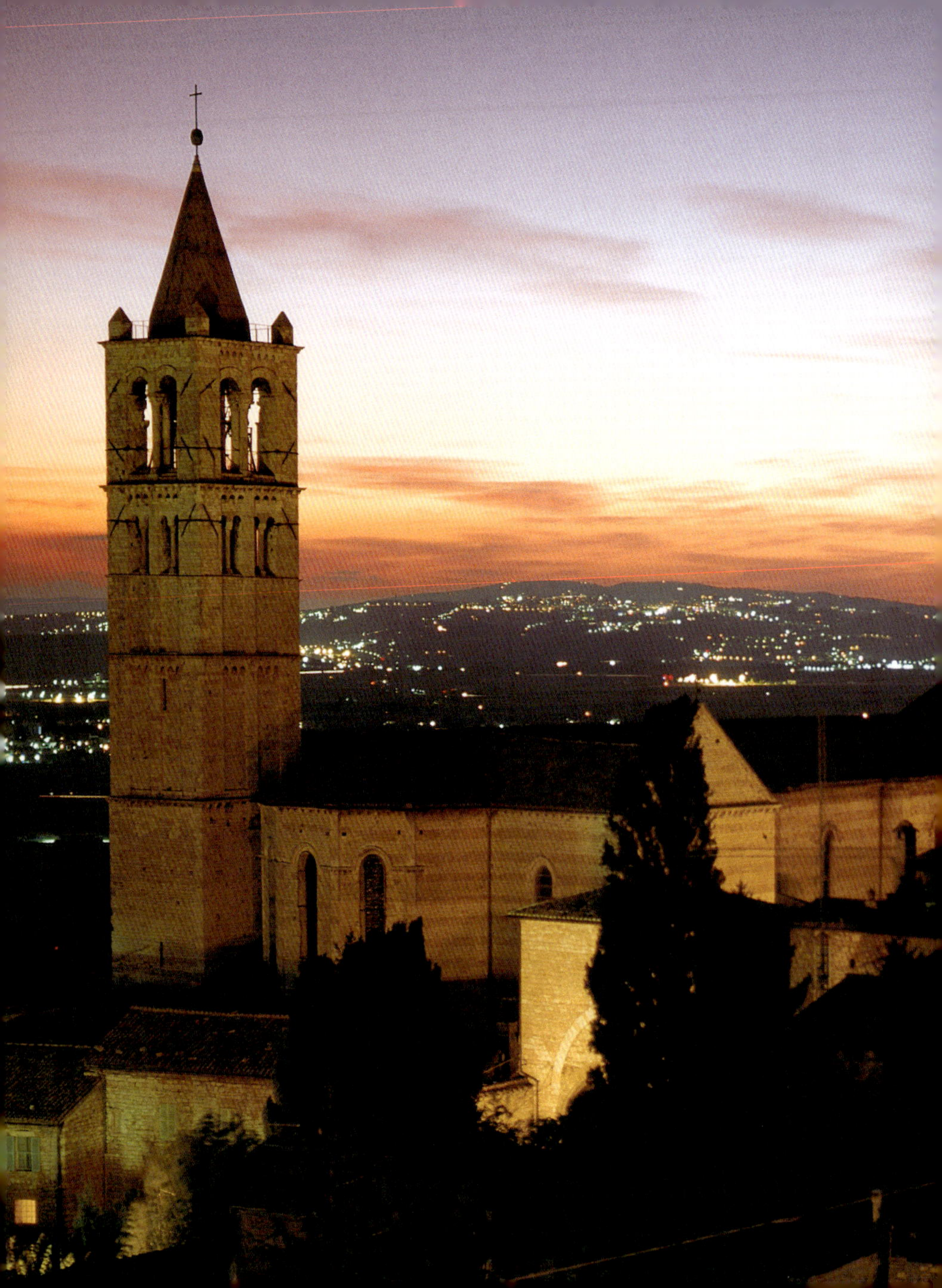

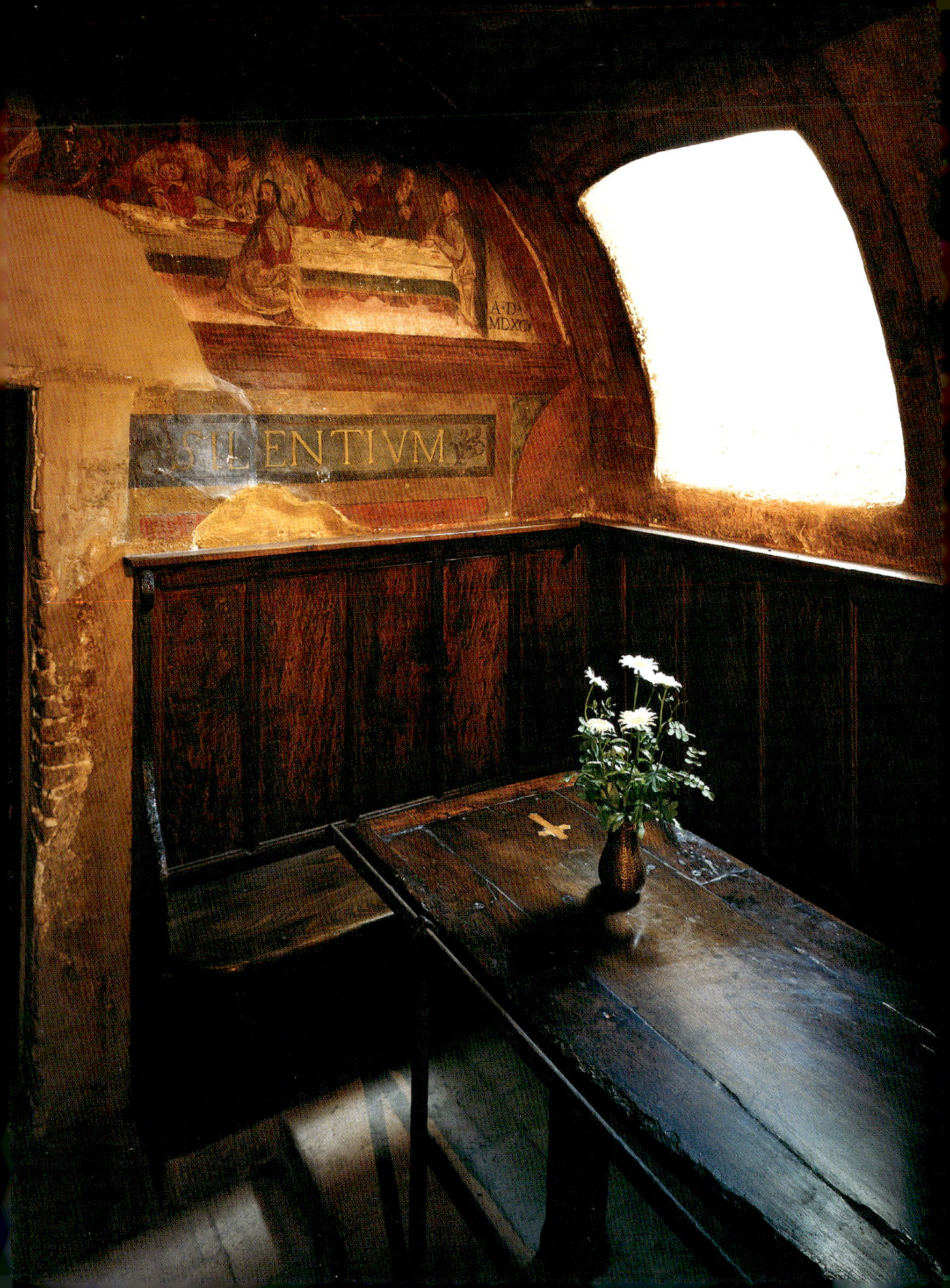
A·D
MDXC
SILENTIVM

ISLANDS, COASTS AND SEAS

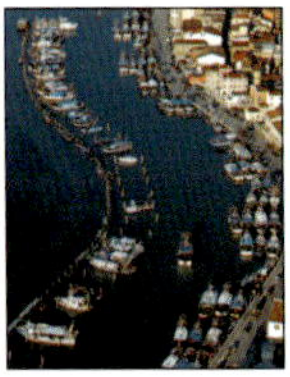

CHIOGGIA spreads over a group of islands located on the southern part of the Venice Lagoon. It is a fishing and seaside resort boasting lovely coloured houses. The streets follow the waving outline of the coast *(p. 233)*.

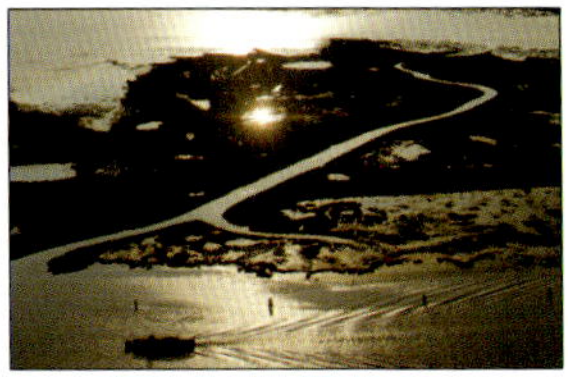

LIGHTS ARE MIRRORED IN THE WATERS OF THE VENETIAN LAGOON. Waterways and sea are hardly rippled by the reflections of the sun or the wake of a boat, and the boundaries between sky and sea merge *(pp. 234-235)*.

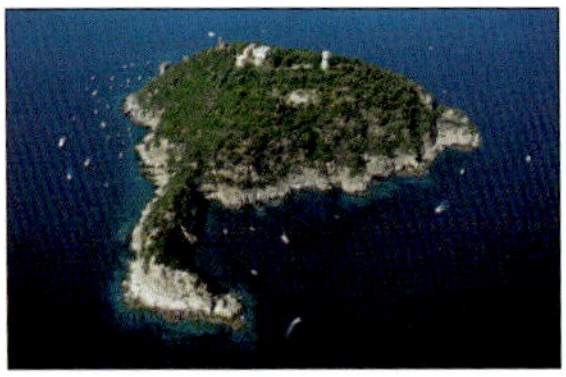

THE GALLINARA ISLAND, two kilometres off the town of Alassio. A private property since 1842, it is a natural protected area, rich in Mediterranean vegetation where rare species of reptiles live *(pp. 236-237)*.

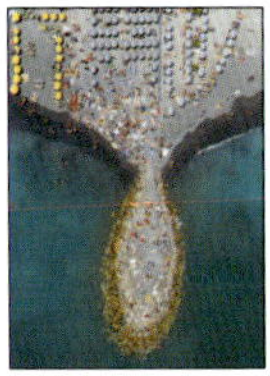

THE BEACH OF LOANO, a tourist resort developed around the 16th-century town's core on the seafront. In this stretch the Ligurian coastline is not marked by a sheer drop from the cliff to the sea, but is sandy *(p. 238)*.

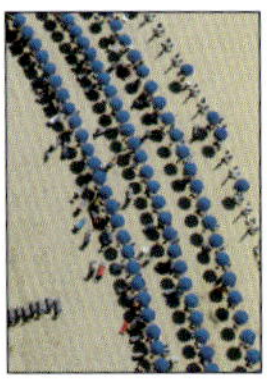

ALONG THE RIVIERA DI PONENTE long sandy shores, narrow coves and wide bays alternate. Therefore one beach is very different from another, and tourist facilities and structures gather on the sandy ones *(p. 239)*.

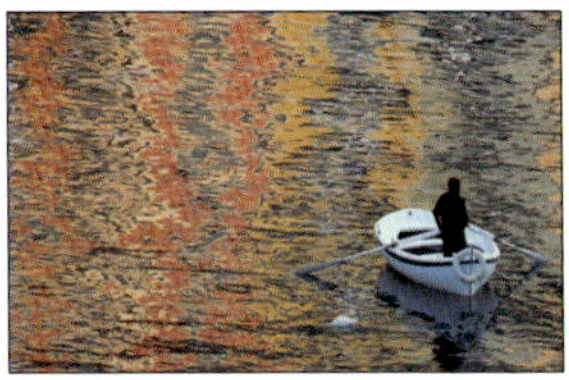

ROWING BOAT TOUR IN FRONT OF PORTOFINO, renowned international tourist destination. The typical tall and narrow colourful houses around the little harbour are reflected in the water *(pp. 240-241)*.

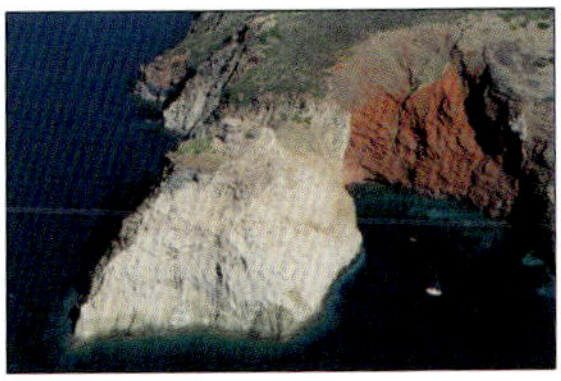

THE CAPRAIA, a volcanic island 65 kilometres off Livorno, is part of the Tuscan Archipelago Park. It is entirely mountainous and characterised by a red and grey rocky coastline *(pp. 242-243)*.

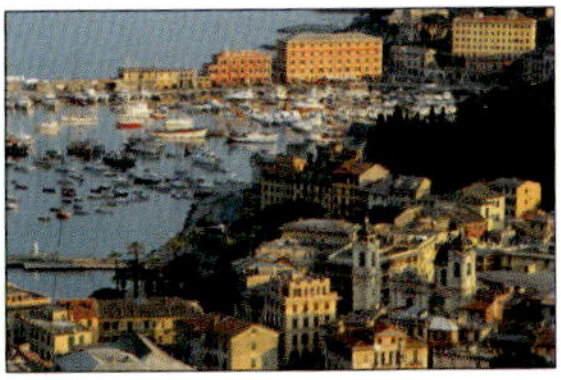

PLACED ON AN INLET OF THE TIGULLIO coast, the town of Santa Margherita Ligure was created by merging two fishing villages: Corte, on the harbour, and Pescino, including a cathedral *(pp. 246-247)*.

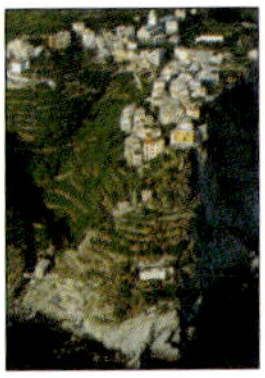

PLACED ON A ROCKY STEEP SPUR on the sea, the village of Corniglia can be reached from the shore via steps. Vines and olive trees are grown in the dry-stone walled terracings around it *(p. 249)*.

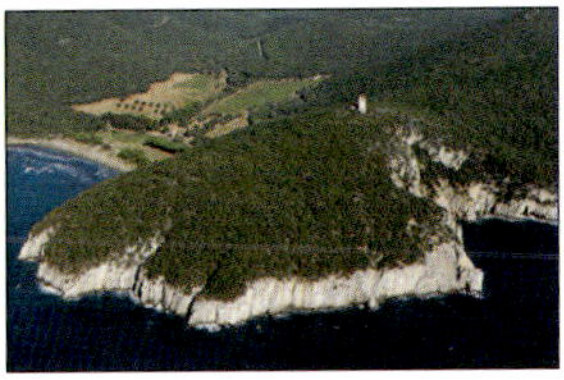

THE UCCELLINA NATURAL PARK expands over about 4,000 hectares on the hills of Tuscany coastline, between Principina a Mare and Talamone. The Medici family built the towers to protect the coast *(pp. 244-245)*.

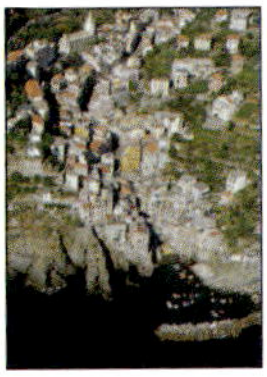

RIOMAGGIORE is the most famous resort of the Cinque Terre. The village, squeezed in a narrow ravine between mountain and sea, expands along tiny streets of colourful houses, very close to each other *(p. 248)*.

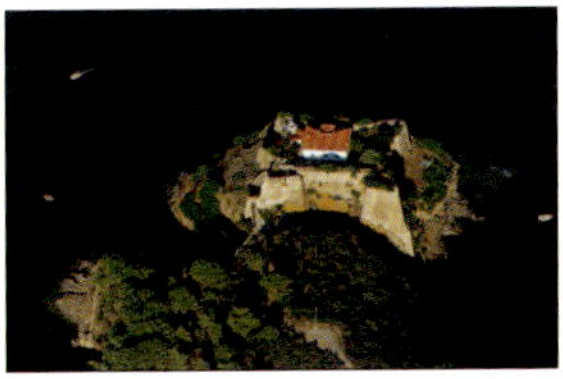

THE 16TH-CENTURY FORTRESS OF PORTO LONGONE, distinguished by the typical star-shaped structure, rises on a promontory on the edge of Porto Azzurro, a seaside resort of the Elba Island *(pp. 250-251)*.

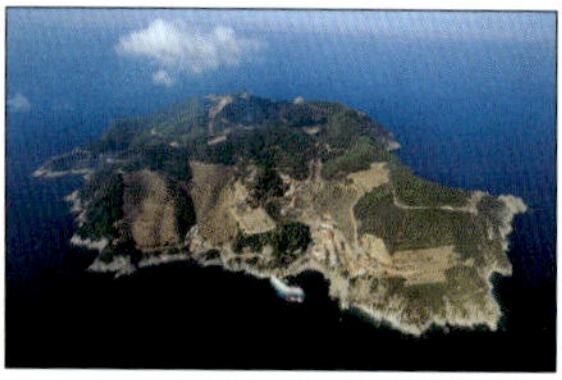

GORGONA, thirty-seven kilometers off Livorno, is a little mountainous island more than two square meters wide. Covered with Mediterranean vegetation, it houses the ruins of old monasteries *(pp. 252-253)*.

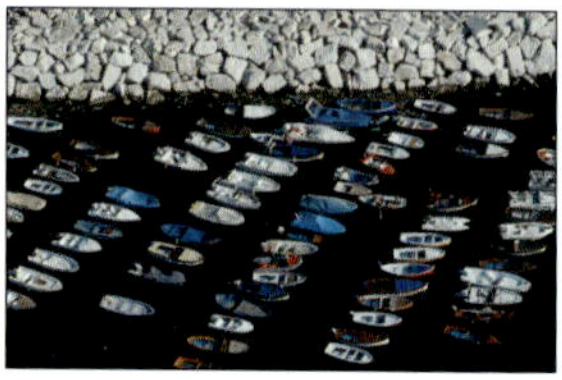

A PICTURESQUE VIEW of small boats in Naples harbour. Both pleasure boats and fishermen coming from the nearby hamlet moor at the port, in proximity of Castel dell'Ovo *(pp. 254-255)*.

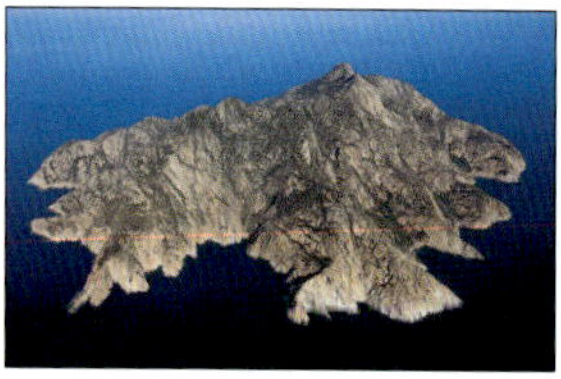

MONTECRISTO IS THE WILDEST amongst the Tuscany islands. It is uninhabited, entirely granitic and 645 meters high at its peak. Alexandre Dumas's 1845 novel *Il Conte di Montecristo* made it known to the world *(pp. 256-257)*.

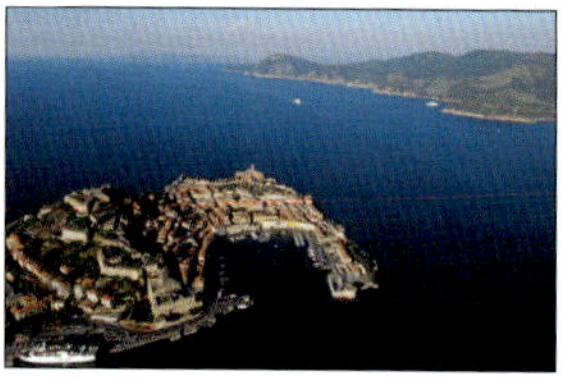

PORTOFERRAIO, the main town of the Elba Island and mooring point for ferries too, rises on an isthmus dotted with ancient fortresses. Luxury hotels face the old harbour promenade *(pp. 258-259)*.

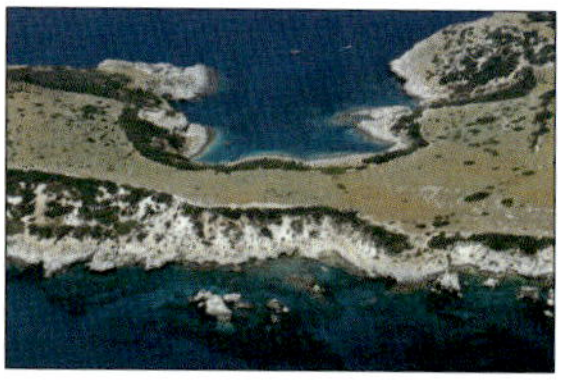

THE TREMITI, a small group of calcareous islands facing the Gargano in the Adriatic sea, have jagged coastlines rich in caves and coves. Saint Nicola's, boasting a 9th-century abbey, is pictured here *(pp. 260-261)*.

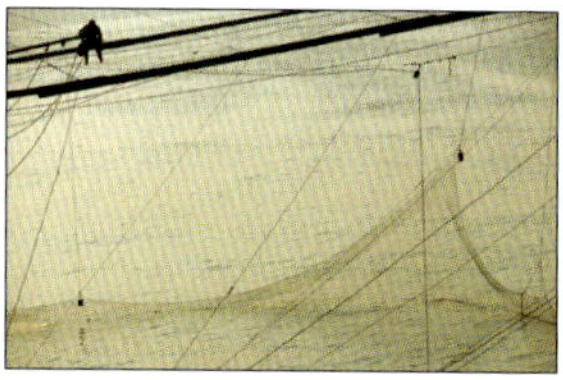

FISHING NETS ON THE GARGANO. Plenty of woods cover this mountainous promontory of Northern Apulia on its inner parts, whereas on the slopes facing the sea olive trees, orchards and vineries prevail *(pp. 262-263)*.

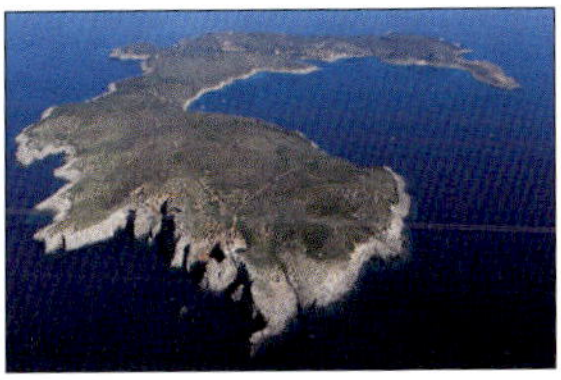

A PRIVATE PROPERTY, the island of Giannutri is two and a half kilometers long and more than one kilometer wide. At Cala Maestra the remains of a 1st-century A.D. Roman villa can be visited *(pp. 264-265)*.

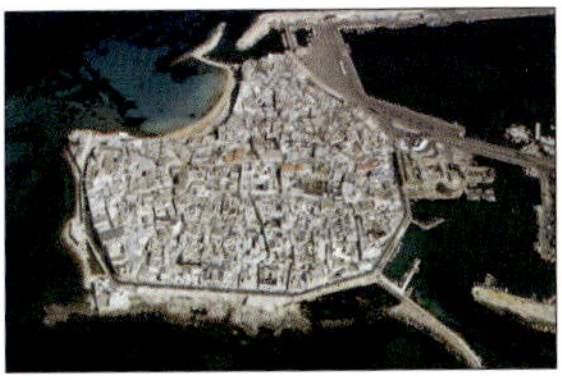

THE MEDIEVAL CENTRE OF GALLIPOLI rises on an island linked by a bridge to the promontory where the modern town expands. A panoramic route runs along the walls surrounding the village *(pp. 268-269)*.

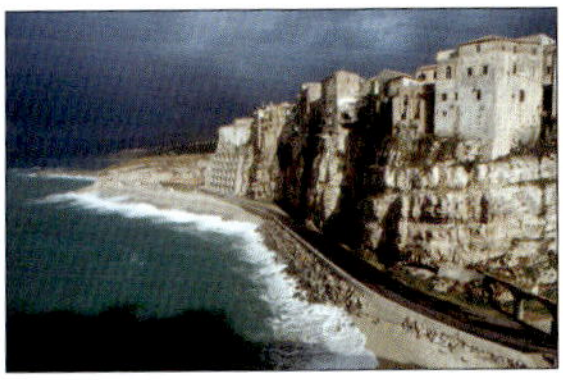

THE ANCIENT CITY OF TROPEA, Calabria, stretches over a headland between the bays of Sant'Eufemia and Gioia. It overlooks the Tirreno sea, which boasts stunning colours here *(pp. 272-273)*.

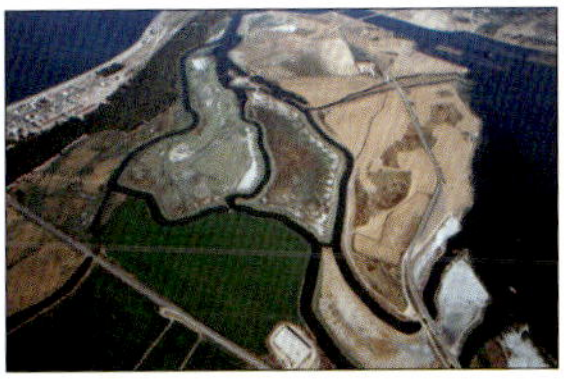

BIRD'S-EYE VIEW OF THE CABRAS POND near Oristano. It expands for around 2,000 hectares creating water effects and it is interspersed by cultivated, brightly coloured fields *(pp. 266-267)*.

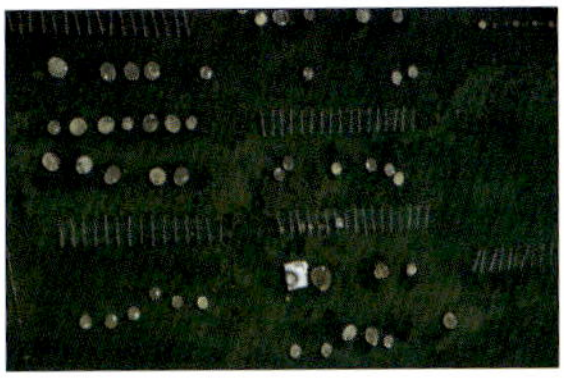

FISH BREEDING in the sea around Sant'Antioco. The island is linked to the Cagliari coast by a three-kilometer-long artificial isthmus. It preserves a necropolis and Punic archaelogical remains *(pp. 270-271)*.

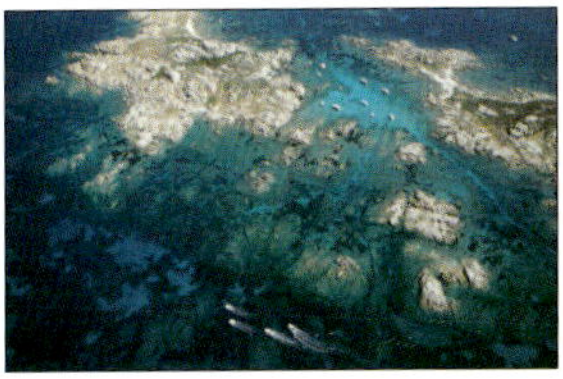

THE REEF OF LECAMERE surfaces from the crystal waters of Costa Smeralda, one of the most fashionable tourist resorts of the Mediterranean sea *(pp. 274-275)*.

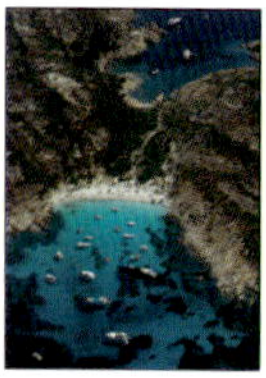

TWO COVES OF MORTORIO ISLAND, divided by a strip of land. Mortorio is near the Costa Smeralda and belongs to the Arcipelago della Maddalena. Wild and uninhabited, it can be reached by private boats *(p. 276)*.

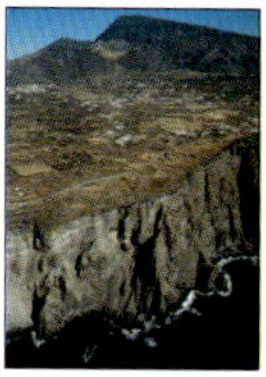

THE STEEP AND DIZZY COAST of Pantelleria, the largest island off the Sicilian coast. In the background there are the mountains, then the cultivated country and the coastal road running along the the entire isle *(p. 277)*.

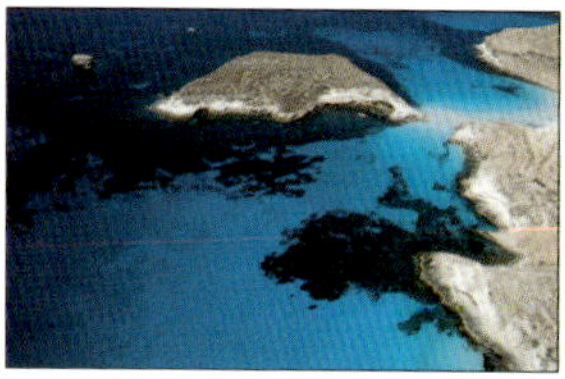

THE RABBITS ISLAND is parted by an expanse of sea, where water rises at knee level. It can be reached from the Lampedusa's bay of the same name, which is also a natural reserve where sea turtles nest *(pp. 278-279)*.

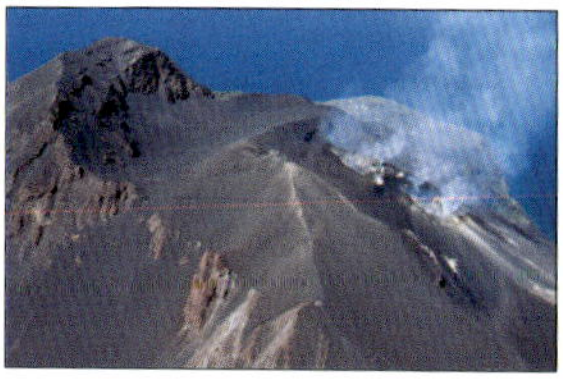

AN IMPRESSIVE VIEW of Stromboli's volcano in the Eolian Islands, here covered with snow. It is always active. The island is marked by high cliffs and the volcanic cone takes its whole area *(pp. 280-281)*.

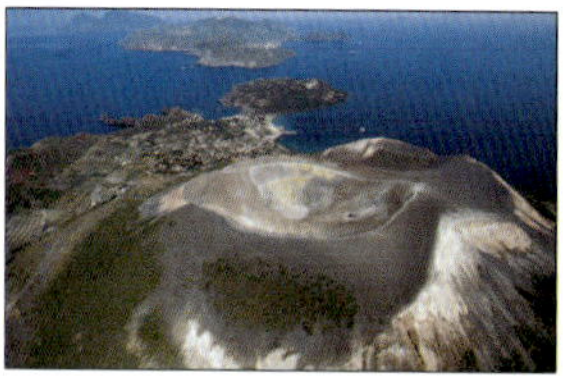

THE HUGE CRATER OF VULCANO, in the Eolian Islands, which last erupted in 1888–90. All volcanoes in the world are named after it. Homer chose the island as the home of Aeolus, the god of the winds *(pp. 282-283)*.

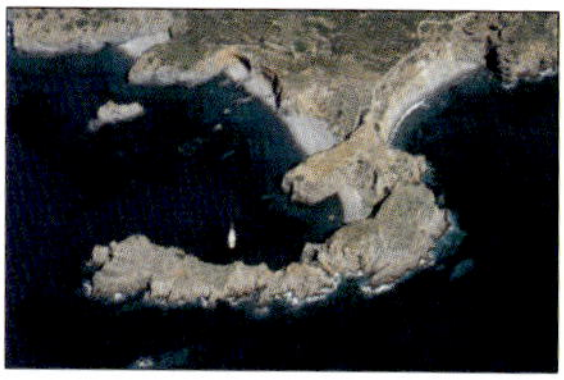

PANAREA is the smallest of the Eolian Islands and is surrounded by rocks and stacks. At Cape Milazzese the remains of a prehistoric Bronze-Age village, made of oval-shaped huts, have been found *(pp. 284-285)*.

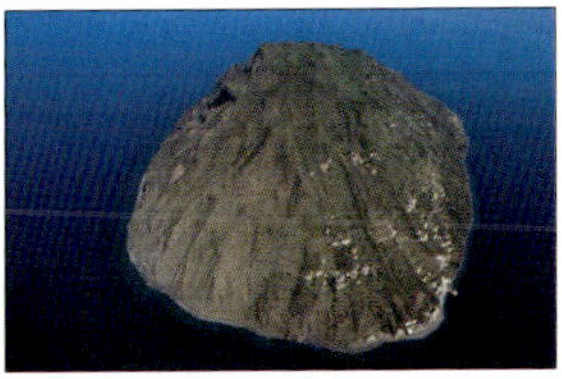

ALICUDI, THE WESTERNMOST ISLAND in the Eolian archipelago, presents a nearly circular shape. It wasn't inhabited during the Middle Ages, and was colonised during the Spanish domination *(pp. 286-287)*.

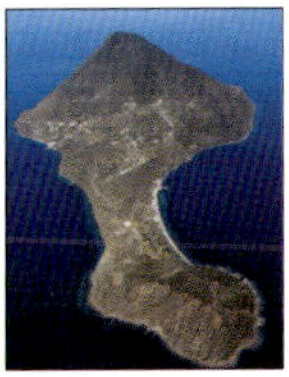

FILICUDI ISLAND is the ancient Phoenicusa, named after the ferns once growing on it. Today it is a cone of naked rocks. The Bue Marino, a huge cave with wonderful reflections of light, is gorgeous *(p. 288)*.

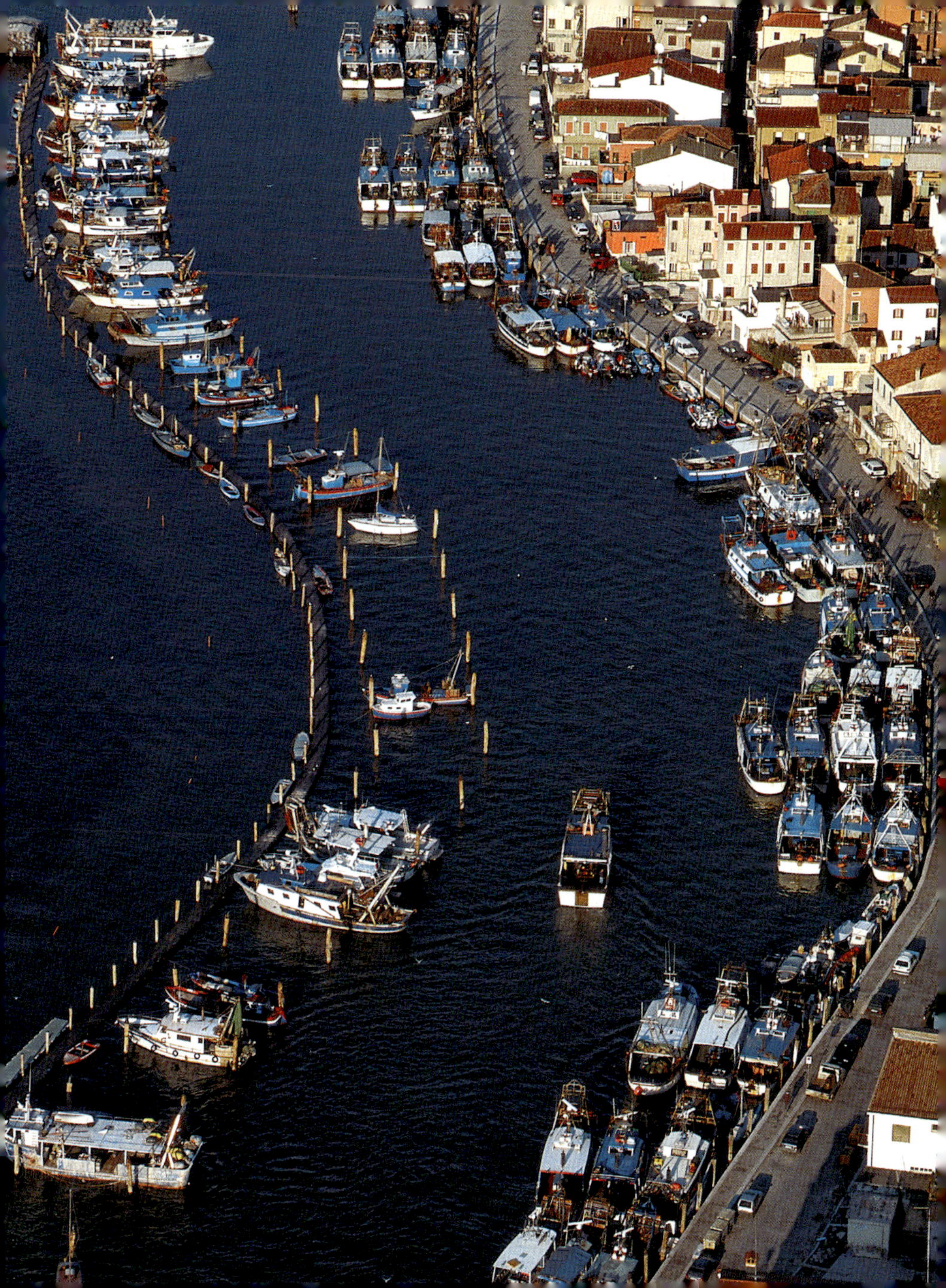

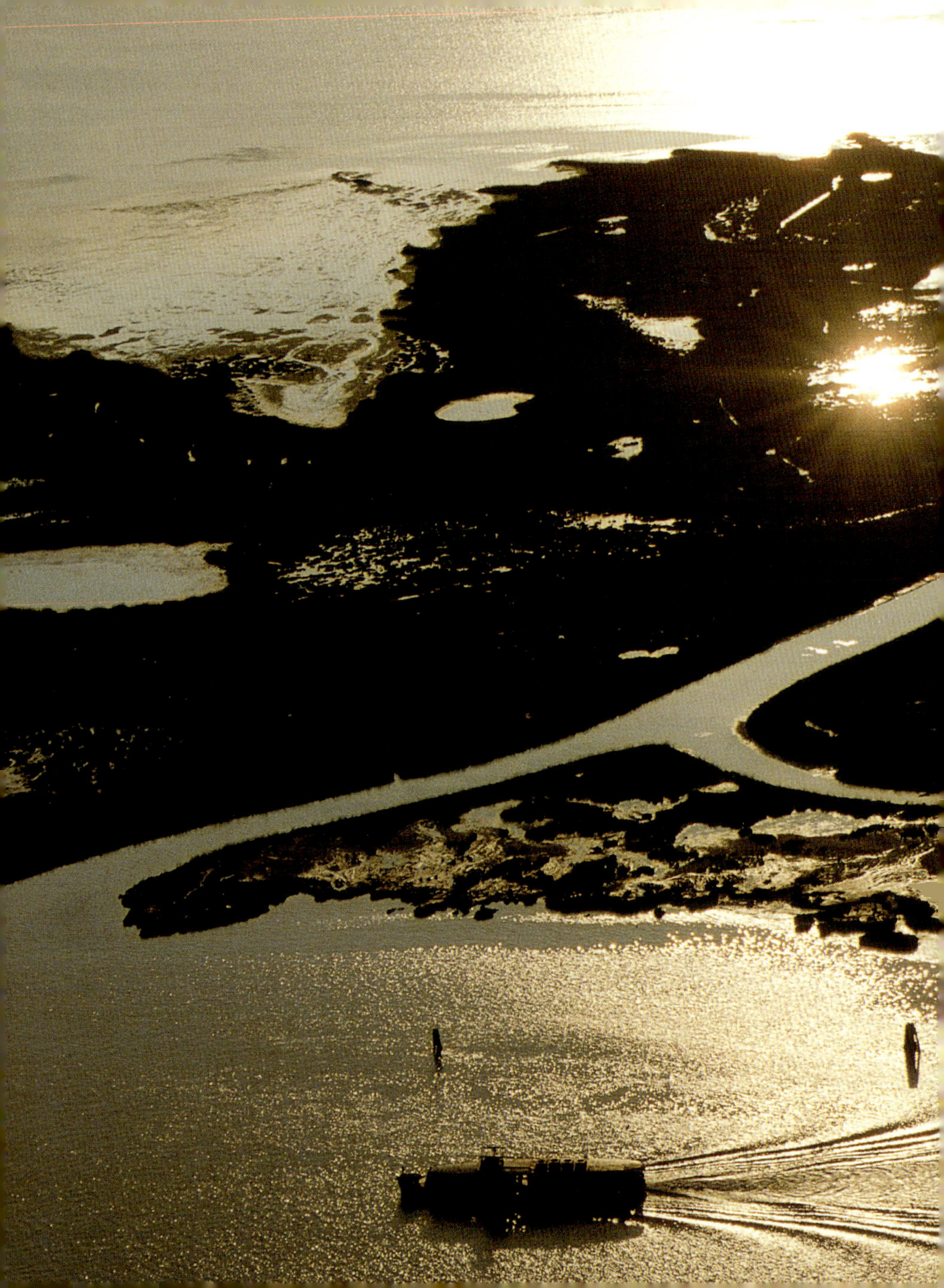

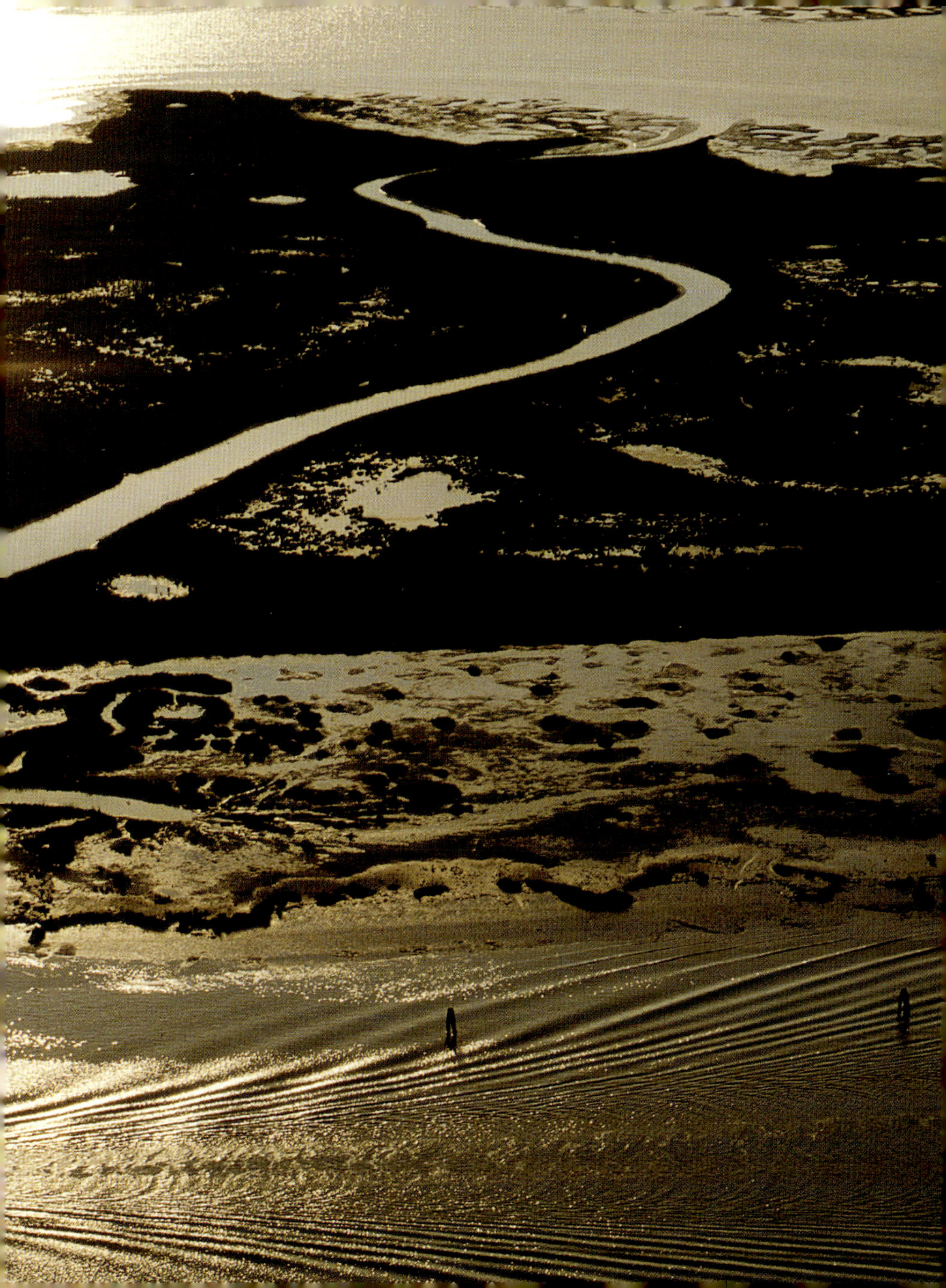

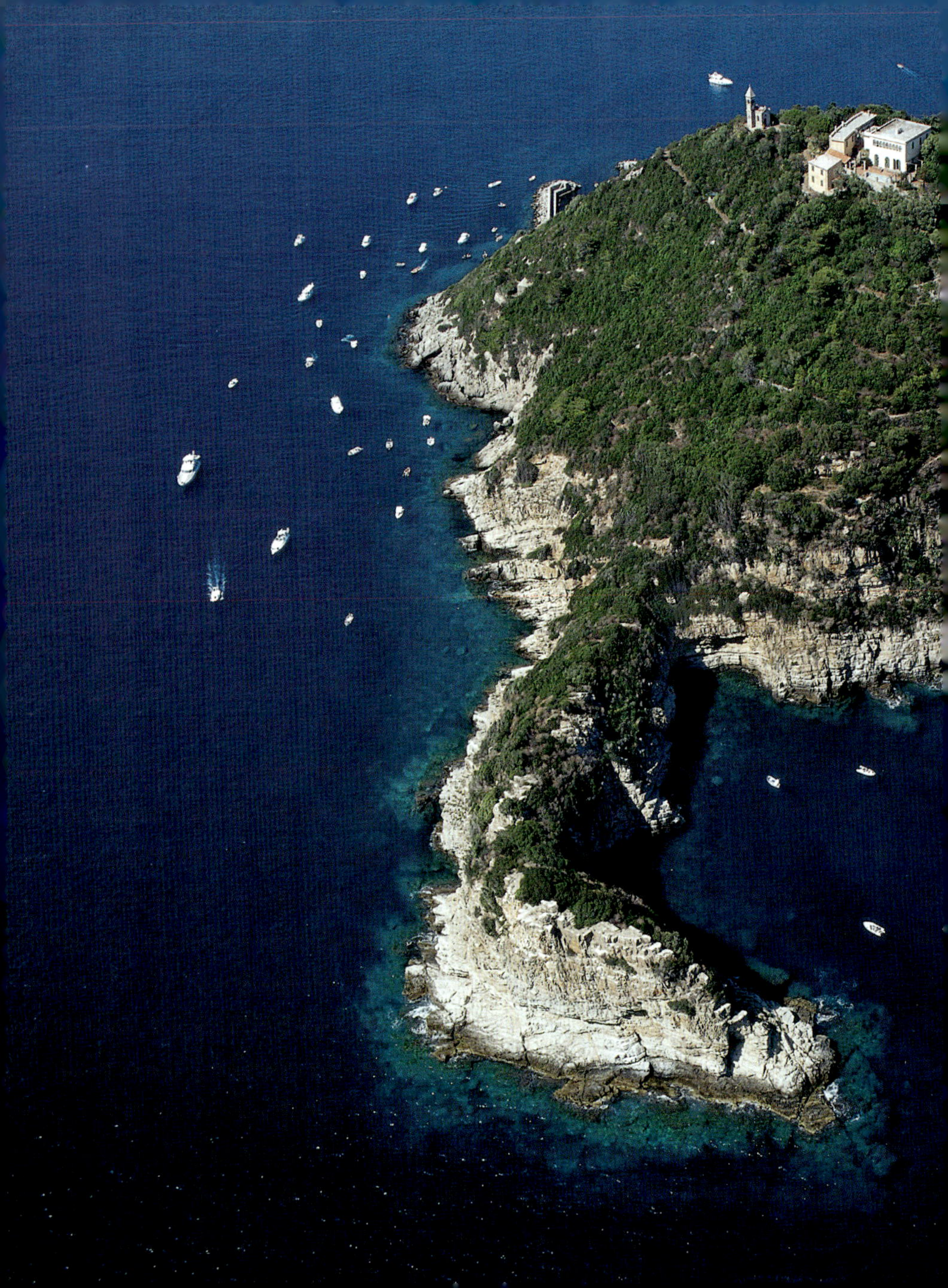

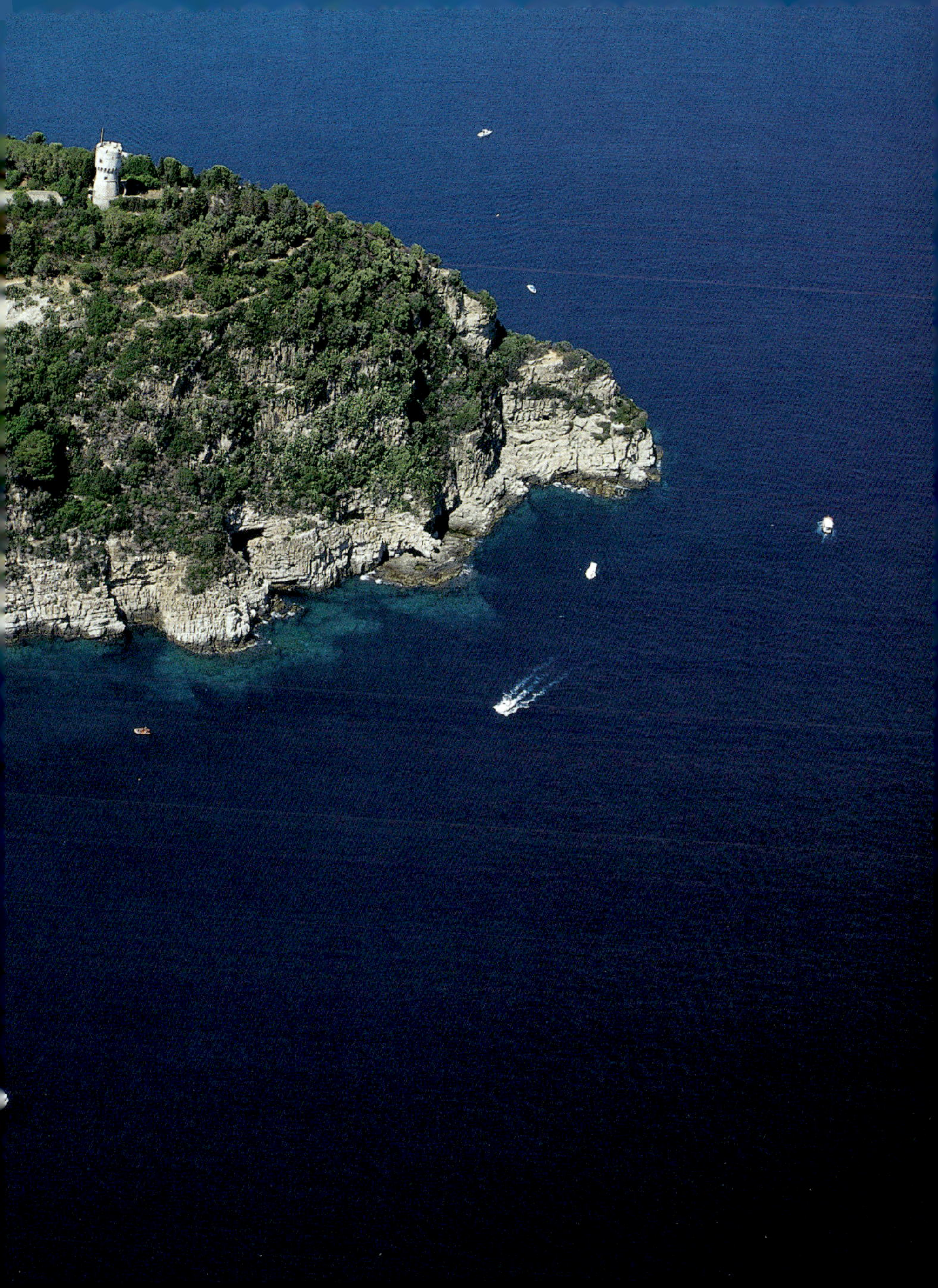

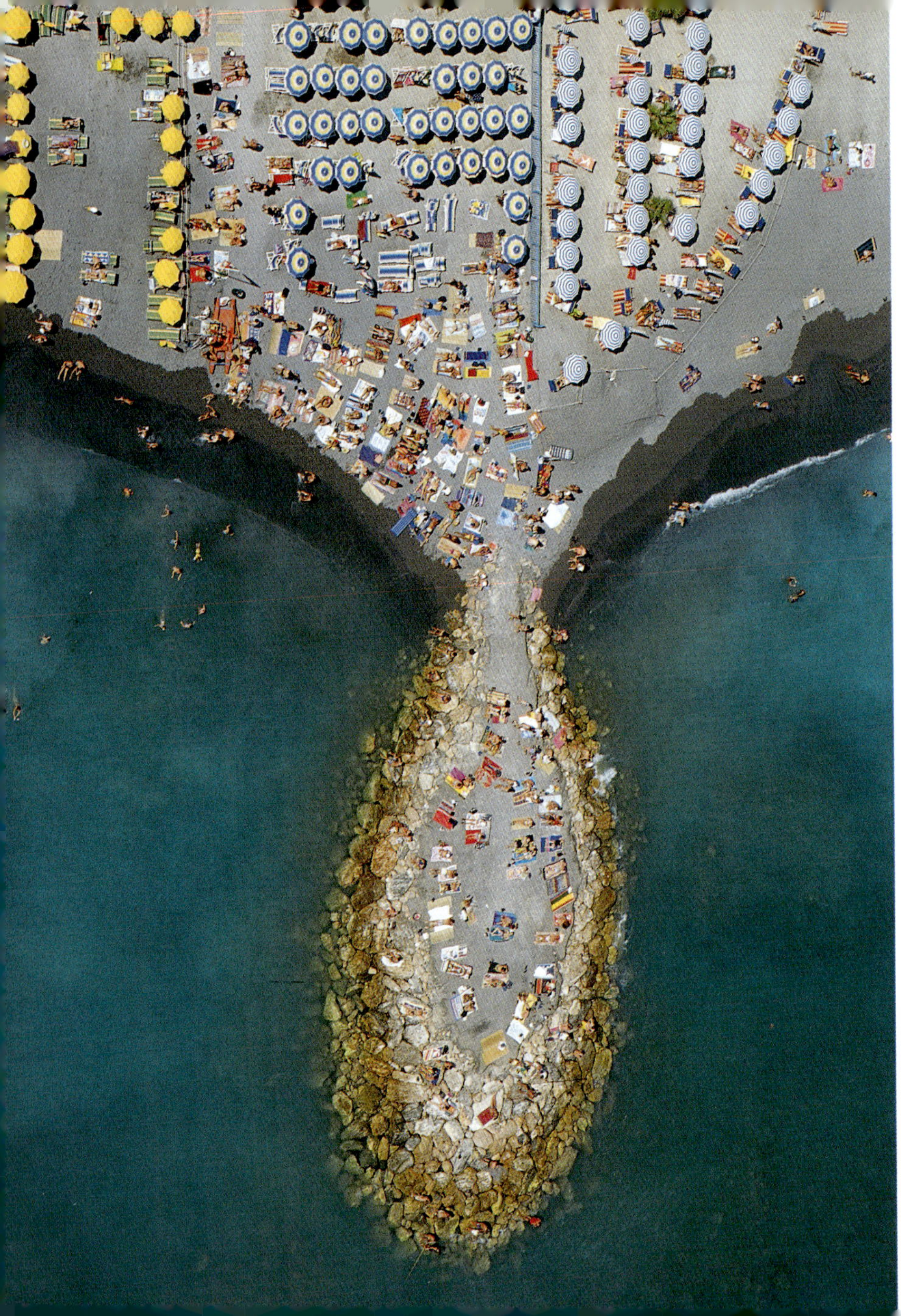

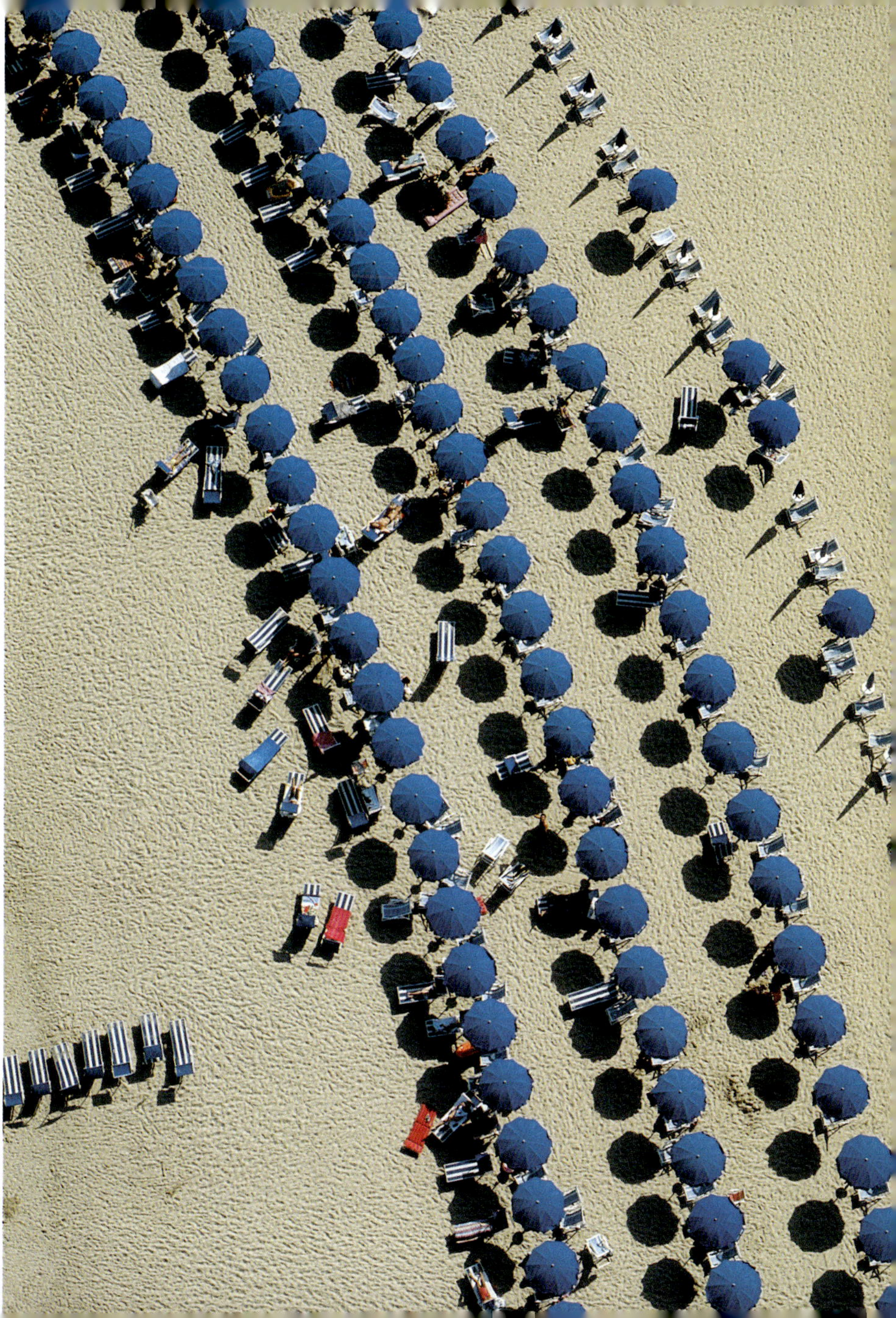

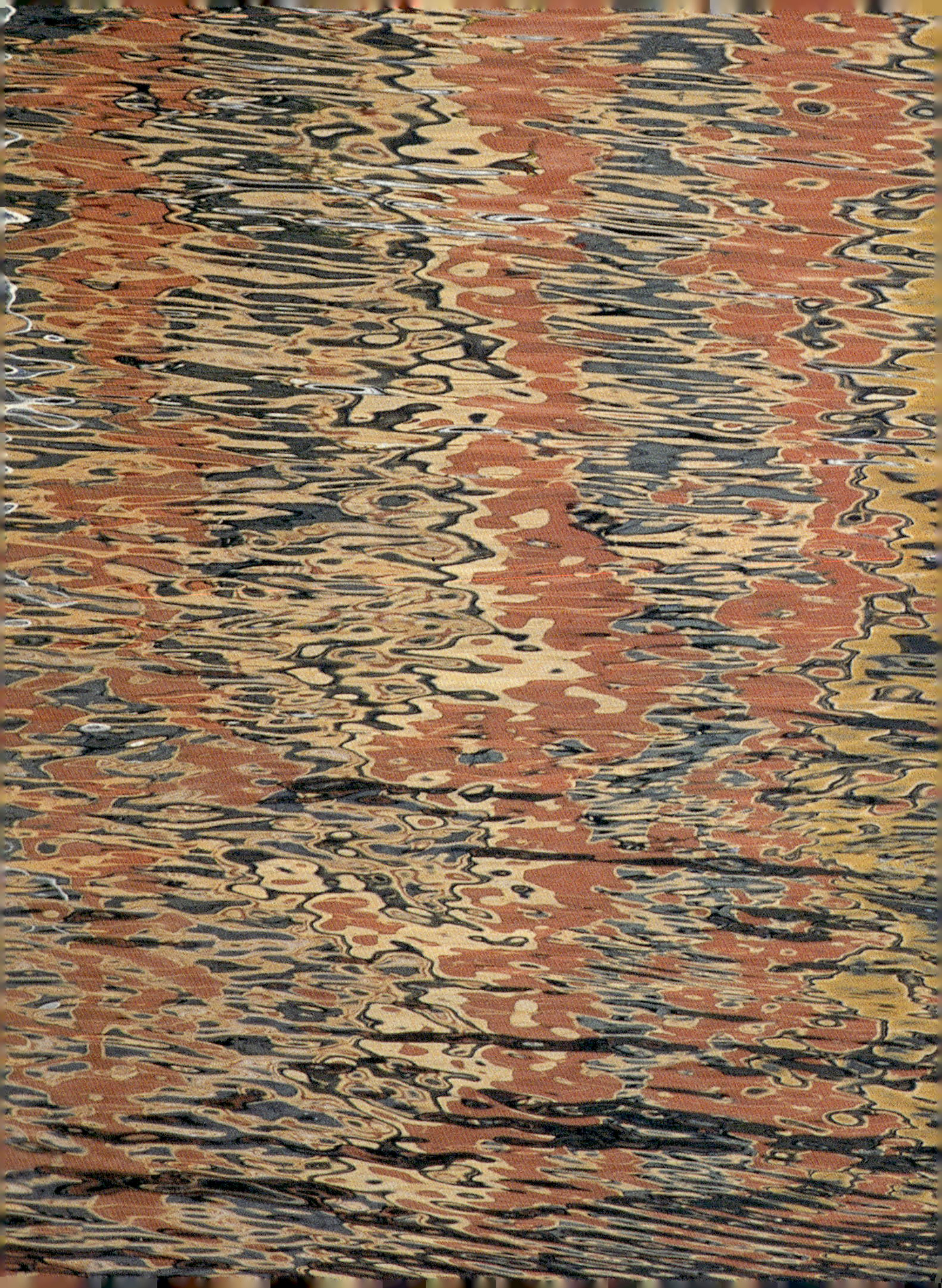

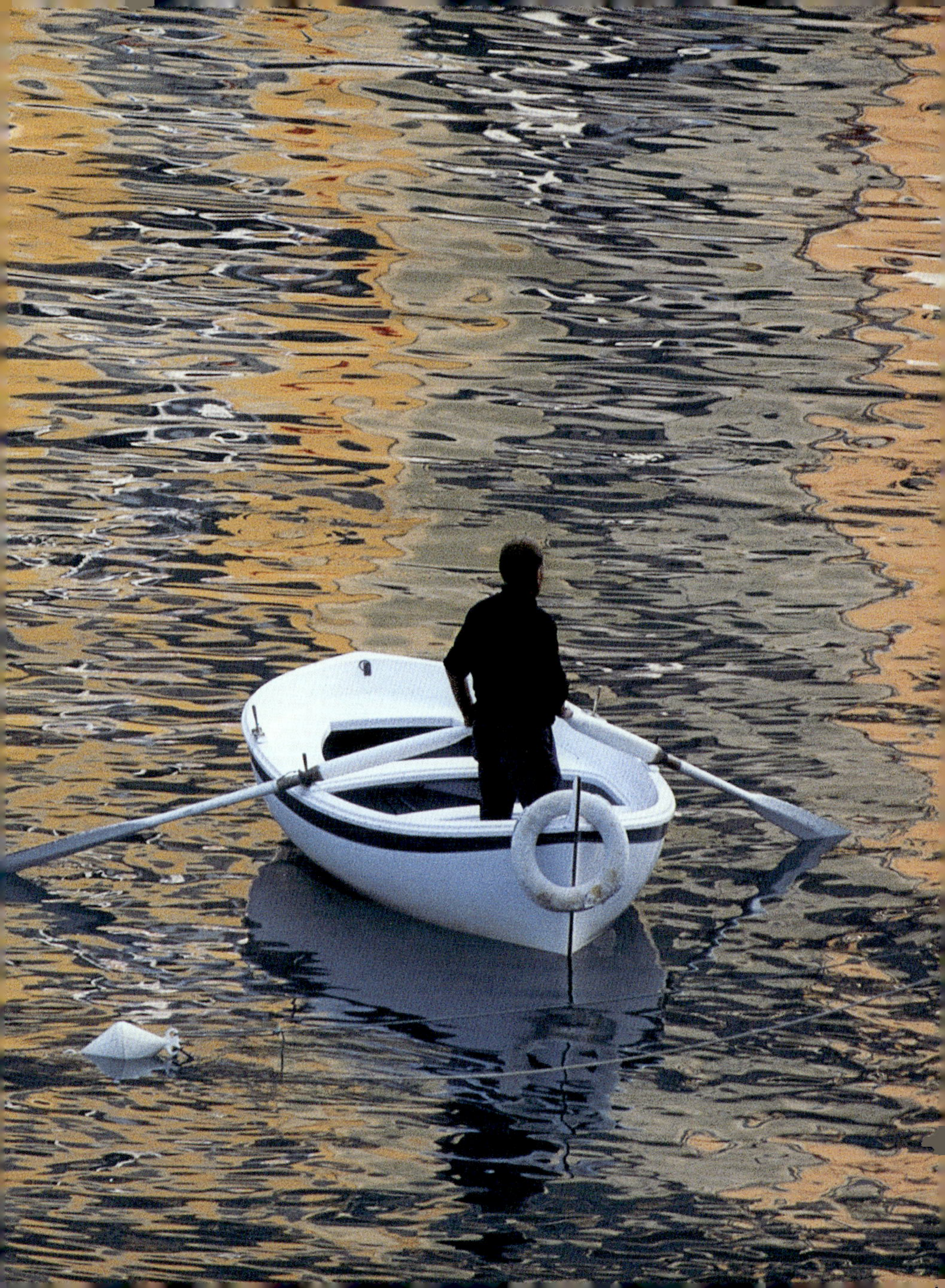

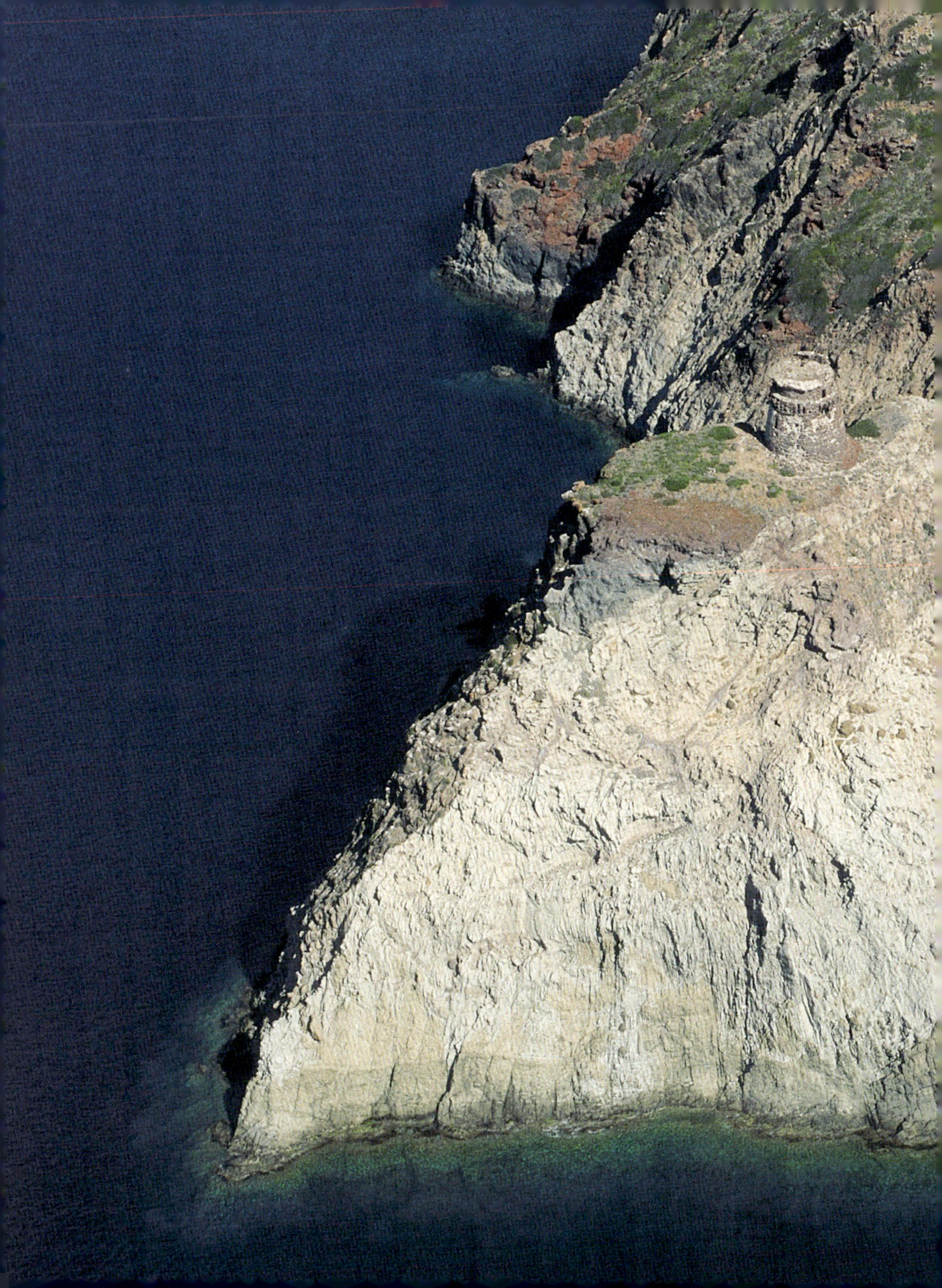

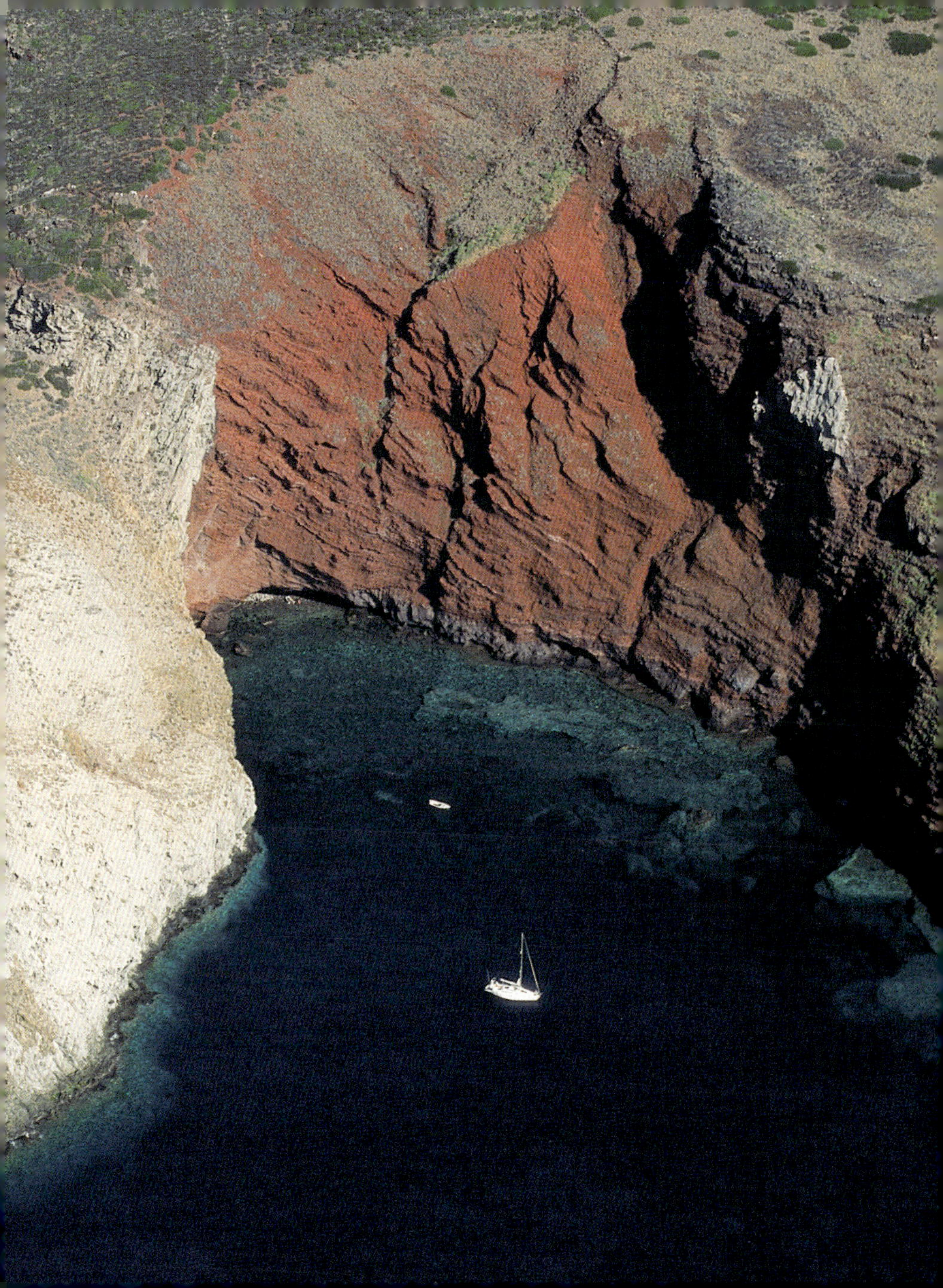

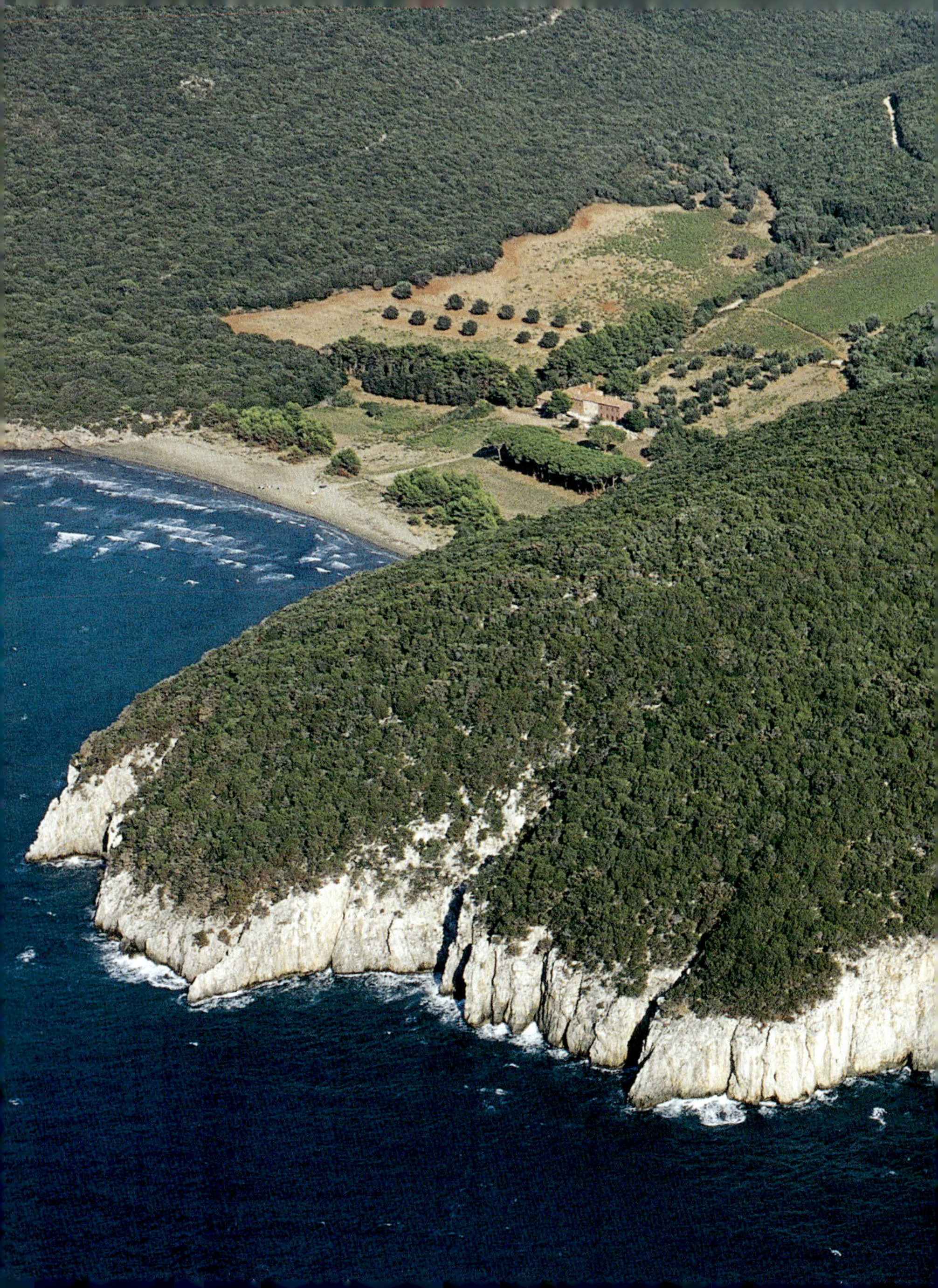

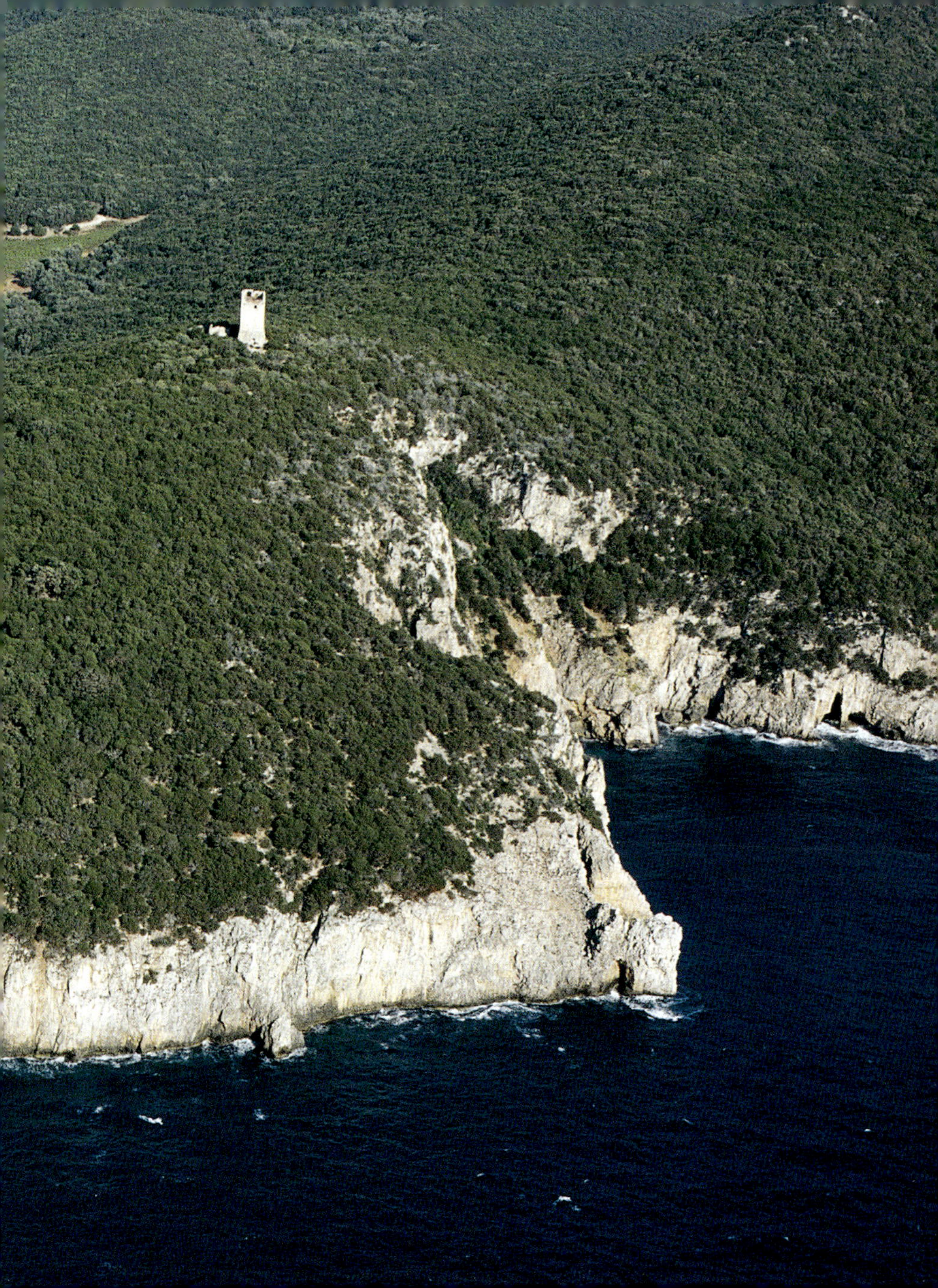

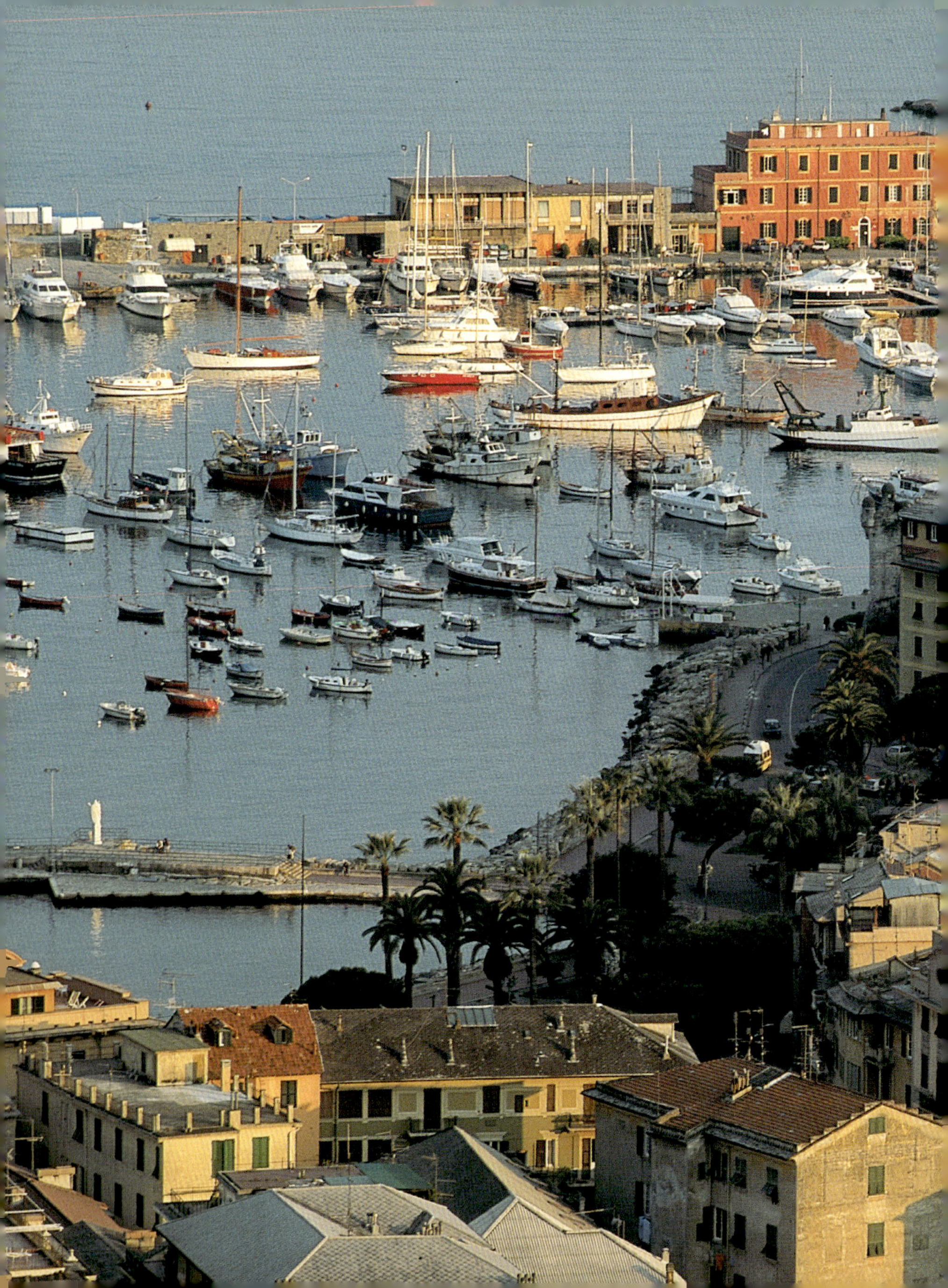

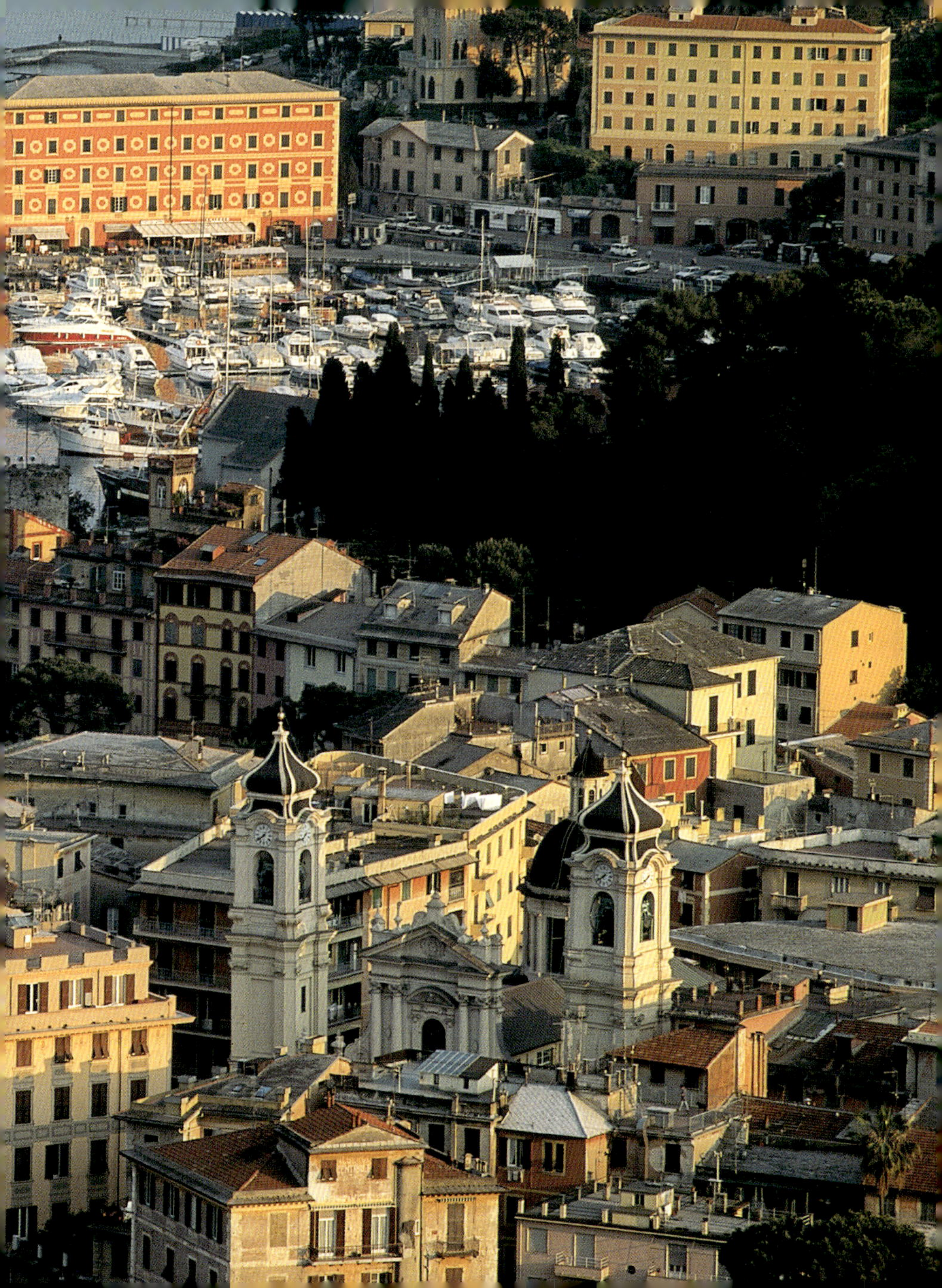

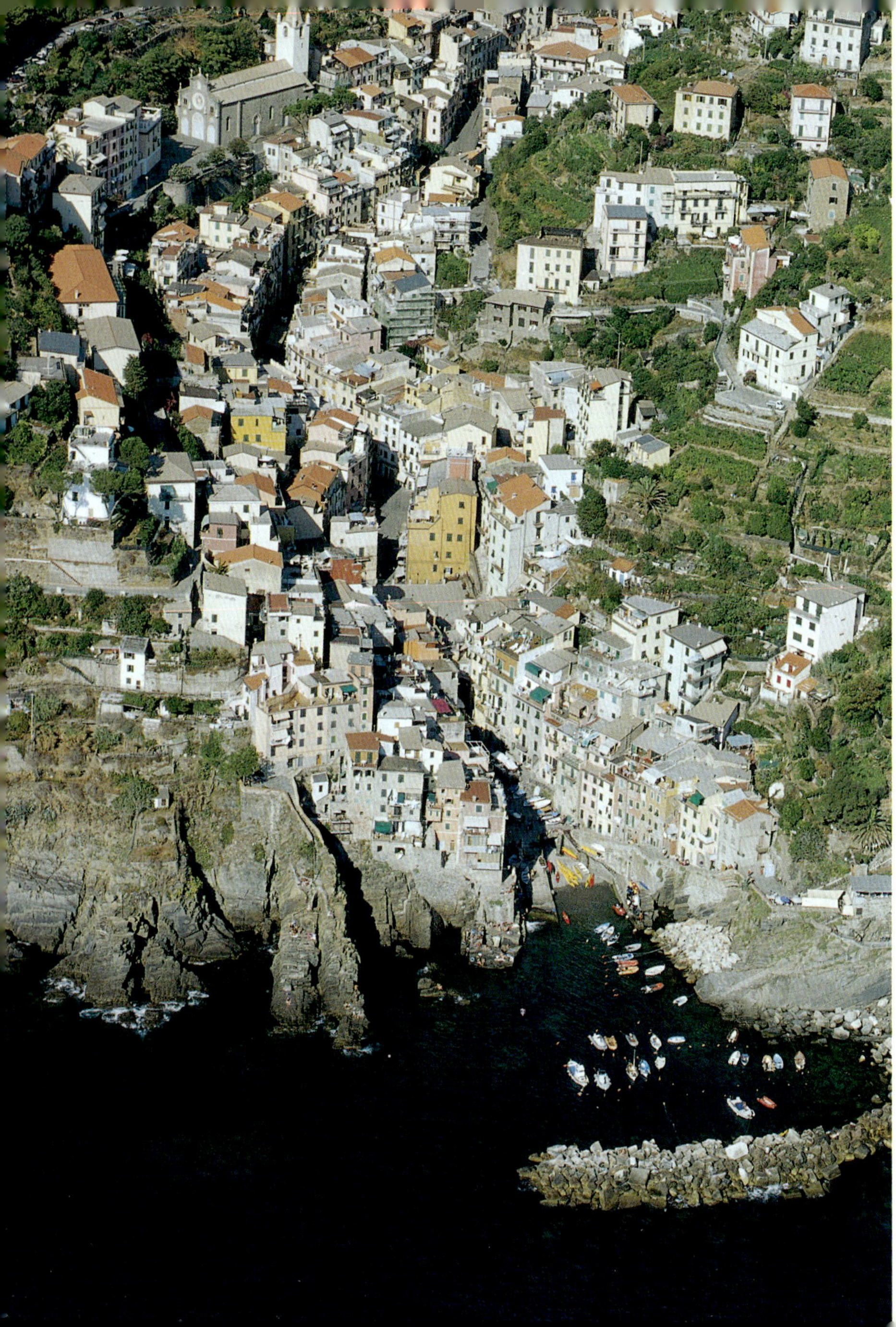

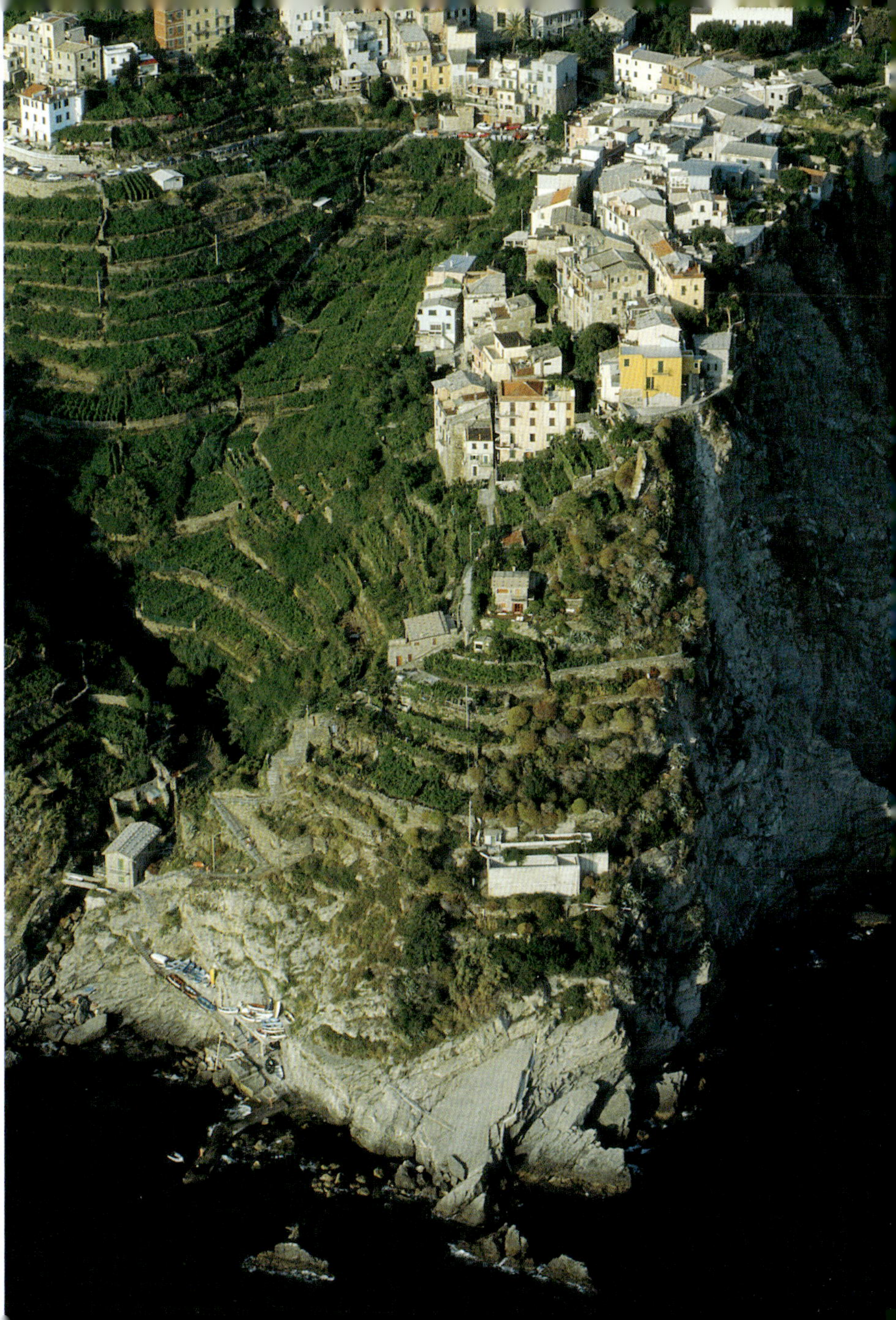

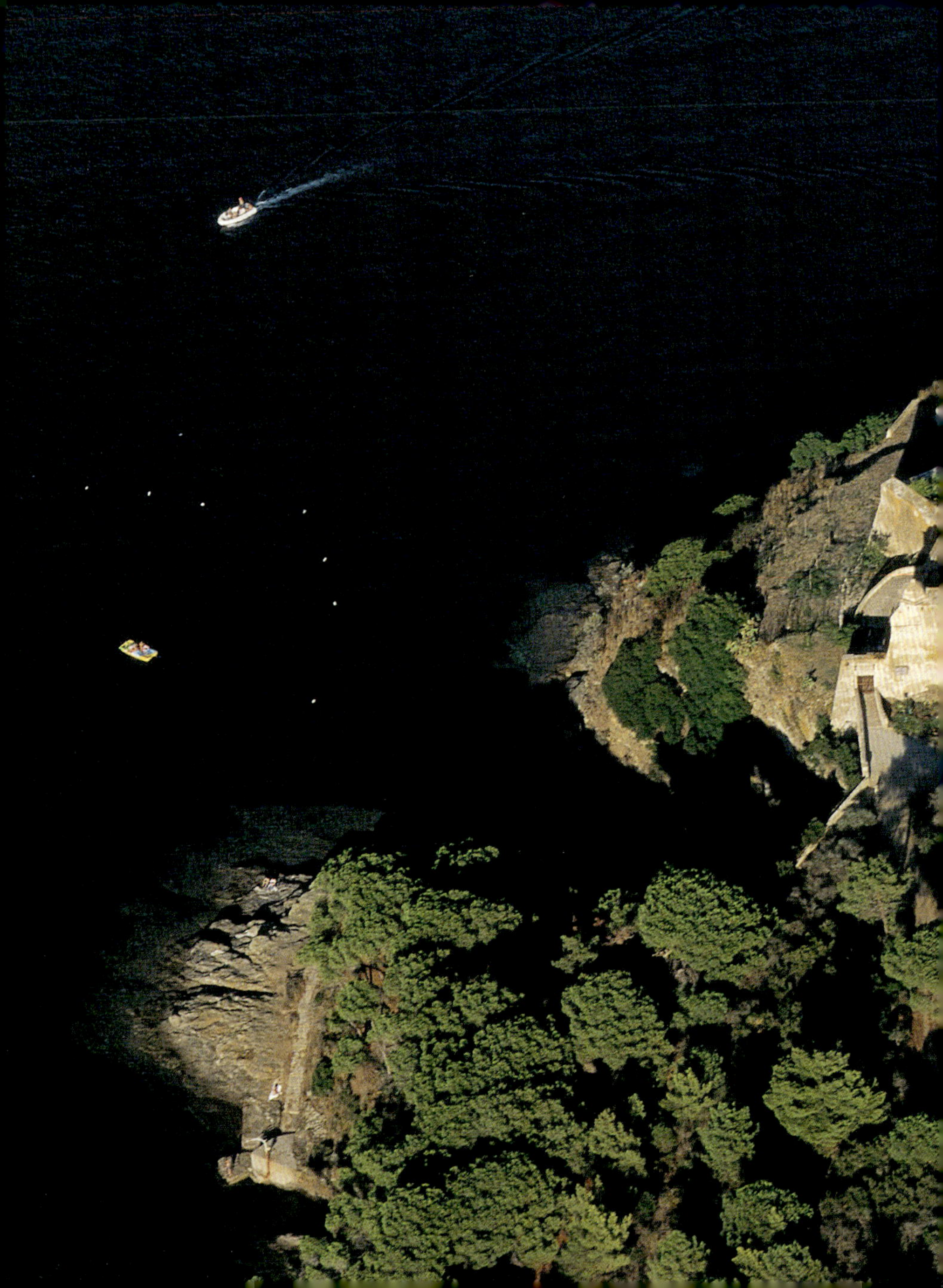

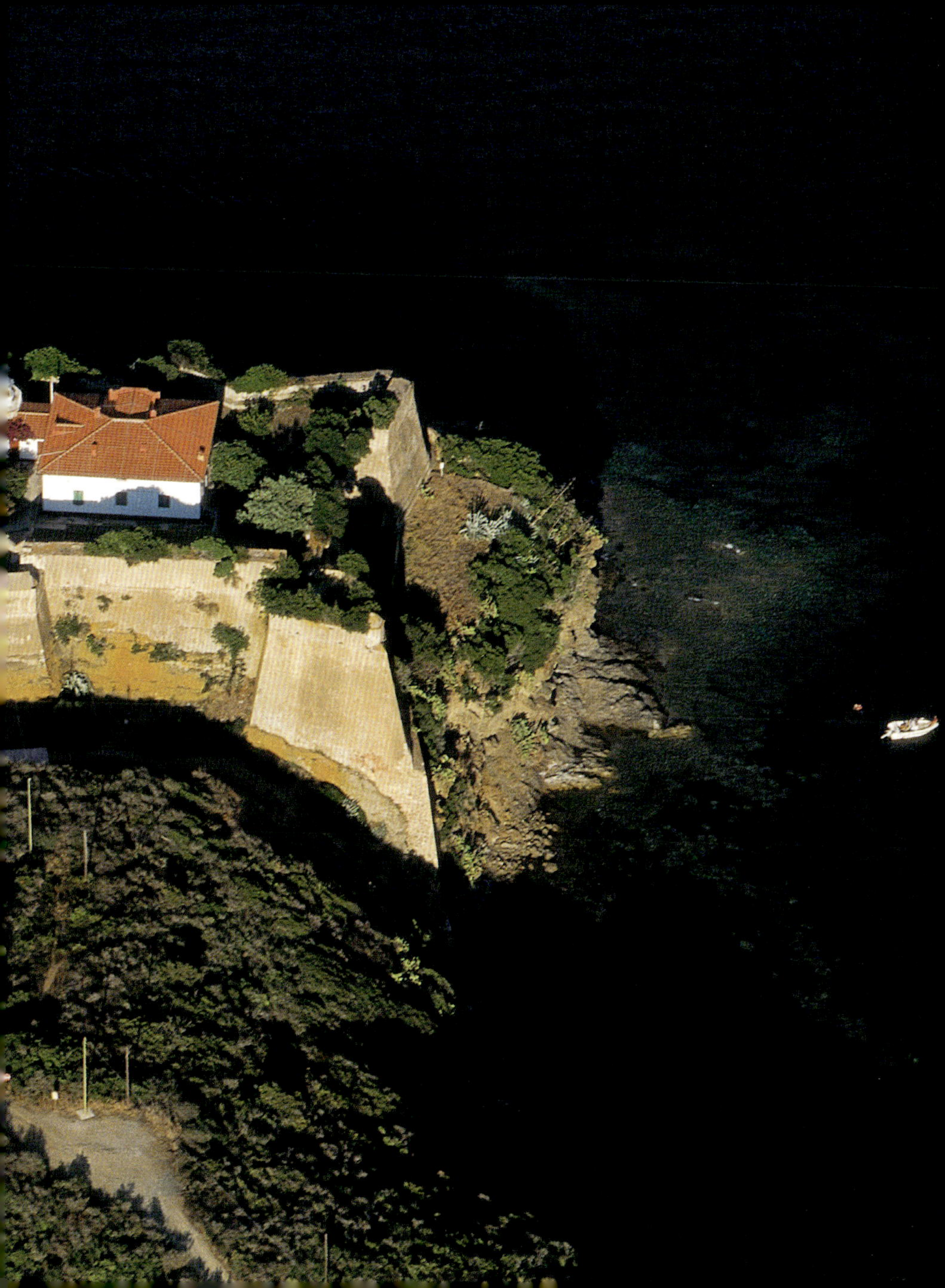

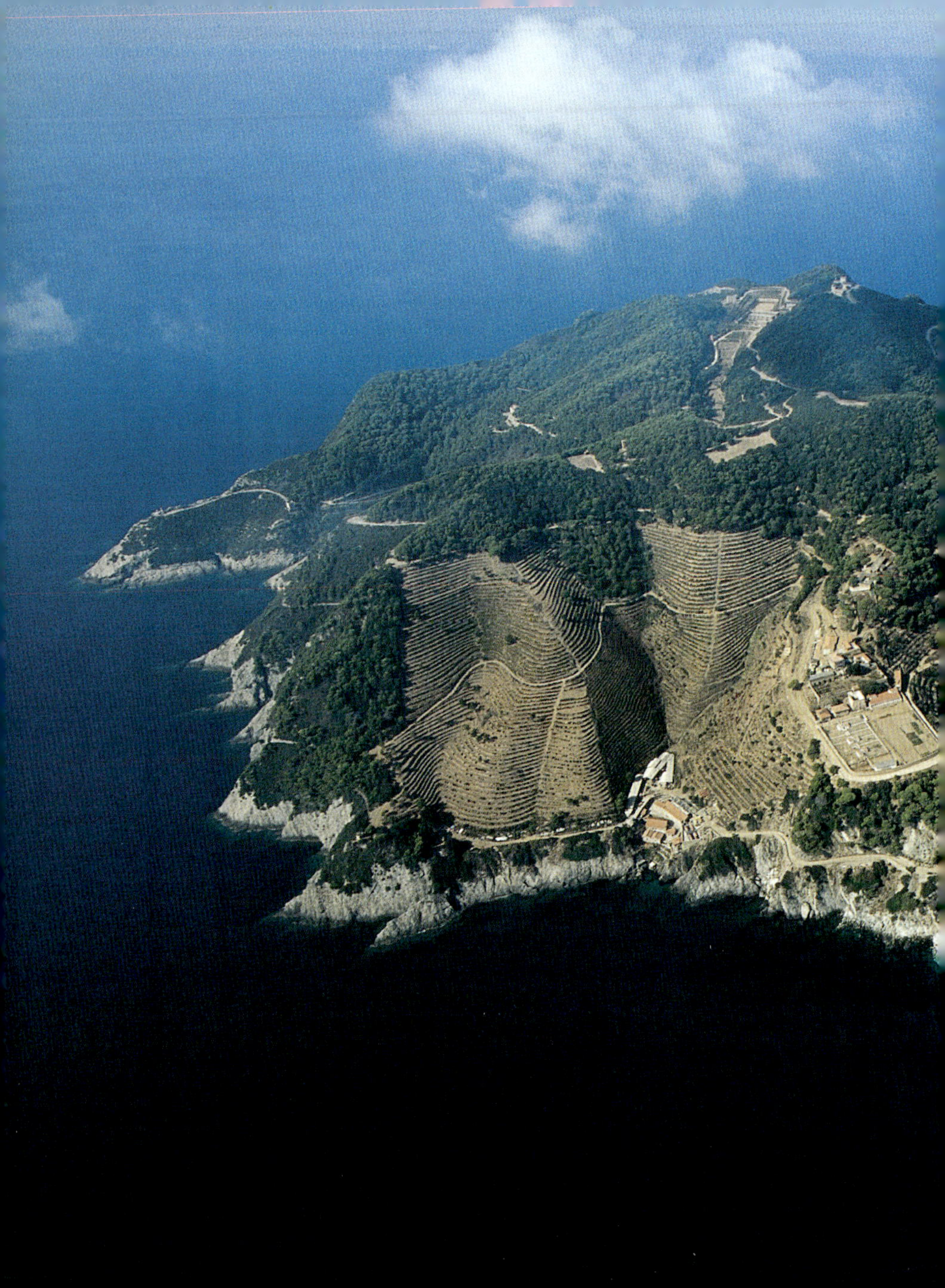

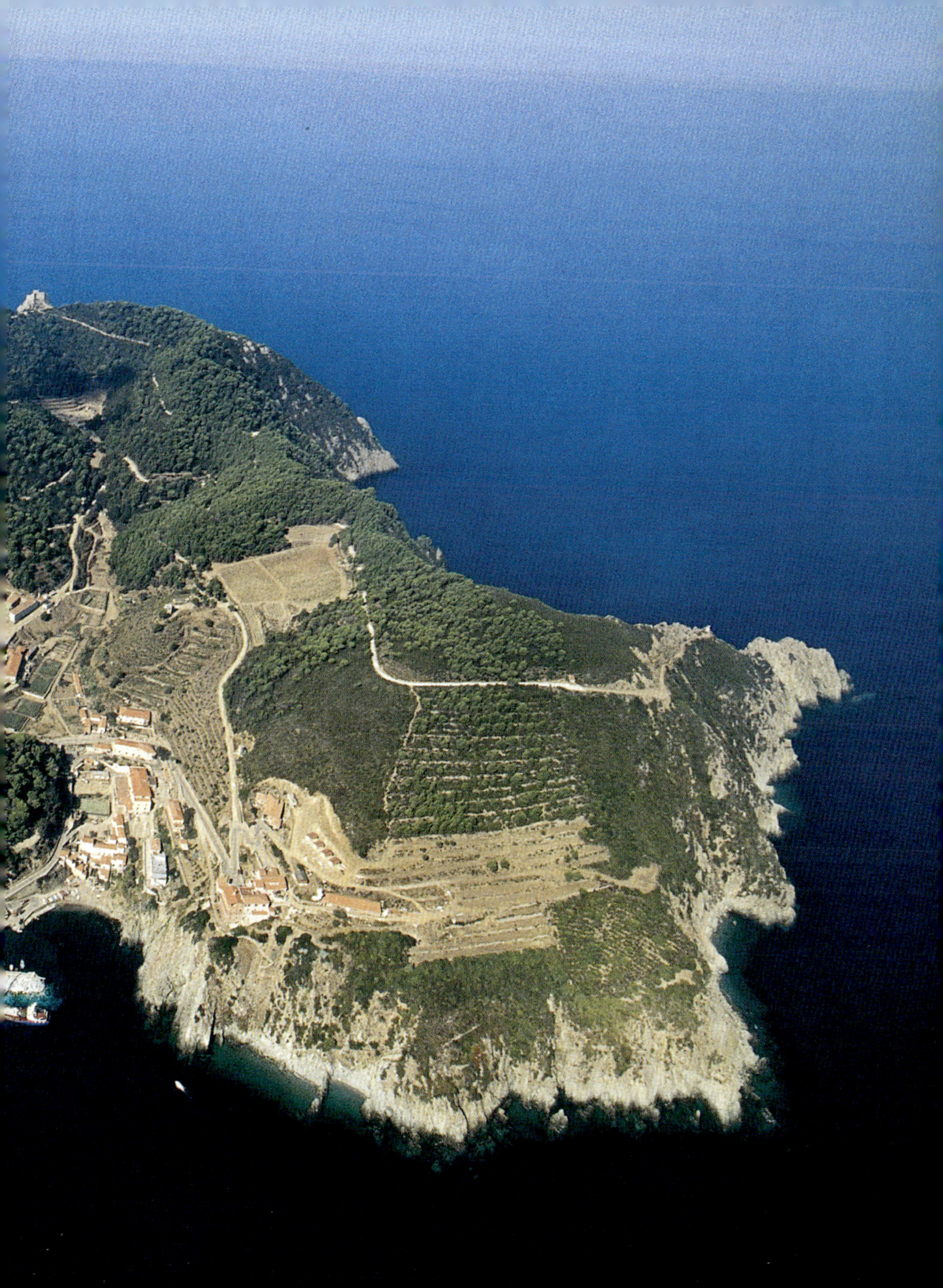

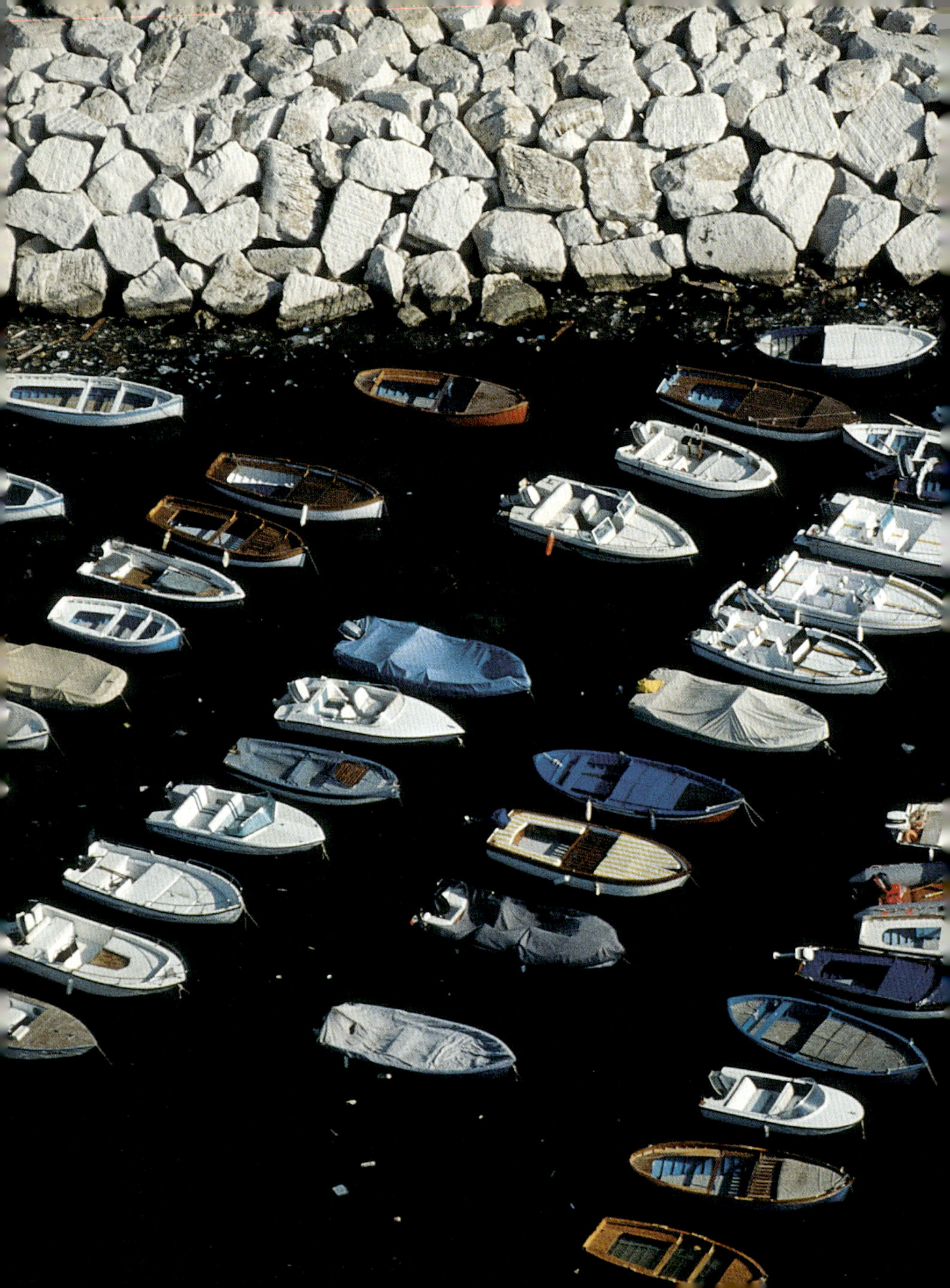

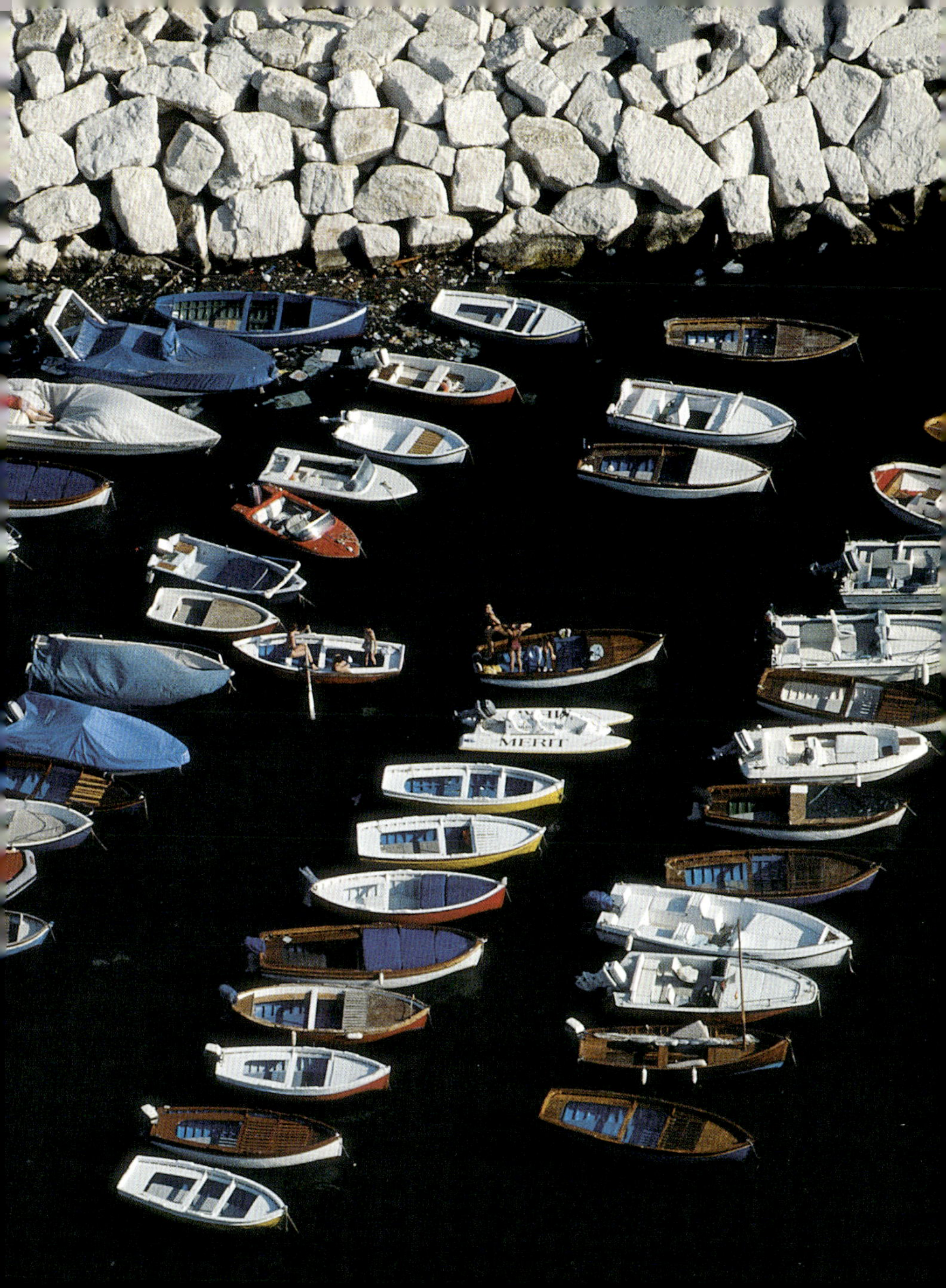
MERIT

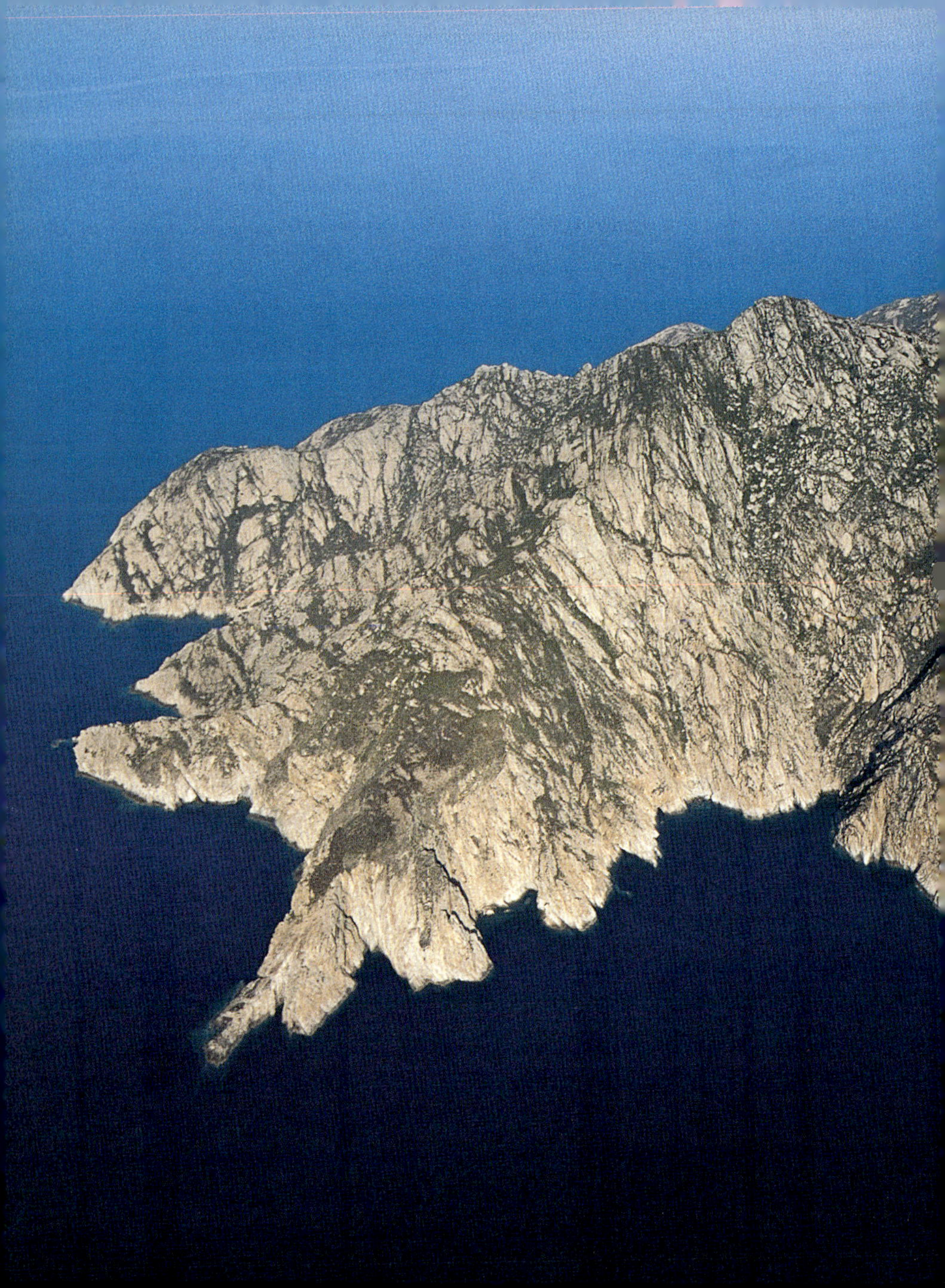

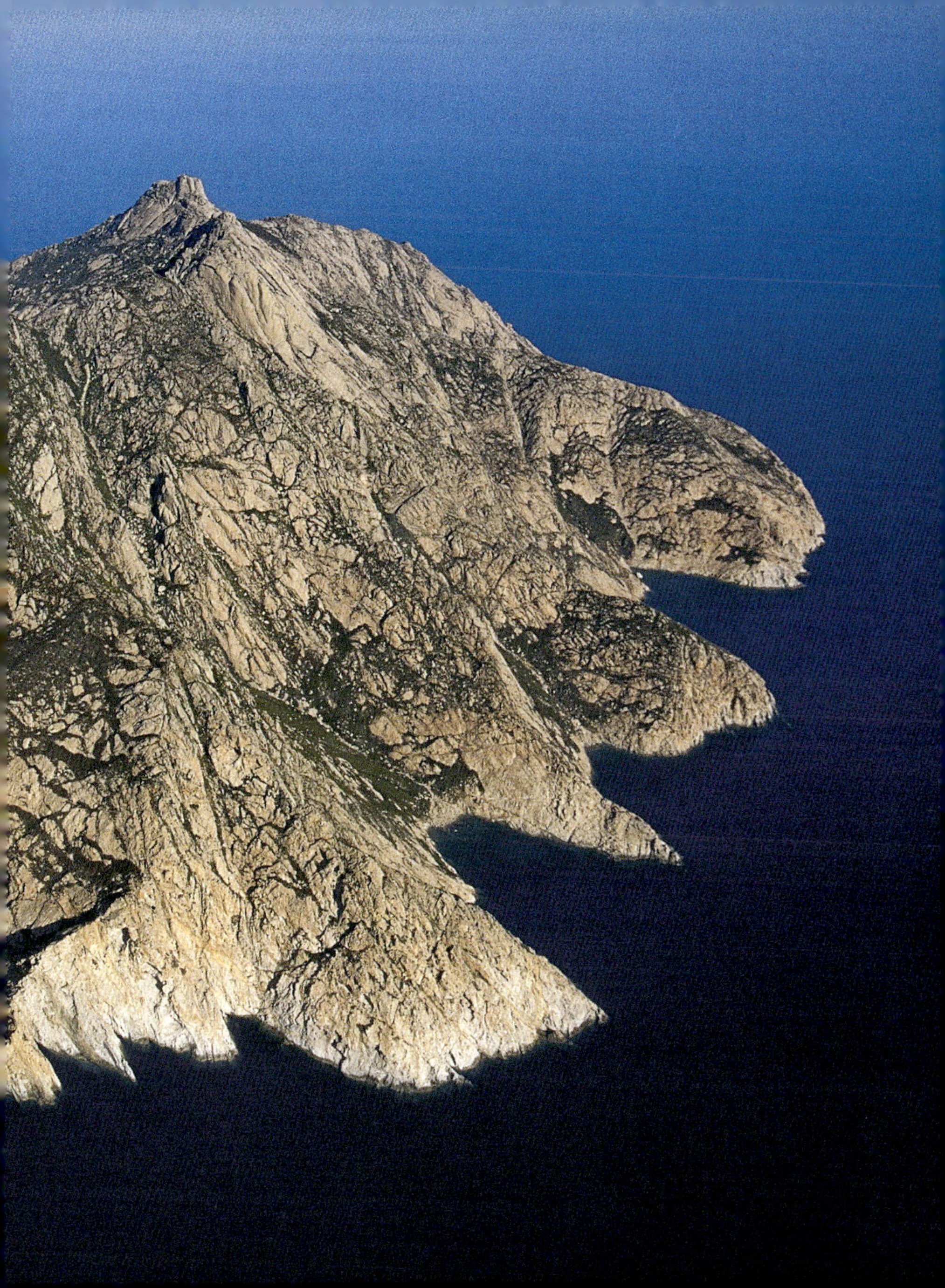

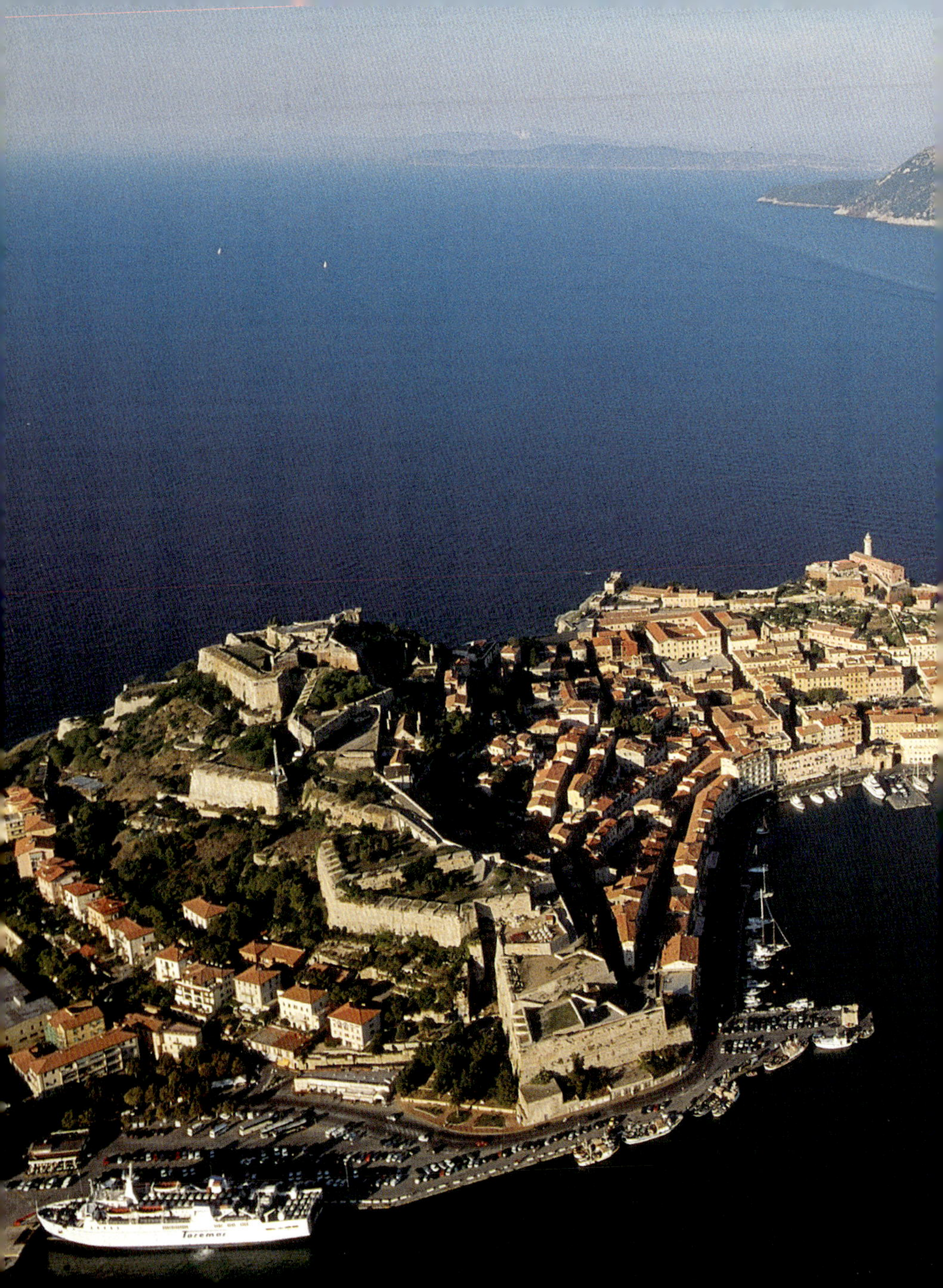
Toremar

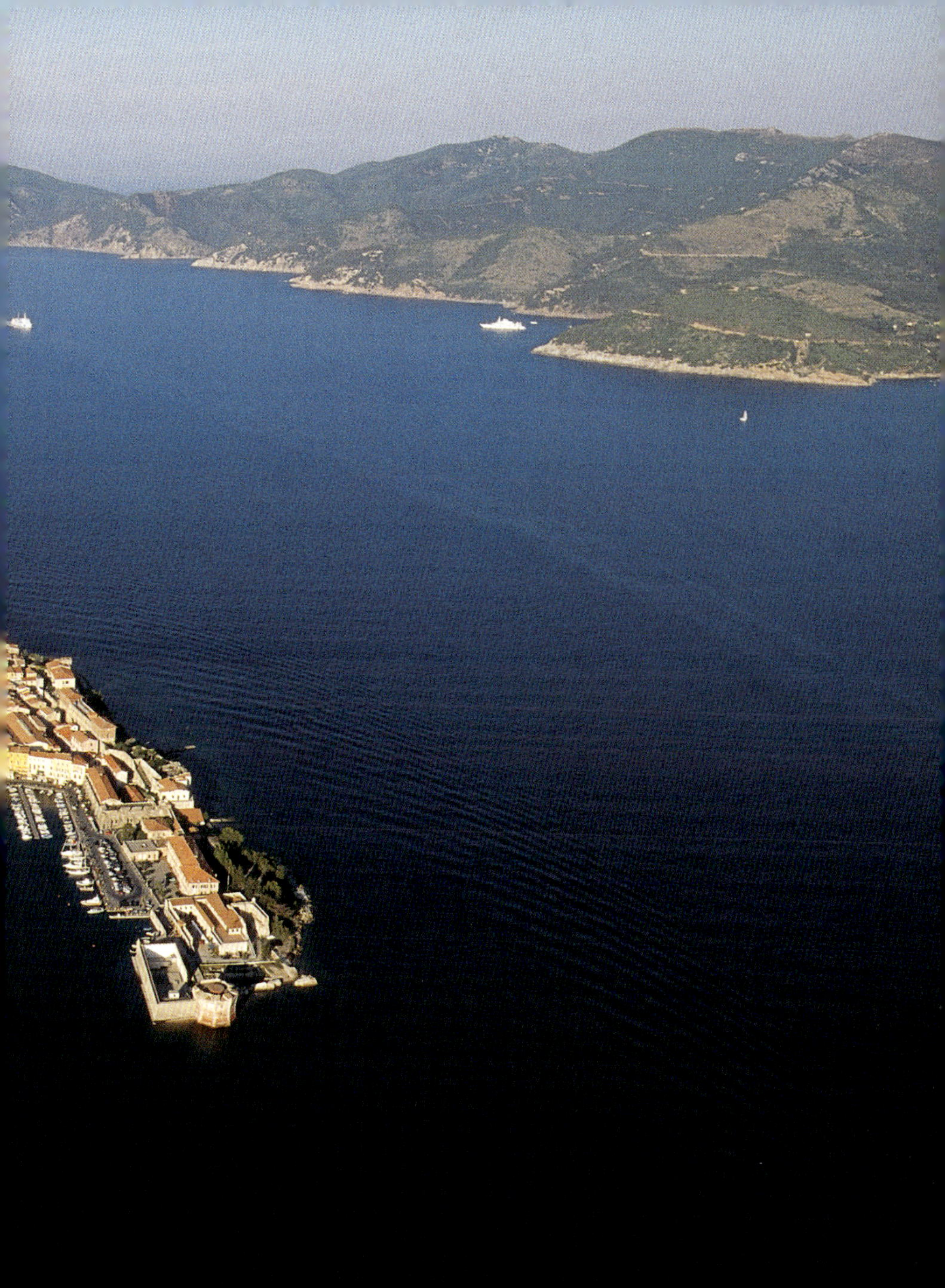

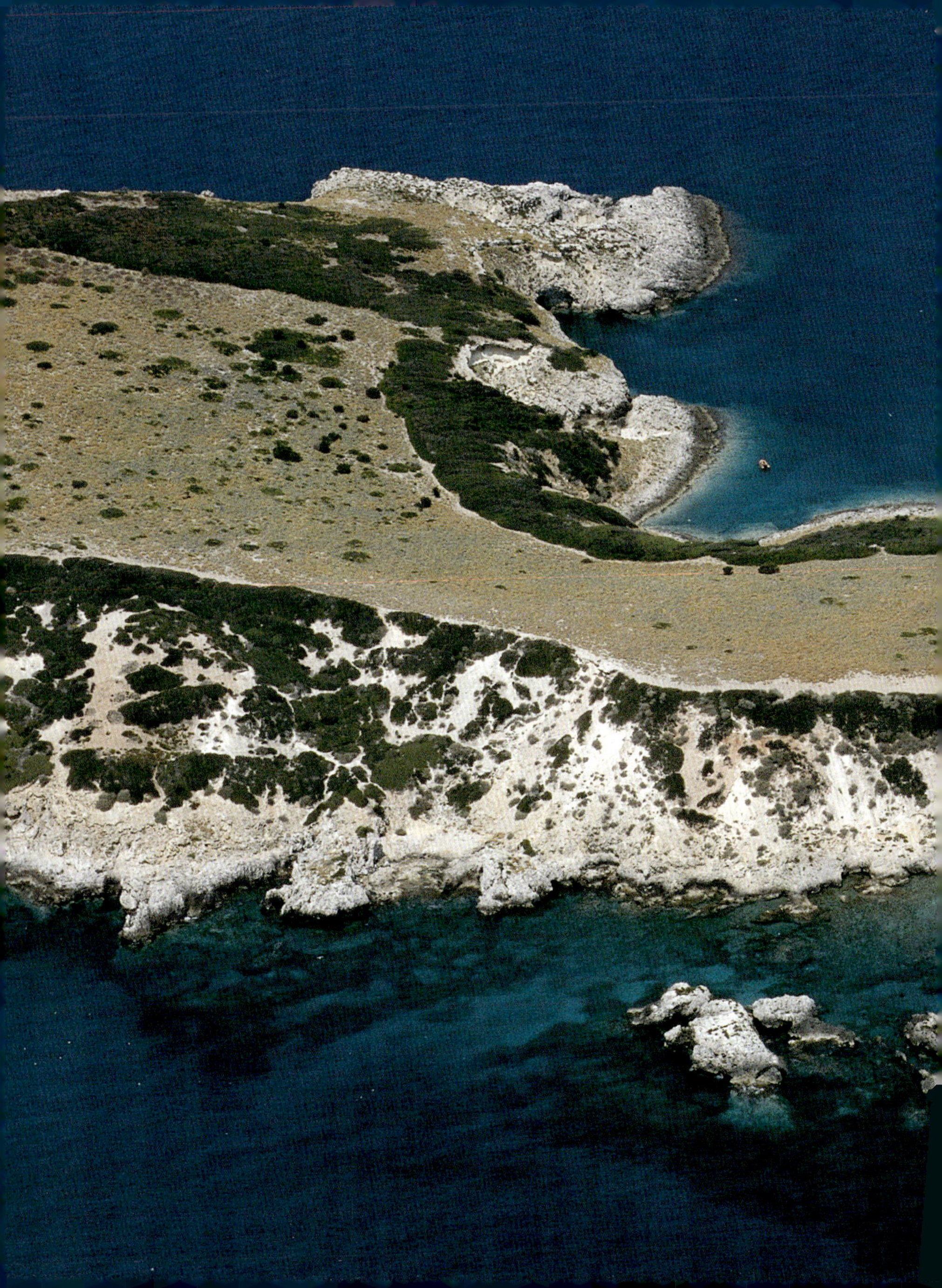

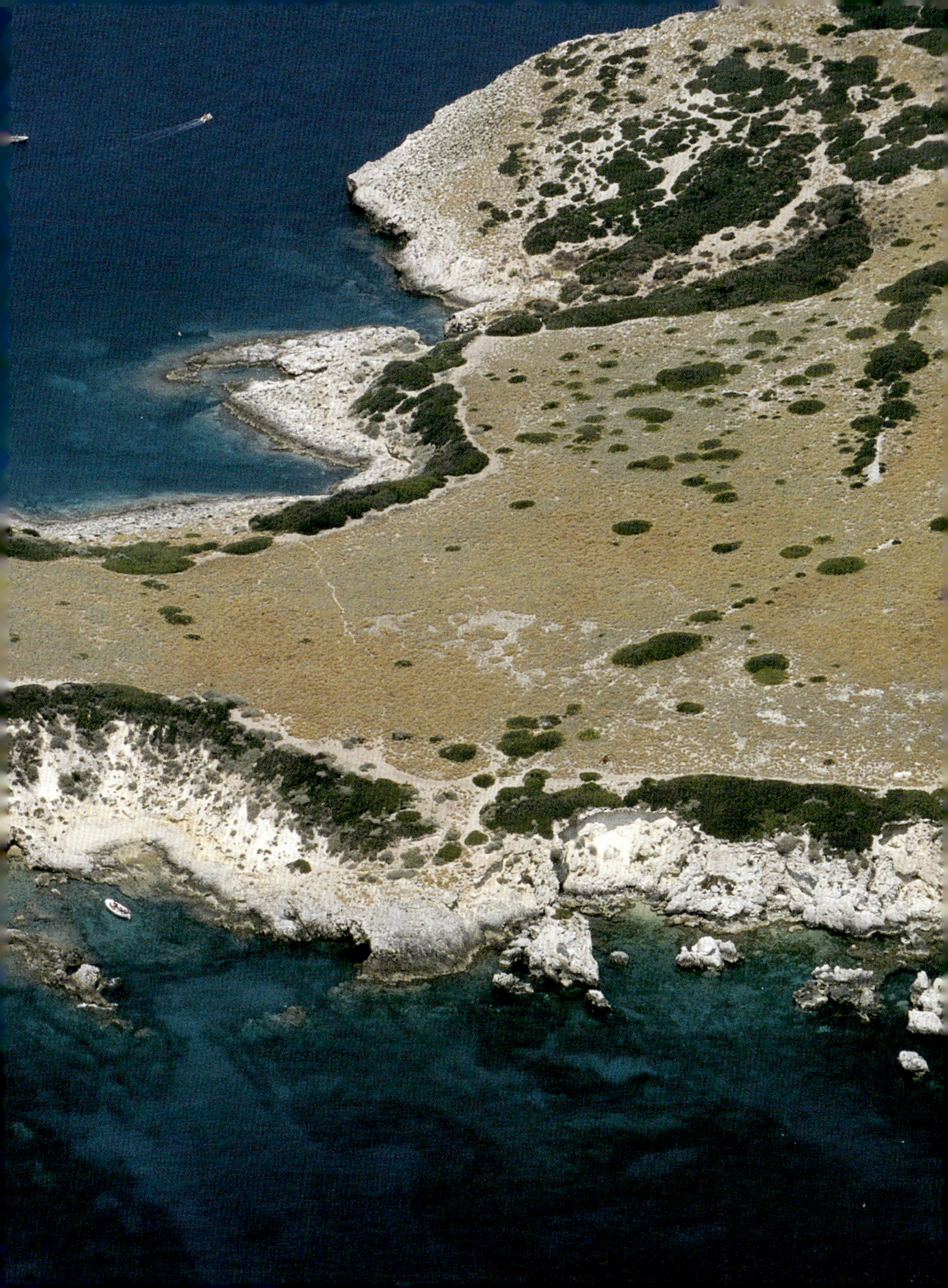

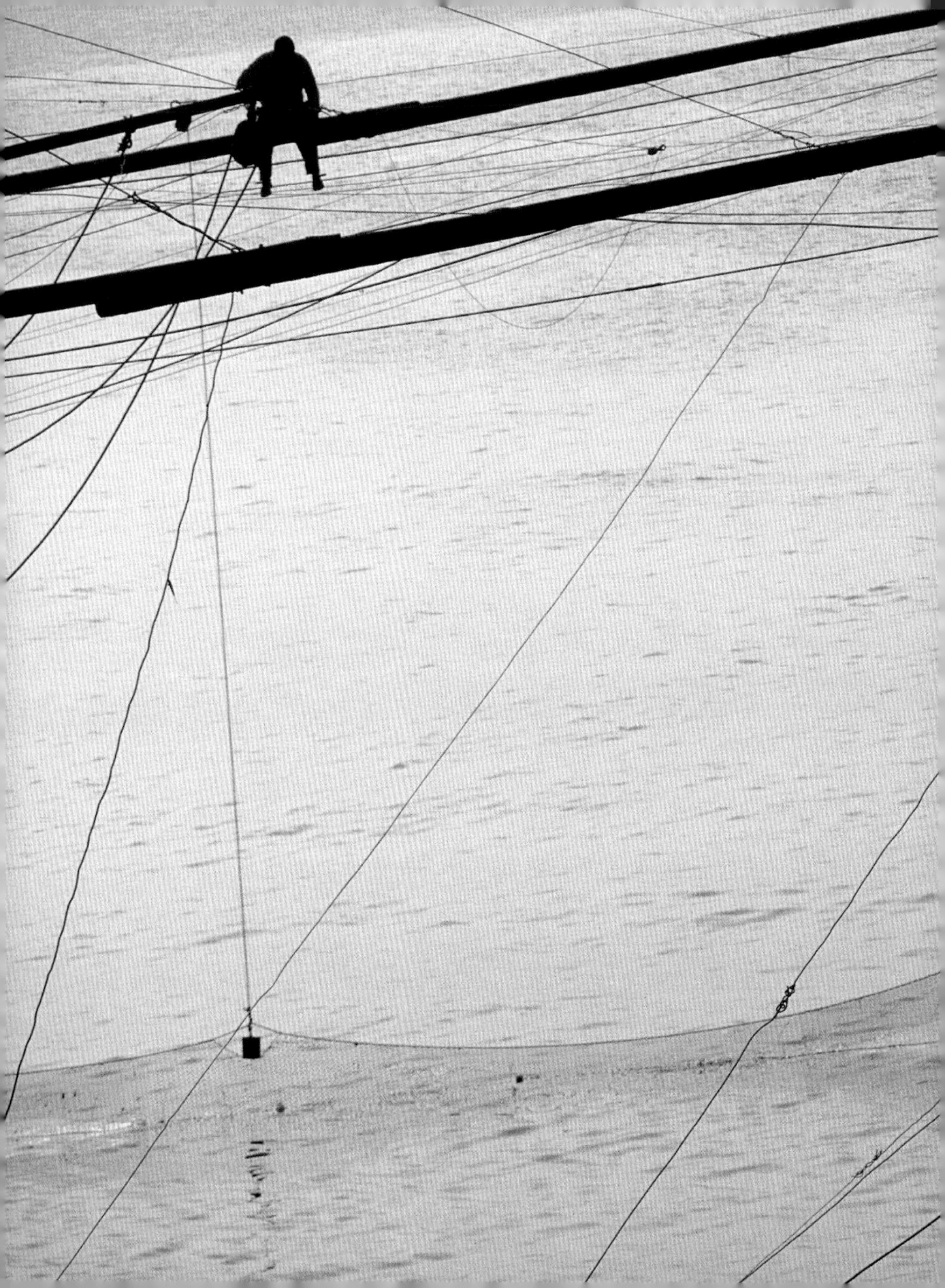

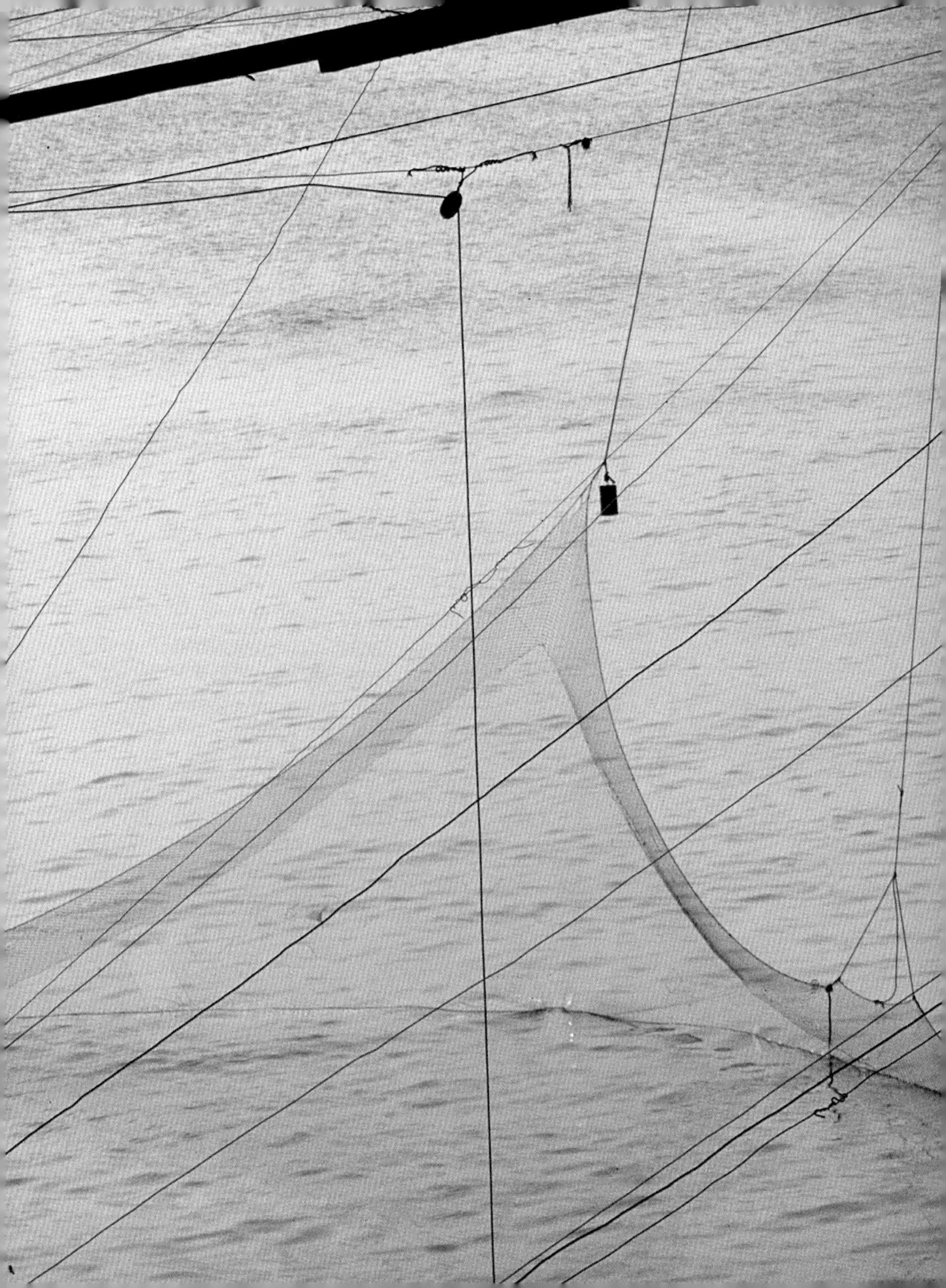

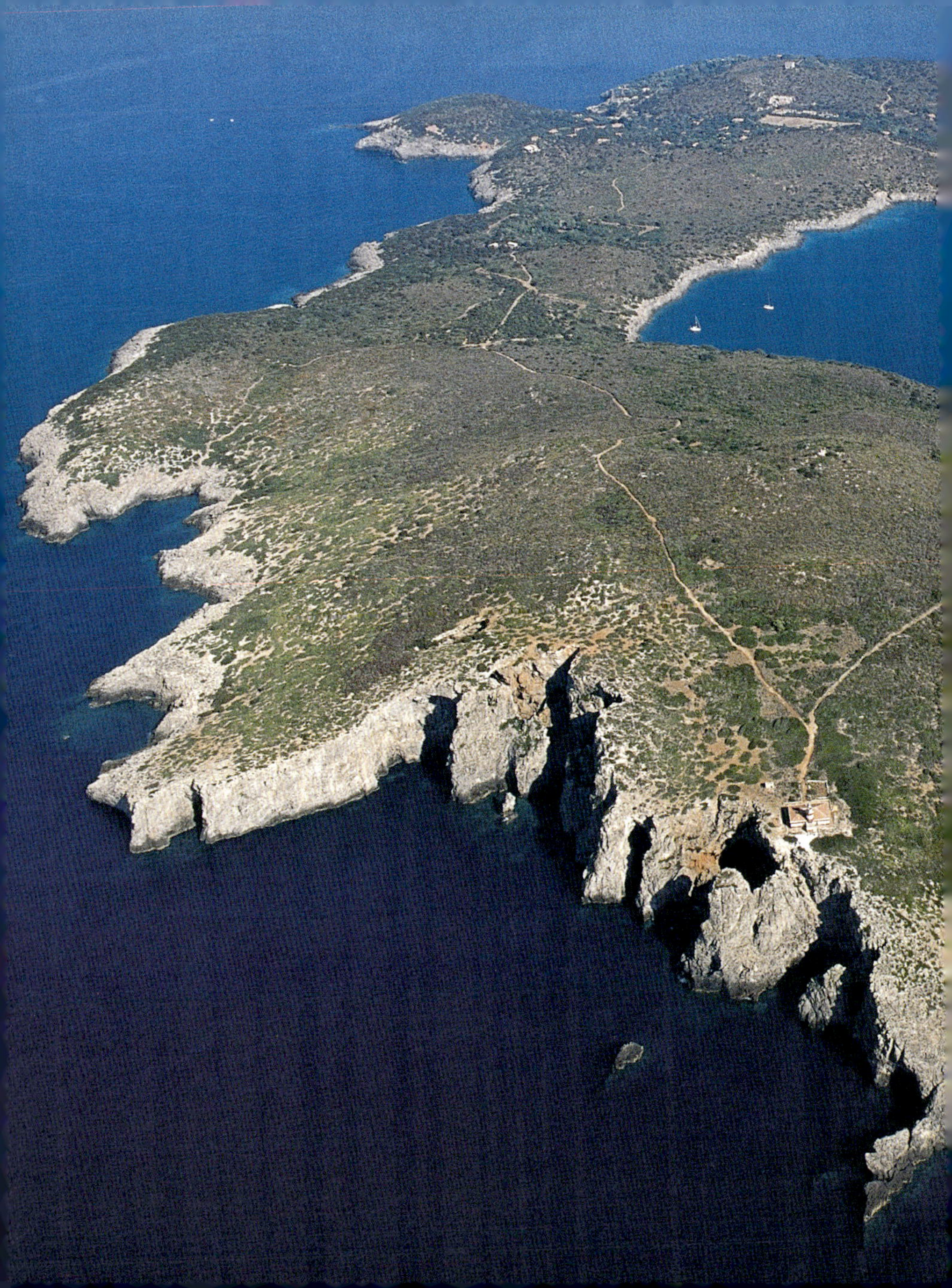

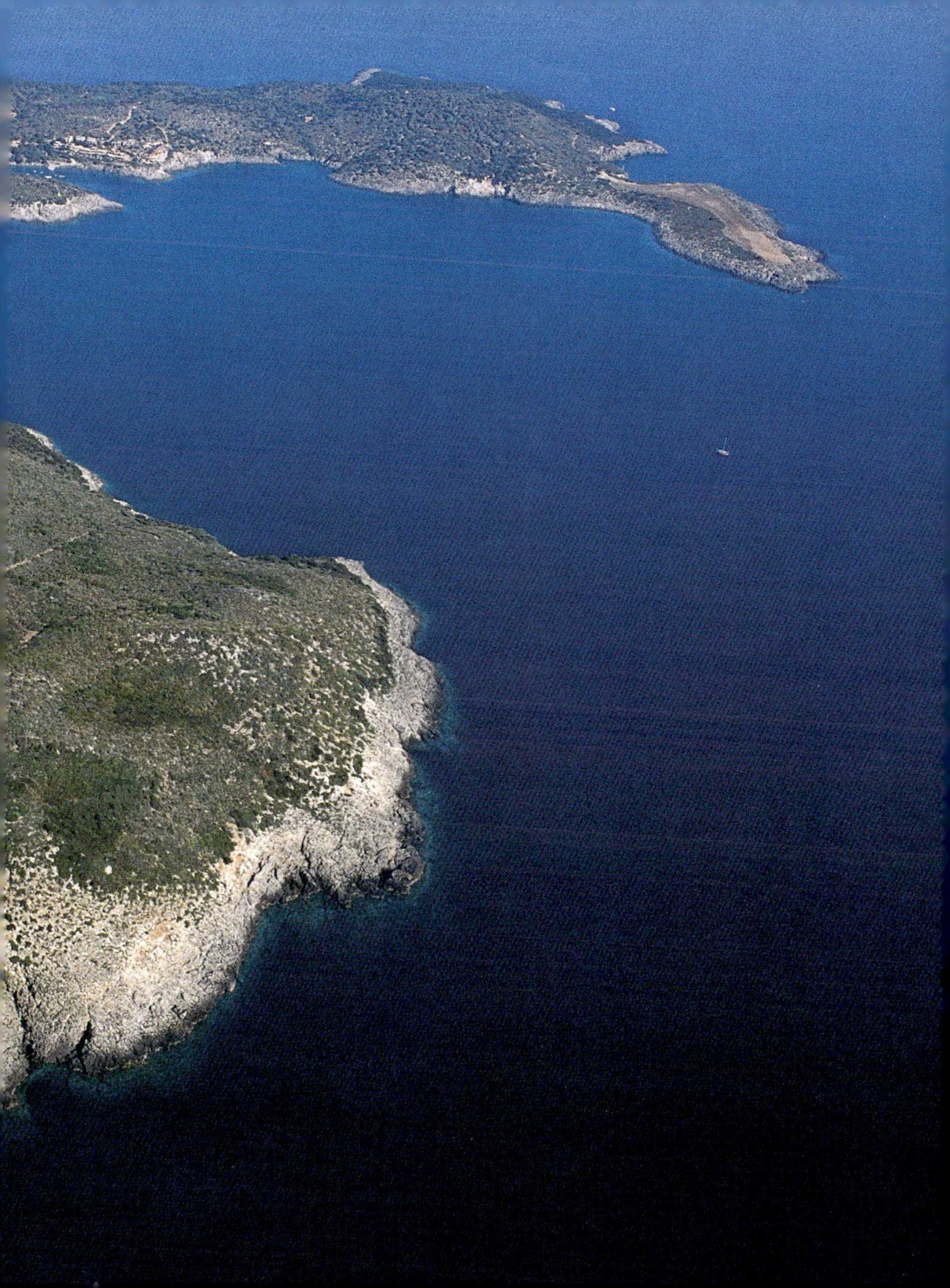

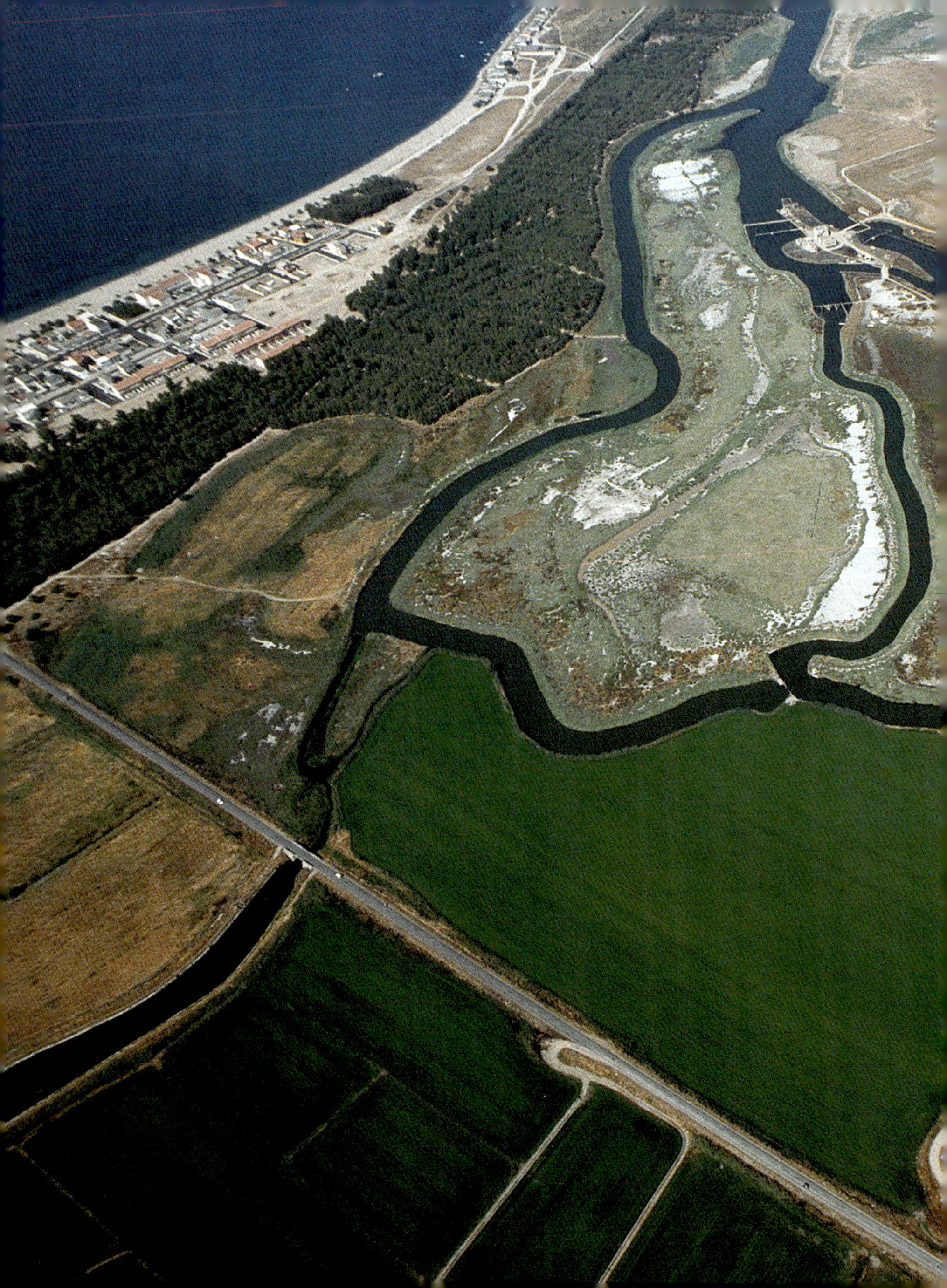

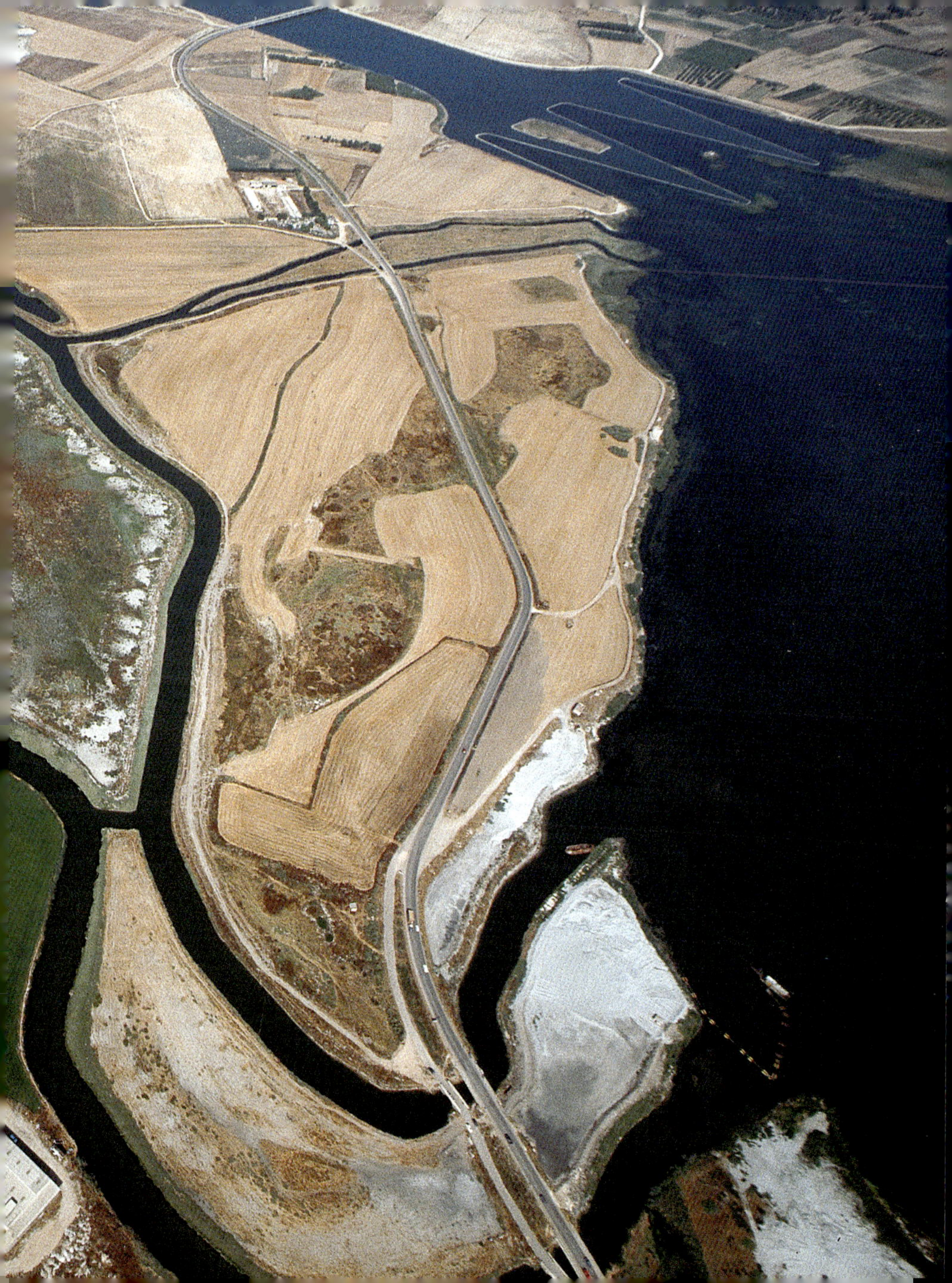

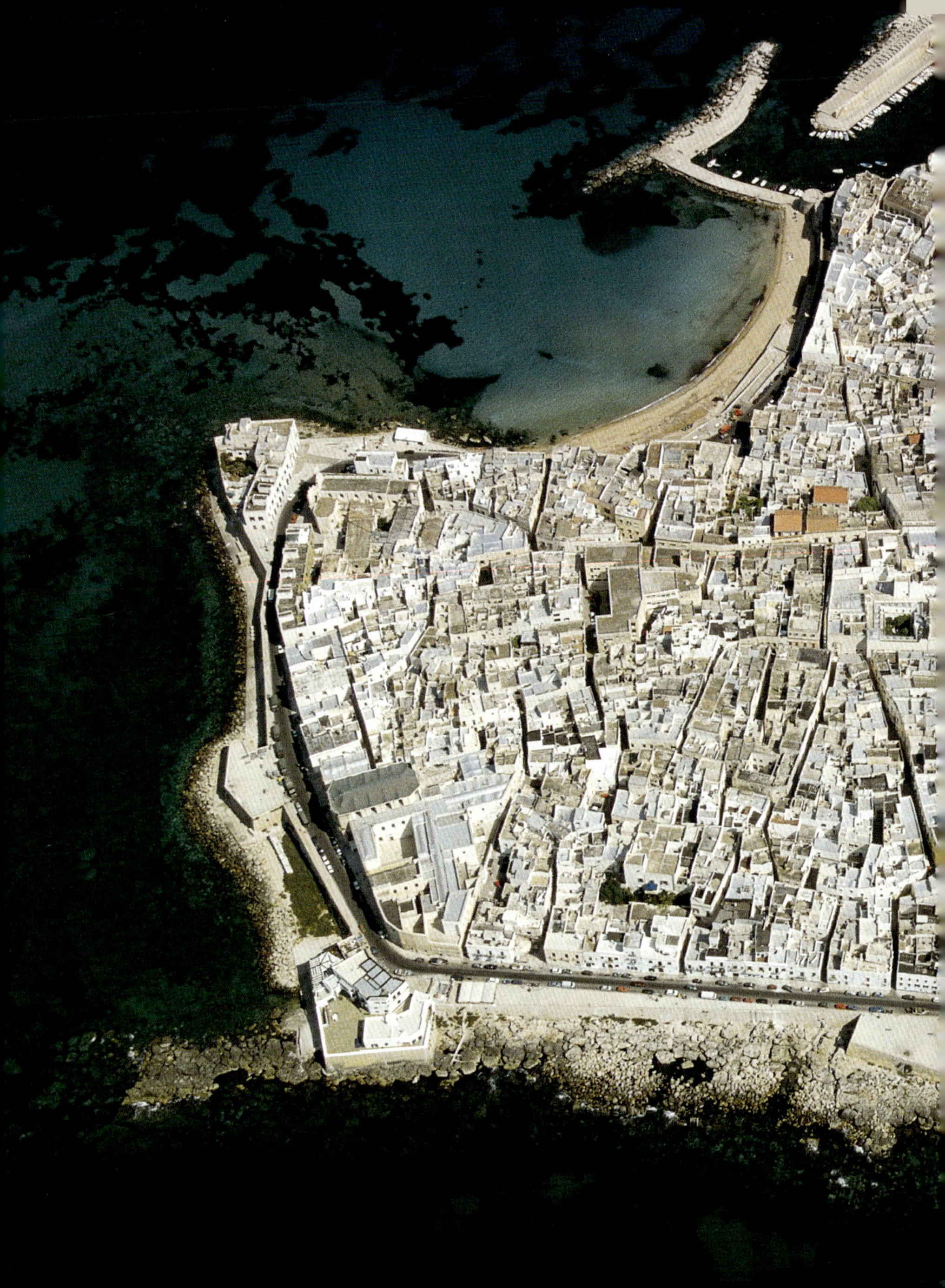

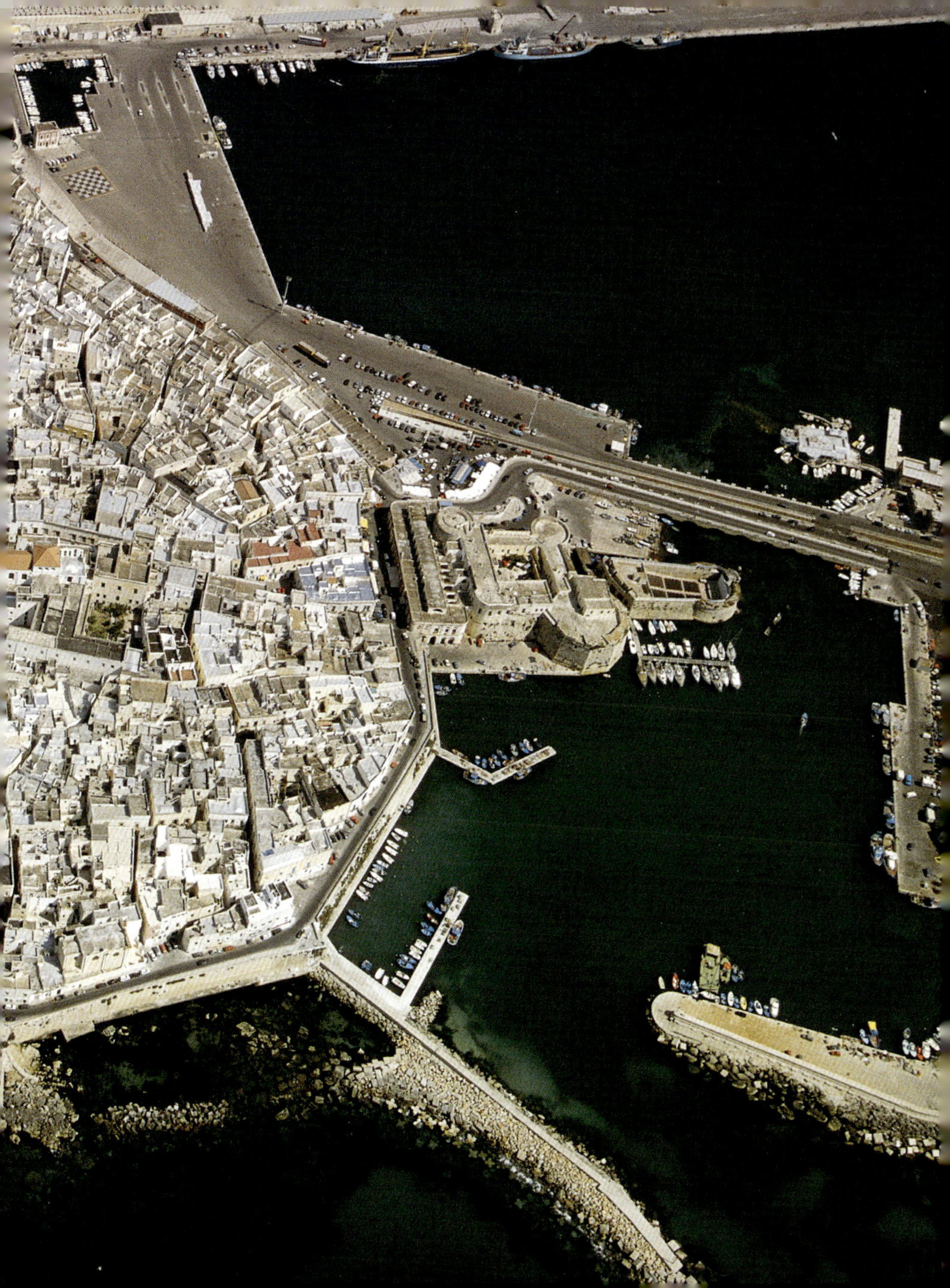

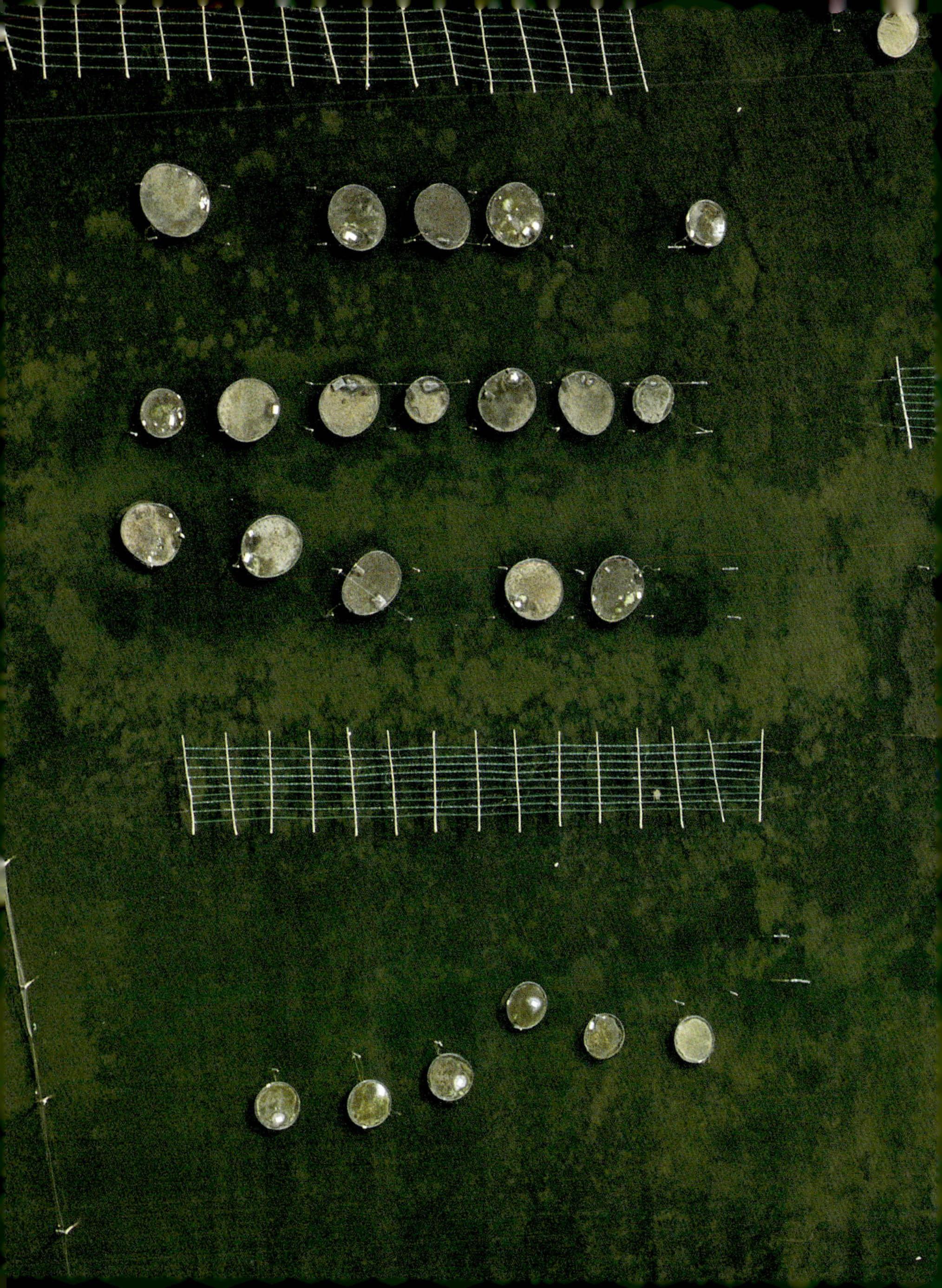

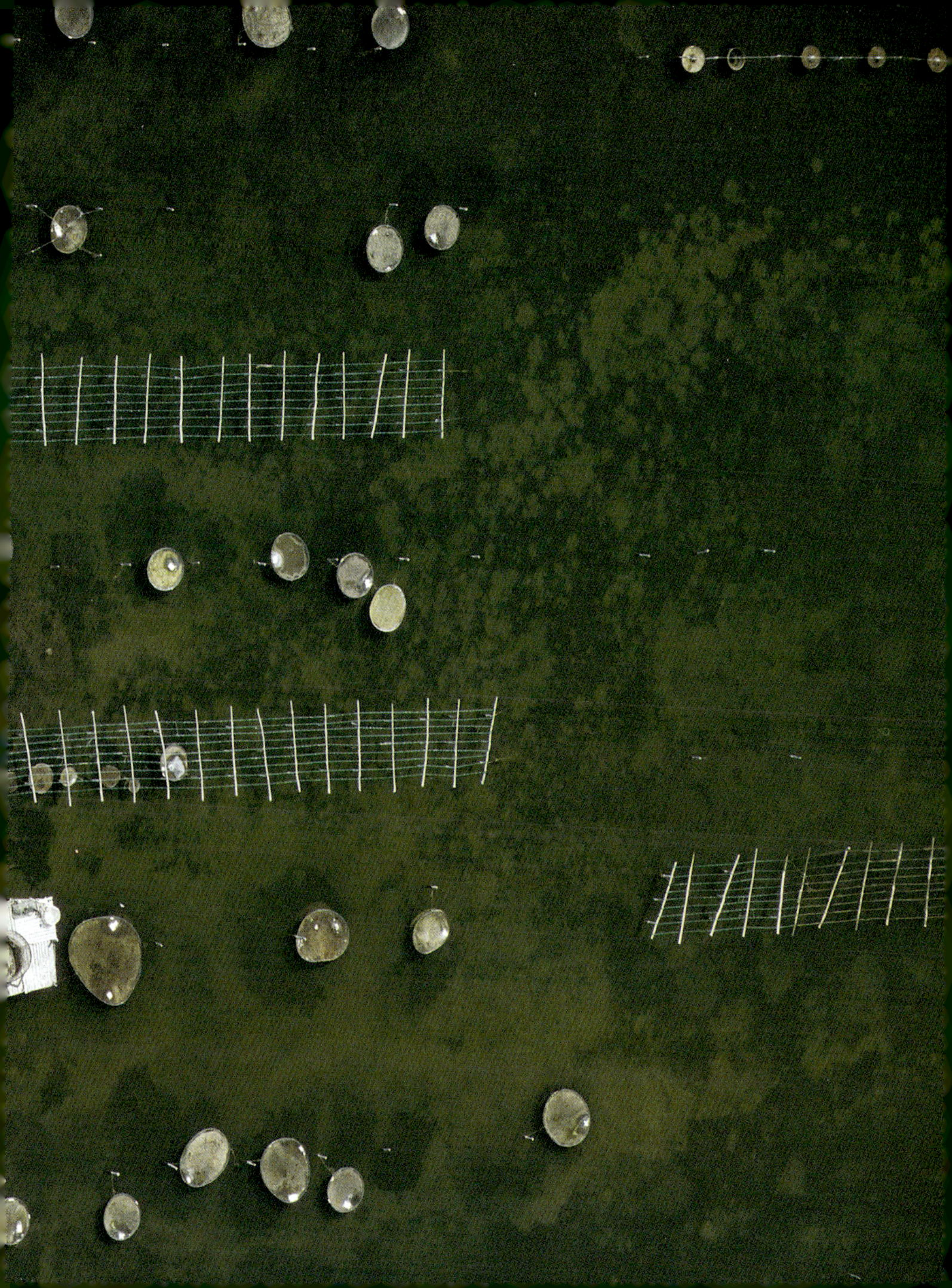

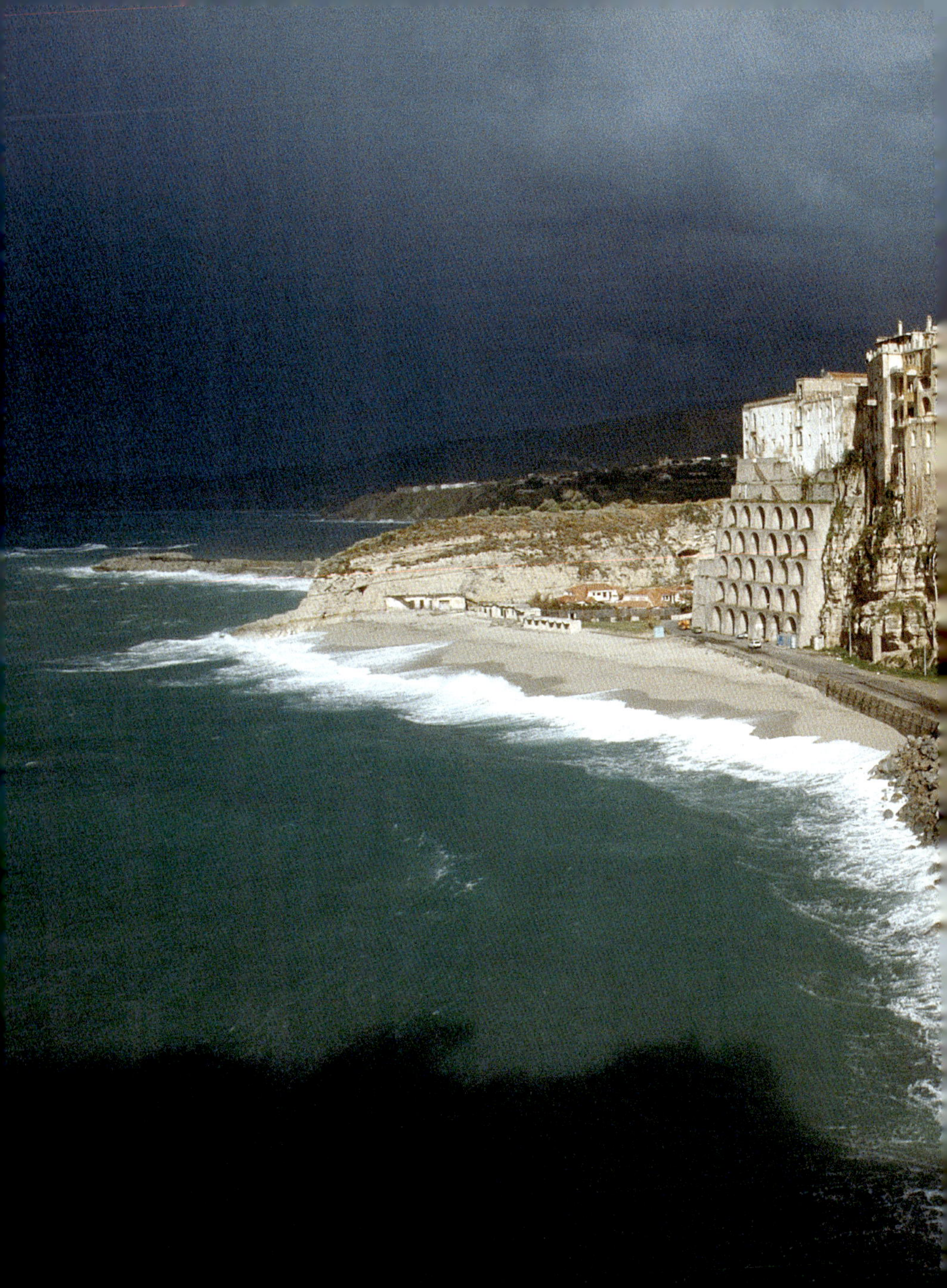

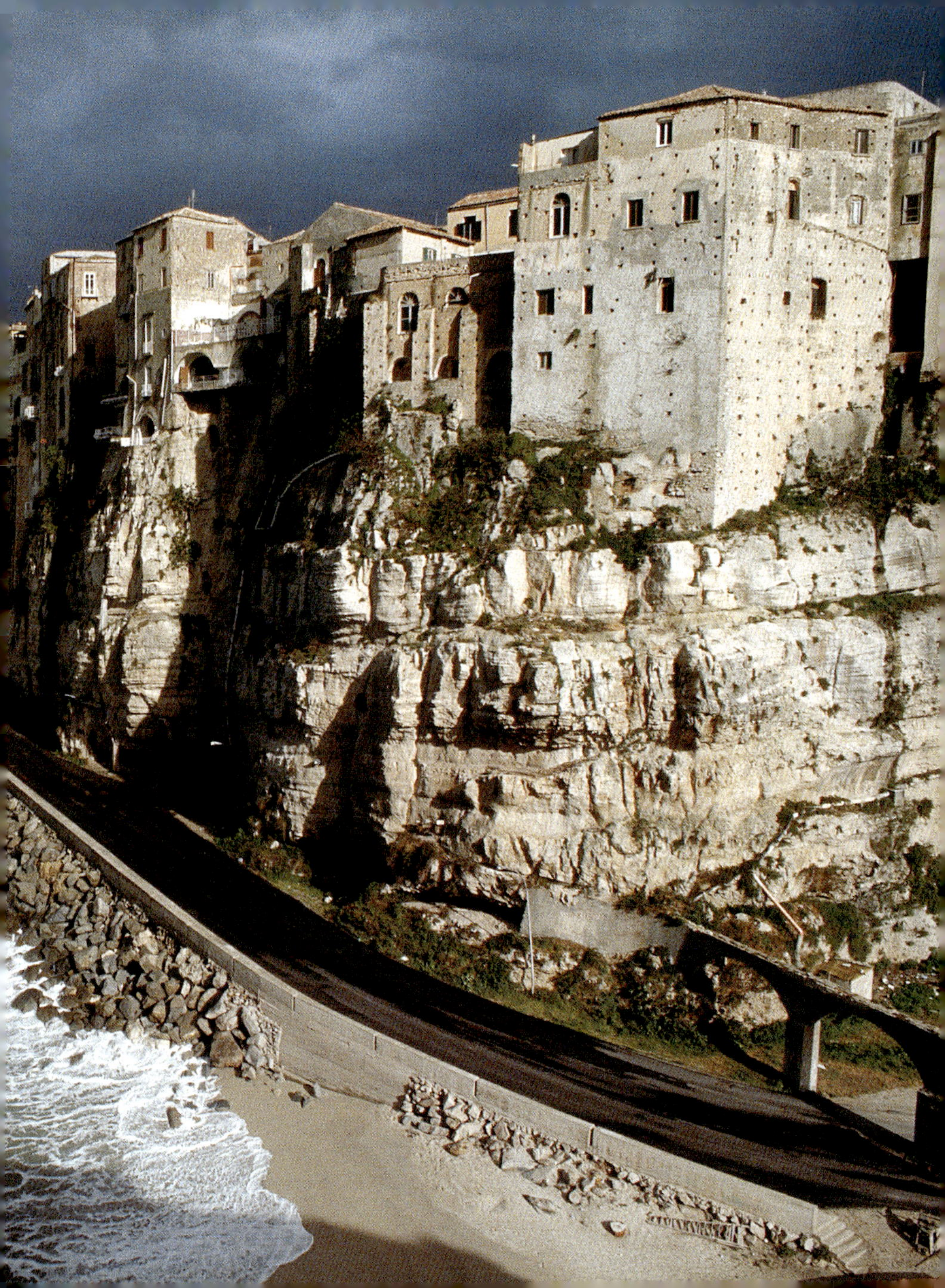

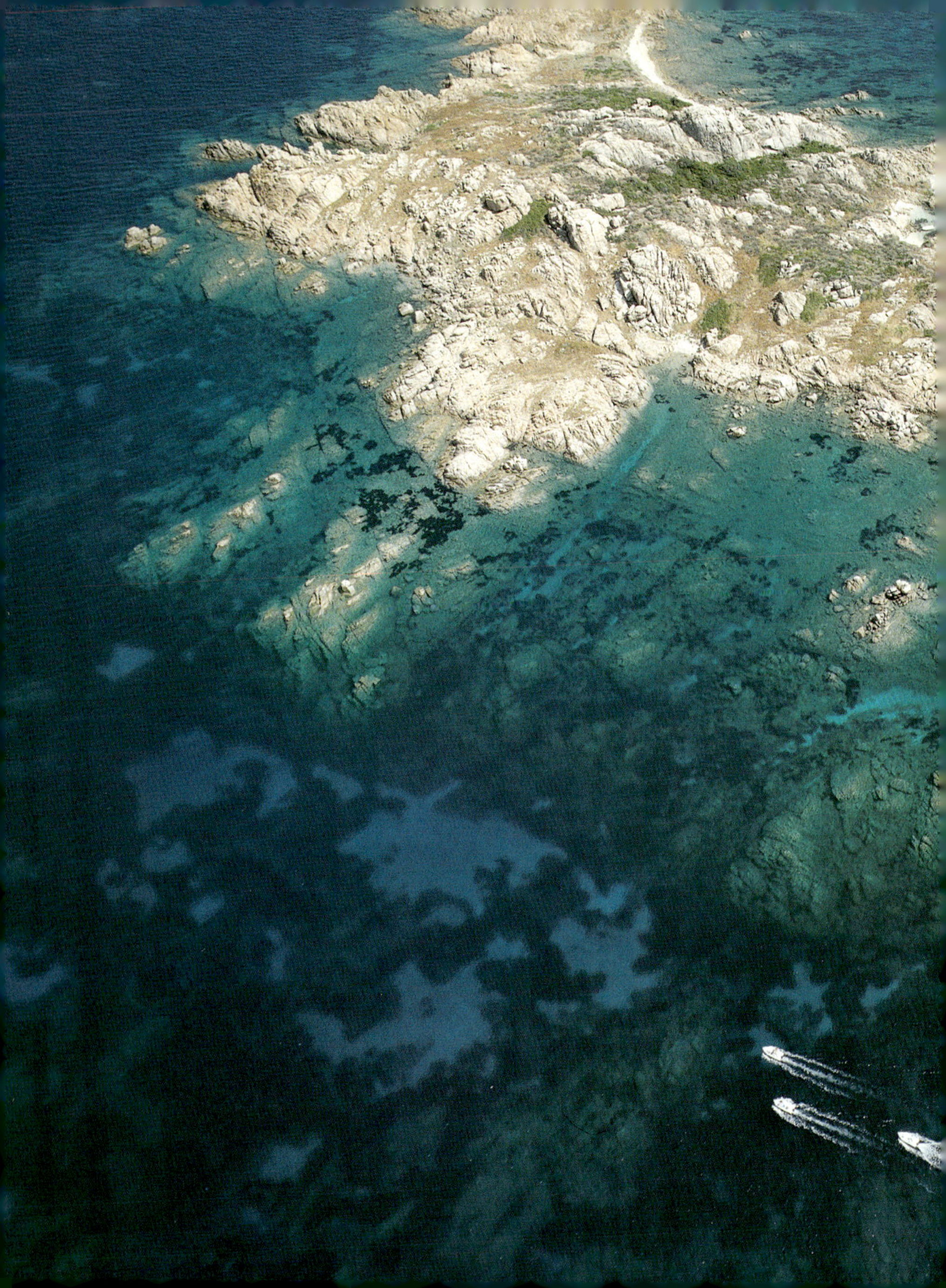

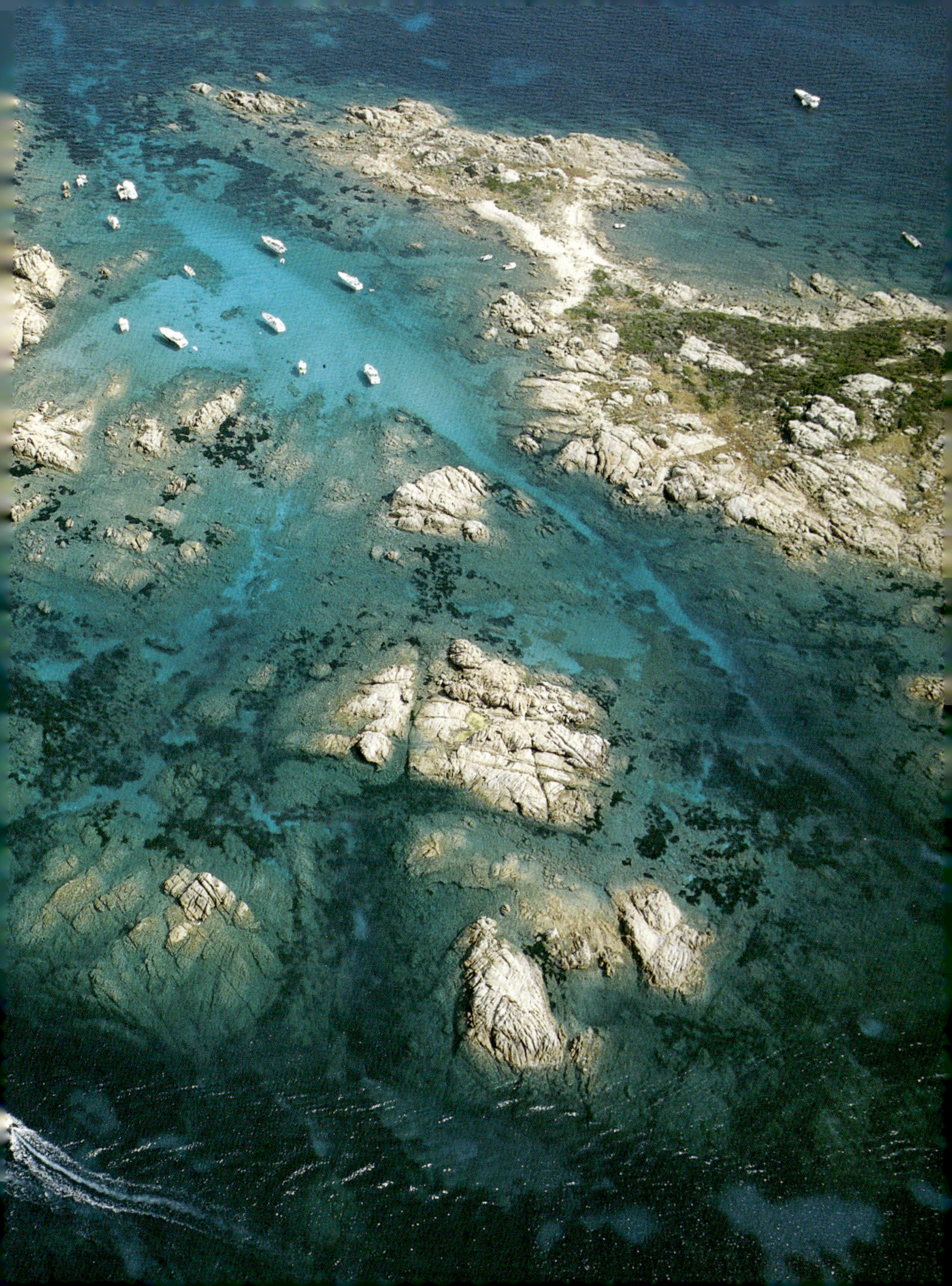

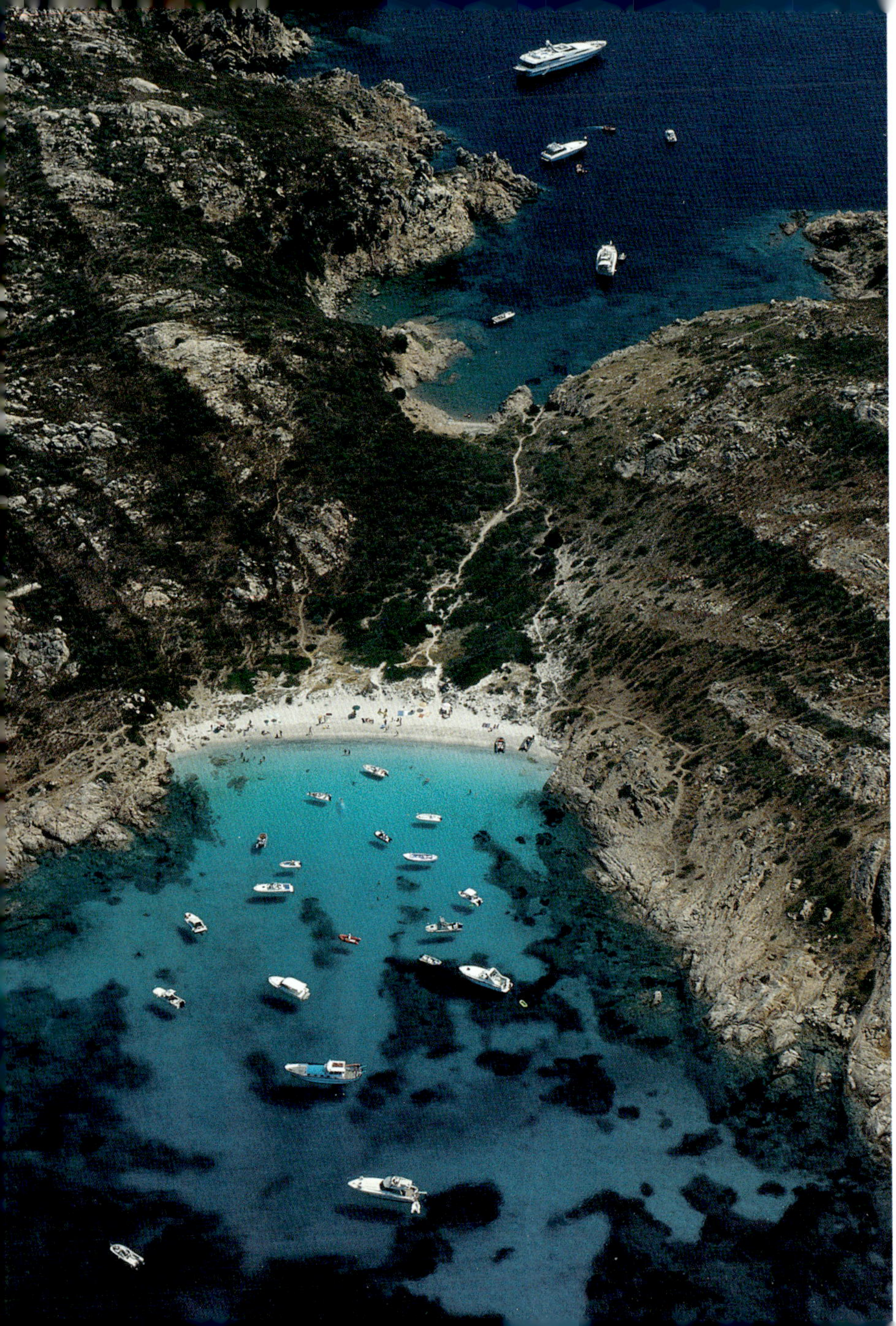

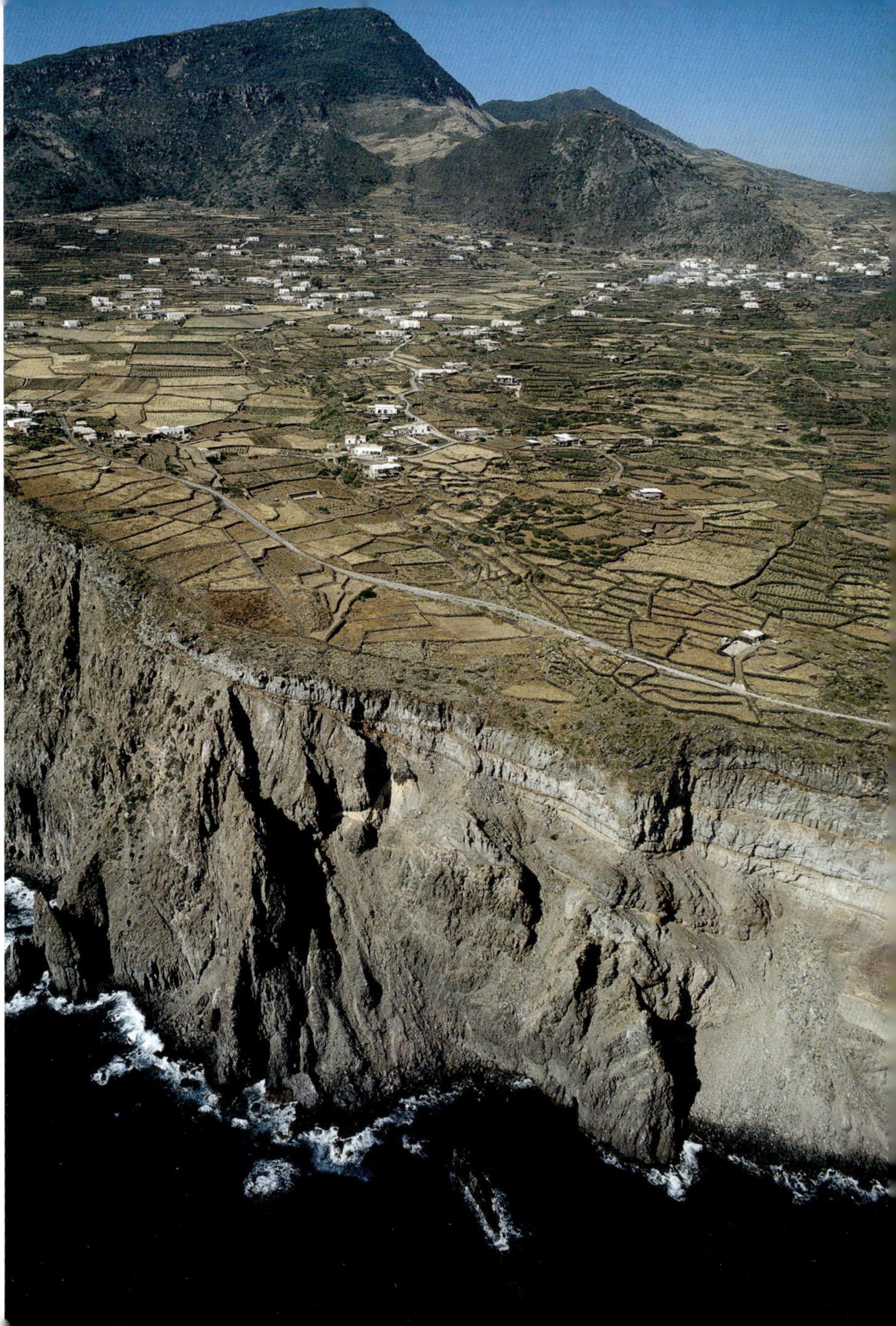

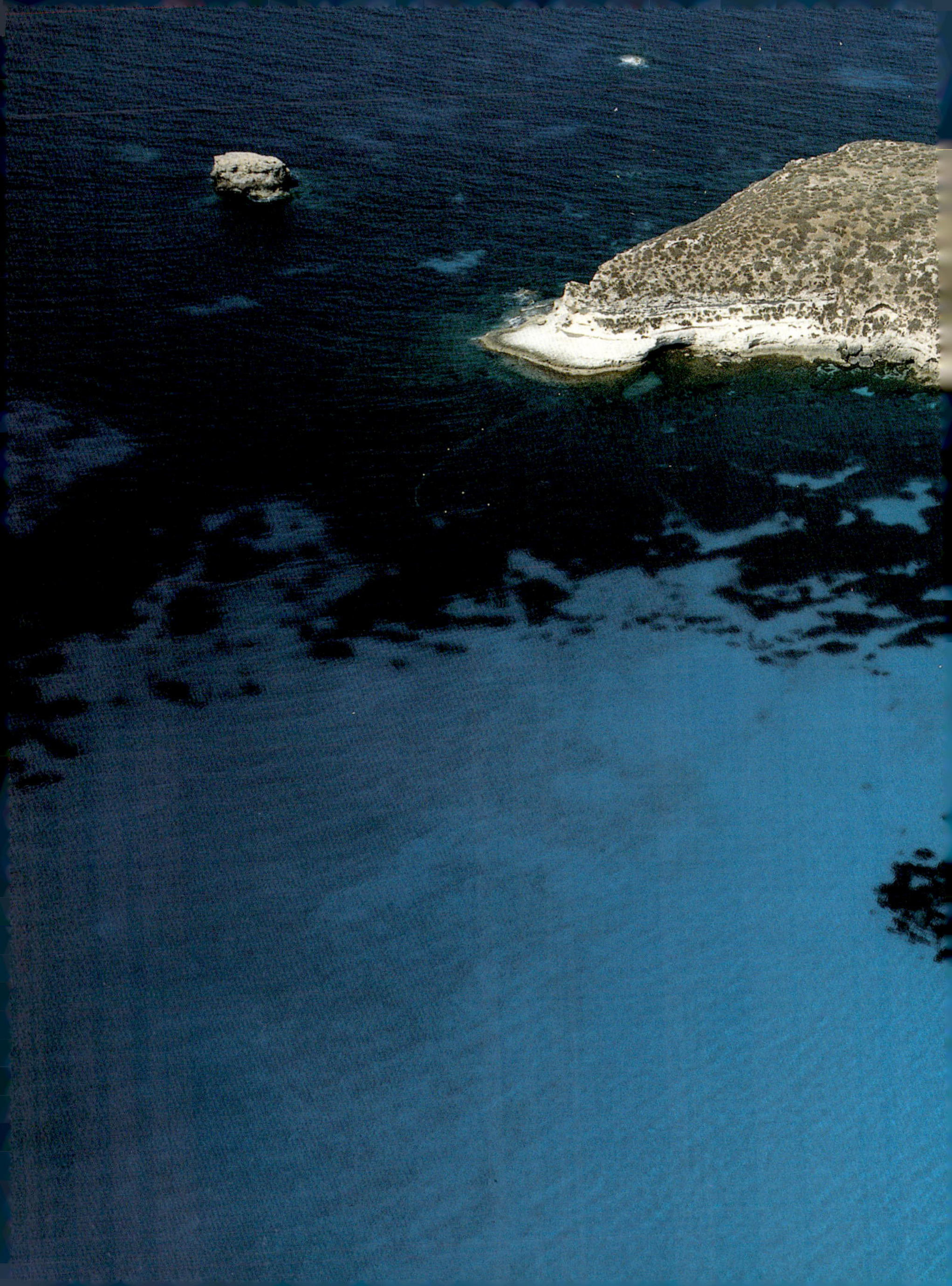

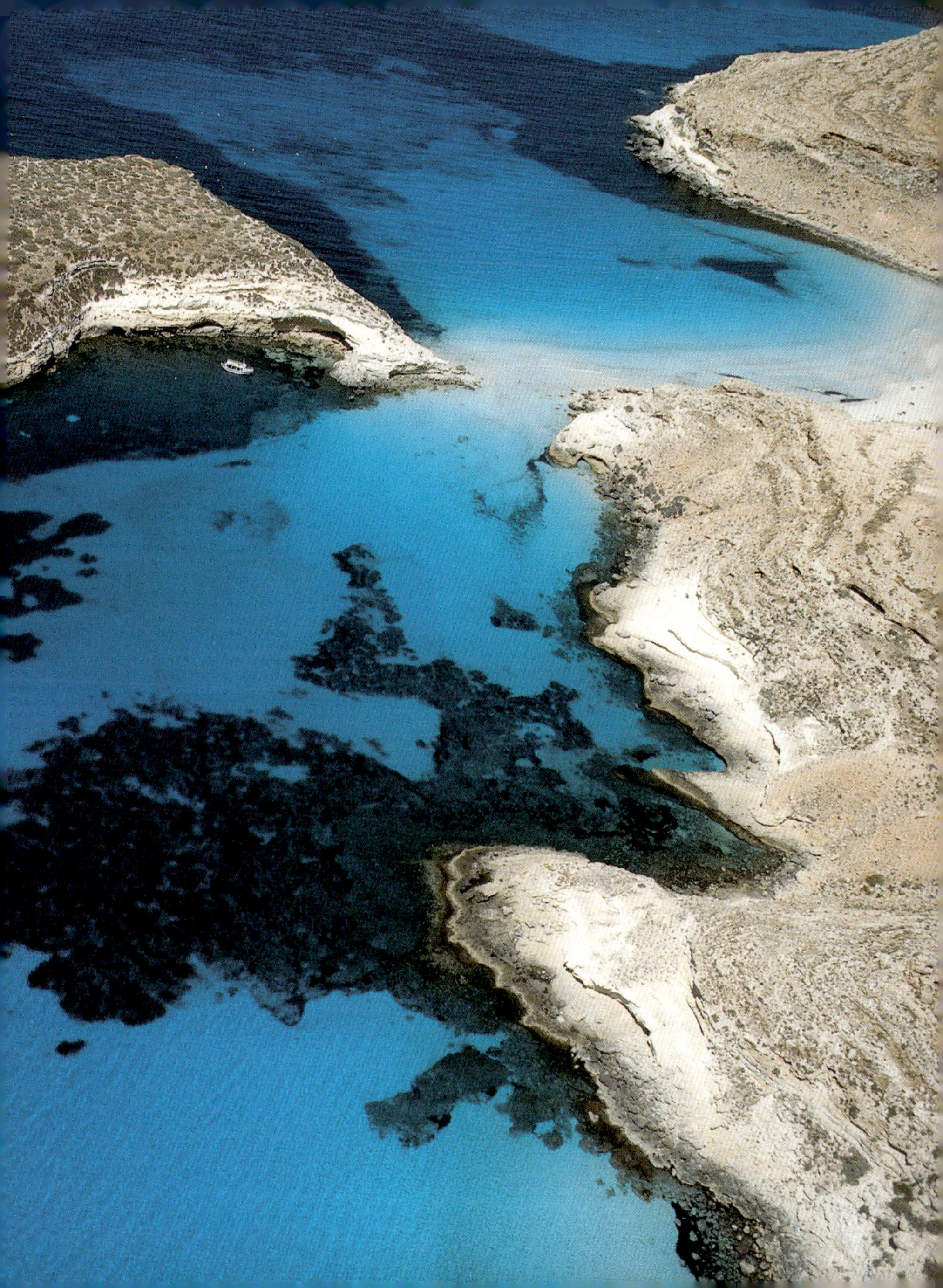

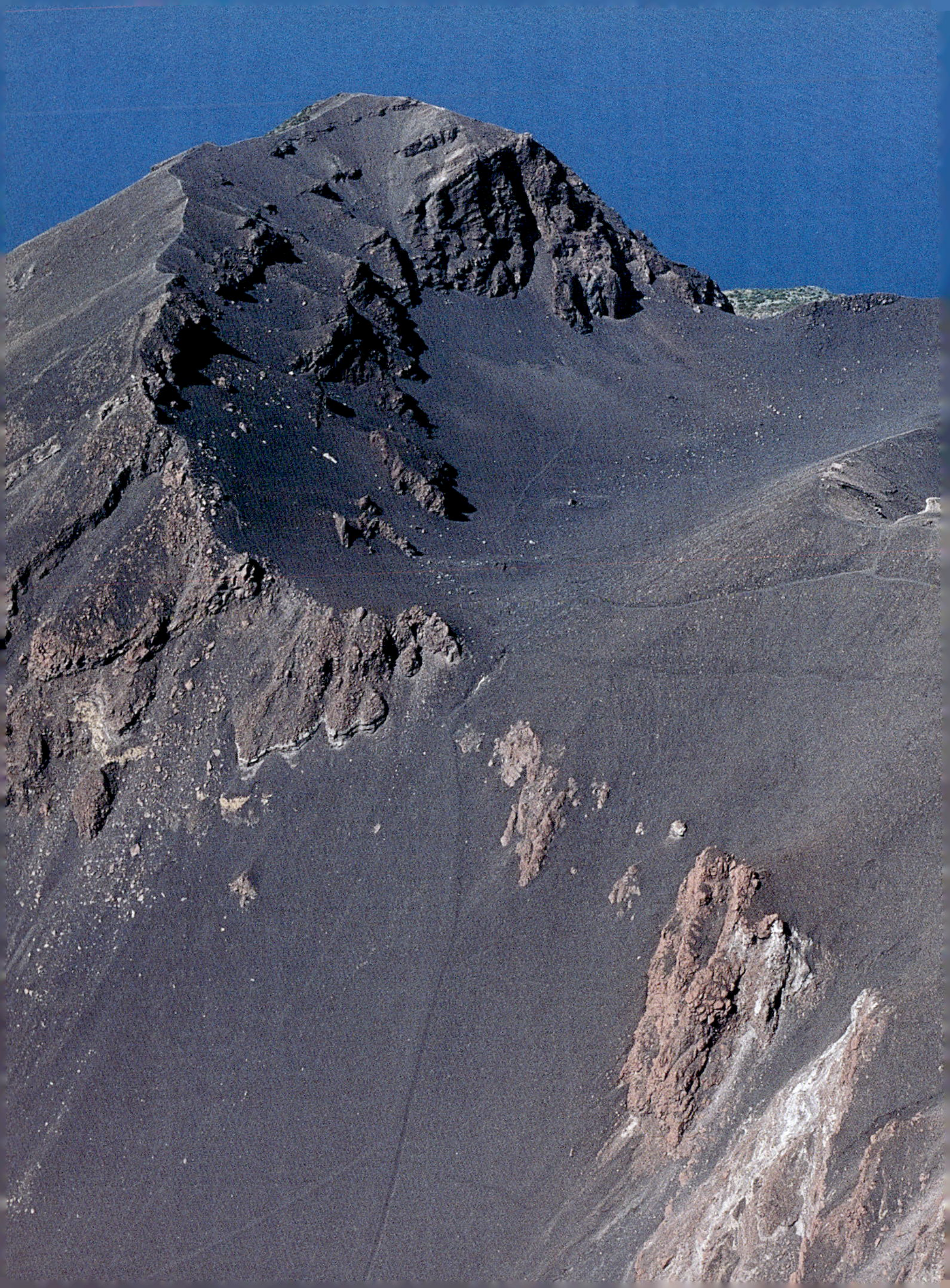

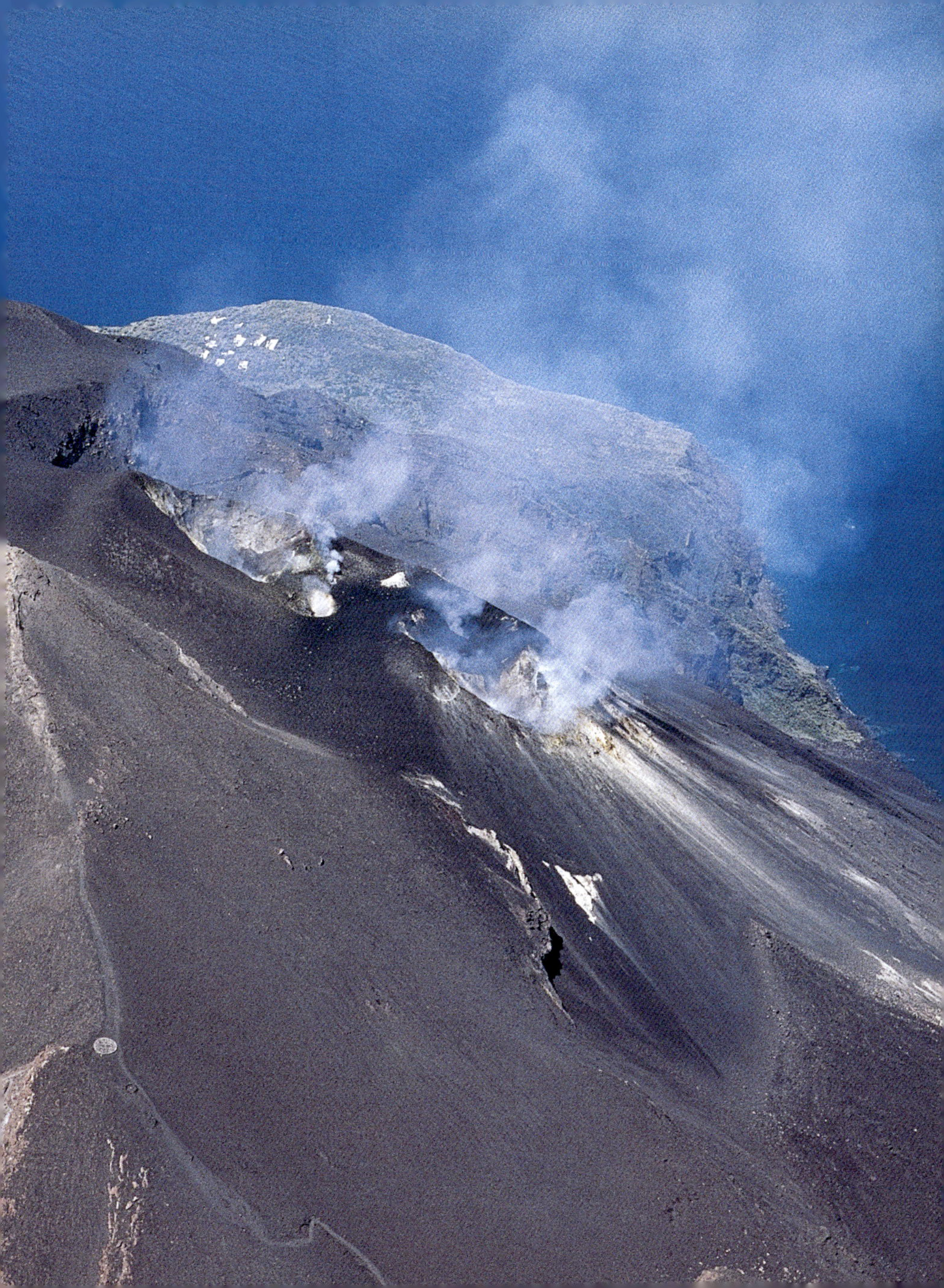

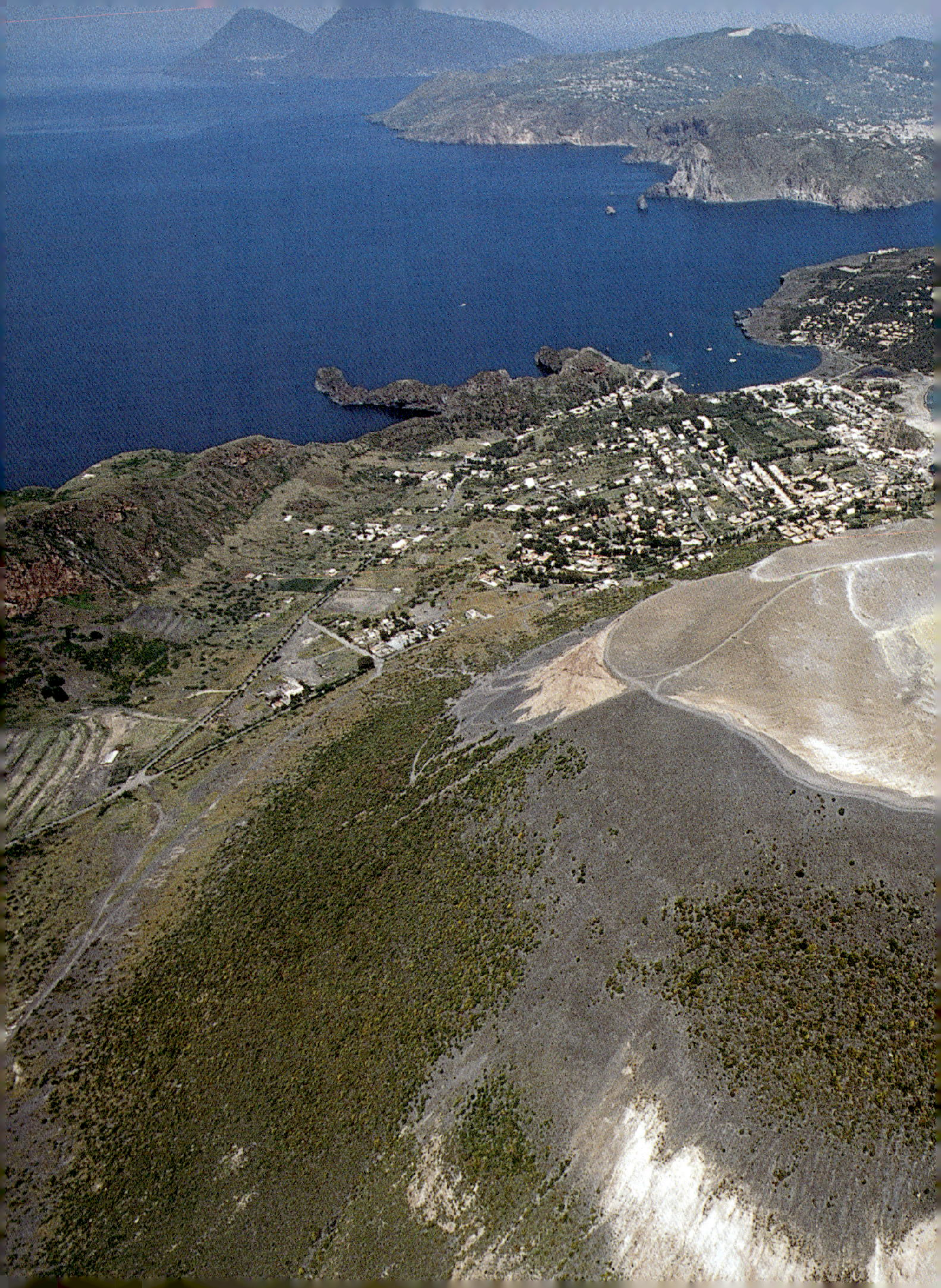

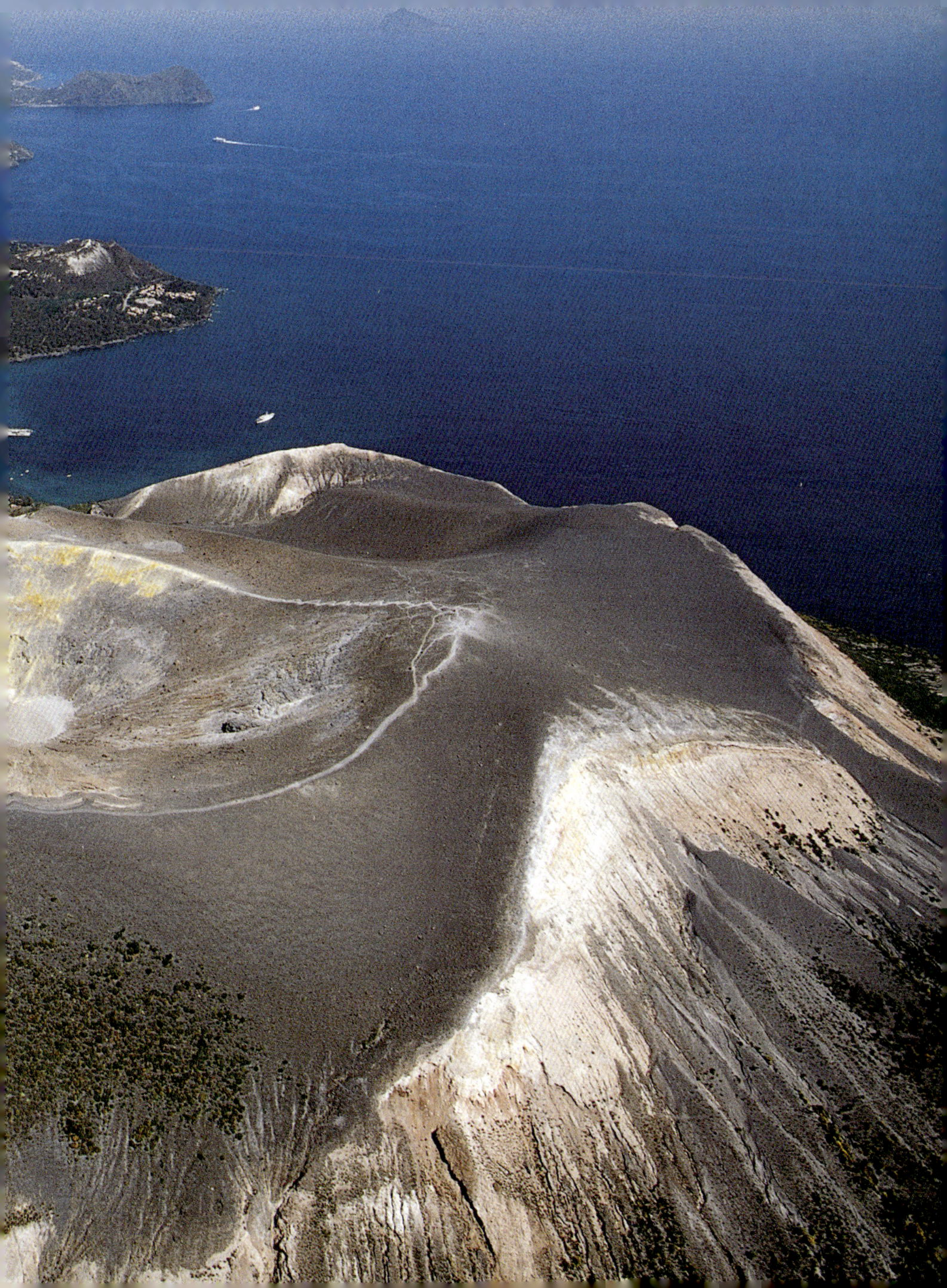

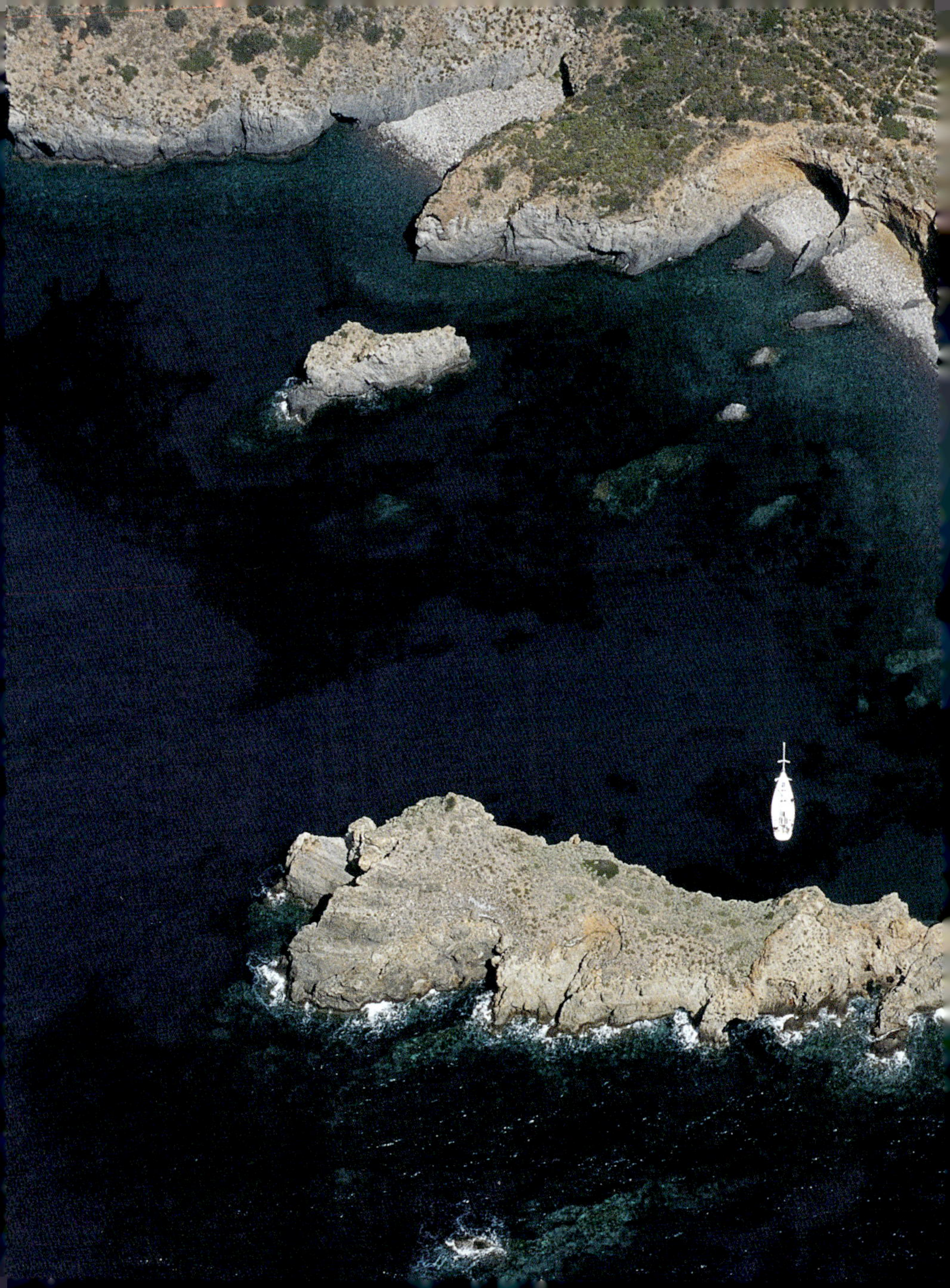

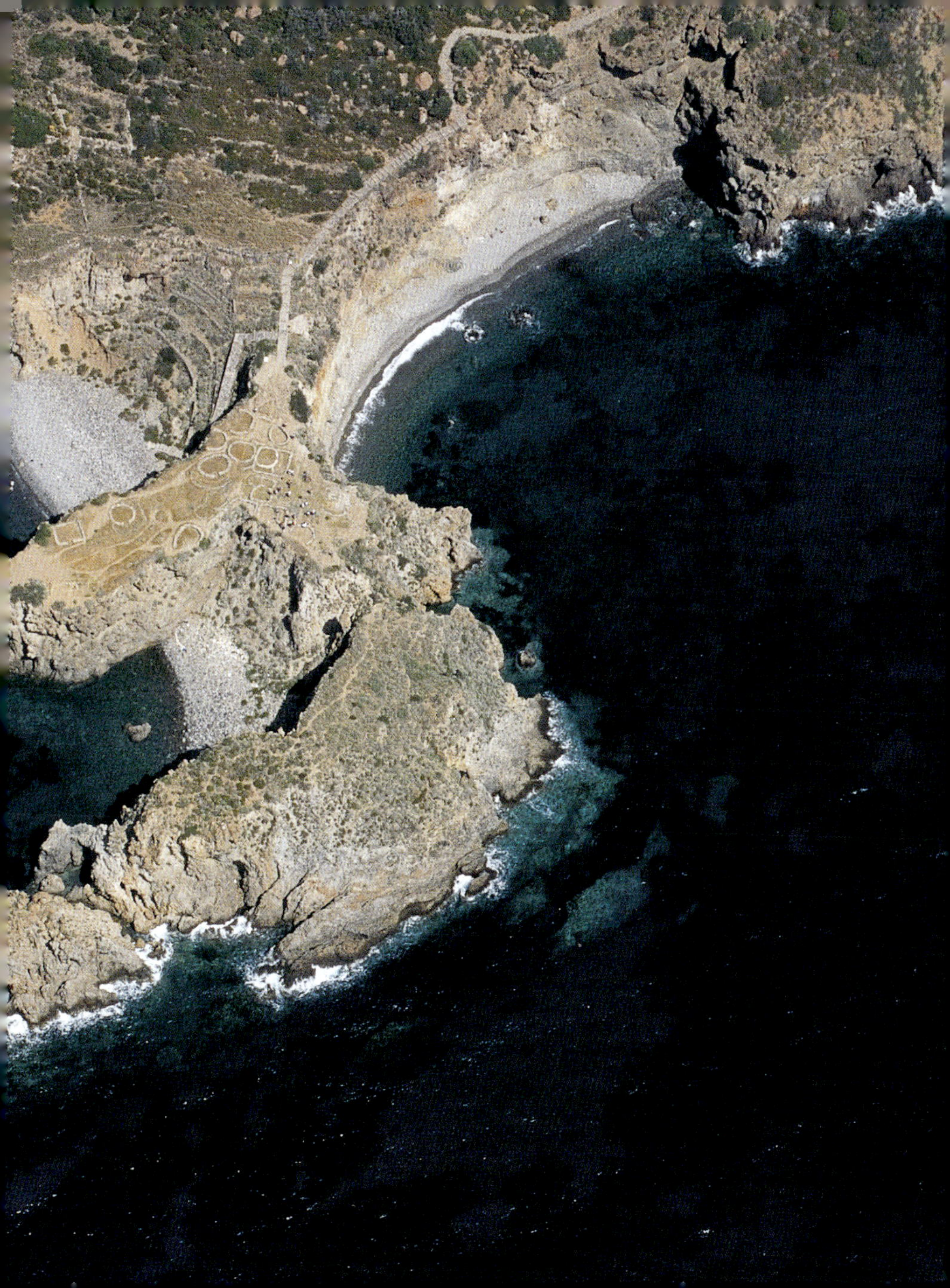

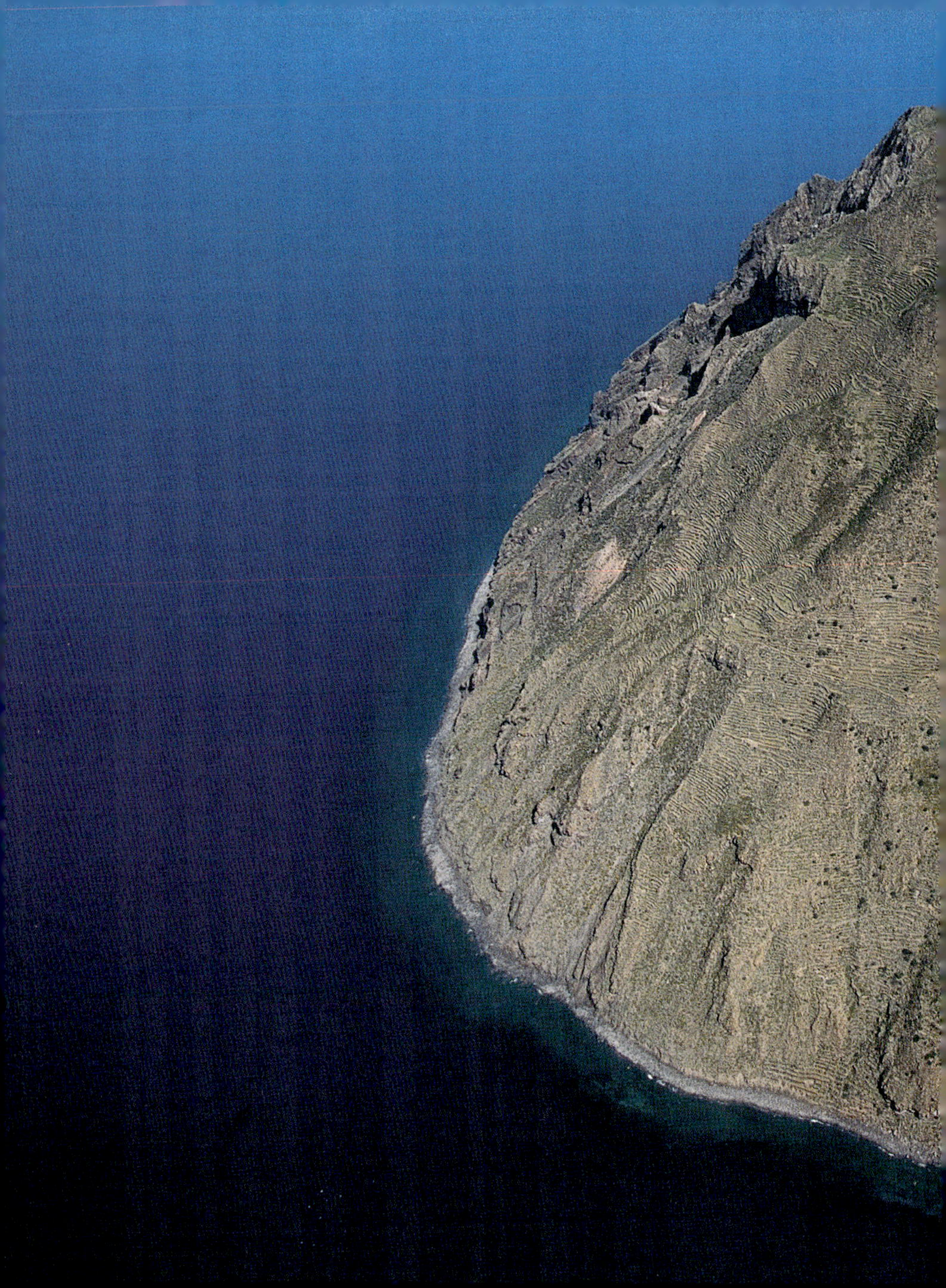

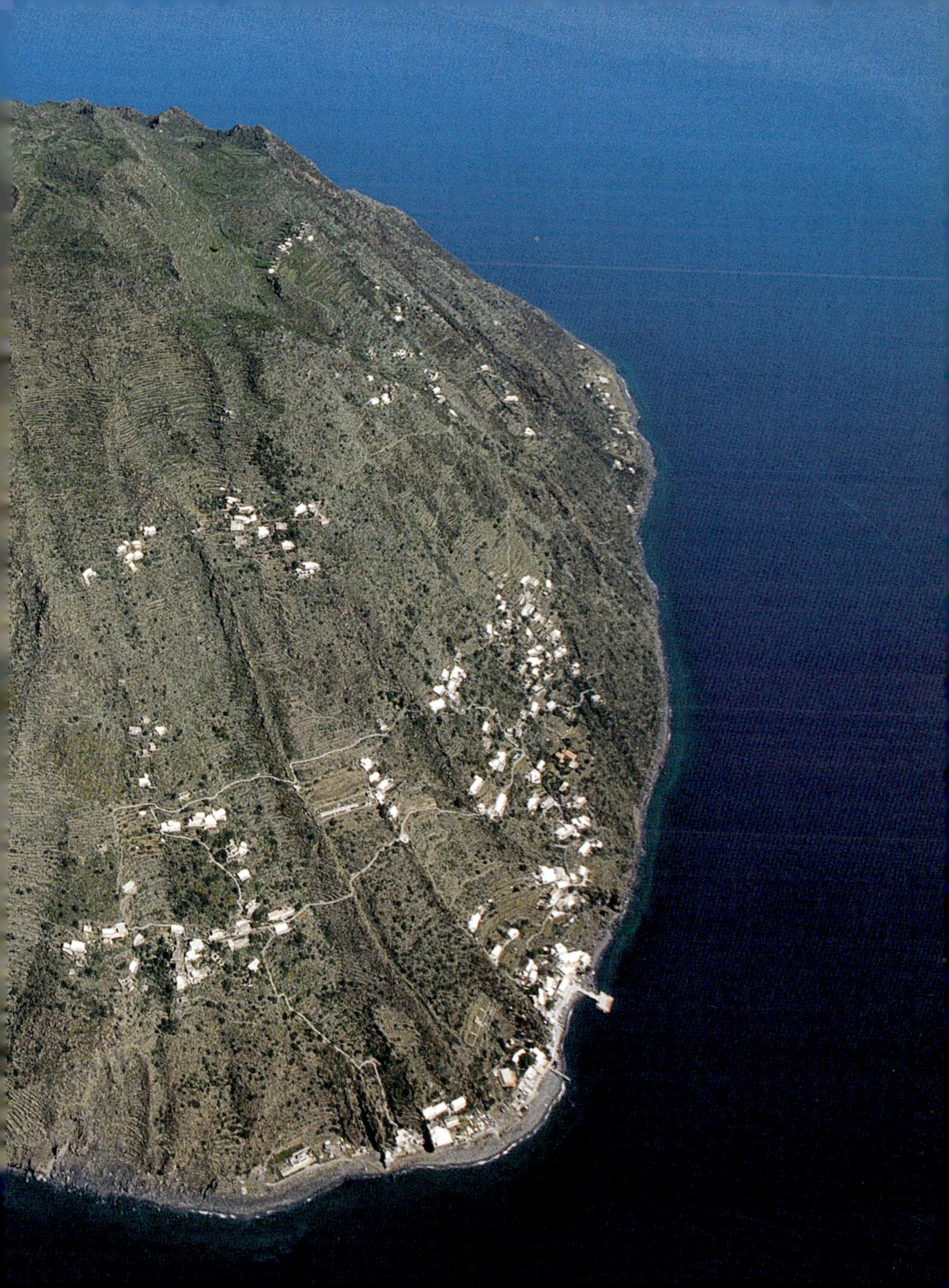

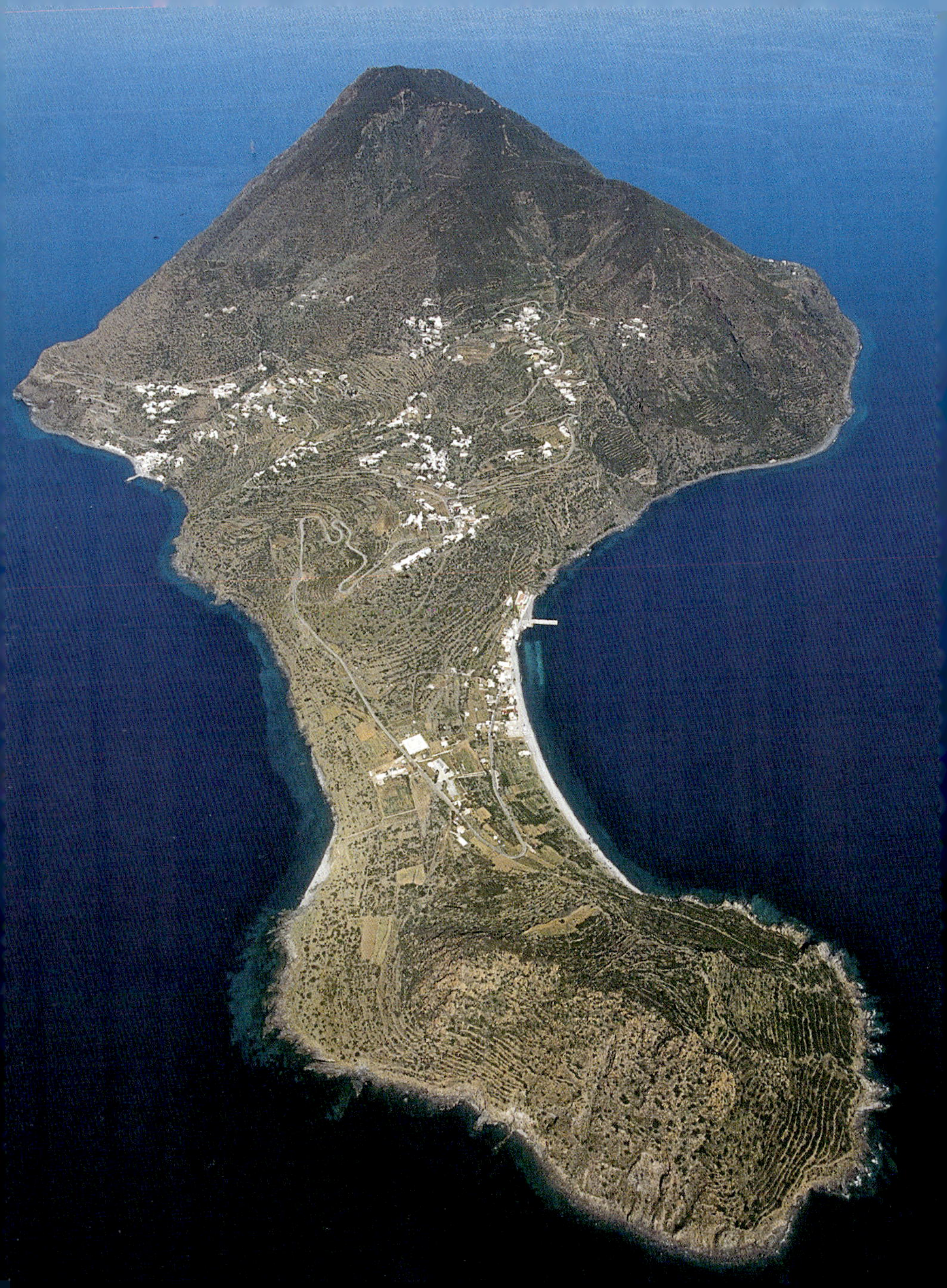

ARCHAELOGY AND MONUMENTAL ART

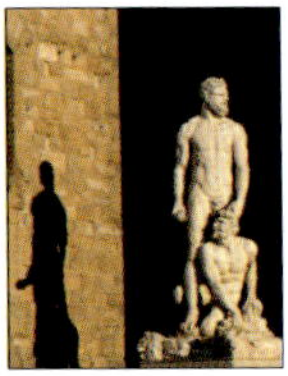

THE 16TH-CENTURY SCULPTURE of Hercules and Cacus by Baccio Bandinelli. This is one of the many statues adorning Piazza della Signoria in Florence, which has always been the town's political centre *(p. 293)*.

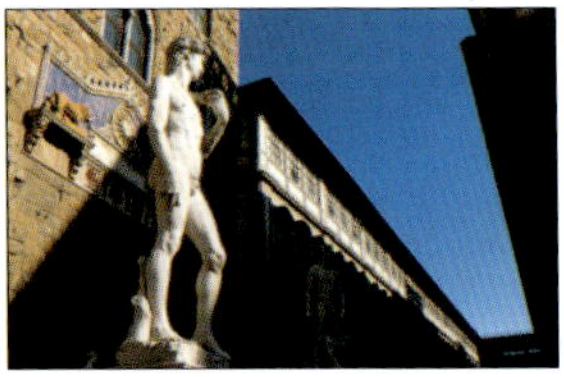

A COPY OF MICHELANGELO'S DAVID can be admired during a visit to Piazza della Signoria, Florence, in front of Palazzo Vecchio. The original work is now on display at the Accademia Gallery *(pp. 294-295)*.

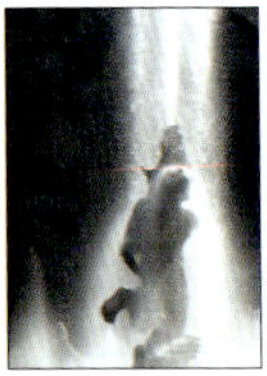

THE SCULPTURE OF THE SEA GOD GLAUCUS hugging a dolphin stands in the middle of the fountain in Piazza della Repubblica, Rome. Four 20th-century groups of Naiads surround the divinity *(p. 296)*.

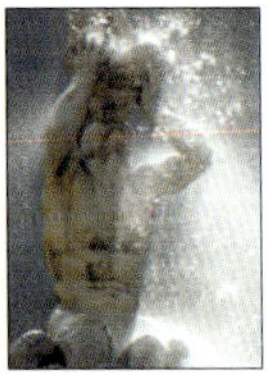

WATER EFFECTS in the Tritone Fountain, Piazza Barberini, Rome. Designed by Gian Lorenzo Bernini in 1642 for Pope Urban VIII, the fountain is located in the middle of the square *(p. 297)*.

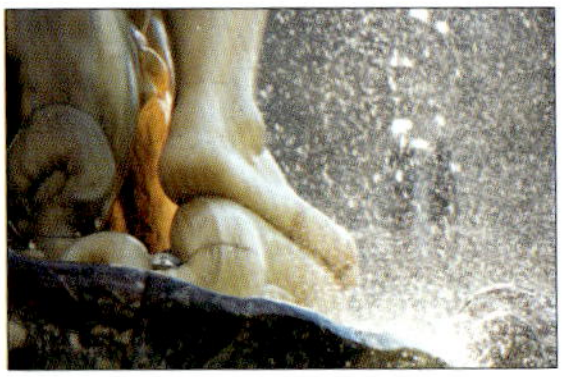

A DETAIL OF BARTOLOMEO AMMANNATI'S NEPTUNE Fountain in Piazza della Signoria, Florence. Amongst the bronze sea gods and satyrs rises the statue of Neptune, known as the "Biancone" *(pp. 298-299)*.

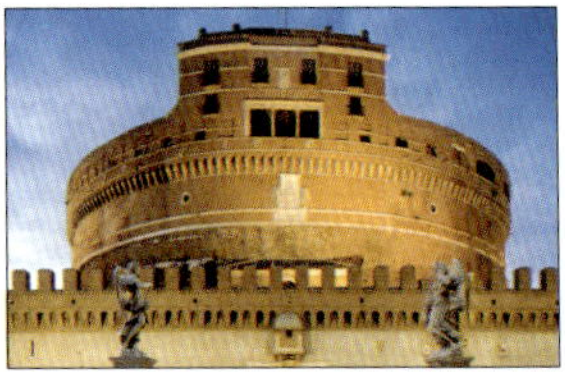

THE IMPOSING CASTEL SANT'ANGELO in Rome was first built as a mausoleum, wanted by Emperor Hadrian for himself and the succeeding Caesars. With the advent of the Papacy it became a fortress *(pp. 300-301)*.

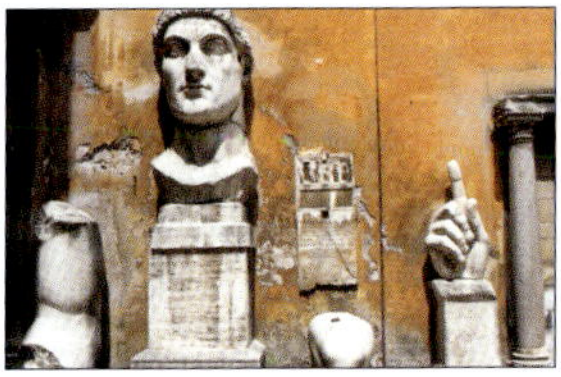

THE ENORMOUS CONSTANTINE'S HEAD at the Palazzo dei Conservatori, Rome. The statue once adorned the Basilica of Maxentius; it had marble head, arms and legs, yet the rest was made of bronze *(pp. 302-303)*.

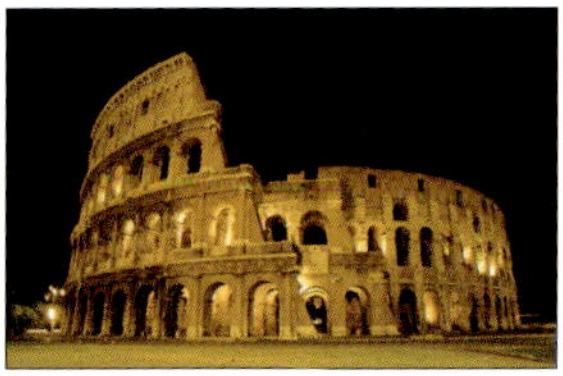

THE COLOSSEUM, ROME, was built by the Flavii as a venue for public entertainment and fights between gladiators and wild beasts. It was inaugurated around 80 A.D. with 100 days of celebrations *(pp. 304-305)*.

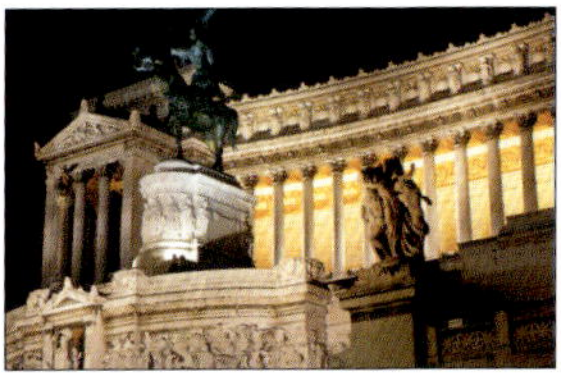

THE WHITE MARBLE VITTORIANO, dedicated to Victor Emmanuel II, was erected in Rome between 1885 and 1911 on the ruins of the Capitoline Arx, destroying a huge part of the medieval city *(pp. 306-307)*.

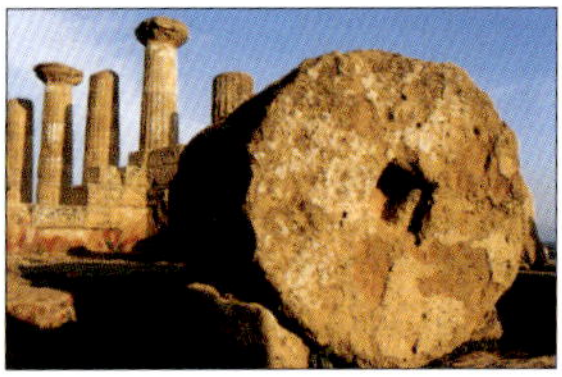

THE TEMPLE OF HERCULES, perhaps the oldest of Agrigento, rises at the entrance of the Temples Valley. Built at the end of the 6th century B.C., it still retains eight columns, four of which have capitals *(pp. 308-309)*.

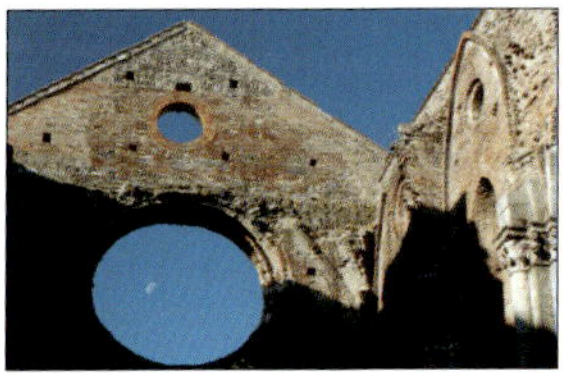

THE ATMOSPHERIC RUINS of the Cistercian Abbey of San Galgano stand on the lovely rise of Mount Siepi, not very far from Siena. The church, started in 1218, is in Gothic style *(pp. 310-311)*.

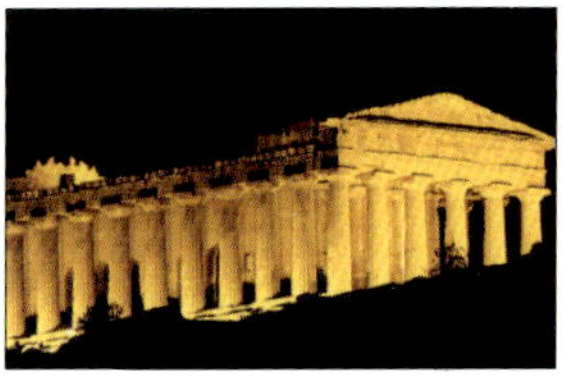

THE TEMPLE OF CONCORD, Agrigento, is a masterpiece of Doric architecture built in the 5th century B.C.. It was transformed in a Christian basilica and reconverted into its original shape in 1748 *(pp. 312-313)*.

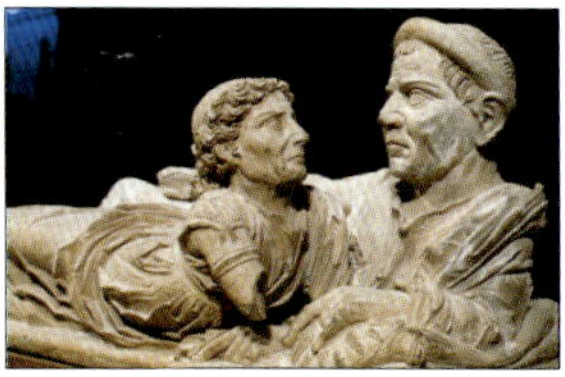

IN THE NATIONAL ETRUSCAN MUSEUM of Chiusi, a small town in Tuscany, are on display important Greek and Etruscan archaeological findings, urns and vases coming from the neighbouring tombs *(pp. 314-315)*.

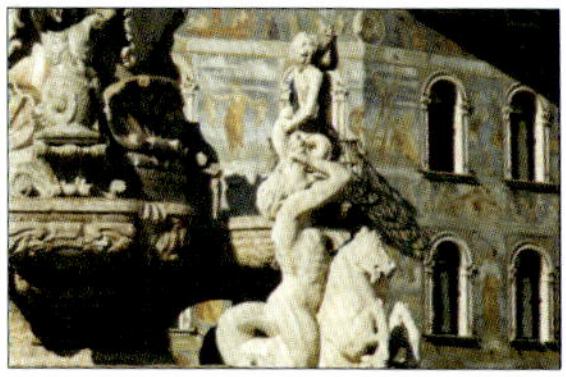

THE FAÇADE OF ONE OF THE CAZUFFI HOUSES – decorated with 15th-century frescoes by Fogolino – in Piazza del Duomo, Trento. In the foreground stands the 17th-century Neptune Fountain *(pp. 316-317)*.

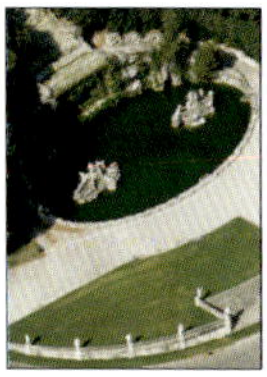

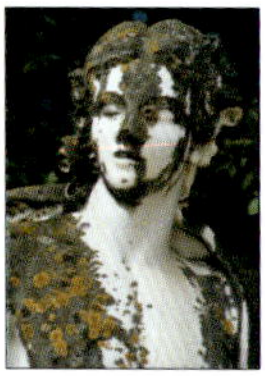

THE HUGE PARK of Caserta's Royal Palace, built for Carl of Borbon in 1752. It spreads over three kilometres. The long descending landscape is interspersed with ponds, fountains, sculptures *(pp. 318-319)*.

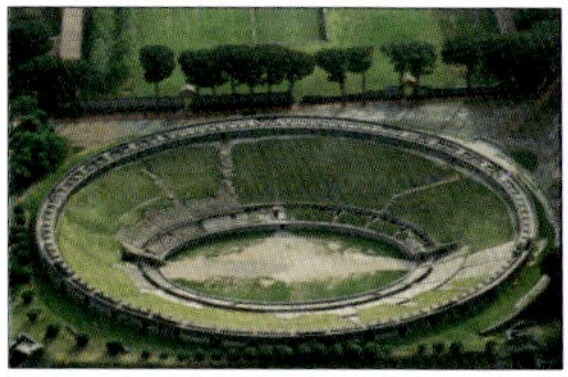

POMPEII AMPHITHEATRE, BUILT AROUND 80 B.C., is the oldest arena known. Elliptically shaped, it has three main and two secondary entrances, three tiers of seats. It could house 12,000 people *(pp. 320-321)*.

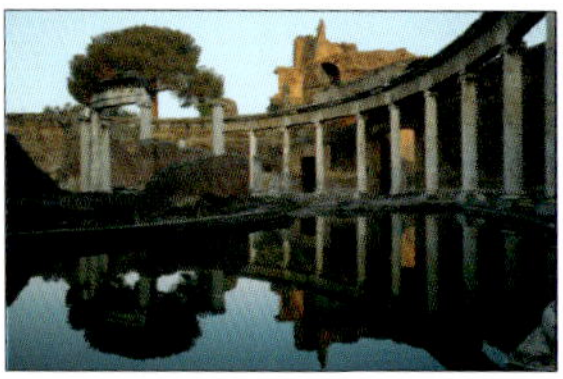

VILLA ADRIANA is one of the most astounding archaeological sites of Italy. Besides the building designed by Hadrian (117–138 A.D.), it includes three spas, a stadium and an ambulatory with a pool *(pp. 322-323)*.

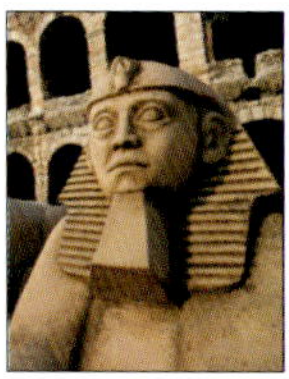

THE ARENA OF VERONA, erected in the 1st century A.D. in limestone blocks, is amongst the best-preserved Roman amphitheatres. It contains up to 22,000 people and offers important opera shows in summer *(p. 324)*.

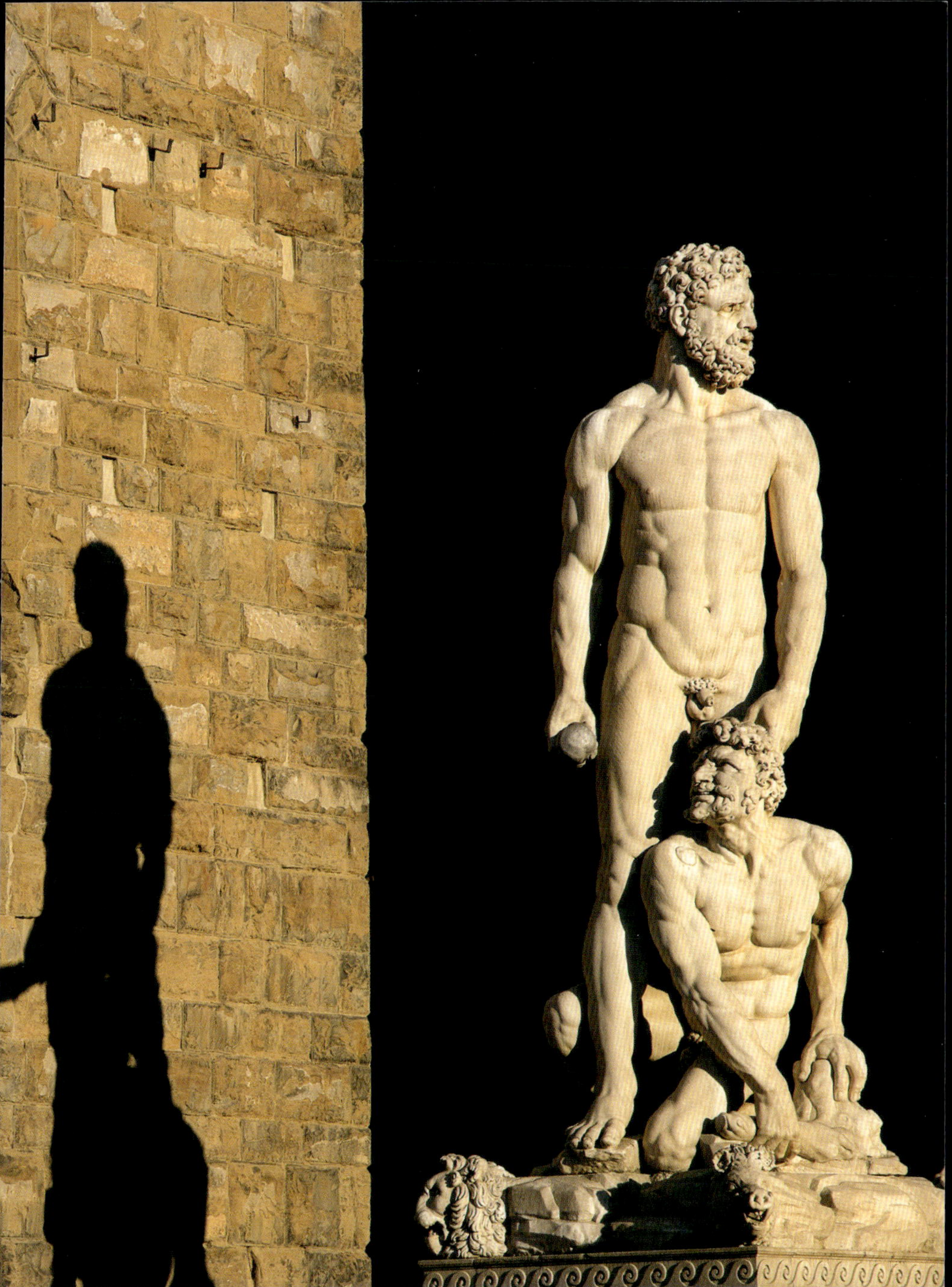

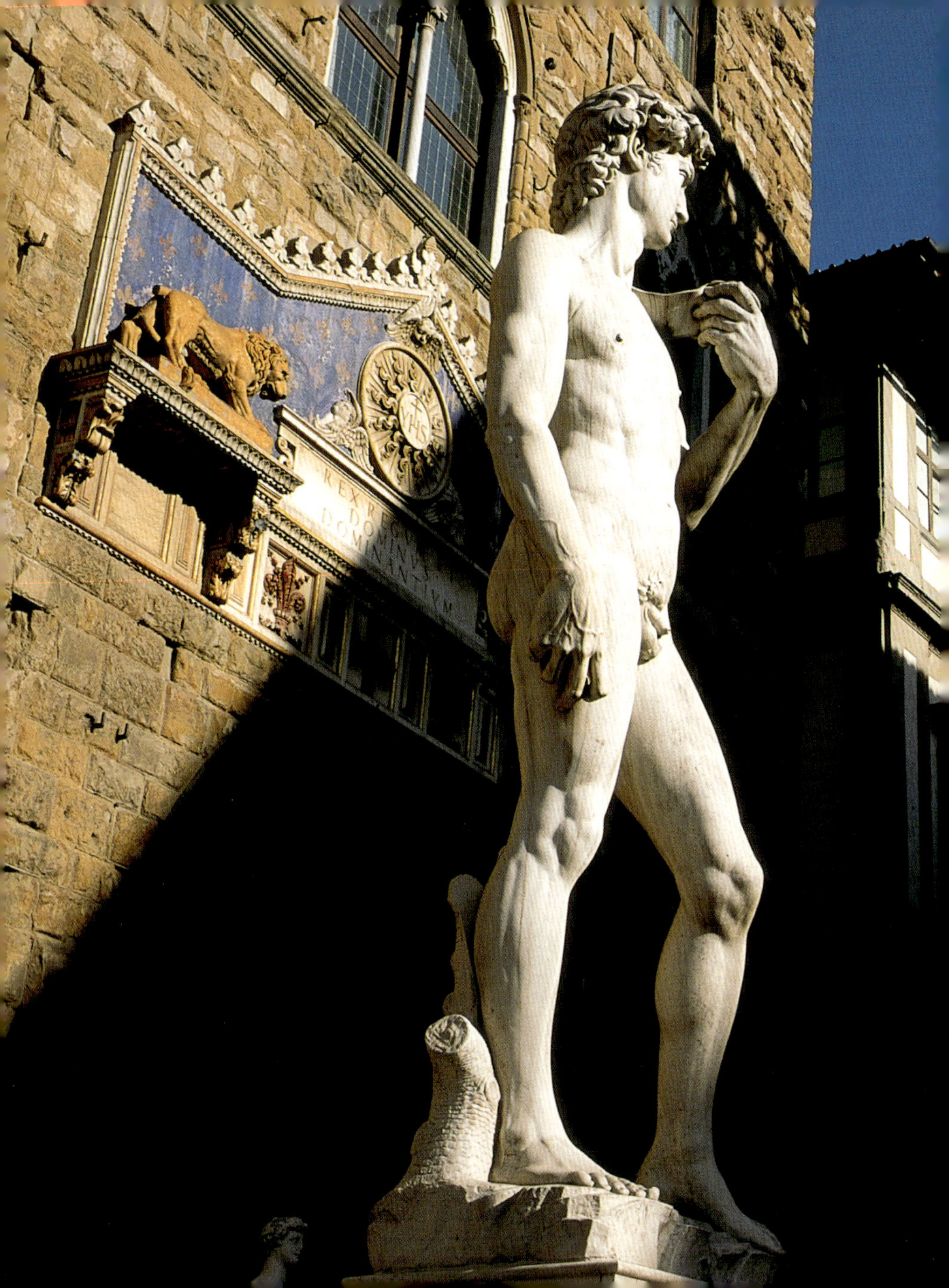
YHS
REX
DOMINANTIVM

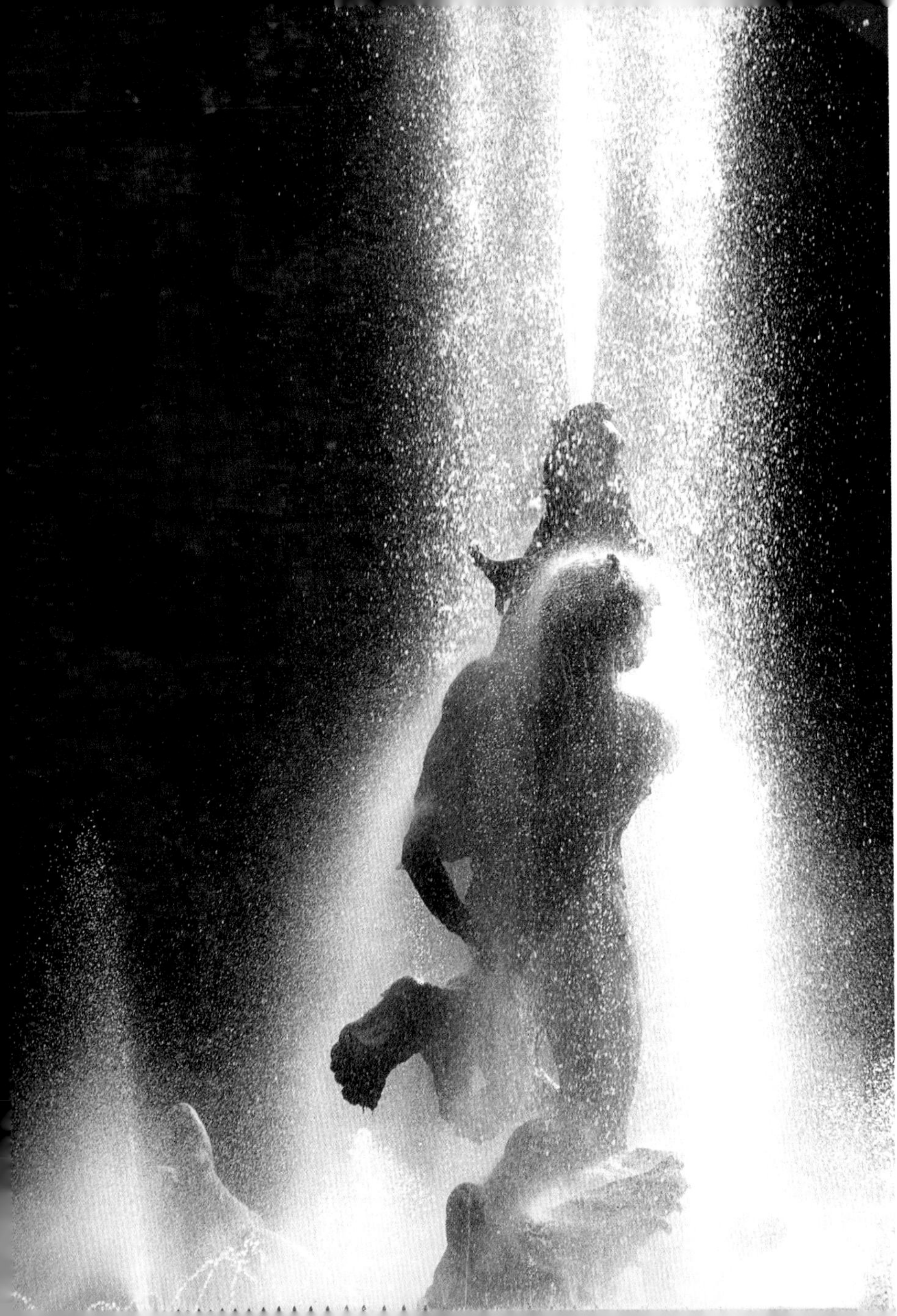

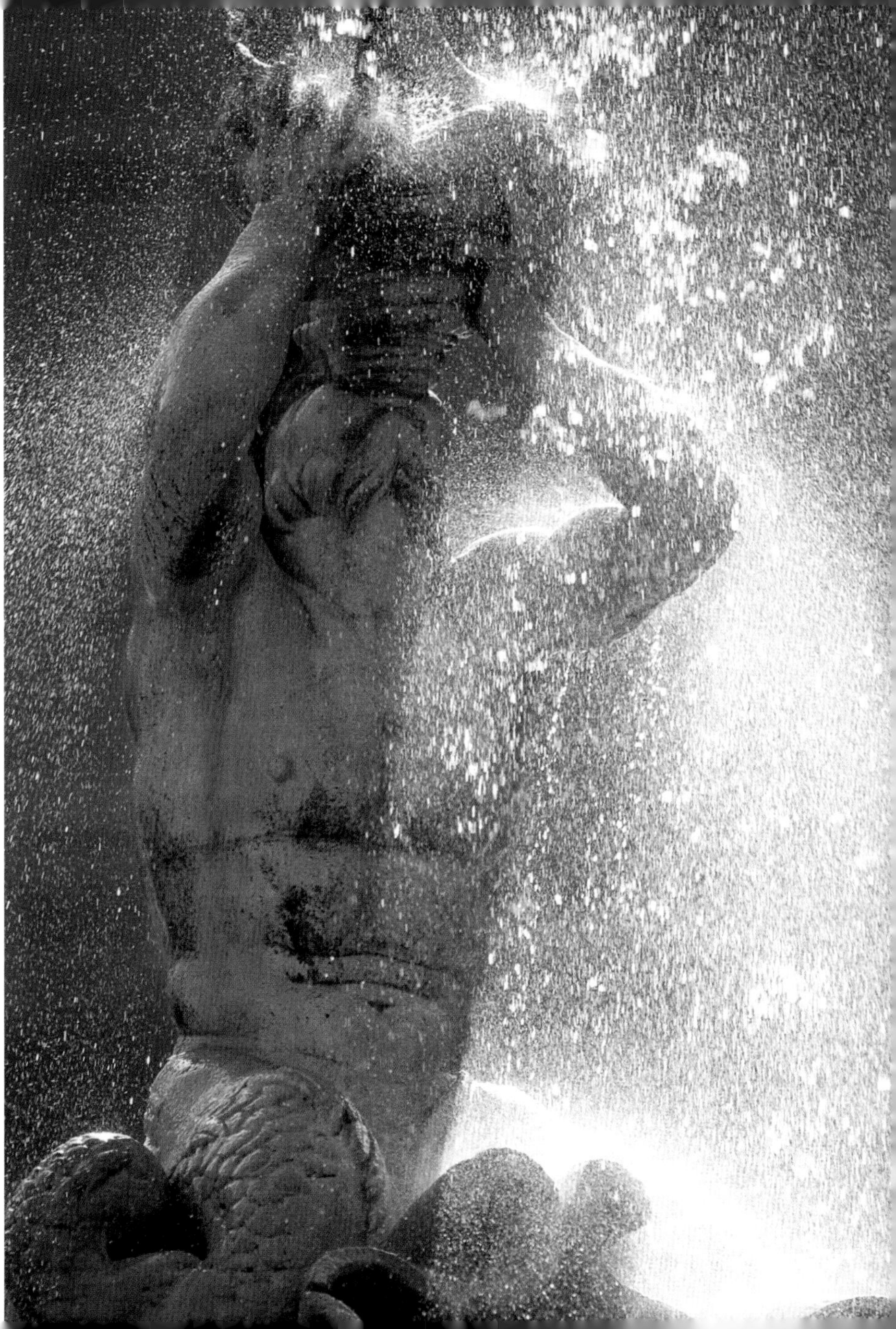

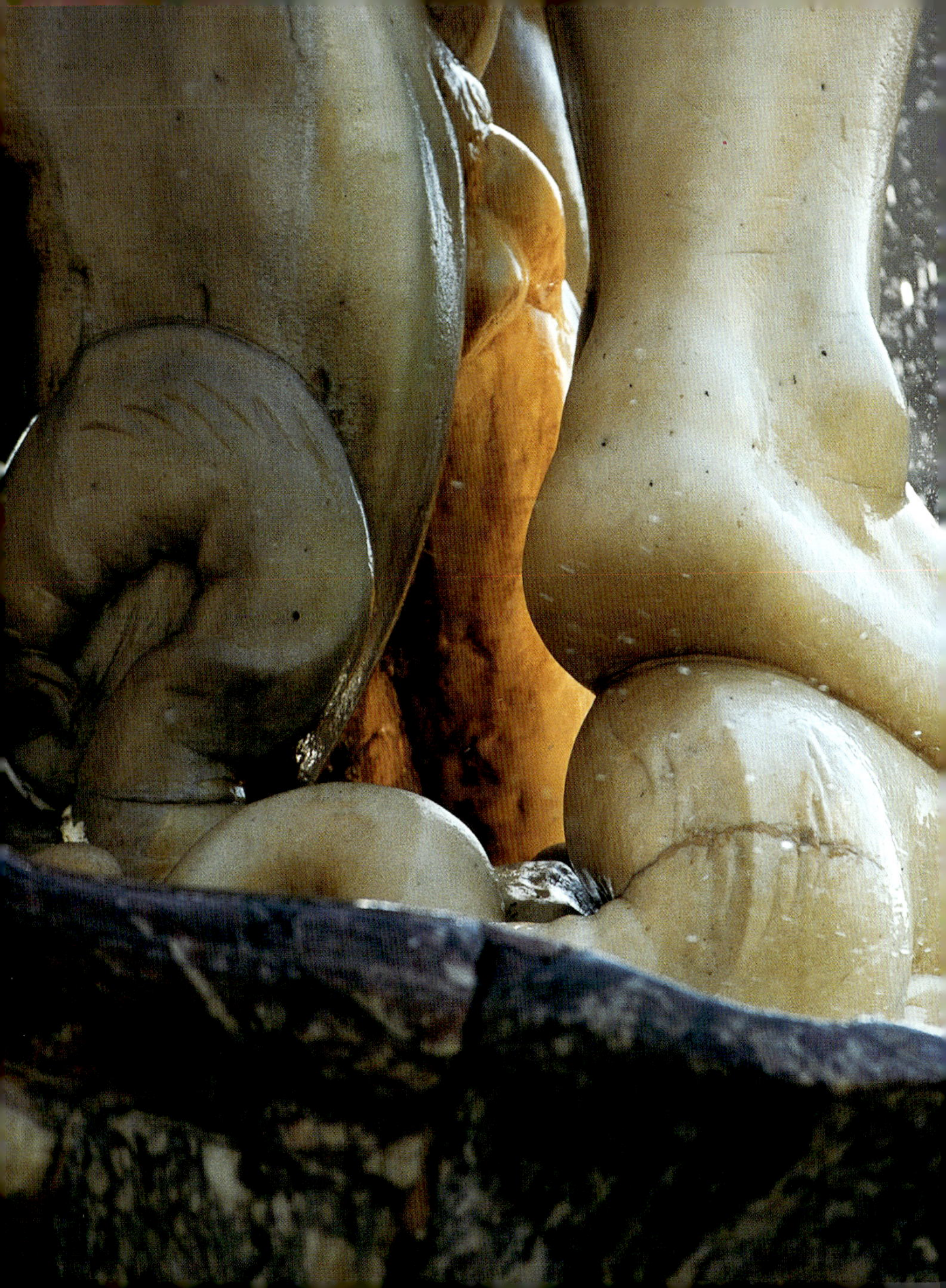

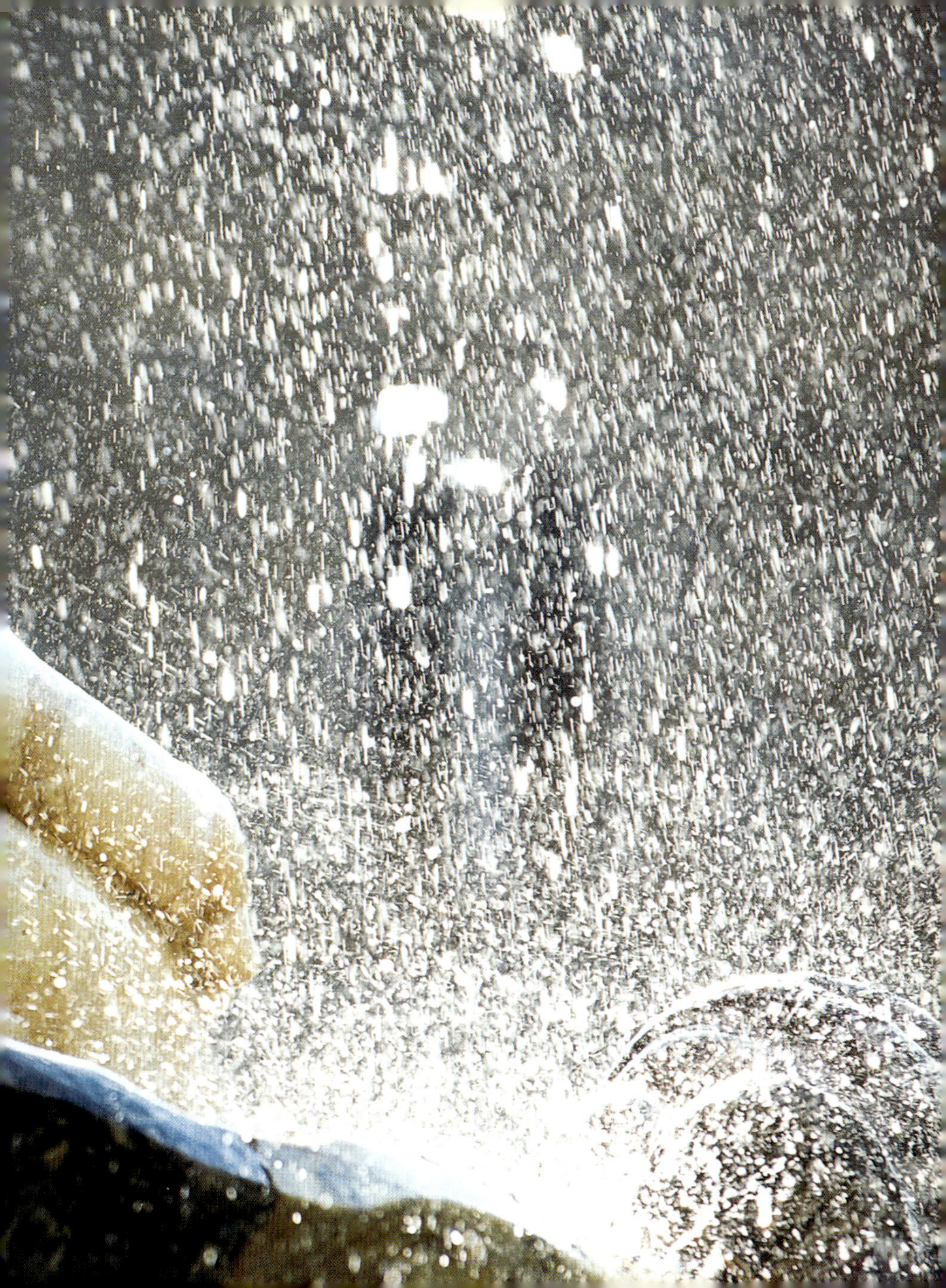

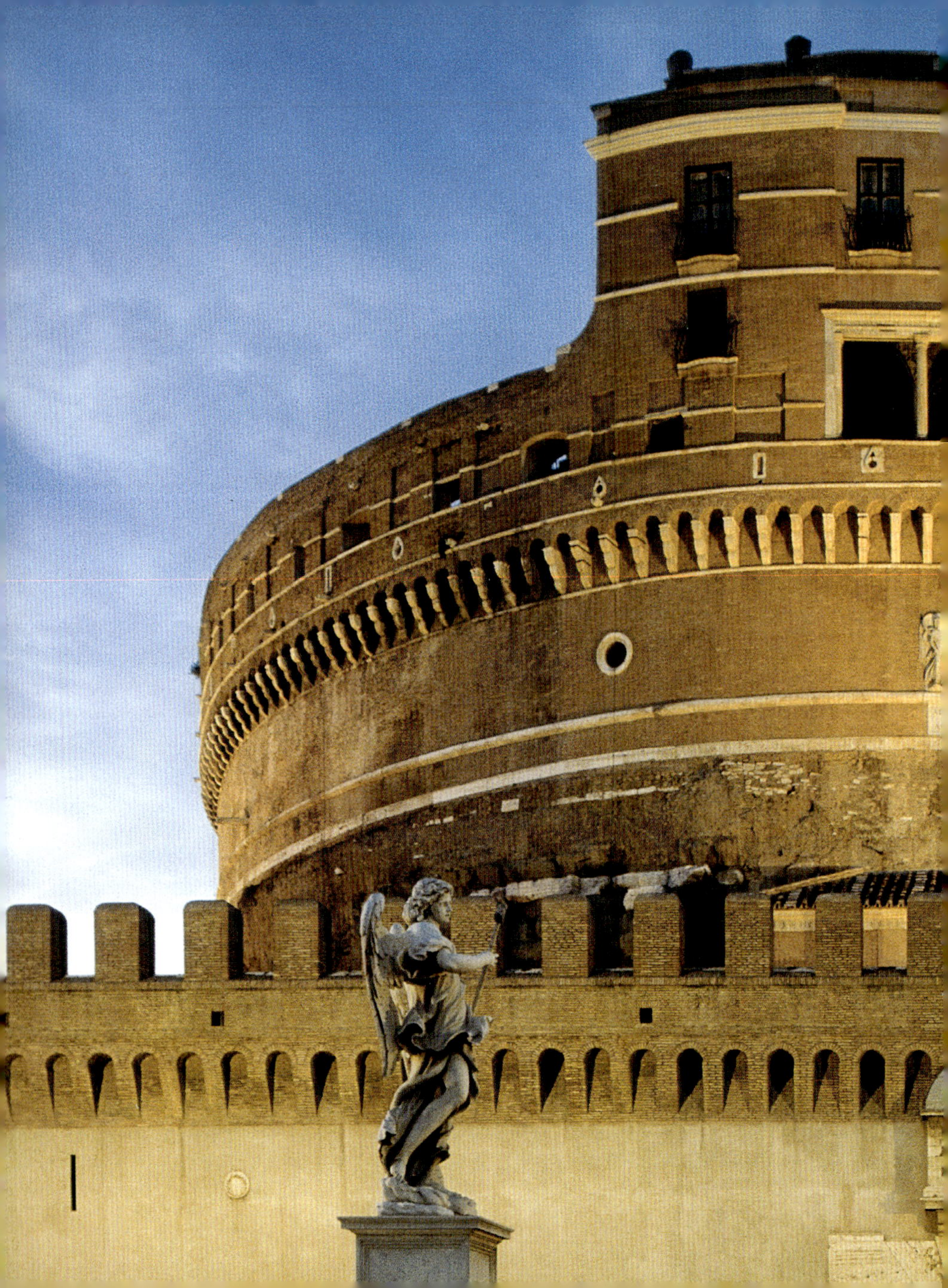

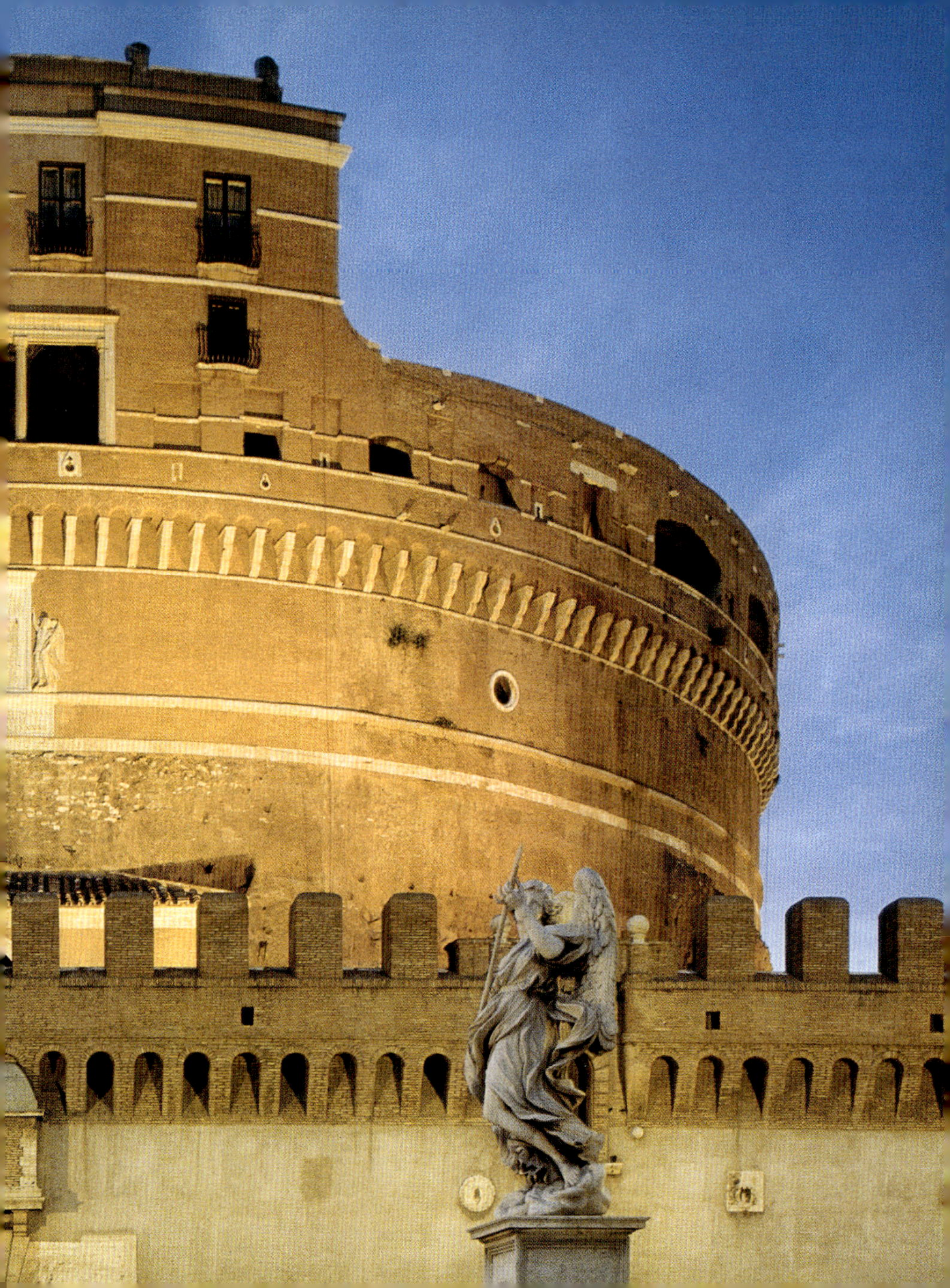

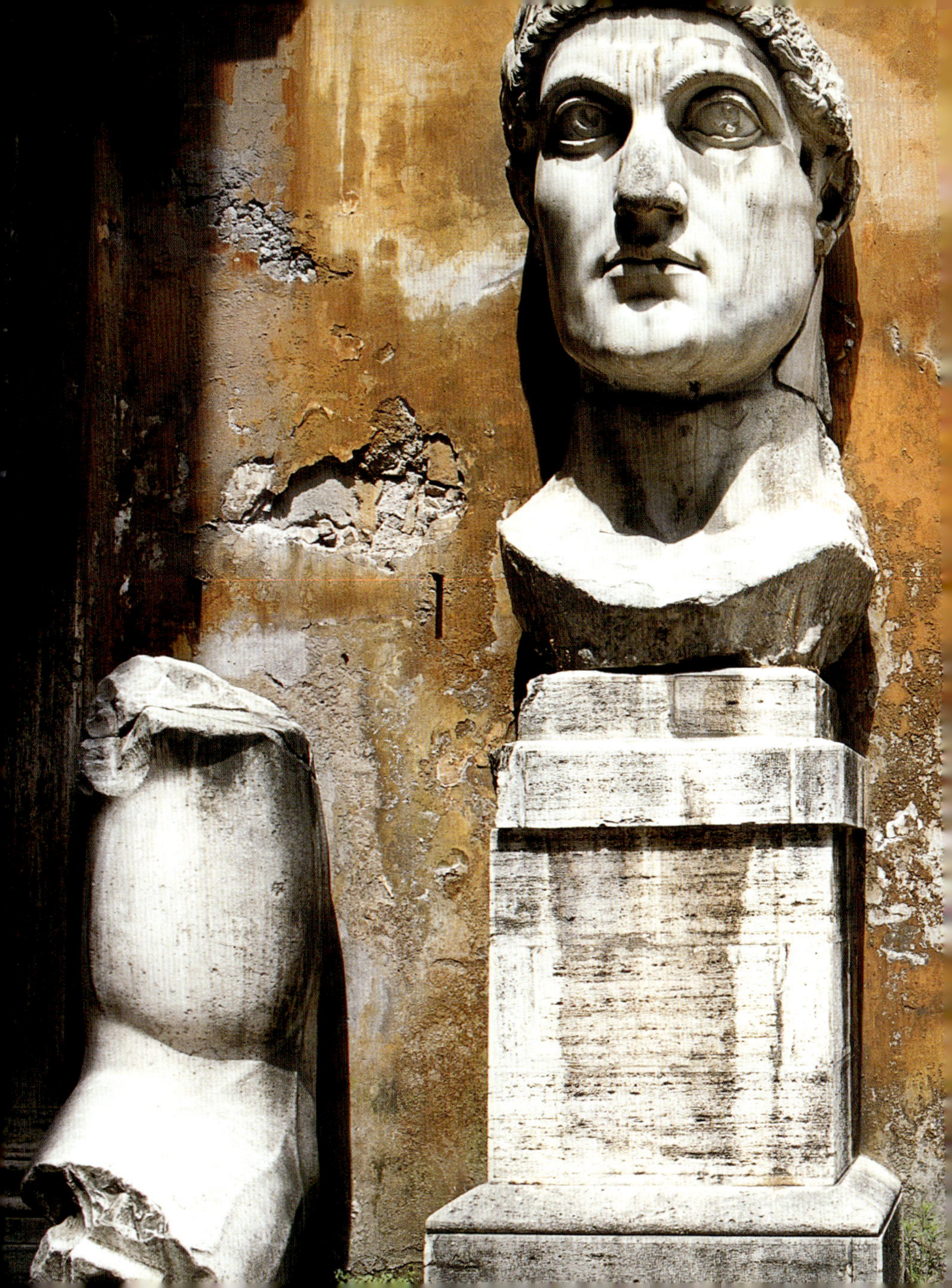

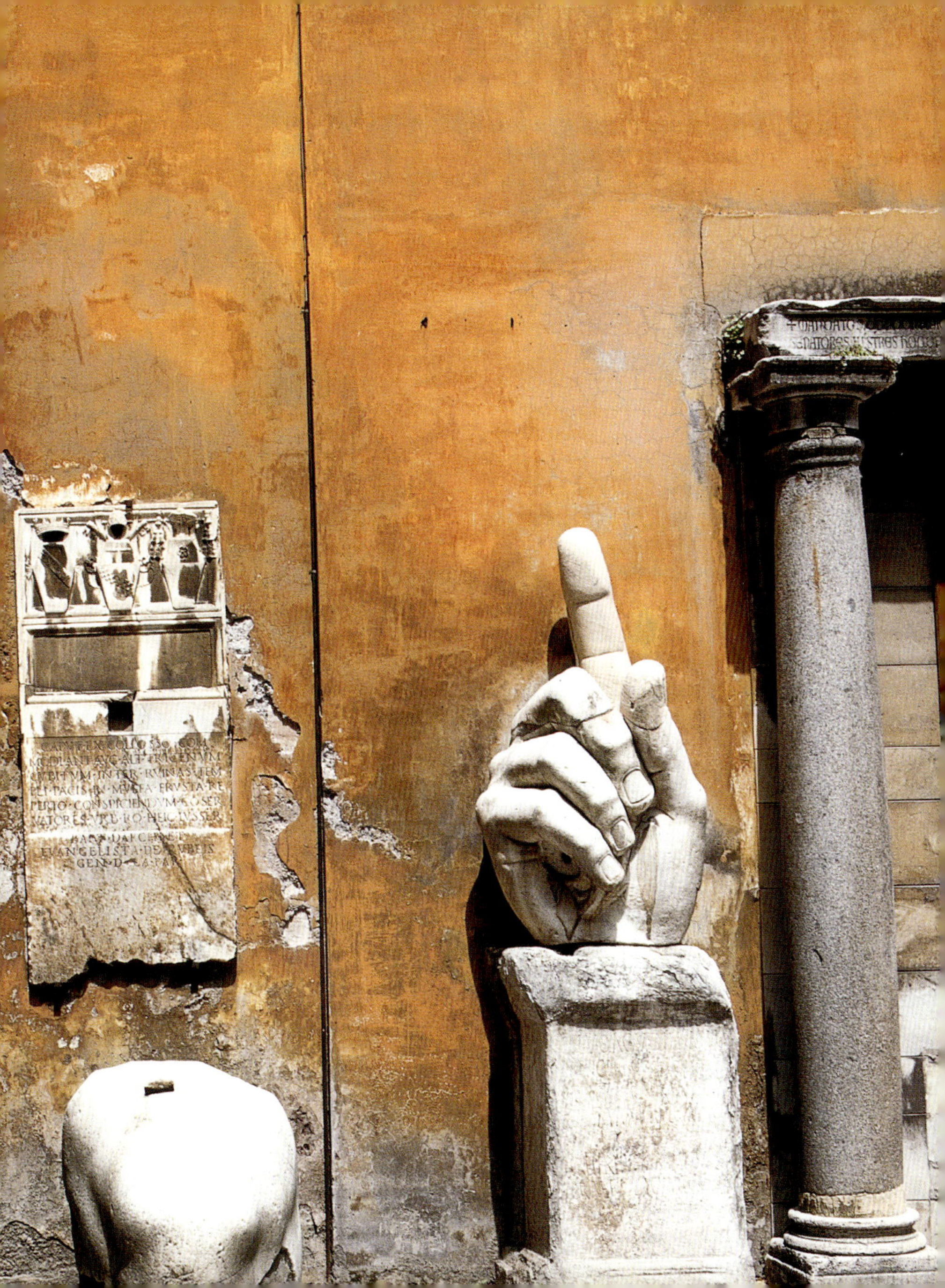

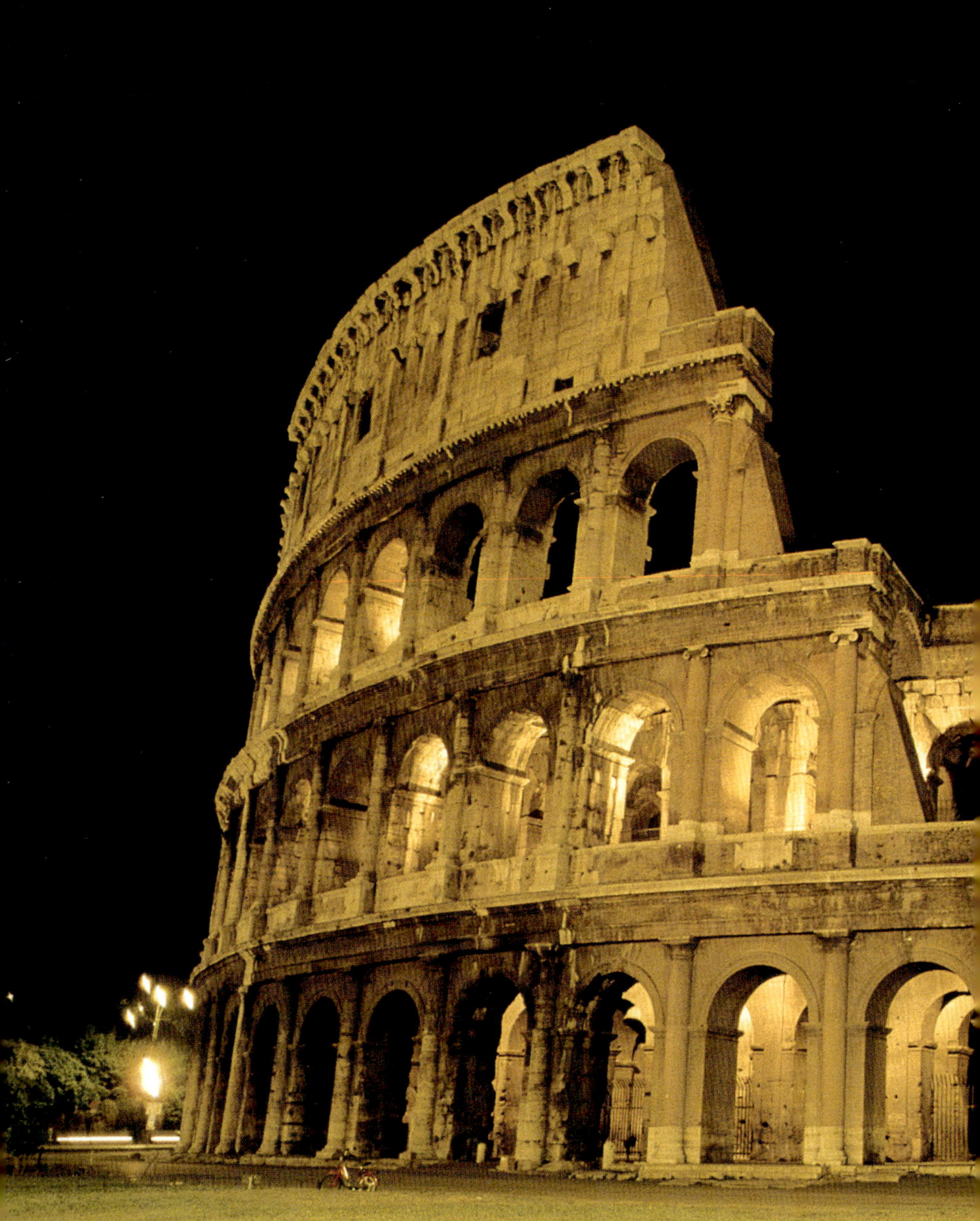

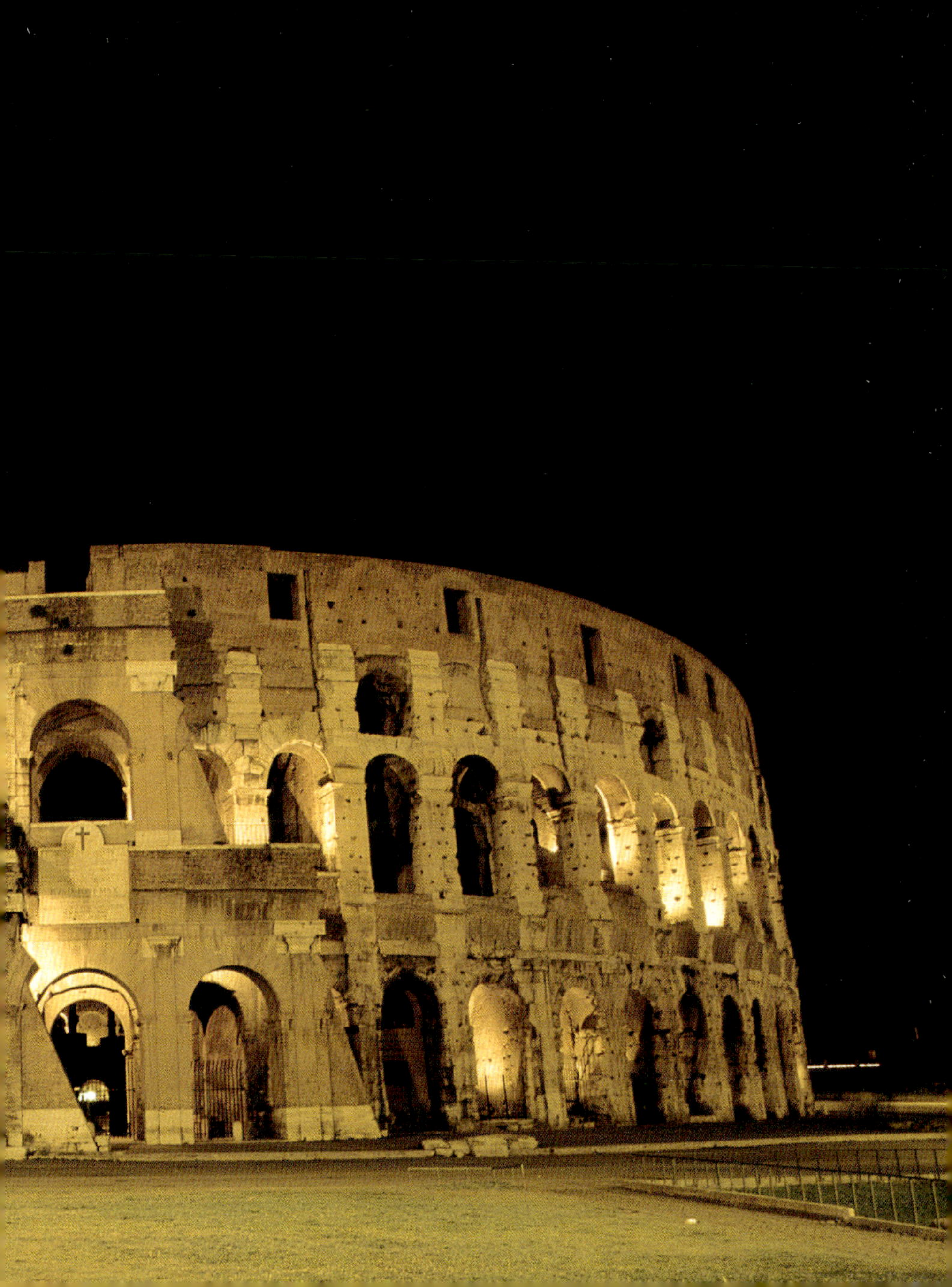

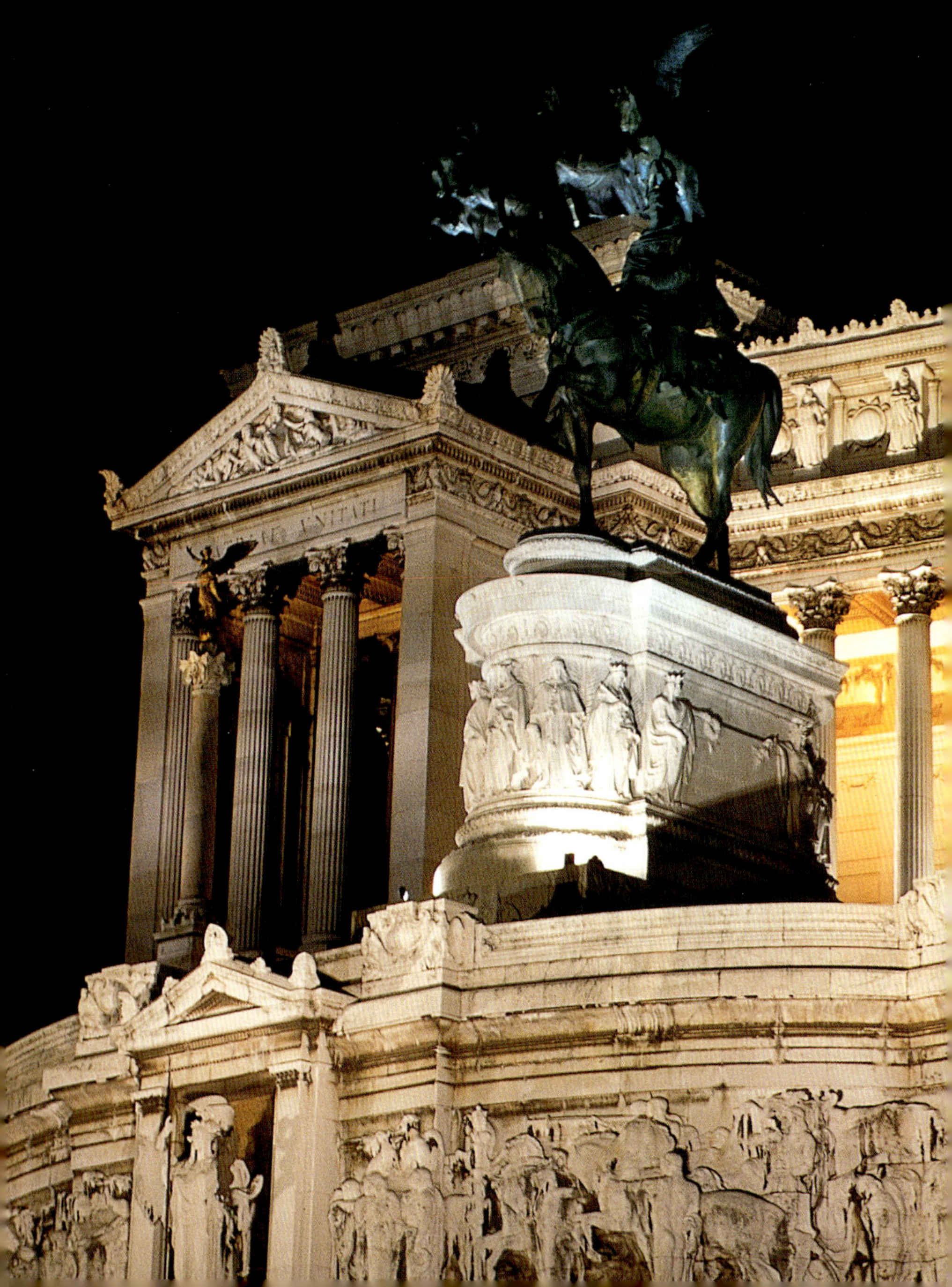

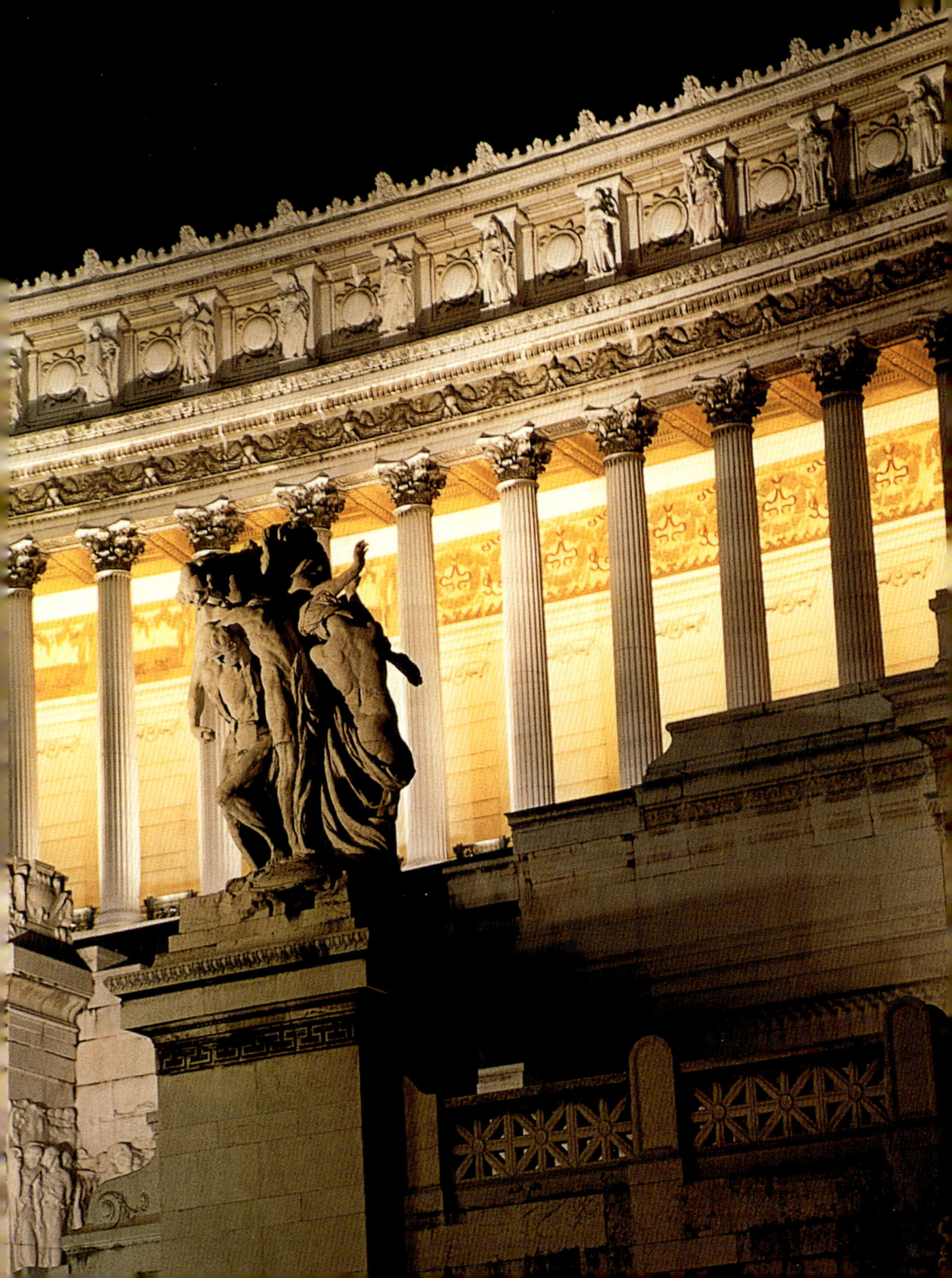

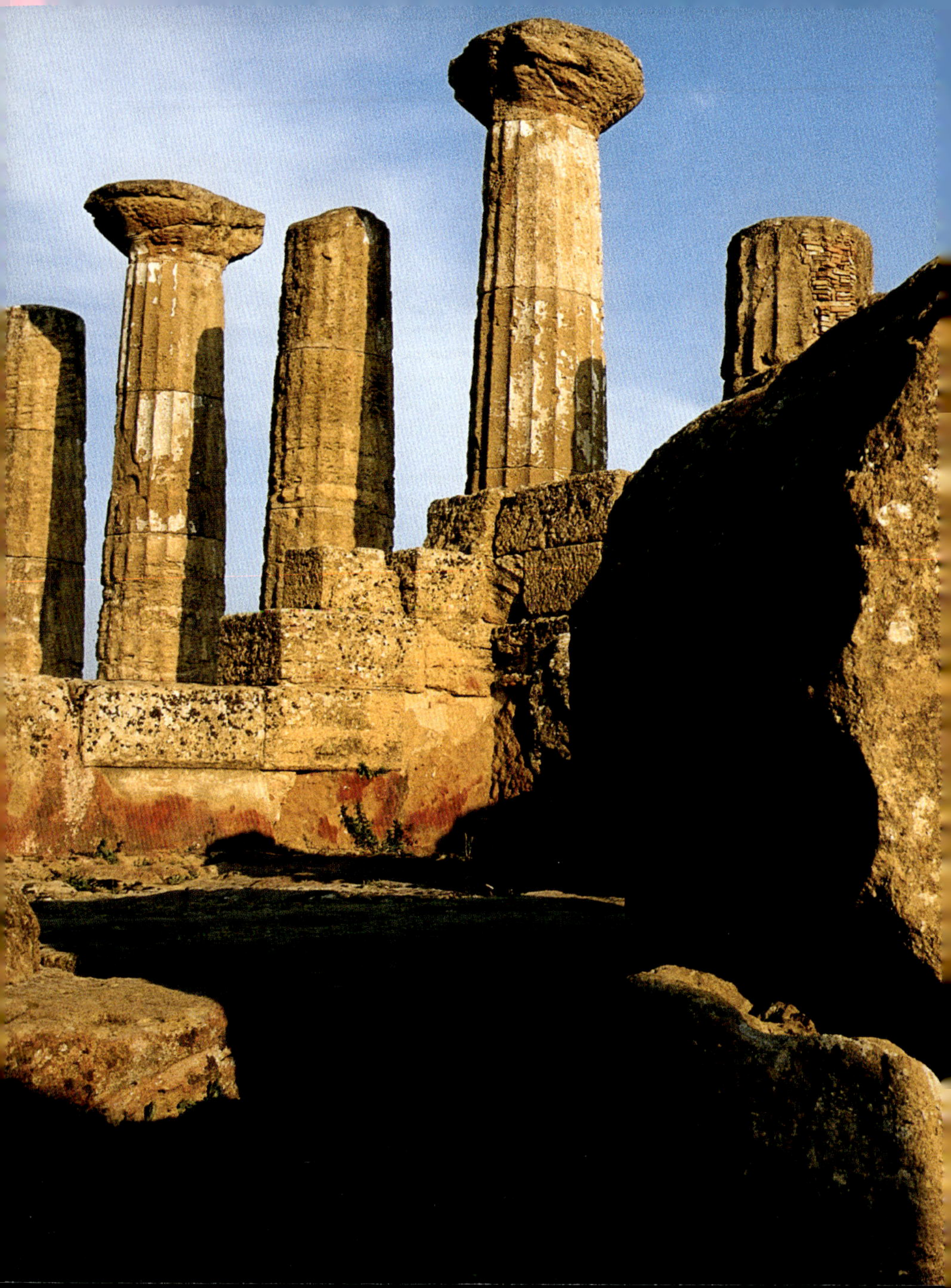

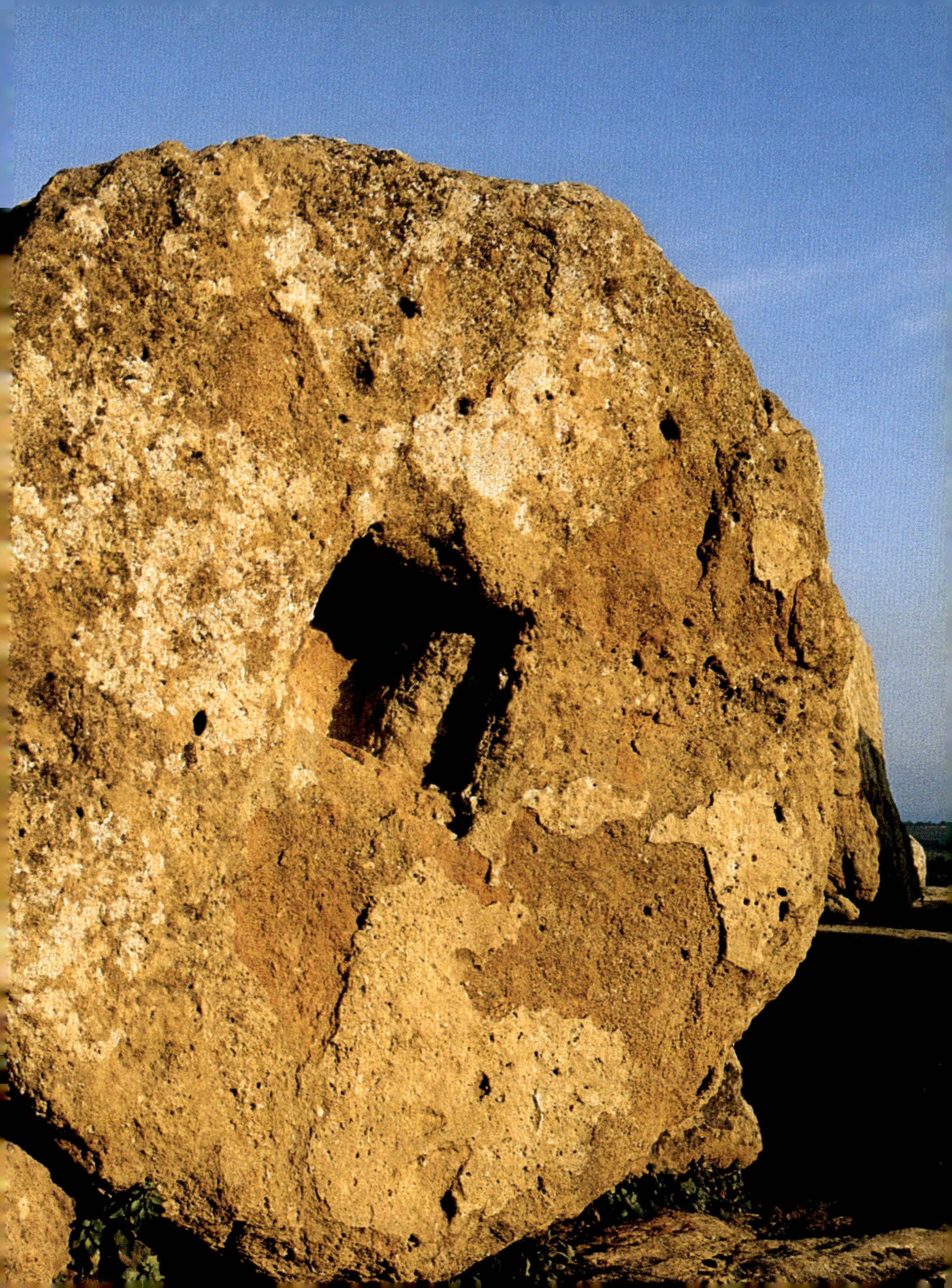

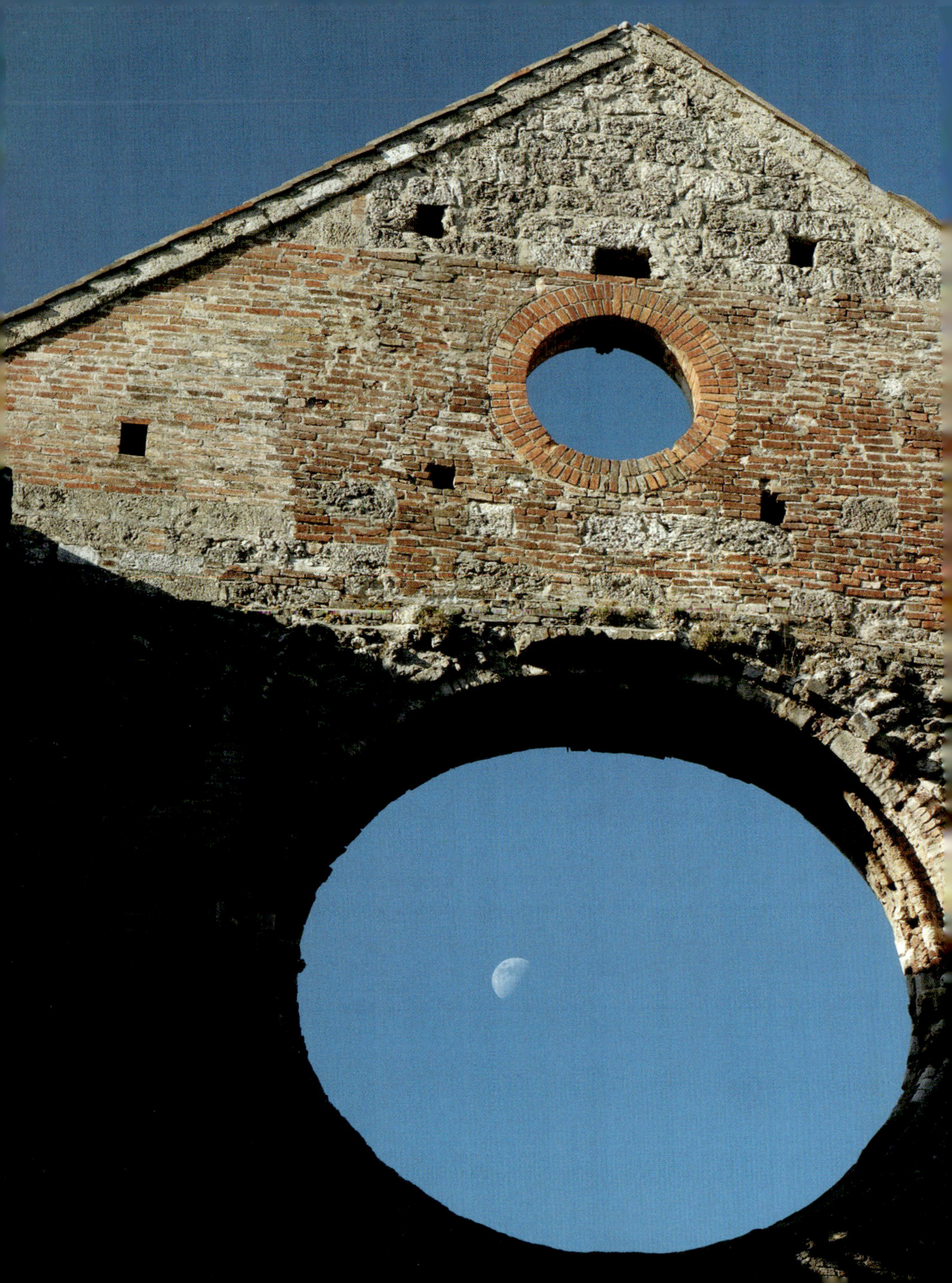

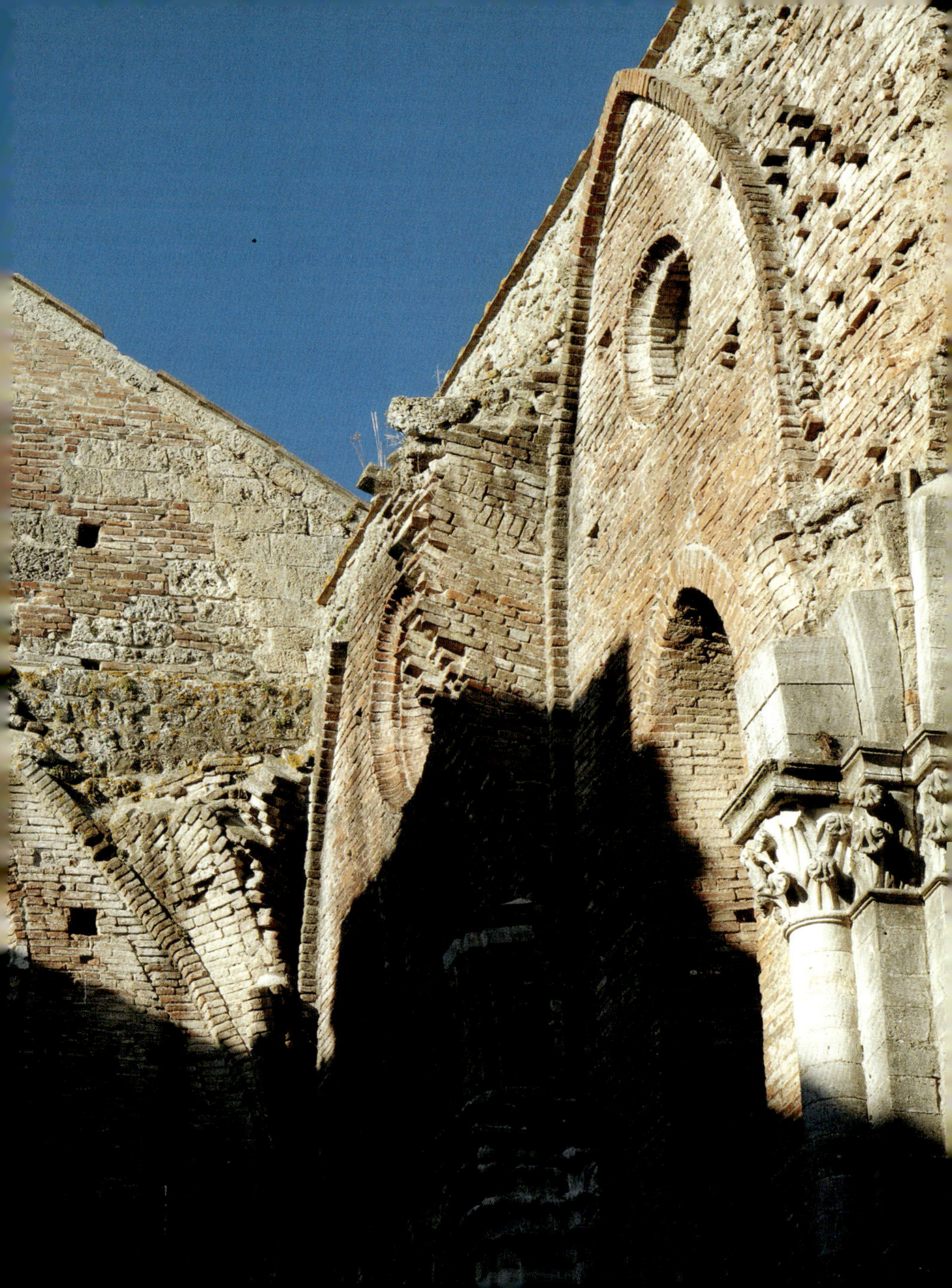

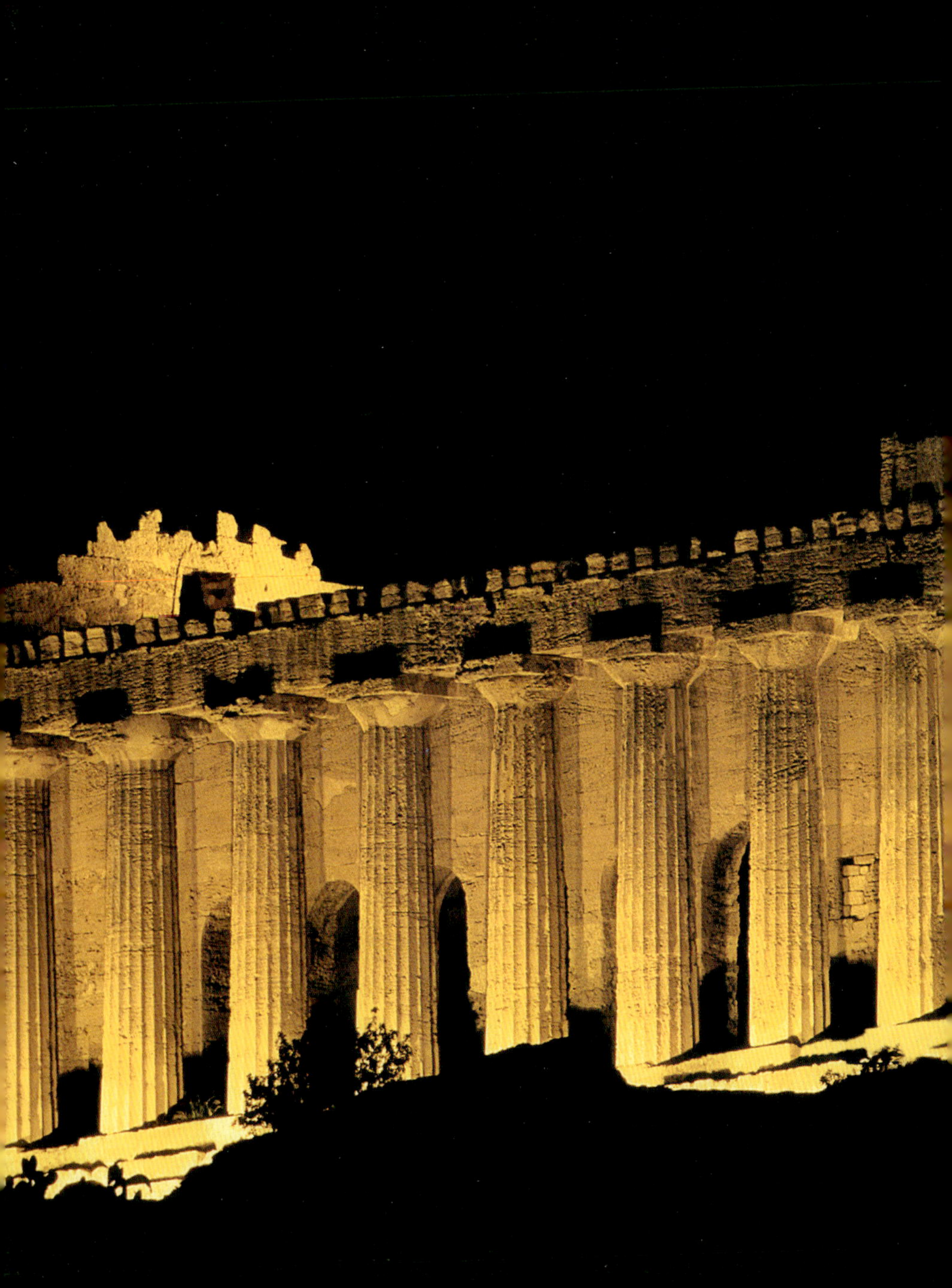

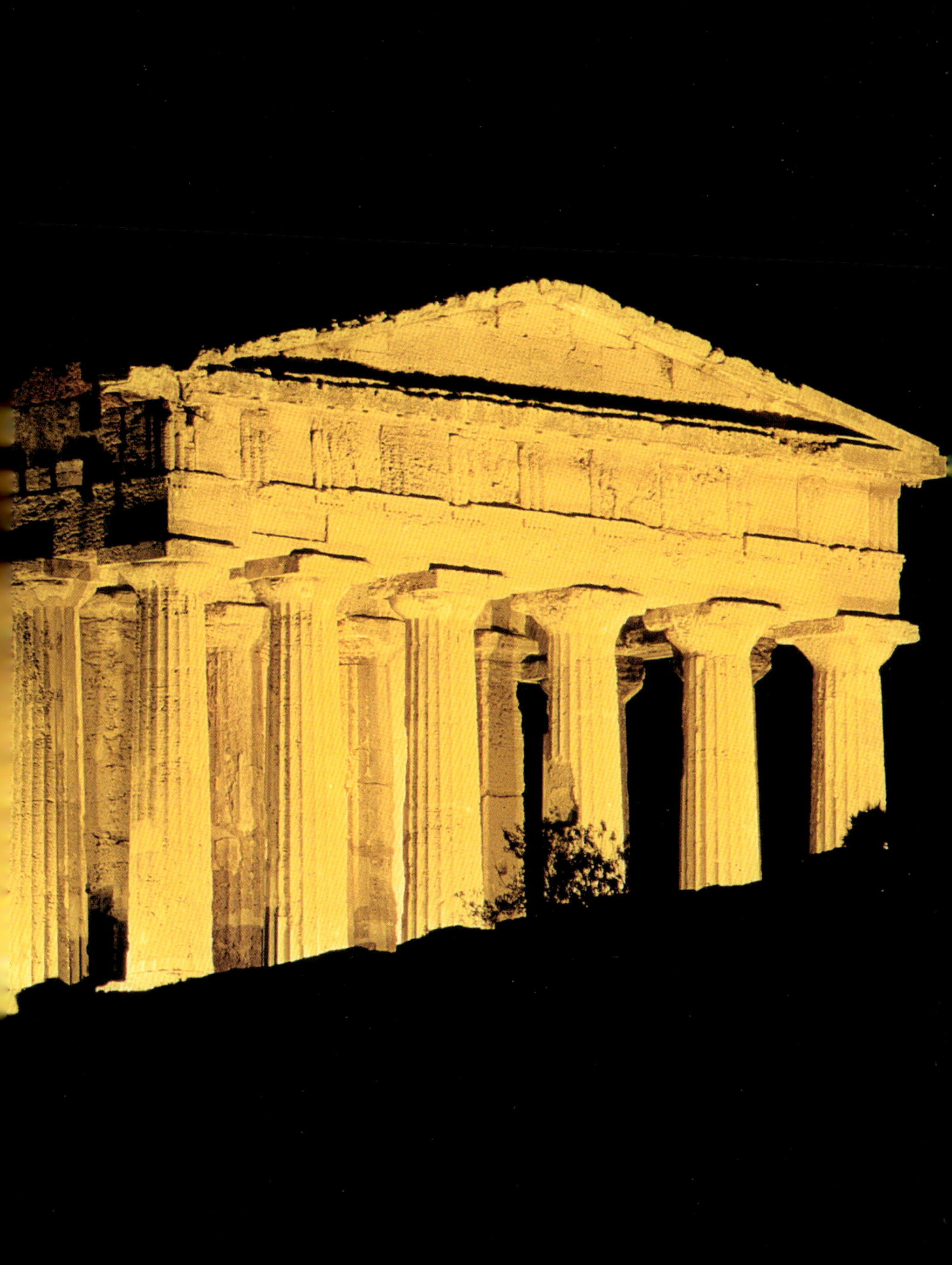

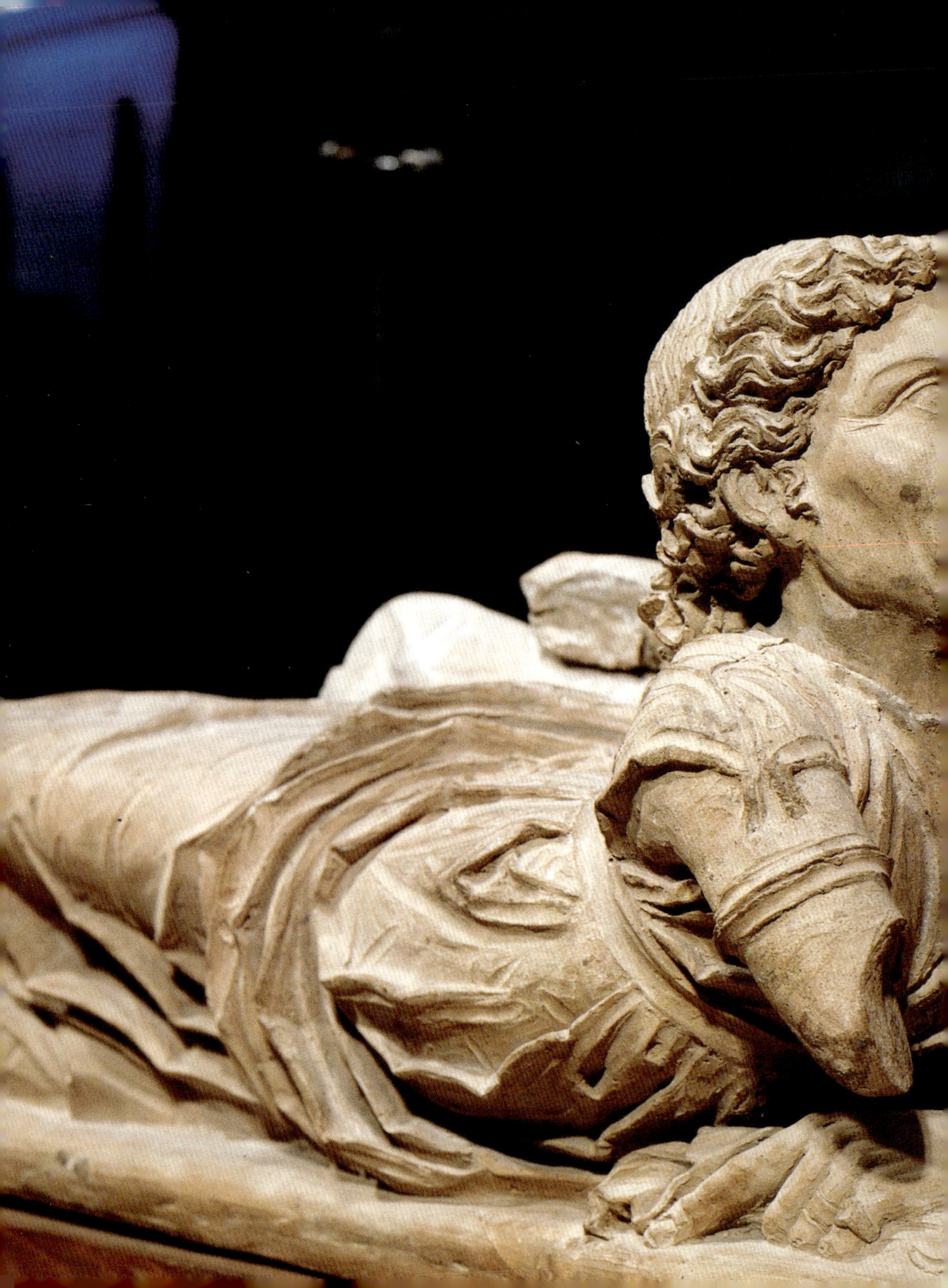

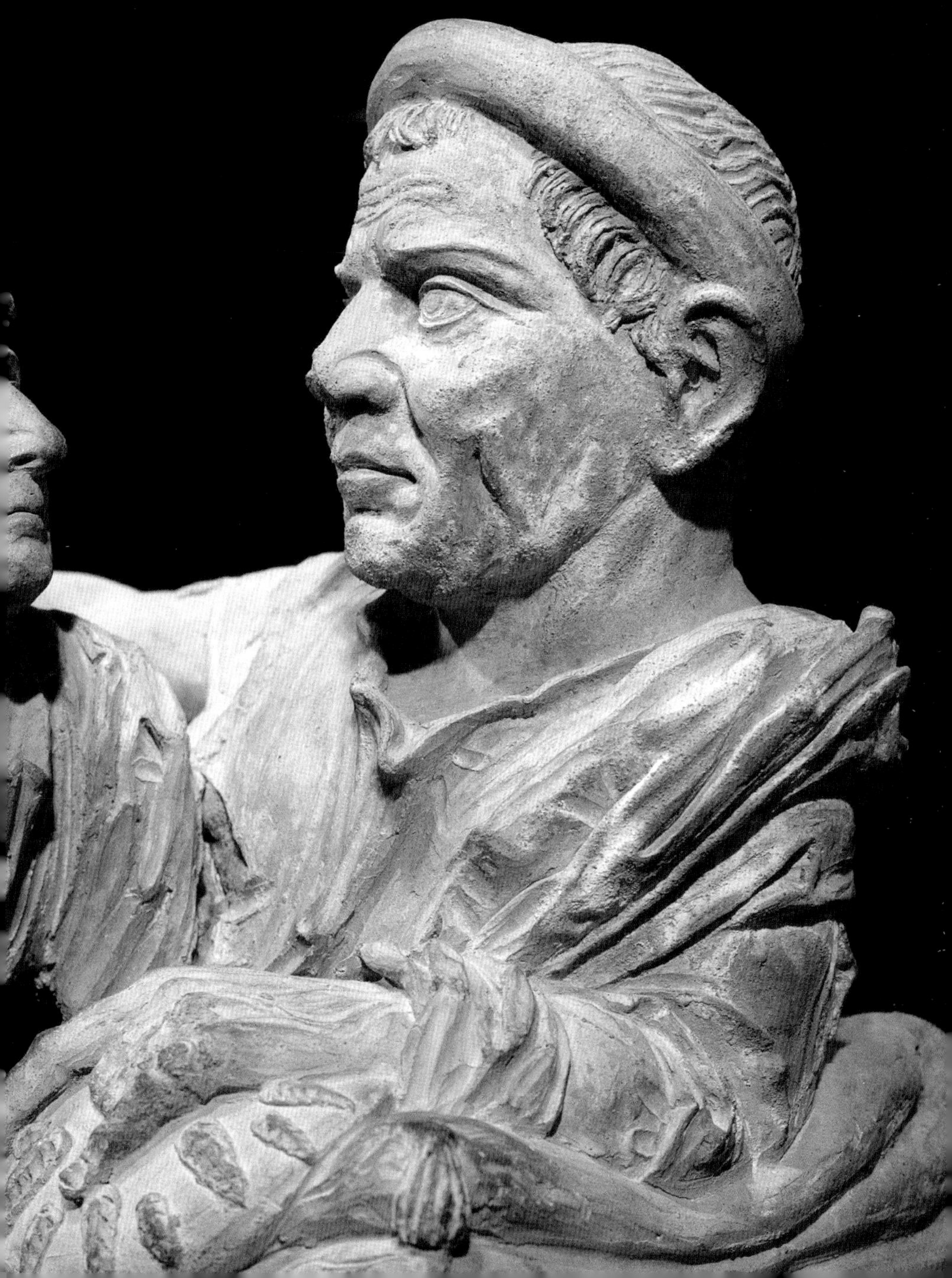

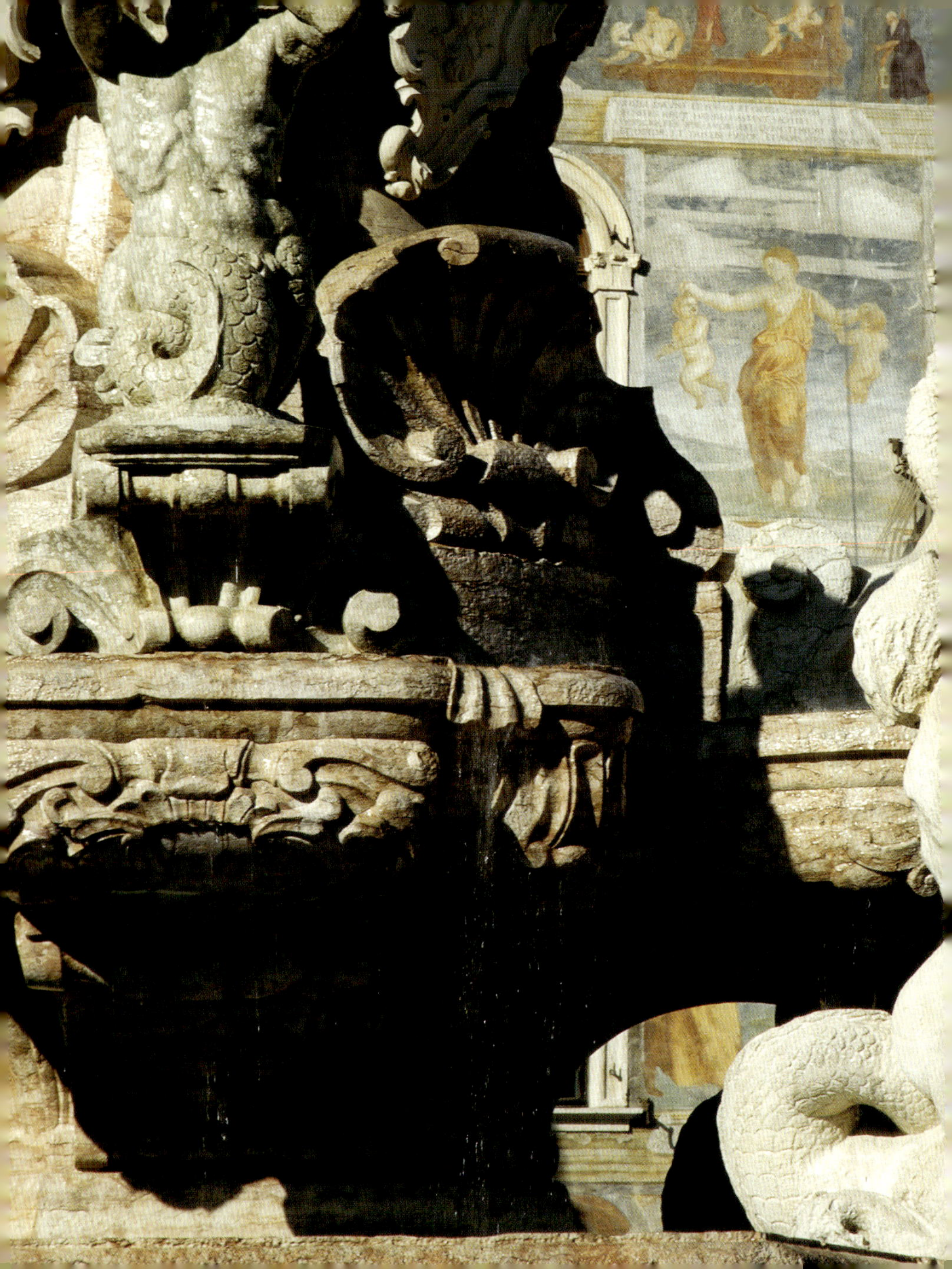

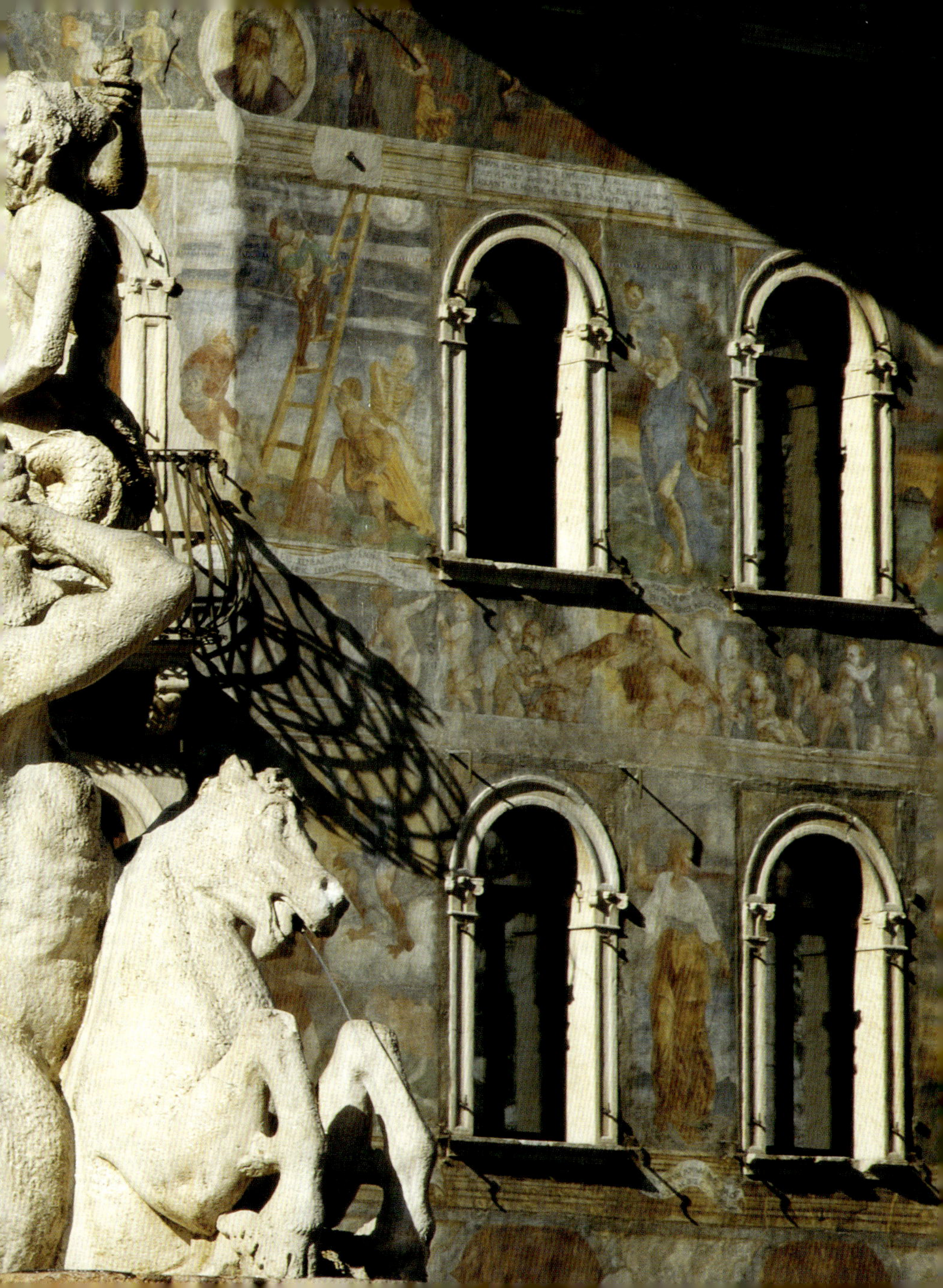

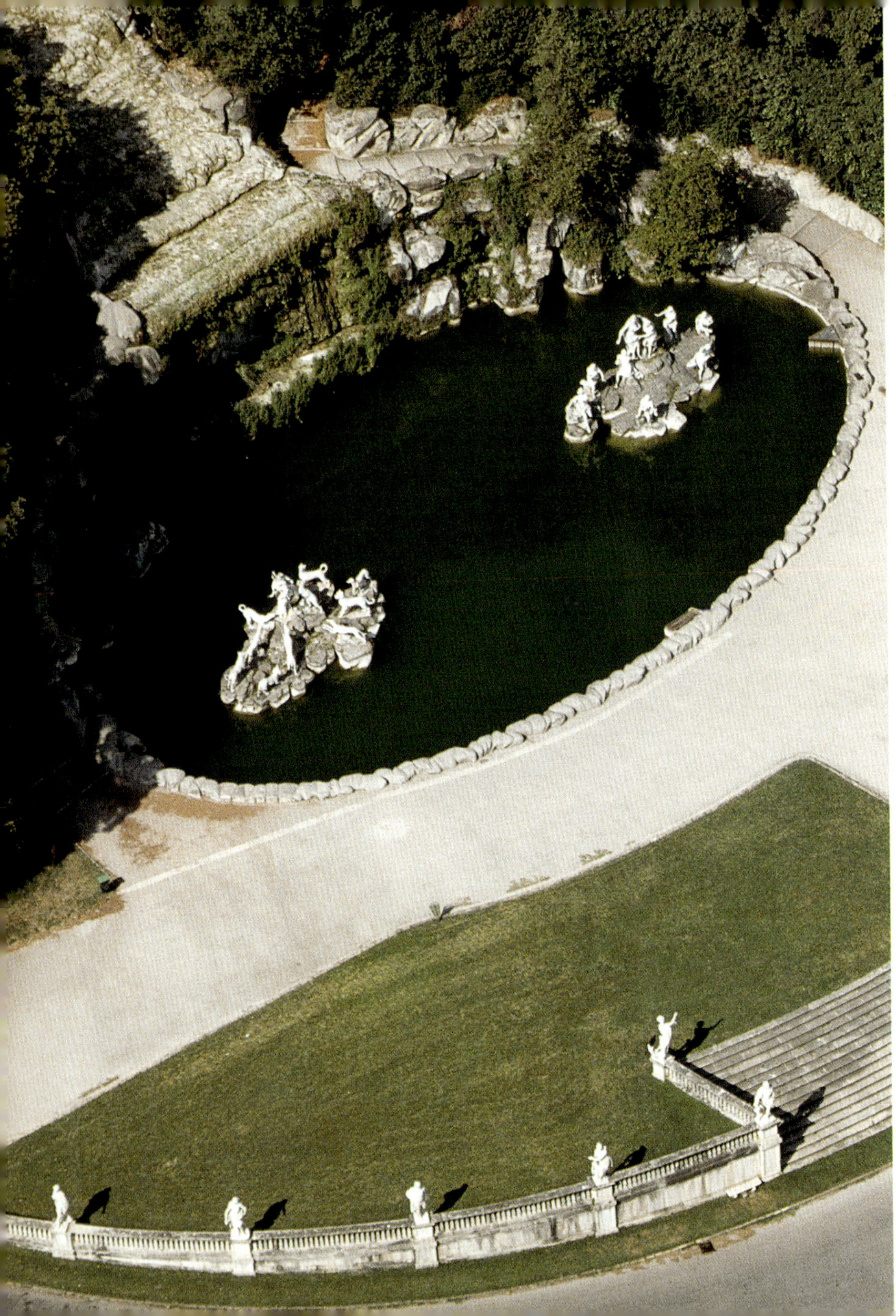

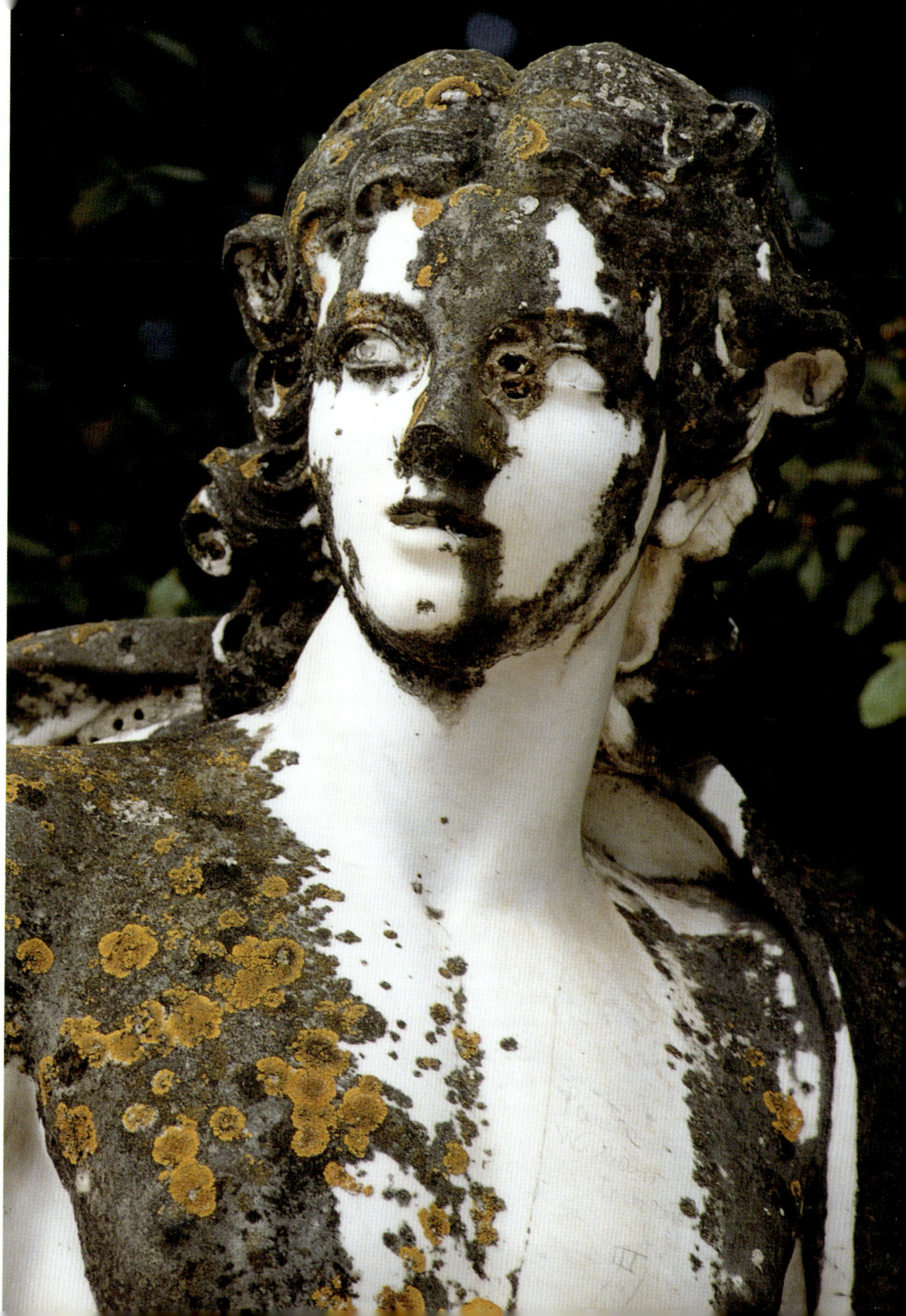

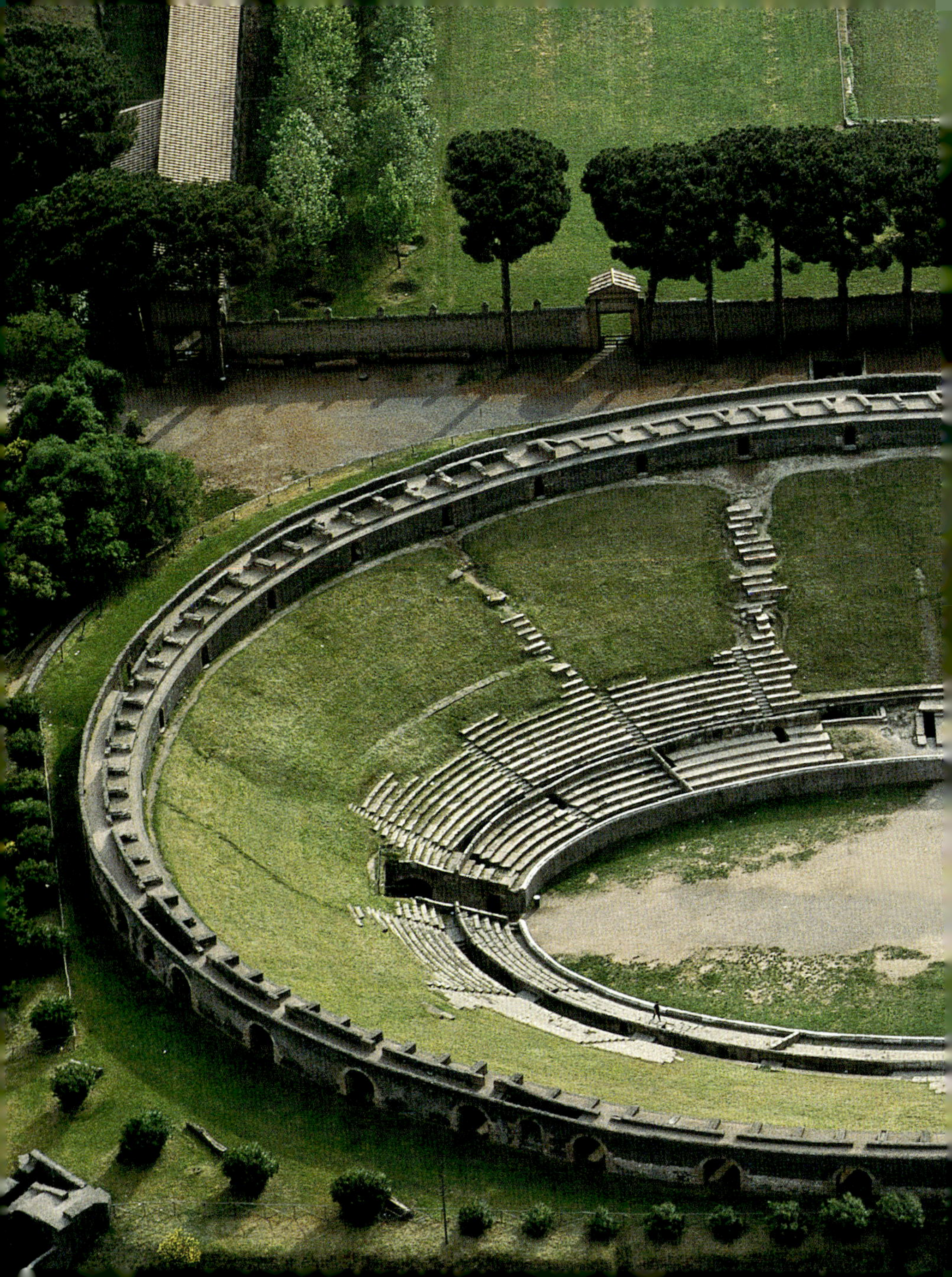

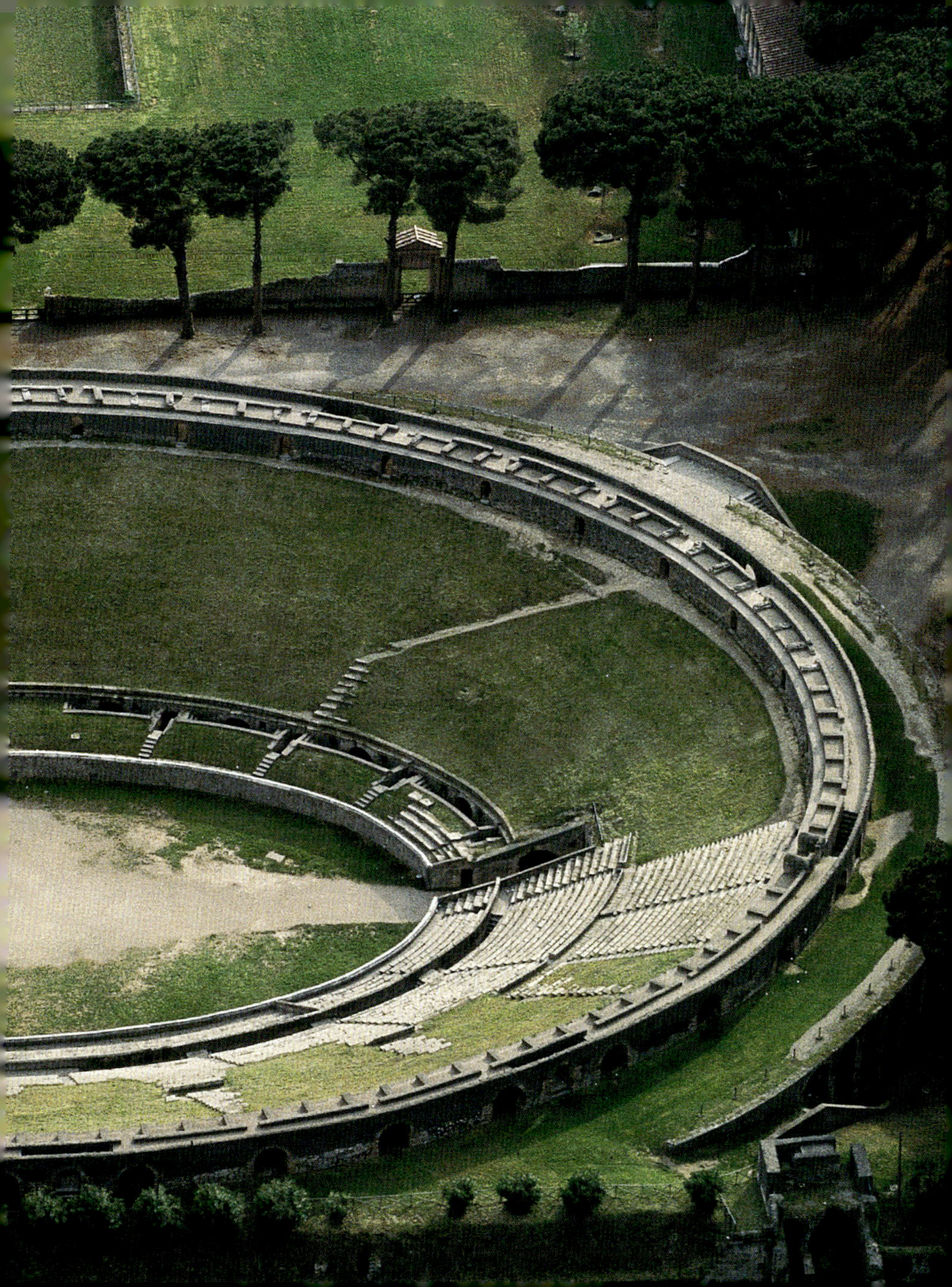

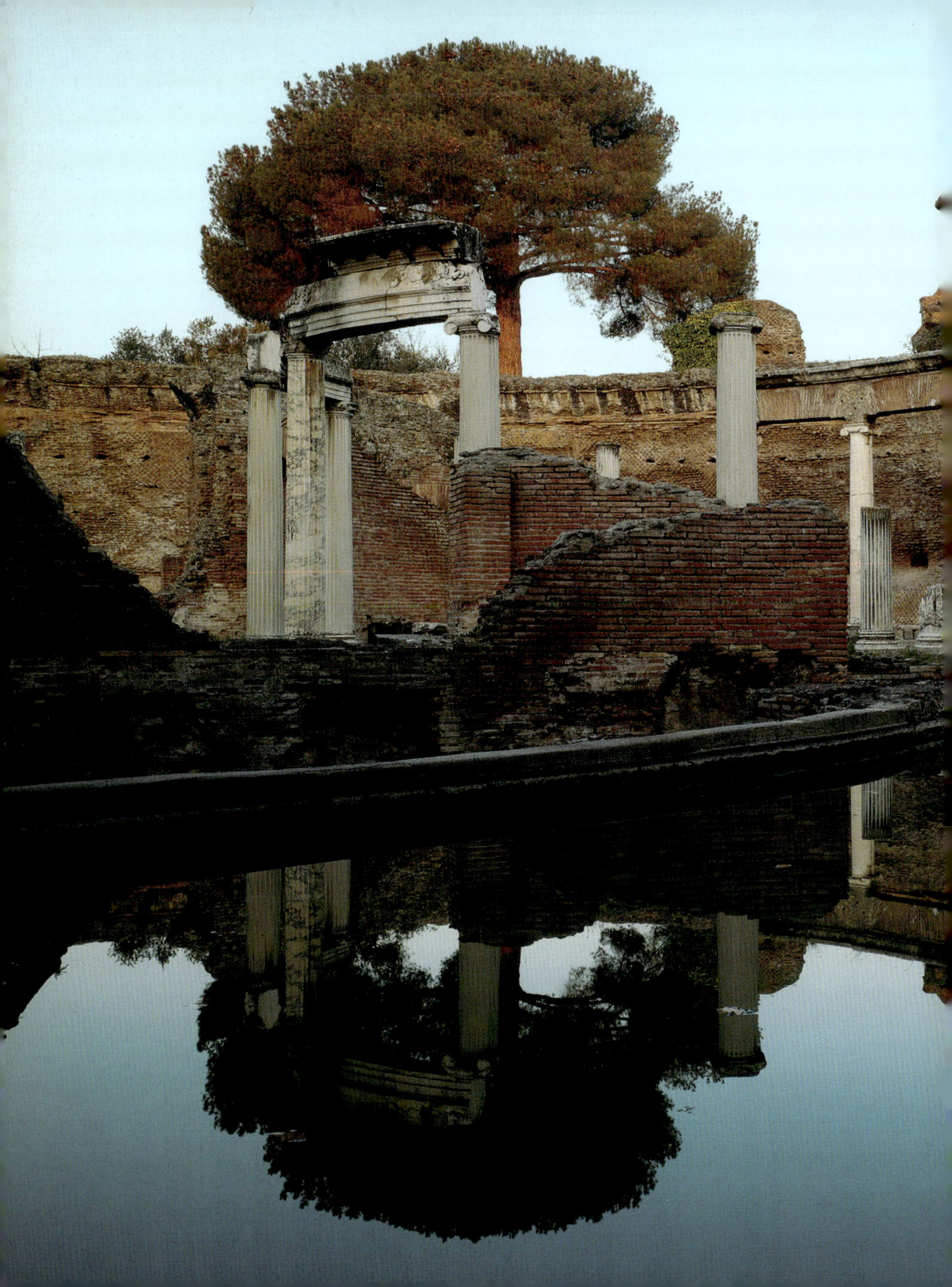

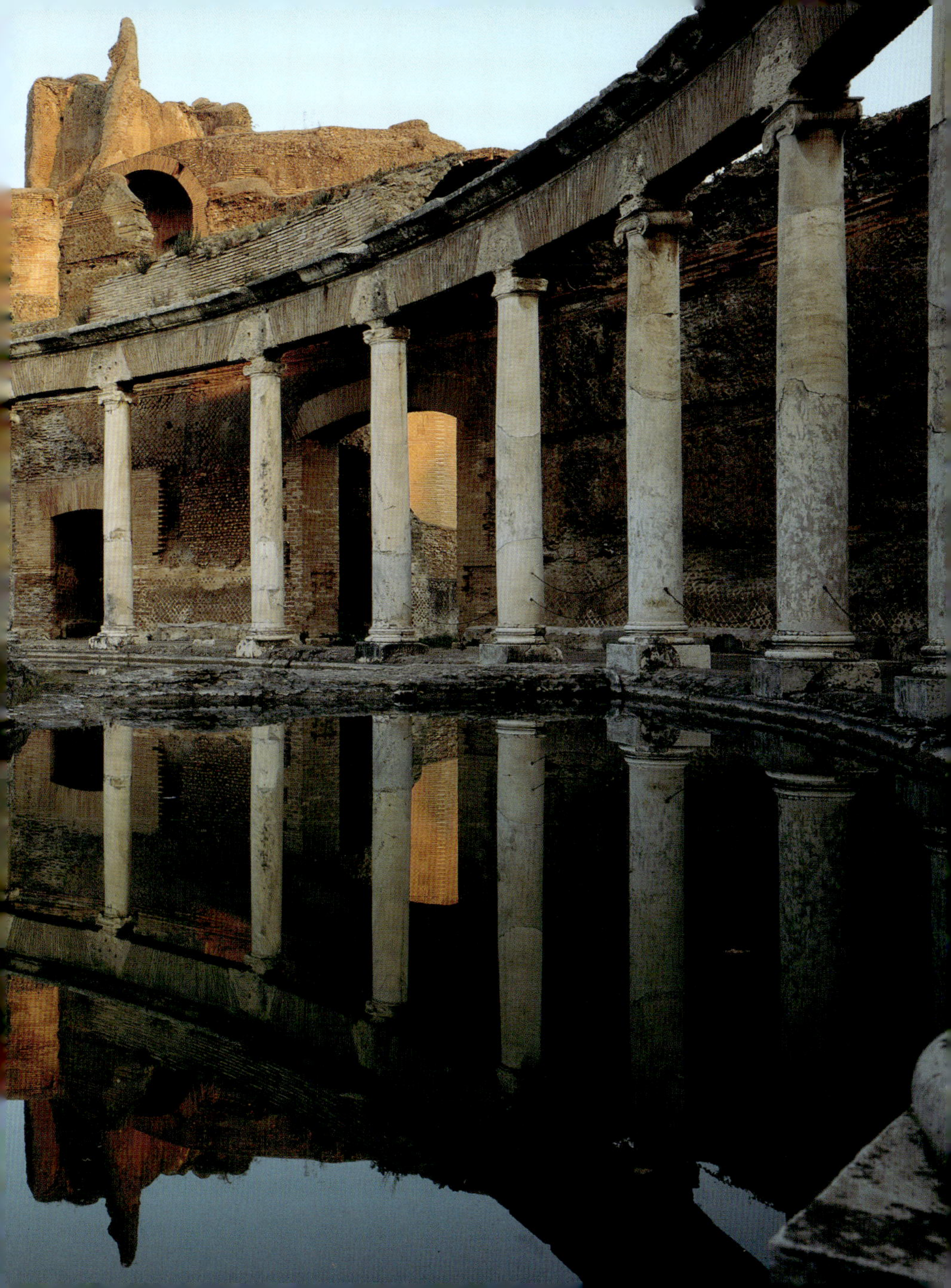

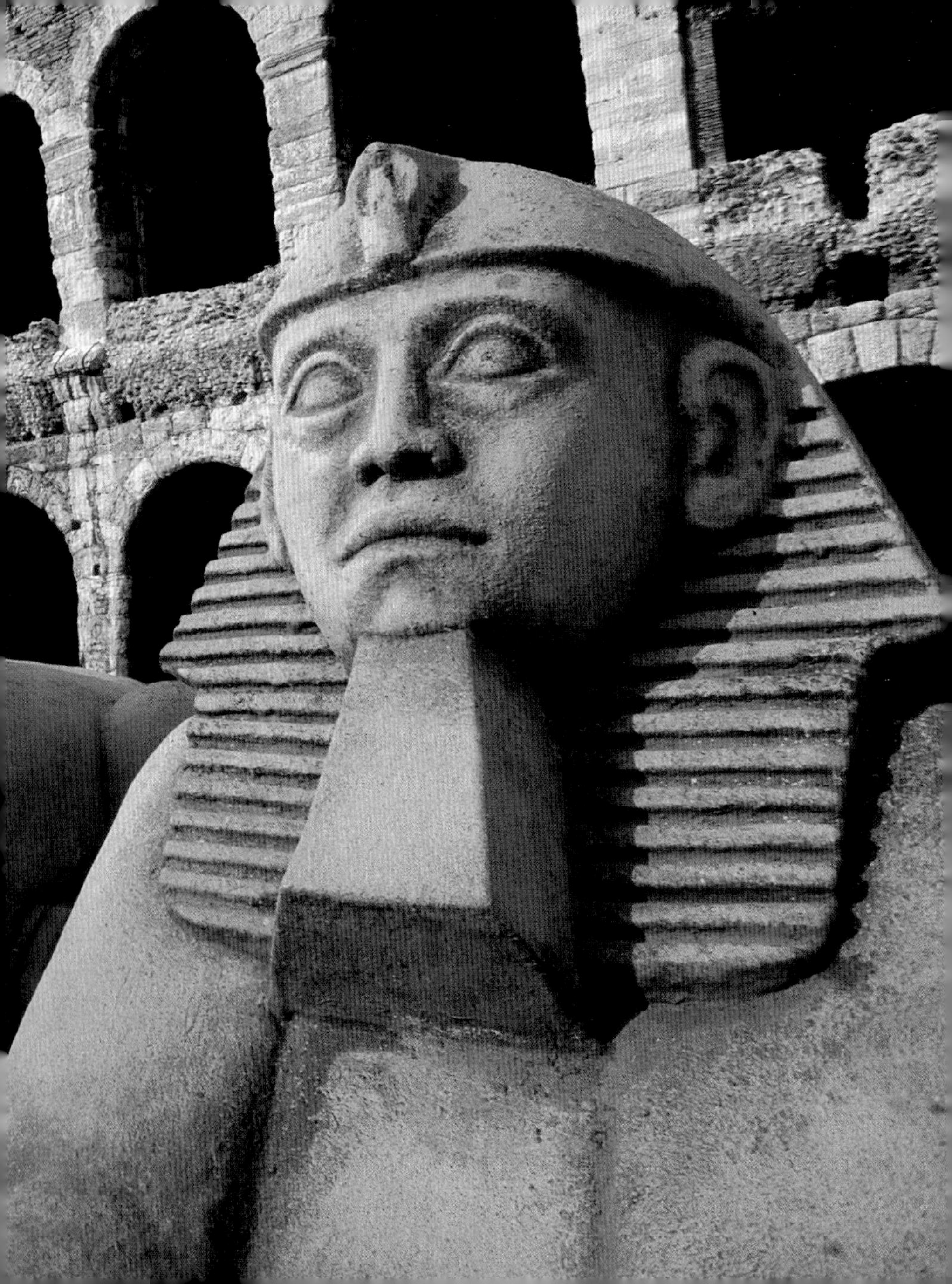

LAKE AND RIVER LANDSCAPES

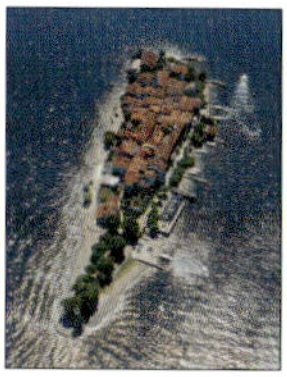

THE ISOLA DEI PESCATORI is the smallest Borromean Island in Lake Maggiore. Also called Isola Superiore, it still preserves alleys and little streets of the old-time route, on which fishermen's houses rise *(p. 329)*.

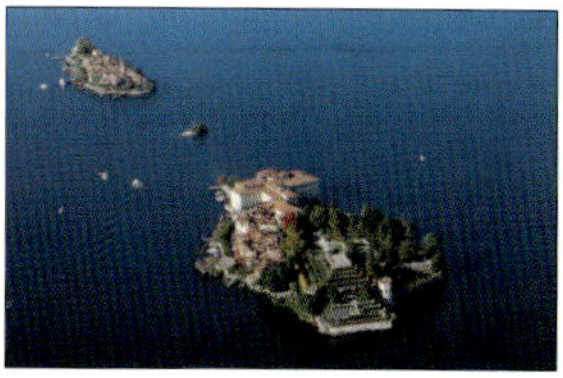

A VIEW OF THE LAKE MAGGIORE and the Borromean Islands. In the foreground stands the Isola Bella, distinguished by a wonderful Baroque palace surrounded by terraced Italian gardens *(pp. 330-331)*.

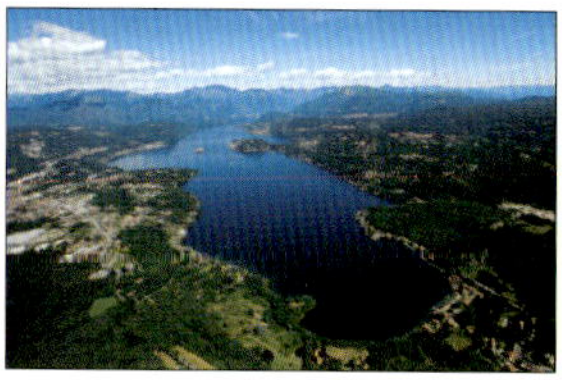

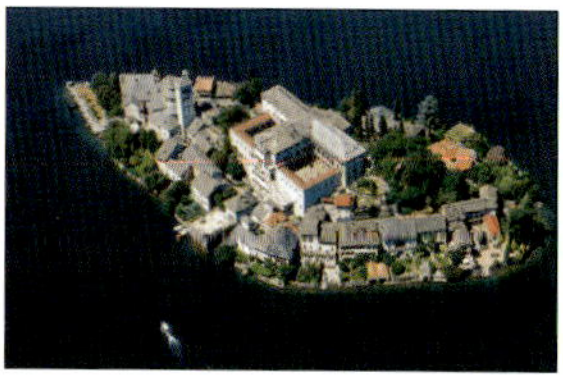

THE LOVELY SAN GIULIO ISLAND, overlooked by the imposing Romanesque basilica rich in art treasures – amongst which a famous 12th-century ambo – and by the 16th-century Bishop's Palace, is one of the most visited resorts of Lake Orta. Set amongst woody hills, the westernmost pre-Alpine lake is named after Orta San Giulio, located on its western shore at the foot of the Sacro Monte *(pp. 332-333, 334-335)*.

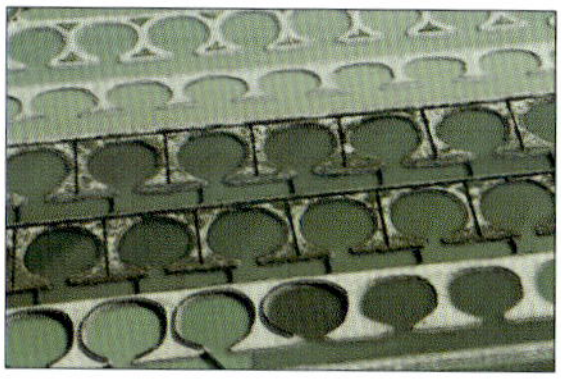

THE COMACCHIO VALLEYS originate from a subsidence which wasn't filled in by river Po, yet by salted water through gaps produced by the tides. Seen from above, the fish tanks show astonishing shapes *(pp. 336-337)*.

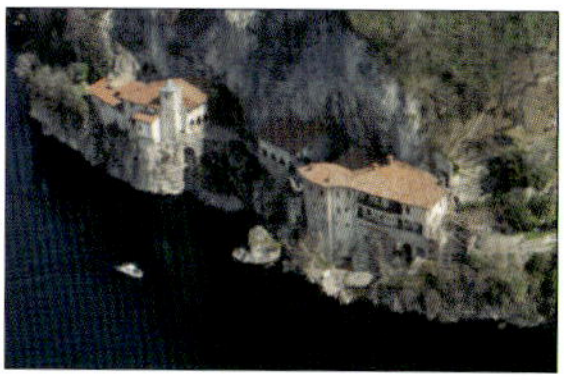

THE SMALL HERMITAGE of Santa Caterina del Sasso was founded in the 12th century on a steep rocky headland on Lake Maggiore. It is one of the most atmospheric sanctuaries of Northern Italy *(pp. 338-339)*.

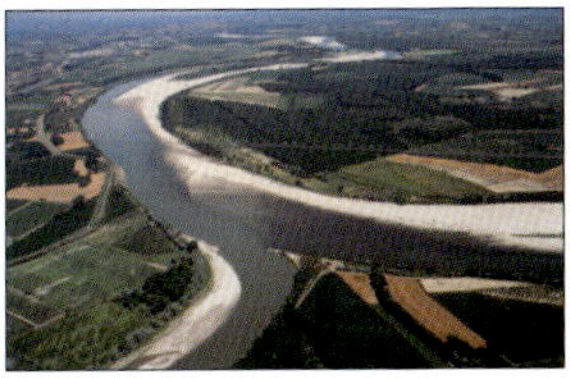

A BIRD'S-EYE VIEW OF THE RIVER ADDA. It rises from Mount Ferro in the Retiche Alps, crosses the Valtellina and flows in and out Lake Como. It finally meets the Po between Piacenza and Cremona *(pp. 340-341)*.

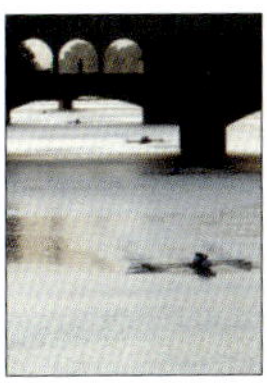

ROWING MEN ON THE RIVER ARNO, which flows through Florence between high walls. The river is crossed by several bridges, the most famous being the Ponte Vecchio *(p. 343)*.

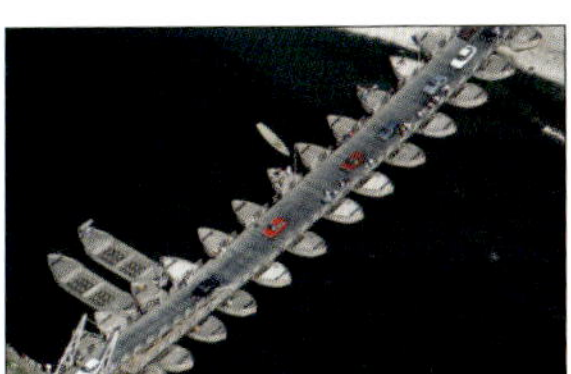

A BRIDGE ON THE RIVER TICINO IN LOMBARDY. The area around the "blue river," named after the colour of its waters, is a natural reserve protecting 90,000 hectares of unpolluted nature *(pp. 346-347)*.

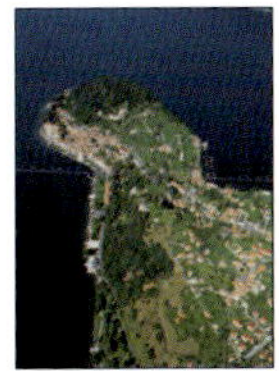

BELLAGIO ON LAKE COMO is known since ancient times for its climate and landscape. In the 18th century it was enriched by sumptuous villas; however, it kept its medieval layout with high-stepped alleys *(p. 342)*.

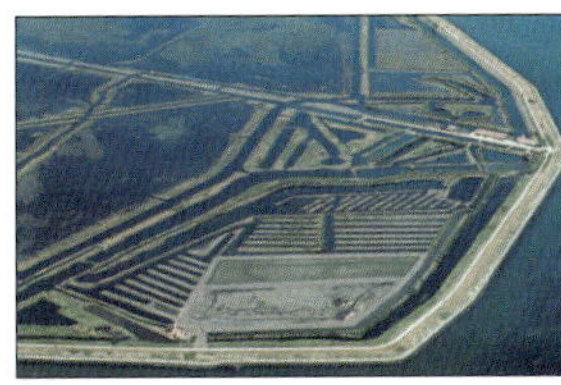

RIVER PO'S UNUSUAL SHAPES watched from above. The landscape created by the river's debris on the way to the Adriatic sea – amongst brakish lagoons, cane fields and dunes – is now a protected area *(pp. 344-345)*.

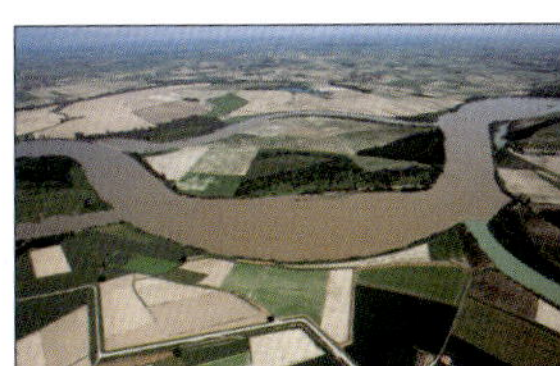

A LOOP OF THE PO. The longest Italian river flows across the entire Padana Plain and is navigable from the confluence with the Ticino up to the mouth into the Adriatic sea, where it forms its delta *(pp. 348-349)*.

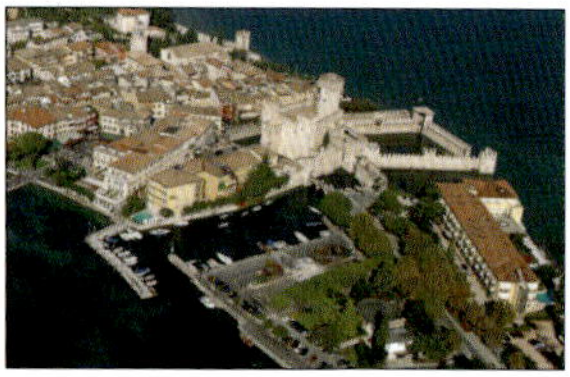

THE HISTORICAL CITY OF SIRMIONE on Lake Garda is built around the fortress erected in the 13th century by Mastino I Della Scala to defend it. The internal dock served as a refuge for the Scala fleet *(pp. 350-351)*.

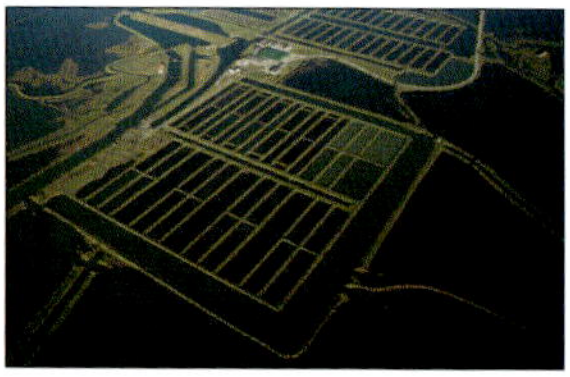

THE COMACCHIO VALLEYS constitute an ideal habitat for fish species. They underwent a complex reclamation programme, which has brought back to farming remarkably fertile lands *(pp. 352-353)*.

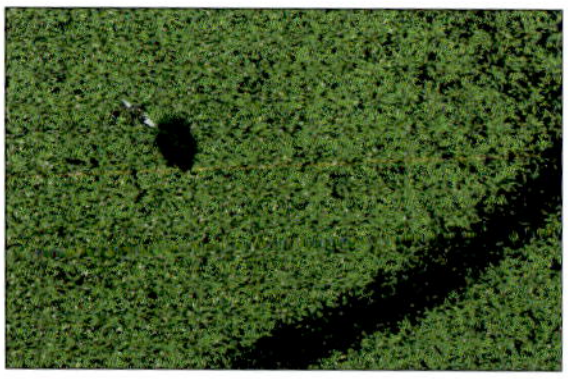

AN EXPAND OF AQUATIC PLANTS covers most of the Lake Superiore, one of the three lakes in the neighbourhoods of Mantua. Formed by the river Mincio, they today belong to the natural park of the same name *(pp. 354-355)*.

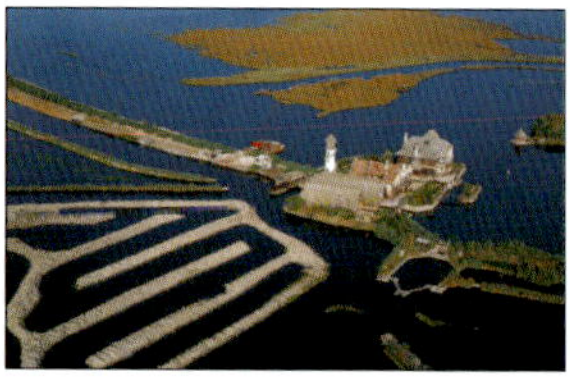

A TYPICAL FISHERY In the Venetian Lagoon. The Lagoon comprises a hundred islets and spreads from the mouth of river Brenta to the Siles's. It was once a rich fishing and hunting area *(pp. 356-357)*.

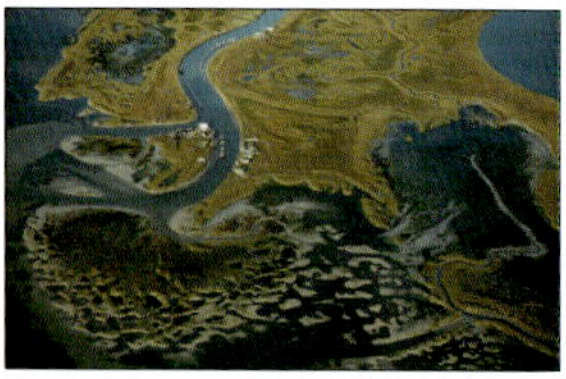

UNA VEDUTA DELLA LAGUNA VENETA, la più vasta zona umida d'Italia che circonda non solo Venezia, ma anche altre isole affascinanti, come Murano, Burano, Torcello, San Francesco del Deserto *(pagg. 358-359)*.

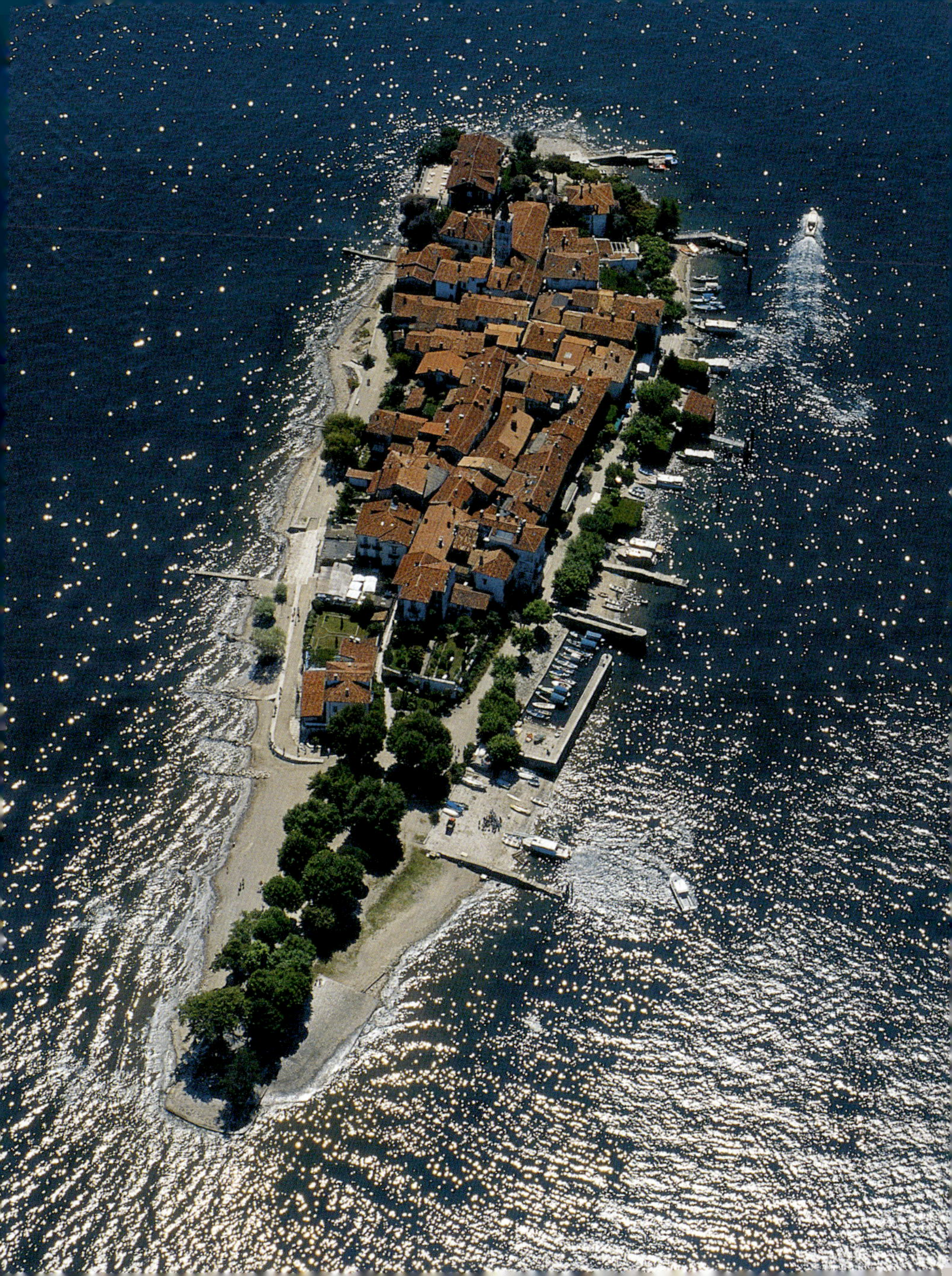

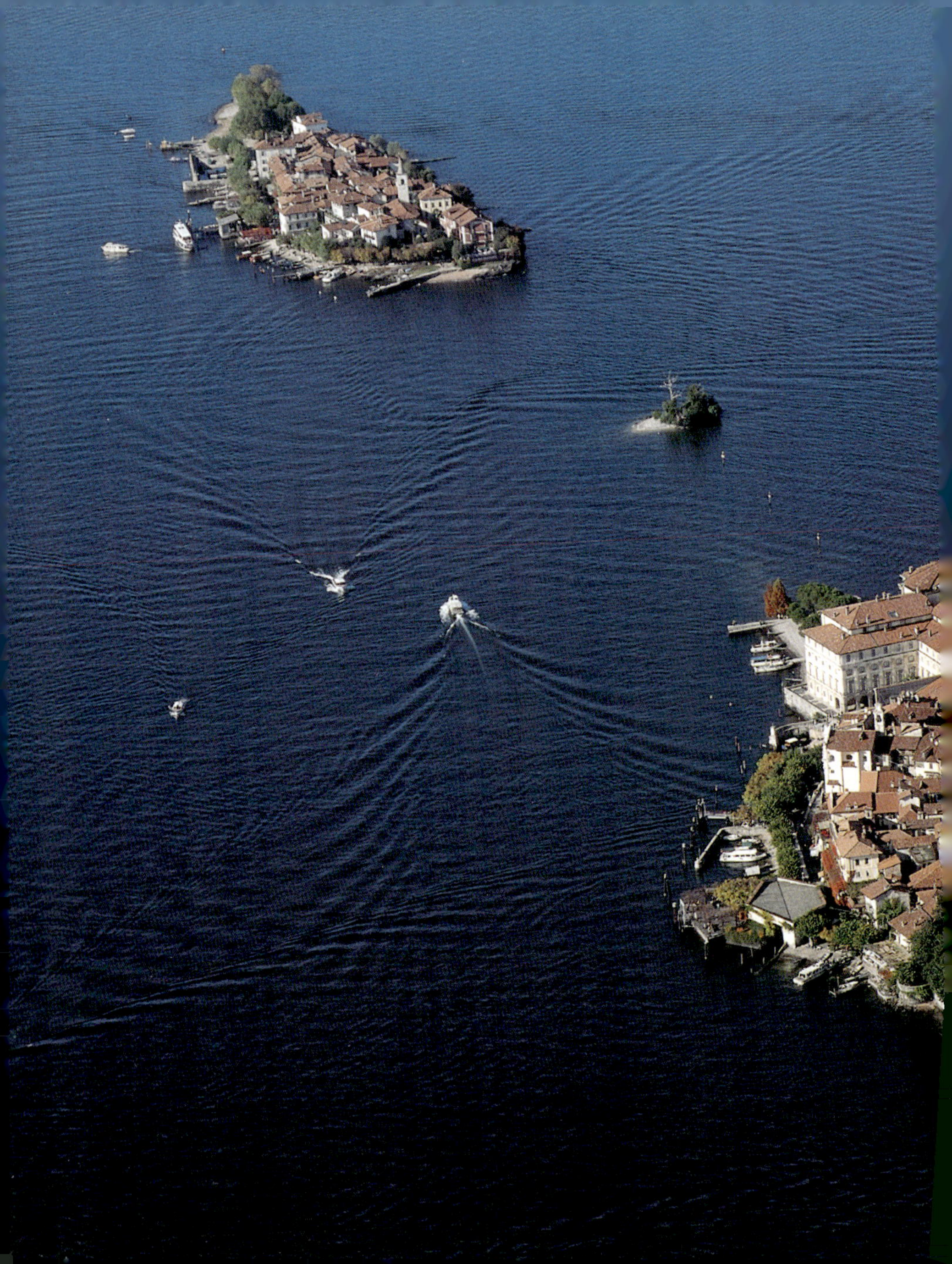

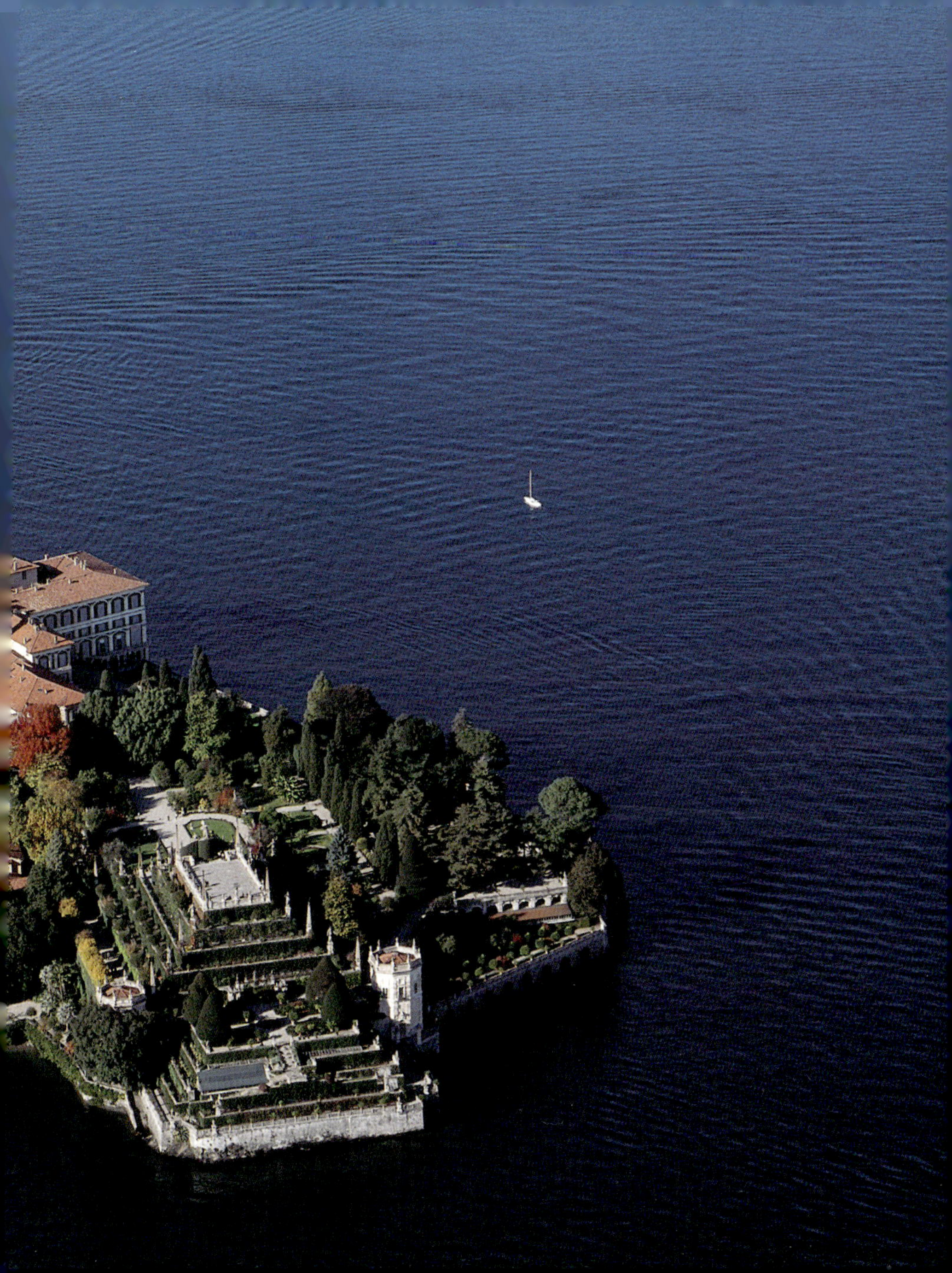

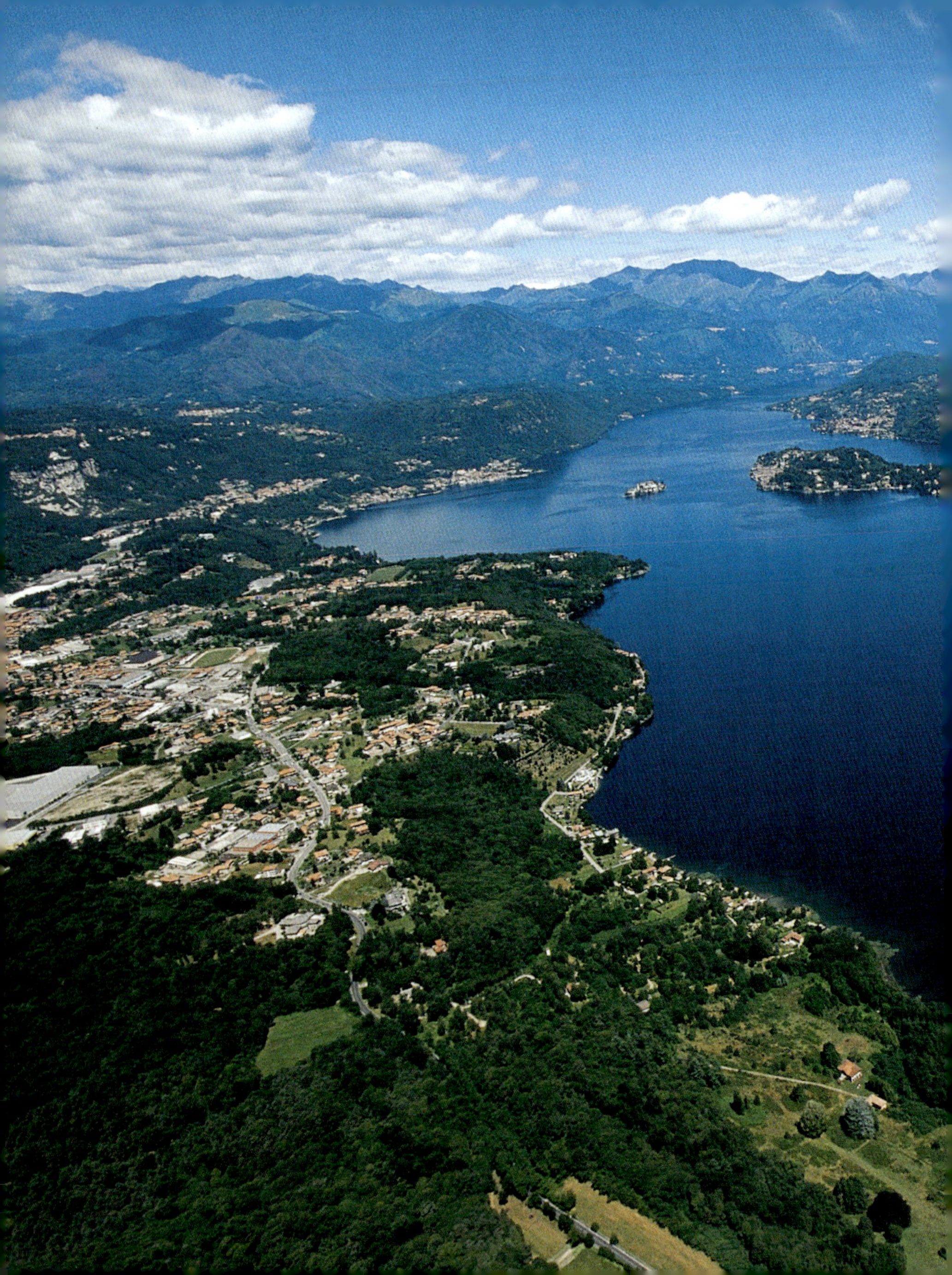

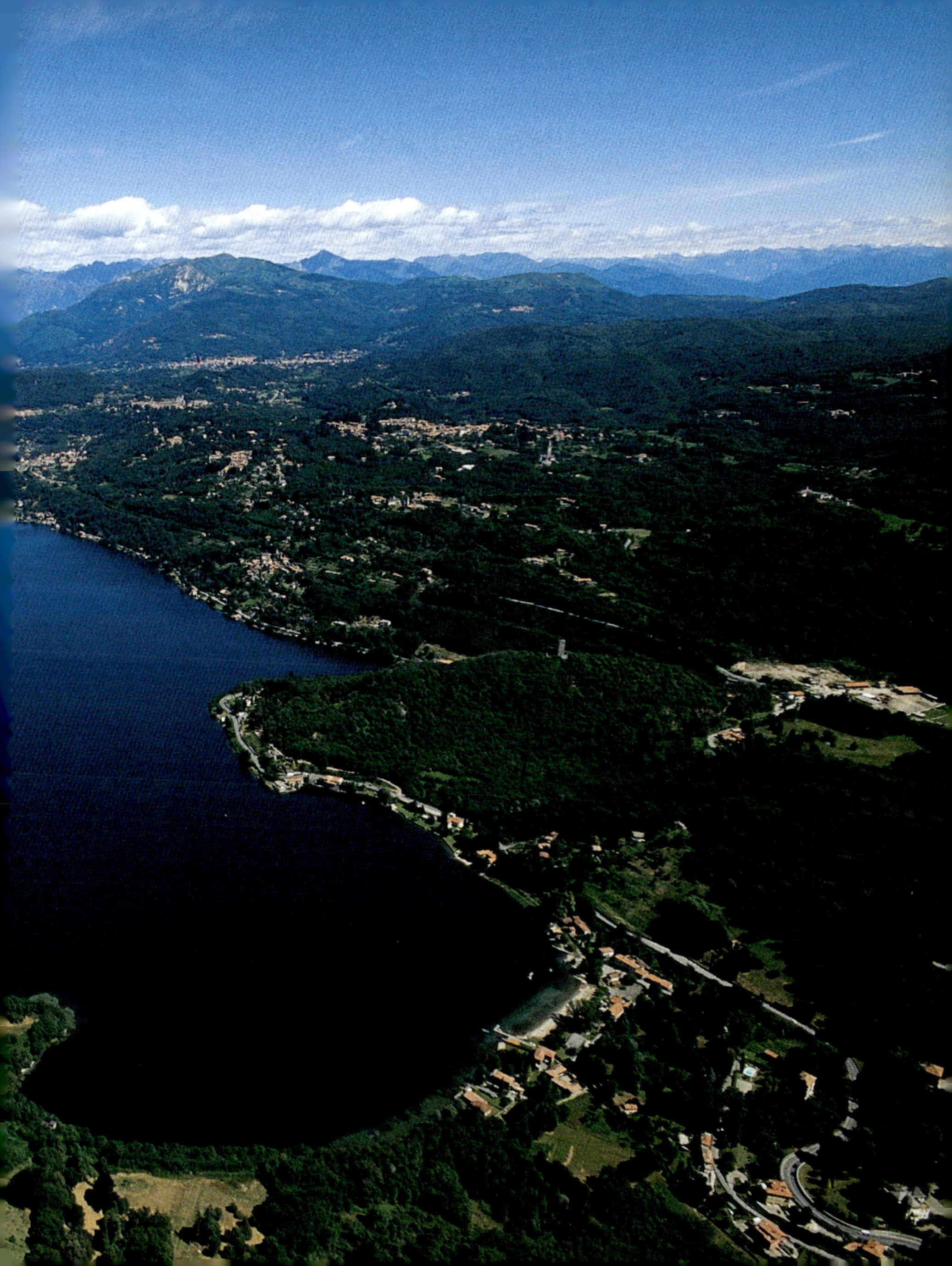

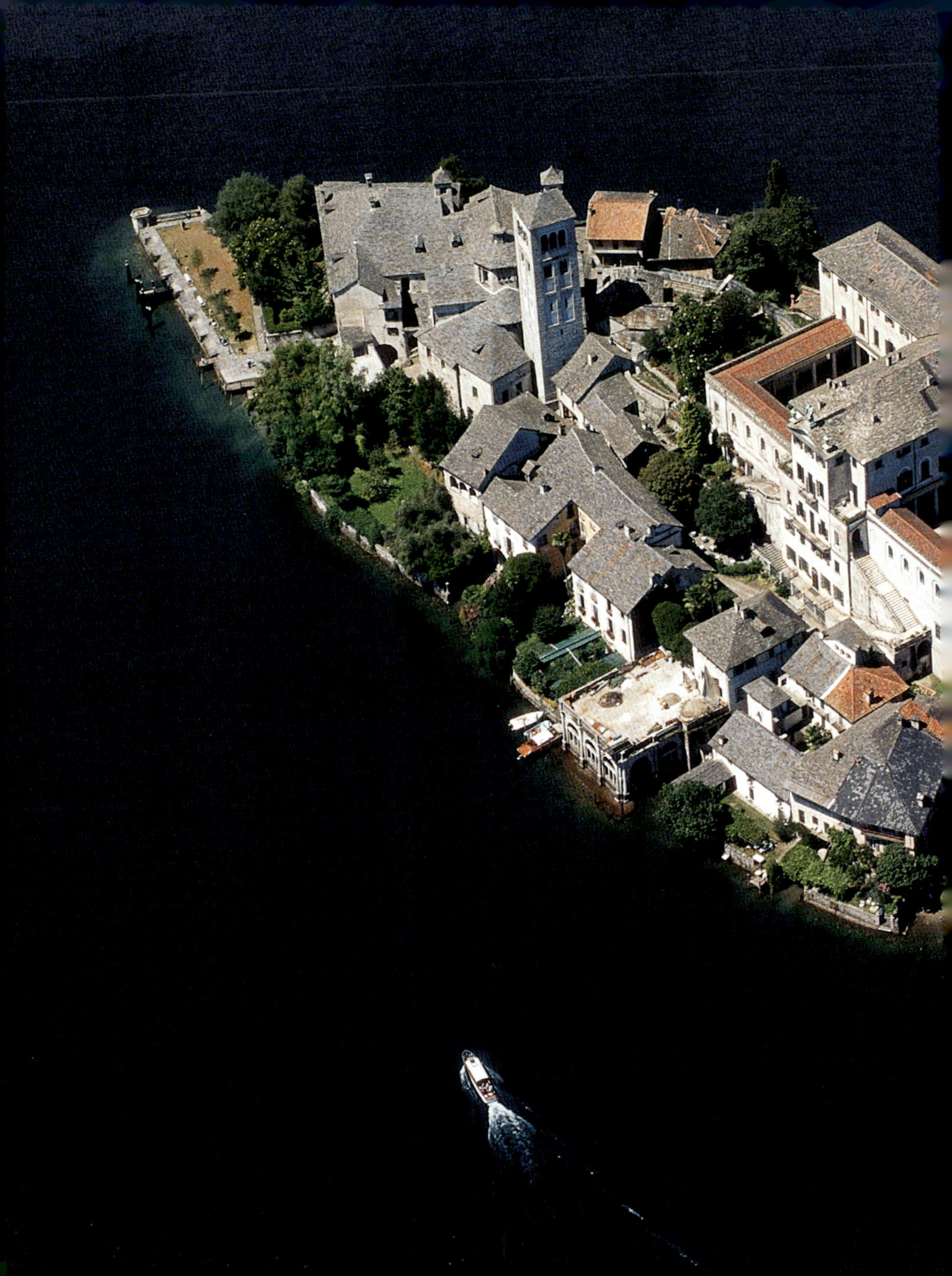

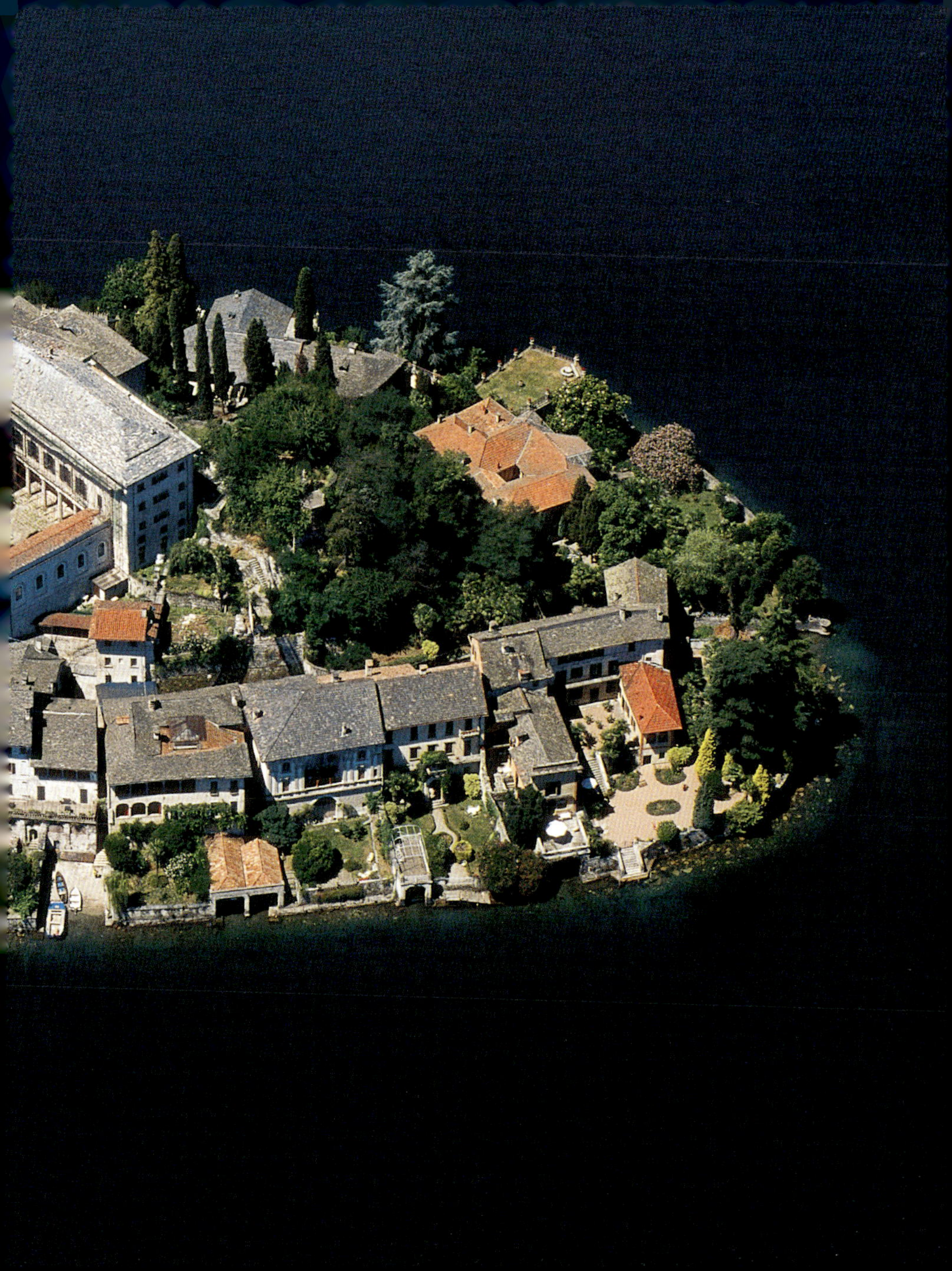

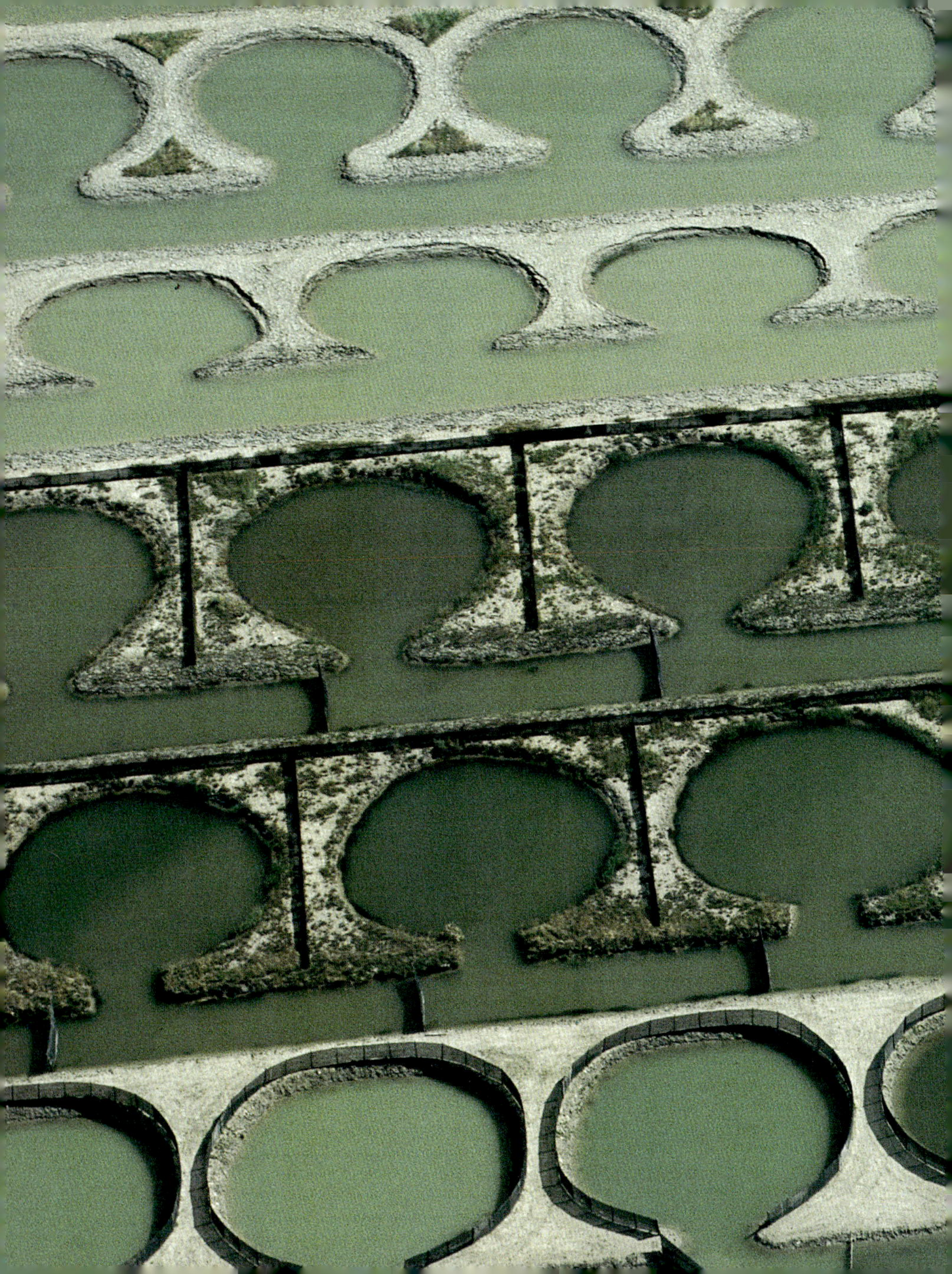

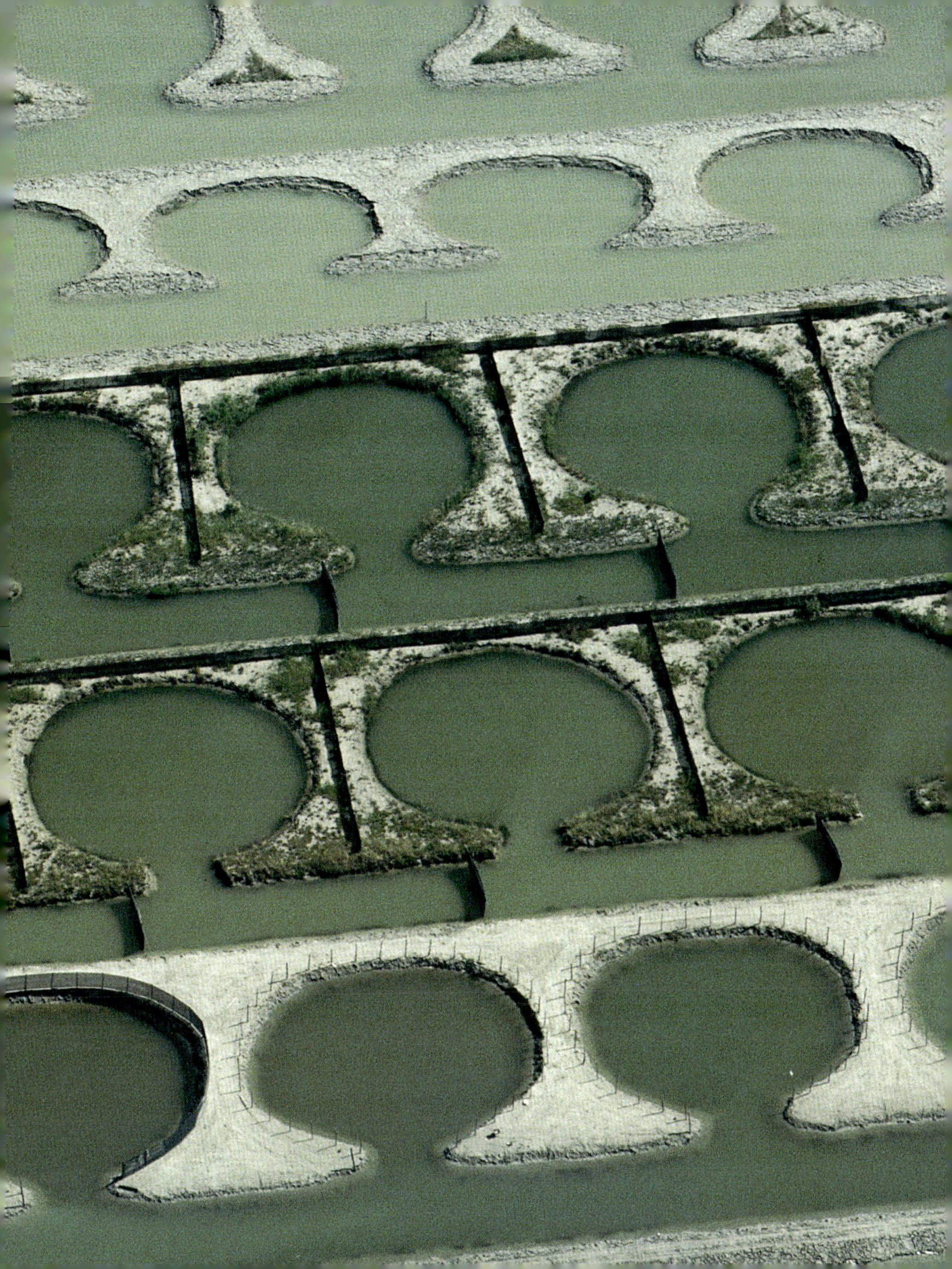

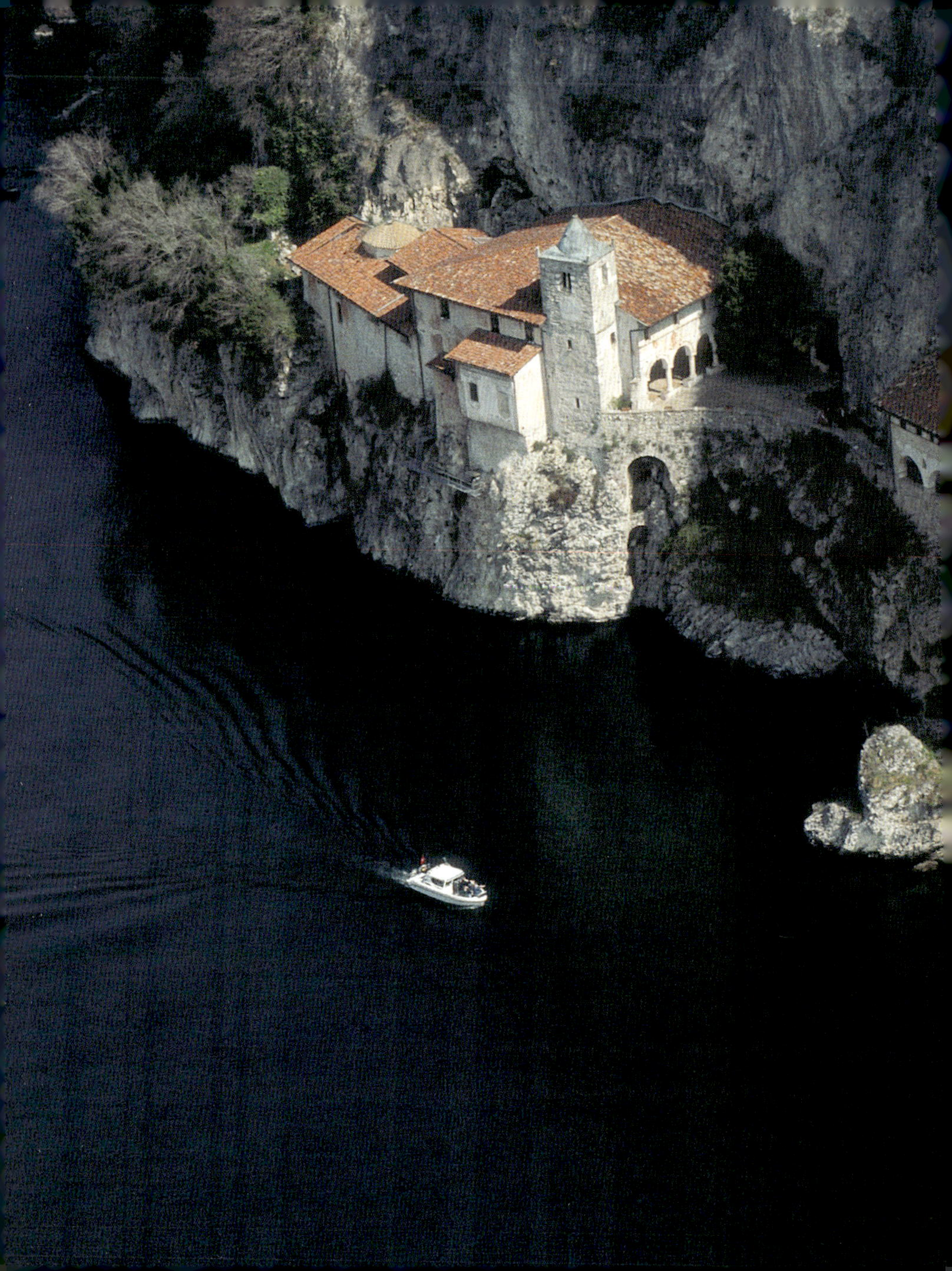

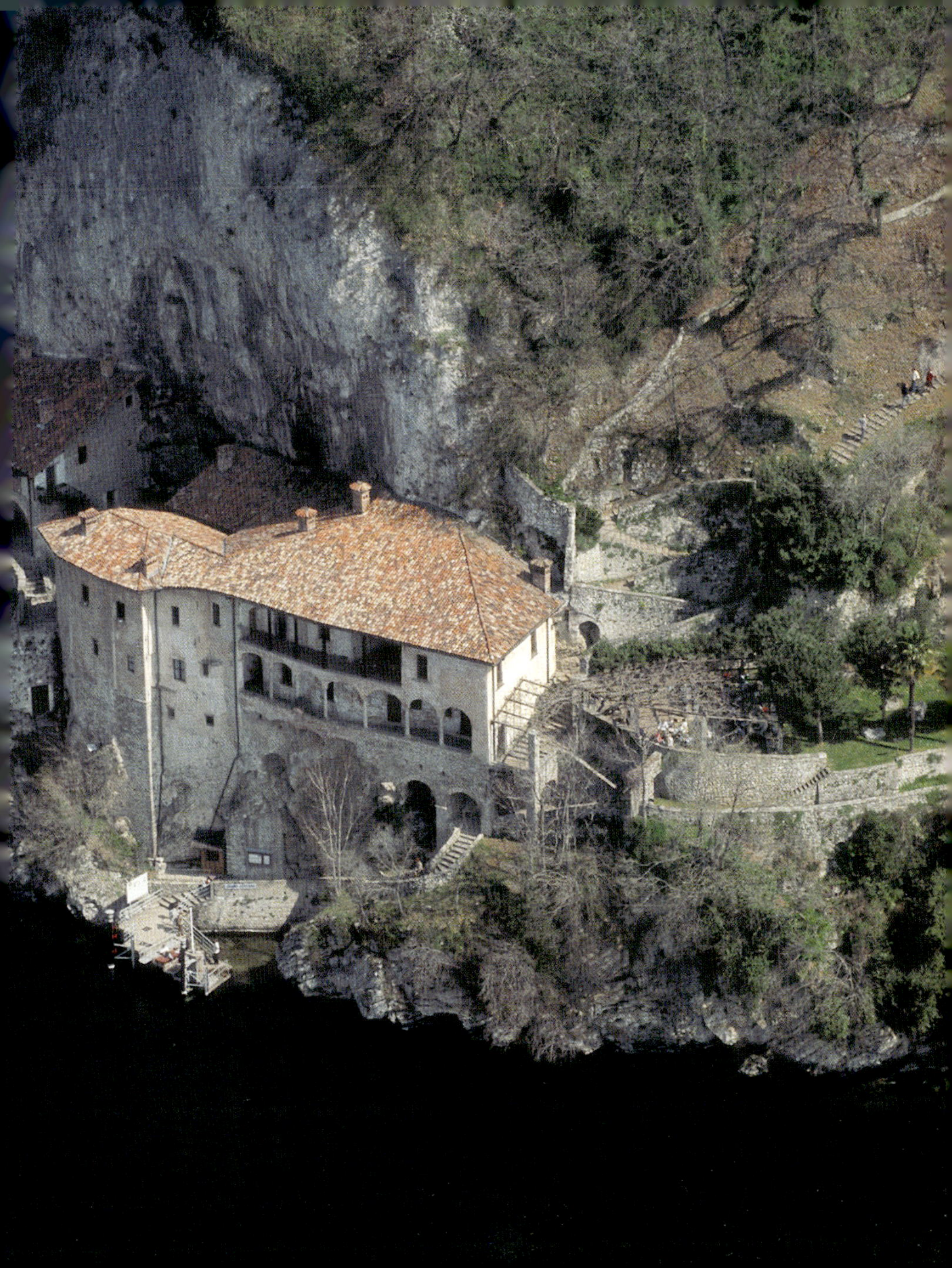

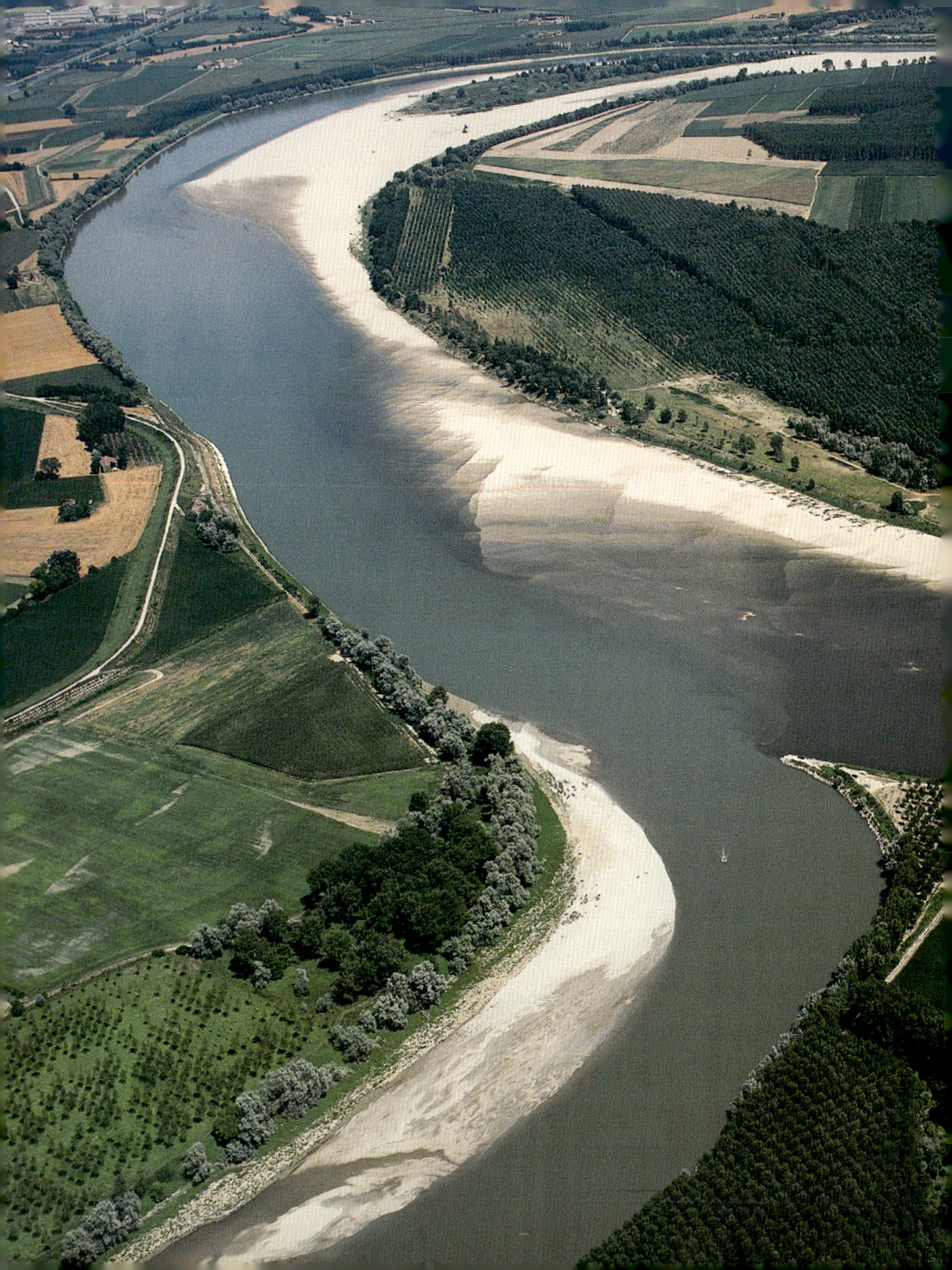

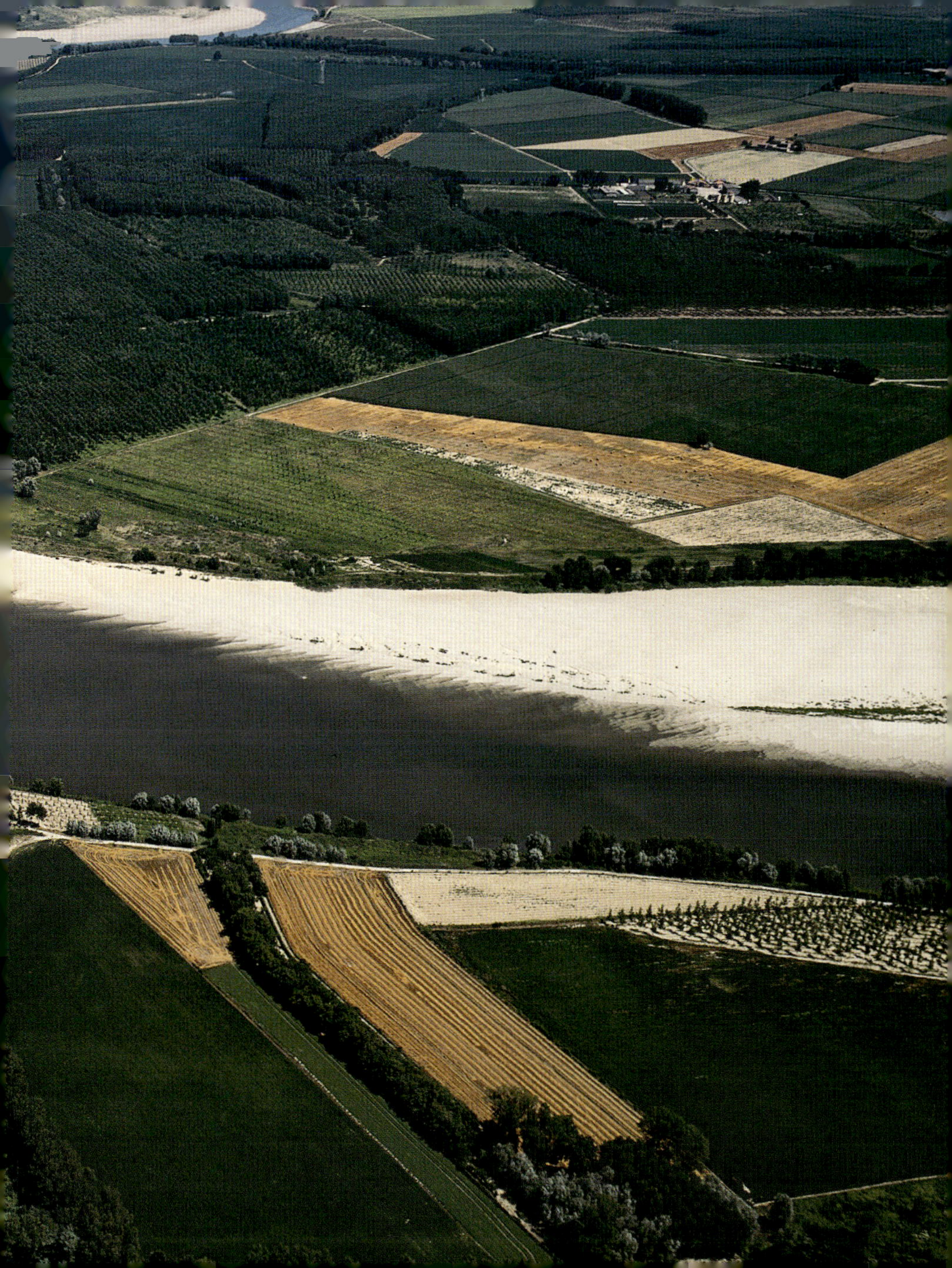

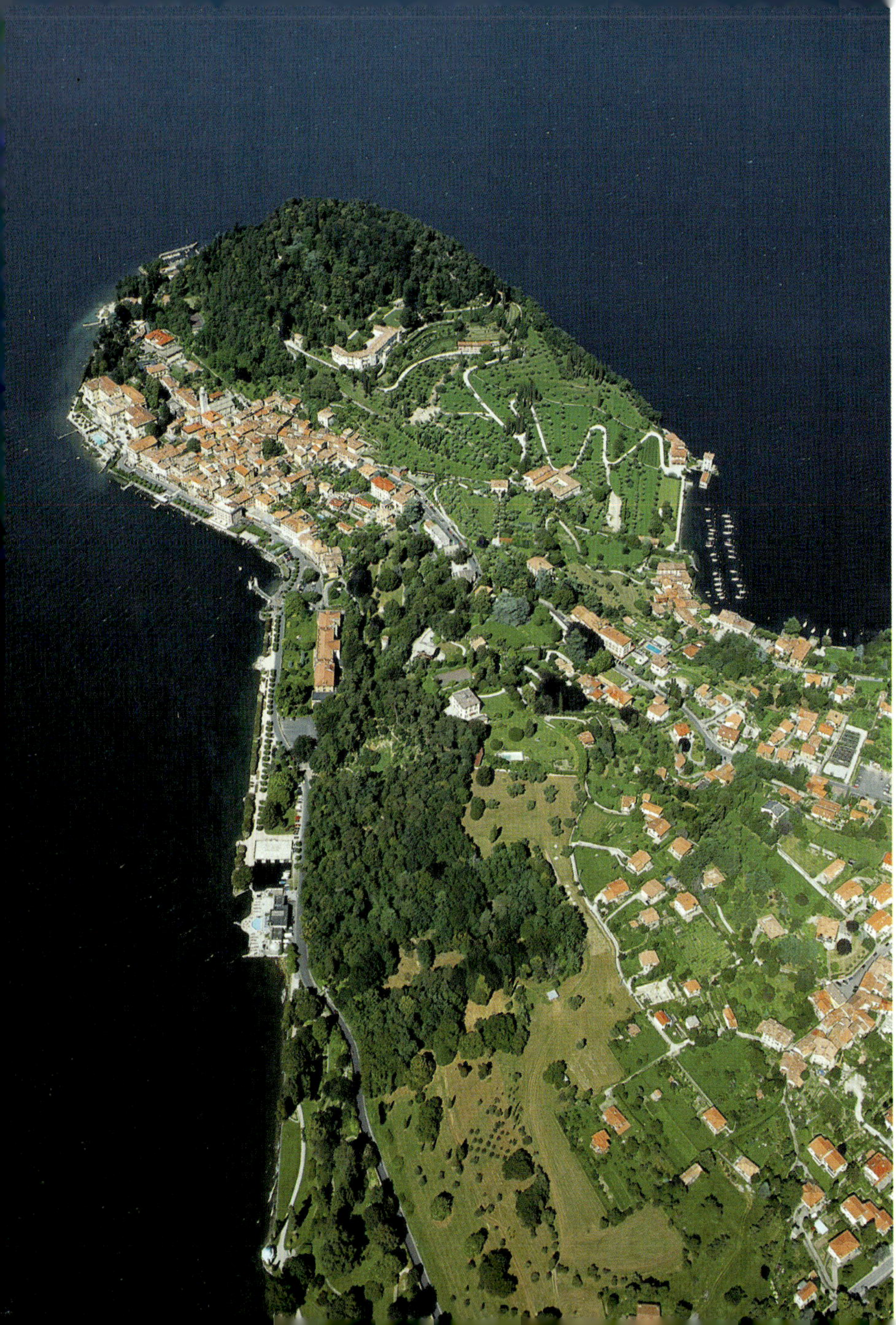

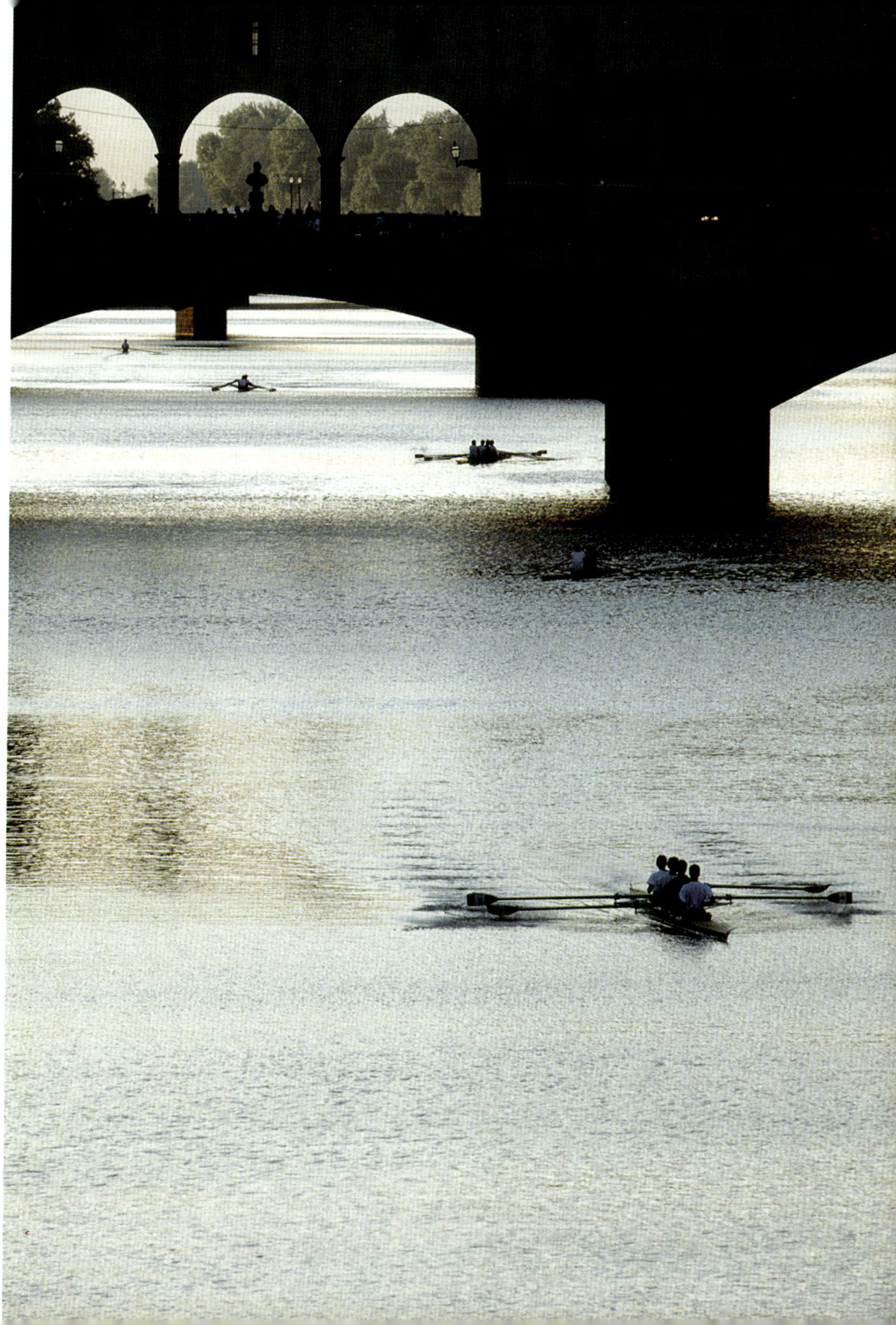

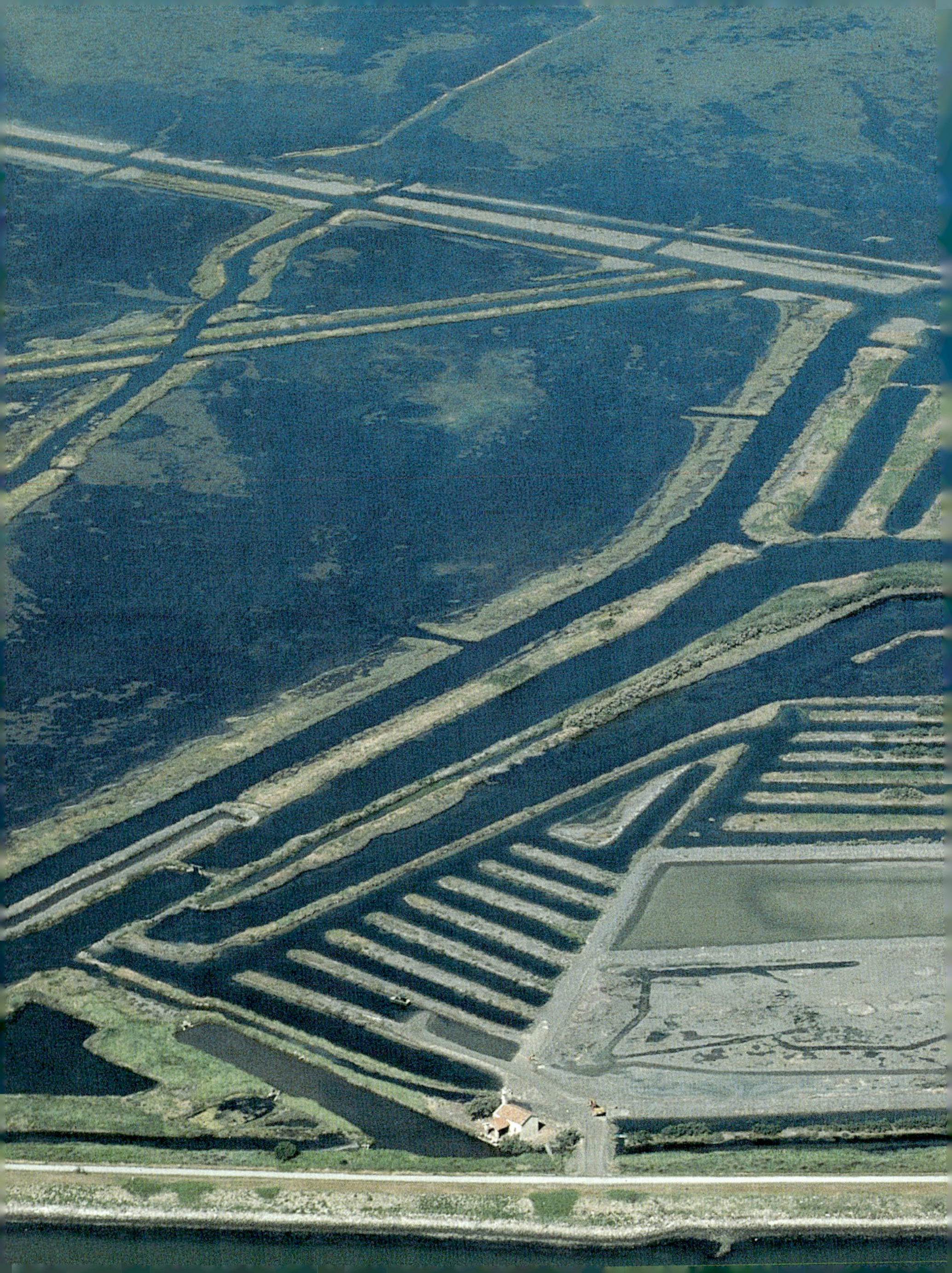

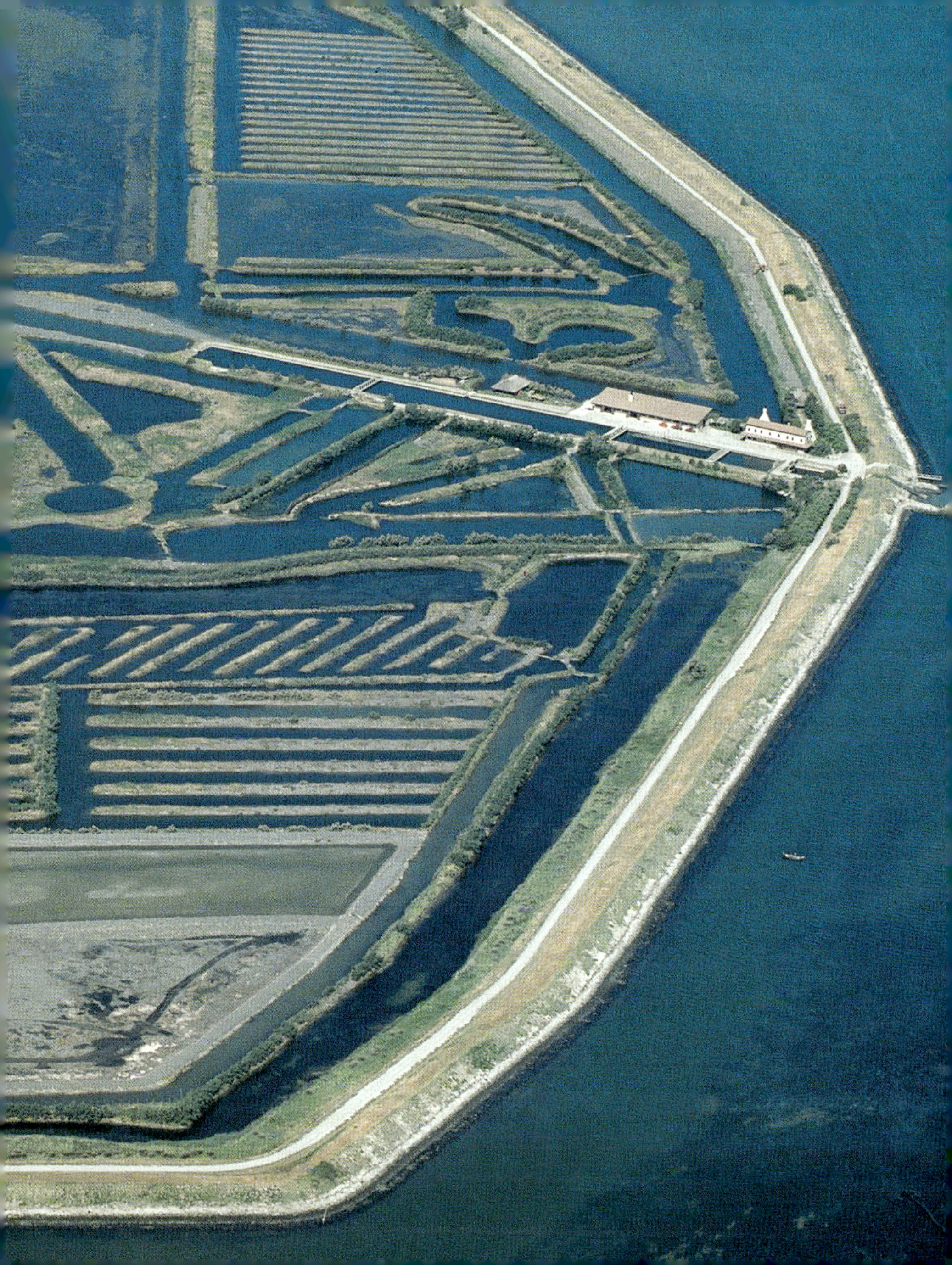

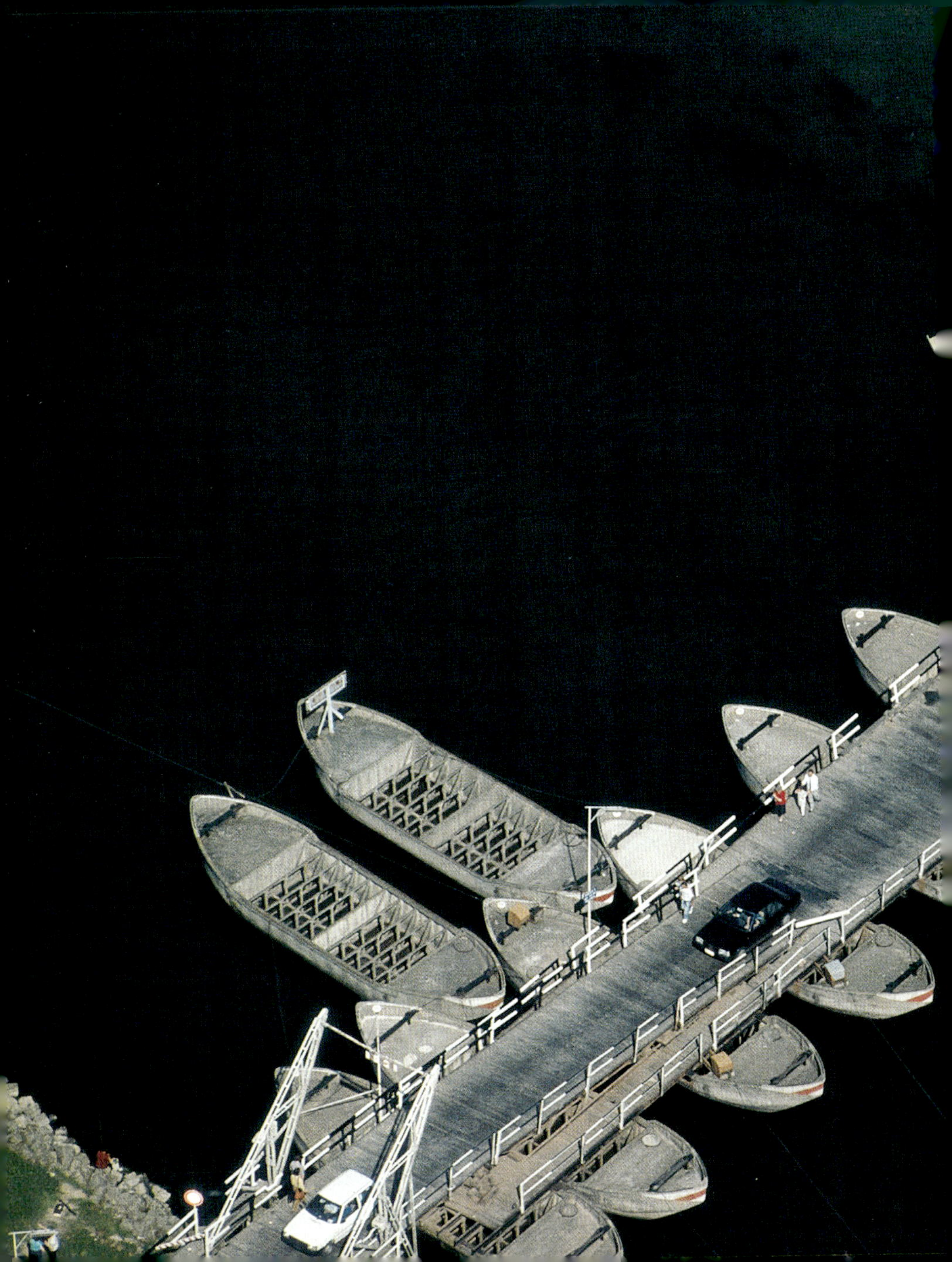

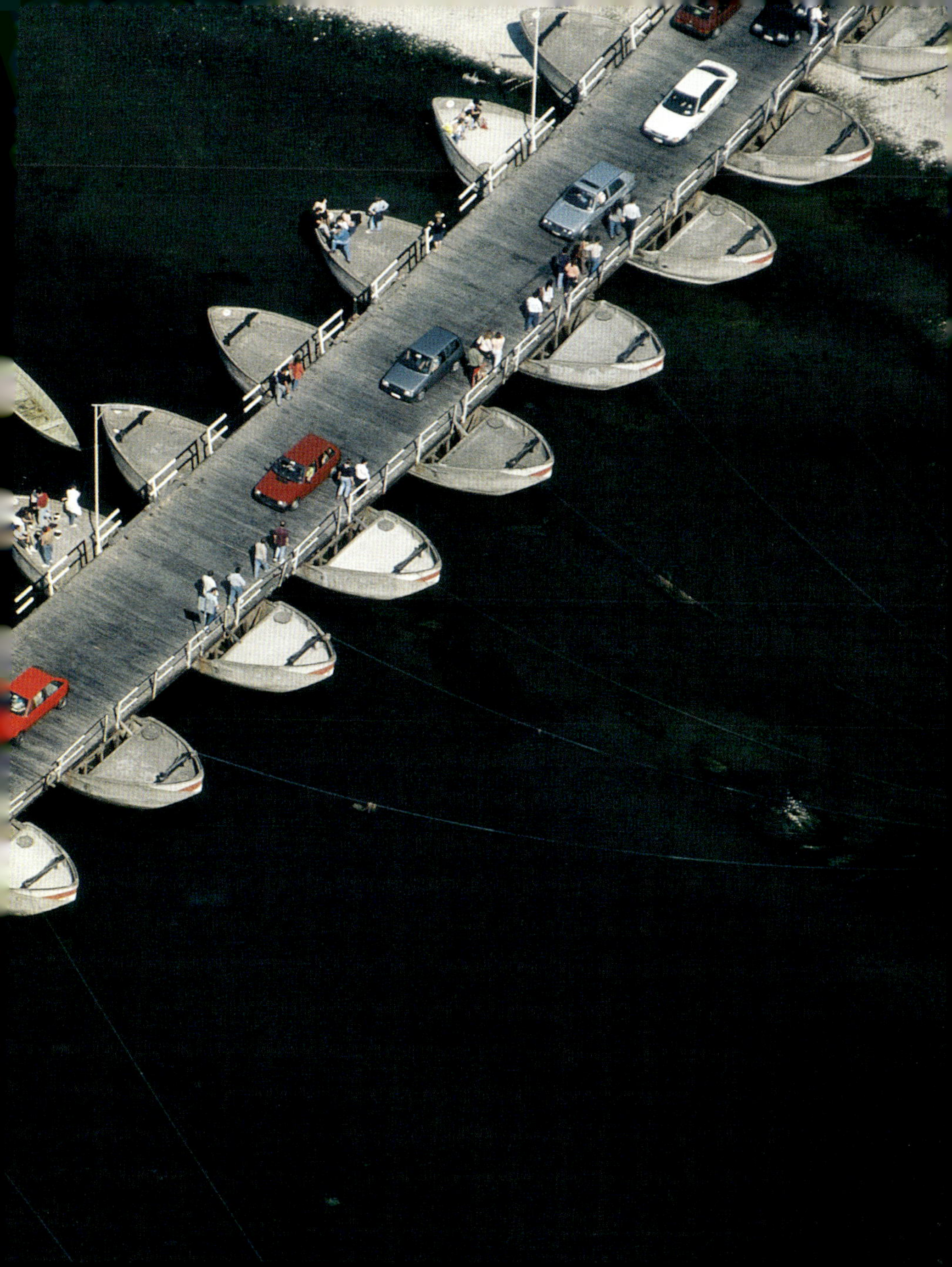

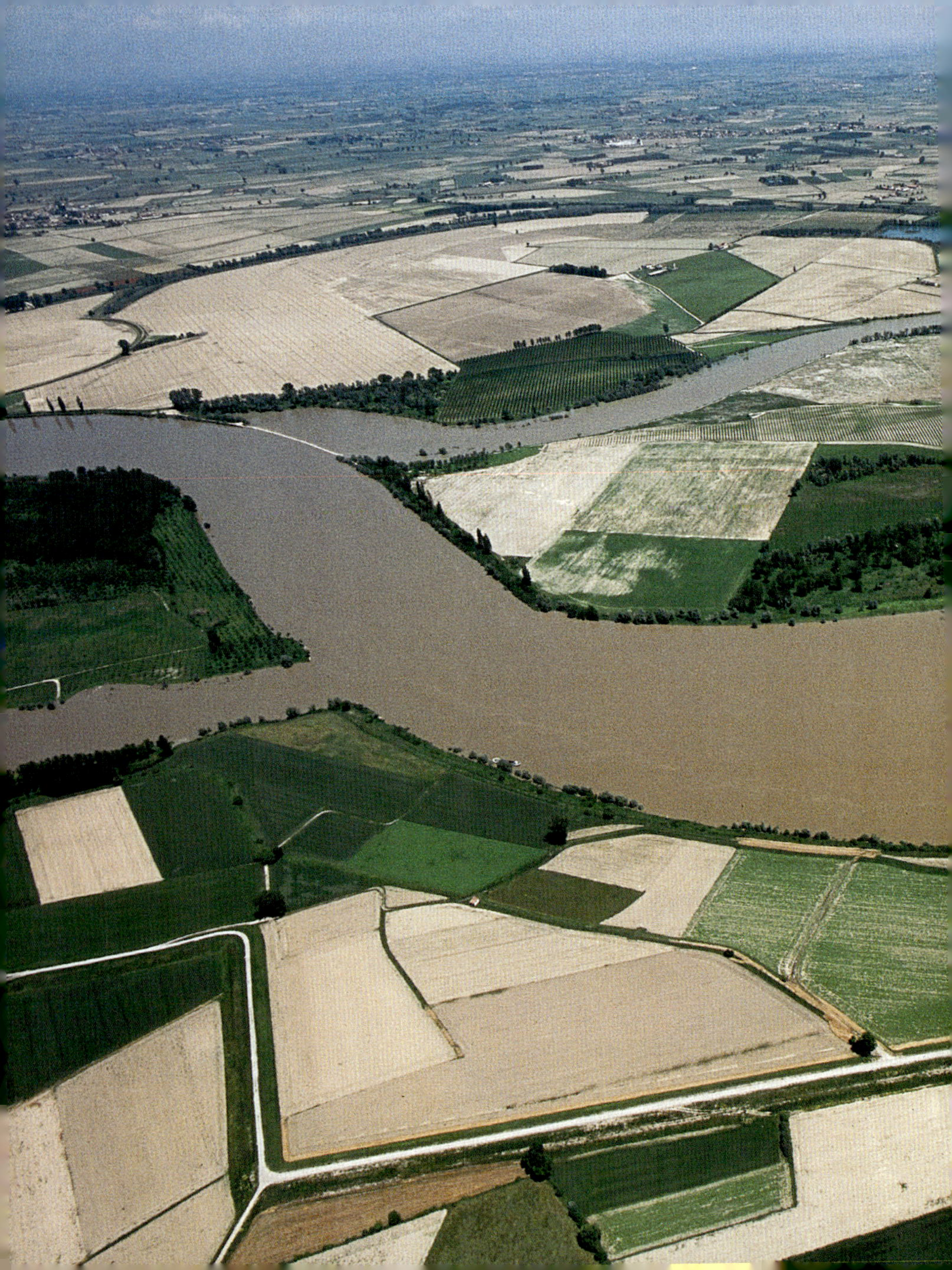

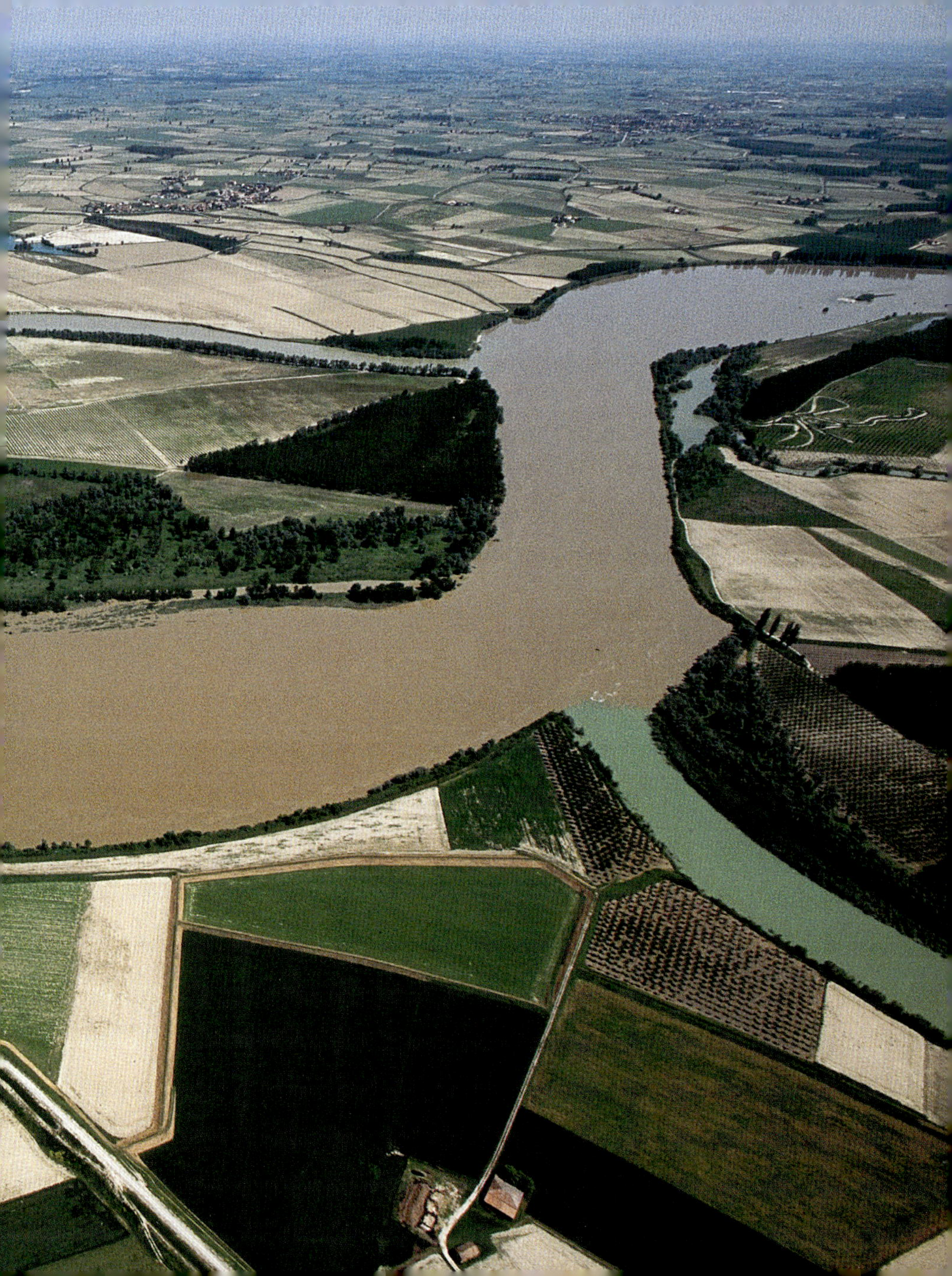

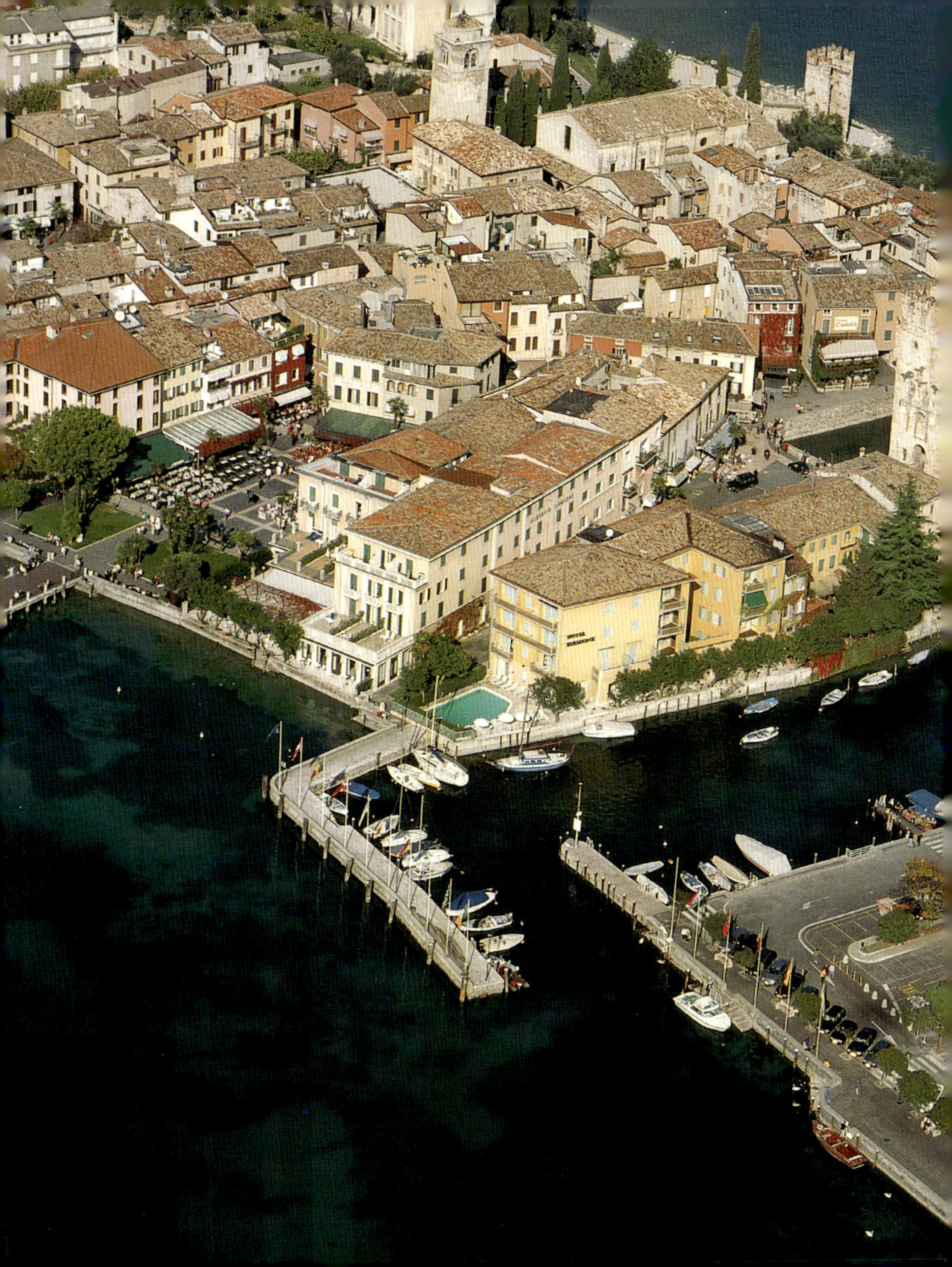

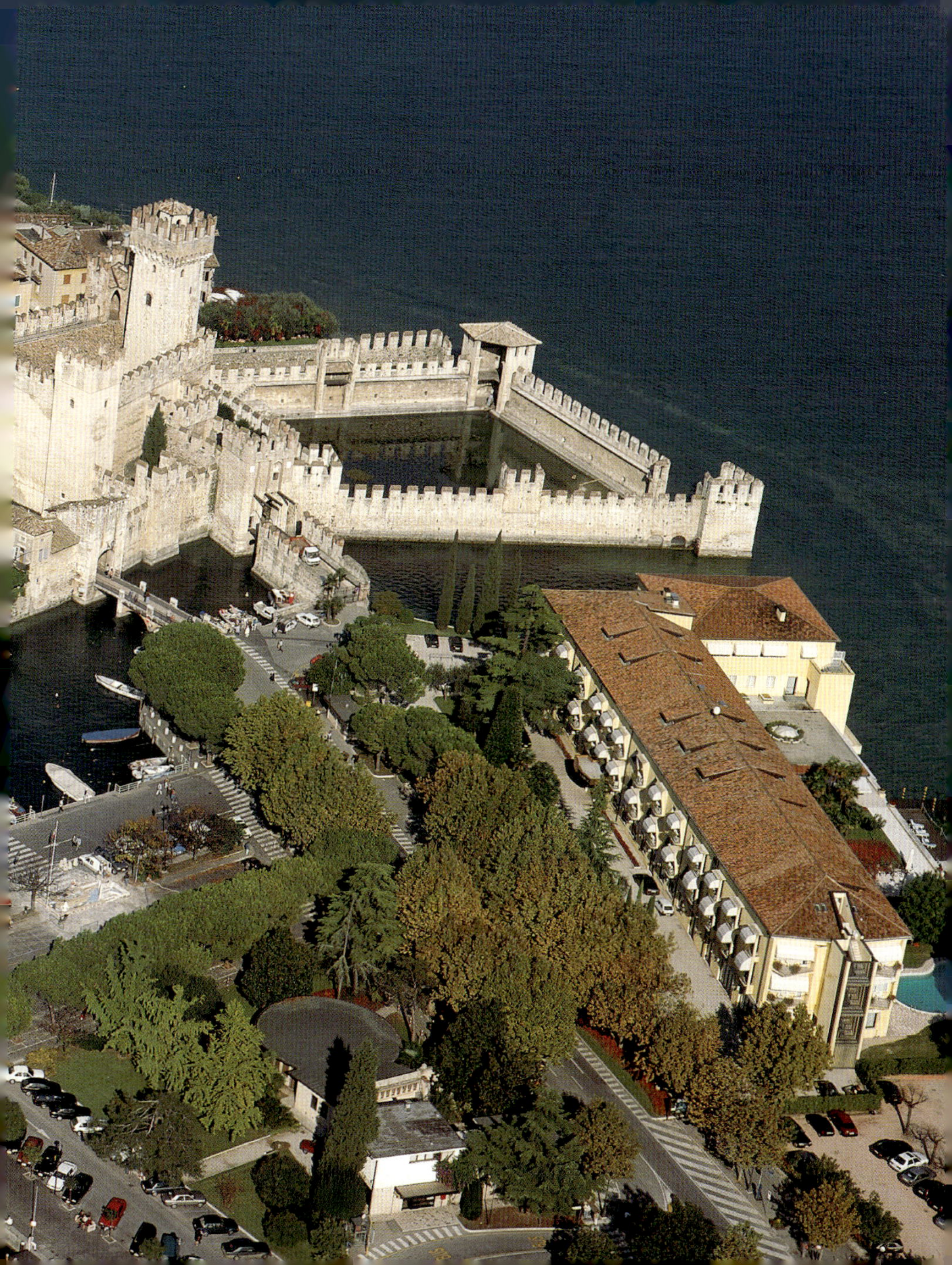

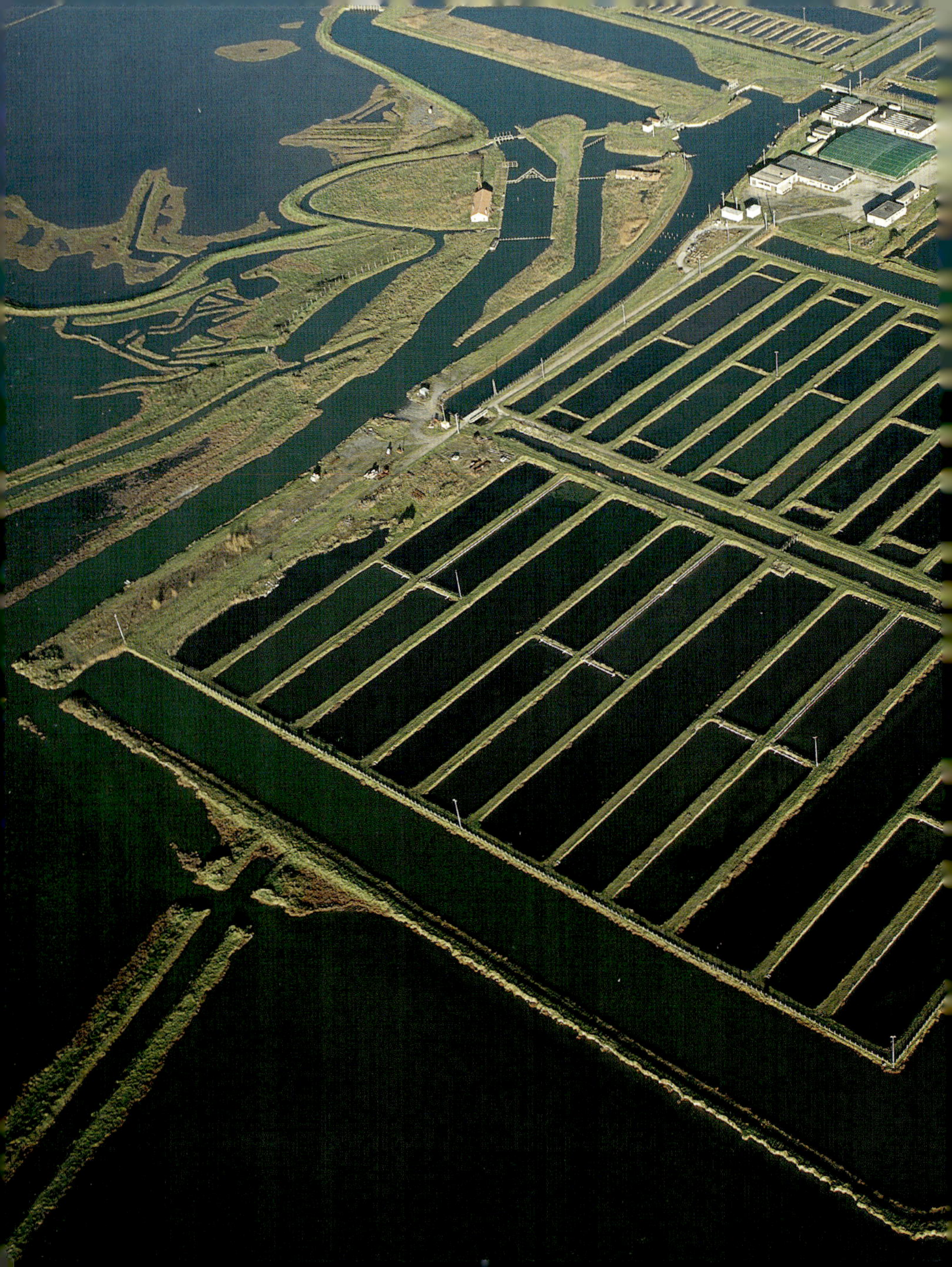

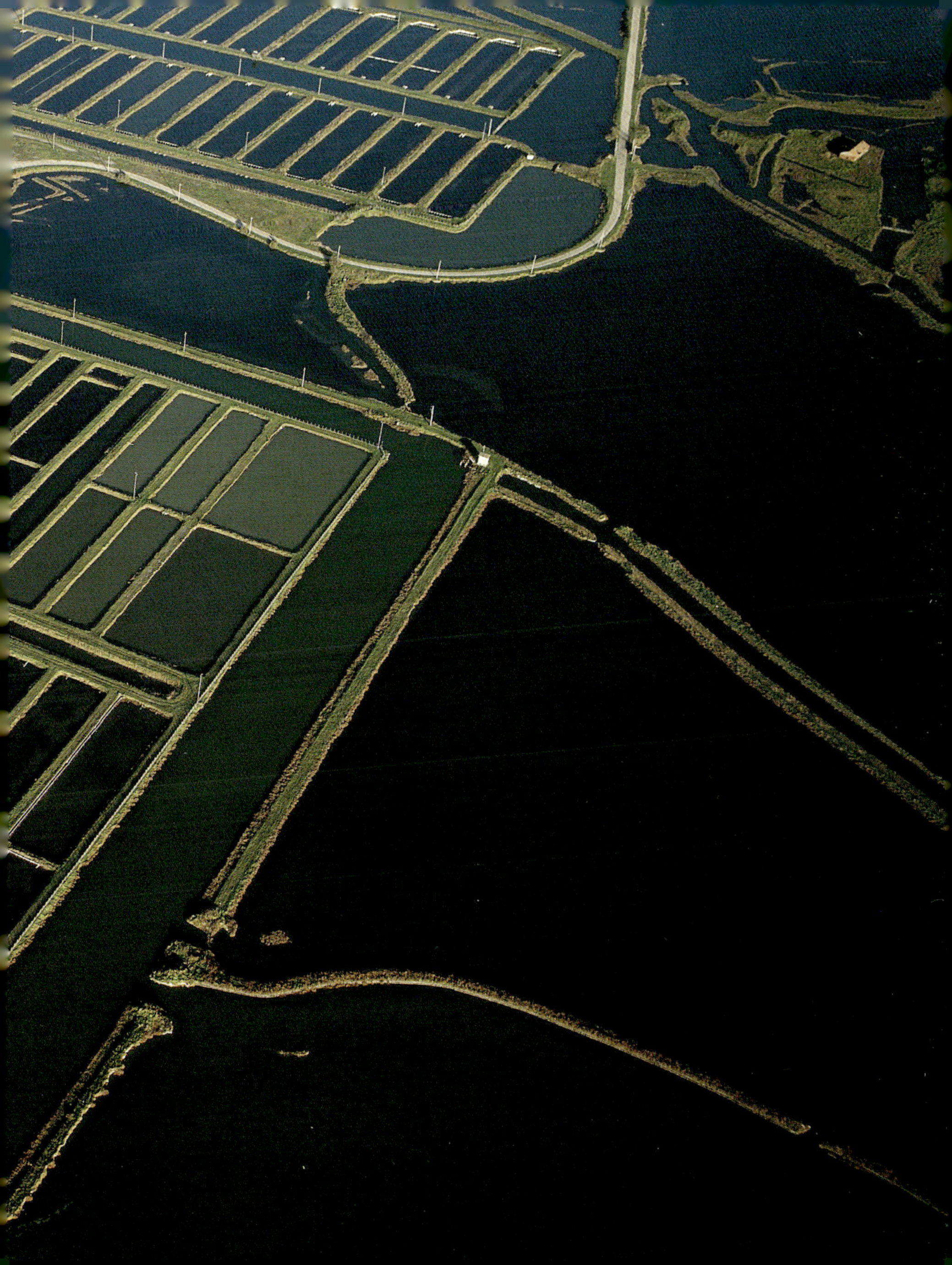

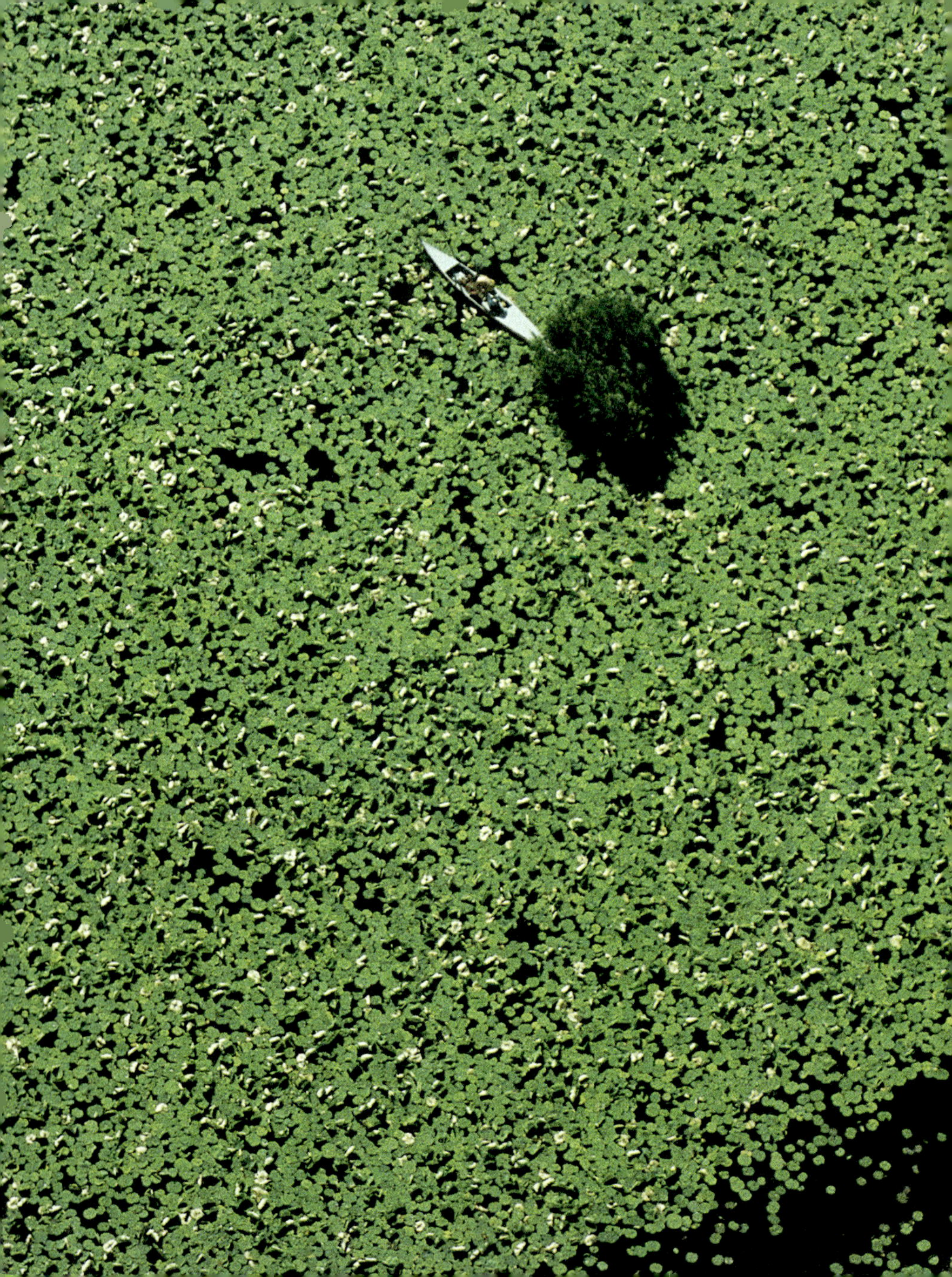

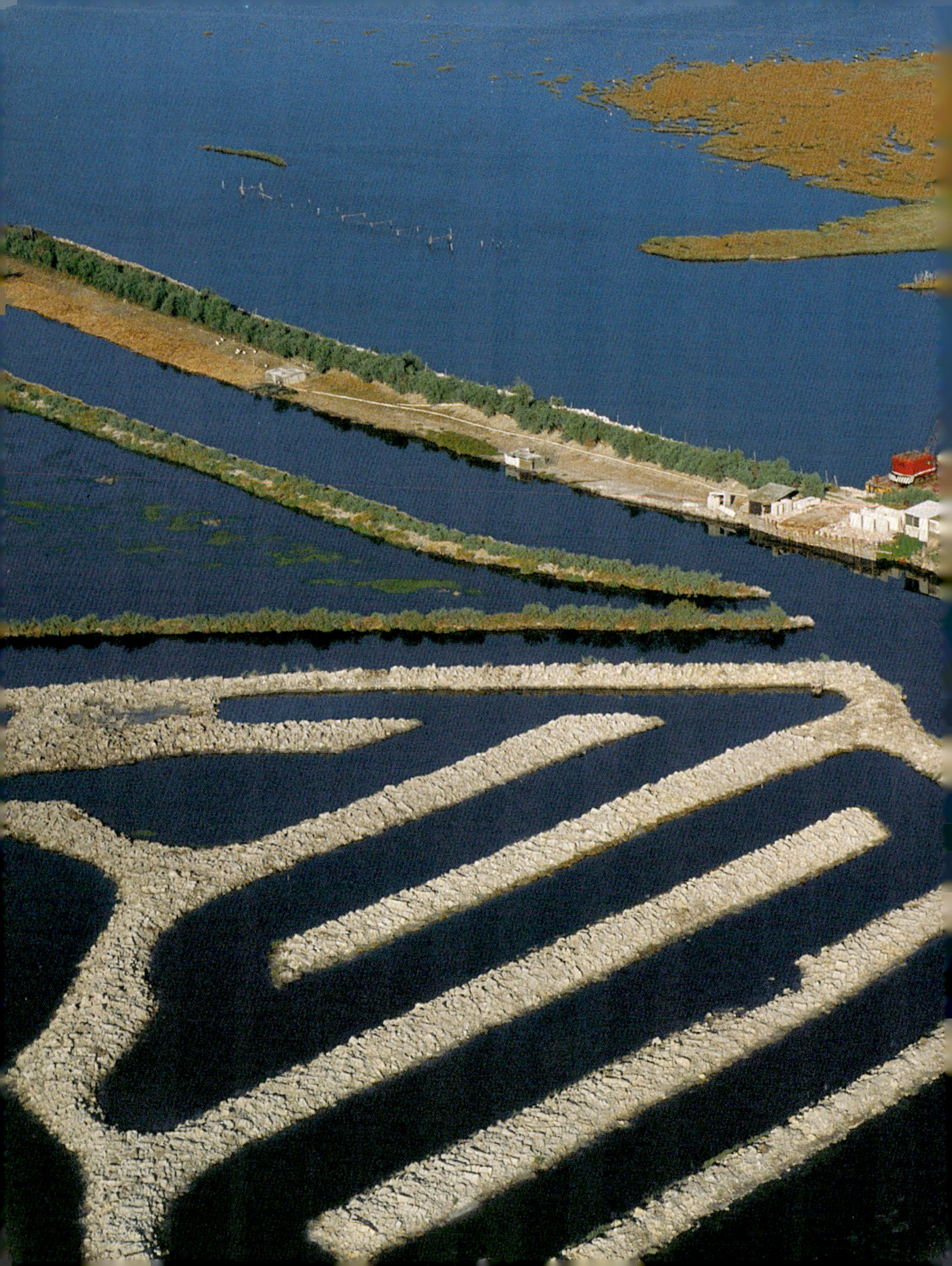

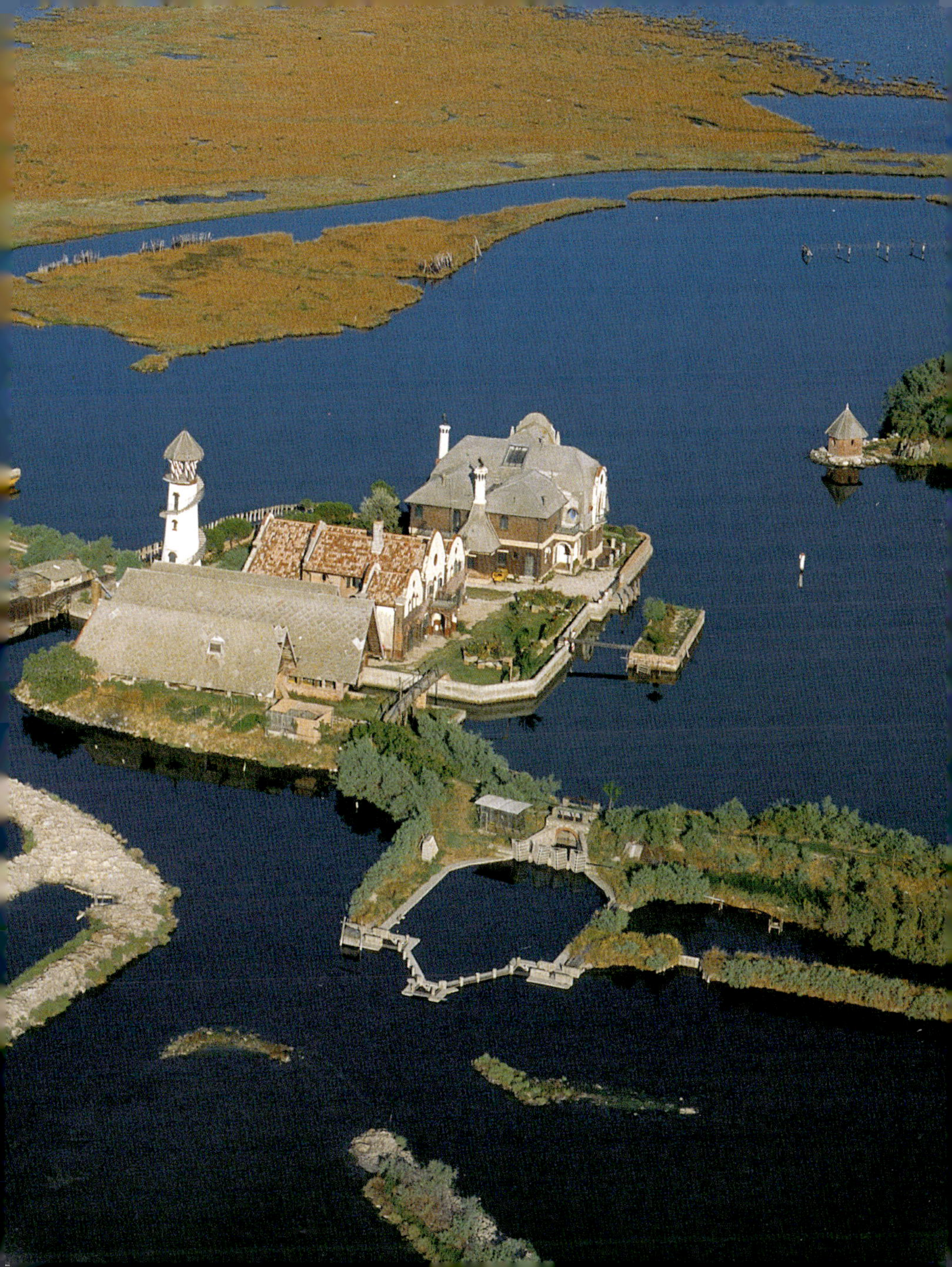

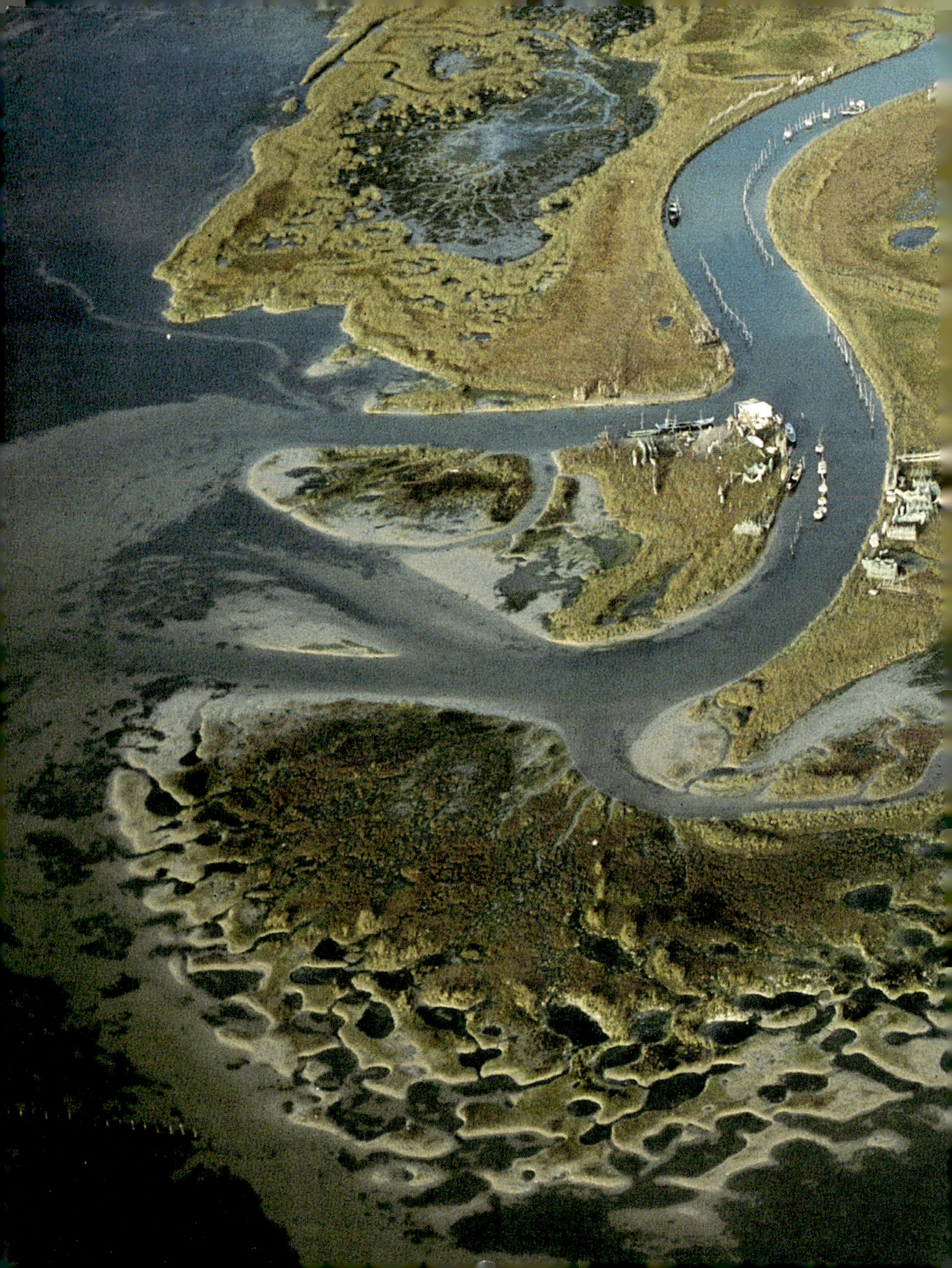

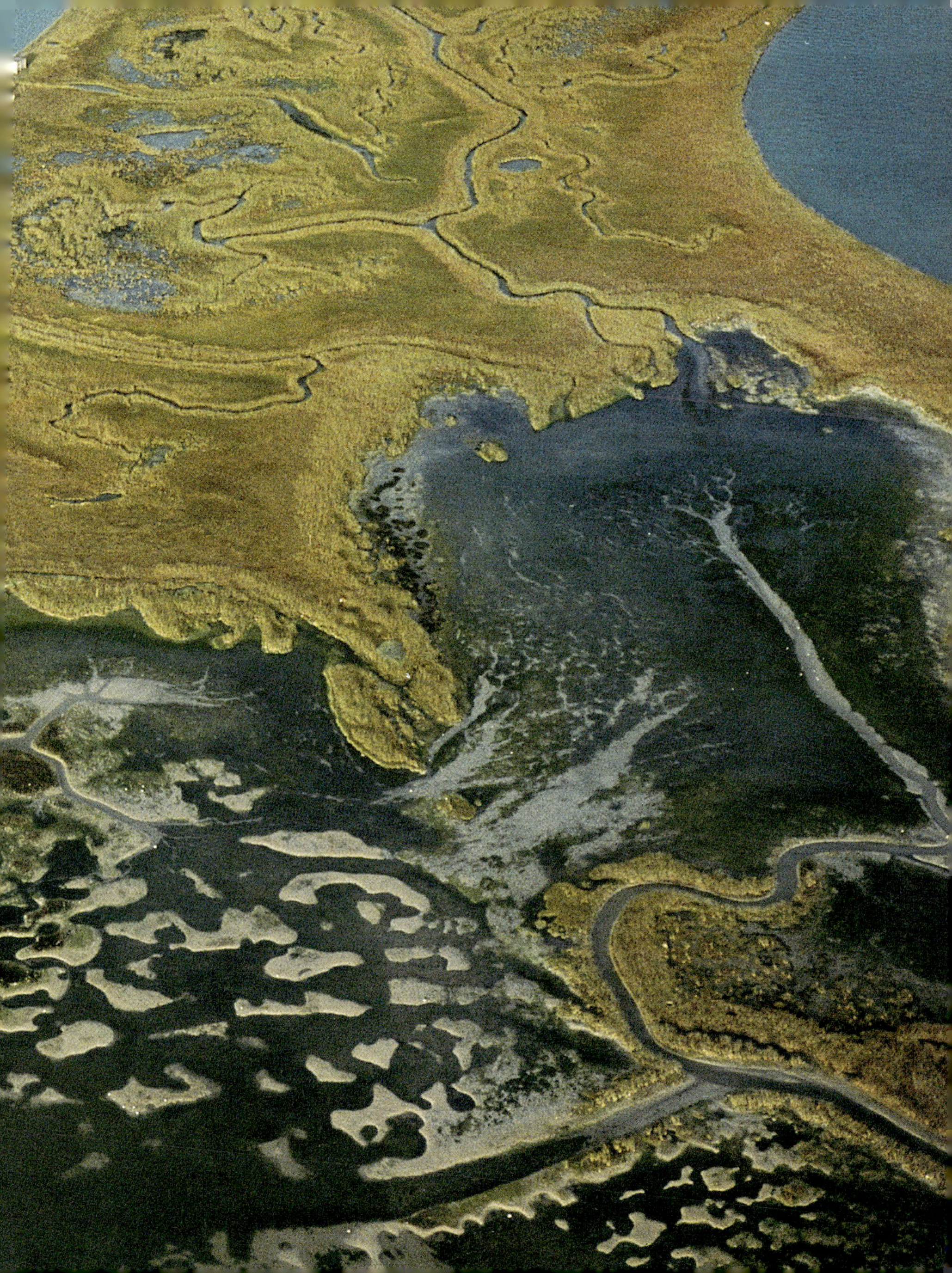

Photographs by Andrea Pistolesi:
Cover; pp. 1, 4-5, 6-7, 10, 14, 22-23, 26-27, 30-31, 32-33, 58-59, 70-71, 74-75, 76-77, 78-79, 88, 100-101, 104-105, 106-107, 118-119, 120-121, 124-125, 126-127, 128-129, 132-133, 134-135, 136-137, 138-139, 140-141, 142-143, 144-145, 158-159, 160-161, 162-163, 164-165, 166-167, 168-169, 170-171, 172, 184-185, 193, 194-195, 196-197, 198-199, 200-201, 202-203, 204-205, 206-207, 208-209, 210-211, 212-213, 214-215, 218-219, 222-223, 224, 246-247, 264-265, 272-273, 293, 294-295, 296, 297, 298-299, 300-301, 302-303, 304-305, 310-311, 314-315, 316-317, 322-323, 343.

Photographs by Guido Alberto Rossi:
pp. 2-3, 21, 24-25, 28-29, 34-35, 36-37, 38-39, 40-41, 42-43, 44-45, 46-47, 48-49, 50-51, 52-53, 57, 60-61, 62-63, 64-65, 66-67, 68-69, 72-73, 80-81, 82-83, 84-85, 86-87, 97, 98-99, 102-103, 108, 109, 110-111, 112-113, 114-115, 116-117, 122-123, 130-131, 146-147, 148-149, 150-151, 152, 157, 173, 174-175, 176-177, 178-179, 180-181, 182-183, 186-187, 188, 216-217, 220-221, 233, 234-235, 236-237, 238, 239, 240-241, 242-243, 244-245, 248, 249, 250-251, 252-253, 254-255, 256-257, 258-259, 260-261, 262-263, 266-267, 268-269, 270-271, 274-275, 276, 277, 278-279, 280-281, 282-283, 284-285, 286-287, 288, 306-307, 308-309, 312-313, 318, 319, 320-321, 324, 329, 330-331, 332-333, 334-335, 336-337, 338-339, 340-341, 342, 344-345, 346-347, 348-349, 350-351, 352-353, 354-355, 356-357, 358-359.

SMA permissions for the aerial photographs published:
SMA 01161 of 17/04/97; SMA 01634 of 04/11/97
RGS 1372 of 22/06/98; RGS 1321 of 15/06/99; RGS 1396 of 14/07/99; RGS 1625 of 07/10/99
RGS 1323 of 25/05/00; RGS 1553 of 20/07/00.

Printed in October 2002
by Artes Gráficas, Toledo